Ad... PE for Edexcel

Frank Galligan
Colin Maskery
Jon Spence
David Howe
Tim Barry
Andy Ruston
Dee Crawford

Edexcel
Success through qualifications

Heinemann

Heinemann Educational Publishers
Halley Court, Jordan Hill, Oxford OX2 8EJ
a division of Reed Educational & Professional Publishing Ltd

OXFORD   MELBOURNE   AUCKLAND
JOHANNESBURG   BLANTYRE   GABORONE
IBADAN   PORTSMOUTH (NH) USA   CHICAGO

Heinemann is a registered trademark of Reed Educational & Professional Publishing Ltd

Text © Frank Galligan, Tim Barry, Dee Crawford, David Howe, Colin Maskery, Andy Ruston, Jon Spence, 2000

First published 2000

04 03 02 01
9 8 7 6 5 4 3

British Library Cataloguing in Publication Data
A catalogue record for this book is available from the British Library

ISBN 0 435 50643 9

Designed by Wendi Watson
Typeset by 𝕋 Tek-Art, Croydon, Surrey
Printed and bound in Great Britain by The Bath Press Ltd, Bath

Acknowledgements
The publishers would like to thank the following for permission to reproduce copyright material:

Addison Wesley Longman for Figure 20.12, p. 70 from *Human Anatomy and Physiology*, 4th ed. By Elaine N. Marieb. Copyright © 1988 The Benjamin/Cummings Publishing Company. Reprinted by permission of Addison Wesley Longman Publishers, Inc., on p. 192; Brown and Benchmark for the graphs on pp. 193 and 384; H.O. & Storm for the graphs on pp. 168, 169 and 170, adapted from J. Bangsbo, *Fitness Training in Football: A Scientific Approach*, 1994; Human Kinetics Publishers for the material on pp. 192, 193, 197, 201, 202, 387, 389, adapted, by permission, from J. Wilmore & D. Costill, 1999, *Physiology of sport and exercise*, 2nd ed. (Champaign, Il: Human Kinetics, 229; The International Olympic Committee for the Games logos reproduced on p. 84; International Paralympic Committee for the logo on p. 91; Lippincott Williams & Wilkins for the extract from *Medicine and Science in Sports*, 1978, on p. 175; McGraw Hill for the material adapted from *Clinical Sports Medicine*, by Bruknerm and Khan, on p. 476; National Coaching Foundation for the Badminton notation sheet (1999) on p. 322; The Observer for 'Georgia v. England', from *The Observer*, 10/11/96, on p. 315; Science in Sport for the graphic on p. 391; *Scotland on Sunday* for the extract, 'Michael Indurain – the physiology of a supreme athlete', on p. 211; The Telegraph for the extract on p. 315, © *The Telegraph* 2000.

The publishers would like to thank the following for permission to reproduce photographs:
Action Images: Figures 4.1, 4.9, 4.13, 4.19, 4.51a, 6.20; Allsport: Figures 1.52, 1.53, 1.70, 1.72a, 1.72b, 1.75, 1.77, 1.78, 1.79, 1.80, 1.81, 1.85, 2.0, 2.11, 2.13, 2.21, 2.29, 2.31, 2.35a, 2.36, 2.38, 2.39, 2.40, 2.42, 2.50, 2.51, 2.52, 2.53, 4.19, 5.3, 5.4, 5.9a, 5.9c, 5.10, 5.17, 5.19, 5.21, 5.22, 5.24, 5.30, 5.32, 5.33, 5.39, 6.124a, 6.124b; Allsport/Anton Want: Figure 4.50; Allsport/David Rogers: Figure 4.57; Allsport/Gary M Prior: Figure 4.59; Allsport/John Gichigi: Figure 4.24; Alan Edwards: Figures 1.33, 1.45, 1.51, 2.18, 3.2, 3.3, 3.70, 5.5, 5.35, 5.40, 5.41, 6.22, 6.27, 6.91a, 6.153, 6.171; Allsport/Hulton Deutsch: Figure 1.66; Ancient Art and Architecture: Figure 1.54; Art Directors and Trip: Figure 4.26; British Library: Figure 1.57; Colorsport: Figures 2.8, 2.19, 2.34, 2.41, 4.32, 4.42, 4.52, 4.55, 4.61a, 4.63, 5.27, 5.31, 5.34, 6.34, 6.36, 6.37, 6.63, 6.92, 6.123, 6.155, 6.156, 6.165; Colorsport/ Agence Temp Sport: Figure 4.51b; Corbis: Figure 1.68; Corbis UK Ltd: Figure 1.67; Empics: Figures 1.34, 1.76, 1.82, 2.1, 2.2, 2.3, 2.5, 2.27, 2.33, 2.35b, 2.37, 2.44, 2.47, 2.48, 2.49, 3.1, 3.9, 4.41, 5.2, 5.8, 5.9b, 5.12, 5.14, 5.20, 5.25, 5.26, 5.29, 5.36, 5.38, 5.40, 5.42, 5.43, 5.45, 5.46, 6.21, 6.80, 6.81, 6.122, 6.129, 6.134, 6.144, 6.147, 6.158, 6.163, 6.164; Empics/Aubrey Washington: Figure 4.61c; Empics/Matthew Ashton: Figure 4.53; Empics/Michael Steele: Figures 4.61b, 4.62; Empics/Neal Simpson: Figure 4.58; Empics/Peter Robinson: Figure 4.15; Empics/Ross Kinaird: Figure 4.20; Empics/Tony Marshall: Figures 4.14, 4.31, 4.44b, 4.60; Hulton Getty: Figures 1.1, 1.5, 1.8, 1.20, 1.60, 1.69, 4.34, 4.48; Hutchison Picture Library/F. Greene: Figure 4.27; Hutchison Picture Library/Mary Jelliffe: Figure 4.33; Mary Evans Picture Library: Figures 1.2, 1.56, 1.73; NUJ: Figure 2.51; Popperfoto: Figures 1.71, 4.44a, 4.54; Popperfoto/Reuters: Figure 4.47; Punch: Figure 1.6; The Military Picture Library: Figure 5.18; Topham Picturepoint: Figures 1.15, 4.56, 6.93, 6.94.

The publishers have made every effort to contact copyright holders. However, if any material has been incorrectly acknowledged, the publishers would be pleased to correct this at the earliest opportunity.

Cover photographs by: Alan Edwards (top), Corbis (middle), Actionplus/Neil Tingle (bottom left), Allsport/Dave Rogers (bottom right)

Tel: 01865 888058 www.heinemann.co.uk

Contents

UNIT 3: EXERCISE AND TRAINING

UNIT 4: GLOBAL TRENDS IN INTERNATIONAL SPORT

UNIT 5: REFINING PERFORMANCE

UNIT 6: SCIENTIFIC PRINCIPLES OF EXERCISE AND PERFORMANCE

General Introduction

Introduction

As a student following the Edexcel GCE Physical Education specification you will share with your fellow students (and teachers) a common interest in, enthusiasm for and enjoyment of the study of physical education and sport.

The study of this subject will provide you with the learning opportunities and experiences which will enhance your understanding of physical performance by learning in, learning about, and learning through physical activities.

You will realise by now that physical education is a multi-faceted discipline which encompasses a variety of practical and theoretical areas. This book is unique in its specification-orientated approach to help you to gain the knowledge, skills and understanding to succeed in both the theory and practical elements of the course. The book is presented in a format which 'mirrors' that of the specification in order to assist you in a methodical approach to study. This format should also assist you in the preparation of a systematic revision programme in the period leading up to AS and/or A2 examinations.

How the book is organized

The text is presented in six Units (or chapters):

Unit 1: The social basis of sport
Unit 2: Enhancing performance
Unit 3: Exercise and training
Unit 4: Global trends in international sport
Unit 5: Refining performance
Unit 6: Scientific principles of exercise and performance.

Units 1, 2 and 3 address the AS components of the Edexcel specification while Units 4, 5 and 6 cover the content relevant for A2. Students following the full A level course should expect to refer back to earlier Units, particularly in connection with the synoptic aspects of Units 4b and 6c.

How the Units are structured

Each Unit has a short introduction which explains the its aims, content and assessment requirements as well as links to other Units of study.

Each Unit contains a number of tasks, most of which ask you for a written or oral response, while others encourage investigation of topics relevant to the specification. These tasks are intended to support and reinforce your learning by testing your understanding of the material to which they refer and in some cases challenge you to apply this understanding to 'real life' situations.

Some tasks will also be appropriate for key skills (available from September 2000) and suggest presentations which may be addressed in a way that complies with key skill requirements in 'communication', 'application of number' or 'information technology'. Key skills address a wider range of activity but the Edexcel specification focuses on the three given above.

In the body of the text in each Unit you will find that certain words or phrases are in **bold**, indicating that they have some particular significance. At the end of each Unit (or in some cases each section within a Unit) you will find a box containing a list of key words and phrases which have occurred in that Unit or section and which should merit your particular attention.

It should be apparent that your success in the modular examinations (AS and/or A2) will depend on how well you can apply your knowledge to practical situations. The review questions listed at the end of each Unit (or sometimes each section within a Unit) provide both an opportunity to review the material in that Unit and an indication of the type of question that could appear in those modular examinations. Where questions are synoptic in nature it is essential that responses embrace the content of other Units (A2 only) and you should be prepared at all times to review the contents of these other Units. It is a good idea to 'read ahead' from time to time so you can develop an awareness of how the content of each Unit interrelates with that of other Units.

This awareness of the interrelation between Units is particularly important when dealing with synoptic questions. It is also important that you understand that synoptic questions will be framed in such a way as to allow your option in Unit 6 to be included in your responses.

Further reading

At best, a course text can be a very good 'signpost' in helping you in your study. Successful students will almost always have done some additional reading in order to broaden their subject knowledge. The text references at the end of each Unit in this book can help here. The first list indicates the sources consulted by the authors in the course of their writing, while the second is there to give you a list of texts to broaden your own study. These lists are not intended to be exclusive or restrictive and your own teachers may be able to recommend others that are either just as appropriate or more easily obtainable

Finally, the Advanced GCE in Physical Education has clear links with the Advanced GNVQ in Leisure and Recreation and the BTEC National Diploma in Sports Science. Students following these courses can utilize the information gained from this book in their other studies.

Unit 1

The social basis of sport and recreation

Introduction to Unit 1

This unit requires you to investigate the historical, cultural and contemporary basis of sport, recreation and physical education. In doing so, you will develop a greater understanding of the role that sport plays in modern society and the provisions that are necessary for this to happen.

The role of physical education is also investigated, in terms of its own intrinsic value and its relationship to sport and recreation. The level and nature of government involvement in terms of material provision and infrastructural development is also crucial. Your study should provide the basis of a sound analysis of both sport and recreation in the UK and a developing awareness of the European perspective, including the role of the European parliament in the development of sporting and recreational policy across the whole of Europe.

Within the context of a social analysis, the identification of likely disadvantaged and/or target groups is central to an understanding of how reformative analysis and policies are formed and implemented.

Social factors influence both élite performance and levels of mass participation and any analysis should examine these social phenomena in both the domestic, European and global contexts. (The latter is covered in Unit 4.)

With this purpose in mind, Section 1B uses the case of the Olympic Games to further examine social issues as they arise in this broader context. Such matters as freedom/ constraint and the consequent opportunity and provision made for Olympic performers varies greatly and often reflects contentious issues such as gender, ethnicity and/or social class.

This Olympic case study is set in a developing historical context. This will allow you to identify, examine and account for such changes that have occurred over time; or indeed those that have not.

In both sections of this Unit you should have access to on-going resource material as many of the areas under review are contemporary and there is plenty of printed and media material around. Local study of current provision and local sports history should prove a very fruitful and rewarding avenue of investigation. It may considerably enhance both personal achievement and satisfaction in addition to potential examination performance.

A knowledge of the provision (both locally and nationally) of your selected activity will be of considerable help with your IPP in Unit 2. The study of this Unit as a whole will provide a crucial link with your chosen alternative social setting within the global context under review in Unit 4.

As in this Unit, Unit 4 will continue the approach through the historical to the contemporary perspective. This will allow you to develop comparisons between two cultures which can then be expanded for synoptic analysis in Section 4B.

Unit assessment

The assessment of Unit 1 will be by means of a one-and-a-quarter hour written paper in which you will be required to answer *one* question from Section A and *one* question from Section B: from a choice of questions.

Section A: UK and the European context

1. Cultural background

Social analysis and mainstream values

Before the **Industrial Revolution**, an analysis of social class in the United Kingdom would have revealed a clear distinction between those who 'had' and those who 'had not'. On the one hand there were the gentry and aristocracy who possessed large estates. Their wealth was produced from their land in the form of harvest and cattle to be sold at market; and in rents from tenant farmers who worked the land on their behalf.

At the other end of the social scale were the peasantry, who owned little apart from a few personal belongings. They worked for an immediate superior in return for a cottage to live in. This was 'tied' to their continued ability to work – if they couldn't work, they lost their home. They earned a paltry income, either from an agreed share of produce; or from selling the small amount that was not considered to be in the master's domain; or from a combination of various sources including, eventually, the payment of a wage in return for labour.

Generally speaking, these two extremes of social class had no bridge between them. The tenant farmer whose operations were on a big enough scale often had pretensions of bettering himself socially. This was sometimes so of the churchman, the estate manager and others who existed in the 'no-man's-land' between these two social extremes.

The class structure became a little more blurred in larger towns, cathedral cities and ports, where the legal and clerical professions and those of the merchant and businessman, inhabited the area between upper and lower class, dependent upon their own success or their immediate past history. Close family connections often meant a climb up the social ladder – or otherwise.

The population of England in the eighteenth and early nineteenth centuries was a largely rural one. Master and peasant were tied to the land by its capacity to produce. For the master, this meant the living he had come to expect and for the peasant the living he had been bred to believe was all he deserved. The remnants of a medieval feudal system ensured that everyone knew his or her place. Neither education nor social reform had arrived with sufficient impact to raise questions about what was often referred to as 'the natural order of things'. The squire or his agents and the local parson knew everyone and everyone knew them. Such men maintained social order, often arbitrarily, in closed and small communities.

The move to the towns

This so-called 'natural order' was to change particularly in the last half of the eighteenth century and the first half of the nineteenth. The development of mechanisation with the Industrial Revolution meant that many thousands of agricultural labourers were no longer needed. Also the growth of foreign imports produced competition and many farming gentry were forced to leave their land or drastically change to the new methods of agricultural production.

The technical revolution that produced steam power and mechanisation as well as the canals to transport both materials and finished goods eventually gave birth to the **railways** and the factories and workshops of industrial England. It also drew men into the towns to find work since they had lost their jobs on the land. It was this process of economic and industrial change that was to have a major influence on social change, and consequently upon patterns of recreation.

Before the Industrial Revolution, the social and church calendar had been the basis of many of the festivities and recreations of the village. This was slowly eroded by the huge demographic shift to the towns and the growing influence of the factory and the organisation of work there. In the countryside, work was regulated by the seasons and the maypole, the harvest festivities, the church wake and various other opportunities for recreation and 'a bit of sport'. Many of these activities did not transport well – if at all – to the smoke and grime of the industrial town. In those towns, particularly in the North and the Midlands, the factory whistle regulated the hours of work and the new masters wanted a return on their invested capital. The landless labourer, newly migrated to an urban landscape of which he knew little, had to work long hours for little pay in order to keep a roof over his head.

The social context

As with most aspects of life nothing takes place in a vacuum. It is crucial to an understanding of the context in which sport and recreation (and later physical education) took place to understand the social and living conditions, first of the rural countryside, and then the industrial town.

For most people, the idyllic and mythical world of the harvest and the meadow was not the reality of rural life. Living conditions were

▲ **Figure 1.1** Life in the slums: Birmingham c.1875

hard and poverty and disease took their toll. There was, however, both space where people could recreate, and the time to do so, within the system of life and work in the countryside. In the expanding towns of the growing industrial revolution people had little time away from the factory. There was also little space, as the urban landscape gobbled up common land and ancient meadow as well as polluting the rivers and streams.

Without these essential components of leisure – time and space – many people found that life with little food, poor water, lack of basic sanitary arrangements and inadequate housing in the slums (Figure 1.1), was harmful to both their physical and spiritual health.

The stress and difficulties faced by the labouring classes caused many men to resort to the public house and the alleyway for their recreation. Drink was for many the only means of escape from a life which had few of its former pleasures. Wives and children went to work in the factory or workshop in order to supplement the family's meagre existence.

The urban middle class

The most apparent change in the social class structure that arose out of the Industrial Revolution was the emergence of the urban middle class.

They filled the gap in the social class system and provided a 'social bridge' between upper and lower classes. In practice, and often to their dismay, they found themselves sandwiched between the traditions and culture of the gentry, to which class many of them aspired, and the boorish and brutish ways of the labouring classes, whom they detested.

Table 1.1 Instruments of control before and after 1800

Rural life (pre-1800)	Urban life (after 1800)
Local squire/gentry	No traditional social hierarchy
Curate/Church	Churches ineffective as control agencies
Local population	Defragmented population

Yet it was out of this new class of industrialists, entrepreneurs, professional men and municipal managers that new ways and values emerged. At first they were self-interested but gradually they assumed the mantle of social and moral responsibility for their communities (see Table 1.1 on page 6). In addition, clerics and the schoolmasters also had a significant influence in the day-to-day lives of their own and subordinate classes.

Attitudes to sport, leisure and recreation

Attitudes to sport and recreation, as well as *definitions* of sport and recreation, changed drastically during this time, particularly in the last fifty years of the nineteenth century.

The seasons and the countryside no longer influenced the recreational activities for most of the people, although the leisured classes (or gentry) continued to hunt, fish and shoot as countless generations had done before them (Figure 1.2).

In the countryside, the hunt, the race meeting, the village or estate cricket match and a whole range of rural sports continued as they had before. Sport was part of a long established pattern – of village and estate – and had continued only partially constrained throughout the Puritan persecutions of the sixteenth and seventeenth centuries. The lord of the manor or the local squire was master of his own domain and the activities there. He was not to be dictated to by some petty, stiff-collared curate who preached and practised abstinence.

The influence of the Church

Often the labourers on an estate would receive some protection from their master when taking part in his own recreational pursuits. However, when taking part in their own, they often fell foul of the clergy and had little choice but to obey their local priest.

The growing influence of the Church meant that many church wakes were closed down when they became too far removed from their original purpose of commemorating the consecration of a church. The same fate befell other traditional festivities whether or not associated with the Church. Recreation had to be purposeful. Any association with drink, gambling or licentious acts were swiftly condemned.

In the towns, many recreations were either banned or severely curtailed through the zealousness of churchmen and local 'worthies'. Those activities that survived did so either by adopting new forms or by going under ground to escape the hard line attitudes of evangelicalism. The local watch committee regulated the use of the streets and the cleric saw that the Sabbath was kept holy.

As a result, unruly and riotous behaviour was removed from view. Consequently the back room or cellar of the ale-house became the place where people could spend their leisure time in the way they chose to.

Bear-baiting, which had once been a public attraction, declined into oblivion. Dog-fighting, cock-fighting and rat-catching, also outlawed by the **Blood Sports Act** of 1834, survived because they were more easily hidden from prying eyes.

'Base and evil pastimes'

It would be misleading to think that these kinds of leisure activities only belonged to the labouring classes. There were those of the

▲ *Figure 1.2* A gentleman at leisure: his wealth and his land gave him two essentials for recreation – time and space

upper classes who took great delight in supporting and patronising what the middle classes often referred to as 'base and evil pastimes'. Local newspapers often reported arrests at illegal cockfights with comments such as, 'and among those arrested were captains, gentlemen and county magistrates'.

Propriety was everything. Public behaviour was moderated until it conformed to the new rules of urban order and the incessant march of 'good manners' spread from town to village. Public drunkenness was frowned upon – indeed penalised – and church attendance on Sundays was necessary in order to gain social acceptability. The new forms of sport had not yet arrived and recreation had become the preserve of those who had time, a little money and were prepared to conform to the new social order, often in order to help secure personal advancement.

An overview of sport before 1800

Man has always needed to survive, and been warlike to defend himself. He has also been drawn to ritual and had the capacity to invent and accept physical challenges. Table 1.2 outlines the way in which these natural skills and activities gave rise to the origins of sport.

Table 1.2 *A simplistic view of the origins of sport*

	Sphere of life	Activity
Survival	The need to hunt, fish and defend personal territory	Weaponry and personal combat
Military	War, service and need to be be skilled in use of weapons	Personal weaponry used used for war
Ritual	Festivals, worship ritual	Ritual, fertility, physical prowess sacrifice, contest
Inventive	From play, challenge and the need to 'contest' and 'invent'	'invasion', throwing, catching, dodging and target games

The development of combat sports

Since before medieval times, combat sports were important both as training for war and in order to prepare young men to be knights in the service of their king or their lord. Their training also included wrestling and gymnastics.

The medieval joust or tournament was part of this preparation but also a festive custom and used to settle matters of honour as well. Whilst the broadsword and the lance figured were the weapons of the knight, the freeman was the master of the longbow and the peasant relied on the quarterstaff, sometimes sharpened to a point for use as a makeshift lance. 'Tilting at the ring' and tilting at human dummy figures was an aspect of a knight's training that was also popular with the lower classes (Figure 1.3). Those ancient fairs that survived both the passage of time and puritanical zeal often had such events. They were held on horseback for those of high enough status and on foot for those who were not.

All these weapons had their uses in recreation and survival as well as in war. While the knight would hunt for sport, the freeman and the serf relied on their weapons for food for themselves and for their masters, as well as for their own defence. The quarterstaff was the poor man's broadsword and along with the back-swording or single stick became a substitute for the finer weaponry of the upper classes.

By late Tudor times the use of gunpowder had caused many of these weapons to be

▲ *Figure 1.3* *Tilting at the sack: a popular nineteenth-century recreation of the medieval tilt yard*

obsolete for defence and the crossbow had superseded the longbow. However, the recreational and ceremonial use of many former weapons of war went on long after they had disappeared from the battlefield. Activities such as archery and broadswording continued as recreational and sporting activities (see Table below).

Recreations of the peasantry

An important point to think about is the developing social setting and how this affected the development of sports for the peasantry (Table 1.3).

Table 1.3 *Peasant recreations before 1800*

Activity	Participation
Blood sports	major participants in bear and bull-baiting, cock-fighting
Contests	back-swording, single sticks, quarterstaff, archery
Cricket	in village games or as invited players in gentry games
Festival games	strength contests, tilting, foot races, smock races for girls
Group/village games	'mob' games: football, hockey, hurling, shinty
Horse racing	jockeys, spectators and/or 'punters'
Hunting	attending the gentry as 'beaters', servants
Pedestrianism	retained professionals with gentry patronage
Prize-fighting	retained professionals with gentry patronage (wrestling in some regions): sometimes as part of festival games
Rebound games	much localised variation: use of church/pub wall, e.g. fives
Swimming (and boating)	boatmen and swimmers with gentry patronage: for cleanliness as well as recreation

Recreational characteristics

- **Localised cultural focus**
  Minimal communications meant that the village, the county town or London was the cultural focus depending on where you lived.
- **Occupational activities**
  Many recreations grew out of agriculture and cottage industries or the nature of courtly/feudal society within a locality.
- **Seasonal and church calendar**
  The rural and church calendar regulated many events. Some events were stopped or died out as a result of industrialisation. There was also limited free time for peasant recreation.
- **Lawlessness**
  Law and order problems grew with urban expansion. Property damage and unruly behaviour became more common and less acceptable.
- **Rituals/festivals**
  Many traditional festivals based on pagan rites (e.g. the maypole) were discouraged or stopped by Puritanism and religious zeal.
- **Limited codification (rules)**
  Poor communications and low levels of **literacy** restricted spread of codification (the rules of a game) beyond the local area.
- **Wagering**
  Both upper and lower classes indulged in betting and this was a feature of many recreational activities of both groups.

Although members of the gentry did not work in the way peasants and tradesmen did, they were often responsible for huge tracts of land – their own estates. Their recreations were centred largely upon these estates with fishing, hunting, shooting, coursing and cricket all available within easy reach.

If early codification (formalisation of rules) did occur it was often in activities patronised by the gentry, such as horseracing and cricket. This was because the gentry were much more freely mobile than the lower classes. This was the case until the development of cheap train excursions in the 1840s and 1850s.

Class and collaboration

Although the activities listed in Table 1.3 are mostly those of the peasant class, a small number involved both upper and lower classes collaboratively. The clearest example of this is cricket, where it was common for both classes to come together, almost as equals for the duration of a game.

Cricket was as much a game of the ordinary people as it was of the upper classes. Village matches would often involve the squire, the parson, the schoolmaster and a number of local village men combining to rebuff the challenge from a neighbouring village. It was also not uncommon for estate workers to be drafted into a team to entertain houseguests on their master's estate; or for men from the nearby village to bolster a team to play against a visiting gentry side.

In horse racing, the gentry rarely rode their own mounts. Retained (or kept) jockeys would ride on their master's behalf, often for a share of prize money in addition to their retainer. This was also a feature of footracing or pedestrianism and prize-fighting.

The gentry mostly took their pleasure from being involved as owners and onlookers rather than as participants, with cricket and hunting being perhaps the only exceptions.

Table 1.4 shows the activities in which the gentry took an interest. They bore some similarity to the peasant recreations listed in Table 1.3 but the gentry's role within them was often significantly different.

Venues for recreation and sport

The places where sporting events occurred were often used by both the upper and lower classes. The inn was a meeting place for local men and the range of pub and inn games was often promoted by the landlord in order to boost trade. Some inns had bowling greens attached or skittle alleys. 'Shove'a'penny' was a popular game and many inns also had quoit beds and held regular competitions.

The coaching inn

The **coaching inn** was particularly important in connection with prize-fights, race meetings, pedestrian matches and animal baiting. Members of the gentry (also known as 'the fancy') who were particularly keen on these

Table 1.4 Gentry recreations before 1800

Activity	Participation
Blood sports	similar to peasant activities but not as major participants: often as onlookers involved in wagers and sometimes as patrons
Combats	fencing as one of gentlemanly arts and for settlement of honour; sparring as form of self-defence only
Cricket	took part: with own class and as benevolent patrons of village/local teams
Fishing	took part: on own estate or on holidays; sometimes combined with swimming/boating
Horse racing	owners, patrons, but only exceptionally as riders
Hunting	took part: social status attached to ownership of land and horsemanship
Pedestrianism	as patrons: for professional runners/walkers, often with gambling for 'side-stakes'
Prize-fighting	as patrons: occasionally gentry took on known champions from outside their own class but this was fairly unusual
Racquets	took part: real tennis, only for the very wealthy, needing specialised facilities

sports would travel great distances to be at an event. The coaching inn, either near to the venue, or as a stopover point on the way, provided accommodation, stabling and possibly some sport. Many inns hosted prize-fights, or were the headquarters for a pedestrian contest. Often the landlord would hold the wagers but bookies would always put in an appearance where there was likely to be a large crowd of would-be punters.

The river

The river was essentially a source of food, and for the labouring classes it provided a place to bathe. However, where there were boatmen there were often races and sometimes swimming contests. Fishing rivers ran through private land and angling was the preserve of the gentry. The poorer classes were greatly restricted regarding where, and for what, they could fish.

The racecourse

Racecourses were on open or common land and not fenced off. Access was therefore open to all but the gentry maintained their distance from the lower classes by erecting grandstands for their exclusive use. Some racecourses were on heathland (e.g. Newmarket) whilst others were next to rivers as the river meadows were often common land. These were also favoured venues for prize-fights and baiting sports.

The road

The road (or path) was the scene of pedestrian contests. Famous pedestrians such as Captain Barclay or 'Deerfoot' would accept challenges with side bets and promised prize money, or they would attempt to beat ultra-distance records for a purse if they succeeded. Barclay once walked 1000 miles in 1000 hours to win a bet of £10,000.

The fairground

Many sports and recreations took place at the fairground. The boxing booth, the wrestling match and the single stick contests were common activities. The onion fair, the goose fair, the hiring or mop fair and the horse fair were all common and went back to the Middle Ages and before. Many of them were **Statute Fairs** held by royal decree and were amongst the most difficult to close down when the new middle class tastes found them unacceptable.

The baiting pit

The baiting pit or cock pit were often located in the inn but before the Blood Sports Act many were built in the open. Fairgrounds and market places were the most common sites of 'bull rings'. These rings were set into the ground and to which the bull or bear would be tethered before being set upon by dogs. Fighting with dogs and cock-fighting did survive (albeit illegally) when the Industrial Revolution brought a mass move to the towns.

The Age of Enlightenment

By the eighteenth century the cultural movement called the **Age of Enlightenment** had spread from the European continent, bringing with it revived interest in classical learning. It also brought about a change in the social structure, including the metamorphosis of the feudal knight into the country gentleman. Social status was everything and for those who wished to be seen as being 'of quality' it became important to acquire a new range of social and recreational skills. European tastes also brought the fencing salon to England and mastery of the epee and the foil (fencing weaponry) were necessary social accomplishments as well as a form of personal defence. Gymnastics was also popular as a means of physical improvement, with Guts Muths' *Gymnastik für die Yugend* (Gymnastics for Youth) published in 1797.

Eighteenth-century sports remained largely rural, which reflected the distribution of the population at that time. The gentry took the opportunities afforded by their estates and hunted both for sport and social status.

The role of the church

For many centuries, celebrations and festivals had traditionally revolved around the Church and its feast days. In the seventeenth and eighteenth centuries, following the rise of Puritanism, the over-zealous clergyman caused many popularised festivals and pastimes to be stopped because they were seen to go against constraining moral values of the Church.

Attitudes varied a great deal locally. It was not uncommon for young men of one parish to move into others on Sundays where the restrictions on Sabbath activities were less rigorously enforced. The church wake was traditionally a festival commemorating the consecration of the church. It was celebrated annually along with a range of activities, many of which were recreational. Often these were stopped because they had become more recreational than religious.

Many of these traditional festivals attracted the less desirable social elements and were associated with such practices as gambling,

▲ **Figure 1.4** *Boys often copied adults – or invented games themselves. A church wall or ruin made an improvised 'court' for a game of fives*

drinking, prostitution and licentious games. This left the clergy with little alternative but to severely restrict their nature or in some cases to close them down altogether. In some rural areas where the wakes did survive, the local gentry may have had influence with the Church authorities; or the fairs were saved to safeguard commercial interests on the basis that trade would be severely damaged if they closed. The **Fairs Act** of 1871, whilst not intended primarily for this purpose, was often used by over-zealous clerics to persuade local magistrates to close down a particular activity.

On a more positive note, church precincts often provided much valued recreational space and walls and buttresses were used for ball games, including localised variations of the game of fives (Figure 1.4).

Types of recreational activities

Festival activities

When people were gathered together to celebrate festivals, they could expect to see various recreational activities going on. These **festival activities**, as they were known, varied from region to region, but would have included some of the following:

- aquatic games
- athletic games
- combat games
- country pursuits
- contest games
- court games
- invasion games
- target games

Court games

Court games, of whatever form, were the province of the wealthy until almost the twentieth century, when the provision of facilities in towns made such games accessible to ordinary people. Real (or Royal) tennis was played only by the very wealthy although peasants set up simplified outdoor versions of the game. Badminton and tennis did not materialise until the 1870s and although not relevant to any analysis prior to 1800, they became the province of the middle class and their suburban lawns when they did arrive.

'Mob' activities

Before the growth and influence of the public schools in the nineteenth century, invasion games such as street football were largely raucous 'mob' activities based on local custom (Figure 1.5). As with other popular recreations, the drinking and gambling that surrounded the games did little to endear them to respectable local residents. They often used this fact, and the considerable damage to property that frequently occurred, to have them stopped. The land on which many games had formerly been played had become enclosed or built upon and owners of property did not want their land being trampled upon by hundreds of dissolute males fuelled by drink and a licence to run riot.

▲ **Figure 1.5** *Street football in the early nineteenth century*

Games such as that in Ashbourne, Derbyshire, survived, as did the Hallaton Bottle Game and the Haxey Hood Game in Leicestershire. Some of these were associated with religious festivals or rites, which may have been their key to survival, but many were lost. Those that continue today probably do so because their value to the local tourist trade outweighs any other considerations.

Sport after 1800

The main thrust of the Industrial Revolution started in the middle of the eighteenth century and continued through the nineteenth. During this time, the population shift to the towns and cities that was triggered by industrialisation saw England move from being an agricultural economy to an industrial one. The changes were not only economic. The structure of society also changed which influenced recreational patterns across the classes.

The urban revolutions

With the move to the towns, the pattern of recreation for the labouring classes changed drastically, but it was some time before their new industrial masters and the authorities in the towns where they lived began to address this fact. The delay in the development of any meaningful municipal infrastructures meant that for some time there was a certain amount of social disorder.

The pace of industrial change

At first many working people refused to be denied the leisure activities they had enjoyed before. The institution of a day of recreation, known as 'Saint Monday' appeared, sometimes in different forms, in industrial towns up and down the country.

With the exception of the large textile areas of the north of England, where steam power did take hold quite quickly, much of England's industrial development took place in small workshops. Many workers were paid by the piece – doing 'piece-work' as it became widely known. They took the day off – often on Mondays – to attend the prize-fights, baiting contests, race meetings and pedestrian races held in the locality – just as they always had. To make up their pay, they simply worked harder towards the end of the week.

Eventually steam power became widespread and workers were then harnessed by the factory whistle for sixty or more hours per week. As the towns grew, the former recreation spaces disappeared to make way for factories, workshops and cheap housing (Figure 1.6). Municipal parks or private pleasure gardens were often strategically placed to provide a screen between slum areas and more genteel ones, allowing the middle classes pleasant walks in pleasant surroundings. Ironically, although intended for everyone's use, such places were often closed on Sundays – the only day the labouring classes were freed from work.

Social change

Eventually the lower classes lost the two most valuable recreational assets they had enjoyed in rural villages – time and space.

In addition to this, the attitude of the new middle class to leisure activities was very different from that associated with the old 'Merrie England'. Their lives were based on serious purpose, the creation of capital, and good Christian living. To this end recreations had to be seen as constructive and worthwhile in order to be acceptable. These qualities became implicitly associated with the term recreation.

▲ *Figure 1.6* Recreational space was in short supply in industrialised areas – a situation reflected (and slightly exaggerated!) in this Edwardian cartoon

▲ *Figure 1.7* A 'respectable' trip to the seaside: with the advent of cheap rail transport such an excursion was no longer only for the upper classes.

Mass transport

The development of the railways in the 1840s and of cheap fares had considerable benefits for the ordinary worker. An escape to the countryside or the seaside became possible. The mountains and the **seaside resort**, both the domains of the upper classes and later the middle classes, had now become accessible to ordinary workers and their families. This was sometimes to the annoyance of those upper classes who found themselves sharing their formerly exclusive resorts with people they considered their social inferiors (Figure 1.7).

The effect of transport on sport

Reliable forms of mass transport also had an influence on the development of sport. Regular fixtures became possible over greater distances, for those who had the time and the money to enjoy them. The growth of popular literature and greater literacy meant that information about events could be spread much more effectively. Organisations such as the YMCA (founded in 1844), and later its sister organisation for young women, the YWCA (1859), played a crucial role in broadening access to sport. Branches in the larger cities, such as Birmingham, Liverpool, Leeds and Manchester, provided gymnasium facilities for their members. They also had a range of recreational sections devoted to activities as diverse as rambling and football; cricket and photography.

The nature of sport, controlled by the new middle class, became codified (standardised into rules). It also embodied the principles of fair play and Christian endeavour espoused in the country's public schools (see pages 14–17). With the gaining of the **Saturday half day** and shorter working hours that resulted from the Factories Act of 1867 and the Industrial Relations Act of 1871, it gradually became possible for ordinary working men to return to their former recreations. These sports were, of course, much changed by the new middle-class guardians of morality.

The move towards rationalised sports

The development of **rationalised sports**, with formalised rules and codes of behaviour, began in the public schools. They were transmitted by 'old boys', returning to their former communities, and by the schoolmaster and the cleric moving to provincial towns and parishes. The controlling middle classes saw to it that the standards of play were their own standards. The new sports governing bodies were set up to ensure that this remained the case. The sanctioning and control of sport had passed from the parson and the squire into new reforming hands.

TASK

a What was the difference between popular recreations and rationalised sports?

b Working in groups of three or four, list *ten* popular recreations and show how they became rationalised.

2. The development of physical education

Sport and public schools in the nineteenth century

Physical education *per se* was not the key factor behind the development of sport in Britain's public schools. It was used by headmasters to gain and maintain social order within their communities.

The 'right to play'

The insistence of boys on their 'right to play' had caused serious breakdowns of control, to such an extent that in some instances the military or militia had to be called in to put down such disturbances.

Their 'right to play' included their wish to carry on their recreational activities but it could also mean 'to do just as they liked', including frequenting the local ale houses where neither their presence nor their behaviour were always welcome:

The riot I mentioned in my last [letter] at Winchester is all over, and no one expelled. It was a formidable thing. For they had several brace of pistols. It began, as I hear by the landlord of the White Hart, desirous of some of the Commoners who were drinking at his house, not to drink any more but to go home ...

MacDonald Fraser,
The World of the Public School

Harsh environment

The masters had little interest – and much distaste – for the rowdy and raucous recreational preferences of their charges. They also had little to do with the boys outside lesson times. Such places were spartan, harsh environments. They were remote in the sense that most boys were boarders and the schools were often criticised for their teaching of a classical curriculum in an increasingly technical world. Beatings were common by both masters and prefects (Figure 1.8). The system

▲ *Figure 1.8* *The English public school was not a place for the faint-hearted*

of fagging, whereby junior boys were at the 'beck and call' of prefects and were expected to perform all kinds of chores, was accepted by most boys on the basis that as they moved up the school 'it would be their turn'.

Channelling excess energies

Thomas Arnold, the legendary headmaster of **Rugby School**, was instrumental in the transformation of such places. He developed a purposeful use for recreations and established a means by which the boys could channel their excess energies. Much emphasis was placed on team games. However, this did not reflect any particular fondness on Arnold's part for such recreations. In fact he preferred swimming, gymnastics and walking in the hills of the Lake District.

Arnold did, however, recognise that the boys placed value on this type of recreation and that it could therefore be most useful as an agent of **social control**. At the same time it developed other desirable character-building qualities in the boys.

Christian virtues

The notion of **athleticism**, where Christian virtues are promoted through the 'physical', emerged from the growing popularity of games and sports. It was used as a way of bringing what were known as **muscular Christian** values into the lives of Britain's public schoolboys. This new form of manly and acceptable exercise taught loyalty, integrity, obedience, magnanimity in victory, dignity in defeat and, above all, fair play. These values were all part of the code by which boys were controlled and by which they in turn would eventually control others.

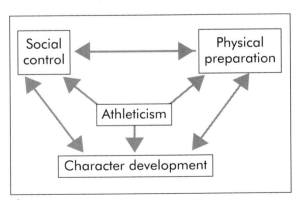

▲ *Figure 1.9* *Components/outcomes of the notion of athleticism*

The idea of Christian virtue had been a central plank of rationalised thinking for some time. To this was added the concept of manly virtue, or **manliness**. The idea that there could be a physical aspect to Christian living was soon taken up in all the public schools, and by the boys themselves out into the wider world. Finally, the quality of **leadership** was tested on the playing field in preparation for the role of many public schoolboys in later life.

The introduction of rules

In order that they should become acceptable, the nature of the games had to change. The image of young 'rowdies' chasing a ball around a field was not one that either Arnold or his contemporaries could support. The introduction of rules was essential to social control (Figure 1.9). The Christian ethic of 'fair play' ensured that it was seen as honourable to play within those rules and unacceptable to do otherwise. Thus, the energies of the boys were diverted into what were seen as worthwhile pursuits: not essentially because they were physical but this happened to provide a useful diversion from alternative 'less desirable' pursuits (Figure 1.10).

The captains of cricket and football were held in great esteem by both masters and boys. The **games ethic** was also important as a training medium for the officers and leaders of the next generation as it helped develop tactical and strategic skills. The harsh existence, the fagging system and the subjugation of oneself to a greater cause were all seen as entirely appropriate in the training of Christian young men.

The growing popularity of the nation's public schools led to the growth of a new generation of such establishments. Insufficient places in the great old public schools meant that others such as Marlborough, Malvern, Clifton and Wellington etc. were founded to fill this need. A whole generation of public schools offered the sons of the newly prosperous middle classes a similar education to that enjoyed by the sons of the aristocracy.

Other ancient grammar schools and foundations were adapted to copy this model and a whole host of endowed establishments took on the image of the new educational ideal. These included those schools endowed by various monarchs, and named after a King Edward, a Queen Elizabeth, a King Henry, etc. They became (largely) 'day-boy' images of their more renowned boarding counterparts.

Although team games remained the central plank of athleticism, the range of activities at these schools (Figure 1.11) also included the purely athletic and combative, as well as swimming and boating, country pursuits, and gymnastic activities.

The image of the Victorian public school is preserved in many contemporary publications. The best known of these is *Tom Brown's Schooldays*, published in 1857 by Thomas Hughes, who was a pupil at Rugby School during Arnold's time. Hughes went on to become part of the great reforming influence of that time. He was instrumental in the foundation of the National Olympian Association in 1866 and in the Amateur

▲ **Figure 1.10** *With the introduction of rules games became constructive. Touchlines and striped tops brought control and identity*

▲ **Figure 1.11** *Players of the Eton field games, 1865. Uniforms were in but the field game still had its own, rather than national, rules*

▲ **Figure 1.12** *Tom consoles Arthur – an illustration from Tom Brown's Schooldays*

Athletic Club, a forerunner of the Amateur Athletic Association, at about the same time.

Hughes was one of three brothers, all of whom went to Rugby School. It is just possible that the character of 'young Arthur' (Figure 1.12), placed in Brown's charge upon his arrival at Rugby, was in fact Hughes' own younger brother who arrived there when only ten years old.

Physical education – by military intent?

It is generally accepted that physical education on the continent influenced its development in Britain. There is debate – as there was in the nineteenth century – about whether the development of physical education in public schools was educationally derived or the outcome of a wider agenda.

During Queen Victoria's reign (1819–1901), the British Empire was involved in some twenty-eight campaigns from the war in Crimea to others that were mere skirmishes in comparison. The army looked to the public schools to fulfil the need for officers. The meeting called by Lord Elcho at the Thatched House Tavern in 1860 (to discuss the introduction of drill into public schools) is often referred to as the point from which physical education (training) began to figure prominently. This, in fact, was more concerned with military than physical training. In the eyes of many, this pointed to the fact that it was militarism which drove the development of physical education in public schools rather than educational concern.

Archibald MacLaren

The outcome of Lord Elcho's intervention was the establishment of the Officer Training Corps as opposed to programmes of physical education. However, the involvement and intervention of **Archibald MacLaren** did much to develop the physical rather than the purely militaristic aspects of training.

MacLaren was a Scotsman who had trained in France. He was a gymnast and a fencer and had opened a gymnasium in Oxford in the late 1850s. His involvement in the formation of the Army Gymnastic Staff at Aldershot did two things. First, it provided trained instructors to work with enlisted men in the regiments at home and abroad. It also created a great number of men who, on leaving the army, were appointed to public schools as both drill instructors and teachers of gymnastics. In one sense, therefore, it might be said that both military and educational agendas were equally well served.

MacLaren was also hugely influential in the building of gymnasia in public schools from the 1860s (Figure 1.13). His model became the norm for all gymnasia constructed before Swedish gymnastics rose to prominence towards the end of the nineteenth century. Although the first known school gymnasium was at Uppingham in 1859, it was closely followed by MacLaren's first school gymnasium

▲ **Figure 1.13** *MacLaren's first military gymnasium at Aldershot in 1861. This was to be followed by many others, including those in several of England's leading public schools*

▲ **Figure 1.14** *The Harrow Shooting Eight, 1875. The influence of the Officers' Mess is fairly evident*

at Radley College, Oxford, in 1860, where he taught gymnastics to the boys. He also built a gymnasium at Rugby School in 1872.

Sport and Oxbridge

The next stage in the development of rationalised, acceptable sport occurred with the passage of public schoolboys along that well-trodden track from school to university.

Early match fixtures between public schools ran up against problems because of the highly localised rules developed within each school. Some standardisation had occurred although much of this was in the form of individualised arbitration prior to each match. Games were played 'by agreement'. In the first half one set of rules was followed and in the second half players followed the rules of the visiting team.

For a truly national range of sports to flourish, some standardisation of both rules and playing area was necessary. Many of these early national rules came out of the **Oxbridge 'melting pot'**. It was so called because the major universities of O<u>x</u>ford and Cam<u>b</u>ridge took boys from all the major public schools, each bringing their own sets of rules. The Football Association (1863) and the Rugby Football Union (1871) and their respective rules emerged largely from discussions and developments at the two major universities.

Further developments

For the rest of the nineteenth century and much of the first part of the twentieth, Oxbridge athletes figured largely in the for-

mation of rules, national associations and international and domestic amateur sports teams. Many of Britain's first Olympic competitors in 1896 had connections with Oxbridge and the English public schools (see page 62).

Most of today's governing bodies of sport were formed during the last half of the nineteenth century with former public schoolboys from Oxford and Cambridge being involved in nearly all of them. The University Boat Race, held on the Thames each spring, together with corresponding fixtures in athletics, cricket, football, and rugby, formed major features of the British sporting calendar for many decades. By the time that participation in sport was again a realistic possibility for ordinary people those sports were now associated with moral values and good breeding and had been stripped of all their former 'mob' characteristics.

It is only relatively recently that these traditional university events have been overshadowed by those with rather more mass appeal, although the boat race continues to hold its fascination as a major viewing spectacle.

The diffusion of the new concept

An appreciation of the role of the public schools and universities in the spreading or diffusion of the new concept of sport is crucial to an understanding of the nature of current sport and sporting issues. A brief analysis gives an insight into the way in which class has influenced sporting development. It also provides

▲ **Figure 1.15** *Rugby School – MacLaren built the gymnasium here in 1872*

Table 1.5 Agencies of diffusion

	Way in which new concept was spread
Masters in non-public schools	Through spread of interest in sport in a wider community of boys
Clergy	Through use of parish/school as a base for spreading the 'muscular Christian' gospel through games
The professions	Through development of 'old boys' clubs to allow a continuing involvement with their own class
Industry	Through the benevolent provision of recreational facilities in the workplace
Civil service	Through the development of civil service and 'old boys' networks
Military service	Through use of sport as training adjunct and the organisation of inter-unit sport

the basis for understanding the cause of many current issues and confrontations in sporting philosophy and infrastructure.

The most obvious means of that diffusion was the practice of former pupils returning to their old public schools as masters and reinforcing sporting values and traditions in doing so. It became customary for masters, particularly housemasters, to be appointed for their sporting ability and enthusiasm. This was to ensure that sporting and athletic values were transmitted to each succeeding generation of pupils.

Some former pupils, or old boys, followed a different career course. In doing so, the diffusion of a sporting philosophy, and the values it encouraged, was extended much more broadly – in both the social and geographical sense.

As can be seen from Table 1.5, former public schoolboys, many of whom would have

been Oxbridge graduates, went into a wide range of callings, and took with them their love of sport and its attendant values of Christian morality and honest endeavour. Although the social diffusion of these principles would not have reached the lower classes directly, a gradual 'trickling down' through the class structure ensured that, eventually, such standards became the norm.

Table 1.6 The diffusion of the new concept in the Empire

	Way in which new concept was spread
Clergy/missionaries	Through work/teaching in the colonies of the Empire and teaching sport to the indigenous population alongside the gospel
Colonial/civil service	Through development of colonial sporting organisations to allow a continuing involvement with their own class and any indigenous comparable class
Military service	Through use of sport as training adjunct and the organisation of inter-unit sport for morale; also the involvement of local recruits of indigenous origin

▲ **Figure 1.16** Playing badminton in India c1900. Note the 'shuttle boys'

Diffusion through the Empire

On a rather broader front, the influence of such young men was taken to the far corners of the British Empire in very much the same way. Careers in the Colonial Service and a range of other callings (as indicated in Table 1.6) ensured that pretty much the same process of diffusion was repeated in India, South Africa, Australia and New Zealand: in fact, wherever the British flag flew.

By the end of Queen Victoria's reign at the beginning of the twentieth century, a vast part of the globe was under British colonial rule. Those who served abroad took with them their sporting philosophy and its values (Figure 1.16).

European and military influences

The process of cultural diffusion was not just one-way traffic out of Britain. Earlier mention has been made of European influences from the Age of Enlightenment (see page 11). Pages 58–61 look at the influence of Baron Pierre de Coubertin that came from his interest in the sports and games of the English public schools and the athletics festivals of Much Wenlock and Dover's Hill.

German gymnastics

Of specific importance to the development of programmes of physical education were the German gymnastics of **Guts Muths** and **Jahn** and later the Swedish gymnastics of **Ling**. German gymnastics arrived in Britain via P. H. Clias in 1822 and Carl Vöelker a little later, in 1825. German gymnastics had the greater following until the work and influence of **Martina Österberg** found favour in the last twenty years of the nineteenth century.

German gymnastics formed the basis of much of the work of Archibald MacLaren at Oxford. It also influenced the style of the gymnasia built in the country's public and proprietary schools prior to the 1880s and 1890s, as well as military gymnasia.

At this time, physical education programmes consisted mainly of gymnastics and drill and were treated as entirely separate from games activities. Some authorities felt that whilst games were fine for the development of such qualities as leadership and 'esprit de corps', they were not an ideal medium for systematised physical development.

In the public schools and the growing number of independent schools it was often the Officer Training Corps (see page 17) with its drill and gymnastics that formed the basis of physical training programmes.

Martina Österberg

Military influences were readily apparent in the early PT syllabuses, not least because military instructors were the only readily available source of expertise – however unsuitable they may have been.

The first widespread attempts at developing physical education programmes in the British Isles came from the appointment of Miss Martina Österberg to the London School Board in 1882. She subsequently opened her own college for the training of women specialist teachers of physical education at Hampstead in 1885. At this time there were no such comparable facilities for men in Britain. With the exception of towns such as Birmingham, which had programmes of teacher training in place from around 1880, men could only gain qualifications by going abroad to Germany, Denmark or to Sweden.

Österberg's college met with immediate success. It trained specialists who worked largely in the new girls' independent schools. These had grown up following the Endowed Schools Act of 1869 in order to provide a similar education for the girls of middle class families to that enjoyed by their brothers.

Swedish gymnastics

The method taught at Hampstead (and later at Dartford) was Swedish gymnastics with some German vaulting. Games such as cricket, hockey, lacrosse and netball were also played. Dance and deportment were considered important in the education of young ladies and were an essential part of the programme. It is Madame Österberg who is credited with the adaptation of the American game of basketball into netball, and the invention of the gymslip.

The 'melting-pot' process which had successfully codified men's sports (see page 18) was not nearly as effective for women. However, old students of Madame Österberg were influential in the national organisation of sports such as hockey, lacrosse and netball.

Some of her former students formed their own colleges, including those at Bedford,

▲ *Figure 1.17* Girls using an exercise wheel (1931)

Chelsea and Halesowen (Anstey College). 'Madame' was apparently infuriated, asserting that hers was to be the only such college in England. In 1899, when thirty-one of her past students formed the Ling Physical Education Association and invited her to be president, she turned them down flat!

Many of the newly established girls' high schools were based in large suburban houses and the garden often sufficed as the games field and the gymnasium (Figure 1.17). Larger establishments, such as Roedean and Cheltenham Ladies' College, were the female equivalents of the boys' public schools and had extensive fields on the same scale.

Sport and physical education in the twentieth century

The developments in sport and physical education in both boys' and girls' schools continued into the twentieth century. However, these developments had little or no effect on the lives of the great majority of children trapped in the industrial towns. For them, the playground and the gymnasium were the streets and alleyways of the slum areas in which they lived.

The **Forster Education Act** of 1870, whilst it made school attendance compulsory, contained no statutory provision for either physical education or games. This did not occur until the formation of the **Model Syllabus** of 1902 and even that was the subject of much heated debate.

In the interim period of approximately 30 years, nothing was done at a national level to institute provision that remotely matched the developing programmes to be found in the private sector of education.

The revised education code of 1885 allowed school boards to employ ex-military instructors to drill their pupils but this was largely seen as a disciplinary move rather than an educational one. Additional grants were payable to school boards with good attendance and discipline records. Ironically, for most ordinary schoolchildren, this was their first contact with anything that could be remotely described as physical education or training.

Some school boards, notably in Birmingham and London, made far more provision than was required of them but these, sadly, were exceptions rather than the norm.

The beginnings of out of school clubs

Whilst statutory provision was so appalling, many individual teachers took it upon themselves to make what provision they could for their children to play organised sport (Figure 1.18). This was often improvised and the playground – where one existed – was used as the venue for athletics, cricket and football matches, either after school or on Saturday mornings.

The South London Schools FA was the first local football association to be formed in 1885. By 1890, others in Sheffield, Liverpool, Manchester, Birmingham and a whole host of other areas followed. There were also cricket,

▲ *Figure 1.18* Granby Road Board School Cricket XI 1901. Many local leagues were run by schoolmasters, but received little official encouragement

▲ *Figure 1.19* *A typical board school of the 1890s. Some had playgrounds, many did not – a central hall may have allowed some drill indoors*

athletics and swimming associations and both Oldham and Leicester had associations for both football codes.

Some senior clubs supported the efforts of local schoolmasters and Leicester Fosse F.C. were among those that allowed school 'town' games to be played on their pitch. They also donated a set of shirts to the local school football association.

One of the few provisions for sporting and recreational involvement for ordinary people was the Baths and Wash-houses Act of 1847 which had allowed municipal authorities to provide public baths. The purpose here was to encourage personal hygiene but such facilities were often soon put to recreational use. Swimming galas were instituted in towns where a public baths had been built and this activity appeared to include girls as well.

In many ways these developments were reflections of the popularity of sports, particularly of football and cricket, outside the sphere of school. Masters were often as keen as boys to be involved. However, such activity – much of which continues today – took place because of personal and professional commitment which received little in the way of official policy or support.

The early syllabuses

The first in a series of physical education (training) syllabuses appeared in 1902 and was accompanied by great disquiet in educational circles. It was undeniably militaristic in content and the teachers' unions and reform groups saw it simply as 'early military training'. At first girls were not included in the earliest provisions, although, as Figure 1.20 shows, some school boards included them in drill activities from an early date.

▲ *Figure 1.20* *A class of girls being drilled in 1902. Girls were not officially included in physical education until 1906.*

The military losses during the many campaigns of the late nineteenth century were seen as a major reason why government had intervened in this way but that was not really the whole story. The appalling physical state of military recruits was a factor and many commentators had also begun to realise that poor diet, bad housing and a host of other social ills were really to blame.

The Inter-departmental Enquiry into Physical Deterioration (1904) found that there was much to do in the realm of social welfare. This was one of the reasons why the second syllabus of 1904 was hastily produced, in an attempt to quieten much of the criticism of 'militarism gone mad' that had accompanied the syllabus of 1902.

The **1904 Syllabus** made distinct moves towards including Swedish gymnastics rather than purely military exercises and this trend continued in the third edition of the syllabus in 1909. The 1909 Syllabus also required local authorities to make provision for the training of their teachers to deliver this syllabus. This meant that the entirely unsuitable drill sergeant, who up to now had taught gymnastics in schools, could be dispensed with as soon as was practicable.

An improved syllabus

The 1919 Syllabus came just after the First World War (1914–18) and was a considerable improvement on its predecessors. Small-sided games were included and playgrounds marked out to accommodate these. Exercises were organised to benefit specific parts of the body. Partner work and group work were also included to augment the dance steps and children's games which had been included in the 1909 Syllabus. In the eyes of many, it was the first syllabus that could be regarded as truly 'child-centred'.

The **Fisher Act** of 1918, out of which the 1919 Syllabus grew, also made provision for local education authorities to set up:

- holiday and school camps
- centres and equipment for physical training, playing fields and school baths (both for bathing and swimming)
- other physical training facilities for use in the day or evening.

Unfortunately those provisions were merely permissive, which meant that there was no compulsory legal requirement for local authorities to put them into practice. It was not until the 1944 Education Act that local authorities were required to make provision for playing field space for all their schools. Some of this provision had to be off-site because many older schools were in the middle of densely built-up areas. As late as 1966, children from inner London boroughs were being transported to facilities on the city's outskirts at a cost of over £550,000 per annum.

In 1918, the demand for women specialists in the new secondary high schools was so great that a one-year course was begun at the University of Reading, in addition to the colleges opened by Madame Österberg and her former students. By then over 1,350 women specialist teachers had been trained with the number of men in comparison being almost non-existent. The only course for men up to 1923 had been at Sheffield Training College and that was closed following the drastic cuts of the Geddes Committee that year.

Primary and secondary provision

In 1926 the re-organisation as a result of the opening of local authority-run grammar schools was a defining influence in the demarcation between primary and secondary education.

The Hadow Report of 1926 recognised the need for physical education to reflect the difference in age groups. Some time was spent in creating the **1933 Syllabus** which was produced with one section for children under eleven and a second for children over that age. It also covered theory and methodology as well as content.

▲ *Figure 1.21* *1933 Syllabus: Group VI general activity exercises – jumping with a pole (informal)*

Broadened interest and provision

A broadening of interest and provision became evident in the period between the two World Wars. Voluntary organisations such as the YMCA and its sister organisation, the YWCA, expanded their programmes of physical recreation. The National Association of Boys' Clubs and the Youth Hostels Association (YHA) also made increased provision for young people in the post-school age groups.

The same period saw the beginnings of the national 'keep-fit' movement for women. In 1929 Mrs Bagot Stack founded the Women's League of Health and Beauty. The increased participation of women in physical recreation is reflected in the fact that this organisation started in London with just sixteen members. Ten years later there were 166,000 members in Europe, North America, Hong Kong, Australia and New Zealand!

The National Playing Fields Association was formed in 1925 in response to the shortage of playing field space. This need had been highlighted, not by the plight of schools, but by that of the many young men thrown into unemployment during the years of the Depression. In 1935, the Ling Association and the National Association of Organisers of Physical Education joined forces to form the Central Council of Recreative Physical Training. This became known by its more familiar title, the CCPR, in 1944.

Carnegie College opened its PE courses for men in 1933. This began to redress the imbalance between provision for men and that of the well established women's colleges, which by then had been open for thirty years or more. This was followed in 1935 by Loughborough College in Leicestershire, and in 1937 by Goldsmiths College in London, also offering specialist courses for men.

This broadening influence continued in the years prior to the Second World War, by which time Directors of Physical Education had been appointed at the Universities of Liverpool, Leeds, Manchester and Birmingham. Also in 1937 the Board of Education had produced a teachers' manual *Recreation and Physical Fitness for Youths and Men* (see Figure 1.22) with a companion volume for girls and women.

The 1944 Education Act

Whilst this Act had no accompanying syllabus to replace that of 1933, it did bring a range of administrative changes which built on the provisions made therein.

Mandatory regulations were laid down in respect of playing field allocation and the provision of gymnasia. The fact that some of these provisions were considerably delayed owing to the shortages resulting from wartime is not a criticism of the Act or its provisions. The school leaving age was raised to fifteen which meant that pupils would benefit from such provisions for a year longer than they had previously. The Act also required that teachers of physical education were to be accorded the same professional status as all other teachers although it was some time before this became a matter of fact.

In the immediate post-war period, seventeen new specialist or 'wing PE courses' were created up and down the country. Unfortunately, all these courses – even where they were part of mixed colleges – were single-sex: ten of them were for men and seven for women. This was, in part, a reflection of the wish of many older women's colleges not to be merged into mixed establishments. The only institution to offer training to both sexes was Birmingham University. Here there was a physical education course as part of a general degree within the Faculty of Arts from 1946. Eventually all these establishments were absorbed by or merged into larger or newer ones. The last of the old women's specialist PE colleges to lose its independence was Bedford College, now a part of De Montfort University.

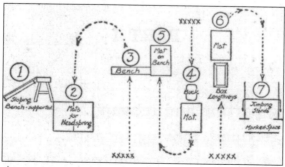

▲ **Figure 1.22** *Apparatus for group activity from Recreation and Physical Fitness for Youths and Men, 1937*

Outdoor apparatus

Another post-war development was the range of experimental initiatives into developing outdoor apparatus (Figure 1.23).

Although militarism had been much criticised in the early days of physical education, it was thought that modified versions of assault-course apparatus might be used to enhance the range of environmental experiences, particularly in inner-city settings. There followed a number of 'experiments' in Bristol, Halifax, Darlington, Manchester and elsewhere to provide such opportunities, particularly for primary school children, who were unlikely to have the benefit of gymnasium apparatus.

There was much concern over the likelihood of accidents but this fear was not realised. McIntosh noted that of 313 accidents recorded in 1951–52 in Bristol schools, only three were caused by climbing apparatus and two of those apparently occurred when apparatus was used against instructions. The more general trend was one of broadening interest in teaching methodology and a wish to extend the experience of children beyond that of regimented gymnastics and team games.

Outdoor education

In the immediate post-war years, attention continued to focus on a much wider setting for physical recreation, both generally and in schools. Cycling and the YHA had allowed a freedom of movement around the country-side and the 'outward bound' school in Aberdovey had opened in 1941. This was followed in 1950 by another in Eskdale. Both were administered under the **Outward Bound Trust** and, by the middle of the 1950s, the testing and building of character was to be based in wild and mountainous settings, as opposed to on the public school playing field. Ironically, the aims were very much the same: the development of courage, initiative, co-operation and leadership.

A sign of things to come in schools took the form of the arrival in Britain of Kurt Hahn, a refugee from the Nazi regime in Germany. His 'county badge scheme', based on that he had left behind in Germany, spread from Gordonstoun School, where he was an instructor, to the rest of Morayshire and beyond. We know it better today as the Duke of Edinburgh's Award Scheme.

Movement and dance

In 1940 **Rudolph** (von) **Laban**'s modern dance first appeared in physical education circles. Isadora Duncan's work had become well known but lacked the organised approach and notation of Laban. Lisa Ullman, who was eventually to become Laban's assistant, had worked at Dartington Hall in 1938. With Laban she made contributions to courses and seminars including Ling Physical Education Association courses and its publication, *The Journal of Physical Education*. Lisa Ullman opened an Art of Movement Studio in Manchester in 1945 but by 1953 moved, with Laban, to new premises in Addlestone in Surrey. Ministry of Education approval and funding was gained the following year and the centre began to offer full-time courses for teachers and PE advisers.

▲ *Figure 1.23* Bristol apparatus, 1944

▲ *Figure 1.24* Matching shapes – ten-year-olds in a primary gymnastics lesson in the mid-1960s

There was much antagonism by many teachers towards what they considered the latest gimmick. The PE profession was divided into two camps with men more resistant (but only slightly) than women.

In 1952 and 1953 the Ministry of Education produced **Moving and Growing** and **Planning the Programme**, both intended to replace the primary age section of the 1933 Syllabus. Educational gymnastics became the new valuable currency in physical education, and 'going with weight', 'taking weight', 'obtaining flight' and 'small parts and large parts' became part of the new language that accompanied it.

There were arguments about the validity of such programmes, particularly when they replaced the original activity of gymnastics. A. D. Munrow's *Pure and Applied Gymnastics*, published in 1955, was an attempt to prevent movement-based lessons replacing traditional gymnastics (Figure 1.24). Munrow also posed questions concerning the replacement of other games-based activities by this new phenomenon of educational gymnastics.

Percy Jones, a PE Inspector in Lancashire, devised a method whereby formal gymnastics movements were broken down into simpler tasks. The 'Percy Jones' or 'platform method' was adopted by many as a satisfactory half-way house between formal and educational gymnastics.

The loss of games and gymnastics was much mourned by many PE professionals. In 1972, some twenty years after the two major government publications of the early 1950s (*Moving and Growing*, and *Planning the Programme*), the then Department of Education and Science produced *Movement – Physical Education in the Primary Years*. This was a fundamental work of revision and re-statement.

Circuit and weight training

Concurrent developments, largely in secondary and further education, were the growth of interest in circuit training, for both sport and general fitness, and in weight training. The trend in secondary education was towards a broader range of options within PE programmes. Such programmes made use of nearby off-site facilities for water-based and outdoor activities and for activities such as squash. The provision of a wide range of activities was a feature of many of the newly developing municipal sports centres and private clubs.

A drawback of this trend manifested itself in the 'inch thick – mile wide' syndrome of the late 1960s and 1970s. The mushrooming range of activities had implications for budgeting and the quality and levels of supervision and instruction – particularly where this was not in the hands of PE-trained professionals.

Towards the National Curriculum

A distinctive feature of the 1970s was the broadening influence of dance as an independent aspect of movement, and the growth of choreographed method and ethnic dance. The 1970s and 1980s have been referred to as a period during which many teachers were 'wandering in the wilderness', with 'fads and fancies'. Government initiatives of the period were thought to have contributed, at least in part, to this apparent search for direction. Consequently, the Education Reform Act (ERA) was passed in 1988 and subsequently, in 1991, the first orders leading to the development of the present **National Curriculum** with Physical Education as one of its 'foundation subjects'.

Reduced curriculum time

The subsequent 'watering down' of National Curriculum Physical Education has included a threatened large-scale erosion of time at primary level to make way for literacy initiatives. Also there has been an incessant erosion of time allocated to PE in the secondary sector. This has occurred to make way for other demands upon curriculum time.

Additional curriculum time has, in many cases, been found for the development of

TASK

a Why were early physical education programmes so heavily militaristic?

b In groups, produce two short lessons of no more than two or three minutes' duration, showing how drill in 1902 differed from a 1933 lesson.

c In co-operation with your teacher, produce a ten-minute gymnastics lesson with an identified 'theme' that could be taught to ten-year-olds.

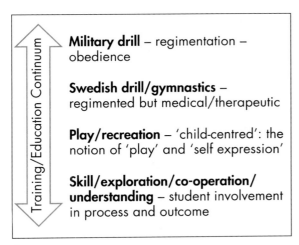

Military drill – regimentation – obedience

Swedish drill/gymnastics – regimented but medical/therapeutic

Play/recreation – 'child-centred': the notion of 'play' and 'self expression'

Skill/exploration/co-operation/ understanding – student involvement in process and outcome

Training/Education Continuum

▲ *Figure 1.25* How policy affects participation in sport

GCSE and A level PE courses. Those are, however, optional subjects and should not be seen as an acceptable alternative to reduced mainstream curriculum time.

Positive developments have come in the from of increased student involvement in their own roles in the learning process – and in the evaluation of outcomes. Figure 1.25 indicates how, in just over 100 years, physical education has moved considerably towards serving the needs of its recipients.

Current and future policies in school sport and PE

School sport has suffered from difficulties in the last twenty years. These include:

- the trend on the part of local authorities to sell off what was seen as surplus land, thus stripping many schools of valuable playing field space
- the growth of alternative sporting activities outside the immediate sphere of education
- the increasing difficulty for teachers of staffing an ever larger range of activities, with reduced budgets, manpower and time.

A reappraisal of the place of school sport is underway, not least because of the difficulties listed above, but also because the increasing pressure of league and exam tables does not reflect either sporting achievements, or the attraction of activities outside schools, which serve to reduce the effectiveness and appeal of school sports programmes.

Many schools still have excellent extra-curricular programmes of sport and recreation but the dwindling of such traditional features as Saturday morning fixtures is an indication of current trends. There are many alternatives to school sport in the wider community and pupils often find them more attractive than school-based activities. Recently the Football Association (FA) has removed the national under 15 group football team from the control of the schools' governing body (ESFA). This move has been received with some disappointment by many teachers but in this case issues of sporting rather than educational excellence are at stake. Many top league clubs are known to prefer that their young talent does not participate in school sport. This fuels further debate as to whether school sport and PE is seen by the wider community as existing only to foster sporting excellence as would appear to be the case in the United States. The demise of the FA's Football Academy at Lilleshall is perhaps a testimony to the higher value placed on sporting outcome than on educational process.

The issue of sporting excellence is closely intertwined with the development of **designated sports colleges**. They are so called because of their acknowledged status as promoters of excellent practice in both physical education and sport. Such schools attract additional funding in order to further improve their programmes. This raises the obvious question whether such programmes have a detrimental effect on other nearby schools. It also asks whether the quest for sporting excellence may in fact divert at least some of the originally intended purpose of this initiative. The intention is that from the 11 schools designated in 1997, the number will eventually rise to over 100, and that the requirement to work in partnership with other schools will ensure the spread of good practice and standards.

The work of the **Youth Sports Trust** and the CCPR Sports Leaders Awards schemes are recent developments and add to the range of tools available to PE professionals – or do they? The TOP Start, TOP Play and TOP Sport programmes are innovative and do not denude educational funding, but is their purpose educational or sporting excellence? And can these two aims be reconciled?

3. Social influences on performance and participation

Cultural setting

In order to participate in physical activity, be it recreational or sporting, you must have **time**, **space** and the **freedom** to participate. The measure in which each of these essential factors is present, and the degree to which they are used, reflects the cultural setting in which they occur.

Factors which are a constraint on physical activity can be categorised as:

- enforced constraints – e.g. political, gender-based, religious or economic restrictions
- natural constraints – e.g. natural and unavoidable restrictions.

Whilst cultural settings can vary enormously, some generalisations can be made as shown in Table 1.7

Table 1.7 *Constraints on participation in sport*

| Setting | Factors affecting participation | |
	Enforced	Natural
Primitive	ritual, tribal constraints	topographic, e.g. desert, remoteness, lack of natural facilities
Emergent	nation-building ethic confers élite status on specific sub-groups or activities. Lack of open access to sport for cultural, political or economic reasons	remote communities; reluctance to abandon ancient cultures. Some technology allows 'target' development
Advanced	largely minority issues, e.g. ethnic, or gender constraints	technology can overcome most natural deficiencies

Resources

All physical activity uses resources. At the simplest level – for example, when a child is playing – activity occurs naturally and incurs little cost. However, with any more formalised physical activity, economic and cultural factors come into play.

The provision and maintenance of resources require both the economic capacity and the political/cultural will to do so. A society, whether it be primitive, newly emergent or technologically advanced, must embrace the notion of freedom to participate in physical activity, even if there are unavoidable economic constraints. Figure 1.26 gives an idealised view of how levels of access can be affected by political and/or cultural policy.

The cost of resources tends to multiply with the increased use of technology. In newly **emergent cultures**, activities using the fewest economic resources are most likely either as recreations or as an attempt to build up a positive national image. The most often quoted example in this respect is that of the Kenyan and North African distance runners. Collectively they use little of their countries' limited economic wealth whilst earning a global reputation as well as much needed foreign currency.

This concept of **nation-building** often focuses on specific activities by identified groups. Figure 1.27 indicates how these easily resourced activities can provide success and

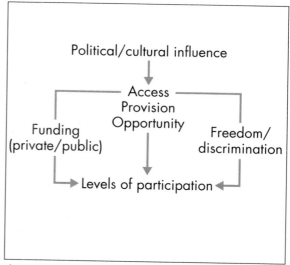

▲ **Figure 1.26** *How policy affects participation in sport*

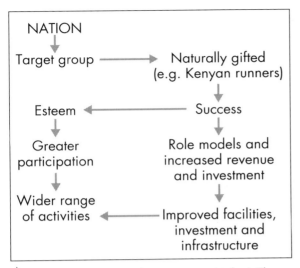

NATION

Target group → Naturally gifted (e.g. Kenyan runners)

Esteem ← Success

Greater participation ← Role models and increased revenue and investment

Wider range of activities ← Improved facilities, investment and infrastructure

▲ *Figure 1.27* Natural resources and talent. These are used to develop facilities, create interest and broaden participation

create **role models** encouraging others to participate. The enhanced profile of both sport and nation brings increased inward investment and subsequent expansion. This can go on to include other areas of recreational/sporting activity.

In technologically advanced societies such infrastructures can be much more easily developed. They are often a reflection of current political thinking, and are funded either centrally, privately or by some combination of both.

Lifestyles in contemporary society

Health concerns

Lifestyles today are becoming far more sedentary than they were before. The physical activity that was once an essential part of everyday living has, in many societies, been left behind with social and technological advancement. As a result in this change of lifestyle the health concerns affecting people of all ages centre largely on fitness, obesity and cardiac problems. The main way of preventing problems in these areas is an increased level of physical activity across all sections of the community.

This pressing medical or health-based concern should add fuel to any existing arguments over issues of access, and/or provision of sporting facilities. Such issues are no longer simply to do with the 'right to play' in

a leisure context but have wider implications for a nation's health.

In the USA, 'fat camps' for young people with obesity problems have been established for some years and in 1998 the first such venture in the UK was seen at Leeds Metropolitan University. Lifestyles are addressed in several ways in such ventures, a central one being a matter of diet and the avoidance of 'junk food' of which there is such an abundance in today's take away culture.

For those who are seriously overweight the assessment of body fat levels is critical and that clearly is within the province of the dietician and the physiologist. Socially, however, there are serious issues to be addressed, including society's perception of body shape and the consequent psychological problems which arise from self-image and self confidence which may be badly affected in those who do not see themselves as reflections of the socially accepted image.

Clearly, the level and appropriateness of exercise regimes are important here but anthropometric variants are also often forgotten, particularly in the case of young people who are 'educated' by media influences as opposed to more rational ones. Where exercise is critical it should be encouraged and in general terms the lobby for increased recreational time in schools could play a most influential part in the physical and psychological well-being of the nation as a whole.

The survey by Sport England in 1999 into young people and sport prefaced its findings with the acknowledgement that:

There is a growing body of evidence which shows that sport can make a significant contribution to individuals and society beyond winning medals. Many of these benefits, for example in terms of health, social regeneration, lifelong learning and reductions in criminal behaviour, are not, however, realised if appropriate skills and a positive attitude to sport are not developed at a young age.

This established medical need for exercise (Figure 1.28) should go some way to justifying claims for the expansion of **mass participation** programmes, which also meet leisure and recreational needs.

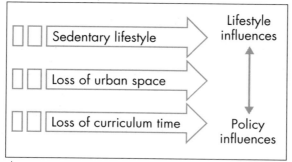

▲ *Figure 1.28* Influences on decreasing activity levels

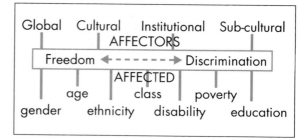

▲ *Figure 1.29* Opportunity and provision

The report referred to above also acknowledges the 'worrying trend that more than a third of 6–8 year olds have less than one hour's PE time per week' and this in connection laments the magnified effect that this is likely to have upon those from materially less comfortable backgrounds. It might also perhaps be appropriate to acknowledge that whilst this would seem to be a most appropriate comment, there are others, such as the obese and other disadvantaged groups, who also suffer.

Clearly, the materially better off can supplement recreational opportunity outside the school environment but the nature, quality and appropriateness of such activity is often in the hands of those less than ideally equipped to monitor and advise upon it.

Beyond school and into adult life involvement in appropriate physical activity is often a function of available free time and previous enjoyable experience. Without both these commodities a physically active lifestyle is far less likely to occur.

Access, opportunity and provision

Access to physical activity, whether recreational or sporting, is a product of **opportunity** and **provision**. These occur (or fail to occur) at different levels.

Opportunity and provision

Opportunity and provision are largely controlled by institutions and agencies and are affected by the cultural setting in which they operate. Figure 1.29 shows that the inter-relationship between cultural values and institutional values is a crucial one as it often determines levels of access. This in turn affects participation levels.

In societies such as the former USSR and the present People's Republic of China, ancient cultural values are often overridden by contemporary political dogma or ideology. In others, cultural or religious values are superimposed on any political policy.

It seems that where political dogma or ideology is the driving force behind policies of sport, recreation and physical education, participation at all levels is encouraged or required. The nature and level of participation is such, however, that it is the political ideology that is best served, rather than individual or group needs.

Where cultural or religious influences dominate, the net result seems to be constraint or discrimination: against either the host culture, or sub-cultures within it. For example, in some Muslim countries, women are discriminated against by their own culture when their religion forbids them to collect in public places, thereby excluding them from most sporting activities.

The two models in Figures 1.30 and 1.31 reflect extreme situations where freedom of access is controlled by limited or engineered policies of access. These are designed to pro-

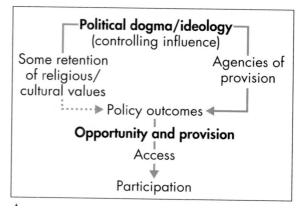

▲ *Figure 1.30* Opportunity and provision: an outcome of political control

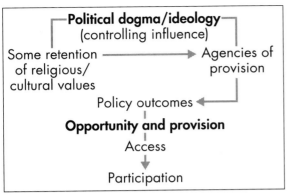

▲ **Figure 1.31** *Opportunity and provision: an outcome of cultural/religious control*

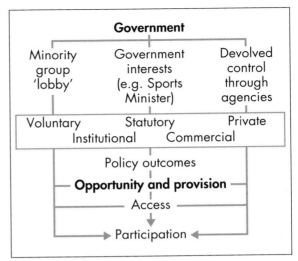

▲ **Figure 1.32** *Opportunity and provision: an outcome of consensus/reformative policy*

mote the values of particular cultural or political beliefs over those of individuals or groups within that culture.

Ideally, in most 'free' societies the political/ideological perspective embraces a range of cultural and sub-cultural values. Opportunity and provision are created on the basis of consensus (the mutual consent of various interested parties) and reform (Figure 1.32). This is reflected in the nature and range of opportunity and provision. Whilst this model is not perfect, it does at least acknowledge that ethnic and minority groups are part of the whole culture and should therefore be considered in policy-making and provision.

Discrimination

Ethnic and minority groups are not always considered at the point of delivery, however. This is as much a reflection of localised discrimination as it is of the failure of policy-makers to ensure full implementation of their intentions. The groups commonly associated with discrimination in terms of access and opportunity include those restricted or excluded because of:

- age
- poverty
- ethnicity/religion
- disability
- class
- gender
- education.

Figure 1.32 gives a simplified view of the various bodies involved in policy-making and provision. It shows how consensus, at least theoretically, can include a range of minority views as part of the decision-making process. There are several shortcomings in this process and, often, implementation is more difficult than policy-making.

Other factors affecting participation

Self-discrimination

Even in a free society, the existence of self-discrimination can restrict participation. Many older people feel that recreation 'is not for them' or that they are simply too old. Asian women, for example, are often either prevented from taking part by sub-cultural values or their own disinclination. There are also certain groups or individuals who do not take part in some activities, feeling that they are too **élitist**. Such constraints can be grouped under three headings:

- economic/physical limits preventing full implementation of policy
- internalised or self-discrimination by a cultural group upon its own members
- the perceived notion of élitism or exclusivity in connection with some activities which acts as a deterrent.

Stereotyping

The stereotypical view either reinforces established perceptions, or questions new ones. Women as tennis players or gymnasts reinforce views on what sports women should do. Women as rugby players, or fighters, on the other hand, fall outside the normally perceived range of stereotypes. This can have an effect on whether or not people take part in sporting activities.

Stereotypes abound within those groups normally considered to be disadvantaged or discriminated against. Ethnic groups, disabled sportspersons and the aged all suffer from rigid perceptions of how they should, or should not participate in recreation. Unfortunately, such views are often held by those in positions of influence, and in some cases by the very groups on whom they are based. Such views are considered to be **negative stereotypes** and do little to advance the cause of these groups.

Positive stereotypes, however, challenge traditional or negative stereotypes, and enhance the image of a particular group. Sometimes this can also be misleading. For example, not all disabled sportspersons compete in wheelchairs and neither do all older people wish to play bowls. Stereotypical views – even positive ones – tend therefore to be generalised, almost caricaturised views. They are often the result of misconception or ignorance.

For example, there is little factual (and conclusive) support for the idea that black people are physiologically inclined to be poor swimmers. There is, however, plenty of evidence to suggest that such a stereotype is founded on

▲ **Figure 1.34** Women's boxing – breaking the stereotype or just the 'rules'?

sociological rather than physiological phenomena (see page 66). In the same way, women's boxing has suffered considerably because of those who simply do not like it, rather than because it has been proved to be any more unsafe for women than men (Figure 1.34).

Esteem

Sports psychologists view self-esteem as an important factor in competitive performance. They are interested in the perception that minority groups have of themselves and how this might affect their inclination to participate in sport, competitively or otherwise. Negative stereotypes work against the development of self-esteem, whereas, positive stereotypes, positive role models, policies of inclusion and increased levels of participation build it (Figure 1.35).

Stacking, centrality and self-fulfilling prophecy

Attitudes to minority groups often include negative stereotypes. Where there is no policy of inclusion of such minority groups, the creation of positive imagery is a response from such groups to improve their self-esteem and present themselves in a better light in the eyes of a hostile culture. Where policies of inclu-

▲ **Figure 1.33** Positive stereotypes can challenge discrimination

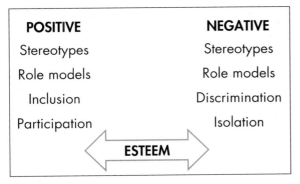

▲ *Figure 1.35* *Positive and negative influences on the development of esteem*

sion do exist, positive images are created by both groups. This is part of a consensus approach to the building of group and individual esteem.

Stacking

Where **stacking** occurs, there is usually a multi-cultural presence (see Figure 1.36) as a result of already broad or expanding immigration policies. This can often create friction between governmental attitudes and those of the dominant culture, whose collective response might be:

- to positively assert its own values
- to reject or select invading cultures in order of coincidence with their own.

Stacking, therefore, acts both as a 'bar' to outside cultural influence and as a 'selection process' to determine the ranking or 'pecking order' in which outside groups should be placed. In the case of both the USA and Australia, stacking has placed in-coming cul-

tural groups in an order that most closely approximates the values of the dominant culture. **Centrality** refers to the centralised control exerted by the dominant (central) cultural influence.

The presence of stacking cannot be taken as an indication of official policy. However, as in Australia where staged immigration policies encouraged first of all British, then West European, followed by East European and other cultural groups, it is hardly surprising that such a system operates in many areas of society, and very much reflects a 'last in, bottom of the pile' situation.

Self-fulfilling prophecy

The self-esteem of cultural groups who find themselves low in the stacking order is hardly likely to be high. Policies of exclusion in sport and recreation simply serve to reinforce what is almost a **self-fulfilling prophecy** of low expectation and achievement. It is alarming to note that in Australia, New Zealand, South Africa and the United States, it is the indigenous native populations that are bottom of the pile in each instance. The desirability of policies of inclusion whether they are purely sporting/recreational or much broader-based cannot be over-stated.

Target groups

The concept of **target groups**, where specific groups are 'targeted' for particular funding or provision, presupposes the presence of policies of inclusion. For any targeting to be effective, such groups are identified as subgroups of a larger disadvantaged group.

In the example in Figure 1.37, 'gender issues' relates to a whole range of 'subgroups' targeted.

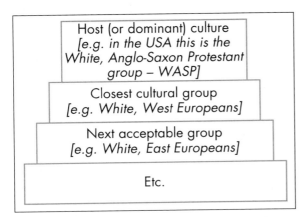

▲ *Figure 1.36* *Stacking exists in many cultural settings but is most evident in areas of high immigration*

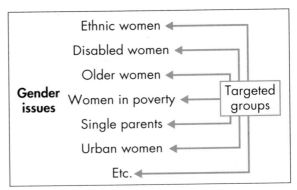

▲ *Figure 1.37* *Target groups within an already identified 'disadvantaged' group*

Targeting policies are much more likely to be effective where a specific sub-group with specific needs is identified. The *Asian Women's Project* in Bradford in the early 1990s was an example of this. By identifying a particular group of women with specific needs, a policy was devised and funding raised which enabled closed swimming pool time to be booked. This meant that participation which would otherwise not have been possible became a reality. Abseiling and canoeing, basketball and netball were other activities presented for women only, by women only, so that a major cultural objection – that of women taking recreation in public – was removed. In such a case, merely providing general access to these sporting opportunities would have been entirely ineffective. Similarly, disabled groups need more than simple provision. They need a level which is beyond that normally required by other groups.

Targeting therefore identifies specific groups for whom normal levels of provision are insufficient, but who, if encouraged, may well develop a capability for self-empowerment. Targeting policies usually face two major difficulties:

- provision of adequate funding
- social, racial or religious prejudice has to be overcome.

Specific interest groups are often set up to promote the interests of such minorities or disadvantaged groups. The Women's Sports Foundation (WSF) was formed in 1984. It works closely with the CCPR and the respective sports councils to ensure that the interests of women and women's minority groups are effectively represented. In the case of disability sport and recreation the **British Sports Association for the Disabled** (BSAD) was formed in 1961 and is responsible for co-ordinating and developing opportunities for its many members. At an élite level, the British Paralympic Association co-ordinates the preparation and entries for the four-yearly Paralympics. Such groups also make an invaluable contribution to the identification and development of appropriate 'target groups' and the framing of reformative policy.

Identification of the issue

Establishment of communication between appropriate groups (e.g. local Asian women's group and community recreation officer)

Involvement of relevant outside bodies (e.g. the CRE or members of disabled sports association)

Establishment of facts – dispellation of myths (What is the *real* issue?)

Process of education/conciliation – rationalising strongly held views; fear appeasement; identification of realistic possibilites

Establishment of achievable targets within commonly agreed parameters both financial and cultural

Agreed outcomes

Enactment

Reformative policy/analysis

▲ **Figure 1.38** *The stages in the reformative process*

Reformative policy

Reformative policies (and the reformative process) are intended to work towards open access to recreation in those areas of society where it is limited. This may be because of inadequate provision or because of cultural beliefs which discourage such access.

For example, the *Asian Women's Project* in Bradford mentioned earlier was set up because a specific group of women were unable to participate in recreational activities. This was not due to inadequate provision for women generally, but to the restriction placed upon some Asian women by their own culture. So that such projects get under way in the first place, an initial identification must be made arising out of communication between such groups and the appropriate agencies. Reformative policy encourages the establishment of groups to represent minority interests. It also ensures that some outcome, where achievable, is obtained. The reformative process is the means by which these issues are addressed, as in Figure 1.38

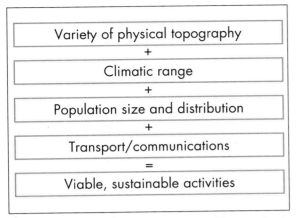

Variety of physical topography
+
Climatic range
+
Population size and distribution
+
Transport/communications
=
Viable, sustainable activities

▲ *Figure 1.39* *Influences on sustainable activities in the natural environment*

Geographical factors

Physical or geographical factors can also influence the nature and scale of provision for recreation and sport (Figure 1.39). In some cases, physical restrictions can be overcome but those national communities possessing a broad range of natural facilities have a distinct advantage over those that do not. Such advantages are not only a function of topography (i.e. the physical characteristics of a place) but also of climate. Large land masses such as the United States or Australia not only have spatial advantage and physical variety but also encompass a range of climatic conditions. So somewhere in the United States it is possible to find appropriate conditions for a wealth of summer and winter sports, as well as for those on land and in water.

This is not always the case elsewhere. In Britain we have a wide range of physical topography but not the climatic extremes to support a full range of winter or summer sports.

Bear in mind that in an age of sophisticated technology, the 'natural environment' can often be artificially created both indoors and out. Facilities such as 'white-water' canoe runs and winter sports facilities can be made where they would not naturally occur. Such developments are, of course, an outcome of policy intent and/or economic capability.

Note: The following sections (Nos. 4 and 5) use the United Kingdom as the basis for study but students should have knowledge of the impact of these issues in the European Union and other European countries. Examination questions may require the use of examples from European countries. (It may be more effective to select a small number of Western European countries as case studies. These could be used for comparative analysis and may provide a possible framework for candidates to undertake an individual study.) [Taken from the Edexcel Specification]

4. Professional (élite) sport

The history of professional sport in Britain centres on three main aspects of development:

- the employment of paid retainers by members of the upper classes (see page 10). They represented their patrons in foot races (pedestrianism), prize-fights and horse racing. This practice was also present in cricket where many estate workers were employed because of their (largely bowling) ability. In all these activities wagering featured largely and has been associated with sporting development ever since – not always legally
- the increase of free time for the labouring classes in the last twenty years of the nineteenth century. This gave rise to the growth of mass spectator sport
- the growth of commercialised sport and media involvement.

Practice of exclusion

The practice of exclusion upheld by many of the UK's amateur sports bodies also had an impact on the development of professional sport. This effectively debarred the vast majority of would-be participants from amateur competition solely on the basis of their means of employment. Although this practice was not intended to bring about the development of professional sport, it did have an effect, as can be seen from the 1893 split between the northern rugby clubs and the predominantly middle-class clubs in the rest of the country.

Many working men were prevented from playing sport if it meant time away from work and the consequent loss of wages. Although the dynamics of change were slightly different in each case, the growth of Northern Union Rugby and the English Football League were both founded upon the need of working men to replace wages lost whilst playing. **'Broken time'** payments were made to compensate for such losses.

In the case of rugby, the number of clubs in the north were not seen by the Rugby Football Union (RFU) as a major threat to its authority. Soccer, however, was far more popular amongst the labouring classes, and the consequences of a rugby-style split in soccer would have been far more threatening to the authority of the Football Association than was the case with the RFU.

Cricket and horse racing had embraced professionalism as a necessary part of their development. The amateur 'ethic', it seems, was not as keenly promoted by the upper class owners within those sports as it was by the middle-class owners in most of the new 'rationalised' sports which became popular in the second half of the nineteenth century. Jockeys were a necessary part of horse racing. The lifestyles of many owners meant they were incapable of riding their own mounts without incurring severe penalties at the hands of the handicapper. Also cricket had long used the professional 'journeymen' – usually as bowlers – without whom teams would have been entirely devoid of their 'work-horses', willing to bowl countless overs in a day.

Because the upper classes liked to promote, patronise and wager on the outcome of matches rather than participate, it meant that the professional was conveniently included in those sports. In other sports, where members of the middle classes liked to participate, paid professionals were looked down on.

Increased free time

The increase of free time in the last twenty years of the nineteenth century created the British **sporting Saturday afternoon**. The massed crowds at football league and cup matches, at rugby league games in the north, major cricket matches, athletic contests and race meetings, particularly those associated with bank holiday and other festive occasions, provided a level of income which allowed those sports to become sustainable. It also meant that these sports began to develop a commercial face. Interest was high enough to encourage the growth of a sporting goods industry, as well as the use of teams and individuals as promoters of commercial goods and services. The growth of interest in cycling, for example, as a recreational pursuit, which boomed in the 1890s, spawned literally thousands of businesses, some of which still survive today (Figure 1.40).

In soccer, many small town businessmen, excluded by virtue of their limited social pedigree from a wider involvement, were drawn

▲ **Figure 1.40** The popularity of cycling as a leisure pursuit in the 1880s and 1890s saw a boom in advertising

▲ *Figure 1.41* Millwall Athletic FC 1894–5
with local businessmen whose financial support
helped create a successful team

into a patronage of their local club. This mirrored the patronage of the upper classes on the wider sporting stage (Figure 1.41). Many of these men had amassed considerable personal wealth in business and could therefore create successful teams with their cheque books. The victory of Blackburn Rovers in the FA Cup of 1883 was seen as evidence of this. It was also a turning point in the ascendancy of working-class sport over its middle- and upper-class counterparts.

Although it is difficult to generalise, early professionalism in sport depended on whether or not it had been traditionally accepted as part of a sport, or on the size of the group involved. In the instance of cricket, upper-class dignity required able bodies to deal with the 'sweaty aspect' of the sport, which meant that the employment of professionals was accepted without question. In soccer, the situation was rather different. It was so popular with the masses that the FA had little option but to concede to the overwhelming weight of opinion. In the case of soccer, what the FA had succeeded in doing, however, was in establishing the nature of the game; its rules and newly 'sanitised' form.

Boxing – the birth of an 'acceptable face'

In boxing, professionalism had also been traditional. Despite the intercession of **Jack Broughton** and the **Marquis of Queensbury**, the sport continued to attract a wholly 'undesirable' element until the formation of the **Amateur Boxing Association** in

1880. This was seen as a definitive move on the part of the sporting establishment to separate the amateur version of boxing from its less reputable professional counterpart. Like many other professional sports, boxing had its stars who did quite well out of their involvement. Countless others however, were rather less fortunate, gaining little except disfigurement and a pitiable old age.

The **National Sporting Club** was founded in 1891, out of the ashes of the former discredited Pelican Club. It was an attempt by the middle class to provide acceptable sport for themselves (Figure 1.42). Colonel Fox of the Army Gymnastic Staff was involved in its formation. He also persuaded the military authorities to have boxing included as part of the training of army recruits. The involvement of Lord Lonsdale and the awarding of Lonsdale belts gave much credibility to both the club and the sport. Contests took place over dinner, with formal dress required and respectable behaviour the order of the day.

Mass spectator sport

The huge crowds at football matches boosted the collective confidence of professional footballers. This gradually led to better contractual conditions. Vamplew, in his study

▲ *Figure 1.42* The National Sporting Club was formed in 1891. It was a successful attempt to give boxing a more respectable face

▲ **Figure 1.43** *As far as the eye can see... The crowd at a Stoke City match in the 1950s*

Table 1.8 *The progress of professionalism in sport*

Stage of development	Outcome
Gentry patronage	Professionals in prize-fighting, pedestrianism, cricket and horse racing
Assumption of 'moral' ownership of the nation's sports by the middle classes	Professionalism used as a means of excluding those not of the leisured classes
The rise in income and leisure time of the labouring classes	Mass influence in the sphere of leisure led to a professional class and the rise of 'shamateurism'
Commercialised sport – a result of the growth of a mass market	Growth of sports-related advertising, goods and media
The 'ownership' of professional sportsmen by club chairmen and promoters in those few sports which supported a professional class	A reasonable but precarious lifestyle for the professional with little or no protection in the event of injury or fall from favour
The period of 'duality' where in some sports amateurs played in the same team as players who were paid to play. In others, professionals were looked down on	Slow but steady rise of professional sport but clear division of ethics. Gradually improving contractual conditions for professionals
The media age: broadening horizons and better deals for professionals	Established mass-market reduces the influence of middle-class morals and the amateur ethic

of the history of professional sport, noted that as early as 1913–14, the average attendance at English First Division football games was 23,100 and that attendances at major cup finals were far in excess of that. The middle-class principle of 'amateurism in all things' was clearly rejected by the mass of ordinary people, who had no objection to honest men earning an honest living doing what they did best. Crowds such as the one in Figure 1.43 (taken in the 1950s) are rarely found at football matches today.

The rise in status of the professional

The rise in status of professional sportsmen, and the growing number of women, was given further impetus with the expansion of broadcasting – particularly television – and the growth of European competition alongside world events. Manchester United's much criticised (and disastrous) entry into European football in the late 1950s may well now be viewed with hindsight as a watershed in terms of the shape of things to come. The relationship between sport and economics is no longer a taboo subject (Table 1.8). In this growing marketplace today's professional sportsmen and women are set to do very well.

In rugby league, there had been no wish on the part of the clubs involved in the breakaway of 1893 to become professional. Their players were almost exclusively working class and simply wished to make up wages lost due to missed work. However, as they were outnumbered by the mass of middle-class clubs in the rest of the country, the RFU was able to

take a much stronger stand than the FA in respect of professionalism in soccer. Today many rugby union clubs now face the harsh realities of economic life in a world governed as much by the laws of business as by the laws of the game.

In 1908, the Football League, alarmed at the escalation of transfer fees to as much as £1,000 in isolated cases, fixed the maximum fee for which a player could be transferred at

£350. Since that time the retain and transfer system has gone. Contractual advantage (players are now 'free agents' at the end of their contractual period, and are therefore free to command their own fees in the marketplace) seems to have swung decidedly in favour of football's professionals as a result of the **Bosman ruling** in 1997. Their rugby union counterparts still have some way to go in developing a market to support their game.

The 1960s saw the arrival of tennis professionals at Wimbledon and the abolition of classifications into **'gentlemen' and 'players'** in cricket. The distinction between officers and gentlemen had been discarded by the equestrian world some years earlier, in 1948. Rugby league players are no longer regarded as the social lepers of the sporting world and only those sports which are intrinsically 'exclusive' remain protected from the ever-rising tide of popularism. For most people, the string of polo ponies or the ocean-racing yacht remain as elusive as ever.

National governing bodies of sport

With the exception of cricket, horse racing and golf, the majority of sports governing bodies in Britain were created in the last 35 years of the nineteenth century. Out of the Oxbridge 'melting pot' (see page 18) the two football codes (rugby football and Association football) emerged, but many other sports were rationalised as part of the same process. Culturally they were all imbued with the same middle-class ethic and were developed as gentlemanly recreations rather than professional pursuits. Oxbridge athleticism was the mainstay of English amateur sport. It was some time before the notion of sport merely as a means of personal improvement was challenged by its rise as mass entertainment and the birth of a professional class of sportsmen.

Today, Britain's sports governing bodies promote and develop their own sports. Their work covers all levels of participation. It includes the framing and enforcement of rules, the organisation of competitions and leagues, international team selection, facility development and liaison with other national and international sports bodies.

Many sports governing bodies, along with many individuals, are also members of the Central Council for Physical Recreation (CCPR) which serves as an umbrella advisory organisation on issues to do with sport and recreation. Contrary to popular misconception, it is a voluntary organisation funded by members' subscriptions, the corporate sponsorship of some of its promotions and some funding from the English Sports Council (now **Sport England**). It acts as a forum for the promotion of initiatives created by its members, which have recently included *The Threat to Sport and Physical Education in Schools; Sport and Drugs;* and *The Loss of Playing Fields and Sports Grounds*. The CCPR also produced *The Fair Play in Sport* charter, which includes a set of basic principles that should influence the behaviour of competitors, coaches, governing bodies and sports promoters.

The global sports arena

In terms of today's global sports arena, the role of the UK's national sporting bodies has had to change in many respects. They have had to embrace – in most sports – the concept of professionalism. They have also had to give up their own once unchallenged authority to that of both European and world bodies. Even those absolute authorities have had to learn to accept that as sport does not exist in a vacuum, their own rulings are occasionally subject to censure. For example, rugby players find that loutish behaviour on the field of play is no longer subject only to the ruling of their own sporting authority but of a civil one as well. Perhaps the most notable example is the recent reinstatement into domestic competition of Ben Johnson. This case underlines the fact that a lifetime ban, normally conferred in the 'wider' world only upon those who commit murder or the like, is highly unsustainable when the 'accused' is effectively prevented from earning a living. Such a philosophy will certainly need reviewing, and the Bosman ruling has perhaps served to remind sporting authorities that sports bodies must behave in a way that is seen to reflect the justice of the 'wider' world.

European and international governing bodies

With the exception of the International Olympic Committee (IOC), it seems that no sports governing body has had the impact upon the sporting world that FIFA has. Soccer appears to have assumed the mantle of 'the people's sport' and control of the game has moved on from the days when Britain gave it – and other sports – to the world.

The Olympic Games and the former Empire and now **Commonwealth Games** were essentially British, the former case by the adoption of British values and in the second by definition. The growth of European and international governing bodies since then has proceeded with Britain not always in the vanguard of development. On a much larger scale, the rationalisation process, which centred upon the universities of Oxford and Cambridge in the last half of the nineteenth century, has been repeated with Zurich, Lausanne and other administrative centres as the 'melting pots' of the twentieth century and thereafter.

The formerly 'British' interpretation of the term 'sport' has now passed into more commercially-minded hands, so that Avery Brundage's famous remark about payment meaning work, which therefore could not be sport, is now almost redundant.

The MCC no longer has the last word in matters cricketing. Similarly, both codes of football, as well as athletics and other once 'British' sports, now have to accept that cultural values other than British ones will determine the nature of what is and isn't 'sporting'. The formerly isolated professional sports organisations (Figure 1.44) are now right in the mainstream of events.

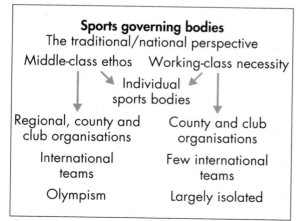

▲ **Figure 1.44** Professional sport in isolation

Changing perceptions

There are, of course, more practical considerations. For example, English Premier League football now lives with the daily shadow of a European Super League, and the unanswered question of how that would affect the authority of the Football Association. If major English clubs spend more time playing under a European authority, at what point will control of them pass out of domestic hands? With the advent of the World Club Championship, will that supersede the European perspective in terms of priority and therefore control? Such problems are not insurmountable. However, they will require a change in the way we perceive a global sporting world, as opposed to a domestic or even European one.

The instance of Manchester United's entry into the first World Club Championships in 1999 highlighted the issue of loyalty in a global world. Should world authorities plan their programmes around existing structures? Is that even feasible? Or should existing and often traditional commitments be put to one side and replanned to accommodate such new developments?

In many respects (and despite the allegations of favouritism, élitism and blatantly 'rigged' selection processes made against it), the IOC has a distinct advantage over many other global sporting authorities. First of all, it is the oldest and it began as the single unquestioned authority. All subsequent 'global Games' have grown from it and many take place under its auspices. As a result, whatever problems occur, solutions are found within a global context and any questioning of the IOC's authority is centred upon quality as opposed to social status.

In many sports, there is often much resentment that a comparatively newly formed body assumes the right to interfere with traditionally established procedures. There is even greater indignation when monetary considerations also play a part. Much of this is to do with 'media money'. Because of media coverage, the income of a Premier League football club is vastly greater than the rest of the clubs in the Football League. The gulf becomes even wider with the advent of a suggested 'European League', and wider still in the event of a 'World' or 'Global' competition.

The nurture of talent in the UK

Traditionally, the search for talent in the United Kingdom has been rather a hit and miss affair. The ethical division between amateur and professional participation has meant that any attempt to centralise the search for talent has been fraught with difficulty. Also the 'recreational' approach to sport has decreed that the early identification and creation of talent is undesirable. The identification of talent by outcome rather than as a result of purposeful process has therefore tended to be the norm in the UK. The idea of directing children into those sporting avenues which might best suit their ability occurred outside the UK more than thirty years ago. In the meantime, we have been struggling with the desirability, even the morality, of such a concept.

School sport

Without too much in the way of gratitude – financial or otherwise – Britain's teachers have, for over a century, worked to provide children with a host of sporting experiences that are the envy of most of the rest of the world. From a standpoint of excellence, the nucleus of a massive programme of talent identification has always been within our grasp. Every child went to school; every school taught sport; so that in all but those activities which required particularly specialised facilities, the framework for talent identification and development has always been in place.

School sport began in the public schools in the last half of the nineteenth century (see pages 14–17), with cricket matches having begun somewhat earlier. By the 1890s many board schools had formed local or district associations (see pages 21–22); notably to provide competition in football (largely soccer), cricket, athletics and swimming. Gymnastics competitions were also a feature where there was local interest and expertise.

Soccer was by far the most popular game in the state education system, with the English Schools' Football Association having been formed in 1904 and the first schools' international (against Wales) being played in Walsall in 1907. Unlike in the public schools, a major drawback in the development of sport in state schools was the lack of facilities. This was not really addressed until provision became a requirement of the 1944 Education Act.

More recently, facility provision has expanded considerably, although the practice by many local authorities of selling off playing field space has caused much concern. Although the more prestigious schools in the independent sector tend to have good provision of facilities, many of the smaller private schools, particularly those in urban areas, are not as well provided for as many state schools.

In some respects, the broadening of opportunity outside sport in school has implications for the identification and nurture of talent. It can be agreed that, if **mass participation** is to be seen a necessary pre-requisite in the quest for **excellence**, then school sport and recreation provide the ideal foundation and infrastructure from which to proceed.

The basis of most school sport in the UK is local inter-school competition, with local area, county and sometimes regional organisations looking after various levels of competition for all age groups. Most sports now have national schools' associations responsible for the selection of representative teams. These bodies are normally affiliated to the senior governing body of that sport. Schools' national associations have performed invaluable work over many years, and the English Schools' Athletic Festival, held in July each year, is the envy of the rest of the world.

Most schools' associations promote coaching and award schemes, often in conjunction with the sport's senior governing body. Such schemes encourage improvement and develop potential sporting talent. They do, however, raise the question of coaching taking precedence over teaching (Figure 1.45).

Sports education initiatives

If done correctly, the development of sports colleges and initiatives such as the Youth Sports Trust (YST) should help to raise skill levels and motivate young people to improve their performance.

BT TOP Sport is run jointly by Sport England and the Youth Sports Trust and is intended to support the National Curriculum. The aim is to have this programme, which is for seven- to eleven-year-olds, established in all primary schools by 2001. Other activities

▲ **Figure 1.45** *Teaching or coaching ... play or sport?*

include TOP Gymnastics, TOP Swimming, TOP Athletics, TOP Ability (for children with disabilities), TOP Outdoors, Fit for TOPS and TOP Dance.

The Sport England programme for schools also includes:

- 'Active schools' programme
- Activemark/Activemark Gold
- 'Active schools' co-ordinators
- Coaching for teachers
- The Panathlon Challenge
- Running sports for schools
- Sporting Ambassadors
- Sportsearch
- Sportsmark/Sportsmark Gold
- TOP Play.

Club sport

The former public schoolboys of the nineteenth and early twentieth centuries, and their slightly later female equivalents, have left their mark on British sport. The old boys' and old girls' clubs founded by many of them as they returned to their former communities, or moved to new ones, have, in the main, stood the test of time.

Similarly, those who went into industry, the church, or education also contributed to the development of a vast network of sports clubs that is probably unequalled anywhere in the world. The 'recreative' ethic, upheld by the muscular Christians of more than a hundred years ago (see page 15), became the foundation of most English sport. Although professionalism is now here to stay, literally tens of thousands of people can participate in sport at all levels 'simply because they enjoy it' on virtually any day of the week.

Many clubs affiliate to an appropriate ruling body and play – at the appropriate level – in competitions and leagues. This provides enjoyment, challenge and occasionally throws up a previously unrecognised talent. Other clubs, formed by groups of friends, simply book a court at the local sports centre and meet regularly for an hour or two of enjoyable activity, supplemented in many cases by an even more enjoyable hour or so 'down the pub'!

Rugby clubs are renowned for the 'Vandals' or the 'Wanderers' VX, formed to allow the 'old un's' to pretend they can still do it – or simply to find an excuse not to go shopping on a Saturday afternoon! For generations of British children, cricket or football in the street has been the cradle of their sporting dreams (Figure 1.46).

Britain is probably the undisputed world champion in terms of recreative sport – or sport 'just for the fun of it'. Traditionally, the British attitude to 'serious sport' has always been hampered by our rejection of 'over-competitiveness'. This rather haphazard structure, founded on a recreational tradition as opposed to the pursuit of excellence, is not an efficient vehicle when it comes to the identification and nurturing of talent. Once young people leave school, assuming that they have not by then been 'identified', their sporting

▲ **Figure 1.46** *The street as the cradle of sport – it has been said that Britons would play or watch a game, of anything, anywhere!*

involvement can take them literally anywhere, and to any level of participation.

In the last twenty years or so, there have been various attempts to develop a network of sports centres and associated initiatives to make the identification and subsequent nurturing of talent a rather less hit and miss affair.

Grass-roots football was given a boost in April 2000 with the formation of the Football Foundation. This body was formed by the Football Association, the Premier League and the Government with some £21 million invested during its first year. Funds are allocated by the FA to assist grass-roots provision of local pitches, changing rooms, parks and schools. In addition, community activities and improvements in stadia safety in lower league clubs are also intended targets for funding.

National sports centres and academies

The facilities of the two National Sports Centres at Bisham Abbey and Lilleshall have now been joined by the Centre at Plas-Y-Brenin in North Wales; also the National Sports Centre at Crystal Palace and the national watersports centre at Holme Pierrepoint in Nottinghamshire (which is also a National Sports Centre). The aim of all these centres was to provide a range of facilities capable of preparing athletes for international competition in line with policies driven by the then still composite Sports Council. The national cycling centre in Manchester has since been added and the Sports Council structure has changed considerably since its inception.

Sports academies and centres of excellence have been developing for some time. The most well known are attached to Premier League football clubs. Rugby clubs of both codes have also set these up, as have county cricket clubs. The intention is to identify talent and provide specific development programmes to meet a club's particular needs. Sports governing bodies such as in cycling and athletics also operate regional and national centres of excellence at appropriate venues for junior and senior development squads.

UKSI in Sheffield and network centres

The recently inaugurated **United Kingdom Sports Institute**, with its headquarters in

Table 1.9 UKSI network centres

Network centres	Based at
East	Sport England Offices, Bedford
East Midlands	Holme Pierrepoint National Sports Centre
North	Gateshead International Stadium
North West	Eastlands near Belle Vue
South	Bisham Abbey National Sports Centre
South Coast	Southampton University
South East	Crystal Palace National Sports Centre
South West	University of Bath
West Midlands	Lilleshall National Sports Centre
Yorkshire	Don Valley Stadium, Sheffield

Sheffield, will head a network of ten regional centres throughout England (Table 1.9).

This network of centres under the centralised control of the UKSI and **UK Sport** will work together with the headquarters in Sheffield to ensure that both able-bodied and disabled athletes are prepared in the best way possible for major international competitions (Figure 1.47). Some specific sports facilities

▲ *Figure 1.47* UK Sport was established in 1997 to focus directly on high performance sport at the national level

will be used by national squads at network centres, for example swimming at the University of Bath, watersports at Holme Pierrepont, gymnastics at Lilleshall and cycling in Manchester.

There is also provision for other parts of the UK.

UKSI in Northern Ireland

The Sports Council for Northern Ireland (SCNI) is creating a network centre in Northern Ireland. This will be based at the University of Ulster and will identify a range of sports for 'targeting'. This will effectively be the UKSI network centre for Northern Ireland and will be run in partnership with SCNI.

UKSI in Scotland

Seven sports have been selected to be part of the Scottish Institute of Sport. This is based at the University of Stirling, which will also be the home of the National Swimming Academy. The other sports initially selected for the Institute are athletics, badminton, curling, hockey, football, and rugby.

UKSI in Wales

The centre of UKSI development in Wales is the Welsh Institute of Sport, with links to facilities at the National Indoor Athletics centre at University of Wales Institute Cardiff, the Plas Menai National Watersports Centre and the Cricket School of Excellence at Sophia Gardens. A network including sports science, medicine, coach support, and the ACE UK programme will also be developed.

Other initiatives

The **Elite Coach Education Programme** is a joint venture between the National Coaching Foundation (NCF) and the British Olympic Association. It is intended to provide for the needs of coaches responsible for performers at the very highest level. The NCF was formed in 1983 and is the coaching arm of UK Sport.

The Success in Sydney Programme is aimed specifically at providing additional support to those hoping to compete at the Sydney 2000 Olympics and Paralympics. It will be available only to those with a proven successful record or who have demonstrated real potential at Olympic and world level. This élite programme will be superseded by others in line with major world events.

The **ACE UK** (Athlete Career and Education Services) programme, run by UK Sport, is quite clearly based on that already in use by the Australian Institute of Sport (AIS). Its purpose is to maximise career opportunities for athletes both during and after their time in sport.

Athletes will have access to educational programmes, career advice and training in personal finance and media management. The programme has been developed by the British Olympic Association, the Scottish Institute of Sport, the UK Sports Council and the home country sports councils.

Sport England

Sport England is the new name for the former English Sports Council, which itself came into being in January 1997. This was following devolutionary changes to the former GB Sports Council when England, Northern Ireland, Scotland and Wales were given their own individual sports councils: Sport England, the Northern Ireland Sports Council, the Sports Council for Scotland and the Sports Council for Wales. This created UK Sport as the senior authority, with the National Sports Councils having authority over developments within each country. UK Sport retains responsibility for development at 'GB' level. Three of Sport England's current slogans are:

- more people involved in sport
- more places to play sport
- more medals through higher standards of performance in sport.

The government policy paper 'Raising the Game', produced in 1997, helped develop a more streamlined structure for the organisation of sport in the United Kingdom. Under the new system the GB Sports Council has been replaced by the UK Sports Council (UK Sport). This now deals with issues at UK level, including doping control and the responsibility for the UK Sports Institute.

How Sport England works

Sport England is accountable to Parliament through the Secretary of State for Culture, Media and Sport. Its work is scrutinised by the appropriate Parliamentary Select Committee as well as the Public Accounts Committee.

Members of its Council are appointed by the Secretary of State for Culture, Media and Sport and are responsible for approving all policy and operational matters for Sport England. They are also responsible for issues of strategy, performance, resources, and standards of conduct, as well as for ensuring that public funds are used properly. A series of panels also advise on:

- lottery issues
- local authority issues
- racial equality
- governing body investment
- women and sport
- disability.

Sport England is funded by the Exchequer and through the National Lottery. It is primarily responsible, through the Sport England Lottery Fund, for distributing National Lottery funds earmarked for the development of sport in England (Figure 1.48).

World Class programme

The **World Class** programme developed by Sport England has two major components:

- 'World Class' events
- 'World Class' performance.

These are intended to ensure that provision is made for infrastructure (organisational) development towards the staging of major sporting events and in preparing athletes for top level competition.

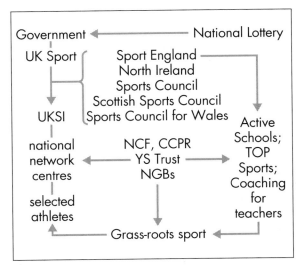

▲ *Figure 1.48* A structure for excellence in sport: how the various bodies work together

European models of sports excellence

France

INSEP (*Institut National du Sport et de l'Education Physique*) was founded at Vincennes on the outskirts of Paris in 1976 to provide training and preparation for France's élite athletes. INSEP is an arm of the Ministry of Youth and Sport (*Ministère de la Jeunesse et des Sports*) which has ultimate responsibility for the development of French sport. This includes deciding which national sports federations receive funding, which sports are classified as élite, and which athletes attend INSEP (Figure 1.49).

INSEP liaises with the various sporting federations, who nominate the athletes chosen to attend. However, the final say in the make-up of each year's élite list rests with the Ministry. Normally some 450–500 athletes are in residence at any one time out of approximately 3,500 élite sportsmen and women. Others attend 'mini' or regional INSEPs and also receive funds to assist with both training and competition. All élite athletes continue to receive funds for up to two years after they retire from competition.

INSEP also provides non-sporting education for young athletes, so that they do not fall behind academically. Athletes take courses in sports medicine and sports science. The Institut also trains professional sports managers and coaches. There is provision for more than 25 sports on its 34-hectare site, housed in facilities which include:

- two swimming pools
- indoor athletics
- indoor velodrome
- a gymnasium and sports hall
- football and rugby pitches
- tennis and basketball courts
- boxing rings
- judo and fencing areas.

French national sports federations provide ninety per cent of the funding required to maintain INSEP, with the other ten per cent coming from the Ministry, through sponsorship and tax. All public companies in France are required to invest a small percentage of their profits in sporting development.

FNDS (*Fonds National pour le Développement du Sport*), or National Sports

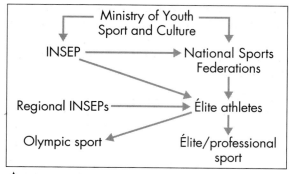

▲ *Figure 1.49* Sporting excellence in France – derived from central government policy

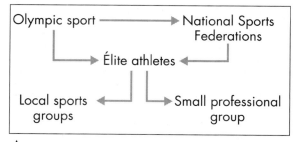

▲ *Figure 1.50* Sporting excellence in Finland – derived from a recreational ethic

Development Fund, is maintained by the Ministry of Youth and Sport (as part of the future development of French sport. It funds sport at grass-roots level and provides equipment for regional sports clubs. It also funds work against drug abuse in sport.

At Olympic level, France won 29 medals in Barcelona in 1992, 8 in Nagano in 1998 and 37 in Atlanta in 1996. Of the Atlanta medals, 20 were won by athletes who had attended INSEP.

With the demise of the 'questionable' sporting ethics of the former Eastern bloc, France is perhaps the most well known European example of a modern, centralised administration that has developed a rather more acceptable approach to the winning of gold medals. The notion of a European model of sporting excellence can, however, be misleading. France is a large nation with a population of over fifty million people and the funding of centralised excellence provision is perhaps more attainable than in smaller countries who have neither the large budget nor the centralised administration that France does.

Finland

In contrast, sport in Finland is run by the Finnish Sports Federation (FSF) without government intervention. Only three per cent of member sports federations have professional athletes in their ranks. Known as 'the Nordic France' because of its dependency upon agriculture, Finland is much smaller than France in both size and population. Figure 1.50 shows a much simpler administrative structure than in France (Figure 1.49).

In Finland, individual sports organisations are responsible for their own élite sports programmes, with the Finnish Olympic Com-

mittee having an overview and influence in Olympic matters only. In such circumstances, it is perhaps not surprising that more than seventy per cent of Finnish professional athletes live abroad.

Public money, in the form of government grants and municipal authority spending, goes largely into the funding of facilities at local level. Government assistance also helps fund facilities for groups too small to be otherwise viable, including provision for disabled and other such groups.

Élite sport does, however, have a high profile in Finland but so does the concept of participation at grass-roots level. The objective of the Finnish Sports Federation is to promote the well-being and ability of local organisations to supply sports services that meet the needs of a physically active population. Four out of five adult Finns consider exercise to be very important in their lives. Ski-ing is part of the way of life and is special amongst the sporting activities (Figure 1.51), as is javelin throwing (Figure 1.52) and distance running.

▲ *Figure 1.51* Children ski-ing: an ability developed as a result of the environment

▲ **Figure 1.52** Finns are known to be excellent javelin throwers and skiers

Sport is the most popular target of Finnish companies interested in sponsorship activity, reflecting a high level of popular interest. Betting and lotteries provide a large proportion of income spent on sport through the public purse.

Commercialisation and Americanisation of UK and European professional sport

Commercialisation and Americanisation are often taken to mean the same thing. In fact, commercialism reflects the changing economic aspects of a sporting Europe that is no longer tied down by amateurism on the one hand or the heavily politicised centralist policies of the former Communist states on the other.

Traditionally, sport in Europe has been championed by the middle- and upper-class amateur and, for the last forty years, by centrally funded national sports programmes. Nowadays, with the declining influence of the former and the demise of the latter, another economic force has stepped willingly into the breach. A growing Europe-wide media industry has also become the channel through which a huge raft of economic activity has been floated. Sporting excellence has become a marketable commodity in its own right. It is undeniable that America is, in many respects, the front runner in this field, hence the term Americanisation. However, the term also carries associations to do with the way that sport is played, as well as the way it is marketed.

The American college system

It has been alleged that the American college system with its sports scholarships was an early form of professionalism without the attendant marketing man – the cynic might well remark that with crowds of up to 50,000 watching college football, who needs marketing? The huge popularisation of sport in the USA via a vast TV network meant that professional sport was born into an ideal environment. Just as significantly, however, this bred an unusual attitude to winning. Vince Lombardi, an American football coach in the 1950s, has been both hailed and ridiculed as the father of this initially unwanted attitude. But it grew, and through the medium of modern communications now has offspring all over the world – including Europe. 'Winning is everything' has now become a much-used expression, which, in its American context, is taken to refer not just to sport but to the rest of life.

Franchise

The franchise – another product of America – was a commercial and media innovation rather than a sporting development. The potential market (i.e. the audience) meant that to uproot a team from its 'home' city became fairly common practice. Television broadcasts meant that games could be broadcast from anywhere, so that local loyalties have become expendable. Whilst this has not yet widely spread into European sport, Europe may have taken this one step further with Europa Cup and Grand Prix athletics (Figure 1.53); a rugby super league and a European football Champions League. In all the above instances, a market has been created via television, giving rise to the humorous saying that '98 per cent of all Manchester United supporters have never been to Old Trafford'. In actual fact they have – via the medium of their television screen!

There are now English Premier League teams that are largely without English-born players, and international athletes whose country of birth seems to have little

▲ **Figure 1.53** *Grand Prix athletics: a market created by television*

influence on which country they represent. Cultural origins, the traditional means by which sporting allegiances were decided, seem to be under threat. It could be said that these cultural associations are now being replaced by commercial ones. Perhaps the FA Cup Final between Tottenham and Liverpool will simply become the Microsoft Cup Final between JVC and Hewlett Packard? It seems that commercial entities are now more important than supporters and that 'virtual' (television) audiences are more important than real ones. Maybe we are in real danger of replacing cultural affiliations with commercial ones?

TASK

a What parallels existed between the paid retainers of early sporting patronage and those of the early 20th century? Discuss.

b To what degree was the Victorian concept of amateurism merely discrimination dressed in acceptable clothing? Discuss.

c Is the nurture of talent more important than the broadest possible level of participation? Discuss this in your group and consider whether the two are in fact linked.

d Does the growth of professional sport, and the importance attached to success, mean that there is a danger that more and more young people will be subjected to inappropriate lifestyles in the quest for sporting excellence?

5. Recreative sport (mass participation)

Commitment to Sport for All

The **European Sports Charter**, adopted by the Committee of Ministers in 1975 and revised in 1992, has 13 Articles. In general terms these endorse the collective view that sport is an important factor in human development.

The Charter embraces the principles of the freedom of every individual to participate in sport in a safe environment. Also to have the opportunity to receive instruction in at least basic sports skills. It further states that those with the capability to do so should have the opportunity to improve their standard of performance at personal and/or publicly recognised levels.

There is also a commitment to protect the **moral and ethical bases of sport**; and to legislate against exploitation for commercial gain, and from abusive or debasing practices including the taking of drugs. The Charter defines sport as:

> *All forms of physical activity which, through casual or organised participation, aim at expressing or improving physical fitness and mental well-being, forming social relationships or obtaining results in competition at all levels.*

European Charter, 1992, Article 2

The European Parliament acknowledges the right of the public/voluntary organisations to establish their own decision-making processes within the law. It also accepts that its own role should be primarily complementary to the action of the sports movement. Article 4 states clearly that:

> *No discrimination on the grounds of sex, race, colour, language, religion, political opinion, nationality shall be permitted in the access to sports facilities or to sports activities, and that where necessary additional measures shall be taken aimed at enabling young gifted people and disadvantaged or disabled people to be able to access such opportunities effectively.*

In relation to young people, Article 5 requires appropriate steps to be taken to:

- develop physical fitness and the acquisition of basic sports skill
- encourage the practice of sport by young people by ensuring that programmes and facilities for sport, recreation and physical education are made available to all pupils
- ensure that appropriate time is set aside for this, including participation after school.

The Charter also requires that the practice of sport, whatever its reasonable purpose, shall be promoted for all sections of communities, by means of appropriate facilities, programmes and instructors.

Improving performance and supporting élite and professional sport

The Charter's requirement that sport at higher levels shall be supported and encouraged includes:

- talent identification and counselling
- the provision of suitable facilities
- sports medicine and sports science support
- scientific coaching and coach education
- other leadership functions
- helping to provide appropriate structures
- competitive outlets.

The appropriate national organisations are required to devise methods of providing support for sportsmen and women who reveal exceptional sporting qualities. This is in order to give them opportunities to fully develop their broader capacities, including a balanced education while in training institutes and a smooth integration into life after sport through the development of career prospects.

Those engaged professionally in sport should have appropriate social status as well as safeguards against exploitation. It is also considered that mass sports participation will be enhanced by the development of training courses leading to diplomas and qualifications. These courses should be appropriate to the needs of participants in different kinds and levels of sport and recreation. Courses should also be designed to meet the needs of those working voluntarily as well as professionally.

Sport and the environment

In terms of future as well as present day practices, the Charter also addresses the need to protect the environment. It requires that sporting activities, whether in urban, open country or water areas, should take account of limited resources and be carried out in accordance with the principles of **sustainable development** and balanced management of the environment. These include:

- taking account of environmental values in the planning and building of sport facilities
- supporting sports organisations in their efforts to conserve the environment
- increasing people's knowledge and awareness of the relationship between sport and sustainable development.

The wider picture

If the aims of the European Charter are to be achieved, appropriate structures for the proper co-ordination of the development and promotion of sport between its various agencies and between the public and voluntary sectors need to be developed. A body capable (in the form of the European Parliament) of the 'wider overview' may serve us well as sport moves from a domestic, through a European and into a global perspective. The co-ordination of sport promotion and development will need to take account of other policy-making arenas. These include education, health, social services, urban and rural environments, the arts and other leisure services. This will ensure that sport is an integral part of socio-cultural development.

The impact of sport for all in Europe

The impact of the European Charter on sport and recreation is likely to be on the means of access to sport and the settings in which such activities occur, rather than directly controlling the administration of specific activities.

The philosophy of Sport for All is embodied in the legislation. At the very least this provides another avenue of redress for those groups or individuals who feel that their legitimate interest is not provided for at a national or domestic level.

Democracy and sport

Towards this end, under a heading of 'Democracy and sport', two policies are currently being given a high priority:

- sport and the law
- sport as a democratic movement.

Policies and systems for addressing issues in high level sport are now well established. Similar provisions for popular sport need particular attention and review. Current European documentation notes that gender equality in sport seems to be a permanent topic of discussion.

The European administration recognises that democratic rights apply just as much to sporting or recreational opportunity as they do in other walks of life. It wishes to encourage more generalised sports participation and the involvement of all age and cultural groups for both social and health reasons. It also notes, sadly, that legislation against doping may also have to be extended.

The role of national agencies

National agencies involved in the provision of sporting opportunity fall into two main categories: first, government departments and national sports bodies and second, clubs and organisations that directly or indirectly promote sport. Those Government departments charged with responsibility for making sport accessible to all must now consider a European philosophy in addition to any domestic mandate or policy undertaking. Outside of Government, those bodies whose specific purpose is to encourage participation include Sport England and the national governing bodies of sports who promote their own sports from grass-roots to élite levels.

Rather less obvious is the part played by those organisations such as the National Associations of Boys' Clubs, Girls' Clubs and Youth Clubs, each of whom promote sport within their own membership and run events and development programmes at both local and national level.

The Guide and Scout movement also does the same, as does the vast army of teachers involved in supporting a wide range of school sport.

In many of these instances, sport is not the primary purpose of the organisation. By providing sporting activities in their programmes, they are nevertheless most influential in broadening opportunity and so enhancing self-esteem. In addition, such organisations as the National Playing Fields Association do valuable work in raising funds for the provision of open spaces for sport and recreation. In a broader context, British Heritage, the National Trust and the Countryside Commission all play their part in the direct and indirect promotion of sporting and recreational activity.

UK Sports Councils

The Sports Councils in the four home countries of the UK are:

- Sport England
- The Northern Ireland Sports Council
- The Sports Council for Scotland
- The Sports Council for Wales.

These organisations are responsible, with other agencies such as local authorities, for the promotion of sporting and recreational opportunities at all levels and in all sections of the community.

They also provide training and education programmes for coaches and officials in partnership with the National Coaching Foundation and at élite level with the UK Sports Institute and UK Sport (see page 43). At school level these partnerships also involve work with school sports governing bodies and the Youth Sports Trust (see page 41).

Other European examples

Many aspects of European sport are derived from the 'Olympian' philosophies of De Coubertin. Victor Balcke, the Swedish Army officer who was much involved in the adoption of Swedish gymnastics by the British army, was also involved in early Olympic developments in Scandinavia. A strong military presence runs through the history of sport there, as well as in physical education.

The role of national authorities in promoting sport in France and Finland was discussed on pages 45–47 in relation to élite sport.

In both Denmark and Sweden physical culture has traditionally been regarded as important and similar views are held in France and Germany. Whilst such activity has formed part of the recreational ethic of many European countries, topography and climate have also been influential. This was particularly so in Scandinavia, where the ability to ski was not simply recreational but fundamental to mobility during the long winter months.

The natural forests and mountainous terrain encouraged the development of hunting, shooting fishing activities, similar to the USA. The winter sports biathlon is a reflection of this.

Grass-roots programmes

Many grass-roots initiatives in the UK have already been mentioned in this section and are also discussed on pages 155–57. Most national sports governing bodies now run their own schemes, often involving highly publicised programmes such as 'Mini-sports', 'Hi-Fives' rugby and 'Quick-Cricket'. There is some minor differentiation between these initiatives and the TOPS, Active Sports and Active Schools programmes funded by Sport England (see page 41). Several of these organisations have had name changes in recent years. The Institute of Youth Sport may also be found under the name of the Youth Sports Trust or the British Sports Trust, whilst the formerly named Sport Aid Foundation is now simply known as **SportsAid**.

SportsAid is not strictly speaking a grass-roots sports scheme. However, its three major aims are:

- furthering the education of young people through sport
- encouraging the socially or physically disadvantaged
- enabling those living in poverty to take advantage of sport.

This means that it effectively catches those groups and individuals who are not catered for by other funding bodies.

In Austria, the youth sport programme does not aim at top level performers but relies on variety and fun. Much of this is competition-free and is run by the country's 53 sporting federations at sports training venues.

There is a strong social commitment to sport here just as in Finland. Other activities range from health programmes for children in primary schools to Youth Sport Days and a polyathlon competition, which includes gymnastics, track and field athletics and swimming for young people aged 13–16.

In France in the 1960s, President de Gaulle's 'five-star plan' endowed many French towns with sports stadia, developed for both spectators and participation. Sport pour Tous (Sport for All) was established in France long before it was thought of in the UK.

Concept of target groups and reforms

Target groups are those groups identified as being in need of specific attention with regard to sport and recreation (see page 33). This might be because of physical needs, as in the case of the disabled, because of social deprivation, as in the case of people living in the inner-city areas, or being unemployed, or because of discrimination either by a group's own sub-culture or their local host culture.

Identification of need for these target groups, and provision for them, may arise either as a result of nationally promoted initiatives and policies, or the more localised identification of a specific need.

Amateur sports and the voluntary sector

The demarcation between **amateur** and professional no longer exists in most sports today. Professionals are no longer looked down on (see pages 35–39). Rugby union football was seen by many as the last bastion of amateurism. In many other sports, competition is now regarded as 'open' (to both professional and amateur competitors). In some sports there are opportunities for both amateur and professional participation, sometimes in the same competition, e.g. golf.

Amateur sport now tends to mean that level of sport which has no pretension to élitism, but which nevertheless caters for thousands of enthusiasts, some of whom take their sport just as seriously as the keenest professional. This area of sport is supported by a vast army of **voluntary officials** and helpers without whom most sporting organisations would grind to a halt. Even at major athletic meetings, where the contestants are now most certainly professional, such extravaganzas could simply not take place without the large number of volunteers who perform a whole array of sometimes thankless tasks for no monetary reward, other than perhaps their travelling expenses.

Wilderness and alternative sports

In recent years there has been a rise across Europe of wilderness and alternative sports. This is perhaps a reflection of a desire to return to nature – in the sporting sense – and the fact that modern com-munications and technologies make such activities possible. This new area of interest is not new in that man has always enjoyed rural and mountain sports.

Previously inaccessible terrain can now be traversed by mountain bike, or even four-wheeled vehicle, because of better communication and technological advances. In addition to the growth of television networks, modern transport allows much easier **access to remote areas** than before.

Competition has been introduced into rock-climbing (although much of this tends to be indoors on artificial walls) and is conveyed to the masses by means of television. The relatively new sport of triathlon, and its attendant 'bi' and 'quad' formats, has become very popular. It perhaps overshadows the more traditional 'modern' and 'athletic' forms of pentathlon competition as it is more dynamic and 'screenable' to Europe's TV networks.

In this respect also, popular culture is once again asserting itself. The traditional winter sports scene is being invaded by the snow-boarders and freestyle skiers with little regard for established etiquette. They refuse, for example, to wear the traditional ski outfits, preferring to be seen in fashion clothing in order to promote a 'cool' image.

Key words and phrases

1. Cultural background
- Industrial Revolution • Railways • Blood Sports Act • Propriety
- Pedestrianism • Prize-fighting • Literacy • Coaching inn • Statute Fairs
- Age of Enlightenment • Fairs Act • Festival activities • 'Mob' activities
- Saturday half day • Rationalised sports

2. The development of physical education
- Thomas Arnold • Rugby School • Social control • Athleticism
- Muscular Christian(ity) • Manliness • Leadership • Games ethic
- Archibald MacLaren • Oxbridge 'melting pot' • Guts Muths • Jahn • Ling
- Martina Österberg • Forster Education Act • Model Syllabus of 1902
- 1904 Syllabus • Fisher Act • 1933 Syllabus • Outward Bound Trust
- Rudolph Laban • Moving and Growing • Planning the Programme
- National Curriculum • Designated sports colleges • Youth Sports Trust

3. Social influences on performance and participation
- Time • Space • Freedom • Emergent cultures • Nation-building
- Role models • Mass participation • Access • Opportunity • Provision
- Élitist • Negative stereotypes • Positive stereotypes • Stacking
- Self-fulfilling prophecy • Target groups • British Sports Association for the Disabled

4. Professional (élite) sport
- 'Broken time' • Sporting Saturday afternoon • Jack Broughton
- Marquis of Queensbury • Amateur Boxing Association • National Sporting Club
- Bosman ruling • 'Gentlemen' and 'players' • Sport England
- Commonwealth Games • Mass participation • Excellence
- United Kingdom Sports Institute • UK Sport • Elite Coach Education Programme
- ACE UK • World Class • INSEP • FNDS

(continued)

5. Recreative sport (mass participation)

- European Sports Charter
- Moral and ethical bases of sport
- Sustainable development
- Democracy and sport
- SportsAid
- Amateur
- Voluntary officials
- Access to remote areas

REVIEW QUESTIONS

1 Explain what a church wake was and its importance in the history of sport.

2 Account for the development of the urban public house as a centre for recreation.

3 The growth of rail transport and the 'Saturday half day' changed the nature of British sport forever. Why was this?

4 How did the 1870 Forster Education Act help in the development of physical education – even though it made no such provision?

5 Was there a difference between 'rationalisation' and 'codification' in sport?

6 Why were the first PT syllabuses so heavily militarised?

7 Who was Rudolph Laban, and what was his contribution to physical education?

8 Why was the training of women PE teachers so far in advance of that of men in the UK?

9 Women had 'wing colleges' whilst men had 'wing courses'. What was the difference and why was this so?

10 What was the 'inch thick-mile wide' syndrome?

11 Explain what was meant by the term 'broken time'.

12 Suggest reasons why the FA did not ban professionalism as the RFU had done.

13 Explain the relationship between UK Sport, Sport England and the UKSI, in terms of provision for excellence.

14 How has European law helped to establish the right to recreation for all its citizens?

15 How has television helped in the creation of a 'global sports arena'?

Texts used in the writing of this section

- Adams, B., *The Badminton Story*, BBC Publications, 1980
- Bailey, S. & Vamplew, W., *100 Years of Physical Education, 1899–1999*, PEAUK, 1999
- Brailsford, D., *British Sport: A Social History*, Lutterworth Press, 1992
- Briggs, A., *The History of Birmingham*, vol. 2, Oxford University Press, 1952
- Clay, G., 'Movement Backwards and Forwards' – The Influence of Government on Physical Education – An HMI Perspective, in *The British Journal of Teaching Physical Education*, vol. 30, no. 4.
- Holt, R., *Sport and the British*, Clarendon Press, 1990
- Lowerson, J., *Sport and the English Middle Classes, 1870–1914*, Manchester University Press, 1995
- Mauldon, E. & Layson, J., *Teaching Gymnastics*, Macdonald & Evans, 1966
- McFee, G. & Tomlinson, A., *Education, Sport & Leisure: Connections & Controversies*, Meyer & Meyer Verlag, 1997
- McIntosh, P., *Physical Education in England Since 1800*, Bell & Sons, 1968
- Munrow, A. D., *Pure and Applied Gymnastics*, Edward Arnold, 1955
- Polley, M., *Moving the Goalposts*, RKP, 1998
- Prestidge, J., *The History of British Gymnastics*, BAGA, 1988
- Rowe, N. & Champion, R. *Young People and Sport: National Survey 1999*, Sport England Research, Feb. 2000
- Tranter, N., *Sport, Economy and Society in Britain 1750–1914*, Cambridge University Press, 1998

Suggested further reading

- Bailey, S. & Vamplew, W., *100 Years of Physical Education, 1899–1999*, PEAUK, 1999
- Brailsford, D., *British Sport: A Social History*, Lutterworth Press, 1992
- Carel Press, *Sports Extra*, Carel Press, 1998
- Clay, G., 'Movement Backwards and Forwards' – The Influence of Government on Physical Education – An HMI Perspective, in *The British Journal of Teaching Physical Education*, vol. 30, no. 4
- Galligan, F. (ed.), *Sports History for 'A' Level*, British Society of Sports History, 2000
- Hargreaves, J., *Sport, Power and Culture*, Polity Press/Blackwell, 1996
- Holt, R., *Sport and the British*, Clarendon Press, 1990
- Lowerson, J., *Sport and the English Middle Classes, 1870–1914*, Manchester University Press, 1995
- Polley, M., *Moving the Goalposts*, RKP, 1998
- Prestidge, J., *The History of British Gymnastics*, BAGA, 1988.
- Rice, J., *Start of Play*, Prion Books, 1998
- Rowe, N. & Champion, R. *Young People and Sport: National Survey 1999*, Sport England Research, Feb. 2000
- Tranter, N., *Sport, Economy and Society in Britain 1750–1914*, Cambridge University Press, 1998
- Vamplew, R., *Pay Up and Play the Game*, Cambridge University Press, 1988

Section B: Issues in sport: The Olympic case study

1. History of the modern Olympics

The games of the ancient world

The sporting connection most readily associated with Ancient Greece is, for most of us, their Games: in particular the ancient Olympiads. Most people have some inkling that the origins of what is today a huge spectacular are to be found long ago, before much of the rest of western civilisation had even reached infancy.

These Games, known collectively as the Panhellenic Games, were an integral part of Greek life. They combined religion, sport and music in festivals that took place throughout the Mediterranean. Not only did they attract participants and spectators, but they helped hold together the various 'city-states' that were Greece at that time.

The Games of Olympia

The Games of Olympia are believed to be the oldest and are certainly the best known. Although now lost in time, it is believed that all the Games began as religious ceremonies. This aspect may have diminished somewhat over time but many of them were held in the name of a god – at least at their outset. Sometimes they were held as 'funeral games' to commemorate the death of famous people. The events served as entertainment for humans but performances were also offered to the gods as appeasement.

The true origin of these Games is lost in the mists of antiquity, although there are reliable references to the fact that the Olympic Games were held in 776 BC. McIntosh, in *Sport in Society* (1963), refers to this date as the first record of an Olympic victor but goes on to say that, 'There is little doubt that festivals and contests were held there [at Olympia] in 1300 BC or earlier'. Harris, in his 'Greek Athletes and Athletics' (1964) suggests that we should take the origin of Greek athletics as far back as the Minoan Age in Crete. He states that, 'The evidence is scanty and inconclusive, but there is sufficient to prevent us accepting unquestioningly, indignant and dogmatic denials of a possible Cretan origin of Greek athletics.' He offers in support of this suggestion the evidence of the famous 'Boxer' vase from Hagia Triada, which has been dated by archaeologists to about 1600 BC.

Greek civilisation emerged from what has been described as its 'dark age' in the eighth century BC. From this point onwards there is much more plentiful evidence to be found in both literature and archaeology. However, this evidence is still scant by modern standards and as a result historians are cautious when it comes to pinpointing events.

Games and athletic meetings were much more a part of everyday Greek life than is often realised. They were also much more widespread. The Olympic Games, although hugely significant and prestigious, were just one of many such festivals held all over the Hellenic world. There were in fact *four* major 'Games' at this time:

- The **Olympic** Games, held at Olympia in honour of the god Zeus
- The **Pythian** Games, held at Delphi to celebrate the festival of Apollo
- The **Isthmian** Games, in honour of the god Poseidon
- The **Nemean** Games, also held in honour of Zeus.

▲ *Figure 1.54* Greek hunters throwing javelins

The reason for the fame of these four Games above all others is unclear.

The Pythian Games

It is probably true to say that they were second in importance only to the Olympic Games. The origin of both of them lies somewhere between mythology and reality. They were dedicated to Apollo and the site of the Games was believed to have been the very spot upon which that god defeated a mighty serpent.

Scholars estimate that the Pythian Games started during the seventh century BC and it is thought that they were originally held every eight years. It is believed that the Games were changed to a four-year cycle early in the sixth century BC. Unlike virtually all the other Games, music remained a central area of activity throughout the history of the Pythian Games. Music always took up the first two (sometimes three) days of competition and also included poetry. Typically, three days of athletic and equestrian competition would then follow, with a final day devoted to the worship of Apollo.

The Isthmian Games

These Games were held near the Isthmus of Corinth. Although the precise year in which they began is unknown, by the sixth century BC they had become a multiple-day festival attracting the same class and number of competitors as the Olympic and Pythian Games. Their origin was also surrounded in myth, including one that they were founded by the god Poseidon in whose honour they were held. The Games were held in the second and fourth years of the Olympic cycle, probably in April. The events were similar to those of the Games at Olympia, including running, wrestling, boxing, the **pankration** (a form of wrestling), and pentathlon. There were also equestrian (probably chariot) events and a festival of music.

The Nemean Games

The Games at Nemea began in the first quarter of the sixth century BC, and like the Isthmian Games they occurred in the second and fourth years of the Olympic cycle, towards the end of the summer. Originally this festival was focused on a divinity about which little appears to be known, other than that it was related to the harvest. However, according to mythology, the festival was founded by Heracles and dedicated to the god Zeus.

Because these Games were established much later those at Olympia, it seems that the programme there was copied at Nemea. It featured athletic, equestrian and music contests. The athletic events included running, pentathlon, running in armour, pankration, boxing, and wrestling.

Prizes at the Games

Originally the prizes in these Games were 'crowns', or garlands of leaves. At Olympia the crown was of wild olive leaves, whilst at Delphi it was laurel. At Isthmia the crown was of pine leaves and at Nemea it was wild celery. Other Games, for example at Rhodes, Eluesis, Argos, Megarta, Sicyon and Marathon, had their own awards. These ranged from shields and cups to leather jerkins at Pellene.

Victors at the major Games would expect to be handsomely rewarded upon their return home. One of the most common myths was that the Games were amateur with participants not receiving payment. Although victors may not have been paid as such, a 'crown' assured any athlete a prosperous living. In later Games, competitors became almost entirely professional and were lavishly rewarded. The rewards offered for victory by many towns were often worth more than the average labourer would make in a lifetime.

In the beginning

Like all the athletic Games, the Olympics had rather humble beginnings, and probably lasted no more than a single day at first. As the Games evolved, the sporting element came to overshadow the religious element, so that by the fifth century BC the two aspects were almost separated. This may have been a result of the increased scope and following of the Games – by the sixth century, competitors travelled from much further afield in order to compete.

The conquests of Alexander the Great (334–323 BC) enlarged and developed the Hellenic world. The practice of Games and athletics contests spread along with the honour and reward gained as a result of such victories. Alexander himself was said to have been a keen athlete but 'avoided taking part in public Games on the grounds that kings should only compete with kings'. He did apparently once compete against a leading sprinter who, with the best of intentions, eased up before the finish to allow the King to win: a gross affront to the King's dignity!

As well as athletics, Greek culture spread across much of the ancient world at this time. It is worth noting that the term 'athletics' was used in a rather different context from the way it is today, although even now we often refer to people who take part in a wide range of sports as 'athletes'. Athletics in the Olympic or Pythian Games would have included running events – as is the custom today – but they would also have included events such as chariot-racing (the only event that was common to the later Roman Games), wrestling and the pankration. The latter was a specialised form of 'no-holds-barred' Greek wrestling and was held in great esteem.

This generalised use of the term 'athletics' is mirrored in the eighteenth and nineteenth century use of the terms 'gymnastic' as well as 'athletic', both words having their origins in those ancient times. The term 'gymnastic' was often used in a generic sense and included such events as the high jump, which we now associate with track and field athletics. The term 'athletics' in the Greek sense not only referred to those events we know under that name today but included a sense of the 'struggle' which was a part of any competitive performance or contest.

The events traditionally included in these major Games in Olympia are given in Table 1.10, together with the first known date of their existence.

Event	Date
Stade	776 BC
Diaulos	724 BC
Dolichos	720 BC
Wrestling and pentathlon	708 BC
Boxing	688 BC
Pankration	648 BC
Boys' running and wrestling	632 BC
Race in armour (Hoplite)	520 BC
Boys pankration	200 BC

▲ **Table 1.10** First known events at Olympia. A boys' pentathlon was held in 628 BC but was immediately discontinued

Stade

The name of this event, **stade**, is taken from the stadium in which the Games were held. The distance was approximately equal to the modern 200 metres, and the race involved running from one end of the stadium, around a turning post at the other end and back again to finish opposite the starting point.

Stadium

The stadia of those days were different from today's. The curve was at one end only, to accommodate a viewpoint for spectators, and competitors ran up and down the centre of what we now call the 'infield' – not around its perimeter (Figure 1.55).

Races of more than one stade in length involved negotiating a turning post at either end of the stadium and all turns were apparently made left-handed.

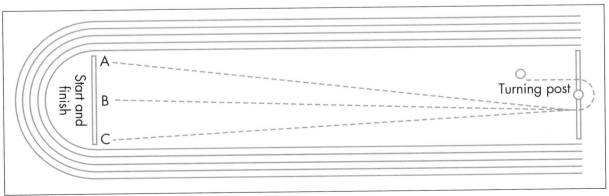

▲ **Figure 1.55** Plan of a typical stadium. The lane-type markings actually represent tiered seating – all competition took place in the centre of the arena. The turning-post needed a judge with a careful eye!

The **diaulos** was a foot-race of approximately 400 metres and involved running two stades, whilst the **dolichos** was a long-distance race that appears to have been held over several distances between seven and twenty-four stades (approx. 1,500–5,000 metres). At the Games of Olympia, the distance would probably have been 20 stades (approx. 4,000 metres).

It is thought that the hippolite/hoplite (race in armour) may at some time have been an equestrian event for warriors, as the word 'hippo' is Greek for horse. There is a clear military connection, as with the javelin event. It is known that at Isthmia and Nemea, and several other Games, there was also an event of four stades, from which the 'race in armour' may have taken its name.

With very few exceptions, only Greek citizens and not slaves were allowed to compete in the major Games. Class was as important then as it was in Victorian times, when the notion of a gentleman trying to better his previous performances and competing against others of equal status was more important than whether or not money changed hands. Some 'ordinary' Greeks (those who did not have 'citizen' status) did sometimes participate: Coroebus of Ellis, the winner of the stade in 776 BC, was reputed to be a cook.

Myron's statue, from the fifth century BC, shows a discus thrower (Figure 1.56). It is reasonable to assume that throwing technique has changed since then. We know from later evidence that the discus was not thrown from a circle as it is today, but from a throwing line. We also know that the landing area was bounded by parallel lines and not by a sector. This suggests that the implement was thrown under-arm or in a straight line – possibly because its weight made a rotational technique impossible. The pose struck by the figure of Myron's statue tends to support this.

There is evidence suggesting discus throws of around 100 feet (33 metres) and also long jumps of 45 feet (14 metres) or more. These are performances that, particularly in the long jump, need explaining.

Like in throwing, technique in jumping has changed considerably over the centuries. Some long jumps in which the ancient athletes carried weights (halteres) are thought to have been two jumps in succession, just as discoi have been found measuring almost twice the diameter of modern implements.

The Games before the modern Olympics

The ancient Games died out some centuries before the birth of Christ. They re-appeared, however, in England in a slightly different form during the sixteenth and seventeenth centuries, with the revival of interest among scholars in the ancient civilisations and their cultures. The **Cotswold Olympik Games**, and the Gog Magog Olympik Games, are so far the earliest known competitions with an 'Olympic' connection.

In 1534 King Henry VIII made himself head of the Church of England. This led to a radical change in university education with professors of Greek being appointed in 1540 at both Oxford and Cambridge. It is thought that there was a revival in interest in ancient Olympic history at this time. It also transpires

▲ *Figure 1.56* Myron's discus thrower. *Myron was a sculptor of the fifth century BC. This is one of the best known images associated with the Games of Ancient Greece and the Olympic ideal*

that the common link between the Gog Magog Olympik Games and Robert Dover's Cotswold Games is Cambridge University.

Robert Dover

Sport was much encouraged at Cambridge in the 1570s and we know there was a football field behind Trinity College where the scholars played a match against the Cambridge town boys. The scholars were soon banned from attending the Gog Magog Olympiks which in fact lasted the whole of May or longer. The ban became a challenge to the scholars who continued to visit the Games.

Throughout England in the early seventeenth century, folk games and festivals were being discouraged by the Puritans and the birth of English Olympianism at Cambridge occurred at a difficult time. It appears that Catholics were more inclined to practise sport than Puritans, and more likely to name a local sports 'Olympik'.

Robert Dover, a Catholic, became a scholar at Cambridge in 1595 and spent a year or two there before becoming a lawyer. He founded the Cotswold Olympik Games in 1612. They lasted until 1852 before being re-convened in 1951. Dover's Games contained a mixture of 'courtly' and 'folk' events, including the smock race, a feature of most English rural festivals. (Figure 1.57)

▲ **Figure 1.57** *Robert Dover presiding over his Games*

Other early Olympics

Symonds D'Ewes, who was also a scholar at Cambridge University, wrote about the Gog Magog Olympik Games in his diary in 1620, but they may have been known by that name as early as 1595 when Robert Dover was at Cambridge.

Further evidence of students naming folk sports as 'Olympik' is found at Oxford University in about 1681, and in 1712 a local games at Cowley were referred to as the 'Olympiad of the country'. There appears also to have been an Olympic Games at Hampton Court, near London, in 1679. In 1771, the writers of daily newspapers were taking Olympic enthusiasm seriously and the *Public Advertiser* likened a cricket match to Isthmian, Pythian or Olympic Games.

The nineteenth century saw an increase in Olympic-inspired sports. Interestingly, in 1801, a five-yearly sports competition began at St Ives, Cornwall, which was repeated at least five more times up to 1826. In November 1832, Baron de Berenger organised a six-day Olympic Festival in London and an Olympic week in 1838. There was also a proposal to hold an Olympic Games to the south of London in 1833, another at Leicester in 1839 and yet another at Lords Cricket Ground in 1846.

Wenlock Olympian Games

The most important contribution to English Olympianism was the founding of the **Wenlock Olympian Games** in October 1850 by Dr William Penny Brookes (Figures 1.58 and 1.59). Prior to this he had formed the Wenlock Olympian Class and in 1859 wrote to numerous town mayors in England urging them to organise their own Olympic Games. A feature of both Roberts Dover's Games and those held in Much Wenlock was that the 'folk' or popular tradition, with entry to many events open to all classes, was retained. This was quite distinct from the Games of Ancient Greece and the modern Olympics, where class was most definitely a key to entry.

The founding of the National Olympian Association

In 1865 a National Olympian Association was proposed in Liverpool with William Penny Brookes, John Hulley of the Liverpool Gymnasium and Thomas Hughes amongst its

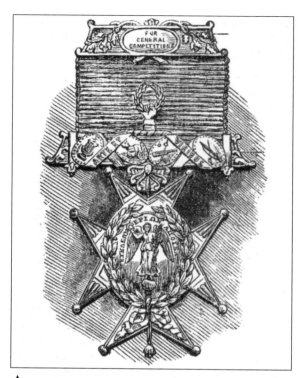

▲ **Figure 1.58** *The Wenlock Medal which was first presented in 1868 for a competition later called the pentathlon*

▲ **Figure 1.59** *The Champion Tilter of the 1887 Games, honoured with his crown of leaves. Right of centre is William Penny Brookes and far right is the herald*

founder members. It was ratified at a further meeting in London in March 1866 and its first Olympic Festival was held in London in July of that year, the success of which was limited. Shrewsbury held games in 1861 and 1864. The Shropshire Olympian Society was formed in 1860 and held games at Wellington in 1861 and 1862, while at Liverpool there were Olympic Games in 1862, 1863, 1864 and 1867.

Subsequent National Olympian Association festivals were held in Birmingham (1867), Wellington (1868), Much Wenlock (1874 and 1876), Shrewsbury (1877) and Hadley (1883), which appears to have been the last of the Olympian Association's festivals. There were also Olympic Games at Manchester in 1864 and 1865, and at Leicester in 1866.

In 1859, William Penny Brookes invited the Greek ambassador in London to attend his Olympics at Much Wenlock. He also sent a silver cross to Athens as a prize for their own Olympics being held in the same year. In 1877 King George I of Greece reciprocated by sending Brookes a silver cup for competition in the pentathlon at the Olympic Games at Shrewsbury.

Despite Brookes' best efforts, the Greek government did not agree to his request that a modern version of the ancient Olympics be inaugurated. That singular achievement was to fall to Baron **Pierre de Coubertin**, whose aristocratic connections possibly allowed him to pursue the matter more effectively. However, the contribution of Brookes and other 'Olympic' innovators should quite properly be acknowledged and applauded.

De Coubertin and the establishment of the modern Olympics

Baron Pierre de Coubertin (Figure 1.60) was born into an aristocratic family in Paris in 1863. He developed an avid interest in both education and sport. Following a conference on education he had organised in Paris in 1889, he received a letter from Brookes inviting him to attend the Wenlock Olympian Games which Brookes had founded nearly forty years earlier. He was particularly delighted with the literary and artistic competitions believed to have been a feature of the ancient Olympiads. He was to find a place for these in his re-creation of those Games in 1896.

English public schools

De Coubertin also took the opportunity to visit some English public schools, including Rugby School, which he had visited on several occasions as a young man. He had been most impressed with the English approach to 'manly sports' and Thomas Arnold, headmaster of Rugby from 1828 until 1841, is said to have been one of the most powerful influences on De Coubertin's later life.

▲ **Figure 1.60** *Baron Pierre de Coubertin, 1863–1937, founder of the modern Olympic Games*

De Coubertin believed that it was the English public schools that had produced the men of character who had built the British Empire. He saw that the philosophy of muscular Christianity (see page 15) and its vehicle of athleticism embodied the way for France to re-build and re-invigorate her youth following the humiliating defeat in the Franco-Prussian War.

He also visited the United States, and by the early 1890s had formulated what has become known as his 'Olympic dream'.

To De Coubertin, what he called 'Hellenic completeness' and the ideals embodied in English sport were the two greatest forces for good and these concepts served as the basis of his 'Olympic dream'. This dream was fulfilled on Easter Sunday 1896 – a paradoxical choice of a day of Christian celebration re-kindling the image of an ancient one steeped in pagan ritual.

The first modern Olympic Games

From 5–15 April 1896, 311 athletes from 13 nations contested the nine sports that made up the modern re-birth of the ancient Games of Greece (Figure 1.61). The countries represented in Athens were:

- Austria
- Australia
- Bulgaria
- Chile
- Denmark
- France
- Germany
- Great Britain
- Greece
- Hungary
- Sweden
- Switzerland
- United States.

This list alone represents the remarkable achievement of De Coubertin in bringing together athletes from four of the world's continents at a time when travel and communications were beset with difficulties. Italy should have had a single representative who, fully embracing the true Olympic spirit,

▲ **Figure 1.61** *The Athens Olympiad in 1896. The poster advertising the Games emphasises a connection with Ancient Greece*

walked from Milan to Athens only to find he was late!

The sports represented at the first modern Games were athletics, cycling, fencing, gymnastics, lawn tennis, shooting, swimming, weightlifting and wrestling. It is interesting to compare these activities with those of the ancient athletes. Such events as the javelin, discus and running races had survived along with wrestling. Much of the rest of the programme, however, was a reflection of the acceptable face of rationalised sport as practised by the middle-class élite of Europe towards the end of the nineteenth century. The ancient Olympic tradition of a laurel wreath for the victor was, however, retained. It is unlikely that the brutish pankration of those Ancient Greek Games would have been acceptable to the refined nineteenth-century middle classes.

Amateurism and the myth of the recreational ethic

The issue of professionalism – or to be more precise what was meant by amateurism – became a subject of contention in the Olympics just as it was in the wider world of sport. History shows that this was not simply a question of whether sportsmen were paid for their endeavours, but whether they were acceptable as gentlemen.

The Victorian recreational ethic embraced the upper-middle class-values nurtured in the English public schools. These were highly esteemed by De Coubertin. To this extent his 'Games for the world' concept was constrained by those values, and restricted to the class it served.

Class and the early Olympics

While little is known of the personal details of many of the early Olympians, we do know the names of the British competitors in the 1896 Games who had entered individually as there were no national teams at that time. They consisted of:

- Launceston Elliot – born in India, where his father was a magistrate; a relative of the Earl of Minto – weightlifting
- John Pius Boland – MP and academic; last-minute entry – lawn tennis
- Edward Battell – footman to the British ambassador – cycling
- Frank Keeping – butler to the British ambassador – cycling
- Sidney Merlin – son of the British consul in Athens – shooting
- George Marshall – reputedly from Oxford University although not verified – 100 metres and 800 metres
- Grantley Goulding – son of a farmer – hurdles
- Charles Gmelin – Oxford University academic, cleric and headmaster – 100 metres and 400 metres
- George Robertson – Winchester College and Oxford University, lawyer – discus (he was a hammer thrower but this event was not held at the 1896 Games).

The importance of social class at the Olympics is perhaps best shown in the example of the two British cyclists, Edward Battell and Frank Keeping, who were based in Athens and worked at the British Embassy. Their entry in the cycling events caused the first confrontation on a point of principle in modern Games history. As employed persons, they could not be accepted by many of their would-be fellow (largely British) competitors as 'gentlemen'. The thinking of the time was that if they were not gentlemen, they could not be amateurs.

With the clear exception of Battell and Keeping, all the other British competitors were clearly of gentlemanly status. De Coubertin himself was known to have open views on the issue of class and sport. However, by definition, those able to travel the world to an Olympic venue would clearly have needed the means and free time to do so.

It was perhaps De Coubertin's love of British sport, combined with the country's role as a world leader, that allowed British middle-class élitist values to dominate the Olympics regarding participation. Harold Abrahams' coach, Sam Mussabini, being banned from the stadium during the 1924 Games in Paris in the film *Chariots of Fire*, provides vivid evidence of what it was like to be 'on the wrong side of the fence'. Mussabini was banned because he was a professional coach. It was some time before De Coubertin's dream truly embraced all classes, colours and creeds.

The Avery Brundage years

Avery Brundage was President of the International Olympic Committee (IOC) from 1952 to 1972 at a time when the pressures on amateur athletes were at their greatest. Prior to that time he had been President of the US Olympic Committee and was known to be a staunch supporter of the amateur principles for which the Games stood. He had been elected to the IOC in 1937.

Some saw him as a stubborn and uncompromising obstacle to the development of the movement, while others hailed him as a defender of the true principles of amateurism against rising commercial and political pressures.

His presidency embraced the political problems of the divided nations of Germany, Korea and China, the Hungarian uprising of 1956, as well as Northern Ireland, the Middle East and Vietnam. The fact that these events coincided with the fastest growth period of the Olympic movement and the most expansive period of mass sport participation drew out the best and worst in a man attributed with the qualities of flint steel.

Angered at the withdrawal of teams from the 1956 Melbourne Games over the Suez Crisis, he raised an issue that was to return to haunt the Olympic movement in years to come:

... if participation in sport is to be stopped every time politicians violate the laws of humanity there will be few international contests ...

Avery Brundage, IOC meeting, 1954

The following year, when questioned on his view of professional sportsman, he replied, after conceding that professional sportsmen were no less honourable than amateurs:

... And there's the difference ... As soon as you take money for playing sport, it isn't sport, it's work.

His assertion that politics had no place in sport has since undergone serious review, particularly in the light of more recent world events. Quite clearly, although there is little argument that playing sport for pay becomes work, the interesting (and relevant) question is whether such work should still be defined as sport.

Brundage convinced both the USA and the rest of the world that the 1936 Games in Berlin should go ahead, despite the views of many of Hitler's opponents. This perhaps best illustrates the single-mindedness of the man who, with hindsight, was not always wise. He is later reported as having admitted to being duped by Hitler's assurances that there would be no vendetta against Jewish athletes in selection of the German team.

Lord Killanin

Brundage was succeeded in 1972 by the much quieter figure of Michael Morris, Lord Killanin. He walked straight into the multitude of wrangles that beset the Montreal Games in 1976, and the first part of the 'tit-for-tat' **boycotts** of the Games in Moscow (1980) and Los Angeles (1984). He bore his relatively short term of office with much fortitude – despite a heart attack in 1977.

Lord Killanin was criticised by many as being weak and lacking the grit and fire of Brundage. However, the quiet manner in which he quelled the furious Soviets – enraged at the disqualification of their fencer, and the disappearance of a young diver seeking political asylum at the 1976 Montreal Games – showed that he simply had a different way of getting things done. The trick in that particular instance was to quietly remind the Russian delegation that if they walked out of the Games (as they were threatening to do) their own hosting of the event in 1980 would be in serious jeopardy.

The rise and reforms of Samaranch

Juan Antonio **Samaranch** is the latest in a line of distinguished IOC Presidents. During his time of office, which began in 1980, he has had to contend with a series of political boycotts and the rise of professionalism as the norm in sport. There have also been a series of challenges to the integrity of the IOC and its commissioners, as well as investigations into his own conduct as the organisation's president. More positively, he has also presided over the return of South Africa to the Olympic fold after many years of isolation due to its policy of **apartheid**.

The result of criticism levelled at the conduct of the IOC and its commissioners resulted in a full review of the commission's operations and conduct. It was passed by delegates in December 1999. The review's most important reforms were:

- a limit to the number of IOC delegates, a fixed retirement age and length of service
- the application of term limits to the period of its presidency
- either the elimination of members' visits to candidate cities, or that visits should be allowed only under certain circumstances
- any organisation receiving funds from the IOC must provide adequate accounts of how those funds are used
- the distribution of 'athlete's passports' in order to aid the administration of doping control.

Ten commissioners were removed following allegations of fraud and dishonesty in investigations leading up to the reforms. However, there are still questions about the validity of an ethics committee that reports to its own president.

There remain potential flaws in the new arrangements. For example, although the tenure (length of service) of delegates is limited to eight years, this is, in some cases, renewable. It is not clear just what such circumstances might be. The increase in the number of delegates from the present 102 to no more than 115 means that, potentially, the

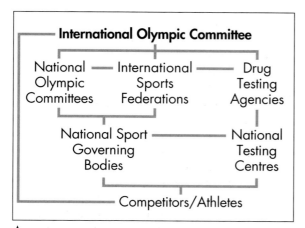

▲ Figure 1.62 *Simplified infrastructure of the International Olympic Committee*

TASK

a In groups, discuss three reasons for the importance of Games in the Hellenic world.

b Using a range of small dumb bells or hand weights, investigate what the effect on performance in the long jump the ancient athletes would have found using 'halteres'.

c Write a short account of the nature of the early Olympic Games and identify any aspects of them that might still be found in the Games of today.

d Write your own short account of the nature of early 'Olympic' activity in Britain prior to 1896.

death of older commissioners and renewable tenure for some others could still leave the major criticism of 'jobs for life' largely unaddressed.

2. Race and ethnicity within the Olympic movement

Race and sport

It has long been part of the Olympic ideal that athletes should be free to participate in the Olympic Games irrespective of race, colour or creed. That this has not yet truly come to pass reflects more on the values of today's world than those of the Olympic organisation.

Mass access to sport is as a result of a broad spectrum of political and cultural values as much as of any particular sporting organisation – however large it may be. The constraints placed upon certain cultural and sub-cultural groups are mainly those of a majority culture over minority ethnic groups. Sometimes constraints are self-imposed, or at least, imposed on certain sectors of a group. Moroccan women, for example are excluded from sporting participation by their own culture. Such self-imposed exclusion is a gender- or religious-based issue, rather than one of race or colour (Figure 1.63).

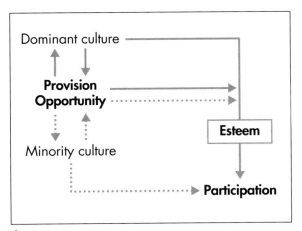

▲ **Figure 1.63** *Provision/Opportunity/Esteem as functions of access/participation in sport*

In order for any minority racial group to have equal opportunity for participation, it must also have equal opportunity for access, and by logical extension, equal provision or equal access to provision. Access can be denied in three ways:

- by a superior (in terms of numbers) culture
- self-imposed cultural constraints
- economic/topographical limitations.

In the ten decades since the white Anglo-American culture has been the dominant force on the world of Olympic sport, things have changed, both within, and even more importantly, outside that world.

The imposition by one culture of its values on a minority or ethnic culture is not the issue here. It is the exclusion of racial minorities from existing access, or the failure to extend such provision in a way that provides access that is appropriate.

Issues of race, religion and/or gender are often intertwined. These issues are referred to more specifically on pages 29–34 in respect of the UK and on pages 300–301 in the global context.

IOC Commissions

As far as the Olympic Games are concerned, the IOC tries to see that member countries are brought into line, where such issues – racial or otherwise – are identified. The **Olympic Solidarity programmes** and the various **IOC commissions** (see below) are responsible for programmes of education and provision in identified areas of the greatest need. The income the organisation receives from television rights funds many of these operations, with 93 per cent of this being invested in programmes of development and education.

Stacking and centrality

These concepts reflect the cultural values within nation groups. The White Anglo-Saxon Protestant (**WASP**) culture that predominates in Britain, the United States and Europe was very much reflected in the Olympic movement when it was started.

The running of the organisation and its development was controlled from the centre. Rules for admission were laid down which were framed to the advantage of the people who ran it. In other words, they decided who would be in and who would not.

Today's International Olympic Committee is, in one respect, a truly cosmopolitan organisation, with 102 delegates from all over the world (soon to be 115). In another respect it can be seen as a self-perpetuating club, designed to ensure the preservation of its own interests.

This kind of discrimination exists in all cultures and in many walks of life. The inclination of a cultural group to perpetuate its own well-being and its values is best served by excluding those of a dissimilar background. Exclusion on the basis of race – particularly of colour – is one of the least subtle forms of such exclusion. In many respects

IOC commissions
- The Ethics Commission
- The Environment
- IOC 2000
- Humanitarian Affairs
- Olympic Games Co-ordination Commission
- Women in the Olympic Movement
- Medical Commission
- Sport for All
- Athletes Commission
- The Olympic Collectors Commission
- CAS – Court of Arbitration of Sport
- WOA – World Olympians Association

what happens in sport is no different from in life generally. This does not, however, make it acceptable or excusable.

Ranking social groupings

The USA is probably the best documented multi-cultural society and it is now almost traditional to rank social groupings there in a pecking order, with the power-holding WASP group established firmly at the top of the pile (Figure 1.64). In Australia, where this model is also found, the maltreatment of the indigenous population has recently received much wider and more sympathetic hearing than before. Hopefully this is a sign of enlightenment and not just 'window-dressing' in the run-up to the Sydney Games of 2000. It may also be less than co-incidental that in both societies, the indigenous populations have been the most abused and figure lowest in the pecking order.

Bar to advancement

One by-product of the predominant culture model and the stacking of minority cultural groups is the concept of the **glass ceiling**. This is the invisible bar that exists to advancement beyond a certain level. It is often associated with issues of gender bias, but applies equally members of racial and ethnic groups. Nowadays, there are many black or ethnic minority coaches in National Football League and National Basketball League teams, but how many teams have black owners? It might be argued that this in itself is an advancement on the times when black or ethnic minority people had little access to sporting scholarships, and that eventually all will compete on a level playing field.

Stereotypes and myths

There are many forms of racial stereotypes. At best they are, however misguided, intended to be positive referrals to specific cultural groupings. The practice of nick-naming US sports teams as 'the Chiefs', 'the Braves' or 'the Savages' is probably ironic because it is a reminder of the ill-treatment of Native Americans by early white settlers.

The mythical association of physical qualities with cultural groups is another form of stereotyping. Some are positive, some negative. More recently, tags such as 'White Men Can't Jump' (the name of an American film

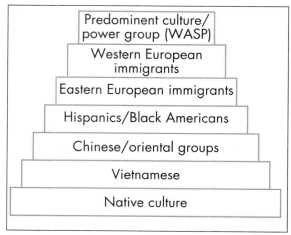

▲ **Figure 1.64** *Cultural stacking in the USA*

about basketball) might even be viewed as retaliatory. There appears to be no evidence for the claim that 'black men can't swim' – at least not physiologically. The reason for this myth becomes clearer if one considers that many blacks have limited access to good swimming facilities and therefore the opportunity to excel in this sport.

The term **white flight** has been used for the disappearance of the white sprinter at top international level. The same might be said to the 'hungry fighter' in the boxing scene. The question is are these preconceptions based on physical fact or sociological phenomena? That such features are evident reflects some degree of social change – including that of access for some racial groups. A disadvantaged cultural group simply has fewer alternatives. It may just be that, when challenged, the white sprinters and boxers simply go to business or law school instead – they at least have that (and several other) choice(s)!

Non-white athletes in the Olympic Games

The first black competitors

The St Louis Games of 1904 was by all accounts something of a 'fiasco'. The organisation was terrible and the presence of the Louisiana Exhibition enticed the organisers into presenting many events as side-shows. An accidental by-product of the shambles was the inclusion of two Zulu tribesmen, who were part of a Boer War exhibit, to run in the marathon. **Lentauw** and **Yamasani** became the first black Africans to compete in the Olympics (Figure 1.65). George Poage of Milwaukee became the first black American to win an Olympic medal, finishing third in the 400-metre hurdles.

Jim Thorpe

The 1912 Games in Stockholm produced Jim Thorpe, who was an American Indian. Thorpe was the biggest star of the Stockholm Games (Figure 1.66). After coming fourth in the high jump and seventh in the long jump, he managed to win both the pentathlon and the decathlon. In the latter event, he managed to smash the existing world record in an event he had never entered before.

Sadly, Thorpe was later stripped of his medals because he had played baseball for money before his Olympic victories. It was not until 1988 that his medals were returned – posthumously – Thorpe having died of drink in 1953.

▲ **Figure 1.66** Jim Thorpe, the great 1912 Olympian. Brundage blocked the return of his medals for decades

▲ **Figure 1.65** Lentauw and Yamasani, two Zulu tribesmen who became the first black Africans to compete in the Olympics

Jesse Owens

Similarly, another great black Olympian, **Jesse Owens**, who returned home to earn his living as a professional athlete, was banned from amateur competition.

Owens angered Adolf Hitler at the Berlin Olympics in 1936 which Hitler thought of as his own. The sight of a black American destroying the pride of the Fatherland was apparently more than Hitler could take. Owens was not the first black Olympian but the significance of his winning was all the greater because of the setting in which it occurred. His victories were seen as important because they challenged Hitler's view of Nordic/Arian ethnic supremacy.

Owens also provided a role model for people of his generation and cultural origin, despite the assertions by some black groups that he had simply been a pawn in the hands of a dominant group who were intent on continuing to oppress his own.

Cassius Clay

In 1960, 18-year-old Cassius Clay ('The Louisville Lip') burst upon the world, winning the light heavyweight gold medal in boxing. Clay was perhaps different from earlier heroes in that he deliberately used his fame to engage in social and civil rights issues as well as campaigning against the war in Vietnam. At the same games, Wilma Rudolph won the women's 100 metres and 200 metres and was also part of the US victory in the 4 × 100-metre relay.

More black Olympians

In 1964, echoing Clay's victory four years earlier, Joe Frazier took the gold medal one division higher when he won the heavyweight title. Bob Hayes won gold in the men's 100 metres and Wyomia Tyus did likewise in the women's event. American Billy Mills, of American Indian extraction, narrowly beat Gammoudi of Morocco in the 10,000 metres.

The black Africans arrived in 1960 with the victory of Abebe Bikila in the marathon, a feat he repeated in the Games of 1964. This was continued in 1968 with Kipchoge Keino's victory in the 1,500 metres and a further win in the 3,000 metres steeplechase in 1972.

The African nations possessed huge natural talent in distance running, and with their nations' destinies in their own hands for the first time, began an assault on the world's distance events which still continues unabated. Had it not been for the boycotts of the 1970s and 1980s, the record books and medal tables may well have recorded an even greater number of achievements than they did.

The Games as a political stage

Towards the end of the 1960s, athletes began to be aware of their potential to influence issues outside the arena of sport. This was demonstrated in **Mexico City** in 1968. The two black sprinters, John Carlos and Tommy Smith, had a political agenda and used the Games as their stage (Figure 1.67).

Concerned at the continued mistreatment

▲ **Figure 1.67** John Carlos and Tommy Smith give the Black Power salute at the Games in Mexico City, 1968

of the black population in the United States, the two athletes used the medal ceremony following their 200-metre final to make a gesture to the world. The Olympic establishment and many outside it never forgave them for it. This was later repeated by Lee Evans and the 4 × 400-metre squad after their victory in that event. As influential role models they, unlike Clay, had made both athletic and political demonstrations upon the same Olympic stage. Ironically, Clay (as Muhammad Ali) is still remembered primarily for his athletic pursuits, whereas two raised black-gloved fists giving the Black Power salute appear to be the legacy of Carlos and Smith.

South Africa, apartheid and the IOC

In 1960 the South African issue came to a head with its eventual exclusion from the 1964 Games. Avery Brundage (see page 63) had hoped that some resolution could be found in time for the Games of 1968. That was not to be as most of the other African nations had made it quite clear that they would boycott the Games if South Africa was re-admitted.

SANOC (the South African National Olympic Committee) was itself a non-racial body, but as Lord Killanin later discovered, it was quite impossible for them to be effective in a hostile political environment. As he remarked in connection with the way that SANOC was attempting to deal with the apartheid issue:

... it could not operate in open defiance of its Government.

Lord Killanin, 1983

TASK

a In pairs, write a short account of racial issues associated with the following games:

1936, 1964, 1968, 1972, 1976, 1980

b Write arguments 'for' and 'against' Avery Brundage's support of the Berlin Games of 1936.

3. Commercialisation and the Olympics

An 'amateur' philosophy

The word 'amateur' comes from the Latin 'to love'. 'For the love of sport' is often used in connection with the principles of amateurism. If that had been the only pre-requisite for potential Olympic competitors then the history of the modern Games may well have been quite different.

When the modern Olympics began in 1896, **amateur status** depended as much on social class as it did on being free from the so-called professional taint of earning money from sport. On the one hand this kept out the declared professional but it also excluded many who were simply not high enough up the social ladder. Certainly in England in the early years of the twentieth century, many of the recently formed national sports governing bodies had clauses in their constitutions that

interpreted amateurism in the most exclusive manner. This kept out would-be participants not only on the basis of whether they had competed for financial reward but also on the basis of how they made their living.

In many respects, it was the success of the Games combined with the growth of marketing that caused the amateur question to become unavoidably enmeshed in Olympic affairs. Nothing takes place in a vacuum and with hindsight it is easy to see how cultural and economic trends in the world at large affect many of its institutions.

Many athletes in various sports found themselves in difficult situations over the question of their amateur status. The pressure of being able to train and compete at the highest level made its demands in terms of time and expense. Tempting offers of financial support became more enticing. The **US scholarship system** (see page 226) ensured that to some degree its own athletes were immune from such pressures, as were the countries of the former Communist bloc such as the Soviet Union and Rumania, with their centralised economies and **state funding** of sport.

Marketing people were excluded from the Moscow Games in 1980 due to the state funding of the Games. The Soviet Union used it as an opportunity to show Communism to the world. However, by the 1984 Los Angeles Games, it was clear that commercial interests were well to the fore, but the signs had been apparent for some time before that. The marketing man's day had come!

Uberroth and Los Angeles

Ironically, it was the IOC, so often penalising athletes who played sport for money, that turned to the market for help. **Peter Uberroth** (Figure 1.68) was appointed to the task of making the 1984 Games viable, for the city and for the IOC. He made such a success of the job that it set the mould for the financing of future Games.

Uberroth estimated that he could run the Games for $500 million and realise a surplus of between $20 million and $50 million. In doing so, he charged $225 million for the television rights and more than double that amount for the radio rights. He persuaded **private enterprise** to build the major

▲ **Figure 1.68** *Peter Uberroth – the man with the golden touch!*

together). However, it side-stepped neatly around the direct acknowledgement of such payments by leaving the matter in the hands of the international bodies of individual sports. Forms of payment through **trust funds** were approved but in many sports full professionalism is now the norm.

Having agreed to accept money for their own product, the IOC could hardly stand in the way of the athletes doing the same. Meanwhile, Los Angeles benefited to the tune of some $260 million in the form of additional sporting facilities from the Games. Afterwards these became available for use by a range of local institutions (Table 1.11).

This was a clear change from Montreal where facilities were either never completed or had been built at critical cost to the city's administration.

facilities, including the Olympic pool, and charged everybody for just about everything else he could. The overriding aim was that the Games should not cost the city's public purse one cent.

It is now generally acknowledged that Uberroth saved the Games – at least in the financial sense. His way of doing business kept the IOC 'in the black' financially. More importantly it demonstrated that big business tied to an attractive package such as the Olympic Games could ensure the future of Baron de Coubertin's dream.

Uberroth also, perhaps unwittingly, triggered associated development that almost certainly came out of the IOC's new courtship with the world of big business. This was the development of the system of payment for athletes. The IOC baulked at officially allowing open competition (amateur and professional being allowed to compete

Table 1.11 *Facilities for the community – a legacy of the 1984 Los Angeles Games*

Facilities	Est. cost $ millions	After the games
Olympic Stadium	160–170	Converted for the use of the Atlanta Braves
Aquatic	17.5	Given to Georgia Tech
Archery, cycling	5–6	Temporary – to be removed
Basketball	7–8	Given to Moorhouse College
Equestrian	18–20	Given to the Horse Park
Hockey	25–30	Shared by a college and a university
Rowing	10–12	Given to the City of Gainesville and Hall County
Shooting	12–14	Given to Fulton County
Tennis	12–15	Given to Stone Mountain Park

The globalisation of sport

Following the financial success of the Los Angeles Games, the organisers of the next games in Seoul simply followed the Uberroth method but were a little too ambitious. TV rights were sold – this time to NBC – for $300 million, plus a share of the profits for the Games organisers. A separate television deal was done with Japan for $50 million. Unfortunately the budgeting had been estimated on a hoped-for TV 'rake-off' of nearly $1 billion and the resultant income was not nearly that amount. Accordingly, costs elsewhere had to be cut in order to trim budgets to a more realistic level.

Amost overnight Olympic sport had become globally financed. Together with parallel developments in other areas of sport, such as soccer in Europe and basketball in the USA, it gave birth to a media market that was to become an advertising executive's dream. The new communications network, made possible by satellite technology and fattened by subscription viewing, put out continuous live broadcasting of major sporting events. Television executives warmed to the task of portraying sports as gladiatorial contests to an increasingly **global audience**. The floodgates that Avery Brundage had spent most of his twenty years as IOC president trying to keep closed were well and truly open!

Multi-national corporations were keen to get a piece of the 'Olympic action'. Now each Games sees a long line of would-be sponsors willing to line pockets and write fat cheques in order to ensure their place at the head of the queue. Of course there are two sides to every strategy. Multi-national corporations, mindful of their markets and of maximising returns on their huge outlay, are keen to get the most out of the IOC in return. The 'Sale of the Five Rings', as it has become known (after the five rings of the Olympic symbol), carries a price for the seller as well as the buyer.

The influence of sponsorship

We have not yet gone as far as 'The Ford Motor Co. Olympic Games', with one company using the Games to promote their goods exclusively. There are, however, a range of 'official Olympic stockists' and 'exclusive Olympic suppliers' selling their wares on the back of their association with the Olympic flag or flame. The Atlanta Games generated thirty-four sponsors and licensed ninety-seven companies to sell products carrying the Olympic logo.

The influence of licence-holders on the Games, organising committees is minimal. Companies pay their licence fee and sell their goods for profit. However, the major sponsors, particularly the American TV networks, want their pound of flesh in return for their millions. It is not unusual nowadays for schedules to be altered to fit in with prime-time broadcasting, or an event delayed until the news broadcast finishes.

The media tycoon Rupert Murdoch has already made inroads into the organisation of some sports around the world, either by buying clubs or developing exclusive contracts for televising their fixtures. A back door into the control of English Premier League football is slowly being forced open – how long will it be before this tactic is tried with the IOC?

The Olympic Programme (TOP)

The Olympic Programme (TOP) was created in 1985 following the Los Angeles Games. This system ensures that main **TOP sponsors** are unchallenged in their category of merchandise and are guaranteed exclusive world marketing rights. All the TOP sponsors are multi-national concerns. They have use of all Olympic symbols and exclusive hospitality opportunities at the Games itself. They also have direct advertising opportunities and preferential access to broadcast advertising. The TOP sponsors are supported by a world wide advertising and public relations programme.

TOP sponsors for the 2000 Games in Sydney are Coca Cola, IBM, John Hancock, Kodak, McDonald's, Panasonic (UK), Samsung Electronics, Swatch, Time International, UPS and VISA. There are also more localised, 'national' sponsorship deals. These are negotiated by the various National Olympic Committees. This is in addition to the sale of broadcasting rights and the revenues from tickets. America's NBC have already paid $705 million in a combined package for the rights to the 2000 Games in Sydney and the 1998 Winter Games in

Nagano. The size of the potential market for advertisers becomes apparent with the viewing figures for the Atlanta Games of 1.2 billion per day, from 214 countries.

It has been estimated that something like $3 billion will be raised as a result of all the marketing programmes associated with the Games of 2000. In terms of its own income, the IOC receives seven per cent of the global figure.

Corruption

Sadly, corruption and sport are not complete strangers to each other. Most of us like to think of sportsmen and women as upstanding role models and in the majority of cases this is certainly true. Some athletes, however, cheat and that is corrupt: that topic is discussed later in this section on pages 85–88, and also in Unit 4 on page 289. Fortunately, it is no longer against Olympic regulations for athletes to accept payment for sport.

The review following investigations into the IOC in 1999 (see page 64) found serious shortcomings. These included the practice of some commissioners accepting material rewards including cash, allegedly, in return for their vote at the appropriate time. In such cases it is interesting to deliberate as to just whom is the most deviant: corrupted or corrupter? Asked what would sway the members in their voting for the venue of the 2002 Winter Games, NOC delegate, Dick Pound, is reported to have replied:

> *Choices can be based on friendship or where your wife wants to go shopping; this time the choice was the boutiques of Salt Lake City.*

> Andrew Jennings,
> *The New Lords of the Rings*

President Samaranch himself had a difficult time convincing the US Senate that the IOC is a fit and proper organisation with which US companies could safely invest their money. He also found it very difficult to explain why, on one occasion, a TV contract was awarded in the absence of any other tenders. He also maintained that he saw no reason why he should not accept gifts, as he took no part in the process of deciding on Games' venues!

There have been various other allegations that medals could be bought and that drug

test results were deliberately lost or misplaced. The 'cash-for-votes' issue clearly rocked the sporting world and did little for the IOC's already tarnished image. Recent changes include the provision for up to fifteen current Olympians to become delegates. Assurances that safeguards are now in place to prevent undesirable activity in future await the test of time.

TASK

a Write a short, generalised account of how Olympic Games were financed:
  i) before the 1984 Los Angeles Games;
  ii) after the Los Angeles Games.

b Identify the reasons

  • why the former methods of financing the Games ceased to be effective

  • why government assistance for Olympic preparation is now more forthcoming than before.

4. Women and the Olympics

The rise of women in sport

Women have been involved in the Olympics since the very first Games in 1896. A Greek woman named Melpomene ran the marathon in 4 hours and 30 minutes, albeit unofficially, and in 1900 Britain's **Charlotte Cooper** was the first female gold medallist – in the tennis singles (Figure 1.69). The use of the term 'gold medallist' in this context is a little misleading, as medals were not awarded to winners until the Games of 1908 in London.

Mildred 'Babe' Didrickson took the 1932 Games by storm, winning two gold medals and losing a third to a fellow American in the high jump (Figure 1.70). At these Games there was a new feature of a purpose-built athletes' village to house the 1,300 competitors – but only 120 of them were women!

The first 'media darling' of the Olympic Games was almost certainly **Fanny Blankers-Koen** (Figure 1.71). She won four gold medals at 100 metres, 200 metres, 100 metres

▲ **Figure 1.69** *Charlotte Cooper, Britain's first female gold medallist in 1900*

▲ **Figure 1.70** *Mildred 'Babe' Didrickson, who won gold in the hurdles and the javelin and silver in the high jump at the 1932 Games*

hurdles and the 4 × 100 metre relay in the 1948 Games in London. Her achievement was considered to be all the more remarkable for as well as being a winning athlete she was also a mother. Even at this time, Arthur Daley, a columnist in the *New York Times*, claimed that there was no place for women in the Olympics – purely on the basis that there had been none in the ancient Games! One of the best-remembered headlines following Blankers-Koen's remarkable achievements was 'The Fastest Woman in the World is also an Expert Cook'.

Discrimination against women

Women's access to sport is, as in other areas of women's rights, a reflection of the culture in which they live. In some very strict **Muslim countries**, women are barred from participating in sport, especially in public, and therefore from the Olympics. Some women's pressure groups feel that such countries should be excluded from Olympic competition,

At the 1992 Summer Olympics in Barcelona, there were thirty-four countries that had no women athletes. When the women's group 'Atlanta Plus' called for these countries to be excluded in 1996, the IOC refused on the grounds that the calls were made against one specific religion and would therefore be on unsafe ground, legally.

Like racial discrimination, gender discrimination means that people are denied the

▲ **Figure 1.71** *Fanny Blankers-Koen, who took the 1948 Games by storm*

Table 1.12 Women competitors – Summer Games 1972–96

	Sports	Events	NOCs	No. of women
1972	8	43	65	1,058
1976	11	49	66	1,247
1980	12	50	54	1,125
1984	14	62	94	1,567
1988	17	86	117	2,186
1992	19	98	136	2,708
1996	21	108	169	3,626

Table 1.13 Women competitors – Winter Games 1972–98

	Sports	Events	NOCs	No. of women
1972	3	13	27	206
1976	3	14	50	231
1980	3	14	31	233
1984	3	15	35	274
1988	3	18	39	313
1992	4	25	44	488
1994	4	27	44	523
1998	4	31	54	827

Table 1.14 Women competitors as percentage of total competitors 1972–96

Year	Men	Women	Total	% of women
1972	6,098	1,058	7,156	14.78
1976	4,838	1,247	6,085	20.49
1980	4,201	1,125	5,326	21.12
1984	5,511	1,567	7,078	22.10
1988	6,279	2,186	8,465	25.82
1992	7,855	2,708	10,563	25.63
1996	7,118	3,626	10,742	33.75

opportunity to take part in the games. There is a clear difference between women who elect not to participate and those who have such decisions made for them – either within their own cultural group, or because of discrimination from outside. Whether or not athletes compete should not be decided by the majority or dominant culture but by the athletes themselves. A key point is whether countries should be left to address cultural constraints within their own culture, or whether the Olympic community has a responsibility to highlight these issues and legislate against instances of discrimination that are brought to its attention.

Tables 1.12, 1.13 and 1.14 present some simple statistics showing the degree to which women generally have made inroads into Olympic equality. There has been much progress but there is still some way to go before improved access, opportunity and esteem are shown in equal participation.

In figures from Summer Games, the percentage of women competitors as a percentage of all competitors seems to support the view that, although women are becoming more involved, there is still some way to go. It should also be borne in mind that a range of political events (boycotts, apartheid, the invasion of Afghanistan and so on) in the 1970s and 1980s may well have delayed progress.

Equal access for women

Equality for women in sport is an issue that cannot be resolved in the sporting arena alone. Cultural and religious mores are complex and this issue underlines clearly that politics and sport are not separate entities. Women have traditionally been denied equal access to Olympic sport on four levels:

- **global** – constraints which exist at a global level. For example, no women's steeplechase in athletics
- **institutional** – constraints applied by certain institutions and organisations. For example, many do not allow women to box
- **cultural** – some religions do not allow women the same freedom as men to compete in sport
- **domestic** – some countries have social traditions which prevent women from being free to compete as they wish.

The once normal assumption in general society that the role of women did not go much beyond a domestic one had happily begun to be challenged before the first Games of 1896. However, this change of attitude was far from universal. Institutions such as the IOC were slow to change. De Coubertin's own belief that the athletics arena was not the place for women did not help.

The first opportunity for women to participate did come: with golf and tennis in the Games of 1900, archery in 1904, figure skating in 1908 and swimming in 1912. De Coubertin's opinions on women and sport may have been influenced by the model of the Ancient Greek Games. There had been no women at the Ancient Greek Games – either as competitors or spectators, and in the early years of the modern Olympics the prevailing social pattern was still inclined towards keeping women very firmly in their (domestic) place.

The early involvement of women

Fortunately, in England, Europe and the United States, women had begun to involve themselves in a range of gymnastic and sporting activities. One of them, tennis, was to be their next stepping-stone to gradually improving their access to the male world of Olympic sport. There were 36 female competitors in the Games of 1908 and, by 1912, swimming and diving events for women had opened the door a little further.

The opening of the track and field athletics events to women at the games of 1928 in Amsterdam was highly significant. In truth this probably only occurred due to the threat of a Women's World Games or Women's Olympics, which was the brainchild of a French woman, **Alice Milliat**.

Annoyed at the refusal of the IOC to include women's athletics in the Games of 1924, she threatened to set up a rival women's organisation. This caused the IAAF (International Amateur Athletic Federation) to step in very quickly and endorse women's athletics. The IOC responded by including athletics for women in the Olympiad of 1928, which put women's sport at the centre of the Olympic and world stage.

Even after the inclusion of women in the athletics events in 1928, at the infamous 1936 Games in Berlin there were only four sports providing women's events. The cause of women's participation was not helped when, in 1928, several runners collapsed at the end of the 800 metres. The race was declared too dangerous for women and banned. It was forty years before it was reinstated, with Britain's Anne Packer winning the gold in Mexico in 1968.

Table 1.15 *The growth of women's Olympic sports: Summer Games*

Year	Venue	No. of women's sports
1900	Paris	2
1904	St Louis	1
1908	London	3
1912	Stockholm	2
1920	Antwerp	2
1924	Paris	3
1928	Amsterdam	4
1932	Los Angeles	3
1936	Berlin	4
1948	London	5
1952	Helsinki	6
1956	Melbourne	6
1960	Rome	6
1964	Tokyo	7
1968	Mexico City	8
1972	Munich	9
1976	Montreal	12
1980	Moscow	13
1984	Los Angeles	15
1988	Seoul	18
1992	Barcelona	21
1996	Atlanta	24

Table 1.15 shows that there was a significant increase in the number of competitors in London in 1948 but twenty years later, in Mexico City, there were still only eight women's sports. Numbers increased again at the 1976 Games in Montreal, but even at the Atlanta Games of 1996 there were 97 events open to women in 24 sports, whereas the total number of events open to men was 163.

Women's involvement in the IOC

Women are currently becoming more involved in the IOC and in national Olympic bodies. Britain's Dame Mary Glen-Haig has been an IOC delegate since 1982, only one year after the first appointment of a woman. HRH The Princess Royal was appointed just two years later, in 1984. Although there have been a number of women appointed since that time, men still outnumber them quite heavily. It is to be hoped that the recent IOC review will lead to the appointment of even

Table 1.15 *The growth of women's Olympic sports: Winter Games*

Year	Venue	No. of women's sports
1924	Chamonix	1
1928	Saint-Moritz	1
1932	Lake Placid	1
1936	Garmisch-Partenkitchen	2
1948	Saint-Moritz	2
1952	Oslo	3
1956	Cortina d'Ampezzo	3
1960	Squaw Valley	4
1964	Innsbruck	5
1968	Grenoble	5
1972	Sapporo	5
1976	Innsbruck	5
1980	Lake Placid	5
1984	Calgary	5
1988	Nagano	5
1992	Albertville	7
1994	Lillehammer	7
1998	Salt Lake City	9

Note: The Summer Games of 1908 and 1920 featured figure skating for women but the popularity of Nordic ski-ing led to a separate Winter Games being established by 1924.

more women. Current serving women delegates are listed here, together with their year of appointment.

- Pirjo Haggman (Finland) 1981
- Flor Isava-Fonseca (Venezuela) 1981
- Dame Mary Glen-Haig (Britain) 1982
- Princess Nora of Liechtenstein 1984
- HRH the Princess Royal (Britain) 1984
- Carol Anne Letheren (Canada) 1990
- Anita DeFranz (USA) 1986
- Vera Cáslavská (Czech Republic) 1995
- Gunilla Lindberg (Sweden) 1996
- Nawal El Moutawakel (Morocco) 1998
- Irena Szewinska (Poland) 1998

Although things are changing, there are many women's issues that continue to confront the Olympic movement. Most notable is the lack of women holding senior posts in Olympic sports organisations. The IOC passed resolutions in 1996 which required that by 2000 10 per cent of all such posts should be held by women, and that by 2005 this figure should be 20 per cent.

The modern sporting female

The overwhelming constraints placed upon early sporting women were those of modesty, propriety and restraint. A young **Olga Korbut**, called into the Soviet team in Munich in 1972 because of injury to a team-mate, began to change all that with a daring and flirtatious floor sequence (Figure 1.72).

The power of the sporting female

It suddenly became acceptable for the sporting female also to be attractive – especially in the newsworthy sense. There were others besides Olga Korbut: Nelli Kim, Vera Cáslavská and, of course, Nadia Comaneci, plus a host of gymnasts from the former Communist bloc countries who moved gymnastics – and women's sport – out of the age of the gymslip and into the world of, first, bri-nylon and then Lycra (Figures 1.72 and 1.73).

Many women would not be glad to acknowledge that it was image rather than ability that brought women's gymnastics into

▲ *Figure 1.72* *Olga Korbut and Nadia Comaneci: two young women gymnasts who took the modern sporting female on to the front page*

▲ **Figure 1.73** *Women's athletic dress had changed quite markedly by the Games of 1928*

| **Achievement** |
| (often by a singularly determined individual or group of individuals in the face of resistance) |
| **Role models/Precedent** |
| **Recognition/Rationalisation** |
| **Acceptance/Conciliation** |
| **Opportunity/Provision** |
| **Access/Esteem** |

▲ **Figure 1.74** *A path towards acceptability*

▲ **Figure 1.75** *Grace and power: an irresistable combination*

the limelight and advanced their cause. Of course, the Communist system had produced athletes of a far higher standard than had been the case before, although the means by which this was were achieved is quite another issue!

Marketability

Beauty and grace are almost unavoidably associated with many women's sporting activities. This, of course, is a societal trait rather than an Olympic one. The proponents of women's sport are divided as to whether the acceptance of women into the sporting arena on the basis of anything other than their right to be there can be condoned.

Some people believe that women have for too long had to rely on other things than 'just cause' to gain advancement. Whilst this is an entirely valid viewpoint, it is important not to confuse the free woman who chooses to exploit the market-place, with her counterpart from former times who was all too often exploited the market-place. There are those who will argue that, within reason, access is the important thing (Figure 1.74). Marketability means power and that can be very influential in the arguments for (in this case) broadened opportunity within the Olympic movement.

Overcoming resistance

Although the resistance of the world's sporting institutions has been overcome generally, some groups of women athletes also have to break down a more localised cultural resistance before they can enjoy the freedoms won by women at an international (global) level. The women of Morocco, for example, led by Nawal El Moutawakel, have to overcome the resistance of a religious culture which discourages women from engaging in open public display. In such cases, the achievement of individuals is often crucial in the breaking down of barriers.

In the wider world, the **image and power** of female athletes is growing continuously. The debate over the failure of some women sports stars to attract sponsorship of the same monetary value as the top men is an important issue that is also evidence that women's sport has arrived in the global market-place (Figure 1.75).

NBC, the American television network, which has contracts in place up to the Games of 2008, is known to be keen that the

Olympics should contain a wide range of events that appeal to male, female and family viewers. It is somewhat ironic that the much-maligned media may be instrumental in broadening still further the scope and number of women's events. If recent history is any guide, it will presumably get its way.

TASK

Produce a series of graphics giving a prediction as to when the number of events and number of participants in both Summer and Winter Olympics, for both men and women, might be equal. Use the data contained in this section and any supplementary material. Present the data in a clearly understandable format to the rest of the group and respond to any questions.

5. Political uses of the Olympics

An overview

International sport has become a powerful political tool. It is hardly surprising therefore that clashes occur between political and Olympic ideals.

The **Olympic Charter** opposes any political abuse of sport but ironically such occurrences are not new. It is therefore necessary to be quite distinct about the nature of political involvements in which the Games has either become embroiled or, in some cases, has voluntarily involved itself.

The Games of 1916 were cancelled due to the First World War and invitations to the Games of 1920 were withdrawn by the IOC from Austria, Bulgaria, Germany, Hungary and Turkey because of their role in that conflict. Similarly, the Games of 1940 were cancelled and invitations to Germany and Japan to the Games in London in 1948 were not extended. The IOC played no part in the two World Wars but decided for themselves – and were under some political pressure to do so – to exclude certain countries for clearly political reasons. There have been numerous other occasions where political events have taken matters outside the hands of the IOC and where it has found itself powerless to intervene.

The development of what became known as the '**East German machine**' grew out of the use of sport by the former state of East Germany as a tool of display and propaganda. The **Soviet system** was also politically motivated, as was the Cuban production line of boxers as is the latest arrival – the gymnasts, swimmers and distance runners of the People's Republic of China.

Very few Olympiads have passed without some political involvement – willingly or otherwise. The Suez Crisis of 1956 prompted the withdrawal of Egypt, Iraq and Lebanon, with Spain and Switzerland objecting to the Soviet invasion of Hungary in the same year.

In the case of the expulsion of **South Africa** (see pages 80–81), the IOC was proactive – if after considerable delay. South Africa was missing from the Games of 1964 in Tokyo and did not return until Barcelona in 1992. The mass boycotts of the 1970s and 1980s grew out of a combination of New Zealand's insistence on maintaining sporting links with South Africa unlike many other countries, and the invasion of Afghanistan by the Soviet Union prior to the Games of 1980.

'Hitler's Games' in 1936

It was however the Games of 1936 in Berlin – 'Hitler's Games' – which caused most political controversy and brought the most indignation down on the head of the IOC and its commissioners. With hindsight this indignation was, of course, justified but there were some people, particularly in Jewish communities, who saw what was to come. They felt that the IOC should have moved the Games elsewhere.

In the event, Hitler used the Games as a display vehicle to show the world the strength of Nazi Germany and its Third Reich. The Games was superbly organised and ironically also produced the finest Olympic film so far produced – *Olympiad* by Leni Riefenstahl.

Jewish athletes were excluded from selection for the German team. However, Hitler failed in his attempt to use the Games as a stage for a demonstration of racial superiority due to the extraordinary performances of Jesse Owens (see pages 67–68), a black

▲ *Figure 1.76* Jesse Owens. He was despised by Hitler but fared a little better back home, where he made a living running against racehorses

▲ *Figure 1.77* Powerful imagery – a poster advertising the 1936 Games in Berlin

American, who won four gold medals in the 100 metres, 200 metres, long jump and the 4×100 metres relay (Figure 1.76). Hitler was apparently incensed at this turn of events, particularly as Owens beat the blonde German, Lutz Long, in the penultimate round of the long jump.

It is easy to see how frustrated the Germans would have been in 1936 from an earlier article in the Nazi Party's own newspaper *Völkischer Beobachter*. This was in its response to the success of black American athletes in the Los Angeles Games in 1932:

Negroes have no business at the Olympics. Today we witness that free white men have to compete with the unfree Negro. This is a debasement of the Olympic idea beyond comparison ... The next Olympics will be held in Berlin in 1936. We hope that the responsible men know what will be their duty. The blacks have to be expelled. We demand it!!

From *Völkischer Beobachter*, quoted in Senn, A. E., *Power, Politics and the Olympic Games*

Owens was afterwards reported as acknowledging the sportsmanlike attitude of the German champion, who, when leading the long jump competition, had pointed out to Owens that his run-up check mark appeared to be in the wrong place. Owens conceded that if it had not been for this unselfish gesture he might well have lost the competition.

As part of the theatrical presentation of the Berlin Games (Figure 1.77), the carrying of the **Olympic torch** into the stadium was introduced for the first time. This was not quite 'invented tradition'. There had been torchlight processions at the time of the Ancient Games but they were often separate occasions, not linked to the Games themselves. The year 1936 was, however, the first time the two had been linked in modern times

World events on the Olympic stage

In 1968 East Germany first participated as a separate nation. Those Games are also remembered for the protest of the American **'Black Power'** salute which was simultaneously both a political and cultural statement (see page 68). Those were the days of the American Civil Rights Movement, of Martin Luther King, the Chicago riots ... all taking place in the larger setting from which the IOC drew its membership – the world and its politics.

The 1972 Olympic Games in Munich saw the horror of terrorism brought to an Olympiad, when eight **Arab terrorists** killed eleven Israeli athletes, nine of them dying after an aborted rescue by the German police. Tight security at succeeding Games has unavoidably removed forever the former freedom and openness of the Olympic village that Baron de Coubertin would have applauded.

There was much opposition to Britain's intention to compete at the Moscow Olympiad of 1980, not least from the then Prime Minister, Margaret Thatcher, and members of her Government. The withdrawal of the US team, directed to do so by its Government, subsequently led to the withdrawal of Moscow and other Soviet bloc countries from the Los Angeles Games of 1984 in retaliation.

Following the break-up of the former Soviet Union, some of the newly independent states initially competed as a unified team in the 1992 Games. By 1996 the Ukraine, Russia and others were entering teams in their own name, having first competed in the Winter Games of 1994 at Lillehammer. The centralised government 'money-pot' was, however, gone. This forced many former Communist athletes into the market-place as professional athletes and sportspersons. Many former ice-hockey players, for example, found their way into National League ice hockey in the USA and Canada, and well-known athletes such as Sergei Bubka, the pole-vaulter, joined the growing European professional Grand Prix athletics circuit where appearance money and prizes could produce much more than a modest lifestyle.

Ping-pong diplomacy

Ping-pong diplomacy was so called because of the visit of American table tennis players and later, swimmers, to China as part of an attempt by the USA to restore diplomatic relations with China. The issue centred very much on China's refusal to recognise the right of Taiwan to compete as an independent nation in international competition but also on its human rights record. Initially China re-entered the international arena by competing in sports in which the Taiwanese had no presence. This issue is still unresolved with the pressure on Taiwan increasing now that first Hong Kong and latterly Macaw have been returned to their former Chinese owners. This leaves Taiwan as the last independent territory, that formerly belonged to mainland China. There is now tremendous pressure on Taiwan to concede its independence to mainland China. It seemingly can only resist this pressure with support from other major powers.

Shop-window policy

This refers to the use of a country's sporting youth to show their political system in a good light. Although not used by Socialist administrations, this was a feature of the former Communist bloc countries. It embraced the notion of the subjugation of the individual to the greater cause of the 'Motherland'. However, most individual nations now recognise that an impressive performance in Olympic competition has 'spin-off' effects for business and commerce, as well as national pride. The Olympic Games has transcended the morality of the purist and become the world's most effective shop window – both ideologically and materially.

Apartheid

The policy of apartheid supported by former South African governments segregated people on the basis of their race – to the distinct disadvantage of the majority black population. After years of international pressure, the IOC finally withdrew South Africa's invitation to compete in the 1960 Olympics. It was to be many years before they returned.

Best remembered for her 'tripping' incident with USA's Mary Slaney at the Los Angeles Games in 1984, South African Zola Budd courted much controversy in the same year by adopting British citizenship to allow her to run in Olympic competition. There were many who felt that she should have been barred, as in other circumstances she would probably have remained a South African, that being the country of her birth. One of the sadnesses of this period in Olympic history was the fact that many fine sportsmen and women

▲ *Figure 1.78* *Zola Budd at the Los Angeles Games in 1984*

were denied the opportunity to compete at an Olympic Games. Budd was one of the few who tried to evade the restrictions and was largely criticised for it (Figure 1.78).

The Olympic movement became involved in the apartheid issue not only because of its initial reluctance to exclude South Africa from membership but because of New Zealand's insistence on continuing its sporting links with that country. Visits of New Zealand teams to South Africa and return trips to New Zealand were seen, particularly by the African nations, as showing approval of the oppressive administration, which discriminated openly against black and coloured people. New Zealand's intransigence in this matter led directly to the African boycotts of the Montreal Games in 1976. It also added to the absences from Moscow four years later, when many other countries objected to the Soviet invasion of Afghanistan.

SANOC, the South African Olympic Committee, was in fact a non-racial organisation but had little influence on its own government's policy. In 1992 South Africa was readmitted to the Olympic fold. Apartheid was ended and – at least in theory – the opportunity was there for all South African citizens, of whatever colour, to represent their country in sport.

The Olympics as a political tool

Almost every Olympics – certainly all those in more recent times – has become associated with various political incidents or motives. The Games can be categorised as a political tool in the following ways:

- **reconciliation** – the awarding of the 1964 Games to Tokyo in an attempt to heal old wounds following the conduct of Japan in the Second World War
- **recognition** – the entry of East Germany as an independent state to the Mexico City Games in 1968, and its subsequent success at the Games of 1972
- **global non-systematic protest** – the Black Power salute in Mexico in 1968; Arab terrorists in 1972; terrorist bomb in Atlanta in 1996
- **global systematic protest** – the boycotts by the African nations of Montreal in 1976; the mass boycott of Moscow in 1980; the 'tit-for-tat' boycott by the Soviet bloc of Los Angeles in 1984
- **propaganda** – Berlin in 1936; Los Angeles in 1984 and Atlanta in 1996 (Americanisation)
- **devolution** – Sydney (2000)
- **corruption** – Salt Lake City (2002)

The 'leave-it-alone' policies adopted by many governments in relation to their aspiring Olympic sportsmen and women now seem to be definitely on the decline. Once the stakes had been raised by the former Soviet bloc countries, without lavish government funding of the efforts of their sportsmen and women, it was perhaps inevitable that the rest of the world would have to follow suit without, it was to be hoped, the attendant allegations of doping and cheating that accompanied their arrival.

Many governments are now funding the Olympic preparations of their national associations, and national academies of sport are becoming the norm rather than the exception. The previous assertions of many (not least the IOC itself) that politics and sport should have no connection, seem to have a very hollow ring in the current climate. **Government support** for Olympic programmes is ever increasing, and the use Games are used more and more as a vehicle for the propagation of a range of politically motivated agendas.

TASK

a Imagine you are a white South African who does not support their Government's policy of apartheid. Make your case for SANOC to be allowed to send a team to the Games, selected in line with the requirements of the IOC.

b Given the situation at the time, how might the Soviet Union and the Communist bloc countries have responded more positively to the USA's boycott of the Games of 1980 than by simply boycotting the 1984 Games in return?

6. The political nature of Olympic bidding

In many ways the political nature of bidding goes back to the first intercalated Games of 1906 (intercalated Games are those that have taken place *between* the normal four-year cycle). These were granted to Athens by De Coubertin to appease the Greek wish for a permanent holding of the Games there. He felt that the prize of Games being awarded to cities all over the world reflected more fully his idea of a true world movement. Since then, politics has unavoidably influenced the nature of Olympic bids.

How the Olympics are awarded

The **bidding procedure** for Olympic venues comes to a conclusion about six years before a Games actually takes place. Normally, for at least two years prior to that time, would-be host cities will have lodged their bids with the IOC. Bidding for the Games of 2000, therefore, will have been underway about the time of the 1992 Summer Games in Barcelona.

Any number of cities may bid to host the Games but the IOC will only accept one bid from any member country. This means that where more than one city intends to submit a bid for the Games, the **National Olympic Committee** of that country will oversee a 'mini-bid' and the winner then goes forward

for submission to the IOC. Any bid must have the support of that country's National Olympic Committee.

The deadline for entry is usually one year before the IOC meet to decide on the successful candidate – which means about seven years before the Games will actually take place.

Normally the city with a clear majority is successful. If, however, as often happens, there is no clear majority, then the city with the least votes is eliminated and a new, or second round of voting takes place.

In comparison to the situation leading up to the Montreal Games in 1976, where bids were thin on the ground, the situation changed fairly dramatically. Of the two recent Games in which **British bids** were involved, the Games of 1992 in Barcelona saw 21 cities prepared to step forward – although not all of them eventually submitted bids. The following Olympiad, eventually awarded to Atlanta, aroused the interest of 26 cities. Again, some fell by the wayside prior to official submission.

The Winter Games of 2002 (which were finally awarded to Salt Lake City) drew an unprecedented ten submissions for a Winter Games. This would have made the elimination of one candidate per round of voting a very long and tedious affair. The IOC's response to this upsurge in interest was to set up a committee to reduce the number of candidate cities to four, prior to the normal voting procedure.

This was the first time such a procedure had been adopted (for 2002) and to the surprise of many, it seemed to work quite well. The trend seems to be towards larger numbers of bidding cities and the intention is that the system will continue for the foreseeable future.

Criticism of the bidding process

It is the bidding process that has attracted growing attention and criticism in recent years. Accusations have been levelled initially at IOC delegates who, in visiting potential host cities to vet facilities and the general suitability of the submission, have allegedly acquired a stream of gifts, cash and other 'favours' as their hosts have sought to extract the promise of votes at the crucial time. The involvement of businessmen and politicians in the bidding process has apparently not been an unknown factor and the recent IOC review has occurred largely as a result of such accusations. Four commissioners have been removed from office, a further six have resigned and President Samaranch has made many concessions in an attempt to restore some credibility to the tarnished organisation.

Such developments indicate that currently the hosting of an Olympics is a much sought-after prize. This pre-empts the question, why do cities bid?

Why cities bid for the Olympics

Prior to the Moscow Games of 1980, the hosting of an Olympiad was seen very much as a great honour for the host city. The popularity of the Games was growing, and increased technological advances made it possible for events to be seen in countries far away from the city in which events were actually taking place.

However, as the Games grew larger, the cost of staging them grew out of all proportion to the capacity of any individual city to finance such a huge series of events. At that time there was little market for advertising and so the potential for such revenue was limited. Television companies were increasingly prepared to pay considerable sums for **broadcasting rights** but without the additional revenues now available the Games could not properly pay their way.

The critical point was reached in 1976 when Montreal, the last city to attempt to finance a Games from its own resources, accumulated massive debts, which nearly bankrupted the city. Many of those debts are still outstanding nearly twenty-five years later. Deficits in the staging of the Montreal Games are estimated to have totalled over $1 billion and some of the construction projects were left unfinished.

The Moscow Games of 1980 were largely underwritten by the Soviet authorities, keen to impress the world. It was therefore the 1984 Games and the emergence of Peter Uberroth (see page 70) which was the first real inkling of how things were to change in the financing of the Games.

The IOC had already seen the writing on the wall. Bearing in mind that some arrange-ments have to be in place several years ahead, on 31 August 1978 a contract was signed between the IOC and the Los Angeles organising committee. This made way for plans to be set in motion that would eventually show that the Games could be run at a profit – although the IOC preferred to use the word 'surplus'.

The change to commercialisation

What followed is now history and the nature of bidding for the Games changed dramatically – and not necessarily for the better. There were now high stakes to be played for, both in terms of potential benefits to host cities and to a whole range of business, commercial and media interests. The nature of the game had changed and now warmly embraced those from the world of big business who had previously been excluded from being anything more than frustrated onlookers.

Potential host cities began to sell themselves for all they were worth. A whole raft of logos (Figure 1.78), publicity events and marketing schemes began to swell budgets to unprecedented proportions. Cities were prepared to gamble millions – or find backers who were prepared to do it for them – in the hope that they might be chosen. It seems that Mr Uberroth had been successful in selling one of America's favourite products – profit!

The Manchester bids of 1992 and 1996

It is now a commonly held belief that the Manchester Olympic bids for the Games of 1992 and 1996 – well prepared and presented though they were – were doomed to failure from the outset.

In searching for an explanation for this apparently illogical statement, it should be said that Manchester was not alone in preparing a bid and being 'led to believe' that it would be a successful one. It is now quite clear that the IOC at that time needed to attend to its affairs. Recent events have gone some way to addressing a whole range of shortcomings and the millennium review of the IOC is discussed on page 64.

Both of Manchester's bids were headed by businessman Bob Scott, who later received a knighthood for his efforts. It is reported that he became so incensed at developments,

▲ Figure 1.78 Games logos and bid logos from the 1980s and 1990s

Atlanta 96

Barcelona 92

Lake Placid 80

Seoul 88

▲ Figure 1.79 Juan Antonio Samaranch, president of the IOC

particularly during the second bid, that his confrontations with certain members of the IOC were finally instrumental in the bid being lost.

It seems that, once again, considerations other than the intrinsic quality of the bids were the foundations of Manchester's disappointment. Newspaper reports and writings on the subject prior to the second bid had the public believing that the deal was as good as done. It later transpired, however, that in the eyes of many IOC delegates, the problem was that Manchester was simply not London.

Manchester had beaten London in a contest to decide which city should be the British entry but there appears little doubt that if London *had* been the city put forward it might have been a different story. There were even rumours that the tendency of Mancunians to vote for left of centre politicians also played its part. This allegation was to surface again in connection with the Olympiad of 1996, which everyone thought should have gone to Athens. Instead it went to Atlanta.

Atlanta not Athens – the controversy

Just about everyone who has any knowledge of the history of the modern Olympic movement thought that the **Centennial Games** would be awarded to Athens. That they were not came as a shock to most – 'and to those in the know this was accompanied by a distinctively and allegedly "fishy" smell!' (Jennings, *The New Lords of the Rings*).

Juan Antonio Samaranch had been known to declare publicly that Athens had always been the clear favourite. This was not surprising and most commentators did not object, despite appearing to be distinctly partisan. It seemed reasonable that one hundred years after Baron de Coubertin's heroic effort to re-kindle the Olympic flame, Athens was most people's favourite venue for the Centennial Games of 1996.

The leading nominations included Belgrade, Manchester, Melbourne, Toronto – and of course, Athens – with Atlanta way down the list. It was a poor city with apparently nothing going for it except that it just happened to be the headquarters of the Coca Cola company. The precise details of why the IOC membership had a sudden change of heart will probably only ever be known to themselves. As in Manchester, there were rumblings about the nature of Greek politics but eventually the deal was done and the Games went to Atlanta.

It should be noted that as far as is known British IOC delegates have always conducted themselves in an entirely proper manner. Princess Anne is known to consistently refuse any gifts she might be offered and has more than once ruffled the feathers of the IOC by attempting to uncover suspect allocation of funds.

At the close of the second millennium President Samaranch was busy trying to heal the wounds of the now apparent misdemeanours of several decades. The IOC, amongst the richest sporting organisations in the world, has good programmes in place for education and provision amongst the needy. It is only right that its efforts should be directed towards those ends rather than otherwise.

TASK

a In groups, make a list of six grievances about the way Games are awarded.

b Select an 'IOC President' (not your teacher) from within the group. With the rest of the group (and teacher) as delegates, proceed to address those grievances.

c Write a summative report, which includes definitive action to be taken in the case of each grievance.

7. Deviance and the Olympics

Deviance and cheating in sport

Definitions of just what is, and what is not cheating are unavoidably subjective. Culture and tradition play a large part in such interpretations and in the non-global sense, localised standards of acceptability do vary somewhat. The now infamous **'Lombardian ethic'**, born of the 'win-at-all-costs' attitude of American football coach Vince Lombardi in the 1950s (see page 47), is often cited as the mould-casting point at which a decline in

sportsmanship occurred. There are others. The early days of European and world soccer saw many British footballers astounded at the antics of their European and South American counterparts. And the Australian attitude to 'positive cricket' and the more recent allegations of 'sledging' have brought censure, both official and communal from the world's cricketing fraternity.

The foundation of the Eastern bloc countries following the division of Europe in the aftermath of the Second World War saw the rise of political ideologies intent upon using sport for political purposes. It devised its own, entirely new, conception of the word **'sportsmanship'**.

The advent of global sport has also highlighted the cultural mores surrounding sporting endeavour in different parts of the world, and in that context it is easy to understand that there are differences. It is, however, considerably more difficult to rationalise such differing attitudes to sportsmanship in the global arena.

The concept of sportsmanship

It is a mistake to assume that the sportsmanship born of Victorian (public) morality is the only definition by which such a concept should be measured. Baron de Coubertin's vision of Olympic competition certainly embraced this philosophy but, as we now acknowledge, the Olympic movement itself, in order to survive, has been forced to work on a much broader ethical canvas.

Consequently, concepts of sportsmanship must be viewed in global terms rather than merely British, European or even American.

Many public schoolmasters of the late nineteenth and early twentieth centuries subscribed to the view that it was better to lose honourably than to win by cheating. Indeed this view found its way into society at large, both in Britain and to all parts of the then Empire and later Commonwealth. Many of today's young people look aghast when confronted with such an apparently naïve philosophy, preferring it seems, the view more commonly held today that, 'you get away with whatever you can'.

As with other contentious areas, sport does not exist in a vacuum. Therefore, changing views and social values must inevitably find their way into any current sporting morality.

The question of sportsmanship is therefore not one that only occurs in the context of Olympic competition. In fact it might be that under the close scrutiny normally attendant at such a major event, many who would normally stretch the rules to the limits may refrain from doing so.

The fact is, however, that the potential rewards for success often outweigh any such **moral considerations**. It is worth considering, however, whether this makes it right.

Sportsmanship replaced by gamesmanship

These can be defined as:

- sportsmanship – the intention to compete within the framework of the rules and the intended spirit of the rules
- **gamesmanship** – the intention to compete to the limit allowed by the rules – and beyond, if that is achievable without penalty.

These definitions, though simplistic, illustrate the essential difference between two moralities or philosophies of sport: the 'win-at-all-costs' ethic versus the recreational ethic. The question is why – apart from cultural considerations – do such differences exist?

Reasons for different sporting philosophies

As in many other areas, the answer lies – at least in part – in history. The reason for the adoption of sport by the English public schools of the nineteenth century was as much a moral one as it was recreational (see pages 14–17). The value of sport was that it contained a code of honour, good behaviour, responsibility and of loyalty and Christian virtue. To the purist, therefore, any deviance from the moral code implicit in such values makes an activity 'non-sporting'. In that context, much of what passes for sport today might at best be considered to be entertainment, but certainly not sport.

However, as always, there are two sides to every story. There are those who argue that just as the Olympic movement has had to 'bend with the wind', today's concept of sportsmanship must also move on from the value-laden idea held by the contemporaries

of Baron de Coubertin and the immovable Avery Brundage.

Sport is no longer the hobby-horse of the wealthy, ridden purely for recreation, but the vehicle on which athletes ride to work. Therein, it seems, lies the difference.

'Be that as it may,' the purists cry, 'gamesmanship is still gamesmanship and cheating is still cheating!' Can we argue with that?

Deviant behaviour

Whether it be the illegal wiring of a fencer's epée so that it registers hits that do not exist, changing an athlete's blood so that it carries more oxygen, or taking a **banned substance** in order to enhance performance artificially, it is cheating and cheating is fraud. It is fraud, in many cases, in the legal sense. In *all* cases it is fraud against one's fellow competitors who (in the main) are trying to compete within a specified set of rules.

There are those who claim that ergogenic aids (drugs) should be allowed, but the fact remains that for the moment they are not. If this sounds clear cut, there are plenty of instances that are not. What about, for example, the athlete who for genuine medical reasons needs to take a certain drug which also enhances performance? Assuming there is no satisfactory substitute, should they be allowed to compete?

How and why rules are framed is clearly an area for legitimate discussion. Deviance, by definition, refers to the behaviour of those who will find their own way *however* the rules are framed. It has been suggested that there should be a separate class of competition for those who wish to explore the boundaries of performance with the aid of what, at the moment, are banned substances. This would leave a drug-free class of competition that would be un-tainted – or would it?

In this context deviance can be defined therefore as any behaviour designed to gain unfair advantage by means of:

- gamesmanship
- deliberate infringement of rules
- interfering with equipment
- knowingly taking banned substances for the purpose of gaining unfair advantage
- being involved in an act, the prime purpose of which is to gain an unfair advantage over one's opponents.

Institutionalised deviance

As became apparent in the massive Communist bloc investment in sport during the Cold War years, deviant behaviour is not only the province of individuals or small groups.

It is now clear that, in respect of the administration of banned substances, many of which were undetectable, the former Soviet and East European governments supported huge programmes of abuse. These were designed purely to win gold medals and enhance their countries' image in the eyes of the rest of the world. Each gold medal won was seen as a victory for the way of life of the Eastern bloc over a decadent and corrupt capitalist West. Horrific stories have come to light, including that East German female swimmers, athletes and gymnasts were forced to become pregnant. They were then told when to have abortions so that the greatest competitive advantage might be gained from the additional vitamin supplies produced by the body in such circumstances.

There are currently alleged reports associating the People's Republic of China with mass drug programmes. Female swimmers and track and field athletes have so far been the subjects of speculation.

Deviant behaviour in sport therefore falls into one or more of the following categories:

- institutional
- group specific
- individual.

It is either:

- voluntary
- co-operative
- enforced.

Ben Johnson

The now famous story of the 1988 Olympic 100-metres champion, **Ben Johnson**, is an example of co-operative/individual deviance, as was the less well publicised example of David Jenkins, the former British 400-metre record-holder who supplied banned substances to those athletes who sought them. Many banned substances are also illegal and Jenkins was sent to prison in the United States as a result of his involvement. Likewise,

▲ **Figure 1.80** Ben Johnson – Seoul 1988. His was a highly publicised case

Johnson, in co-operation with others, decided to gain advantage from the use of steroids. Although he did not go to prison, he was eventually banned from athletics for life (Figure 1.80).

Johnson's story continues to court controversy. In 1998 he took Athletics Canada and the IAAF to court on the basis of restraint of trade. As a result he has been reinstated to compete domestically in Canada, some eleven years after his fall from grace.

Petra Schneider, gold medallist

Sharon Davies, now a well-known TV presenter and former 'golden girl' of British swimming, has much sympathy for the East German swimmer who relegated her to the silver medal position in the 400-metres individual medley final in the 1980 Moscow Olympics. Although Petra Schneider, the East German swimmer, deprived Davies of a gold medal, she also acknowledges that Schneider was a victim of an iniquitous **institutionalised system** of drug abuse in which she had little choice but to participate.

The question of personal culpability (at least in the moral sense) therefore is somewhat reduced where athletes have clearly been placed under some institutionalised duress.

Davies' anger is now directed at the IOC. Despite being in possession of evidence sup-

▲ **Figure 1.81** Kornelia Ender, the spearhead of the 'East German machine' in 1976 in Montreal

discovered that a state-sponsored plan, (Plan 14.25) had ordered the systematic doping of East German athletes during the 1970s and 1980s. Such widespread doping has thrown much doubt over the validity of Olympic medals won by East German athletes during this period and is still the subject of much controversy.

The IOC and international drug control

Doping is cheating. Doping is akin to death. Death physiologically, by profoundly altering, sometimes, irreversibly, normal processes ... Death physically, as certain tragic cases in recent years have shown. But also death spiritually and intellectually, by agreeing to cheat and conceal one's capabilities, by recognising one's incapacity or unwillingness to accept oneself, or to transcend one's limits. And finally death morally, by excluding oneself de facto from the rules of conduct required by all human society.

Juan Antonio Samaranch,
President of the International Olympic Committee

The issue of drugs in the Olympic Games has grown enormously since the first drug-related death of a competitor – the Danish cyclist **Knud Jensen** in the 1960 Games in Rome. The IOC's current interpretation of drug abuse includes the deliberate *and* inadvertent use of substances that enhance performance.

Along with the Union Cycliste International (UCI), the IOC was a leader in establishing a medical control, responsible for drug testing, which was operative at both the Summer and Winter Games of 1968.

The IOC code of eligibility requires that all competitors abide by its requirements, including testing for banned substances. A list of both banned and allowed substances is published and updated regularly. The role of the **IOC Medical Commission** involves establishing all the routines and practical aspects of the collection of urine samples and ensuring that they are securely transported, sealed and numbered, to the

porting these allegations and an admission on Schneider's part of her own (albeit reluctant) complicity, they refuse either to proclaim Davies as the real gold medallist or to remove Schneider's name from the record books. The reason given is that there are apparently so many such instances that to address them all would be impracticable.

When it comes to 'institutionalised doping', the former East Germans must surely lead the field. Kornelia Ender spearheaded their assault on the Montreal Olympics of 1976, leaving many much-fancied Americans in their wake (Figure 1.81). Shirley Babashoff, then a fifteen-year-old, who herself won two gold and six silver medals, left Montreal feeling cheated: 'They were beating us by yards,' she said. 'They looked like men.'

Following the disintegration of the German Democratic Republic (GDR) in 1989, it was

accredited laboratory for that Games. The Commission also works closely with the international federation concerned as well as the accredited laboratory, which operates under its total authority. The IOC rules do not prevent further sanctions against guilty parties being taken by the international federation responsible for an individual sport.

Since 1994, testing procedures have been expanded to include blood as well as urine samples This is an attempt to maximise the effectiveness and broaden the scope of testing procedures. All international sporting bodies are now under pressure from the IOC to adopt its medical code for all their international competitions. This includes 'random' testing, both in and out of season, so that top athletes can now expect to be tested for banned substances at any time during the year. Some fifteen per cent of the samples tested by the IOC's lab in Lausanne in Switzerland are taken out of season.

A major concern continues to be the on-going battle against the chemists who manufacture new drugs and seem to stay just that one jump ahead of the testers. The IOC's list of banned substances has now grown to around 150 and any athlete taking these is liable to disqualification if found guilty.

The latest challenge centres on the use of **erythopoietin** (EPO), which increases blood oxygenation by forming additional red blood cells. This improves stamina and the drug can be produced comparatively cheaply. The first testing for EPO was in Lillehammer in 1994. It was instrumental in the inclusion of blood sampling into testing procedures.

The IOC's anti-doping campaign is based upon three principles:

---

1 The protection of the health of athletes.

2 Respect for medical and sports ethics.

3 Ensuring an equal chance for everyone during competition.

TASK

a Consider and discuss the following contradictory approaches to addressing the question of drug abuse in the Olympics:

i If modern sportsmen and women are professionals (i.e. they earn their living from their sport), is a lifetime ban justifiable as it is also effectively a 'restraint on trade' for life?

ii If members of national Olympic teams are found guilty of drug abuse, then the entire team sport they represent – not just the individual(s) – should be banned from Olympic competition for a specified period. In the case of abuses occurring in several sports, invitation to that country's NOC to compete in future Games should be withheld for a specified period.

b Discuss and vote on the above proposals from the point of view of individual and collective responsibility.

8. Paralympics

History of the Paralympics

In 1944 **Dr Ludwig Guttmann** opened a spinal injuries centre at **Stoke Mandeville** Hospital in Buckinghamshire. He pioneered a new approach to rehabilitation, centred on sport. The **Paralympics** movement, as it is known today, began life as an organised sports competition for veterans of the Second World War who were suffering from spinal chord injury four years on in 1948. The opening day of that first competition initiated by Guttmann coincided with the opening day of the 1948 London Olympic Games. Within a short time competitors from Holland were also taking part. It was the first organised competition for wheelchair athletes.

It was not, however, until 1960 that a Games on the Olympic pattern was first organised and a further sixteen years elapsed before competition was expanded to include other disability groups at the Toronto Games in 1976. The Games for the disabled were

▲ **Figure 1.82** *Wheelchair athletes are just that – athletes in wheelchairs!*

initially held as an independent event but have shared the main Olympic venue since the 1988 Summer Games in Seoul and the 1992 Winter Games in Albertville, France. It was not until 1988, however, that a commitment was made by the full Olympic Organising Committee to assist the **International Paralympic Committee** (IPC) with the organisation of the Games.

Impairment classifications

The current impairment classifications include athletes with:

- cerebral palsy (CP-ISRA)
- spinal cord lesion, spina bifida and polio (ISMWSF)
- blindness (IBSA)
- les autres or amputations (ISOD).

The first Games to be known as the **Olympic Games for the Disabled** took place in Geilo, Sweden in 1980, and the first use of the term 'Paralympics' was at the Games in Seoul in 1988. Yet, even this apparently simple progression of status is not without its own measure of rancour and distaste.

IOC support of the disabled movement?

Although Samaranch was known to support the disabled movement, it also became apparent that he preferred the association not to interfere with the IOC's prospects of developing relationships with would-be sponsors.

It became fairly clear that it was felt that too close an association with disabled sport might harm the **market potential** of the Games. If this was true then either Samaranch or the marketing people he was hoping to attract seem to have had little esteem for the athletes themselves or for the millions of ordinary people who marvel at the exploits of disabled sportsmen and women.

There were allegations that in a series of meetings in 1983 with Dr Jens Bromann of the IPC, Samaranch made three things clear:

1 He did not want the title 'The Olympic Games for the Disabled' used again – for marketing reasons.
2 He would not allow the Olympic flag or symbols to be used in connection with disabled events.
3 The IPC were not to ask for the inclusion of disability events in the main Olympic programme.

Clearly, the third item above was open to change, as Paralympic events have consistently been included in the main Olympic programme for some time, although not perhaps to the degree that many would like to see. The flag of the Paralympic movement is now **three teardrops** in red, blue and green, giving some credence to the second point above (Figure 1.83). The IOC was not happy with the first choice of *five* teardrops in the same colours and configuration as the Olympic flag. It remains to be seen whether the IOC's professed change of direction as a result of the millennium review will eventually see all athletes under *one* Olympic flag.

It was five years after these reported meetings with Dr Bromann that the IOC officially embraced disabled sport. It is worth considering why this has come about. Perhaps there has been a change of heart on the part of its leader; perhaps marketing opportunities now embrace disabled sport; or maybe the pressure of world opinion has penetrated the previously impenetrable?

▲ **Figure 1.83** The IPC logo has three teardrops in red, blue and green

Table 1.17 Summer Paralympics, 1952–96

Year	Venue	Nations	No. of competitors
1952	Stoke Mandeville	2	130
1960	Rome	23	400
1964	Tokyo	22	390
1968	Tel Aviv	29	750
1972	Heidelburg	44	1000
1976	Toronto	42	1600
1980	Arnhem	42	2500
1984	Stoke Mandeville (UK and USA)	42	4080
1988	Seoul	61	3053
1992	Barcelona	82	3020
1996	Atlanta	103	3195

Table 1.18 Winter Paralympics, 1976–98

Year	Venue	Nations	No. of competitors
1976	Örnsköldsvik (Norway)	14	250
1980	Geilo (Sweden)	18	350
1984	Innsbruck	22	350
1988	Innsbruck	22	397
1992	Albertville	24	475
1994	Lillehammer	31	1000
1998	Nagano	32	571

Jennings, in his somewhat scathing view of the machinations of the IOC, was concerned to note that whilst the IOC's **funding** of disability participation in the Olympics rose from $20,000 in 1984 to $60,000 in the following year, investment in the Olympic stamp collection rose from $40,000 to $200,000 in the same period. This last activity is known to be a personal hobby of the IOC President. Again, it underlines the concern that has been growing over the hidden agendas that seem to surface almost continually in connection with the organisation.

Links with the Olympic movement

The Paralympics represent the pinnacle of achievement in disability sport. As the movement itself has grown, the number of athletes involved has increased from 400 in 1960 to just over 3,000 in Atlanta in 1996 (Table 1.17). Similarly, there has been a small but significant rise in the number of competitors in the Winter Games (Table 1.18). It is anticipated that in the Sydney Games of 2000 these numbers will be even higher. The general opinion seems to be that the Sydney organisers will ensure that disability sport has the appropriate high profile it warrants.

Venues are now shared with the 'big brother' Games of much longer standing, and since 1988 the IOC has, at least officially, acknowledged and embraced the Paralympics.

The range of issues that affect other cultural minorities also have an impact on disabled athletes, whether within the sphere of Olympic competition or in the wider world. The opportunity to participate is, as shown on page 29, dependent upon levels of access and provision and upon transmitted and perceived esteem in relation to that group or groups. Outstanding performances by one or two dedicated athletes – as in the United Kingdom – can act as 'pump primers' for the development of **recognition and acceptance**. In turn, this serves to improve

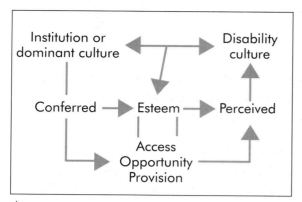

▲ **Figure 1.84** Achievement by one leads to opportunity for others

▲ **Figure 1.85** Is there any real reason why this woman should not represent herself and her country as able-bodied athletes do?

provision and thereby broaden **opportunity**. As Figure 1.84 depicts, the 'disability culture' exists very much at the whim of the dominant culture in which it exists. Any successes it can gain will confer upon it some esteem (however reluctant) from that dominant culture, which it takes to itself. Such success can act as a catalyst in the provision of facilities and thereby increases access for others from the minority (disability) group.

As in other areas of discrimination, such problems do not exist solely in the area of sport, and certainly not only in Olympic sport. They are reflections of **societal values**, which leave much to be desired and are held and practised in a range of cultural settings, and at all levels: global, institutional, cultural and domestic.

If the Olympic family is to truly embrace disability sport, perhaps there is an argument for the range of cultures it brings together to make it clear by their own practices that **inclusion** is the only way forward.

TASK

Create a time-line chart showing the development of Paralympic sport from Stoke Mandeville in 1948 to Sydney in 2000. Show disabled involvement in both Winter and Summer Games and the years in which distinct progress was made (e.g. Seoul 1988 – first use of the term 'Paralympics').

Key words and phrases

1. History of the modern Olympics

• Olympic • Pythian • Isthmian • Nemean • Pankration • Stade • Diaulos
• Dolichos • Cotswold Olympik Games • Wenlock Olympian Games
• Pierre de Coubertin • Boycott • Samaranch • Apartheid

2. Race and ethnicity within the Olympic movement

• Olympic Solidarity programmes • IOC commissions • WASP • 'Glass ceiling'
• 'White flight' • Lentauw • Yamasani • Jesse Owens • Mexico City • SANOC

3. Commercialisation and the Olympics

• Amateur status • US scholarship system • State funding • Peter Uberroth
• Private enterprise • 'Trust funds' • Global audience • TOP sponsors

4. Women within the Olympics

• Charlotte Cooper • Mildred 'Babe' Didrickson • Fanny Blankers-Koen
• Muslim countries • Global • Institutional • Cultural • Domestic
• Alice Milliat • Olga Korbut • Image and power

5. Political uses of the Games

• Olympic Charter • 'East German machine' • Soviet system • South Africa
• Hitler's Games • Olympic torch • 'Black Power' • Arab terrorists
• Ping-pong diplomacy • SANOC • Reconciliation • Recognition
• Global non-systematic protest • Global systematic protest • Propaganda
• Devolution • Corruption • Government support

6. Political nature of Olympic bidding

• Bidding procedure • National Olympic Committee • British bids
• Broadcasting rights • Centennial Games

7. Deviance and the Olympics

• 'Lombardian ethic' • 'Sportsmanship' • Moral considerations • Gamesmanship
• Banned substance • Ben Johnson • Institutionalised system • Knud Jensen
• IOC Medical Commission • Erythopoietin

8. Paralympics

• Dr Ludwig Guttmann • Stoke Mandeville • Paralympics
• International Paralympic Committee • Olympic Games for the Disabled
• Market potential • Three teardrops • Funding • Recognition and acceptance
• Provision • Opportunity • Societal values • Inclusion

REVIEW QUESTIONS

1 What is the meaning of the word 'Panhellenic'?

2 What was the difference in the prizes awarded at the 'Crown' Games as opposed to other Games?

3 What influenced the reborn interest in ancient and classical history in Britain?

4 What was the influence of William Penny Brookes in:

    a The Wenlock Olympian Games

    b The National Olympian Association?

5 From where did Baron Pierre de Coubertin get the motivation that led to his founding the modern Olympic movement?

6 Outline Hitler's political motives in the staging of the Olympics in Berlin in 1936.

7 Why did Avery Brundage resist moves to give back medals to Olympian Jim Thorpe?

8 Describe the essential difference of approach to solving problems between Brundage and his successor, Lord Killanin.

9 What part did South Africa's policy of apartheid play in Olympic boycotts?

10 Discuss the connection between the WASP culture and the Olympic movement.

11 Why was SANOC so ineffective in its dealings with its own government?

12 What essential change in philosophy overtook the Olympic movement following Peter Uberroth's involvement in the 1984 Games in Los Angeles?

13 Develop arguments 'for' and 'against' the withdrawal of Olympic medals from former Eastern bloc athletes.

14 Is there a moral justification for 'gamesmanship' in Olympic sport?

Texts used in the writing of this section

❏ Anderson, J., 'Disability Sport', in *Sports History for 'A' Level*, British Society of Sports History, 2000

❏ British Olympic Association, *Education Pack for Schools*, BOA, 1999

❏ Coakley, J. J., *Sport in Society*, 5th Edition, Mosby, 1990

❏ The Daily Telegraph, *Gold Medal Legends – The Olympic Games, 100 Years in Pictures*, The Daily Telegraph, 1996

❏ Guttmann, A., *The Olympics – A History of the Modern Games*, University of Illinois Press, 1994

❏ Jennings, A., *The New Lords of the Rings*, Simon & Schuster (Pocket Books series), 1996

❏ Lucas, J., *The Modern Olympic Games*, A. S. Barnes, 1980

❏ Prestidge, J., *The History of British Gymnastics*, BAGA, 1988

❏ Senn, A. E., *Power, Politics and the Olympic Games*, Human Kinetics, 1999

❏ Terry, D., 'Early English Olympism', in *Sports History for 'A' Level*, British Society of Sports History, 2000

❏ Tyler, M. & Scott, P., *The History of the Olympic Games*, Marshall Cavendish, 1980

❏ Wenlock Olympian Society, *William Penny Brookes and the Olympic Connection*, Wenlock Olympian Society, 1996

❏ Whitfield, C., *Robert Dover and the Cotswold Games*, Henry Sotheran, 1962

Suggested further reading

❑ British Olympic Association, *Education Pack for Schools*, BOA, 1999

❑ British Society of Sports History, *Sports History for 'A' Level*, BSSH, 2000

❑ The Daily Telegraph, *Gold Medal Legends – The Olympic Games, 100 Years in Pictures*, The Daily Telegraph, 1996

❑ Guttmann, A., *The Olympics – A History of the Modern Games*, University of Illinois Press, 1994

❑ Jennings, A., *The New Lords of the Rings*, Simon & Schuster (Pocket Books series), 1996

❑ Senn, A. E., *Power, Politics and the Olympic Games*, Human Kinetics, 1999

❑ Wenlock Olympian Society, *William Penny Brookes and the Olympic Connection*, Wenlock Olympian Society, 1996

Unit 2
Enhancing performance

Introduction to Unit 2

This introduction will enable you to meet the requirements of Unit 2 more successfully. It provides you with a clear understanding of:

- the knowledge required to enhance a performance
- how to complete the assessment assignments
- the processes of examination you will be required to complete.

Unit 2 of the specification seeks to provide you with the opportunity to enhance your knowledge, skills and understanding central to the performance of practical activity through three sections: a, b and c. By being able to apply, acquire and evaluate your knowledge and understanding, the Unit seeks to provide you with the learning experiences necessary to enhance your own understanding of performance by learning in, learning about *and* learning through physical activities.

> **enhance**: to make better, to improve (i.e. a performance)

Physical performance involves movement. This Unit is concerned with performance within a sporting and physical recreation environment.

In Unit 2 you are given the opportunity to select your own study route and choice of practical activities for assessment. The Unit requires all students to take part in practical activities in Section B but you have two options. With Option A you offer two practical activities for final assessment, whereas with Option B you undertake a research project. All students will be required to cover the topics contained in Section A Acquiring skill and Section C Performance: Analysis and Provision.

Unit weighting

The following weighting for Unit 2 forms 40 per cent of the total marks available for the Advanced Subsidiary course and subsequently 20 per cent of the final Advanced Level award:

- Section A: Acquiring skill – 12%
- Section B: Option A: Practical application or Option B: Research project – 20%

- Section C: Performance: Analysis – 4% Local and national provision – 4%

The essential nature of Unit 2, and subsequently Unit 5, is to give you the opportunity, through a variety of experiences, to gain a wider and deeper understanding of how to prepare for, improve and evaluate your own performance and that of others.

The most important principle to remember when doing Unit 2 and later Unit 5 of the Advanced course is that you have experienced progression in your practical performances, your knowledge and understanding of the Unit content.

Key Skills

The Unit provides opportunities for you to extended all your Key Skills but in particular in the following three areas:

- communication
- application of number
- information communication technology.

How do I record my experiences?

Unit 2 requires you to construct an Individual Performance Portfolio (IPP) as the focus for all your studies. This can be described as the document that contains a record of all your work carried out, not only during Unit 2, but also Unit 5 for those continuing on to the Advanced Level course. The IPP will be discussed later in this Unit.

Unit overview

Section A: Acquiring skill

This section requires you to make the connection between theoretical knowledge and its application to practical activity. Your centre will be required to select a minimum of three activities from the categories of Team games, Racket games and Individual activities with at least one activity from each category. These activities will be used as a medium through which you develop an understanding of the knowledge contained in Section A which covers the subject area of skill acquisition.

This section is worth 12 per cent of your AS course.

Section B: Option A: Practical application or Option B: Research project

For Section B you have two options:

- Option A – to be assessed in two practical activities
- Option B – to undertake a research project of 1500–2000 words.

For individual activities performance is assessed against objective measurements. If you choose Option A, the two practical activities must be from two different categories. Your teacher will help you make the best choice of which two you will be most successful in. In team and racket activities you will be assessed on your ability to perform within structured practices and in a competitive situation.

Alternatively you may decide to undertake Option B, the research project, which will enable you to research, analyse and evaluate an area related to practical performance. Further details of the research project are on pages 139–47.

This section is worth 20 per cent of your AS course.

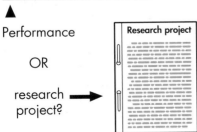

Performance

OR

research project?

Research project

Section C: Performance: Analysis and Provision

In this section you will be required to demonstrate an enhanced understanding of an activity through two study routes.

Analysis of performance

You will be required to undertake an analysis of performance in one activity selected from your two chosen practical activities. If you have chosen to do the research project for Section B, you will select one activity from those in the full list of activities contained in the Edexcel specification document. Your selection will enable you through direct observation, research and by viewing recorded performances, to acquire the knowledge and understanding that will help you to answer oral questions in five key areas:

- rules/laws of the game or activity
- terminology and tactics
- recognising strengths and weaknesses
- planning, practices and training
- the perfect model.

Local and national provision

Next you will carry out a small-scale research project entitled 'Local and national provision'. This will concern the development of sporting excellence in one of your chosen activities to show that you have an appreciation of the social context in which the individual may begin at grass-roots level and progress to the level of the élite performer. Drawing on various resources you will be required to evaluate provision with regard to enhancement of performance. This will be

▲ **Figure 2.1** Analysis of performance in action

presented in the form of an analytical written assignment that will be assessed by your teacher. It will be part of your IPP and be externally moderated.

This section is worth 8 per cent of your AS course. The Analysis of performance and the Local and national provision assignments are worth 4 per cent each.

Key features of Unit 2

The following key features summarise the content and direction of study of this Unit:

- the production of an Individual Performance Portfolio (IPP)
- the enhancement of your performance in two practical activities *or* the undertaking of a research project
- the analysis of performance of one activity
- the understanding of a small-scale project on the local and national provision of one activity from grass roots to sporting élite.

The rest of this unit explores and outlines the requirements for each section and how you can develop your knowledge, skills and understanding throughout the Unit and maximise your examination grades.

The foundations you lay in the Advanced Subsidiary course will enable you to progress into the Advanced Level course more successfully and provide you with the practical experience to further refine your knowledge, skills and understanding. You will also gain the experience necessary to give suitable practical examples for the written examination papers of Units 1 and 3, the written assignments of Unit 2: Sections A and C and, if selected, the research project in Section B.

In essence you will view Unit 2 as your *practical coursework*.

The Individual Performance Portfolio (IPP)

From the beginning of the Advanced Subsidiary course it is important for you to begin formulating your own Individual Performance Portfolio or IPP. The IPP will stay with you throughout your Advanced Subsidiary course and will be carried through into the Advanced Level course. The portfolio is a file or folder used to hold your worksheets, records or examples of work. It is the focal point for all students undertaking the course.

The IPP provides you with an opportunity to gather together evidence of your practical activities, written assignments and sporting experiences. The IPP itself has no direct assessment but the components contained within it form part of the assessment requirements of Unit 2.

The IPP has no common format and you are free to design and formulate your own unique portfolio either as an individual or as part of a particular examination centre. An A4 folder is the most obvious choice.

Each student's IPP must record information that reflects the course requirements of Unit 2. You will still be able to devise your own personal elements and unique style of IPP although there is a requirement for it to contain the following components:

- an account of your playing record in your two chosen practical activities
- a record of the progress/experiences you have gained from your two practical activities offered for assessment through practices and competitive situations or against objective measures of assessment
- a record of and evidence of your knowledge and understanding in your choice of activity for the analysis of performance
- any coaching, leadership or refereeing awards you may have obtained
- the written assignments for Sections A and C of the Unit – that is the three assignments for 'Acquiring skill' and the analytical account of the development of sporting excellence in one activity to include 'Local and national provision' of an activity
- a section for the recording of the physical fitness tests related to the measurement and evaluation of exercise and training in Unit 3
- if Option B is selected for Section B, the research project will be contained in your IPP prior to moderation.

The need to build up the IPP from the outset of the Advanced Subsidiary course will help you acquire the knowledge and understanding of practical activities as well as develop the skills required to analyse performances. It is from this first year base that you will be able to construct a Personal Exercise Plan as part of the coursework requirements of Unit 5.

▲ **Figure 2.2** *Preparation is vital to a successful outcome*

Many students will have experience of practical activities that take place away from their school or college. These activities may also involve undertaking planned, programmed and formulated training regimes and specific activity enhancement sessions, along with appropriate competition. It is acceptable to include in the IPP any record or account of these experiences that will reflect the standard of performance obtained and the related experiences that will have shaped and developed a student's knowledge, skills and understanding of a practical performance.

The IPP is completed at the end of Unit 2, and then at the end of Unit 5. It will contain the required coursework material and centre-assessed components, which are then externally moderated by Edexcel.

Section A: Acquiring skill

Although this section of the Unit is not directly examined as a written paper, the content is essential as an element of the practical assessment and analysis of performance, as well as an element of the synoptic paper. The teaching of this element will be of a practical nature. Your learning involvement should be active and must include constant application of the theories.

1. The classification and teaching of movement skills

Skill versus ability

When discussing the acquisition and development of **skill** in the sporting environment, it is essential that we understand the different types of skill, the difference between 'skill' and '**ability**' and how these link with a term commonly used in sport: **technique**.

Skill is a commonly used word which has a variety of interpretations. In sport, we tend to use skill more as a concept than a word. We talk in terms of skills existing within a sport (for example, a serve in tennis) or in terms of a sport itself being a skill.

In sport, a skill is seen as a co-ordinated act, involving complex movements brought together in a consistent and smooth manner. We have different interpretations of what constitutes a skilful movement as analysis is based on our own experiences and performances. An expert performer will have a different view of a performance from a novice. The following definition should help you understand the concept of skill:

An organised co-ordinated activity in relation to an object or situation which involves a whole chain of sensory, central and motor mechanisms.

Welford

A number of key qualities are needed in order for a performance to be skilful:

- consistency
- accuracy
- control
- an intention
- fluidity.

▲ *Figure 2.3* *Measurement is an example of a cognitive skill*

Different types of skill

It is important to remember that there are a number of different types of skill.

Cognitive skills

Cognitive skills are also often known as intellectual skills and involve thought processes. An example would be the adding up of judges' scores in ice skating, the measures of a length of a long jump (Figure 2.3) or the calculation of batting averages at the end of a cricket season).

Perceptual skills

Perceptual skills involve interpretation of stimuli. We may see the same information as someone else, but our brain might interpret it differently from them. In Figure 2.4, you may be able to see two faces looking at one another or an old fashioned 'goblet', depending on your interpretation.

Motor skills

Motor skills involve the muscular system and concern movement and muscular control. For example, walking or running are motor skills as they involve movement and muscular control (Figure 2.5).

Perceptual motor skills

Performance in sport is an extremely complex process. It does not just involve one type of skill, but several. Most skills are referred to as **perceptual motor skills** as they involve thought, interpretation and movement: cognitive skills, perceptual skills *and* motor skills (Figure 2.6).

▲ **Figure 2.4** *Perceptual skills – what can you see?*

▲ **Figure 2.5** *Motor skills involve movement and muscular control*

See → Interpret → Think → Move

▲ **Figure 2.6** *Perceptual motor skills: the process involved in a performance*

Ability

In order to be able to learn and perform any skill, especially in sport, we must have the abilities required. Abilities are generally seen as being innate. That is, you are born with them or they are developed early in life. Abilities are often seen as the building blocks of sport. Without the basic building blocks or movement vocabulary, we will never be able to develop skill fully.

Examples of specific abilities required in sport would include: hand/eye co-ordination, flexibility, speed, etc. Without these abilities, it would not be possible to learn skills such as a smash in badminton. Later in this book we will see that it may be possible to develop basic skills with the correct learning environment. However, without innate ability you will never become a superstar.

TASK

In pairs or individually:

a give a sporting example of each type of skill.

b explain the difference between a skill and an ability.

c list the skills and abilities required for a specific sport.

Technique

A term commonly associated with skill and ability is technique. Technique is often confused with skill. In fact there is a strong relationship between the three terms: skill, ability and technique. In order to perform a particular skill in sport, we must learn the required technique. In order to learn the technique fully, we must have the necessary abilities.

SKILL = ABILITY + TECHNIQUE

If you consider the definitions of skill and ability, you will see that performers at the élite level must have been born with natural abilities and then develop the specific techniques for them to perform the skills at such a high level.

TASK

Select a skill in sport. Outline how abilities will influence the development of the technique and, ultimately, the skill and the sport itself.

Classification continuums

Many theorists have attempted to analyse the wide range and diverse skills involved in sport. Every sport requires a different type of skill and so each has very different requirements. The importance of being able to categorise skills becomes evident when we look at the teaching/learning and practice of different skills. If we know the general requirements of a particular skill, we can then decide the most appropriate learning and practice environments.

Identifying the requirements of each skill is important if we are to optimise the learning and development of sporting skills, which is the main focus of this section.

There are various methods for categorising skills, all of which demonstrate the need for a flexible and analytical approach. **Classification continuums** is not an exact science and there is room for individual interpretations. Many of the theories are based on the concept of continua, that is: skills can be classified on a sliding scale depending on their requirements.

Knapp's open–closed continuum

Barbara Knapp recognised two basic classifications of skills. She suggests that skills can fit on a continuum between open and closed (Figure 2.7).

Open skills are those which are directly influenced by the environment in which they are performed. They are skills that require adaptation each time they are performed. The adaptation may depend on a range of environmental conditions such as the weather, the pitch conditions, the speed on a ball, the position of an opponent etc. Thus an open skill is never performed in exactly the same way twice. We must use our knowledge, experience and perceptual skills to analyse the situation before performing the required skill, as in, for example, a tackle in hockey. This

▲ *Figure 2.8* The shot putt – an example of a closed skill

skill requires consideration of a whole range of factors before the correct variation of tackle is executed.

Closed skills are those that have no outside physical influences acting upon them. They are the same each time they are performed. The performer will go through 'a pre-learned sequence of motor activities' with no reference to the environment in which the skill is being performed. Once learnt, closed skills should be performed in exactly the same way each time (Figure 2.8). In a basketball free-throw, the performer's skill is the same each time; there are no outside physical factors interfering with the performance. There is no need to adjust the skill because no one is blocking the shot, the basket remains stationary and the environment remains stable.

Skills can be categorised on the continuum in Figure 2.7 on the left, between 0 (closed) and 10 (open), depending on the degree to which outside factors influence the performance of a skill.

(Note: In an exam question it is vital that you explain your thinking. No marks will be given for just placing a skill on the continuum. You must give reasons.)

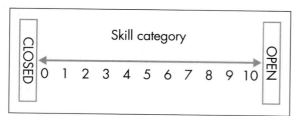

▲ *Figure 2.7* Knapp's open–closed continuum

TASK

Classify the following skills according to Knapp's open–closed continuum:

- a through vault in gymnastics
- a golf drive
- a rugby tackle
- a catch in rounders.

Remember to explain your thinking.

Pacing continuum

As with Knapp's method of classification, the pacing continuum recognises two extremes of skill with other skills fitting between the two extremes (Figure 2.9). This method is based on the degree to which the performer has control over the timing of the skill performance. That is, who instigates the performance of the skill? Is it the performer themselves or is it an outside factor?

Self-paced skills are those that are instigated by the performer. They control the timing of the performance, taking as much or as little time as they want. In a golf drive, for example, a player hits the ball when he or she wants to. They are not told to play the shot at any particular time.

Externally paced skills are those where the timing of the performance of the skill is not controlled by the performer, but by an outside instigator. This could be an official or another performer, such as at the start of a 100-metre sprint, or the service return in tennis. In the first instance, the starter controls the start and in the second the return is played when the ball reaches the opponent. In this case the return is not completely externally paced as the opponent can choose to take the ball either early or late.

Discrete/continuous/serial skills

This method of skill classification relies on the existence of an obvious beginning or end to the skill itself. In other words, is the skill a separate aspect of a sport, which can be removed and practised alone, or is it an element that cannot be identified as having an obvious point at which it starts or ends?

Discrete skills have a clear beginning or end. It is obvious when that skill is being performed and it can be taken out of the sport as a whole and practised on its own as in, for example, a free-throw in basketball. This is a discrete skill as it is obviously a separate element of the game of basketball.

Continuous skills are those that have no obvious point at which they start or finish, in other words the skill just continues to flow from element to element, as in running. This is a continuous skill as each step flows into the next. It is not clear where each phase begins or ends.

Discrete and continuous skills are again often shown on a continuum (Figure 2.10).

Serial skills are those which are made up of a number of discrete or continuous skills put together. These are skills that make up a routine or a sequence, such as in a gymnastics floor routine, or a running forehand in tennis. An example would be a javelin throw (Figure 2.11).

Which method of classification?

The method of classification used depends on the purpose. Classification is often seen as a starting point for the planning of teaching strategies and approaches to learning. A combination of methods may be used in order to identify the range of requirements of the skill.

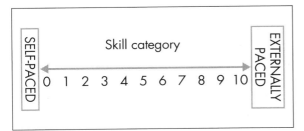

▲ **Figure 2.9** The pacing continuum

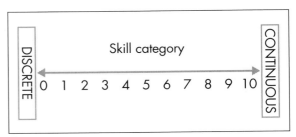

▲ **Figure 2.10** Organisation continuum

▲ Figure 2.11 *The javelin throw is an example of a serial skill*

Closed ....✓......Open

Self-
paced ....✓..................... paced   Externally

Discrete ...✓.............................Continuous

▲ Figure 2.12 *A profile of the skill requirements of a rugby tackle*

All three continua are sometimes shown in one representation of a skill, in order to build a profile of the skill requirements as in Figure 2.12.

It will become more apparent that the requirements of the skill will influence greatly the appropriate teaching, learning and practice conditions.

Individual versus coactive versus interactive skills

The skills we perform in sport are many and various: sometimes we are alone, sometimes others perform around us and sometimes others perform along with us.

Individual skills are those performed in isolation. These are skills where we are the only performer at a particular time. For example, in a diving competition, we perform alone and are then followed by another performer.

Coactive skills are those performed at the same time as others but without direct confrontation. In a 100-metre race, for example, we perform alongside, but cannot physically influence other runners.

Interactive skills are those where other performers are directly involved. There is a direct influence on skilful performance in the form of active opposition. In rugby, for example, the skill involved in tackling meets with avoidance skills on the part of an opponent.

Each skill has different performance requirements. Individual and coactive skills require concentration and often performance of a pre-learned routine/sequence of movements. Interactive skills will require interpretation and variation depending on the situation. An obvious link can be drawn between these and open–closed skills.

TASK

Compare the skills performed in a game activity, an individual activity and a racket activity. Are the skills:
- individual
- coactive
- interactive?

TASK

Create a classification profile of:

a a badminton smash

b a netball centre pass

c a basketball rebound.

Factors affecting practice

A major factor influencing the development of a skill is practice. A commonly used phrase is 'practice makes perfect'. In reality practice can only lead to improvement as very few of us are perfect! The type and appropriateness of the practice will influence the skill development. As discussed earlier, different types or classifications of skill require different learning environments.

There are two main types of practice.

Fixed practice

Fixed practice involves repetition of an activity. This allows the skill to become 'over learned' or automatic to the learner. Repetition will allow the movement pattern to become second nature. This type of practice is ideal for skills that are always performed in the same way, that do not require adapting to the environment. Closed skills, interactive skills and coactive skills all tend to require fixed practice to allow the motor sequence to be perfected, since they will remain the same in practice as they are in a competitive situation (Figure 2.13).

Variable practice

Variable practice involves a variety of activities/situations. The learner applies the skill to a number of different environments in practice, allowing both the development of the skill and the ability to adapt that skill to a range of possible situations. This is vital for open and interactive skills, as they are never the same twice. Initially the movement pattern required to perform the skill is learned and then the adaptations required.

It is a common and sensible approach for open and interactive skills to be taught and practised initially in a closed environment. Once mastered, the environment can be made more and more open, e.g. dribbling in hockey. This is usually taught as a stationary skill with the ball being moved from side to side, then at walking pace, then jogging etc., then the dribble is practised with defenders and ultimately in a game situation.

▲ **Figure 2.13** *Fixed practice involves the repetition of an activity, such as this golfer practising putting*

The organisation of a practice session will depend greatly on those involved and the activity being practised. Depending on the amount of experience, the skill level and the fitness of the performers, practices may be organised in two ways.

Distributed practice

Distributed practice involves the division of a practice session into sections. It is usually associated with variable practices. The overall session involves breaks between each section during which the activity may be changed, feedback given, performers given a rest and the next activity explained.

Distributed practice sessions are good for those with less experience and lower levels of fitness as they allow extrinsic **feedback** (see page 111) from the coach, periods for recovery and development of the practices.

Massed practice sessions

Massed practice involves a continuous session with no breaks. It tends to be used for experienced performers who have higher levels of fitness and is most suited to fixed practice. The performers will work constantly, allowing the skills to be tested under fatigue conditions as in a game situation. This suits experienced performers, as they are able to act on intrinsic feedback (see page 112) to improve their performance. An example of this type of session would be a circuit where the performers move from activity to activity without a break; or a session where they spend the whole session shooting in basketball.

TASK

Plan and run a practice session for an open skill, developing from a closed to open environment.

The practices should be progressive and develop the ability to adapt.

Other aspects of the requirements of a particular skill which need to be considered when organising practice are pacing and serial/discrete skills.

Pacing

Externally paced skills can be learned and perfected as self-paced skills and then gradually external pacing can be introduced. This allows the technique to develop without time pressures. The sprint start can be learnt by performing the start in 'free time' rather than with a stop-watch. Once the correct technique can be reproduced without difficulty (driving low, short explosive strides etc.), external pacing influences can then be introduced.

Serial/discrete skills

Serial skills, being made up of a number of discrete parts, are **low organised skills** (easily divided into parts). They can be practised in parts and then linked together, preferably progressively, thus allowing links to be developed between each part. A floor routine in gymnastics can be learnt as a series of skills with links – handstand, forward roll, cartwheel etc.

TASK

Discuss why the type of skill being developed and the stage of learning an individual has reached will influence the type of practice introduced by the teacher.

Styles of teaching

You should already be familiar with this area of work as you will have experienced various approaches to teaching throughout your schooling and in different areas of the curriculum.

Researchers have analysed approaches to teaching and identified a number of different styles. **Mosston and Ashworth** identified ten different styles, or variations on styles, used by teachers/coaches. These are known as Mosston and Ashworth's spectrum of teaching styles and are represented in Figure 2.14.

Each letter in the model represents a different style of teaching. Styles at the left-hand side of diagram represent a large teacher input with little room for learner interpretation. Styles at the right-hand side involve learner control rather than teacher input.

Some of these teaching styles are self-evident but it is important that those given below are understood.

Command style: A

In the **command style**, the teacher is in total control. The pupils do what the teacher tells them to and they are given no freedom to make decisions for themselves. It is based on the connectionist approach, where the learner acquires skills by learning to associate a stimulus with a particular response, e.g. aerobics sessions.

This method of teaching has both strengths and weaknesses. It allows a lot of information to be given to large groups in a short period of time. It also ensures that the learners perform the skill as they are told, thus avoiding danger. Its weaknesses are that the learners may become de-motivated as they are not given responsibility for their own learning. They are treated as a group, with little or no individual attention or feedback.

TASK

Discuss the type of skill and situation in which the command style of teaching may be most appropriate.

Reciprocal style: C

Reciprocal style allows the learner slightly more freedom. The teacher is still setting the tasks, but the learner is more involved. The teacher outlines a task and will then give coaching points for the skill to be performed, pointing out any particular areas to watch for and any common faults. The learners then split into pairs with one performing and the other watching and giving feedback.

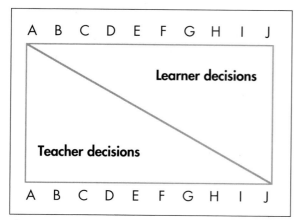

▲ **Figure 2.14** Mosston and Ashworth's spectrum of teaching styles

This method obviously overcomes the lack of individual attention in the command style, for example, and ensures all members of the group are involved throughout. The weaknesses, however, are that the feedback (from fellow students) may possibly be incorrect and learners may not be keen to listen to advice from other learners.

Discovery/problem-solving approaches: H, I and J

Styles H, I and J are all **discovery or problem-solving approaches**. They involve the teacher setting a task and the learner(s) creating or discovering their own solutions. These approaches differ from each other in the degree of freedom given to the learner.

In style H the teacher may give fairly tight guidelines as to the requirements of the task, for example, create a dance to a specific piece of music with a specific theme and certain required elements. In style J the learners may be given complete freedom to create their own dance.

These discovery methods link closely with a Gestalt and whole approach to learning, where the learners will develop a solution through insight and understanding.

Guidance and presentation of information

Teachers must constantly consider what teaching approach will suit the learner and the activity. They must also think about how they are going to put that information across to the learners and how they are to guide the learner to improve and hopefully perfect the skill.

Both the learner and the task need to be analysed carefully to ensure that the most appropriate methods of guidance and presentation are used.

When considering the requirements of the skill, we need to decide if it is appropriate to present it as a whole or if it can, and needs to be, broken into more manageable parts. Skills that it is appropriate to split into parts and which can easily be divided are referred to as 'low organised skills'. Those that are difficult to divide up are '**highly organised skills**'.

Highly organised skills tend to be continuous skills (see page 105) as it is difficult to divide them up. There are no obvious **subroutines** to highly organised skills as, for example, in running.

Low organised skills tend to be serial skills (see page 105) as they are made up of discrete parts, such as in a high jump or a triple jump. Skills that are low organised are often best taught a piece at a time, or as a whole followed by concentration on specific parts. There are three specific approaches that may be used to divide the skill into parts:

- **pure-part**
- **whole-part-whole**
- **progressive-part.**

Pure-part method

This method identifies the subroutines of the skill. The learner then learns, practises and perfects each separate part before moving on to the next and, ultimately, the whole skill. For example, the tennis serve is made up of four main subroutines:

A – toss
B – racket back
C – strike
D – follow-through.

Using the pure-part method, this skill would be introduced as shown in Figure 2.15.

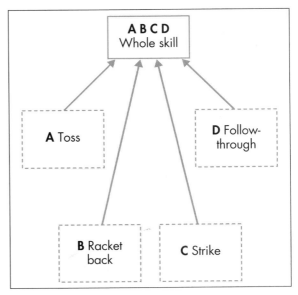

▲ **Figure 2.15** The tennis serve: using the pure-part method each subroutine is taught separately

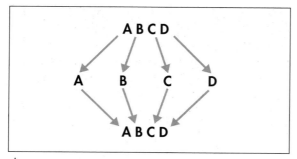

▲ **Figure 2.16** *The whole-part-whole method*

This approach has both strengths and weaknesses. The major strengths are that it allows each part to be perfected without worrying about the others. It allows any problem areas to be identified and worked on. It also avoids the possible danger and worries associated with attempting to initially perform the whole skill in one go.

Whole-part-whole method

This method is similar to the pure-part method, but it involves an initial introduction to the whole skill before breaking it into its parts and then putting it back together (Figure 2.16).

Progressive-part method

This method overcomes the problems of the other two, in that it allows an initial experience of the skill, which allows a clear mental picture during the cognitive phase. It also encourages flexibility in approach, allowing the method to be developed appropriately for the particular skill (Figure 2.17).

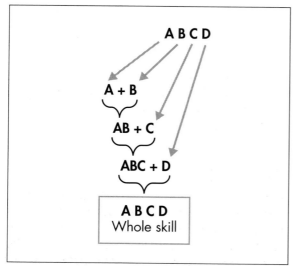

▲ **Figure 2.17** *The progressive-part method*

What are the strengths and weaknesses of each of these methods of skill learning? Which would more effectively encourage the flow of skill?

Consider the stages of learning when answering this question.

Whichever approach is used, the benefits must outweigh the drawbacks. Many theorists believe that although parts methods are helpful, teaching and learning a skill as a whole is ultimately better. They argue that by dividing skills into subroutines, the performer is unable to picture the ultimate learning aim. They are unable to link the separate parts and do not gain an understanding of the sport as a whole.

As the learner progresses, the teacher must consider what form of guidance will allow them to understand and develop a particular skill.

Guidance

When learning, one of the major factors influencing whether we progress through the stages will be the guidance given by the teacher or coach. There are various ways in which this may be given. The best method will again depend on the learners and the activity being learnt. The following types of guidance may be used:

- **visual guidance**
- **verbal guidance**
- **manual/mechanical guidance.**

Visual guidance

This type of guidance involves the transfer of information through the use of demonstrations, video images, visual aids such as posters, modification of the display, manuals etc. Visual guidance is of particular use for beginners. These performers are at the cognitive phase and therefore need to form a mental picture of how to perform the skill. This form of guidance allows this to happen much more easily than an explanation which they may not fully understand.

Modifying the display involves changing the focus of the skill, giving visual cues to assist with skill production, for example, placing footprints on the floor to help a dancer learn a new dance, or placing a target for a badminton player to serve at. Both of these examples allow the performer to use the visual stimuli as a guide when performing the skill.

Verbal guidance

Spoken information about performance can be very beneficial as long as it is clear and concise. Beginners often have problems with verbal guidance, as they may not understand the information being given, especially if it concerns technical aspects of skill production. It is often difficult to explain complex elements of skill performance and it may be best to use verbal guidance to support visual guidance. For example, before or after a demonstration a coach may explain the important elements of the skill such as feet position and then demonstrate again.

Performers in the later stages of the learning process benefit more from verbal guidance as they already understand the basics and will be fine-tuning their techniques. Those in the autonomous stage benefit most, as they are able to concentrate on what has been said, not needing to think about how to perform the basic skill.

Manual/mechanical guidance

This form of guidance involves physically moving or restricting the performer. This can either involve physically manipulating the performer into the correct position so they gain the 'muscle memory', or kinaesthetic awareness of how the skill should feel (see page 117). When they then perform the skill again on their own, they can feel if it is correct and if not adjust the performance. For example, a tennis coach may stand behind a player and move the racket into the correct position to play a forehand (Figure 2.18).

The other form this may take is by restricting the movements to only allow correct action, thus again developing **kinaesthesis**. For example, a butterfly swimmer who is having problems keeping their legs together could have their legs tied together. This is obviously not suited to beginners as they are likely to sink!

Each type of guidance has advantages and disadvantages depending on the skill and the

▲ **Figure 2.18** *Mechanical guidance helps the learner be aware of how the skill should feel*

learner. Often a combination of methods is the most beneficial and enables the skill to be developed efficiently.

TASK

a The most commonly used form of visual guidance is a demonstration. What factors are important in a good demonstration?

b Discuss why verbal guidance would not be given during a demonstration.

c Give an example of each form of mechanical guidance.

d Discuss the advantages and disadvantages of each guidance method. Give examples to support your arguments.

Feedback

Feedback is very much associated with guidance. In order to learn and develop skills both guidance and feedback are necessary. Whilst guidance is information related to the task ahead, feedback is information about what we have done.

As with guidance, the most appropriate form of feedback depends on the learners and the activity being learnt. Whichever form is used, it is important that it is given or received as close to the performance as possible. It must be accurate, understandable, concise and constructive. Feedback can be:

- positive
- negative
- extrinsic/augmented
- intrinsic
- terminal
- concurrent
- knowledge of performance (KP)
- knowledge of results (KR).

Positive feedback

Feedback about a performance should outline what was performed correctly. This is essential for learning: we need to know what was correct so that we know what to repeat. If we do not receive positive feedback, we are likely to change what we do until we are told it is correct. For example, having performed a tennis serve, a coach may tell us that the technique was good because the throw up was the correct height, the preparation was correct and the strike was good because we reached up high. It is essential that beginners are given positive feedback so they know what to repeat. It also motivates them to participate further.

Negative feedback

Negative feedback is more than just what is incorrect about a performance. It should include this, but also how to improve/put right any errors in technique. Although this type of feedback can be used with both beginners and experts, it must be used carefully. Too much negative comment can de-motivate, even though it is a constructive form of criticism. To an expert, this type of feedback is essential if they are to fine-tune their technique.

Whether positive or negative, feedback can take different forms.

Extrinsic/augmented feedback

This comes from outside the performer: from teachers, coaches, peers etc.

Intrinsic feedback

Comes from within the performer. This is in response to the feel of how the skill was performed through the kinaesthetic sense.

Terminal feedback

Feedback after (or even before) a performance.

Concurrent feedback

Gathered during the performance of the skill. This may be extrinsic – a coach shouting information, or intrinsic – the feel of the movements.

Knowledge of performance (KP)

This form can be either intrinsic or extrinsic. It is information about technique and performance. A coach will talk to his team after a game about the way they played. This will be both positive and negative feedback.

Knowledge of results (KR)

This form of feedback is generally extrinsic. It is information concerning the outcome of the activity. A 100-metre sprinter would be told his time, or a gymnast will be given a score by the judges.

Traditionally performers have been more interested in results rather than the way they were achieved. Research now suggests that KP is much more effective in improving performance than KR. The wide use of video has enabled specific information to be used to improve performance.

TASK

Discuss why 'knowledge of performance' may be better for the learning process than 'knowledge of results'.

Leadership

In sport the role of the leader can be essential. A team without good leadership can lack direction and ultimately may fail. The position, the approach and role of the leader will often depend on the situation and the group itself. There has been a great deal of research on the role of a leader and also on group dynamics.

The most obvious leaders in sport are those with specific leadership titles: coach, captain, etc. However, we also see unofficial examples of leadership, where an individual may be seen to be a leader even though they are not a designated captain.

Often success as a leader depends on the acceptance of the leader by the group/team. So it is important to understand where the leader has come from and how they gained the position of leader. Carron (1981) investigated how the leader gains the position of power and suggested there are different types of leader.

Prescribed leaders

A **prescribed leader** is somebody who has been put in the position by an outside body; they are not selected by members of the group/team, for example, the chairman of a football club will employ a manager to lead the team but does not usually consult the team. This is not necessarily the most successful way to appoint a leader, but it is sometimes the easiest and in some situations it may be the most appropriate. It may cause difficulties, however, within the team if they resent an 'uninvited intruder'. This resentment often occurs if the team already have good cohesion (work well together) or if there is an individual within the team structure who the members feel should be their leader.

Emergent leaders

Often, but not always, the most successful leader is the one who emerges naturally from within the group. **Emergent leaders** are selected by their peers from within and will show specific leadership characteristics. The reason emergent leaders tend to be successful is that they have the support and respect of the team.

Often leaders are a mixture of emergent and prescribed. Candidates for a team captain may be selected by the manager and then voted by the players.

Leadership characteristics

The subject of leadership characteristics has given rise to a great deal of research and debate. This focuses around whether leaders are born with leadership qualities or if they develop through experiences. There appears to be no right or wrong answer to this question, with a mixture being most likely. Traditionally, 'trait theorists' believed that some people are born with the personality and attributes required to lead. More recently it is more widely agreed that although this

may be the case, it is 'social learning' which will influence a person's development as a leader.

There is no hard or fast rule as to what makes a good leader. For a sports leader to succeed, it appears that some of the following factors need to be present:

- sport-specific skills/knowledge
- interpersonal skills
- peer respect
- good communication skills
- empathy
- consistency
- fairness.

Although it is not possible to identify all of the specific elements of leadership, researchers have attempted to produce scales to rate leaders. These include the Coach Behaviour Description Questionnaire (CBDQ) and the Leadership Scale for Sport (LSS). These are both questionnaire-based approaches that are used to identify from team members what characteristics they require in a leader.

TASK

a Give examples of the different leaders seen in the sporting situation.

b Discuss why a club might feel that a prescribed leader is most appropriate for them. Why might this be the best method of appointing a manager/coach?

c Discuss examples of emergent leaders in sport. Identify the characteristics which may be the reason for their selection.

d What other characteristics do you think good leaders demonstrate?

Types of leader

Fiedler (1967) investigated the role of the captain in gaining maximum productivity in a group. He identified two categories of leader:

- task-orientated
- person-orientated.

Task-orientated leaders are those leaders who have good activity-related skills/knowledge. They are those who can lead the team because of their understanding of the task and who lead because of this knowledge or experience. To be the leader of a group climbing Mount Everest would require a leader with previous experience and knowledge of the environment, routes, climbing techniques etc.

Person-orientated leaders are those with strong inter-personal skills. They are motivators and will be aware of how to get the best out of each individual rather than concentrating on just completing the task. A group lacking in motivation will require a person-orientated leader to gain the best performance from them.

The approach adopted by a leader varies with both the individual and situation. Three specific styles of leadership have been identified:

- autocratic
- democratic
- laissez-faire.

Autocratic

Autocratic leaders take control. They dictate what should be done and the group are expected to follow. This style is often suited to dangerous situations where decisions need to be made quickly. It also seems to suit individuals who are confident (and often task-orientated), as little notice is taken of individuals when decisions are made.

Democratic

Democratic leaders are person-orientated. They will tend to listen to and act on the opinions of the group. They will often go with the majority opinion and may even go as far as taking a vote. Voting is often difficult in the sporting situation, but this type of leader will take advice from others.

Laissez-faire

It could be argued that this style of leadership does not involve leading. Anything goes – the group will be encouraged to do what they want to. There is little direction from a laissez-faire leader.

Successful use of this style will depend very much on the members of the group. If they are highly motivated and experienced, then this can lead to greater motivation as the group feel that they are trusted to make their own decisions (Figure 2.19).

▲ *Figure 2.19* Mountain leadership: no place for laissez-faire?

Identifying leadership characteristics

A number of methods have been devised to try to identify leadership characteristics and to measure the influence of the leader. Some of them are based on trait theories (we are born with particular characteristics) and others are based on a social learning perspective. These include:

- path-goal theory
- normative theory
- situational leadership theory.

There are others which link many of the concepts from a range areas of thought. One such is Chelladurai's multi-dimensional model of leadership (Figure 2.20).

This model shows the relationship between the leader's personality, the group and the situation. This relationship will produce behaviours that may or may not deviate from 'expected' or 'preferred' behaviours and will, in turn, influence the outcome or performance satisfaction experienced by both group and leader.

Consideration of Chelladurai's model of leadership suggests that:

1 The satisfaction of the team with the approach of the leader is influenced by many factors.

2 The way a leader behaves is dependent on a number of factors:

- how the leader wants to behave
- how the team want a leader to behave

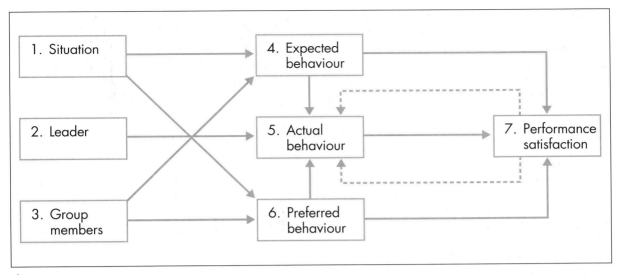

▲ **Figure 2.20** *Chelladurai's multi-dimensional model of leadership*

- the situation
- the personality of the leader
- how the leader is expected to behave.

All of the above make the task of leading difficult. A leader must satisfy a range of different people, often with conflicting requirements. The team may expect the leader to do one thing, the manager another and the officials another. A successful leader may not always be popular, but will require the support of those around them.

We all have different opinions as to what makes a good leader. We will prefer different approaches in different situations and ultimately it may be argued that a good leader is the one who wins.

▲ **Figure 2.21** *A leader must satisfy a range of different people, often with conflicting requirements*

TASK

a Discuss various leaders in sport. Are they person-orientated or task-orientated? For example, Ken Bates, Chelsea FC Chairman. Which type is best?

b Identify and discuss examples of each style of leadership in sport. For example, autocratic – Will Carling.

c Discuss the qualities of each of the examples above. Add any attributes you feel are important in a leader.

Below is a list of some of the characteristics that may be important in a good leader:

- good communicator
- respected
- empathetic
- knowledgeable
- a role model
- high-level performer
- confident.

2. Information processing and the learning of motor control

In sport we must learn and perform a wide range of skills, but being skilful is not always enough. Because sport involves mainly perceptual motor skills (see page 100), it is vital that we select the correct skill for the situation. The process by which we make that skill selection is through the **information processing system**. This system is often known as the **DCR process**. We **D**etect information, **C**ompare it with previous experiences and then **R**eact. In other words, we take in information (input), we decide on a course of action and then we perform the skill (output) (Figure 2.22).

Theorists have investigated this process, identifying key elements to decision making. Welford produced a more complex analysis based on the above idea. He suggested that we take in information through our senses and temporarily store all of these inputs prior to sorting them out. The inputs that are seen as relevant to the decision are then stored in

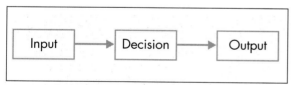

▲ **Figure 2.22** The decision-making process

the short-term memory. A decision is made by comparing the information in the short-term memory with previous experiences stored in the long-term memory (Figure 2.23).

The decision is carried out with reference to the long-term memory to see how to perform the selected skill, and the action and the results are stored for future reference. The whole process then begins again.

Sensory input

There are three main ways in which the information is taken in through the senses prior to a decision being made. These are:

- **vision**
- **audition**
- **proprioception**.

Vision

This is information taken in through the eyes. It is essential in most sports. We see objects, team mates, opponents, etc. We tend to react much more quickly and take in information better if the visual stimuli are bright.

Dull information is sometimes ignored or not noticed. An example of this was when Manchester United wore grey shirts. The brightness of stimuli was seen to influence the decision process – the players claimed that they found it difficult to identify team mates easily and the shirts were never worn again.

Audition

This is information taken in through the ears, i.e. what is heard. In sport this might be a

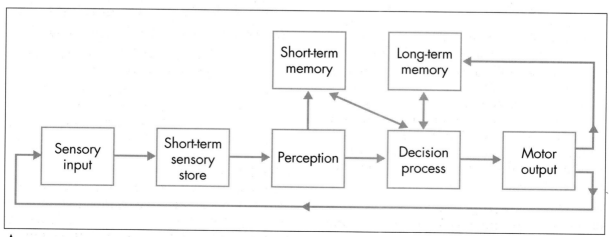

▲ **Figure 2.23** Welford's model of information processing

team mate calling for the ball, or a ball striking a bat. As with visual information, the stronger the stimulus, the more quickly we react to it. In other words we respond to loud sounds more than quiet ones. This might suggest why a gun is used at the start of a race.

Proprioception

There are a number of different methods whereby the body itself gathers information with the muscles and body parts acting as proprioceptors or carriers/receivers of information.

Equilibrium is the awareness of balance or body positioning. We are able to feel if we are off-balance or are about to fall over and we can tell our body position in relation to other objects. Awareness of both of these can be seen as abilities, but they can be developed with practice. A sporting example where we use our sense of balance is in an activity such as the beam in gymnastics, or when we are being tackled in rugby. We can feel that our body is overbalancing and needs adjusting. An example of awareness of body position is in trampolining, when we are able to judge when we are at a point in a somersault where we need to open out to land on our feet.

Kinaesthesis is a vital element in the development and performance of sporting skills. It is the feeling of movement of the body and its parts. It is sometimes known as 'muscle memory'. It is the feeling of movement and is often used to feel if an action is correct – if it feels right or if adjustments are needed. An example in sport would be when playing a golf shot you might feel that the back swing was too far 'inside the line' and adjust the stroke accordingly. We develop this 'kinaesthetic awareness' through practice and experience. The more experienced we become, the more we can feel if a skill is correct, without having to see or be told the results.

Tactile sense, or the feeling of pressure, is the final method of proprioception. We use our sense of touch to tell if we are touching or controlling an object. In a drop-shot in badminton, we use our tactile sense to control the delicate touch of the shot.

Short-term sensory store

All information that is taken in through the senses is stored for a split second in the short-term sensory store before it is processed. This includes both the relevant information (e.g. where team mates are) as well as irrelevant information (the sound of an aeroplane overhead). After a very short time, this information is replaced and lost.

Perception

The **perception** stage of the information processing system is vital. It is at this stage that there are considerable differences between beginners and experts. Experts can identify and sort the inputs quickly and effectively.

The perception stage is the sorting of relevant and irrelevant sensory inputs. Those that are required for decision making are kept and transferred to the short-term memory whilst those that are irrelevant are discarded. This process is called **selective attention**. In order to make a rapid and correct decision, we must attend to key information and not be distracted by irrelevant inputs. For this reason and because of **channel capacity** (the amount of information which can be stored – usually 7–10 pieces of information: see below), we sort through the inputs using selective attention. In a basketball game, we would store the positions of players, calls for the ball etc. but would discard a whistle on another court, or an aeroplane overhead.

TASK

a Following a practical session, identify a situation you were in, e.g. dribbling towards the basket in basketball.

Outline all of the sensory inputs you will have taken in. Include those that may not be of relevance to your decisions.

b Using the sensory inputs listed in **a**:

i which inputs would be held in the short-term sensory store?

ii which inputs would be chosen to continue through the system following selective attention?

Short-term memory

The information selected during the perception process is then stored in the short-term memory. This storage area is also referred to as working memory. It is here that the inputs about the current situation are stored.

It is suggested that the capacity of this memory store is roughly seven pieces of information and it is only kept for less than a minute. The definition of a piece of information is difficult. To a beginner, for example, the position of each player may be different pieces of information, whilst to an expert these may be 'chunked' – the position of all other players is stored as one piece of information. This might explain why experts make better decisions in sport.

Long-term memory

The long-term memory contains a large quantity of information relating to past experiences. It has a limitless capacity and holds information for a lifetime. The information stored includes previous experiences, actions and results as well as movement patterns learnt for the performance of skills.

There are various theories relating to the way information is stored in the long-term memory. Some of these will be discussed later.

Decision process

The decision process takes place by comparing the current situation (short-term memory) with previous experiences (long-term memory) to find similar situations and then deciding what is the best action to perform.

The decision will depend on the success/failure of previous actions, experience, personality etc. When looking at the psychology of sport on pages 423–5, we will consider how personality factors can influence decisions, with extroverts often opting for a difficult action and introverts the easy option.

Motor output

The motor output is the performance of the action selected in the decision process. The output is performed with reference to the movement pattern stored in the long-term memory. Once it has been performed, the situation and the result are stored for future reference. Any feedback is also stored for future reference, both in terms of the result and the performance.

The whole process (Figure 2.24) will then begin again as the performer is now in a new situation.

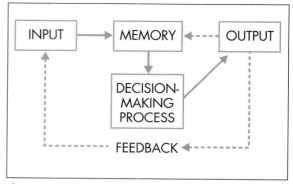

▲ **Figure 2.24** Information processing

There are several different models and representations to show information processing. All of them have similar meanings even if they are not the same visually, or if the terms used are different. Note the following:

- receptors/perceptual mechanisms = input
- translatory mechanisms = memory
- effector mechanisms = output.

TASK

Explain how Whiting's model in Figure 2.25 equates with the Welford model in Figure 2.23 (page 116). Use examples to help your discussions.

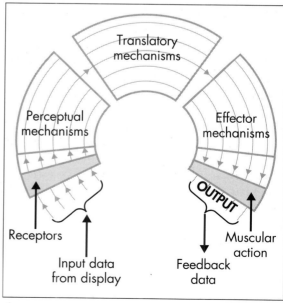

▲ **Figure 2.25** Whiting's model of information processing

The application of processing models

The information processing system is an essential element of performance in sport. If a performer makes the wrong decision, or makes the decision too slowly, the sporting performance will suffer.

If the performer must make a decision under time pressure, the decision may not be the most appropriate because not all possibilities can be considered. The performer may select the first action he or she come across. For example, if a rugby player receives the ball and is about to be tackled by a huge forward, they may decide to pass the ball as quickly as possible, rather than considering the range of other possibilities.

Processing models not only help to explain the difference between the decisions made by different performers, but also how we manage to create time and space. The **Psychological Refractory Period (PRP)** shows how a 'dummy' works to create time. The PRP is the result of the information processing system being a **single channel mechanism**, so that only one decision can take place at a time. Once the process is begun for one decision, it cannot be interrupted or another cannot begin until that one is complete (Figure 2.26).

In Figure 2.26 below, 'stimulus 1' could represent a hockey player seeing another player moving to his left. The defender will begin to make a decision about the best action. If, whilst the player is making the decision, it becomes clear that this was a dummy and the player is moving to the right, this new information cannot begin to be processed until the first decision is completed. Thus there is a delay in the second decision during which time the player has dribbled past the

▲ **Figure 2.27** *The defender's dilemma: when to make the tackle*

defender. The double arrow represents the delay involved in deciding whether, for example, your opponent is really going to pass the ball or just pretending to (dummying).

To make the best use of the PRP in the sporting environment, the second set of stimuli must be timed correctly. If they are too late, the first process will be near to completion and the delay will be short. If the second stimuli follow too quickly, the defender can ignore the first set and simply pick up on the second.

TASK

Outline what makes a good 'dummy'. Don't just think in terms of invasion games. Dummies are also used in activities such as badminton to deceive an opponent.

Implications of response time and reaction time

The amount of time it takes us to complete the DCR process varies from individual to individual and situation to situation. In most sporting situations, the quicker a decision is made, the better, whilst in other situations we can take longer over the decision, for example in chess. The time it takes to make a decision is called reaction time; the time taken to perform the action once you have made the decision is called **movement time**; and the whole process from taking in the information to the completion of the action is called **response time**.

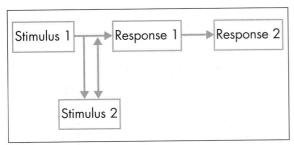

▲ **Figure 2.26** *The Psychological Refractory Period (PRP)*

$$\boxed{\begin{array}{ccc} \text{RESPONSE} = & \text{REACTION} + & \text{MOVEMENT} \\ \text{TIME} & \text{TIME} & \text{TIME} \end{array}}$$

It appears that more experienced and better sporting performers are able to respond both more quickly and more accurately. They seem to have more time to perform the skills and they also appear to make fewer mistakes in their selection of the appropriate action.

Factors influencing response time

Some of the factors that govern the speed and accuracy of decisions can be controlled and improved by the performer; others cannot. These factors include:

- time available
- intensity of stimuli/efficiency of sense organs
- anticipation/readiness for stimuli
- experience
- stage of learning
- psychological state
- number of possible responses
- level of fitness/tiredness.

Time available

If a performer has a long time to decide what to do, they can consider a range of possible actions and the implications of each action. If not, they must make a quick decision and may not consider all possible actions. For example, in a game of chess, a player will consider all possible moves and what the opponent will do in each case. However, in a game of rugby, a player receiving the ball with an opponent close by will need to make a quick decision and cannot afford to spend time weighing up the options. Therefore in the first example, the response time will be slow, but in the second it needs to be very fast.

TASK

a Discuss the problems with having to make a rapid decision.

b Why are performers in activities where decisions have to be made quickly more likely to make mistakes than when doing activities not under time pressures? Give examples.

Intensity of stimuli/efficiency of sense organs

The stronger the stimuli from the display, and the better our sight and hearing, the quicker we react. In other words, if the visual stimulus is bright or the audible stimulus is loud, we are likely to respond more quickly than if it is dull or quiet. This is the case in many sports, where we tend to make the stimuli strong if we want quick responses: a gun at the start of a race; a bright red/white cricket ball; brightly coloured shirts in team games, etc.

TASK

Give some other examples of strong stimuli in sport.

Anticipation/readiness for stimuli

If we are expecting a particular stimulus and are able to anticipate its arrival, we are going to respond more quickly as we are prepared to begin processing the information. For example, at the start of a race we respond quickly because we are given a warning prior to the gun; and in tennis, more experienced players are able to anticipate a particular shot and begin to process the information even before it arrives.

Experience

Experienced performers have been shown to respond more quickly and more accurately than those with less experience. The reasons for this centre on their ability to focus on just the important stimuli. This means that they don't take in as many irrelevant inputs and so have to spend less time sorting them during the perception process. They are also quicker and more accurate in their selection of relevant information during selective attention. They are also more likely to anticipate accurately and they are faster and better at selecting the correct response during the decision process.

TASK

It could be argued that the more past experience we have, the longer a decision will take. Why is this not the case and why do experts respond more quickly than novices?

Stage of learning

Performers in the autonomous stage of learning will respond more quickly than those in the earlier stages as they do not have to think how to perform a particular skill. They just do it.

Psychological state

A performer who is at their psychological peak for performance is likely to perform more quickly and more accurately. If they are under-prepared, they are likely to be slow at reacting and careless in their movements, whereas if they are over-stressed, they are likely to rush a decision and make the wrong choice.

Number of possible responses

When responding to the information from the display (the situation we are in), the more choices we have, the longer it will take us to respond. If there is only one possible response – **simple reaction time** (SRT) – it will only take a short amount of time to decide what to do. If there are several possible responses – **choice reaction time** (CRT) – it will take longer to respond, as we have to decide which of the various possibilities to carry out. **Hick's Law** relates to the amount of time it takes for a performer to respond compared to the number of possible responses. Hick discovered that the time taken increases proportionally to the number of possible responses until a point at which the response time remains constant despite the increase in possible responses (Figure 2.28).

In Figure 2.28, Subject 1 has more possible responses than Subject 2. Subject 2's response time is correspondingly faster.

The point at which the graph levels off varies from individual to individual and from situation to situation. The factors affecting this point are the same as those that affect the overall response time.

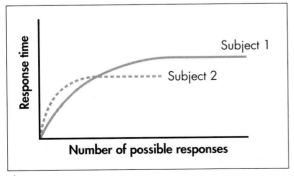

▲ **Figure 2.28** Hick's Law

Often we will make a wrong decision because we decide on an action too quickly without considering all of the options.

Motivation

Motivation can influence our decisions, our learning and our performance in sport. If we are not in a positive psychological state, we will make mistakes in performance and will not learn to perform at our best. Motivation, its effects and its development are considered fully on pages 430–33.

> Motivation = the drive to strive

It is important to be aware of the influence of motivation on the acquisition of sporting skills. Those who are highly motivated are more likely to learn and practise skills than those who are not.

Motivational factors

We are motivated to learn and perform by many factors. Teachers, coaches and the performer themselves need to be aware of the factors which motivate an individual first to participate and second to strive for improvement.

Motivational factors can be intrinsic or extrinsic. Intrinsic motivations are those that come from within the performer themselves. They are factors such as personal satisfaction or enjoyment. Biddell (1984) suggested that performers who are intrinsically motivated are more likely to continue participating than those who are not.

Extrinsic motivators are factors from outside the performer. They give the individual an extrinsic reward such as money, trophies or recognition. Biddell suggested that extrinsic motivation is of benefit at first and can drive individuals to participate and work hard initially, but in the long term extrinsic motivation is not enough on its own. There must also be elements of intrinsic motivation.

Examples showing what Biddell is suggesting can often be seen in sport. If football players were solely motivated by money, many of them would not continue to perform well once they had gained a contract paying them £50,000 per week. Money is no longer an issue. It can also be seen in the case of some boxers who do not train as hard once they have reached a point when they have made enough money to set them up for life.

TASK

With a partner, discuss what motivates you to play the sports you play and whether you are still motivated by the same factors as when you first began to play.

Arousal

The level to which we are aroused will influence both our performance and our ability to learn skills. The influence of **arousal** specifically on performance is considered on pages 444–47. At this stage it is important to understand what is meant by arousal and how it can affect us.

Arousal is the level of psychological readiness. We can be both over- and under-aroused which can lead to a decline in performance and concentration. Motivation will affect our level of arousal, as motivation leads to a state of arousal, depending on the levels of adrenaline produced.

The level to which we are aroused can affect us greatly. If we are aroused to our optimum level, we will perform and learn at our best.

Influence of over-arousal

If, for some reason, we are placed under so much pressure that we become over-aroused, our performance can be influenced greatly. This over-arousal is often referred to as stress and it can influence our ability to think clearly. When over-aroused, the decision process becomes erratic, with poor and rushed decisions. Within the information processing system, our selective attention becomes inaccurate and the decision process confused. If we are in this state, we will not perform to our best and we will also be unable to learn productively. John McEnroe, a

▲ *Figure 2.29* McEnroe: unnecessary tantrums or over-arousal?

talented tennis player who gained some notoriety in the 1970s due to his outbursts on court, was considered by some sports psychologists to have been a victim of his own inability to control and/or channel arousal levels (Figure 2.29).

It is vital that a coach and individual can identify this state in a performer and find ways in which the arousal can be reduced to achieve the best results. The snooker player, Jimmy White, has demonstrated the effects of arousal many times in the World Snooker Championships. Up until the final, White produces his best performance and gradually improves as the rounds go on. However, on several occasions, he has reached the final only for the pressure to lead to him under-performing. He misses shots he would usually hit and he attempts shots he would not usually attempt. His level of arousal is too high and he under-performs.

Influence of under-arousal

If we are under-aroused, not motivated, we perform below our best because of a lack of effort. A performer will lose concentration and take less care over what they are doing. They are likely to make incorrect decisions as they are not concerned with the outcome. They make performance mistakes for similar reasons. We often see teams from higher divisions lose to much lower opposition in this way.

It is important to consider motivation and arousal together as motivation tends to influence arousal levels.

Motor memory

Whatever the skill, when we learn it we must develop the particular movement pattern for that skill. The movement pattern or **executive/motor programme** is made up of different components (subroutines) that have to be controlled and performed in the correct order and at the correct time (Figure 2.30). The skills in the game of badminton require a number of 'executive programmes' – one of which is the smash. Each of these programmes is broken down into a series of subroutines – 'mini-skills' – which may also be subroutines of other executive programmes.

Our motor memory is the storage of how to perform a particular skill and is accessed in the long-term memory whenever we want to perform.

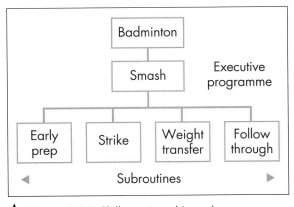

▲ **Figure 2.30** Skill structure: hierarchy

The more experiences we have, the wider our movement vocabulary. Therefore if we can develop a detailed and correct motor memory, we will be fully equipped to learn and perform skills in a variety of sports.

Schema and loop theory

The learning of skills has traditionally been seen in terms of behaviourist concepts, that is, that we learn to respond to particular stimuli in particular ways. Schmidt (1975), however, suggested that the learning of skills was a more cognitive process. He suggested that we learn by grasping four areas of information:

- the initial conditions – this refers to the situation and the initial position, e.g. what was the starting position for the serve?
- the motor programme – the general pattern of movements required to perform a task, e.g. the subroutines of the throwing action
- knowledge of the outcome – what was the result of the action? e.g. did you score or what was the time?
- sensory feedback – what were the sensory outcomes of the action? e.g. how did the performance feel?

Quite simply, what Schmidt is suggesting is that we learn a number of movement patterns, or schema, which we then adapt depending on the requirements of a particular situation. The basic schemas tend to be developed early in life and are then used to develop a wide range of activities (Figure 2.31). As children we learn how to run and how to jump. This can be modified later into long jump, hurdles, heading in football etc. It is purely a case of using the basic movement pattern and adjusting it depending on the situation.

Depending on the type of skill and the stage of learning achieved, the control or performance of the skill will take different forms. Some skills are performed automatically with no conscious control and with no attention needed, whilst others require concentration, thought and care. Martenuik (1973) investigated the control mechanisms involved in the performance of skills. He suggested that we can perform with three distinct levels of control.

▲ **Figure 2.31** *A throwing schema: in time this may be refined into a number of high-level throwing skills*

Level 1 – open loop control

At the **open loop** level of control, skills are being performed at a subconscious level, *without conscious control*. The performer will not need to pay attention to the performance and the performance will not be influenced by any feedback received. In other words, the skill is performed the same way no matter what happens. This level of control occurs when the activity is so fast that there is no time to take in and adjust to feedback. For example, an experienced cricketer will instinctively respond to a short-pitched ball appropriately and without undue delay.

Level 2 – closed loop control

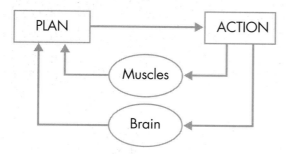

At this level of control, the performer will pay more attention to the requirements of the task. Although it still involves *subconscious control*, there is also attention paid to any

errors and these are adjusted without thinking. Because the control and adjustments are not conscious, the skills remain smooth and fluent. The brain is told an adjustment is being made but it does not control the performance. An example of this is a small adjustment made by a slip fielder in cricket when taking a catch.

Level 3 – closed loop control

At the **closed loop** level of control, the performer is *consciously* performing and adjusting to the feedback received. Because the performer has to pay attention, think and adjust, this makes the performance slow and jerky. So at this level, rather than the brain being told of adjustments, it is responsible for thinking about and controlling the adjustments (Please also see the diagram for Level 2).

TASK

Give examples of open and closed loop control.

Learning phases

In this section of the course we are concerned predominantly with the development and learning of skills. Learning in its simplest form is the development from a position where we *can't* perform a skill to a stage when we *can* perform it. The following is a widely accepted definition of learning:

> *Learning is a more or less permanent change in performance brought about by experience.*
>
> Knapp, 1973

This is saying that we learn to perform skills through practice and performance. It is important to note that Knapp is suggesting that once something is learnt, it remains with us, thus supporting the statement: 'Once you learn to ride a bike, you never forget'.

Learning in sport involves the development of skills through practice, hence the saying: 'Practice makes perfect'.

A theoretical understanding of **learning phases** and skill development should lead us to consider this statement in more detail. As perfection is very rare and not all practice is always productive, a more accurate statement would be: 'Correct practice leads to improvement'.

Fitts and Posner (1967) recognised that as we learn, we do not move directly from 'can't' to 'can'. They suggest that the learning process is sequential – we move through specific stages/phases as we learn (Figure 2.32).

These stages are hierarchical. In other words, each stage must be passed through before the next one is achieved. Also, the learner may possibly move back a stage, depending on the situation.

Cognitive stage/phase

This is the initial stage of learning and is essential if the learner is to progress successfully through the other stages and is to move to a stage where the skill can be performed consistently well.

The **cognitive** stage involves formation of a mental picture of the skill. The learner gathers information about the requirements of the skill from a range of sources. The most efficient is from a demonstration, which allows them to see the key requirements and to work through the performance mentally. They will then attempt to perform the skill.

The more complex the skill, the longer it will take for the learner to understand the requirements. If the skill is to be learned successfully, the mental picture must be correct. If not, the skill will develop incorrectly.

Associative stage/phase

During this stage the learner will practise the skill, according to the information gathered during the cognitive stage. It is essential that the learner gains feedback about their performance at this stage, in order to understand what they are performing correctly and also what elements need to be changed. Often learners will need to return to the cognitive stage to reform and check the mental image they have of the skill.

Whereas visual guidance is essential in the cognitive stage, verbal guidance will be used more in the **associative stage**.

Autonomous stage/phase

When the performer reaches this stage, tasks are performed with little or no conscious thought and attention can be paid to tactical and other considerations. In tennis, for example, a player would be able to serve whilst contemplating what their opponent will do next, rather than be unduly concerned about the mechanics of serving. Not all performers reach the **autonomous stage** in all skills. For those who do, if practice is not maintained, reversion to the associative stage will occur.

▲ **Figure 2.33** *Throwing the hammer: a very complex but closed skill, allowing an autonomous level of control to those who persevere*

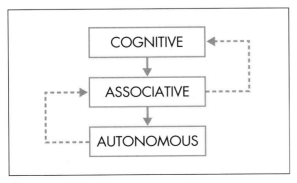

▲ **Figure 2.32** *Learning stages/phases*

This is an advanced stage of learning where the elements of the skill have become part of long-term memory and are automatically produced in response to an appropriate stimulus. Cognitive elements remain where fine adjustments are required for specific situations and will only become part of the autonomous skill if they occur regularly or are practised. Closed skills such as those involved in throwing events can be finely honed so that a highly consistent level of performance can be produced (Figure 2.33).

Transfer of learning

Often we find that performers who are good in one sport will also be good in a range of sports. This may be because they have natural sporting ability, but it will also be based on the concept of skill transfer. This means that skills that have been developed in one situation can be used in other situations. Teachers and coaches will constantly use this concept when teaching and developing performance in sport.

Transfer of learning can take place in the following ways:

- skill to skill
- training to game
- theory to practice.

Skill to skill

This is where a skill developed in one situation has an influence on a skill in another situation. If the influence is on a new skill being developed then this is said to be **proactive**. For example, if a badminton player learns and practises a particular skill in squash, this will be proactive transfer, as the skill developed in badminton will be transferred to squash.

If the influence is on a previously learnt skill then this is said to be **retroactive**. For example, if a squash player learns the skills required in tennis and then returns to squash, the transfer from tennis back to squash will be retroactive.

Training to game

There is constantly transfer from the training situation to the game situation. We spend hours in training, perfecting skills and moves that we then want to transfer into a game. For example, a hockey team will practise penalty

corner moves that they will then attempt to replicate in a match.

Some sports rely almost entirely on this form of transfer. American football is based on set plays that are called by the coach. These have been practised in training until they have become autonomous, with each player knowing exactly what he should do (Figure 2.34).

Theory to practice

We often will use theoretical concepts to improve our performance. A coach will ask his team to follow a particular tactical approach. This will be discussed and the theory outlined and it will then be transferred from the theory session into a game. A coach of a basketball team, for example, may feel that the opposition cannot perform well under pressure so will tell his team to mark man-for-man or use a half-court press.

▲ **Figure 2.34** *Training to game transfer – the basis of American football*

▲▼ **Figure 2.35** *Negative transfer – some skills that appear to be similar do not transfer well*

The effects of transfer

When discussing transfer, it is important to understand the different forms it can take. The effects are not always good.

Transfer can be **positive**. This is where a skill developed in one situation has a beneficial effect on the performance of the skill in another situation. For example, if a performer learns how to perform a somersault on a trampoline, they will be able to use that experience to help with the learning of a somersault in diving. In this case the transfer is both positive and proactive.

Transfer can also be **negative**. This is where a skill developed in one situation hinders the performance of a skill in another situation. If a tennis player attempts to play badminton, they have difficulty because the skills are different in each sport. At first glance the skills are similar, but in reality the techniques are very different (Figure 2.35). Tennis requires a solid wrist action, whilst badminton requires vigorous use of the wrist. If a tennis player does manage to learn the skills required for badminton, they will

then have problems returning to tennis. In this case the transfer is both negative and retroactive.

Transfer can be **direct**. This is where a skill can be taken almost exactly from one situation and used in another. Catching a rounders ball is almost identical to catching a cricket ball. There is very little difference in the techniques used; the only difference is a slight variation in the size of the ball.

Transfer can be **bilateral**. This is where a skill can be transferred from one side of the body to the other. In many sports, those who are able to use both feet or both hands are seen to be at an advantage. They have managed to transfer the skill from the dominant side of the body to the other. With practice a footballer who can control the ball with his right foot will develop the ability to control with his left. This type of transfer is positive as it is beneficial to performance. It also often requires transfer from theory to practice – the player will need to analyse how the right-footed skill is performed in order to work out how to do it left-footed.

Sometimes a skill developed in one situation helps another situation more than the reverse. For example, netball has more skills that help in improving basketball than in the reverse scenario. Netball players can use their accuracy when shooting, movement and passing skills in basketball, whereas basketball players will automatically want to dribble and use a backboard to shoot when playing netball. This type of transfer is called **unequal** transfer.

When considering the theory of transfer it is important to note a link between this and schema theory.

TASK

a List the factors that enable positive transfer to take place and reduce the effects of negative transfer.

b Watch a sporting event and pick one individual to watch and record. Before watching, create a list of the skills likely to be used on a skill analysis sheet. Record skills as they are performed and the success/failure of shots.

c Use the results from **b** to produce a statistical analysis of the performance.

Prepare and give an oral presentation of your findings with visual aids, including:

- discussion of the methods used
- statistical analysis
- conclusions about the performance
- discussion of areas to be improved in the performer.

Key words and phrases

1. The classification and teaching of movement skills

- Skill • Ability • Technique • Cognitive skills • Perceptual skills
- Motor skills • Perceptual motor skills • Classification continuums • Open skills
- Closed skills • Self-paced skills • Externally paced skills • Discrete skills
- Continuous skills • Serial skills • Coactive skills • Interactive skills
- Fixed practice • Variable practice • Distributed practice • Feedback
- Massed practice • Low organised skills • Mosston and Ashworth
- Command style • Reciprocal style • Discovery/problem-solving approaches
- Highly organised skills • Subroutines • Pure-part • Whole-part-whole
- Progressive part • Visual guidance • Verbal guidance
- Manual/mechanical guidance • Kinaesthesis • Prescribed leader
- Emergent leaders • Task-orientated leaders • Person-orientated leaders
- Autocratic • Democratic • Laissez-faire

2. Information processing and the learning of motor control

- Information processing system • DCR process • Memory • Vision • Audition
- Proprioception • Equilibrium • Tactile sense • Perception
- Selective attention • Channel capacity • Psychological Refractory Period (PRP)
- Single channel mechanism • Movement time • Response time
- Simple reaction time • Choice reaction time • Hick's Law • Motivation
- Arousal • Executive/motor programme • Open loop • Closed loop
- Learning phases • Cognitive stage • Associative stage • Autonomous stage
- Transfer of learning • Proactive • Retroactive • Positive • Negative
- Direct • Bilateral • Unequal

REVIEW QUESTIONS

1 What factors influence performance in sport?

2 What characteristics of the task should be considered when deciding how to organise a training session?

3 What aspects of those taking part should be considered when deciding how to organise a training session?

4 What factors influence the style of teaching used?

5 Why is the decision process so important in sport?

6 Explain, in theoretical terms, how a 'dummy' works in sport.

7 Why is feedback so important in the learning process?

8 Discuss the benefits for different people and different skills of the various forms of guidance.

9 Why do some people become better at sport than others?

10 How can the learning process be made simpler?

Texts used in the writing of this section

❑ Biddell, S., *European Perspectives on Exercise and Sports Psychology*, Human Kinetics, 1995

❑ Carron, A.V., *Social Psychology of Sport, An Environmental Approach*, Mouvement Publications, 1981

❑ Davis, D., Kimmet, T. & Auty, M., *Physical Education: Theory and Practice*, Macmillan (Aus.), 1986

❑ Fiedler, F.E., *A Theory of Cognitive Dissonance*, Harper & Row, 1967

❑ Fitts, P.M., *Human Performance*, Brooks/Cole, 1967

❑ Knapp, B., *Skill in Sport: The Attainment of Proficiency*, Routledge & Kegan Paul, 1967

❑ Proctor, R. W. & Dutta, A., *Skill Acquisition and Human Performance*, Sage, 1999

❑ Schmidt, R. A., *Motor Learning and Performance*, Human Kinetics, 1999

❑ Sharp, B., *Acquiring Skill in Sport*, Sport Dynamics, 1992

❑ Welford, A. T. & Traviss, A., *Fundamentals of Skill*, Methuen, 1968

Suggested further reading

❑ Davis, D., Kimmet, T. & Auty, M., *Physical Education: Theory and Practice*, Macmillan (Aus.), 1986

❑ Proctor, R. W. & Dutta, A., *Skill Acquisition and Human Performance*, Sage, 1999

❑ Schmidt, R. A., *Motor Learning and Performance*, Human Kinetics, 1999

❑ Sharp, B., *Acquiring Skill in Sport*, Sport Dynamics, 1992

❑ Welford, A. T. & Traviss, A., *Fundamentals of Skill*, Methuen, 1968

Section B: Option A: Practical application

Introduction to Option A

This option requires you to select two practical activities for assessment. These two activities are to be chosen from the three different categories of team games, racket games and individual activities. The two chosen activities must be from two different categories. This section requires you to take part in practical activity that focuses on two key areas of performance in structured practices and competitive situations. Individual activities are assessed against objective measurements. Each of these two required forms of activity form the base of your practical assessment. As such they are the medium through which you will be able to improve your playing standards and activity knowledge, leading to better understanding of the wider concept of performance enhancement.

Any performance requires the foundation of productive practice and appropriate competition (Figures 2.36 and 2.37). By combining these elements in a planned and programmed way you will be able to improve the quality and standard of your selected practical

▲ **Figure 2.37** *A competitive situation*

activities and gain not only higher marks from assessment but also greater reward from your achievements.

2. Progress through practice and performance

Structured practices

Structured practices may be best described as your ongoing coursework which is designed to *enhance* your ability to perform. This is not a simple question of 'practice makes perfect'. It is the medium through which you can develop a range of associated performance components that underpin movement and the application of a **skill repertoire** (a range of skills) within the sporting arena. These components will in part be familiar to you. They relate to the interaction and influence that physiological, psychological and technical developments bring to the sphere of performance.

Expanding on this theme, Sharp (1992) views the learner as being able to acquire:

the precise movement patterns which, if executed at the right time and in the right manner, reveal fluent, skilled performance

▲ **Figure 2.36** *Any performance requires the foundation of practice …*

as only one component of the process of learning – the other two being attitude and knowledge. The interplay of these three ingredients is central to enhancing performance. According to Sharp, skill belongs to the individual and is the link between intention and action. Once a skill is learned a permanent change in behaviour will occur (Figure 2.38). This relationship will subsequently form the basis of study in Unit 5, Section A of the Advanced Level course.

The practical work that you undertake will be designed to allow you to make progress in your ability to perform at a higher level. It will also incorporate a wider knowledge and understanding of how this can be achieved.

Learning the correct technique

Structured practices by definition require you to engage in situations where you will be tested under increasing pressure. Through careful coaching you will learn to enhance the **technical components** which underpin skilful performances. Learning the correct technique of a skill through structured practices and learning strategies is the cornerstone to enhance performance and technical training, which is central to this Unit. Dick (1992) explores the concept of technical training as a process built in stages. As your performance improves you focus your efforts using the knowledge and understanding reflecting the work covered in Section 2A.

Some sportsmen or women appear more able to perform a range of skills (a skill repertoire) at a higher level and to a higher standard due to their technical proficiency. How long you spend perfecting a skill may depend on the quality of technical coaching you receive. Your knowledge of the 'skill versus ability' debate gained from Section 2A (page 102) will help you to understand the concepts involved here.

As sports performers, we all have different combinations of abilities, such as strength, speed, co-ordination, balance, dexterity etc. which are *internal* to the performer. These combine with structured practices to enhance skills, which are *external* to the performer, and aid performance. Skills can be broken down into subroutines although opinion has suggested that those skills that are high in complexity and that are highly organised are very difficult to break down into subroutines, and so such skills need to be learned as a whole.

You will be familiar with the concept of '**drilling**' a particular movement into a performer. For some activities it is easier for them to be enhanced, and even judged, by movement replication, such as in gymnastics or karate. The constant repetition of a 'set' movement or series of movements which mirror the competitive environment easily fit into this format. However, the use of the word 'drill' is too rigid and limiting to describe the variety of experiences that structured practices involve. Barrow and Brown (1988) support the view that the key to learning is practice that must be followed by feedback. Learning is achieved by 'doing' and 'skill is learned only through one's own responses repeated over and over again'.

Developing a wider understanding

Structured practice enables you to develop a wider understanding of how to improve performance. Knowledge of the technical building blocks, which form a motor programme, will not only directly help you to successfully perform a skill, but also provide you with the basis of *understanding a movement* for Section 2C in the Analysis of performance.

Some activities are assessed on technical merit whilst others, such as trampolining, also include a 'tariff' system that defines the degree of difficulty in a routine or skill. Structured practice can replicate this and your experiences should be designed to prepare you for competition.

▲ *Figure 2.38* 'Practice makes permanent'

▲ *Figure 2.39* *A safety harness allows difficult skills to be mastered in a safe environment*

The requirements to perform successfully in a racket or a team game are not as straightforward. From your experiences gained in Section 2A Acquiring skill you will be able to apply the theoretical knowledge of the *classification and teaching of movement skills* and that of *information processing and the learning of motor control* to the practice environment. By understanding the technical components specific to an activity and then developing a performance through guided and structured practice, you can produce enhanced performances.

Structured practice considerations

It is important to remember that all practices in some way need to reflect the 'real' conditions and circumstances of competition. When structuring a practice the following factors need to be considered:

- Is the playing area appropriate to the numbers of players involved?
- Are the established rules of the activity applied?
- Are any imposed conditions enhancing the practice objectives or hindering them?
- Can a performer cope with the speed and pressure being applied to the practice?
- Is it possible to extend the practice to further enhance technique and skill production?

- Can the practice increase the performer's knowledge and understanding of when, where, how and why to perform skills? Will it enable the performer to demonstrate tactical awareness, decision making and movement?
- Practices need to be competitive even if the performer is being competitive against themselves.
- Practices have to mirror playing/performing conditions with appropriate equipment.
- Practising with and against players of a slightly higher standard can 'lift' your own performance.

The old adage of 'train well play well' works!

When, where, how and why?

It is important to view the performance of skills as a process requiring more than just a movement with a label. All skills have a perceptual element (see page 102) and by definition demand that learning has and is taking place. The application of skill to a practice or competitive situation cannot exist without the interaction between the context in which it is being performed and the intention of it. Therefore, you will need to develop the understanding of *when* to perform a skill or movement, *where* to perform it, *how* to perform it and *why*.

- *When* to perform a skill involves tactical and strategic considerations reflecting the knowledge and experience you have of the activity.
- *Where* to perform a skill extends this knowledge on to a more specific appreciation of location and circumstance.
- *How* to perform a skill or movement defines the technical detail of production.
- *Why* demands the knowledge of perception. Perceptual motor skills lay the foundation for enhanced performances that in their own right are dependent upon additional physiological and psychological influences.

Using the example of a tennis player (Figure 2.40) involved in a rally from the base line, the player has to perceive the relationship between themselves, the opponent and the ball. They have to interpret the delivery of the next shot and decide tactically their return

▲ **Figure 2.40** *All skills have a perceptual element*

and why to select it. The performance of the shot will be to the best of the player's technical capability, using feedback to judge its success. Not forgetting the concept of anticipation and the need to learn from the entire process!

This interaction is more readily applied to team and racket games but still has some value in its application to individual activities. The canoeist interacts with the flow of water; the gymnast with equipment and music; the karate or judo player with an opponent. You will need to link your knowledge and understanding gained from Section 2A to this area of performance.

What do I need to achieve through structured practice?

As a result of your development through structured practice, it is expected that your performance will be enhanced as skill is learned correctly. Positive enhancement can be observed through the following changes in performance:

- improved technical proficiency in the performance of skills
- increased consistency – fewer errors
- decreased energy expenditure
- increased timing and ease of movement
- improved anticipation/automation of task
- increased focus on tactics and strategies
- decreased self-talk (see Unit 5, Section A – Techniques for enhancing performance: stress management techniques and goal setting)

- growing confidence, creativity and composure
- a wider and more advanced skill repertoire
- the increased use of appropriate motor abilities
- a developed 'fitness for purpose'.

Competitive situations

All the work you undertake through structured practice needs to be tested in an appropriate competitive situation (Figure 2.41). This will invariably mean the full version or requirements of your activity staged in the appropriate setting. However, at times it is also possible that an amended version of the activity may also allow you to test your skills, abilities and techniques competitively.

The application of the appropriate Governing Body rules or laws, the need to perform against opponents of a comparative standard and the opportunity to employ tactical awareness are all fundamental requirements.

Within the sphere of a competitive performance, additional factors will affect the outcome. The characteristics and components that contribute to and make up a successful performance are inter-dependent and this relationship at times can be compensatory. The performer will therefore use a combination of all the following characteristics and abilities to some degree when performing competitively:

- be able to apply technique and skill
- use tactics and strategies of an appropriate nature

▲ **Figure 2.41** *All work through structured practice needs to be tested in an appropriate competitive situation*

- exhibit game/activity awareness
- display decision-making ability
- demonstrate an ability to play in different positions or perform in different disciplines/mediums
- cope while performing under increased pressure
- possess a 'fitness for purpose'
- influence a situation and be able to improvise.

Activities conducted away from your centre

You are able to undertake an activity that is not catered for at your centre as long as it is under the direction of your PE staff and contained in the category listing. Staff will need to liaise with the club or centre overseeing your instruction and monitor the progress you are making. For assessment they will need to be familiar with the examination requirements, the criteria for assessment and the standardisation of activity performances. Video evidence is required of your performances in both structured practice and the competitive situation.

How will I be assessed in Section B: Option A?

During the course of Unit 2B: Option A, you will be focusing your enhancement of performance in two areas:

- structured practices
- competitive situations.

Each of these two components will be assessed against a set of descriptive criteria. These criteria will be used to make both ongoing judgements about the level of performance seen in these two areas, as well as a summative judgement at the end of the course. This will be carried forward to signify the level of attainment that you have reached.

The subject criteria on the pages that follow give details of those elements which underpin the progress and development which can be achieved through practice and performance in an appropriate competitive situation.

The criteria will enable you to make judgements about your performance enhancement in relation to the activity-specific key aspects within the spheres of practice and competition.

These allow for the differences between team games, racket games and individual activities, which have their own individual assessment requirements and subsequent criteria, while still allowing for some comparability between all activities. Your performance will be assessed by your own centre and then moderated by an external examiner (see box on page 135).

It is important for you to remember that the standard of performance at the Advanced Subsidiary level will be judged against a different set of criteria from those for the Advanced Level course.

Candidates will be measured in the assessment of performance at both AS and A level. Although in each case the criteria will be different, assessment will be made in two areas:

- for all team and racquet games: in structured practices and competitive situations
- for individual activities: two assessments that mirror the same division of practice and competitive performance.

The Advanced Level criteria require a higher standard of performance in structured practice and competitive situations than those of the Advanced Subsidiary course.

Assessment scores

Each set of criteria uses a scale from 1 to 15 with a mark of 15 being the highest score that can be awarded to a candidate for either their structured practice or competitive performance. The maximum mark that a candidate can achieve therefore is 30. Each set of criteria is grouped into bands: 1–3, 4–6, 7–9, 10–12 and 13–15. Each band is used to judge a performance and to distinguish between performances. Once a candidate is assessed into a band then the exact mark out of 15 can be decided.

Maximising your opportunities

As your experiences develop and you play at a higher level of competition, how you adapt and enhance your performance will be reflected in the degree of application that you show.

Be prepared to take every opportunity to compete, not only for your centre, but also for clubs outside your educational environment as your performance may be judged in an official tournament or competition. If selected to represent an area, district, region or to compete at national level, then this will be reflected in the marks awarded to you. Your performances will be assessed and the marks awarded subject to moderation.

> **moderation**: the process through which an independent examiner, by direct observation or scrutiny, is able to judge and compare your standard of performance against recommended national standards, using appropriate assessment criteria

Assessment in team games

In team games at AS level, you will be able to improve your marks by focusing your enhancement of performance in structured practice in the following key areas:

- levels of technique and skill demonstrated
- ability to maintain technical accuracy under pressure
- application of tactics and strategies as appropriate to the practice or competition
- level of perception demonstrated
- level of progress, learning and understanding shown.

In your competitive performance, the major requirement is for you to transfer what you have learned in practice to an appropriate competitive situation. In addition to the factors above you should also demonstrate:

- a level of 'fitness for purpose' – that is, a developed level of the fundamental fitness components that your team game requires in order for you to compete, e.g. strength, speed, agility or co-ordination
- the level of influence you have within your competitive situation
- the ability you have to play in more than one position (excluding specialist positions such as goalkeepers)
- the ability to show improvisation
- the application of a game plan.

Assessment in racket games

The assessment of performance in racket games at AS level follows a similar pattern to that of team games at this level. The assessment criteria however, will highlight those aspects of a racket game that should be the target for enhancement. Assessment will require you to focus upon structured practices in the following key areas:

- level of fitness for purpose – that is, a developed level of the fundamental fitness components that your racket activity requires in order for you to compete, for example, strength, speed, agility and co-ordination.
- level of technique in each stroke
- degree of advancement in a skill, e.g. the addition of spin
- level of consistency of technique when working under pressure
- use of tactics and strategies
- level of perception demonstrated
- level of progress in learning and understanding shown.

Extending your performance into the competitive arena will require you to further demonstrate the following aspects:

- the influence that you can make to an appropriate competitive situation and, where applicable, to the singles and doubles game
- your level of court awareness
- your consistency and number of unforced errors
- the ability to employ variation to shot or stroke through the use of disguise, power and touch
- the ability to perform under pressure and influence an appropriate competitive situation.

Assessment in individual activities

The range of individual activities open to candidates and the diversity of their nature requires each performance to be assessed against a set of separate criteria at AS level.

Some of the assessments will take the form of completing a prescribed list of movements or actions. Many of these reflect the requirements of Governing Body awards. The format for assessment will be similar to that of your team game or racket selection – that is, the maximum mark available to you will be 30 made up of two performance marks out of 15.

In athletics and swimming, you will be required to perform events which will then be judged against standard performance tables. This will accompany a judgement based on the technical merit and proficiency of your events developed through structured practice. Your centre will make these tables available to you and offer advice how best to enhance your performance. Your centre staff, or an appointed club official under their guidance, must authenticate all records of performance.

You will need to familiarise yourself with the requirements of your particular activity choice, as their diversity does not allow for detailed explanation here. The following guidelines may be of help to you as they are relevant to all individual activities:

- Focus on improving your core techniques to the highest possible standard as they are often marked on their own merit.
- Do not rely on a 'one-off' performance as part of any assessment – it may just be an off day for you!
- Sometimes it is better to perform a skill which carries a lower 'tariff' well than one which carries a higher 'tariff' badly.
- Make allowance for the winter training and playing season – grab every opportunity you can.
- Ensure any activity conducted off-site has the appropriate qualified instructors and/or coaches as recommended in the full specification document.
- If possible, train with another student as you can encourage and coach one another where appropriate.
- Never put performance above safety.
- Make use of any technical support – video analysis is vital.
- Ensure you are assessed competitively on at least three 'formal' occasions.

Performance components

Any performance requires a combination of inter-related factors that together help enhance the quality of it. Central to the assessment criteria of Section 2B is the concept of 'fitness for purpose'.

> **fitness for purpose**: the application of a range of fitness components relevant for the performance of a given activity

Fitness for purpose

Any sporting performance relies upon physiological, psychological and technical strengths combining together. The word 'skill' is often misunderstood and you need to think of it in a much wider conceptual framework. Skill is a shortened word for what Sharp (1992) describes as:

> ... *a continuous interplay between the technical ability of a performer, the perceptions and judgements that he or she makes and the fitness or degree of preparedness the performer possesses.*

Essentially you will need to enhance, through structured practices and competitive situations, the interplay between attitudes, knowledge and movements. Revisit Section 2A Acquiring skill and relate the understandings gained from the text to your own practical experiences.

Linking work studied in Section 2A to that of Unit 3 Exercise and training will be of benefit. Training is easily incorporated into your structured practices and fitness for purpose, for it is a clear target for enhancement.

The use of fitness testing to measure any improvements acts as a benchmark to the progress you are aiming to achieve. The elements that are part of the core physiological make-up of an athlete can be identified and specifically improved to meet the requirements of the activities that you have selected. The components include:

- strength – static, explosive and dynamic
- speed
- cardio-vascular endurance
- local muscular endurance
- flexibility – dynamic and static
- co-ordination – gross body, hand/eye and eye/foot
- balance – gross body, static and dynamic
- agility
- reaction time
- power – strength and speed
- visual – activity and tracking.

Refining your performance

Your work in this section of Unit 2 will be extended in Unit 5 if you continue to complete a full A level. This will require you not only to extend your own knowledge and understanding of 'Factors affecting performance' but also to draw together the specific content of Unit 6 when exploring 'Exercise and energy systems' and 'Sports psychology' or 'Sports mechanics' in order to *refine* a performance.

▲ **Figure 2.42** *Weight training increases strength: strength underpins all movement*

You will need to identify the core elements of your activity, such as speed and co-ordination, discuss the requirements with your centre staff and then progressively aim to enhance them in order to maximise the potential for success in an activity. By linking this to the 'Analysis of performance' part of Section 2C, you will begin to understand the process by which performance is enhanced through the five areas of analysis. Typically, you will need to understand:

- how to improve through training
- how to apply the principles associated with training
- the different practice conditions under which learning enhances performance.

The foundations that you lay in this Unit will provide you with the base for your Personal Exercise Programme (PEP) in Unit 5B. You should be able to apply the correct training methods, understand the physiological and

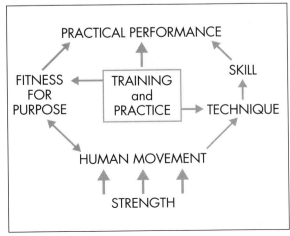

▲ **Figure 2.43** *Components of improved performance*

psychological benefits so derived and evaluate the programme. (Further explanation of the PEP occurs in Unit 5 on pages 346–51.)

It is important for you not to view each Unit of the specification in isolation. Linking and relating the subject content of other Units to your ability to perform practical activities is a central theme of the specification.

Figures 2.42 and 2.43 illustrate how strength underpins all human movement and how, through a combination of training and practice, you enhance performance.

Common technical components

The focus of your work in this option will be to enhance your performance in two practical activities. Whilst developing a 'fitness for purpose' you will also need to focus on your technical proficiency in those skills which will enable good performance. All activities have a range of skills that require fundamental techniques to be mastered, and by relating technical development to the assessment of these skills, a clear common approach is maintained.

The assessment of skills in isolation forms part of the examination requirements for those students continuing with the course at Advanced Level.

Team and racket games

In team and racket games the assessment focuses on three key components:

- preparation
- execution
- recovery/result.

Each component of skill requires technical detail for its successful completion. In the *preparation* phase, focus on aspects of:

- stance/body position
- feet and/or hand placement
- alertness.

For the *execution* of a skill, a more detailed knowledge of the specific technique(s) involved are required, although these can commonly be based on:

- body position and the transfer of weight
- positional and **spatial awareness** throughout the movement
- technical accuracy and control
- use of timing, power and touch.

The final phase of *recovery and result* is concerned with the outcome in the performance of a skill but it still requires a technical input. Central to the successful completion and technical proficiency in a movement is the recovery from it. Here, three key factors need to be considered:

- the consistency of the movement/skill
- the result of the movement/skill
- the technique employed and the recovery allowing further movement.

In your own activity you may easily identify this process and apply it to your activity:

a the fitness components

b the technical detail necessary for skills to be mastered

c the tactical knowledge that provides the understanding required to complete the training, practice and competition undertaken throughout Unit 2.

Individual activities

The diversity of individual activities does not detract from common core technical components. Although you must be aware of the more exacting demands of individual activities as they will be assessed on technical proficiency, it is still possible to focus on common, generic, detail which will allow you to concentrate on activity-enhancing practices.

You should concentrate on breaking down a skill into a number of segments that are specific to each individual activity. This enables you to more easily isolate the techniques as appropriate. As with your team and racket games, the foundations built here are essential for the refinement of performance in Unit 5 and the requirement to offer skills in isolation for assessment in that Unit. You should focus on the central technical components appropriate to your activity, which should in turn address the ordering and timing of:

- control of a movement
- the quality of a movement
- timing of sequenced techniques
- entry into/out of a movement
- body, hand, arm and leg movement
- any repulsion and/or height
- recovery and control.

The above points focus your ability on analysing a skill and/or movement, which reflects how you as a performer will also be assessed. While providing a 'frame of reference' for technical improvement it is impossible to devise a generic series of components that suitably fits all activities. You should pay careful attention to the appropriate practical guidelines contained in the full Edexcel specification. For example, in canoeing the requirement to develop activity-specific techniques is clearly identified both as part of the activity requirements and the subsequent assessment of a performer. Through instruction, the canoeist will develop technically in their ability to perform a variety of strokes, manoeuvres and movements. By successfully replicating a recommended technical model, the performer adds accuracy and successful performance to the learning of a basic skill (Figure 2.44).

▲ **Figure 2.44** Correct technique enables skilled performance

Section B: Option B: Research project

1. Introduction to Option B

This option offers you the ideal opportunity to identify, elaborate and analyse a performance-related aspect of the AS level specification of your own choosing. In doing so, it provides a further opportunity to cover the theory from other modules related to a specific practical area, and also the chance to input your own material and ideas. A well conducted research project can also act as an ideal foundation for the investigative study carried out as part of full A level.

The research project represents 20 per cent of the marks at AS level or 10 per cent of the marks at A level.

The task

In the process of carrying out the study you should:

- identify an aspect of practical activity suitable for a small-scale study
- locate and review literature and documentation
- develop a reasoned analysis of the area of study
- interpret and draw meaningful conclusions
- organise and present findings in a coherent manner.

Unlike the investigative study option in Unit 5, the research project does not have to involve empirical research. Instead secondary sources of information can be used. For example, if the study were to investigate the different systems of play used in hockey, the researcher could reinforce a point or argument by including information analysing the systems used by national league hockey teams.

This information might be already available from coaching magazines, books, videos or the Internet. However, care must be taken to compile a list of all sources of information and ensure that they are acknowledged.

For many students, the task of carrying out a project of some 1500–2000 words will be a major challenge. *Success will depend on good planning and organisation*. The use of a **project diary** throughout the research process will be invaluable.

RESEARCH TIP

The project diary should include:

- planning dates and deadlines
- a log of progress and problems
- a compendium of references
- sources of guidance.

---

2. Identification of the activity

Getting started and choosing a suitable topic for study can be the hardest stage of the research process. Therefore it is important that you spend sufficient time investigating potential areas for study and analysing their suitability for a project of this size. *This stage of the research process should not be attempted in isolation*. Discussing ideas with teachers and friends can avoid seemingly obvious mistakes later.

In order to make the process easier, it should be broken down into the stages identified by the **Research process diagram** (Figure 2.45). It can be used as a template for carrying out the research project.

Deciding what would suit you

This initial stage involves a degree of self-analysis. First, you need to identify which areas of physical education or sport you are interested in.

Quite clearly, embarking on an eight-month-long project is going to be made easier if you have already developed an interest in a particular area or have a particular expertise.

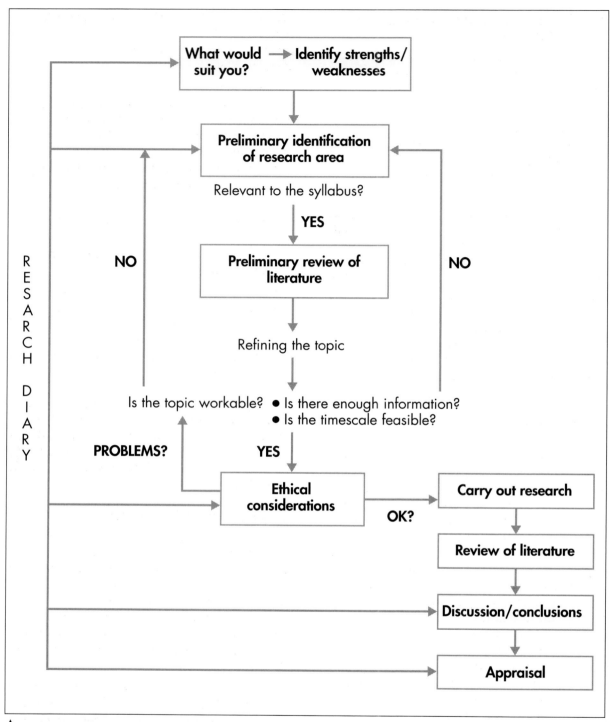

▲ **Figure 2.45** *The research process*

Coaching or training experience or even regular spectating experience could help you focus on a specific research topic.

Second, you also need to take into account your particular academic strengths and weaknesses. If you are better at the scientific rather than the socio-cultural aspects of the specification, it makes sense to focus on the physiological, psychological or bio-mechanical areas where your particular strengths can be better utilised.

Preliminary identification of research area

This stage involves refining your broad area of interests and identifying them with specific aspects of the syllabus. This can be achieved by:

- cross referencing your area of interest using a variety of textbooks
- checking against the specification
- discussing your ideas with your tutor and/or friends.

For example, volleyball might be your initial area of interest. This interest could be extended and applied to the 'Exercise and training' aspects of the specification through an analysis of the fitness components required by élite players in volleyball; or by investigating the training methods used by élite athletes.

Alternatively, such an interest related to the 'Acquiring skill' section could involve reviewing the most effective methods of teaching the 'dig' or 'volley' to novices.

Preliminary review of literature

A library search is required at this point to refine a particular idea and to look at its feasibility. The initial idea may need some further refinement or you might find that there are not enough reasonably available resources relating to the area of interest therefore making it unworkable from the outset.

On the other hand, the scope of your idea might be too large. For example, you might have chosen deviance in sport as an initial area of interest. Despite (or indeed because of) the massive breadth of resources on this topic, it would be clearly unmanageable to cover it as a whole. It must therefore be refined so that it becomes a more manageable undertaking. A study analysing deviance of a specific group, in a particular activity, might prove a more realistic option.

RESEARCH TIP

If you haven't used the library before, ask the library staff to introduce you to the resources available and show you how to access them.

Examples of suitable areas for study

The suggestions below are meant to act as a starting point and guide rather than as a definitive list.

- **Social aspects**

  A study reviewing how to increase the participation of a select group in a specific activity, e.g. women in football.

  A study investigating the importanc of finance in the development of élite performers in a specific activity.

- **Exercise and training**

  A comparison of systems of play in a specific sport.

  A comparison of different training regimes to improve endurance for a given sport.

- **Acquiring skill**

  A study reviewing the different types of feedback used in a specific sport.

  A study of motivational techniques used by athletes in a specific sport.

Once you have refined your research topic, determined that it is manageable and feasible in the allotted timescale, *and* ascertained that there are sufficient resources to work from, you now need to address potential **ethical** considerations.

Ethical considerations

Research is fraught with ethical considerations. Many of the problems listed below refer to the conduct of researchers when carrying out research, or occur as a consequence of research involving other people.

Although the research project does not have to involve empirical research, it is as well at this stage to be aware of some of the potential pitfalls:

- *Consent* – subjects' (or parents') consent should be sought at all times. Subjects of your research should also be made aware of the nature of the research beforehand and have the right to withdraw their support at any time.
- *Plagiarism* – this is copying someone else's work so closely that it can be recognised clearly as theirs rather than yours. All work presented should be your own.

- *Acknowledgement* – other peoples' work should be acknowledged at all times.
- *Safety* – psychological and physiological discomfort to anyone involved in the research should be avoided at all times. All research should be safe for all parties concerned. It is most important that proposed research procedures should be discussed with, and approved by, an appropriate member of staff.
- *Fabrication and falsification of records* – all researchers should report their findings honestly and accurately.
- *Confidentiality* – subjects should not be named. Personal data (unless in a case study) should be treated confidentially.
- *Competence* – the researcher should be fully qualified to carry out the particular research. Again, prior discussion with appropriate member(s) of staff should involve your being 'approved' to carry out your particular research methodology.

KEY SKILLS

If you undertake a research proposal presentation (no set length) to your tutor or class, the records of the presentation, together with records of the formative stages, provide a good means of satisfying the criteria for the Level 3 Key Skills Unit on Communication.

3. Locating literature and documentation

By this stage you should have a clear idea of your research proposal. Your preliminary literature review should have confirmed that enough resources are available and any ethical issues have been considered and resolved.

The review of literature is important for the project in that it aims to synthesise all of the information relevant to the research topic.

On a practical level, the review involves researching all relevant information from a variety of resources. You will need to be imaginative and diligent when doing this. Sources of information include:

- *Books* – general physical education texts are the obvious starting point but more

'topic-specific' publications will need to be studied in order to demonstrate that a wide range of resources have been consulted.
- *Journals* – an excellent source for up-to-date research. These contain research papers covering a wide range of research disciplines. Examples include, *The British Journal of Physical Education* and *Research Quarterly for Exercise and Sport*. However, these might not be available in the school/college library.
- *Newspapers* – newspapers can provide useful quotes, information and analysis of current issues and developments in sport.
- *Videos* – coaching and documentary videos.
- *CD-ROM databases* – newspaper CD-ROM databases are available, which provide information from selected newspapers e.g. *The Times*, and the *Guardian*. Specific topic information can be accessed by a key word search. Alternatively, the library might have access to sports-related CD-ROM databases such as DISCUS.
- *Internet* – a wealth of sports-related information is available which can be accessed through general searches for a particular activity (e.g. hockey) or by accessing information from sport-specific sites.

RESEARCH TIPS

1 Begin your research using general PE textbooks or encyclopaedias and then focus in on primary sources such as research papers or articles.

2 If your school/college is under-resourced in any of the above areas, you will need to make a trip to a university or local library.

3 Remember as you go along to write down the references for all your sources of information in your project diary.

4 Make notes summarising the information from each source as you go along. This not only saves time but also helps to avoid plagiarism.

4. Developing a reasoned analysis

Review of literature

For the research project, the literature review and discussions/conclusions sections make up the main body of the study. This is where all of the information relevant to your research topic is **identified**, **elaborated** upon and **analysed**.

It is not possible to just sit down and write these sections off the top of your head. They must follow a distinct pattern as well as follow logically from the plan given in 2. Identification of the activity (Figure 2.45). Writing these components will require considerable care and attention in order for you to produce a clear, coherent piece of work that follows a logical structure.

Identify

This stage takes the form of a general introduction to the area of study. In most cases it involves setting your research topic into its wider context whilst also defining any relevant technical terms.

For example, the study might involve a comparison of different training methods used to improve cardiovascular endurance in hockey. Therefore, at this stage, you would need to introduce the reader to the broad area of training for physical activity. Then you would need to go on to define what is meant by cardiovascular endurance and explain its relevance to sporting activity in general. Finally you would identify the importance of this type of training in hockey.

Elaborate

This involves expanding on the themes identified in the first stage and relating them to the research topic. Using the above example, you would present information explaining the different cardiovascular endurance training methods used in hockey. Your sources might include research articles, coaching articles or players' own accounts.

Remember that research information included here has to be summarised rather than repeated word for word. You should also try to link or synthesise similar themes in order to present a particular point of view or argument. Your aim in this section should be to demonstrate that you have researched (from a variety of sources), read and understood all of the information related to your research topic.

5. Discussion/ conclusions

Analyse

This stage of your project involves critically assessing or analysing the merits of the information already presented. In other words, you are explaining just what the information conveys. You might want to include any information of your own here in order to refute or support an argument. For example, you may have amassed case-study data on the training methods of an élite hockey player in your school/college, which might either support or contradict a research article summarised earlier.

If you have included data of your own it needs to be presented in a form that can be easily read and interpreted. This can be done using **descriptive statistics** as a means of summarising trends in the raw data collected. Common descriptive statistics include:

- measures of central tendency (average)
  - the mean
  - the median
  - the mode
- measures of dispersion
  - standard deviation
  - variance.

Graphs or charts could also be included in order to enhance the clarity of any results (Figure 2.46). These might include:

- bar charts
- pie charts
- histograms
- frequency distribution curves.

Whichever graphic device is used it should be clearly labelled and an explanation of the main findings given below it.

When you have completed the discussion section it should read as a logical flow of analytical argument. The writing style should be clear and fluent. According to Thomas (1996):

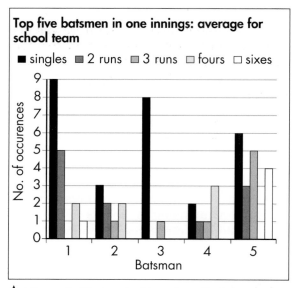

Figure 2.46 *A typical bar chart display*

If after reading the discussion the reader asks, 'so what', then you have failed in your research reporting.

Conclusions

This is a brief synopsis of the outcome of the study. The conclusions should be meaningful and comment on the overall findings and their relevance to the theories or information that you have presented in the review of literature.

6. Organisation and final presentation

The length of the project should be between 1500 and 2000 words (not including tables, charts or graphs). It should be submitted on A4 paper in a form that makes it easy to read.

Appraisal

Prior to submitting your study it would be advisable to seek some informed opinion as to its suitability for purpose. Any feedback gained at this stage may still allow you to make appropriate additions or alterations to your study.

The layout of the project

Introduction and planning

The purpose of this section is to introduce the reader to the topic being studied. It aims to attract the attention of the reader. The area of study should be clearly described together with its relevance to the candidate.

A clear coherent plan should then be included, which sets out the main objectives of the study and how the study is to be conducted.

Review of literature

This section should involve identifying, elaborating and evaluating the information that is directly relevant to the research area.

Discussion/conclusions

The literature reviewed as part of the research for the study should be analysed. If data has been collected to highlight a point or argument it should be presented here in an appropriate form. Conclusions should be drawn from the interpretation of the data and related to the focus of the study (see also page 143).

Appraisal

In this section the researcher analyses any difficulties encountered in the study and suggests how they might be addressed if the study were to be repeated. If any wider implications or issues are raised they should also be addressed here. For example, the project may have unearthed implications for schools/colleges or other sports groups.

This section should conclude by suggesting possible directions for future research. Specifically, suggestions for an investigative study for A2 could be presented here.

Bibliography

All sources of information and references must be listed in this section. References for books should be given alphabetically by author using the Harvard system. For example:

Author (initial first names); *Date* (in brackets); *Title* (in italics if word processed); *Publisher*. E.g. Galligan, F. et al. (2000), *Advanced PE for Edexcel*, Heinemann Educational.

References for articles in journals should include the author and title of the article, the name of the journal, the volume and the relevant page number(s). For example:

McCrone, K.E. (1984), 'Play Up! Play Up! and Play the Game! Sport at the late Victorian Public School', *Journal of British Studies*, Vol. 23, No. 2, pp.106–134.

Appendices

Information that interrupts the flow of the study should be included in the appendices, i.e. raw data, instructions, calculations and questionnaires. Your project diary should also be included in this section.

It is also good practice upon completing your project to double-check both the content and written style. There is a project checklist on page 147 to help you with this process.

Key words and phrases

Option A: Practical application

1. Introduction to Option A

(There are no key words and phrases in this sub-section.)

2. Progress through practice and performance

• Skill repertoire   • Technical components   • Drilling   • Spatial awareness

Option B: Research project

1. Introduction to Option B

• Project diary

2. Identification of the activity

• Research process diagram   • Ethical

3. Locating literature and documentation

(There are no key words and phrases in this sub-section.)

4. Developing a reasoned analysis

• Identified   • Elaborated   • Analysed

5. Discussion/conclusions

• Descriptive statistics

Texts used in the writing of this section

❏ Coolican, H. *Research Methods and Statistics in Psychology*, Hodder & Stoughton, 1995
❏ Dick, F., *Sports Training Principles*, 2nd Edition, A.&C. Black, 1992

❏ Heyes, S., et al., *Starting Statistics in Psychology and Education*, Weidenfield & Nicholson, 1986
❏ Thomas, J. K., 'Physical Activity', in Nelson, J. R., *Research Methods*, 3rd edition, Human Kinetics, 1996

Suggested further reading

❏ Coolican, H., *Research Methods and Statistics in Psychology*, Hodder & Stoughton, 1995
❏ Dick, F., *Sports Training Principles*, 2nd Edition, A.&C. Black, 1992

RESEARCH PROJECT CHECKLIST

NO ✗   **YES ✓**

Presentation

☐   Is the project the right length? (1500–2000 words)   ☐
☐   Has the spelling and grammar been checked?   ☐

Title

☐   Does the title reflect the nature of the study?   ☐
☐   Is it succinct? Not too short – not too long?   ☐

Introduction and planning

☐   Has the general purpose of the study been introduced?   ☐
☐   Are the reasons for studying this topic given?   ☐
☐   Is the purpose of the study clearly stated?   ☐
☐   Is a plan provided, highlighting the stages to be carried out?   ☐

Review of literature

☐   Are all the sources acknowledged?   ☐
☐   Is there evidence of research from a variety of sources?   ☐
☐   Are all the sources relevant to the study?   ☐
☐   Does the review of the literature show a clear progression   ☐
    from the plan?

Discussion/conclusions

☐   If your own data is utilised, is it displayed in a suitable form?   ☐
☐   Have the findings been discussed with reference to the   ☐
    review of literature?
☐   Are the conclusions presented clearly and in detail?   ☐
☐   Is the writing style clear and fluent?   ☐

Appraisal

☐   Are any of the limitations of the study referred to?   ☐
☐   Have the wider implications of the study been discussed?   ☐
☐   Have suggestions been made concerning future research?   ☐

Bibliography

☐   Are all the sources acknowledged?   ☐
☐   Are the sources listed in a clear and consistent way?   ☐

Appendices

☐   If used, is a table of raw data included?   ☐
☐   Has the research project diary been included?   ☐

Section C: Performance: Analysis and provision

In Unit 2 Section C you will be required to undertake two further activity-specific studies which will enhance your knowledge and understanding of practical performance:

- an analysis of performance
- an account of the local and national provision of an activity.

Introduction: Analysis of performance

The first of the two requirements in Section 2C is for you to carry out an analysis of performance of one of the two practical activities you selected for Section B: Option A. If you have chosen Option B, then you will analyse an activity selected from the practical activities list in the Edexcel specification document.

There is a requirement that the analysis of performance is from an individual, and, if appropriate, a team perspective. You are advised to start the processes involved in this section as early as possible and use every opportunity to gain a wider appreciation, knowledge and understanding of the activity selected. This analysis will require you, through evaluation, to demonstrate specific knowledge and understanding in five sections:

- rules/laws of the activity
- **terminology** and **tactics**
- recognising strengths and weaknesses: giving summative analysis and evaluation
- planning, practices and training
- **the perfect model**.

The performance observed may be that of your own along with the performances of others. You will need to make full use of direct observations, recorded performances, some independent research and the knowledge and understanding gained from Unit 1 and the content of Unit 2 Sections A and B as well. In addition, you are encouraged to attend coaching courses and clinics, undertake leadership awards and experience specialist instruction from national governing body award courses.

> The analysis of performance is a two-dimensional concept. You will not only analyse a performance, but the activity from which the performance emerges.

In this section of the course you will acquire new skills that will be of direct benefit to you in completing this Unit overall. The ability to analyse a performance is in its own right a skill which has to be learned. You will have to be certain of what you are looking for in a performance – the strengths and weaknesses, the perfect model, how tactics shape a performance and what planning, training and practices support and enhance the performer. An activity cannot be performed without the existence of rules or laws and the terminology that defines the activity shape, style and procedure.

Essentially, through observation you will study a performance but this does not fully explain how to analyse a performance. In order to analyse you must have a specific purpose in mind. There is no secret to this and by focusing your analysis on key areas you will be more accurate in your observations. These areas have been identified and described by the NCF (1999) as:

- technical
- tactical
- behavioural
- physical.

By analysing *technique* you will see how body movements are executed and whether these conform to an accepted or prescribed movement pattern. *Tactically* a performer needs to understand where and when to perform skills, movements and deploy strategies. *Behavioural* analysis reveals that it is impossible to observe mental factors. We only see the physical responses from them. A performance is always conditioned by the mental processes that shape our behaviour through such aspects as attitudes, arousal, body language or concentration. These aspects are not directly assessed in this section but they cannot be ignored when analysing the performance within an activity.

Finally, *physical* factors are crucial to any performance and form the platform from which the performer is able to participate in an activity. Fitness, diet, health and injury control are all significant components of the performer's fitness profile.

These four key areas do not fit exactly in with the five sections of analysis as listed in the specification document (see page 148). However, they do offer an explanation and focus that will help provide a framework of how to analyse.

The matrix of criteria, which grades the assessment of your analysis, measures the extent of your knowledge and understanding. It is advisable to obtain a copy of this matrix, which is found in the full specification document (Appendix B, Section B). More details of the assessment procedure are given on pages 151–54.

Note that in order to gain maximum marks for the section of rules/laws of an activity, a candidate has to be 'qualified to officiate in a competitive event or able to apply all the rules and laws in a match situation'. This clear statement signifies the depth of the knowledge and understanding you require and the experiences that you will need to gain. By exploring, at this point, the detail that you will require for this part of the course you will be more able to undertake your analysis.

WRITTEN PROJECT

You may wish to undertake a written project for your Analysis of Performance. This can be kept in your Individual Performance Portfolio (IPP). However, this is no substitute for understanding the required content and being able to demonstrate the depth of your knowledge through oral examination.

Rules/laws of activity

It is neither appropriate nor realistic for you to learn all the rules and laws of your activity. In reality very few players, coaches, officials or spectators are knowledgeable enough to claim that they do.

It is also unrealistic for you to know the finer points of all the rules and laws of your activity and all their possible applications. The number of offences that could be committed at a line out in a rugby match, if multiplied by the thirty players on the field of play, is a case in point! Also part of the sphere of rules/laws is your possession of some knowledge of refereeing, official signals and an understanding of recording procedures.

What is appropriate is that you have the ability to take part in an activity and not be hindered by lack of knowledge or ignorance of its rules/laws. This also includes the unwritten rules and methods of procedure that go hand in hand with the more formal written rules and laws.

Marking

However, the assessment criteria are clear in their statements. In order to gain maximum marks for this first section of your analysis (a mark out of 6), you will need to 'be qualified to officiate in a competitive event or able to apply all rules and laws in a match situation'.

This implies that you not only have a knowledge of officiating but also the confidence and management skills to be responsible for a performer or group of performers. An appropriate standard of competition would not exceed that appropriate to your own age group and would possibly be below it. However, if you are officiating above your age group, even outside your own centre, this reinforces the opportunity to receive maximum marks.

A mark of 2 out of 6 is awarded to a candidate for a 'basic appreciation of rules and laws'. Such a candidate will clearly have a limited knowledge of appropriate rules and laws.

It is a clear intention of this unit to credit candidates for their achievements in obtaining external awards. If you qualify as an

▲ **Figure 2.47** *If you qualify as an official in an activity you will be able to gain the maximum 6 marks*

official in an activity, that is as a referee or adjudicator or similar, you will have prior accreditation and therefore you will be able to gain the maximum 6 marks (Figure 2.47).

TASK

Offer to officiate an event or match for your centre at a junior level. Build up your knowledge and experiences by doing this more than once. It is always different seeing the action from the other side of the fence!

Resources

You will be able to supplement the depth of your knowledge by observing live performances, using video, studying law books or manuals and gaining as much experience as possible from officiating at events or matches.

Terminology and tactics

For this section of your analysis you will need to develop a clear appreciation of the specific terminology for your chosen activity and how the selection of tactics are fundamental to the enhancement of a performance. The range of terminology used by any activity varies enormously, from obvious and simple, to obscure and difficult, and through your own playing experiences you will have a reasonable degree of knowledge of appropriate tactics and terminologies.

Terminologies

The terminologies associated with an activity might include words and phrases that form a 'language' which is almost unique to it. In the Task below some examples are given from each of the activity categories. They help explain the tactics employed and, of course, define aspects of both team and individual performance, team plays, sequences and manoeuvres. In addition, they also describe technical detail and movements as a whole.

TASK

a In team games say which activity has the following specific terminology:

'second phase', 'off the top', 'back row', 'tight head', 'in the loose', 'at the restarts', 'ruck', 'maul', 'no. 8 move' and 'double scissors'.

b In a racket game, what activity involves the following terminology:

'top spin', 'slice', American serve', 'cross court' and 'drop shot'?

c In an individual activity the terminology used can be more specific. Which activity do the following come from: 'crash dive', 'corkscrew', 'rudi' and 'randi'?

For some activities there is far more terminology to get to grips with than for others. You will have to begin to build up a 'vocabulary' for your activity from the outset of the Unit.

Tactics

Tactical ploys in sporting activities can only be used to advantage if the level of competence of the performer permits. The use of tactics and **strategies** in team games is perhaps more obvious than would appear to be the case in many individual activities. However, racket games, which may appear one-dimensional, do contain numerous instances where introducing a change in tactics and/or strategies can affect the outcome of a match.

It is a requirement of this section that you have developed a wider appreciation of the types of tactics and strategies of your activity.

In many cases you will have the opportunity to contribute to their development and implementation in a live performance or match situation.

> **tactics**: a plan or scheme used to organise a group, or used by an individual, in order to achieve an objective and/or overcome an opponent
>
> **strategy**: a similar word to tactics – both tactics and strategies can be seen as specific actions of individuals or groups employed during a performance, or as part of longer-term plans or schemes.

Marking

The assessment of this aspect will involve the application of criteria that define the extent of your knowledge and understanding.

To obtain a maximum mark of 6 a student needs to be able 'to coach to a high standard their part in an activity', the intention being that you will have the ability to help others incorporate tactics and strategies in their own performances and to 'self-coach', influencing the appropriate practice or competitive situation (Figure 2.48). A mark of 2 only requires you to have 'a sound knowledge of basic tactics and use simple terminology'.

The following task is designed to make you think about and decide how you would respond to changing situations by altering your tactics and strategies.

TASK

a In a gymnastics competition with one vault left, you need to perform a near perfect vault at a higher tariff in order to win. Do you continue with the planned vault that you have practised or decide to perform a slightly harder one that if completed successfully would give you victory?

b As a canoeist, how do you cope with a white water run which, due to the weather, is now becoming more difficult?

c As a judo player, what throws, holds and tactics can you use to overcome an opponent who has never beaten you but is now ranked much higher in a tournament?

If you have no experience in any of the above activities, ask other members of your group to set similar tasks for other activities that you know about.

Resources

For this part of the analysis full use should be made of national governing body publications and videos. Use match and player analysis, programmes and coaching manuals, as well as drawing upon your own playing experience. Coaching awards and an appreciation of playing systems and tactical scenarios add depth to your knowledge and understanding.

Observation and evaluation of performance

This section of the analysis requires you to be able to appreciate a whole performance, from which you can isolate the individual components that contribute to it. This will involve an understanding of playing systems, styles and tactics employed and the levels of skill and technique involved. For example, a game of basketball may be assessed simply on the basis of offence and defence. To that may be added the ratio of successful scoring shots to attempts, rebounds, steals etc. In addition, some activities will require an understanding of aesthetics and choreography.

▲ *Figure 2.48* *The game plan is not working!*

Some individual activities may have quite specific components not found in other sports but a performance can still be analysed as a whole and then broken down into the required divisions. A gymnastic routine may focus more on the technical merit of the performance, the interpretation of music in a sequence and the degree of difficulty involved in the vaults and agilities. In some activities, the aesthetic element will be far more prominent than in others.

The need to provide summative statements based on the performance observed requires you to focus upon the strengths and weaknesses within the performance and the performer themselves. This is not to be seen as a complete in-depth analysis of every player in a team game but rather an ability to identify the positive and negative aspects contributing to a performance. You can begin this process by keeping a record of your own performances in your selected activities and try to evaluate the reasons behind the performance.

An analysis of a game of soccer at half time, for example, could include reference to the following areas as a focus to the state of the game at that particular time, and how your team is performing:

a How many goal attempts has each side had?

b Which players are the opposition's best? How can we reduce their influence?

c Which sections of our team – and theirs – are performing well: attack, midfield or defence?

d Is the opposition stronger on the right or left flanks or through the middle?

e Have our goal attempts come from distance or close to the goal?

f How many unforced errors have we made?

g Is our speed of passing effective?

h From where are we forced to defend?

i Which team has put the ball out of play most often?

j Set plays – which team is doing better?

You will extend this aspect further in Unit 5 when considering the factors that affect a performance; and in Unit 6 Section B, 'The psychology of sport.'

Marking

The assessment criteria require you to be confident in your ability to analyse and a maximum mark of 6 requires you to 'be able to give an in-depth match performance analysis using various methods i.e. videos, structured reports, analysing individual performances … supported by evaluation programmes'. A mark of 2 would be given for a basic knowledge of strengths and weaknesses relying on a 'commentary' rather than an explanatory analysis.

In order to fully develop in this section and score well it will be necessary to bring together all the knowledge and understanding you have gained from other aspects of the course.

TASK

In pairs, construct match or activity sheets for an actual activity. Discuss its design with your partner and your teacher and feed back to the group. Use video to support your analysis.

Planning, practices and training

This section requires you to demonstrate the application of knowledge gained from your own playing experiences and that acquired from Unit 3. Any performance is built upon the combination of ability and preparation (Figure 2.49). In order to prepare for a performance you will need to plan how to enhance skill and, if applicable, group cohesion, and your physical ability to compete.

Correct training practices will combine physical developments and improvements to the techniques that underpin skill. The application of the 'Principles of training' studied in Unit 3 and a knowledge of the specific training methods best suited to your activity should provide the basis for answers on this aspect of study. The knowledge and understanding learned from this will provide you with a firm foundation for the completion of a Personal Exercise Programme (PEP) in Unit 5.

▲ **Figure 2.49** *Any performance is built upon the combination of ability and preparation*

Marking

The assessment requires you to apply your knowledge to observed performances and reflect upon your own experiences. A maximum mark of 6 demands that you are 'able to plan and implement a programme for élite performers. Evidence of such an undertaking will be required'.

The use of the word 'élite' can be off-putting. It means those who, by virtue of ability and application to a particular activity, have been chosen to represent an institution, area, county or region. This will have required them to be involved in planned practice and training programmes. You may not personally have undertaken these programmes but will have knowledge of them obtained through observation and research.

A lower mark of 2 requires an ability to plan simple activities in order to improve an individual skill. The level of knowledge and understanding needed to gain this mark is very basic and limited in respect of depth and detail.

Resources

The use of the knowledge and understanding gained from Unit 3 and that of your own personal involvement in sport can be your biggest resource. In addition, you may wish to observe the practice and training sessions of an individual or team who play at a high level. You will be surprised how much they work on quite basic skills and techniques, although at high speed. There are some very good videos of top players and teams training and your centre may have some of these. The media also cover this topic in detail through activity-specific journals, magazines and specialist sports documentaries.

The perfect model

Knowledge of the perfect model is an invaluable tool to the performer (Figure 2.50). The perfect model is the technical mastery obtained in the performance of a skill as defined by a **recognised coaching scheme**, awards programme, governing body publication or a coaching manual. You will have already read about a 'recommended technical model' and this essentially refers to the same thing. If you have a detailed understanding of the perfect model you will be able to enhance not only your own performance but that of others as well.

Marking

In order to gain a maximum mark of 6 for this section you will be required to 'have a detailed knowledge of the parts of the perfect model ... and have an up-to-date understanding of élite performance'.

The terminology here can again be slightly daunting. Concentrate your studies on the core skills involved in your performance and the techniques that underpin them. A mark of 2 simply requires you to 'describe the basic elements of the perfect model'. As you begin

▲ **Figure 2.50** *Knowledge of the perfect model is an invaluable tool to the performer*

to specialise in your activity and performances and draw together all the knowledge and understanding of Unit 2, the perfect model evolves rather than suddenly appears!

Resources

Video analysis, governing body publications, coaching manuals, media analysis and observation of élite performers will enable you to build a technical understanding of how to perform a skill perfectly.

Assessment procedure: Analysis of performance

The assessment procedure for the Analysis of performance element requires candidates to be examined orally on their knowledge and understanding related to the analysis of performance of an activity.

Each candidate will be given a centre-assessed mark out of 15, made up of the 6 marks available for each of the 5 individual sections. This gives a mark out of 30 which is then divided by 2.

An external examiner will moderate the mark awarded by your centre and the oral examination will focus on **direct questioning**. Evidence contained in your IPP can also help form a judgement about the level of knowledge and understanding you have related to the five sections of the analysis.

The questioning of candidates will reflect the marks awarded by a centre. Those candidates gaining marks towards the top end of the scale – marks 12–15 – will therefore receive a level of questioning pitched at a higher level than those marked at a lower level.

Candidates will therefore be required to show an understanding of the following components:

- individual skills, team situations, tactics, routines and sequences
- strengths and weaknesses in any performance related to skills, techniques and tactics
- correct use of activity-specific terminology
- knowledge of how to improve performances through practice
- knowledge of how fitness and training procedures can improve performances
- rules and regulations.

Exemplar questions

Using the individual activity of swimming as an example, the following questions could be asked of a candidate being marked at 12–15:

1 What safety rules should be borne in mind by swimmers at all times?
2 Give the laws associated with the start and turn of your strongest stroke.
3 Break down any stroke and explain technically how it is performed.
4 Outline a specific drill or practice that might improve part or the whole of a particular stroke.
5 Explain the technique(s) of breathing in your prime stroke.
6 Explain the difference in take off/start between the front crawl, breast stroke and butterfly.
7 What are the physical benefits of a planned, programmed and systematic training programme performed over a long period of time?
8 Outline a typical training session for your event.
9 Give reasons why everyone should learn to swim.
10 What corrective methods might be used to correct a lazy leg action in the back crawl?

KEY SKILLS

The 'Analysis of performance' is an ideal opportunity for you to develop in the Key Skill of Communication and the use of Information Communications Technology.

The questions below refer to the team activity of cricket. The questions are of a level appropriate for a candidate marked between 10–15. A more capable candidate, scoring towards the top end of the mark range, would be able to answer in more detail and with a greater depth of knowledge and understanding.

1 What is meant by a no ball/wide/short run with the appropriate umpire signals?
2 What is the difference between a leg-bye and a bye?
3 How would you coach a young cricketer who is unable to find either line or length in his bowling?

4 What does having a balanced bowling attack in your side mean?

5 What tactics might a seam/spin bowler use in a game when the batting side is chasing a small target?

6 Comment on the essential requirements of a good batter, fielder or wicket keeper.

7 Give any fitness components necessary for cricket and describe the practices used to enhance either a batter, bowler or fielder.

8 A typical warm-up session would include what elements for a cricketer?

9 Select any attacking/defensive stroke and explain how you would execute the skill if seeking the perfect model.

10 Explain how you would utilise field placing to restrict scoring from an off-spin bowler.

Using the examples given, you should familiarise yourself with the level of questioning and then build your own bank of potential examination questions and answers related to your specific activity. In this way you will further extend your knowledge and understanding.

2. Local and national provision

This second part of Unit 2 Section C requires you to undertake a small research project of between 600 and 800 words on the development of sporting excellence based on the local and national provision of an activity. The activity should be chosen from one of the two activities offered for practical assessment for Option A of Section 2B. If you are undertaking Option B, the research project, the choice of activity may be made from any of the practical activities contained in the practical activities list in the Edexcel specification. There is no restriction on a candidate selecting the same activity that they chose for assessment in the 'Analysis of performance'.

You will be able to build on your existing knowledge of the provision for your activity at grass-roots level – that is, the first level of participation, usually locally, where the performer is playing for fun and recreation – and how a performer progresses to representative level and the provision for élite performers. The assignment draws together the knowl-

▲ *Figure 2.51* *Local provision: your knowledge may be usefully broadened by visiting a local club or facility.*

edge and understanding gained from Unit 1 Section A. You will be able to apply your understanding of mass participation in sport (Figure 2.51) and the élite performer coupled with the development of excellence.

Sporting agencies and bodies

You will be required to describe the **agencies and bodies** involved in these processes and the funding of any projects. The processes involved in talent development invariably follow defined pathways based on established structures and processes.

Central to these processes is the role of the national governing bodies. It is now commonplace for these organisations to have their own development plans, incentive schemes and resource provision for all abilities.

Any study of such provision will touch on issues related to gender, age and ability. You will be required to make some reference to these and to the provision for disabled performers.

Development programmes and sports aid initiatives

In today's modern sporting arena, a whole variety of programmes and initiatives to encourage sports participation and to develop excellence have been introduced. The desire to balance mass participation with élite sport provision is not a new one and your assignment may reflect how this dilemma has been resolved for your chosen activity.

In 1992, for example, the Sportsmatch Scheme was launched. This business sponsorship incentive scheme matches pound for pound the amount of investment sponsors are prepared to put into grass-roots sport. It is funded by the Government through Sport England and administered in England by the Institute of Sports Sponsorship. Rugby union is one sport that has made good use of this and has schemes to promote their game at grass-roots level sponsored by Lloyds TSB and the Ford Tag Rugby initiative.

In comparison to England, all public companies in France are expected to invest a small percentage of their profits in the National Sports Development Fund which takes care of most of the country's sports needs below international level.

In the UK, the Top Play and BT TOP Sport schemes have been developed to support teachers, leaders, coaches and adults in introducing young people to sport. This is aided by the Youth Sports Trust. Most sports have benefited from these initiatives (see page 41 for more on this and other initiatives of this type).

Sport England is now even more active in the help and guidance it offers in all spheres of sport. The vast majority of performers need the support of volunteer helpers in small clubs based in the local community. In 1999 an **Awards for All** programme was launched to aid voluntary sector organisations specifically at grass-roots level.

Active Schools and Active Sports are programmes aimed at providing every young person not only with the opportunity to learn foundation skills, but also to provide a nationwide programme to help young people to improve their sporting skills and to gain access to organised sports opportunities. The Football Foundation has been launched for the express purpose of funding the sport at grass-roots level. Such initiatives may have affected your chosen activity and reference to them may be included in your assignment.

Sporting excellence

Sporting excellence and élite development has similarly been subject to many new initiatives and strategies to provide sporting success on a world stage. These range from the developments which are in place for the 2002 Commonwealth Games and the exciting Sportcity in Manchester, to the UK Sports Institute and the ten regional Network Centres with sporting provision for world class athletes.

National governing bodies, the Government and Sport England have been involved in the World Class Performance programme for all athletes including those with disabilities. Élite athletes will benefit annually from over £25 million of capital and revenue funding. Further research into these areas of provision

▲ *Figure 2.52* Local facilities are not only provided for the development of sporting excellence

▲ *Figure 2.53* Investigating provision should include all social groups will enable you to fully complete the provision assignment. From 1999 Sport England aim to invest £200 million annually in England's sporting future. A total of £150 million will be invested in the Community Projects Fund and £50 million in the World Class Fund. You will need to carry out some independent research in this area to find out how this investment has affected your particular activity.

Remember that any investigation of provision should include *all* social groups. There are a number of specialist sports organisations, for example, which cater for disabled athletes. You may wish to contact them to discover the level of their involvement in your chosen activity. These include:

- The British Sports Association for the Disabled
- The British Paralympic Association
- The British Amputee Sports Association
- The UK Sports Association for People with Mental Handicap.

You will be able to draw further on your knowledge and understanding gained from Unit 1 of the course when studying the 'Social influences on performance and participation'. It is important to remember that sport does not exist in a vacuum. Provision occurs just as much because of activity *outside* the sporting arena as it does due to activity inside it.

Figure 2.54 represents an overview of élite development in association football. It traces the ladder of progression, from grass-roots to Under 18 to élite performer, which is open to a performer as excellence develops. You should be able to construct a similar model for your chosen activity.

Resources

In order to complete this part of Section C you will need to draw information from a variety of different sources. The assignment can be broken down into two parts, namely local provision and national provision. However, the two do not exist independently. As indicated in Figure 2.54, the progression that a performer can make from the initial grass roots level as a novice performer through the levels of excellence to élite performer is dependent on both local and national provision.

Local provision
- LEAs
- schools
- local networks
- county councils
- regional associations.

National provision
- NGBs and coaching schemes
- National Network Centres
- UKSI
- BOA.

The range of resources available will vary from activity to activity. The following resource avenues may be useful:

- the appropriate national governing body coaching development scheme
- the local district or borough council leisure department
- area, county or regional associations for your activity
- Sport England for Sports Mark and Sports College provision etc.
- school sports structure at district, county and regional levels
- academy developments in sports such as rugby union, association football, cricket etc.
- the United Kingdom Sports Institute and its regional centres of excellence and élite athlete programmes
- sponsorship schemes used to promote excellence through development programmes and élite performer aid

▲ *Figure 2.54* An overview of élite development in association football

- local and national agencies responsible for the provision and development of sport for the disabled.

The scope of this project is such that in some respects you will only be outlining the provision and development pathways. However, it is important that you include specific examples to highlight a particular element while aiming to maintain a wider appreciation of provision.

Assessment procedure: Local and national provision

When completed, your assignment will initially be marked by your own centre against an established set of criteria. The assignment will be contained in your IPP and offered for moderation by an external examiner. The assignment carries a total possible mark of 45, which will then divided by 3 to give a mark out of 15. This carries the same weighting as your 'Analysis of performance'.

The mark scheme on which the assessment of your assignment on 'Local and national provision' will be based has four criteria:

1 Introduction and planning of the areas to be investigated – 5 marks.
2 Review of related topics and literature – 15 marks.
3 Discussions and conclusions – 15 marks.
4 Appraisal of the study and implications for improvement in performance – 10 marks.

Full details of the criteria and marking bands are contained in the specification document which should be made available to you.

Key words and phrases

1. Analysis of performance
- **Terminology**   • **Tactics**   • **The perfect model**   • **Strategies**
- **Recognised coaching scheme**   • **Direct questioning**

2. Local and national provision
- **Agencies and bodies**   • **Awards for All**

REVIEW QUESTIONS

1 In reality does 'practice make permanent'?

2 Explain the difference between skill, technique and ability.

3 Review the conditions that make practice most effective.

4 Discuss the importance that a developed 'fitness for purpose' plays in enhancing a performance.

5 Select a motor skill that you are familiar with and list its subroutines.

6 'Correct practice enhances a performance.' What changes in a performance would you expect to see following a period of structured practice?

7 What do you understand by the term 'components of fitness'?

8 Any performer who is successful in competition would be able to apply and cope with 'pressure'. What do you understand by the word 'pressure'?

9 How would you analyse an activity of your choice?

10 Does the perfect model exist?

11 What is meant by the term 'tactics and strategies'?

12 Make a list and explain any sports initiatives you are aware of that have aided the development of sport at grass-roots level.

Texts used in the writing of this section

- Davis, Kimmet & Auty, *P.E. Theory and Practice*, MacMillan, 1986
- Dick, F. W., *Sports Training Principles*, 2nd Edn., A & C Black, 1992
- Edexcel, *AS/A2 Physical Education Specification*, 2000
- Lyons, K., *Using Video in Sport*, Springfield, 1988
- National Coaching Foundation, *Observation, Analysis and Video*, NCF, 1999
- Pereni, A. & Di Cesare, M., *Zone Play*, Reedswain, 1977
- Reilly, T. et al, *Science and Football*, E. & F. Spon, 1988
- Wirhed, R., *Training To Win Football*, Wolfe, 1992
- Wuest & Bucher, *Foundations of Physical Education and Sport*, Mosby, 1991

Suggested further reading

- Davis, Kimmet & Auty *P.E. Theory and Practice*, MacMillan, 1986
- Dick, F. W., *Sports Training Principles*, 2nd Edn., A & C Black, 1992
- National Coaching Foundation, *Observation, Analysis and Video*, NCF, 1999

Unit 3
Exercise and training

Unit 3: Exercise and training

1. Introduction to Unit 3

This Unit will advance the understanding of anatomy and physiology you gained at Key Stage 4 through a mix of theoretical and practical work. The Unit is designed so that its various components are integrated and not treated as entirely separate areas.

The opportunity to be involved in practical testing should be offered as part of the Unit and will help you to relate theories to practical applications.

The Unit is concerned with applied physiology and the adaptations of the body to various levels and periods of exercise. Various types of training will be examined in the light of a range of intended purposes, from basic healthy living to preparation for élite competition.

Practical work should be carefully recorded and kept in your Individual Performance Portfolio (see page 100) as a basis for your Personal Exercise Plan. The latter is part of Unit 5: Section B for those who go on to complete the full Advanced level course.

Assessment of this Unit will be by means of a one and a quarter hour written paper. You will be required to produce two answers from a choice of questions.

The body and exercise

The integration and self-regulation of the body's systems ensures that under normal circumstances a safe range of equilibrium is maintained so that there is no damage to the body in the short or long term. This is known as **homeostasis** ('unchanging') and refers to the body's ability to maintain stable internal conditions during heavy or prolonged activity. It is sometimes referred to as a *dynamic state of equilibrium*.

The disturbance of homeostasis through exercise/training is a form of **exercise stimulus or stress**. At the end of exercise we remove this stimulus/stress and trigger the **recovery** process. By undertaking regular exercise we allow the body to adapt and become better able to cope with exercise stimulus.

It is important that the active sportsperson understands this fundamental aspect of homeostasis in the special context of high level exercise and training.

2. Immediate effects of exercise – a practical introduction

The human body responds to exercise before any discernible movement has taken place. In response to the need to provide the working muscles with adequate supplies of oxygen and nutrients to fuel movement, the body enters the evolutionary state of readiness – the state of **'fight or flight'**.

The body prepares for an increase in physical activity by making physiological adjustments that enable an immediate motor response to sensory stimuli.

Warm up

The sporting body will not perform effectively if it is not operating at the optimum temperature for its systems to function at their best. As resting body temperature (normally 36.1°C – 37.8°C) rises, an approximate 10 per cent increase to the rate of chemical reactions occurs (catalysis). Warm up should therefore be gradual and initially of a low intensity, leading into the more intense level of the proposed activity. In extreme conditions, if core body temperature rises beyond 41°C (106°F), a suppression of nervous system function may occur, causing convulsions. A body temperature of 43°C (109°F) is normally fatal.

Body temperature is controlled by an area in the brain called the hypothalamus within a very narrow range as indicated below:

- at rest > 36.9°C (98.6°F)
- moderate exercise > 37.7°C (>100°F)
- severe exercise > 41.1°C (>106°F).

▲ **Figure 3.1** *Exploding out of the blocks!*

▲ **Figure 3.2** *Positive early habits ensures good practice later in life*

At the end of a correct warm up, the appropriate body temperature should have been reached and you should be in a state of physical and mental readiness for the activity to follow (Figure 3.1).

Any study of the warm up and the immediate effects of exercise begins with a clear understanding of the principles of performance preparation. This requires an appreciation of how we may best prepare our body for the stress we place on it during exercise. This is essential so that we optimise our physical performance, whether in training or competition.

To prepare the body's systems to meet the demands of exercise or training you must make sure that the warm up contains specific activity appropriate to what is to follow in competition. This is an essential feature of any preparation and should never be overlooked by the coach, trainer or sportsperson.

Encouraging good habits from an early age is key to ensuring the development of good practice into later life (Figure 3.2) when, as research shows, the ageing process makes us more prone to physical difficulties. (See planning of fitness and training programmes on page 204).

A properly structured warm up should consist of three component activities:

- gross motor activity – this should involve all the major muscle groups and acts as both pulse and respiratory rate raiser (Figure 3.3.). There should also be some gentle mobilisation of the joints in order to loosen and lubricate them by the secretion of synovial fluid at the joint (McCutchen's weeping lubrication theory)
- flexibility activities – to warm, loosen and relax muscles by increasing blood flow; also general preparatory stretching
- activity specific or sport-specific stretches – these should link to the demands of the activity.

▲ **Figure 3.3** *Gross motor activity: pulse raising and joint mobilization*

A further aspect of warming up preparation is **skills practice**. This is particularly relevant in games activities, which should only be undertaken after a proper warm up. How often has an individual strained a muscle by beginning with this type of activity? Excessive or sudden eccentric lengthening of muscle fibres, without following the correct warm up sequence, may lead to muscle tears!

Similarly, plenty of time should be allowed for a warm up before any intense performance activity takes place. Lack of physical preparation time means the body is unable to meet the increased demands placed upon it, perhaps leading to unnecessary and avoidable injury.

The benefits of such preparation can be lost if there is a prolonged delay between the warm up period and the start of activity. A delay of more than five minutes will result in the benefits being significantly reduced. Muscle temperature losses should be minimised and attempts must be made to regain any such losses. Similarly, during a break in play, such as half time in a team game, temperature losses may inhibit performance at the restart. Studies have shown that running distances at the start of the second half in football are considerably shorter than those of the time period at the start of the game (Bangsbo, 1994).

Gross motor activity

Gross motor activity, designed to mobilise the joints and warm the muscles, should begin at a low intensity. A slow walking to jogging pace will initially stimulate the heart and respiratory rate rises that will gradually increase as intensity of activity increases. Avoiding exercises that are predominantly performed on one spot is essential here to avoid placing high impact or strain on musculo-skeletal structures such as joints and ligaments.

Stretching

Stretching describes the process of increasing the length and flexibility of the soft tissues, especially muscles and tendons. It also includes ligaments, nerves and skin. Different approaches to stretching can be adopted to suit individuals and the activity they undertake. However, it should always be based on the following fundamental principles.

Stretching improves the length–tension relationship of a contracting muscle to enable the production of force over a greater muscle length. Over-stretching should be avoided at all costs to prevent tearing the muscle and tendon soft tissues. Stretching also benefits the individual in a number of ways in addition to preparing the body for exercise:

- to prevent or decrease the risk of injury
- to enable full development of opposing muscle groups; muscles need length and strength – a long and strong muscle can exert more force
- natural shrinkage with age is linked with stiffness and lack of mobility
- to improve relaxation/relieve tension/decrease stress
- to enable postural improvement
- to allow blood flow through relaxed muscle fibres, thus improving circulation.

Static stretching involves gradual stretching of a muscle to a position where it is then held steadily for between 10 and 30 seconds. There must be proper alignment of body structures and no twisting of joints. This must be done without bouncing and there should be a feeling of being 'comfortably uncomfortable' with no sense of pain. There should be no sudden movements. This type of stretch does not provoke the stretch reflex so commonly activated by **ballistic stretching** (see page 177), which would be dangerous in this situation.

Active stretches are static stretches performed only by the individual with no partner assistance. The London Central YMCA's acronym of **SEAM,** for remembering two mechanical principles of alignment, applies equally to stretching:

S Stability
E Effectiveness
A Alignment
M Momentum

Passive stretches use an external force to allow movement. The individual is assisted by a partner to exert the movement or by using a pull on their own body part thus using gravity or momentum to gain stretch. Partner stretches require care and understanding of what is required by both individuals. In this form of static stretching, there is a danger that the individual may over-stretch and cause muscle fibre damage. Control and care must be taken to ensure that the exercise is both safe and effective.

We are frequently told not to bounce whilst stretching, and this is true to a point. Bouncing or swinging without sufficient control of movement or warmth in our soft tissues can easily damage these structures. When an insufficiently warmed muscle and associated tissues contract and shorten as a result of over-stretching or sudden **dynamic** or ballistic movement, fibre damage can result. This is known as the **stretch reflex** and is obviously undesirable. However, the bouncing and swinging movements of ballistic stretching can be useful, provided they are built up progressively and executed properly. Activities such as the long jump and triple jump that demand explosive and dynamic movement will require ballistic stretching as part of the latter stages of the warm up programme.

Safe and effective stretching must follow some basic rules:

- before stretching, muscles must be warm
- joints must be mobilised
- always use controlled, slow, smooth, rhythmic movements and do not attempt a bouncing action
- joints of back and legs must not be locked straight
- stretch major joints before minor ones
- slowly bring the muscle to a fully stretched position, drawing the two ends of the muscle away from each other. Hold the position for an initial count of 10–20 seconds and then relax
- carefully stretch the muscle some more and hold for a further 10–20 seconds
- preparatory stretches should be accompanied by some linking pulse–raising activities to avoid body temperature dropping too much during this time

- stretch the entire body in a sensible sequence, avoiding too much time on the same area
- breathe normally in a relaxed and regular way – do not hold your breath
- be aware of the importance of gradual build-up in the warm up so that body temperature is raised without your becoming out of breath.

Proprioceptive neuromuscular facilitation (PNF)

PNF involves the use of muscle contraction before the stretch in an attempt to achieve maximum relaxation. It is often described as the 'contract – relax and hold – relax' technique. After a muscle is asked to work hard (i.e. in muscular contraction), it tends to relax immediately due to a reflex triggered by nerve sensors in the muscle.

These nerve centres are called **Golgi tendon organs (Gtos)**. Combined with **muscle spindles**, found between muscle fibres or cells, they inform our brain via the central nervous system of the body's position and/or that of a limb or joint and can give a degree of spatial awareness. In the case of a stretching muscle, Gtos are sensitive to:

- resting muscle length
- changes in muscle length
- speed at which muscle fibre lengthens.

Awareness of this **myotatic** response (*myo* = muscle; *tasis* = stretch) enables us to stretch more effectively. This response describes the different structures within muscles that enable them to change shape and length.

Stretch reflex

If muscles are stretched too fast, the stretch reflex comes into operation. As the muscle is stretched, distortion of the muscle spindle initiates the stretch reflex, contracting the muscle and preventing muscle damage. However, the amount of contraction possible in this stretch reflex is proportional to the rate and amount of stretching. The faster and greater the stretch means the subsequent reflex contraction is more forceful and therefore more damaging to a cold or untrained muscle. Muscle tears are possible.

Inverse stretch reflex

The **inverse stretch reflex** allows the muscle to relax in the stretch and go beyond its normal range. It is initiated via sensory nerves in Golgi tendon organs found in the muscle tendons. The Gtos respond more to increased tension from forceful contraction and extreme stretch than muscle length. When a muscle is fully stretched for the minimum recommended stretch time of 6 seconds, maximum benefit is achieved. The Gtos initiate action of the antagonist (non-stretched muscle) to relax, thus allowing the stretched muscle to do so with less resistance from its antagonistic opposite. Due to their progressive controlled nature, static stretches are a beneficial way of initiating the inverse stretch reflex.

Reciprocal innervation

Reciprocal innervation describes the ability of opposing (antagonistic) muscles to reflexively relax. In general movement terms, reciprocal innervation allows the rhythmical self-co-ordinated movement of opposing sets of muscles. In terms of stretching, this reflex inhibition allows us to contract one muscle while its antagonist automatically relaxes. For example, by laying in a supine position and contracting the quadriceps muscle group, the hamstring muscle group will relax.

Motion and mobility

All forms of stretching are designed to extend an individual's **range of motion (ROM)**. **Mobility** is described as the capacity to perform a range of joint actions through a wide range of motion. Movement at joints is considered in more detail on page 178. In aerobics or exercise classes, ROM warm up is an accepted way of beginning the warm up since it is a safer way of preparing the muscles for the actions of such workouts.

Preventing injury

In addition to the basic warm up guidelines within which an individual should operate, safe and effective exercise also requires protection against both chronic and acute injuries. These can occur with progressively increasing training loads. Coaches or trainers must ensure that individuals are screened for any physical anomalies. These include history of heart disease or high heart-disease risk (smoking, overweight, blood pressure), diabetes, habitual inactivity in the case of untrained participants. This screening may be done by means of a **Physical Activity Readiness Questionnaire (PARQ)**.

PARQ

You may wish to design your own PARQ and take part in a one-to-one or group discussion about the issues of readiness for activity. You could then be asked to lead different phases of the warm up and explain your session in practical and theoretical terms to the rest of the group. Both tasks are suitable for Key Skills evidence (Communication) and provide evidence of participation and individual experience.

Repeated or continual stress of one body part can lead to chronic injuries. Common lower leg injuries, such as 'shin-splints' (inflammatory reaction of the musculo-tendinous unit of the front of the lower leg caused by over-exertion of the muscles during weight-bearing activities), are due to continuous high-impact movements such as running or jumping. The amount of training that an individual carries out plays a key role in determining the risk of injury. Fatigued muscles do not protect the associated connective tissues as effectively.

Research has shown that running more than 40 miles a week markedly increases the risk of injury. Exercise and training has a way of discovering weak areas of the body with consummate ease! Your chances of injury increase greatly if:

- there has been previous injury
- training takes place over many consecutive days
- there is an weekly increase of over 10 per cent in training volume.

Injury prevention can take the form of:

- alternating between high-impact and low-impact exercises
- avoiding the repetition of exercise to exhaustion which can lead to physiological damage
- reducing the number of 'foot strikes' (Figure 3.4); many track athletes now

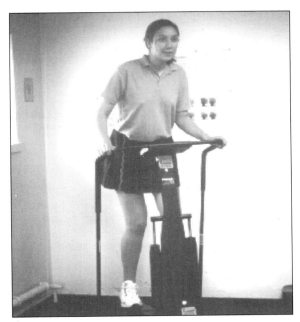

▲ Figure 3.4 The use of a 'stepping machine' reduces high quantity/high-impact foot strikes

use 'aqua-joggers' (running in swimming pools), which creates similar intensity without repetitive high-impact foot strikes
* avoiding the maxim 'no pain, no gain' – exercise may sometimes be uncomfortable but should not be painful.

Contra-indicated exercises

These are exercises that contravene mechanical principles of alignment (SEAM – see page 164) and place unnecessary strain on physiological structures, causing discomfort or pain. Such exercise and training methods should obviously be avoided.

TASK

Organise and video an exercise circuit session demonstrating safe and effective principles of exercises. Hold a group discussion on the physiological reasons for doing so. Use a database to record and update individual progress of group members.

'SMARTER'

The study of exercise and training can be a complex one, yet exercise and training in practice should be economic and simple.

KISS – Keep It Simple *otherwise you'll look* Stupid!

Exercise methods should be straightforward, avoiding complex movement, which allows more room for error and therefore injury. Exercise and training should have specific set goals that follow sound coaching/training principles. Target-setting using the **SMARTER** acronym is:

Specific
Measurable
Achievable
Recorded
Time-planned
Effective
Reviewed

It is the job of the coach or trainer to devise exercise and training programmes that develop progressively over time (see Planning of fitness and training programmes on page 204).

Ensuring the correct exercising surface can minimise the risk of various injuries. The ideal indoor surface should be shock absorbing yet not too soft since this allows instability of the ankle in particular. Sufficient friction should be allowed between foot and surface, but not so much that the foot has difficulty moving.

The suitability of footwear is largely determined by individual need and the type of activity to be undertaken. Generally speaking, footwear must provide stability at the heel and forefoot, with sufficient shock absorption throughout. The sole should grip the floor/ground to avoid slip, but should not 'stick' when the player is turning quickly.

Completing the warm up

The completion of a structured warm up should allow seamless transition into activity; the body is fully prepared for the forthcoming increase in intensity. In simple physiological terms (discussed in more detail on page 169) there is an increase in:

* heart rate
* cardiac output
* ventilation/respiratory rate
* blood supply to the working muscle
* heat generation
* nervous stimulation of the muscles.

Cool down

Just as the body needs to prepare for exercise, it also needs to be given the opportunity to readjust to a normal resting state at the end of it. A gradual reduction in intensity of activity after cessation of exercise allows the body systems to recover as efficiently as possible.

Cool down should consist of active recovery exercises of decreasing intensity and stretches (mainly active). As well as a return to the normal resting state, it also allows the following adjustments to take place progressively and safely:

- a slow decrease of the cardio-vascular and respiratory rates
- a slow decrease of the metabolism.

Post-exercise cool down also:

- aids faster dissipation of waste products, including removal of lactic acid, which inhibits muscle action (Figure 3.5); it lessens the potential for delayed onset muscle soreness (DOMS), which is due to partial microscopic tears in the muscle cell membranes
- can assist in preventing muscle soreness caused by spasms/involuntary contraction with the inclusion of active stretching activities
- reduces the chance of dizziness or fainting by encouraging venous return (blood returning to the heart) thus preventing venous pooling at the extremities
- encourages the lowering of blood levels of adrenaline; such adrenaline levels can place strain on the heart if allowed to remain high.

If cool down activity is not undertaken after moderate or vigorous exercise, depending

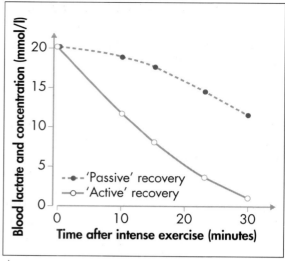

▲ **Figure 3.5** *Blood lactate concentration following intense exercise followed by either 'active' or 'passive' recovery, showing how lactate concentation decreases at a faster rate with 'active' recovery.*

on an individual's fitness level and body position, the following effects can be seen:

- a lowering of blood pressure
- a subsequent decrease in stroke volume.

See the circulatory, vascular and respiratory (CVR) systems in action' on page 190.

Any cool down activity should last for at least five minutes of decreasing intensity before complete cessation occurs. The aim should be to achieve a recovery heart rate of at least 120bpm 3 minutes after cessation of exercise. After 5 minutes the heart rate should be around 100bpm.

The rate at which an individual recovers is dependent on their current level of fitness, the intensity of the main activity and the intensity and duration of the cool down. Accurate measurement of an individual's recovery heart rate such as in the Harvard Step Test is a very good indicator of the existing level of fitness.

Immediate effects of exercise

The **physiological changes** that take place at warm up continue during exercise, allowing the body to adjust and meet the varying demands of physical activity. Physiological changes that are demonstrated before exercise may be described as **anticipatory effects**. These include increases in **heart rate** and in the **depth and rate of ventilation**.

Circulatory, vascular and respiratory (CVR) rate rises occur as a result of the engagement of the nervous system. The body's 'fight or flight' early warning system alerts the body to prepare for exercise. It is the balance between the sympathetic and parasympathetic nervous system activity that dictates any adjustment of the circulatory, vascular and respiratory (CVR) systems needed to meet these changing physiological demands. The sympathetic nervous system speeds up heart rate while the parasympathetic system slows it down. These two systems originate in the cardiac centre in the medulla oblongata of the brain.

Adrenalin affects every tissue and the 'fight or flight' description of the body's response refers to the stimulation of this increased supply of oxygen by adjusting **blood flow patterns** to the working muscles.

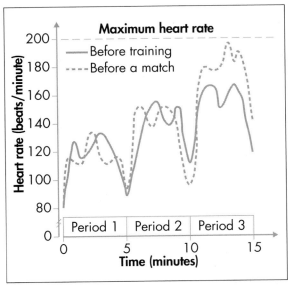

▲ **Figure 3.6** Heart rate of a football player during a warm up before training and before a match

Figure 3.6 shows variation in the heart rates of a footballer measured during a warm up prior to training and again prior to a match.

As can be seen in the graph, when combined with the effects of a structured warm up, cardio-vascular and respiratory values increase in a linear fashion according to the intensity of the activity. Near maximum heart rates are achieved towards the end of the warm up, preparing for the potential maximal values that may be reached during competition.

During preparation for training, the heart rate values well below maximum. The coach/trainer can control the individual's training exercise intensity and only needs to reach maximal values at the end of the warm up for training if such values are to be reached during the session. After warm up, as exercise continues beyond the initial stages, the intensity of the activity dictates the response of the body to the demands being placed upon it.

Aerobic (steady state) exercise

This occurs when the body is able to meet the physiological requirements to maintain activity continuously:

- the heart rate increases to a level plateau, beating faster and stronger, and pumping more blood per beat than at rest (stroke volume increases). Cardiac output is correspondingly increased to the level necessary to meet the demands of the muscles
- certain blood vessels constrict to allow blood flow to be re-directed away from non-essential areas such as the gut and non-exercising muscles
- blood vessels in the active muscles dilate to increase blood flow
- blood vessels near to the skin surface dilate so that blood cooling from the evaporation of sweat is enhanced
- ventilation rate and activity rises. This is evidenced by the active use of a greater range of respiratory muscles.

As exercise intensity increases to near maximal aerobic demand (VO_2 max), there is a range of physiological responses as the heart and lungs struggle to provide oxygen-rich blood quickly enough for the working muscles:

- maximal heart rates are reached even though intensity may still increase
- stroke volume may actually decrease at maximum heart rate since the rate is so fast the heart chambers do not have sufficient time to fill and empty with each beat – thus the heart's efficiency drops
- the lungs reach a maximal rate and depth as they work faster and harder to sustain gaseous exchange
- more and more blood is being shunted to the skin surface to prevent over-heating, thus less blood goes to the muscles
- energy production cannot be maintained.

As the point of **aerobic capacity** (aerobic fatigue) is reached, one of the body systems fails to keep up with demand. The body now begins to meet its energy demands **anaerobically**:

- the ATP/PC (alactic anaerobic system) provides the immediate energy source for short duration (around 10 seconds), high intensity exercise
- the lactic acid system provides a high intensity energy source after depletion of the ATP/PC system until accumulation of lactic acid eventually increases in such quantities that it inhibits muscle action.

Energy systems are covered in more detail in Unit 6A: Exercise and energy systems.

Performance and body temperature

As muscle temperature increases, so does muscle performance. At a muscle temperature of 41°C, performance can be as much as 15 per cent greater than at a temperature of 37°C (Figure 3.7).

Heat generation, through increases of both body temperature and deep muscle temperature (by means of a warm up), in turn leads to:

- increases in the potential force exerted by muscle
- increases in the speed of muscle contraction (nerve messages travel faster at higher body temperatures)
- reduction of viscous resistance in a muscle (internal friction is reduced), therefore muscular contraction and relaxation is more rapid.

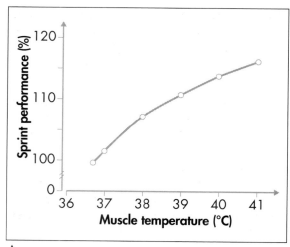

▲ **Figure 3.7** The relationship between muscle temperature and sprint performance

Like machines, the body is not 100 per cent efficient – much more energy is generated than is actually required. Depending on the type of exercise performed, only 20–30 per cent of energy produced is actually used for work. Most of the rest is lost as heat!

Mechanical efficiency also varies enormously from sport to sport. In swimming, for example, mechanical efficiency can be as low as 10 per cent. The energy not used in muscular contraction and lost as heat creates a considerable heat load in the body. Only major physiological adjustments will reduce or regulate body temperature to prevent the body over-heating.

Blood flow patterns alter in response to exercise. As exercise intensity increases, blood flow to the body periphery (shell) increases, flushing the appearance of the skin. This allows heat loss by:

- evaporation – at a high body temperature and dry environment (i.e. not humid), water evaporates and cools the skin
- convection – cool air over a warm body
- conduction – heat loss by contact with a cooler object
- radiation – heat loss by electro-magnetic waves.

During strenuous performance in extreme heat conditions, the body is placed under additional stress. If the body is exercising in conditions where the air temperature equals or exceeds skin temperature, the body temperature rises extremely quickly. If activity must take place in these conditions, the sportsperson must prepare for this by:

- drinking plenty of fluid before, during and after exercise
- wearing as little clothing as possible to increase the surface area of the skin exposed to the air to encourage evaporation
- wearing light-coloured clothing which reflects heat (some athletes now wear scientifically designed 'cooling vests')
- replacing water-related weight loss after exercise.

If air humidity is extremely high, in addition to an air temperature above that of the exercising body's skin temperature, the cooling effect of sweat is lost. The body cannot lose heat effectively since sweat cannot evaporate effectively as the air is partially saturated with moisture.

It should also be noted that cold temperatures also cause certain problems to the athlete. The body will respond to the cold by constricting blood vessels at the skin and shunting blood away from the body's periphery back to the

body core to protect the main organs. Hypothermia means that the body's core temperature has fallen below 35°C (the average core temperature being around 37°C). Signs of ill effects include:

- shivering (as the body tries to keep warm)
- slurred speech
- lack of co-ordination/stumbling
- slowing of mental and physical activity
- behavioural changes.

Preparing for activity in cold conditions in winter sports, such as ski racing, requires thoughtful consideration of different environmental conditions. A warm up preparation must allow for the rapid cooling of the body. If there is any delay between the end of the warm up and the start of the activity, this could be disastrous for an athlete, not only in terms of performance, but also in terms of potential injury. In cold weather conditions, individuals should wear additional clothing to decrease heat loss and allow body temperature to be maintained and increased more effectively.

TASK

Investigate the effects of temperature on muscle performance. Use either skin thermometers in a practical session, library-based research with data collected from reference texts, or data collated by your teacher.

3. Musculo-skeletal structures in action

The ability of the skeletal structures to generate the forces required to perform physical activity is provided by the muscular system. It is fired by the nervous system and fuelled by the cardio-vascular and respiratory systems. Movement considered here is that involving the **gross musculo-skeletal structures**. These facilitate the vast range of human movement. The term 'musculo-skeletal system' is used here to refer to the action of the combined muscles and skeleton, i.e. the muscle and **connective tissues** attached to the skeletal structures.

▲ *Figure 3.8* Additional clothing decreases heat loss and aids warm up preparation

▲ *Figure 3.9* The musculo-skeletal system in action

In terms of exercise and training for sport, it could be argued that muscles are the most important part of our anatomy. It is not that other body components are not vitally important – but that muscles are the key to successful movement (Figure 3.9). Muscles enable the performance of a vast range of movement in sport and exercise. They respond quickly to correct exercise and training, although, conversely, we do see deterioration when exercise and training ceases.

Musculo-skeletal structure and function for sport and exercise – gross structures

Muscles have three functions:

1 to provide movement of the skeleton
2 to provide a pump for blood circulation
3 to provide slow rhythmic contraction for digestion.

The term 'muscle' refers to all three types of contractile tissue found in the body.

These are all made up of elongated cells or fibres and all have the special ability to contract.

The three types of muscle demonstrate structural and functional differences:

- **skeletal muscle** (also known as striated, striped or voluntary muscle) is stimulated by voluntary contractions controlled by the nervous system (neurogenic contraction). Skeletal muscle is capable of contractions ranging from those producing very rapid and powerful movements to those of a much more gradual, less powerful and controlled nature
- **smooth muscle** (also known as involuntary, visceral or non-striated muscle) is located in walls of viscera (walls of hollow organs) and blood vessels. It is stimulated by involuntary neurogenic stimulus and is the least specialised of the three muscle types. It has slow, rhythmical contractions and is associated with the control of internal organs rather than athletic movement.
- **cardiac muscle** is found only in the heart and has a special cell structure, which generates its rhythmic (myogenic) contractions. This cell structure is found only in the heart wall and its contractions are not under voluntary control.

The cardiac (heart) muscle is covered in section 4 of this Unit. In this section we will consider only gross skeletal muscle structures. Of over 600 skeletal muscles in the human body, fewer than 100 are regularly studied in relation to exercise, training and sport. In this Unit you only have to study those muscles acting on the major joints. To understand the location and action of muscles on the skeleton you first need to be familiar with the gross musculo-skeletal structures.

Connective tissue

The broad sheet or band of fibrous connective tissue that surrounds a muscle is known as a **fascia**. Fasciae (plural) appear as glistening white sheets, which are made up of irregularly interwoven collagen fibres. They can tolerate tension from dif-

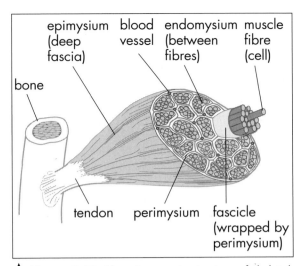

▲ *Figure 3.10* *The microscopic structure of skeletal muscle*

ferent directions. They are structured to be adaptable to the changing size and shape of muscles.

The connective tissues of muscle form component layers that have different functions (Figure 3.10).

Individual contractile muscle fibres or cells are covered by **endomysium**, a thin layer of connective tissue that wraps itself around the fibres and binds them together to form bundles. These bundles are known as **fasciculi**, which in turn, are themselves bound together by a layer of white fibrous connective tissue mixed with elastin fibres known as **perimysium**. Finally, the external layer, made up of smooth collagen fibres is called the **epimysium**. The epimysium gives the muscle its shape and binds it together. The external layer is moist, which allows other muscles to slide against it.

Muscle shapes and movement

Although all skeletal muscles are made up of **fasciculi**, the alignment or arrangement of these varies. Muscle shapes are determined by the arrangement of these bundles of muscle fibres:

- **parallel** arrangement of the fasciculi, where the long axes of the bundles run with the longitudinal axis of the muscle, are known as **strap-like** (e.g. the sartorius of the thigh), or **fusiform** (e.g. the biceps) (Figure 3.11).

- where the muscle fibres are short and there is angled attachment of the fasciculi to a central tendon running the length of a muscle in feather-like pattern, these muscles are known as **pennate**. Fasciculi attachment to only *one* side of the tendon is a **unipennate** muscle (extensor digitorum longus), whereas those attached to both sides of the tendon (a feather-like appearance) are known as **bipennate** muscles (rectus femoris).

- **convergent** muscles are broad at their origin (nearest to the centre line of the body) but converge to a single tendon at their insertion (furthest away from the centre line of the body) as in the pectoralis major.

- external body openings are controlled by **circular** muscles where fasciculi form a circle of muscle fibres allowing the opening to open and close, for example the orbicularis oculi muscle of the eyes.

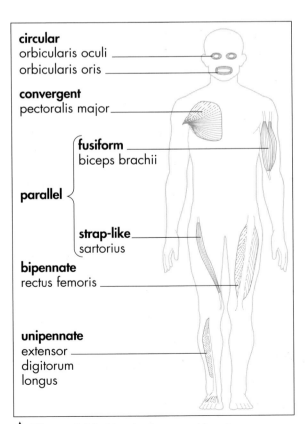

▲ *Figure 3.11* *Muscle shape and location*

The patterns of the fasciculi influence the range of motion and power of a muscle. Muscle fibres shorten to about half their resting length when contracted, so that the longer a muscle fibre, the greater its range of motion. Parallel (strap-like or fusiform) fasciculi arrangement provides the greatest degree of shortening but these muscles are not usually very powerful. Muscle power is, however, dependent on the number and type of muscle fibres rather than their length. Bipennate muscles, which actually shorten very little, demonstrate this by being very powerful. Thus, **muscle size** does not always relate to strength. Strength is directly proportional to the cross-sectional area of the muscle as well as the type of fibre. It is important not to confuse the roles of muscle fibre length and muscle cross-section in relation to a) the range of movement and b) muscle strength.

Muscle strength

People often begin a strength-training programme with the aim of building muscle size (**hypertrophy**), 'bulking up' at the expense of everything else. An understanding of the different strength qualities shows that hypertrophy training may not significantly improve the strength performance of muscle for a particular sport or activity.

Appropriate strength training will develop specific strength qualities vital for success in a specific sport. **Maximum strength** is the maximum amount of force that an individual can produce during a given movement of unlimited length. Some sports, such as powerlifting and wrestling, require maximum strength. Explosive strength is the ability to use this muscular force at speed. It is required by sprinters exploding out of the blocks and footballers shooting for goal.

Reactive strength allows the individual to absorb heavy impacts and explode out of the impact or landing with great force. This allows the long jumper, for example, to take off from the board or for a sprinter to propel herself along the track.

Sustained strength allows the individual to maintain maximal forces over repeated contractions over 20–30 seconds. A rugby player in a ruck or maul will try to exert a high force for several seconds at a time as he or she tries to push off his or her opponent towards the try line.

Strength endurance is similar to sustained strength. However, strength endurance is more concerned with strength that is maintained over longer periods of continuous activity, such as rowing, triathlon or élite marathon running.

The adaptation of the nervous system in muscles is vital for successful development of maximal and explosive strength. In addition, increased muscle size may be a hindrance in terms of the additional body mass to be moved. Increases in speed of strength must be developed to enable the potential of a muscle to exert maximal force.

The natural resting length of a muscle does not give a muscle the maximum tension that it can develop. Increasing **muscle length** by partially stretching before movement increases the forces generated. This is sometimes depicted as the length-tension curve and is seen in the use of the inverse stretch reflex in stretching (see page 166) and plyometric training. Increased tension from the partial stretch, together with the contraction of the stimulated muscle, increases the degree of force that a muscle can produce. An optimum position of stretch increases the elastic recoil of the muscle – you can only stretch so far prior to combining this stretch with contraction to increase muscular force. This is often called the 'pre-jump' and is utilised in jumping events. In throwing, it is sometimes called 'winding up' the throw.

Characteristics of skeletal muscle tissue

As a result of muscle structures (see Figure 3.10) and their specialist molecular struc-

TASK

Produce a short presentation on muscle types and their relevance to sporting performance, using diagrams to assist your explanation. Your presentation could include discussion of muscle shape, size, location and type appropriate for a variety of sporting performances.

tures (see also Unit 6A: Exercise and energy systems) skeletal muscle tissue demonstrates four main characteristics when stimulated by the nervous system:

- excitability – the ability to receive and respond to stimuli
- contractability – the ability to shorten and thicken when sufficient stimuli have been received
- extensibility – the ability to stretch
- elasticity – the ability to return to the original shape after contraction or stretching.

These four characteristics enable muscles to provide:

- energy for movement
- heat
- improvement of the circulatory system
- maintenance of posture.

Not all skeletal muscle fibres (cell types) are alike in either structure or function. For example, skeletal fibres contract at different speeds and vary in colour depending on the myoglobin content. These and other factors combine to inform us about the **muscle fibre type**.

Muscle fibre types

The two main muscle fibre types are **slow twitch** (Type I) and **fast twitch** (Type IIa and Type IIb).

Type I (slow twitch) fibres:

- are red
- are connected to slower-firing nerve fibres (slow oxidative fibres which split ATP at a slow rate (see page 379)
- have the right chemical components (enzymes) to produce energy for long periods of time
- have large amounts of myoglobin, mitochondria and blood capillaries
- have a good supply of fuel to produce the energy required for endurance
- have a slow contraction rate but are very resistant to fatigue and are therefore better suited to endurance events.

Type IIa (fast twitch oxidative fibres – FOG):

- are red
- contain large amounts of myoglobin and mitochondria and have many

blood capillaries
- have a high capacity for regenerating ATP by oxidative processes
- have a high contraction velocity and are resistant to fatigue
- are infrequently found in humans.

Type IIb (fast twitch glycolytic fibres):

- are white
- are relatively low in myoglobin content, with few mitochondria and blood capillaries but large amounts of glycogen
- are connected to fast-firing nerve fibres – fast glycolytic
- have the right chemical components (enzymes) for the production of large amounts of energy (splits ATP quickly) in the shortest possible time, allowing rapid muscular contraction
- are therefore better suited to short duration, fast powerful activities but fatigue quickly
- are considered the 'true' anaerobic fibre.

Molecular fibre type structures are discussed in more detail in Unit 6A on page 373.

The different skeletal muscle fibre types in the body vary in quantity and differ from individual to individual. We inherit these different **muscle fibre type proportions** in our muscles from our parents. Proportions can vary according to the action of the par-

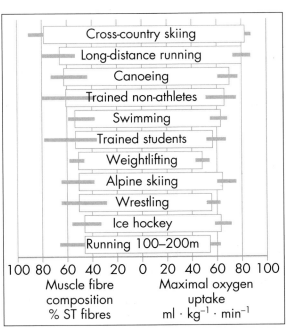

▲ **Figure 3.12** Percentage of fibre type proportions

ticular muscle. Muscles involved in providing posture, particularly those of the back, neck and leg, are found to have a high proportion of slow twitch fibres. Typically, muscles such as those of the shoulder and upper arm, which are used in more dynamic actions, high intensity/short duration activities like throwing and lifting, are found to have higher proportions of fast twitch fibres.

A muscle biopsy can be a painful and expensive way of determining muscle cell type. The combination or proportions of muscle fibre type can more easily be determined by your **suitability** for certain types of activities or events. Thus, in exercise and sporting terms, different muscle fibre types in different proportions determine a range of suitability for different sporting activities.

As a rough indication, good endurance and a slow progression to full speed indicates slow twitch fibre predominance, whereas good explosive strength or sergeant jump height indicates a likelihood of fast twitch fibre predominance.

Typical muscle fibre type proportions in relation to suitability for various sports are illustrated in Figure 3.12.

By structuring specific training activities an individual can develop and bring about changes in skeletal fibres. This can be described as the **effects of training fibre type**.

Suitable training can train slow twitch fibres to operate more quickly, for example. However, it is not possible to convert them completely to fast twitch fibres. Similarly, fast twitch fibres can be trained to develop more endurance. This is based on knowledge of the properties of the Type IIa fibre or FOG (Fast Oxidative Glycolytic).

Note that concentrating training on one fibre type will probably result in losing some of the characteristics of the other fibre type. An élite 100m sprinter would therefore struggle to run effectively in more endurance-based events. The molecular detail of these physiological changes in fibre type is described in more detail in Unit 6A: Exercise and energy systems.

Types of bone

The different **bone types** also enables a wide variety of movement:

- long bones (arm, leg) act as levers
- short bones (wrist, ankle) give strength
- flat bones (cranium, ribs, sternum, scapulae) are protective
- irregular bones (vertebrae, facial) provide a large surface area for muscle attachment
- wormian bones (cranial sutures/joints) act as wedges or joins
- sesamoid bones (patella) inside a tendon – allow the tendon to slide over the joint.

Additionally, the variety of surfaces on bones provide:

- attachment for ligaments and tendons (projections)
- variety to articulating (joint) surfaces (processes).

Cartilage types

There are three **cartilage types** which, like bones, are stiffened forms of connective tissue. The various forms of cartilage function according their structure:

- **fibrous** white fibro-cartilage is resistant to stretching and acts as a tough shock absorber between vertebrae. It also reinforces the **hyaline** cartilage of the knee and hip
- hyaline cartilage is firm yet resilient. It is the most common form of cartilage and is found in air passages and at the articulating surfaces of bone
- **elastic** (yellow) cartilage is flexible and resilient and is found in structures that require the cartilage to move such as in the larynx and the external ear.

Posture

Posture is maintained by the sustained partial contraction of portions of skeletal muscle. This results in **muscle tone**, which is essential in maintaining posture. Static posture (correct standing or sitting) and dynamic posture (walking, running, lifting, etc.) are best performed when the body is correctly in alignment. Physiological structures work best when the body is in this position of alignment.

With poor posture, the centre of gravity shifts and affects the ability of the body to perform efficiently. This can cause long term structural damage (Figures 3.13 and 3.14).

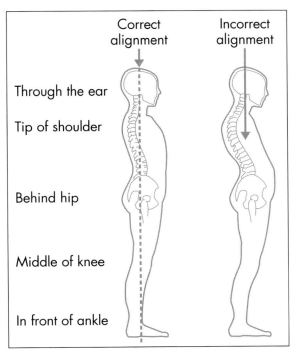

Figure 3.13 *Posture: correct and incorrect alignment*

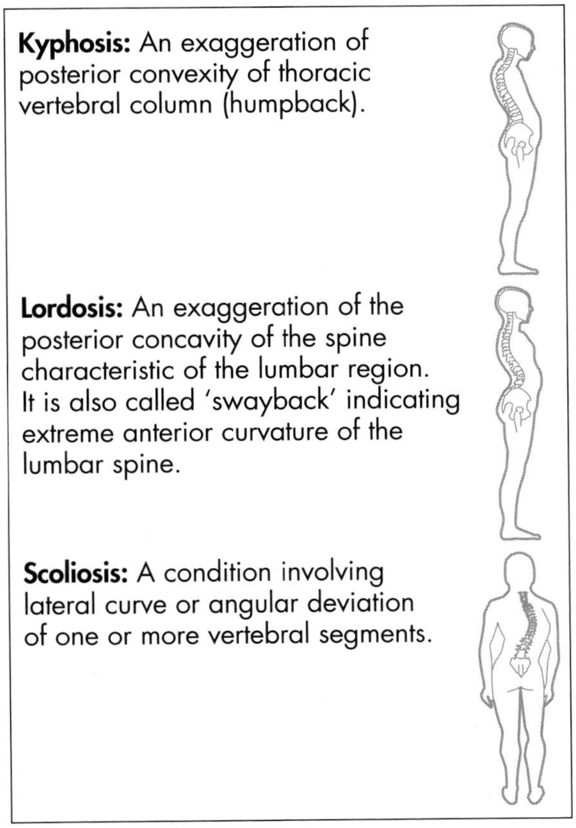

Correct alignment | Incorrect alignment

Through the ear

Tip of shoulder

Behind hip

Middle of knee

In front of ankle

Kyphosis: An exaggeration of posterior convexity of thoracic vertebral column (humpback).

Lordosis: An exaggeration of the posterior concavity of the spine characteristic of the lumbar region. It is also called 'swayback' indicating extreme anterior curvature of the lumbar spine.

Scoliosis: A condition involving lateral curve or angular deviation of one or more vertebral segments.

Figure 3.14 *Typical postural defects*

Postural defects occur for various reasons:

- soft tissue damage causes functional defects – these can be corrected
- structural defects involve permanent changes to skeletal structure that require remedial action in the form of braces or even surgery.

The effects of exercise

The **effects of exercise** for **short-term responses** of the musculo-skeletal system were described on page 169. **Long-term adaptations** are listed on page 196.

The inability of a muscle to maintain its strength of contraction is called **muscle fatigue**. This is dependent on the fibre type being used, which in turn is determined by the intensity of the activity. Gross musculo-skeletal structures demonstrate long-term musculo-skeletal adaptations in response to exercise and training. These adaptations enable these structures to cope with the increasing demands of future workloads.

In relation to structure and function, flexibility is gained via the two main categories of stretching (see page 164). **Static flexibility** refers to the combined efforts of active and passive flexibility exercises that lengthen the skin, muscle fibres and muscle fascia in a smooth and controlled manner.

Dynamic flexibility relies on momentum to gain advantage in the over-stretching of a muscle to achieve a physical performance or task. This is achieved by ballistic stretching and some consider it necessary for those sportsmen and women in explosive speed competition, where there is a need to gain the largest range of motion possible to enhance performance, e.g. sprinters. It has been suggested that this encourages the stretch reflex response to 'propel' the athlete from the blocks.

Compared to someone who is normally fit and healthy, an active sportsperson requires an appropriate greater amount of dynamic flexibility in order to perform the specific, and often more exuberant, movements of sport. For example, the normal range of movement would not be sufficient for a tennis player to serve as fast and as accurately as possible in a competitive situation. Dynamic flexibility (ballistic) training may enhance the range of motion considerably so that the required performance demands can be tolerated.

Any sport or activity that requires dynamic, explosive movement at speed must embrace ballistic stretching as part of the exercise and training programme. This is in order to both improve performance and prevent/minimise the risk of injury.

The variety of approaches to **resistance training**, such as weight training, produce specific strength results that should complement the sportperson's requirements for performance in their sport.

Aerobic (low intensity/high duration) endurance-type training produces the following effects on skeletal muscle:

- increase in fuel stores (glucose and triglycerides)
- increase in O_2 extraction due to increased concentration of myoglobin
- increased vascular activity enhancing O_2 delivery
- increased number and size of mitochondria meaning greater aerobic energy production
- increase in the number of the oxidative enzymes
- increase in the size of slow twitch fibres.

Anaerobic training (high intensity/low duration) produces:

- an increase in the size and number of fast twitch cells
- an increase in creatine phosphate stores giving extra duration of high intensity energy (exercise duration of approximately 10 seconds)
- greater glycogen stores and quantity of anaerobic enzymes resulting in greater anaerobic energy production.

In addition, exercise and training in general produces:

- muscle hypertrophy (growth), mainly in fast twitch fibres
- increased capillary density per fibre
- increased strength of connective tissues
- increased ability to recruit more motor units (a motor neurone and the muscle fibres that it stimulates) which produces more forceful muscular contractions.

TASK

a Produce a report on a sportsperson of your choice and focus on the key muscles used in their performance. The report should highlight the major muscles used in specific actions and the type of muscle fibres predominantly used. Your explanation of the fibre shape, length and size must also be related to the sporting function of a particular performance action (e.g. David Beckham striking a free kick with force). You could use video analysis evidence to support your explanation.

b Design a training programme to develop flexibility using the principles outlined in this Unit and developed by further research of relevant resources. Assess the effects of the programme on muscles.

Hypo-kinetic musculo-skeletal disorders

Hypo-kinetic disorders arise (and deteriorate) as a result of lack of exercise or movement. They may also be described as lifestyle factors that can be altered by increases in physical activity. They include a range of musculo-skeletal and cardio-vascular and respiratory factors:

- obesity or overweight
- joint structure damage
- osteoporosis
- high levels of blood fat and cholesterol
- coronary heart disease
- high blood pressure.

Musculo-skeletal locations and action

When the nervous system initiates **muscular contraction**, this allows the skeletal system to perform as a comprehensive set of levers. The sportsperson can then undertake a wide range of motor movements at their disposal in a purposeful and co-ordinated way.

There are several descriptors for types of muscle action, each relating to the contraction of the muscle and its effect on the skeletal system at joints.

Types of muscle action

Isotonic muscle action involves the movement of any joint by the increasing contraction of a muscle against a resistance.

There are two forms of isotonic muscle action:

- **concentric** muscular action can be considered as the initiator of movement against a resistance, accelerating the movement of the body part. The **prime mover** (or **agonist**) muscle shortens and thickens, reducing the joint angle and moves the insertion towards the origin, providing the force to produce movement.
- **eccentric** muscle action involves an opposing, or **antagonist** muscle developing tension against the agonist muscle. It lengthens as it tries to resist the movement initiated, pulling the origin and insertion apart. This 'braking' action is known as eccentric action.

Isometric muscle contraction occurs when the muscle stays the same length – there is no movement of the joint, but there is resistance against an object. Such contraction frequently occurs in activities like wrestling or judo.

Only specialist equipment, mainly used in rehabilitation, produces **isokinetic** muscle action whereby a joint is moved through a constant angle at a constant speed and with constant force, ensuring resistance equal to the force through a full range of movement. This is an effective means of developing muscular strength.

A range of muscular action also exists to support the work of the agonists and antagonists. **Fixators** allow stability of the joints at the origin and insertion of the active muscles. The action of **synergists** is to assist the active muscles of a movement. For example, the muscles of the lower arm (brachialis and brachio-radialis) assist the biceps in the action of elbow flexion.

Joints

Kinesiology is the structural analysis of movement at joints and considers:

- the size, shape and surfaces of the articulating bones
- the skeletal muscles that act on them.

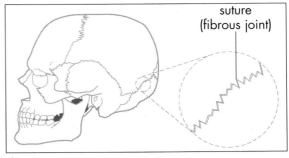

▲ **Figure 3.15** Skull suture – a fibrous joint

Some joints only allow a limited range of movement, while others allow a wide range of movements (Figures 3.15, 3.16 and 3.17). There are over 600 muscles in the human body and many of the deep (non-surface) muscles are not necessary to know for study at this level. It is, however, essential that we see muscles as part of a wider picture – that they operate in partnership with other physiological structures to produce a whole range of gross to fine movements. By studying the major joints you will understand how the musculo-skeletal structures work in action.

Articulations (joint movements) occur in three main categories according to the degree of movement permitted:

- **immovable/fibrous** (synarthrodial) **joints** are where bones are joined by fibrous tissue and allow little, if any, movement. Examples are the skull and pelvic bones (Figure 3.15). These joints need to be rigid to function effectively, but must provide some

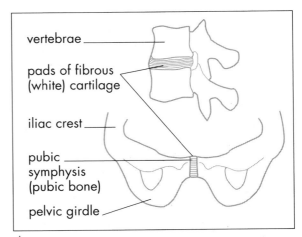

▲ **Figure 3.16** The vertebrae and pubic symphysis – cartilaginous joints that are only slightly movable

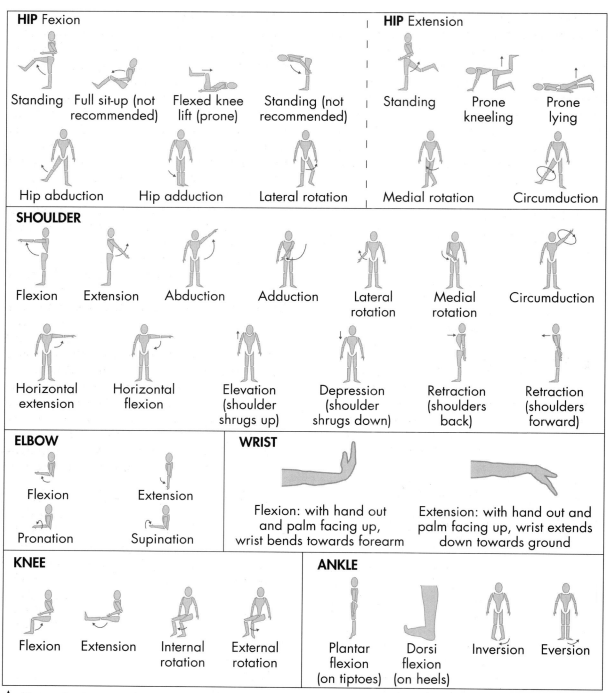

▲ **Figure 3.17** *Types of joint movements*

'give' to allow shock absorption and to allow for a degree of tissue swelling

• **slightly movable/cartilaginous** (amphiarthrodial) **joints** are where bones are separated by pads of fibrous (white) cartilage. Examples are the cervical, thoracic and lumbar sections of the vertebral column and the pubic bones

• **freely movable/synovial** (diathrodial) **joints** are characterised by their mobility, which is provided by key characteristic structures. These are discussed in more detail on pages 181–82.

The shape of the bones at an articulation determines the range and therefore the type of movement.

Type and range of movement is similar in all humans but is limited by the ligament, tendon and muscular supporting structures at each joint. The range of movement available to the sportsperson is increased by correct flexibility and mobility training that enables the musculo-skeletal structures to perform to their optimum range. However, different bone structures can limit the type and range of movement at each particular joint (see Figure 3.17).

Table 3.1 *Range of movement patterns*

Movement	Description
Flexion	reduction in a joint angle (bending)
Extension	increase in a joint angle (straightening)
Abduction	movement away from the midline of the body or other body part
Adduction	movement towards the midline of the body or other body part
Lateral/external rotation	rotation away from the midline
Medial/internal rotation	rotation towards the midline
Circumduction	a combination of flexion, extension, abduction and adduction: the body part describes a circle
Dorsal flexion	bringing the toes towards the tibia
Plantar flexion	pointing the toes
Eversion	turning the sole of the foot outwards
Inversion	turning the sole of the foot inwards
Supination	turning the palm up
Pronation	turning the palm down

The knee joint

Detailed study of the knee as an example of a freely movable hinge synovial joint illustrates this (Figure 3.18). The knee exhibits a range of structures that are quite complex. They allow the joint to withstand the tremendous forces that are often encountered in all dynamic sports. Due to this complexity, several of its delicate structures are highly vulnerable to injuries. The hinge of the knee is formed by the femur and the tibia, with the distal end of the femur sitting on the proximal end of the tibia, like a ball sitting on a table. The structures illustrated in Figure 3.17 provide passive stability for the joint. That is to say, they stabilize the joint but do not move it. The muscles illustrated in figure 3.18 are active stabilizers. They can stabilize the joint but also move it.

The quadriceps muscles provide active stability and extend the joint (straightening it from a flexed position) with the **anterior and posterior cruciate ligaments** attempting to prevent hyperextension and rotation (passive stability). The anterior and posterior cruciate ligaments prevent anterior and posterior translation (twisting) of the tibia). A frequent sporting injury is damage to the anterior cruciate ligament caused

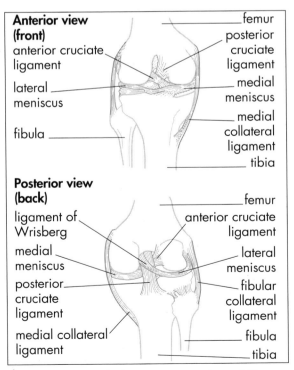

▲ **Figure 3.18** *The knee joint – passive stabilizers*

by forcing the knee backwards or by falling on a twisted or bent knee.

The **fibular collateral ligament** (lateral ligament) prevents the knee from flexing away from the mid-line of the body. The **medial collateral ligament**, which joins the insides of the knee, is damaged by excess stress and load being placed on the inside of the knee causing it to sprain or worse, tear. In both cases the knee becomes unstable and then reconstructive surgery may be necessary followed by extensive rehabilitation of the knee and the muscles surrounding it. (Figure 3.19).

Menisci (extra layers of fibrocartilage) deepen the joint to enable joint stability. They act as wedges between the articulating bones. There are two cartilages, the **medial and lateral menisci**, inside the knee to give joint stability, shock absorption and friction free movement. They also aid slight rotation of the joint. This rotation allows us to change direction at speed but heavy twists may result in a torn cartilage. This can be described as internal or external rotation of the knee whilst the knee is in a degree of flexion.

Anatomical structures in the knee also include:

- femoral condyles which increase the surface area of the joint and give stability
- the **synovial fluid/capsule** which gives stability from the pressure of the fluid: synovial fluid also lubricates and provides nutrition for hyaline cartilage
- pads of fat which cushion the joint giving shock absorption
- **bursae** which prevent wear and tear of the different structures that glide against each other as the joint moves.

The muscles illustrated on the next four pages concentrically contract (shorten) in the direction shown by the arrow to initiate the movement concerned. (O = Origin, I = Insertion).

The shoulder girdle

This consists of two scapulae (shoulder blades) and two clavicles (collarbones). The clavicles articulate with the sternum so that the girdle forms an incomplete ring around the upper thorax.

There are five main muscles involved in movement of the shoulder girdle:

- trapezius (Figure 3.20)
- levator scapulae (Figure 3.21)
- rhomboids (minor and major) (Figure 3.22)
- pectoralis minor (Figure 3.23).

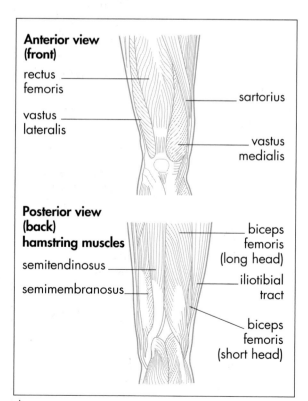

▲ **Figure 3.19** Muscles that act on the knee joint – active stabilizers

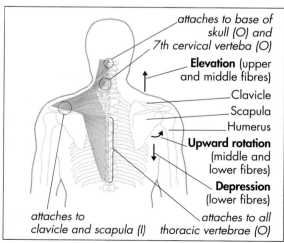

▲ **Figure 3.20** The shoulder girdle showing the trapezius muscle

These muscles produce the movements of:

- abduction/adduction
- flexion/extension
- elevation and depression
- internal and external rotation.
- upward and downward rotation

These and other types of joint movements are illustrated in Figure 3.17 on page 180.

The shoulder joint

This consists of the scapula, clavicle and humerus. There are nine main muscles involved in the movement of the shoulder joint, listed on the next page:

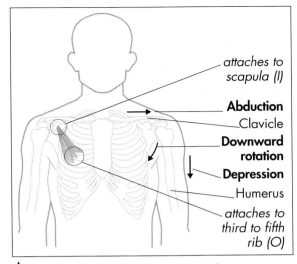

▲ **Figure 3.23** Pectoralis minor muscle

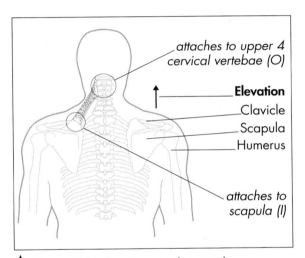

▲ **Figure 3.21** Levator scapulae muscle

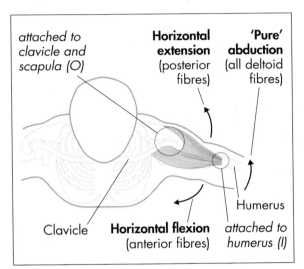

▲ **Figure 3.24** Deltoid

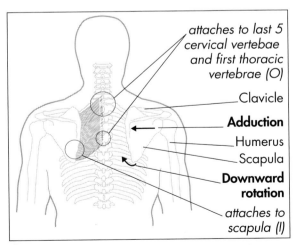

▲ **Figure 3.22** Rhomboid muscles (major and minor)

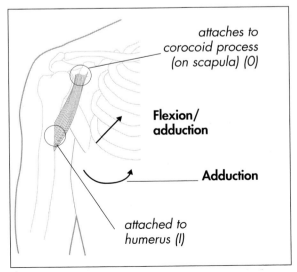

▲ **Figure 3.25** Coracobrachialis

- deltoid (Figure 3.24)
- coracobrachialis (Figure 3.25)
- supraspinatus (Figure 3.26) ⎫
- infraspinatus (Figure 3.27) ⎬ rotator
- teres minor (Figure 3.28) ⎬ cuff
- subscapularis (Figure 3.29) ⎭ muscles
- teres major (Figure 3.30)
- latissimus dorsi (Figure 3.31)
- pectoralis major (Figure 3.32).

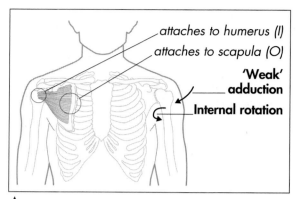

▲ **Figure 3.29** Subscapularis

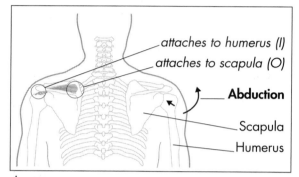

▲ **Figure 3.26** Supraspinatus

The rotator cuff muscles hold the head of the humerus in the glenoid cavity during movement.

These muscles produce the joint movements of:

- flexion/extension
- adduction/abduction
- rotation (internal and external)
- horizontal flexion/extension
- circumduction.

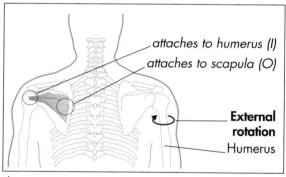

▲ **Figure 3.27** Infraspinatus

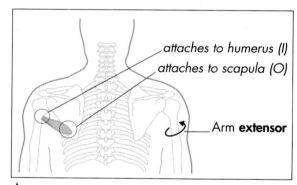

▲ **Figure 3.30** Teres major

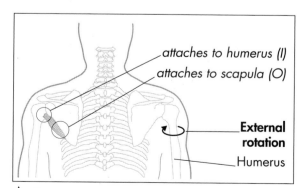

▲ **Figure 3.28** Teres minor

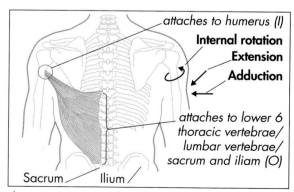

▲ **Figure 3.31** Latissimus dorsi

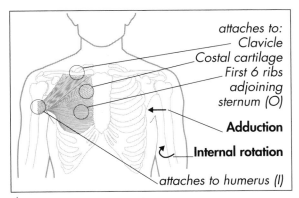

▲ *Figure 3.32* Pectoralis major

attaches to:
Clavicle
Costal cartilage
First 6 ribs adjoining sternum (O)

Adduction

Internal rotation

attaches to humerus (I)

The elbow and radio-ulnar joints

These joints consist of the humerus, radius and ulna. There are seven main muscles that are involved in their movement:

- biceps brachii (Figure 3.33)
- brachialis (Figure 3.34)
- brachioradialis (Figure 3.35)
- triceps brachii (Figure 3.36)
- supinator (Figure 3.37)
- pronator teres (Figure 3.38)
- pronator quadratus (Figure 3.39).

These muscles produce the joint movements of:

- flexion/extension
- pronation/supination.

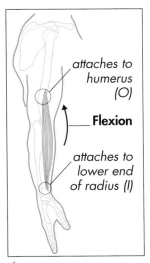

▲ *Figure 3.35* Brachioradialis

attaches to humerus (O)

Flexion

attaches to lower end of radius (I)

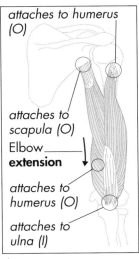

▲ *Figure 3.36* Triceps brachii

attaches to humerus (O)

attaches to scapula (O)

Elbow **extension**

attaches to humerus (O)

attaches to ulna (I)

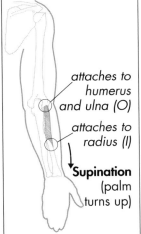

▲ *Figure 3.37* Supinator (posterior view)

attaches to humerus and ulna (O)

attaches to radius (I)

Supination (palm turns up)

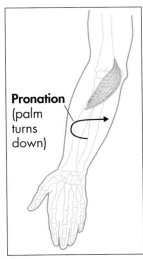

▲ *Figure 3.38* Pronator teres

Pronation (palm turns down)

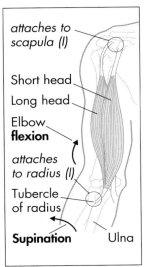

▲ *Figure 3.33* Biceps brachii

attaches to scapula (I)

Short head

Long head

Elbow **flexion**

attaches to radius (I)

Tubercle of radius

Supination

Ulna

attaches to humerus (O)

Flexion

Radius

attaches to ulna (I)

▲ *Figure 3.34* Brachialis

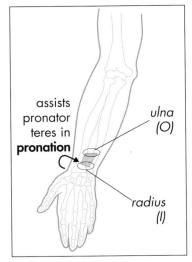

assists pronator teres in **pronation**

ulna (O)

radius (I)

▲ *Figure 3.39* Pronator quadratus

The wrist and hand joints

These joints are made up of 29 bones in all, including the radius and the ulna. There are eight carpal bones arranged in two rows of four from the wrist and five metacarpal bones with fourteen phalanges (two for the thumb and four for each of the fingers).

A range of muscles, including intrinsic muscles (muscle within muscles), produce movements of the wrist and hand. These include:

- flexor carpi radialis (Figure 3.40)
- palmaris longus (Figure 3.41)
- flexor carpi ulnaris (Figure 3.42)
- extensor carpi ulnaris (Figure 3.43)
- extensor carpi radialis (Figure 3.43).

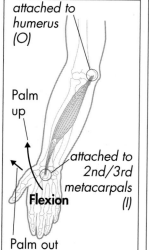

▲ **Figure 3.40** Flexor carpi radialis

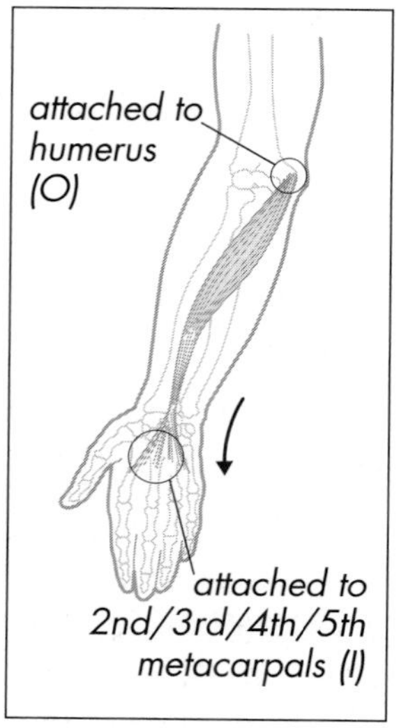

▲ **Figure 3.41** Palmaris longus

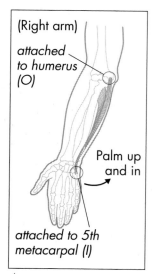

▲ **Figure 3.42** Flexor carpi ulnaris (wrist flexor)

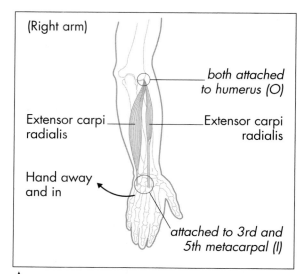

▲ **Figure 3.43** Extensor carpi ulnaris and extensor carpi radialis (wrist extensors)

The muscles produce the following movements:

- flexion/extension
- adduction/abduction
- extension of the forearm.

The hip joint

This consists of the femur and the pelvic girdle. The hip girdle is made up of the left and right pelvic bones joined together at the rear by the sacrum. The large and strong muscles that act on the hip and pelvic girdle include:

- § sartorius (Figure 3.44)
- iliopsoas (iliacus and psoas major) (Figure 3.45)
- rectus femoris (Figure 3.46)
- tensor fasciae latae (Figure 3.47)
- gluteus medius (Figure 3.48)
- gluteus maximus and minimus (Figure 3.49)
- biceps femoris (Figure 3.50)
- semitendinosus
- semimembranosus
- pectineus

- adductor brevis (Figure 3.51)
- adductor longus (Figure 3.52)
- adductor magnus
- gracilis (Figure 3.53).

Muscle location determines their action on the skeletal structures. These muscles produce the joint movements of:

- flexion/extension
- abduction/adduction
- internal/external rotation.

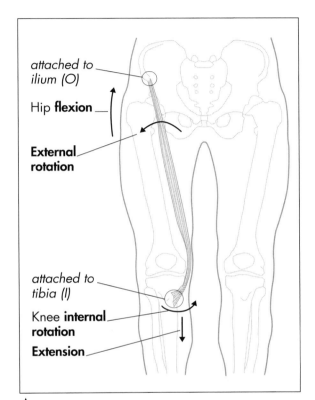

▲ **Figure 3.44** Sartorius

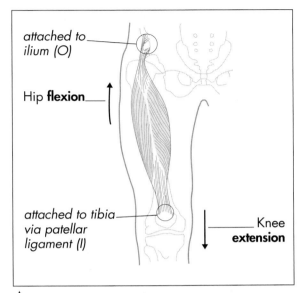

▲ **Figure 3.46** Rectus femoris

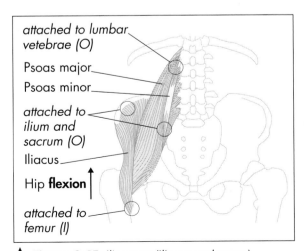

▲ **Figure 3.45** Iliopsoas (iliacus and psoas)

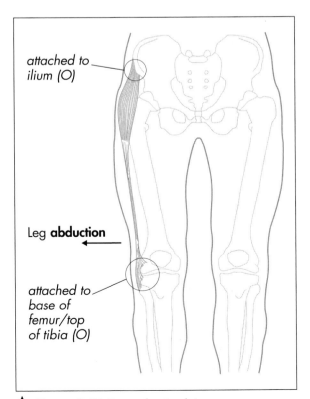

▲ **Figure 3.47** Tensor fasciae latae

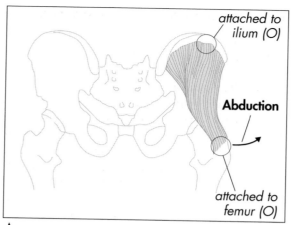

▲ **Figure 3.48** *Gluteus medius*

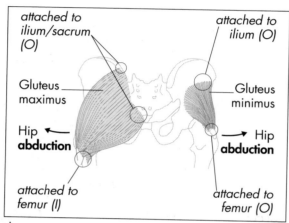

▲ **Figure 3.49** *Gluteus maximus and minimus*

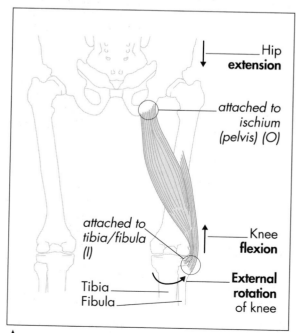

▲ **Figure 3.50** *Biceps femoris*

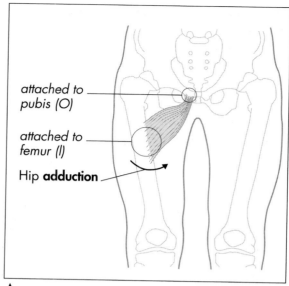

▲ **Figure 3.51** *Adductor brevis*

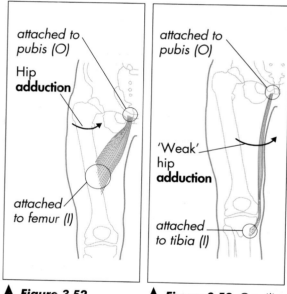

▲ **Figure 3.52**
Adductor longus

▲ **Figure 3.53** *Gracilis*

The ankle joint

This joint is made up of 26 bones, 7 tarsal bones and 14 phalanges. During movement body weight is transferred from the tibia to the two bones found at the heel – the talus and the calcaneus.

Muscles that act on the ankle and foot include:

- gastrocnemius (Figure 3.54)
- soleus (Figure 3.55)
- tibialis anterior (Figure 3.56)
- peroneus brevis (Figure 3.56).

These muscles produce the joint movements of:

- inversion/eversion
- planar flexion/dorsal flexion
- knee flexion.

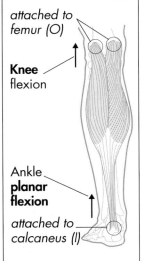
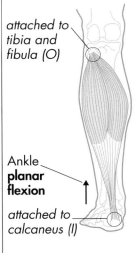

▲ **Figure 3.54**
Gastrocnemius

▲ **Figure 3.55** *Soleus*

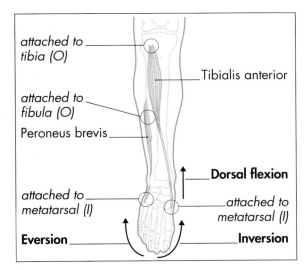

▲ **Figure 3.56** *Tibialis anterior and peroneus brevis*

The abdominal region

The abdominal region (or trunk) is made up of the muscles that act on this area. These are:

- internal oblique (Figure 3.57)
- external oblique (Figure 3.58)
- transverse abdominus (Figure 3.59)
- rectus abdominus (Figure 3.60).

These muscles produce the movements of:

- flexion
- right and left rotations.

Proprioception

Proprioception kinaesthetic awareness describes a person's continual awareness of their balance, their whole body position or the position of any of its constituent parts. Sensory organs allow the transmission of information, via the central nervous system, about individual joint movement, without the need for visual confirmation or feedback.

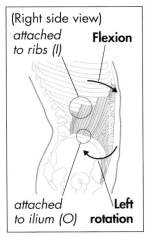
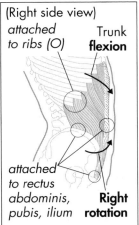

▲ **Figure 3.57** *Internal oblique muscles: assist trunk flexion and left trunk rotation*

▲ **Figure 3.58** *External oblique muscles: assist trunk flexion and right trunk rotation*

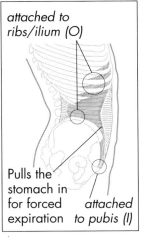
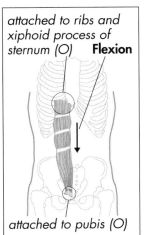

▲ **Figure 3.59**
Transverse abdominus

▲ **Figure 3.60** *Rectus abdominus*

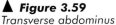

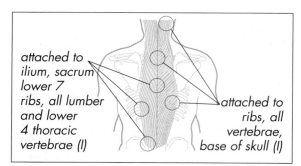

attached to ilium, sacrum lower 7 ribs, all lumber and lower 4 thoracic vertebrae (I)

attached to ribs, all vertebrae, base of skull (I)

▲ **Figure 3.61** *The lower back region. The muscles that act on the spine include the erector spinae (sacrospinalis), this enables spine extension/hyper extension*

As previously discussed in the section on warm up (pages 165–166), two sensory organs – Golgi tendon organs in partnership with muscle spindles (located between muscle fibres or cells) – are sensitive to muscle movement. They can determine from its resting state, both muscle length changes and the speed of this change in length. This gives an individual this sense of bodily awareness. Tone and posture is also maintained through the operation of this sensory partnership.

TASK

In pairs, take a specific joint and its associated muscles and produce a wall display showing the location and action of each.

Produce large, labelled diagrams, with explanations of the movement patterns at each joint, suitable for display in the classroom, the gym or sports hall.

4. The circulatory, vascular and respiratory (CVR) systems in action

The delivery of oxygen and nutrients to the working muscles and the removal of waste products is the responsibility of the cardiac, vascular and respiratory systems (CVR). They work together to ensure that the body can meet the demands of exercise. Homeostatic adjustments (see page 162) are made to CVR systems in response to dif-

ferent levels of exercise (training stimulus) which are demonstrated at rest, sub-maximal and maximal exercise intensities. CVR systems also adjust to different environmental conditions. The CVR systems are best developed by continuous, Fartlek and interval training methods.

Response and regulation to exercise of the CVR systems

Cardiac cycle

Exercise increases blood flow through the heart so that the **cardiac cycle** accelerates to accommodate the increased demand for oxygen. The normal cycle is around 0.8 seconds per heartbeat. This accelerates with faster and more powerful atrial and ventricular contraction, which is stimulated by the cardiac centre in the brain. Heart rate is defined as the number of heart contractions in each minute. During exercise this rises as the heart increases the supply of oxygen and nutrients to the working muscle sites, whilst allowing the return of waste products more quickly back to the lungs.

There are two distinct periods in the cardiac cycle – one of heart muscle relaxation (**cardiac diastole**), the other of contraction (**cardiac systole**):

- During the cardiac diastole, the bicuspid and tricuspid valves are closed and the atrium is full. Once full with blood, the atria force the bicuspid and tricuspid valves to open and fill the ventricles. This lasts for about 0.5 second at rest.
- During the cardiac systole, the atria contact and send blood via the bicuspid and tricuspid valves into the ventricles. When full, these contract causing blood to be expelled from the heart via the semi-lunar valves (the bicuspid and tricuspid valves are closed at this time). This lasts around 0.3 second at rest.

Stimulation of the heart originates in the cardiac centre in the medulla oblongata. The sympathetic and parasympathetic nervous systems work antagonistically and provide the stimulation for acceleration and deceleration of the heart rate. Cardiac systole (contraction) is initiated by the electrical cardiac impulse from the sinu-atrial node (the pacemaker, found in the right atrial wall). This distributes electrical stimulus through the myocardial (heart muscle) wall between the heart chambers, where the atrio-ventricular node (between the right atrium and right ventricle) continues distribution of the electrical signal across to the ventricles.

This change in heart rate is another example of homeostatic regulation of the body to adjust to changing demands. During exercise, the impulses from the sympathetic nerves increase in frequency and the sinu-atrial node is stimulated by the release of noradrenaline so that the heart rate increases. There is greater venous filling and more efficient emptying of the ventricles. Deceleration of the heart rate occurs via receptors in the aorta and carotid arteries (the arteries supplying the heart with blood) following dramatic rise in blood pressure. The parasympathetic nerve system sends impulses to the sinu-atrial node to slow heart rate down. This is known as **negative feedback control**.

Other influences on heart rate include:

- hormones e.g. adrenaline from the adrenal medulla
- increases in temperature
- gender – women have a higher heart rate than men
- age – heart rate decreases with age
- size – a larger person has a larger heart and the heart rate is slower
- posture – variations in sitting, standing, laying down
- altitude – the heart beats faster at a higher altitude.

The heart functions as two pumps (though effectively beating as one), one pump dealing with oxygenated and one with deoxygenated blood (see Figure 3.62). Deoxygenated blood returns from the body's systems (the systemic system) via the vena cavae. It enters and fills the right atrium of the heart. At the same time oxygenated blood returns to the heart from the lungs (the pulmonary system), via the pulmonary vein, and enters and fills the left atrium. When both atria are full, atrial contraction, stimulated by impulses sent from the cardiac center, forces blood into the

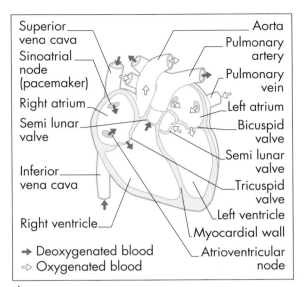

▲ **Figure 3.62** The heart

ventricles. Deoxygenated blood flows through the tricuspid valve into the right ventricle. Oxygenated blood flows through the bicuspid valve into the left ventricle.

When this ventricular filling is complete, the tricuspid and bicuspid valves (known collectively as the atrio-ventricular valves) close. The full ventricles then contract, forcing blood out of the heart via the semi-lunar valves. Deoxygenated blood from the right ventricle enters the pulmonary artery and goes to the lungs where it is oxygenated by gaseous exchange. Oxygenated blood from the left ventricle enters the aorta for transmit around the body.

Cardiac output

Cardiac output (Q) is the volume of blood pumped out of the heart by each ventricle in one minute. It can be calculated by multiplying the **stroke volume** (SV), or the amount of blood pumped out from the ventricles with each beat in cm^3, by the heart rate (HR) (bpm – beats per minute). For example; if an individual has a stroke volume of $75cm^3$ and a heart rate of 72 bpm:

$$Q = SV \times HR$$
$$Q = 75cm^3 \times 72bpm$$
$$Q = 5400cm^3/min$$
$$Q = 5.4 \text{ litres/min}$$

Variations in stroke volume and heart rate are discussed on pages 192–94.

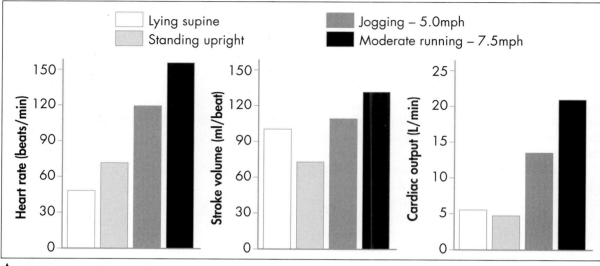

▲ **Figure 3.63** *Changes in heart rate with changes in posture and levels of exercise*

Exercise increases cardiac output and therefore velocity and blood flow into the systemic system (Figure 3.63). Blood is redistributed to the skeletal muscles, where it is needed, by means of **vascular shunting** – the smooth muscle wall of arteries/arterioles relaxes, reducing peripheral resistance, or contracts, increasing this resistance. The **vasomotor centre** brings about stimulation to vaso-dilate (widen) arterioles in active areas of the body and vaso-constrict (narrow) them in less active areas of the body so that blood can be redistributed according to need. In later stages of exercise, the blood may be diverted to skin arterioles as a way of cooling the body.

Blood pressure

A rise in **blood pressure** is caused by the resistance of blood vessels to blood flow. Blood pressure can be defined in three ways:

- peripheral resistance × blood flow (cardiac output)
- the pressure of blood exerted on the vessel walls
- the force per unit area exerted on the wall of a blood vessel.

It is expressed as:

systolic pressure (higher no.)
diastolic pressure (lower no.)

Peripheral resistance describes the relative obstruction to the passage of blood

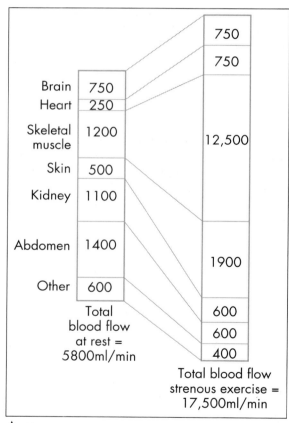

▲ **Figure 3.64** *Distribution of blood flow at rest and during exercise*

through the main arteries of blood exiting the heart at ventricular systole (systolic pressure) when the ventricles send blood out at the highest force and at ventricular diastole (diastolic pressure) when the heart is at rest.

As exercise levels increase, a rise in blood pressure must be assessed in terms of both systolic pressure or diastolic pressure as they demonstrate different changes. In endurance activities, systolic blood pressure rises in direct proportion to the increasing intensity of exercise. The rise in cardiac output, with exercise, increases the systolic blood pressure surging the blood through blood vessels. Diastolic pressure (Figure 3.64) changes little.

Blood vessels

Blood vessels vary in their structure depending on their role in blood transport. Arteries and arterioles (smaller vessels with a decreased diameter) are responsible for the delivery of blood from the heart to the body tissues. Vaso-dilation or vaso-constriction of arteries regulates blood flow through the systemic system and at muscles and other tissues. This regulation of blood flow by means of vasomotor control is allowed by the sympathetic nerve fibres which control the contraction of smooth muscle in the thick middle layer – the tunica media.

Veins have a similar structure to arteries, although they have less of the smooth and elastic muscle tissue which is necessary to allow some expansion of the vessel as blood surges back to the heart. Since much of the blood is returning to the heart against gravity, it is helped along the way by pocket valves which close at regular intervals to prevent a backflow of venous blood.

Capillaries are vessels designed to allow ease of gaseous exchange by their one thin (epithelial) layer of cells. The cross-sectional area, that is to say the area of all the ends of all the capillaries, found at a typical muscle site, would be larger than that of the largest artery – the aorta. This allows efficient and rapid transfer of the oxygen carrying red blood cells to the muscle where it is needed for muscle action.

As blood travels away from the heart under high pressure the sub-division of the blood vessels into arterioles and capillaries increases the total cross sectional area that the blood will flow through. This means that blood pressure falls and the blood slows down markedly as it enters the capillary system (tissue-capillary net). Blood will speed up slightly as it leaves the capillaries due to the reduction of the cross-sectional area (see Figure 3.65).

Blood plasma volume

Blood plasma volume is the proportion of plasma relative to the other constituent parts of the blood. Fifty-five per cent of the blood is plasma (ninety per cent of this is water), whilst forty-five per cent is made up of the blood corpuscles. **Red blood cell (RBC) count** or number and therefore **haemoglobin** (the carrier of oxygen on the RBC) concentration can increase by legal and illegal means (e.g. the use of **recombinant erythropoeitin** or **RhEPO** – see page 199). This can be measured by means of a **haematocrit**. A haematocrit measures the current state of hydration of the blood (i.e. amount of fluid/plasma) and relates the number of solids such as blood cells to the amount of plasma. As red blood cell count rises, so will the haematocrit. Thus a 'normal' haematocrit may register at around 42–43 per cent, yet an athlete using EPO may develop a haematocrit nearer 50 per cent. Since levels of haemoglobin are a deciding factor in an individual's athletic performance, any increase by legal or illegal means can be of benefit to the individual.

However, increases in red blood cell count cause a reduction in the amount of

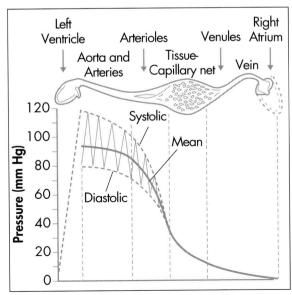

▲ **Figure 3.65** Blood pressure differential along the systemic tree

blood plasma. Decreases in blood plasma increase the viscosity (thickness) of the blood and therefore reduce its ability to flow. This is serious, particularly in exercise conditions where the body is under stress and water loss also reduces blood plasma levels.

During any exercise, the heart works hard to provide the muscles with the quantities of oxygen-rich blood they demand to keep functioning efficiently. As exercise intensity increases and more blood is required, the heart either has to increase the stroke volume (the amount of blood being pumped out per beat) or to beat more frequently. Since blood plasma volume decreases during exercise, the heart has to beat more rapidly to compensate for a lower stroke volume. There are greater increases in heart rate in exercise that is prolonged and done in hot conditions. This causes fatigue and dehydration, thus increasing losses in blood plasma. This effect is sometimes called the 'cardiac or heart rate drift'.

Oxygen transport

The transport of oxygen into the muscle cell takes place as **myoglobin** receives oxygen from haemoglobin. Myoglobin has a higher affinity for oxygen than haemoglobin and thus will deliver oxygen to the muscle cell **mitochondria**. The microscopic mitochondria, found in muscle cells, are the centres of aerobic respiration: using oxygen, resynthesizing ATP and producing CO_2 and H_2O as the by-products of the oxidation of glucose.

Gravity helps deoxygenated blood return from body parts above the heart to the right atrium, but hinders the return of such blood from below the heart. During exercise, this process, known as **venous return,** is assisted by:

- pumping or 'milking' action of the active muscles, known as the skeletal pump, to return blood to the right atria:
- surges of pressure in arteries alongside veins cause an additional pumping effect on veins
- 'pocket valves' prevent backflow of blood, or venous pooling

- thoracic pressure decreases, caused by the increases in thoracic volume during exercise and the veins around the thorax expand as a result, 'sucking' the blood up
- cardiac contraction 'sucks' blood up
- hydrostatic pressure (the attraction between fluid molecules moving in a particular direction) causes blood to be drawn to the heart.

Exercise increases venous return and cardiac output is dependent on this. Greater venous return caused by increasing physical activity stretches the myocardium and it then contracts with greater force – the cardiac fibres themselves are the stimulus which cause greater force of contraction. This is known as **Starling's Law** of the heart.

Respiration

Inspiration involves the diaphragm and the external intercostal muscles. The external intercostals move the ribs up and out and the sternum swings up and forward at the same time as the diaphragm contracts, flattening towards the stomach. With the lung expansion that follows and resultant lowering of air pressure in the thoracic cavity, air rushes in to fill the lungs.

Expiration is the passive process involving the relaxation of the inspiratory muscles and elastic recoil of the lungs. As thoracic pressure decreases, air is forced out. The mechanics of breathing, both at rest and during exercise, alter in response to changing demands, such as in exercise. The rate and depth of breathing is determined by the frequency with the respiratory centre stimulates the appropriate muscles. **Ventilatory control** is governed by the respiratory centre in the brain, which stimulates a combination of chemical, nervous and hormonal changes that stimulate breathing:

- proprioceptors (see page 189) in the muscles and joints detect movement
- chemoreceptors inform the brain of excessive levels of carbon dioxide and insufficient oxygen at the working muscles and, as the most powerful respiratory stimulant, cause increases in respiration

Table 3.2 *Respiratory volumes and capacities for an average 20 year-old male*

Respiratory volumes	Value (ml)
Tidal volume	500
Inspiratory reserve volume	3100
Expiratory reserve volume	1200
Residual volume	1200

Respiratory capacity	Value (ml)
Total lung capacity	6000
Vital capacity	4800
Inspiratory capacity	3600
Functional residual capacity	2400

adapted from Marieb, 1999

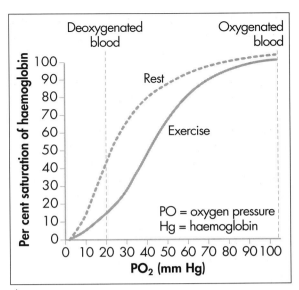

▲ **Figure 3.66** *Oxygen dissociation curve*

- other receptors can detect stressors such as emotional and pain stimuli and respiration can be controlled voluntarily for a short time
- stretch receptors in the lungs which respond to excessive inflation (possibly damaging to lung structures) by initiating inhibitory impulses. These stimulate expiration until the lungs recoil to safe size (Hering-Bruer Reflex)
- when stimulated, irritant receptors promote reflexes to keep the airway clear by means of coughing (such as caused by smoke or other air pollutants).

There are three main **respiratory volumes – tidal volume**, the volume inspired or expired per breath; **inspiratory reserve volume**, the maximal volume inspired from end-inspiration and **expiratory reserve volume**, the maximal volume expired from end expiration. These three main respiratory volumes vary according to the demand placed upon them by the conditions of inspiration and expiration. **Residual volume**, the volume remaining at the end of maximal expiration, remains the same, even after the most strenuous exercise, to prevent lung collapse.

Respiratory volumes and **capacities** for an average 20 year-old male (Table 3.2) demonstrate the range of lung volumes possible to accommodate the demands that may be placed on the lungs. Total lung capacity, in this table, is the volume in the lungs at the end of maximal inspiration; vital capacity is the maximal volume force-fully expired after maximal inspiration; inspiratory capacity is the maximal volume inspired from resting expiratory level, and functional residual capacity is the volume in the lungs at resting expiratory level. Lung volumes and capacities in women tend to be lower due to size difference in size.

Gaseous exchange

This occurs between the blood, lungs and tissues and is the term given to the movement of gases in opposite directions. Each gas, within a mixture of gases, exerts pressure which is equal to its percentage in that mixture (**partial pressure**). When oxygen pressure levels are highest, following its release from saturated oxy-haemoglobin (see Figure 3.66), it will be transported to areas of lower concentration – as would be the case in exercising muscle. **External respiration** is the process of gas exchange at the lungs. Oxygen passes

TASK

Carry out an investigation into heart rate, blood pressure and respiratory rate before exercise, during various levels of exercise and during recovery.

Write up your results, discussing and evaluating your findings in terms of the theoretical aspects of cardio-vascular and respiratory systems discussed in this section.

through the pulmonary capillaries and carbon dioxide leaves the blood and enters the lung alveoli. **Internal respiration** is the process of gas exchange between the systemic capillaries and the tissues. Carbon dioxide enters the blood and oxygen leaves the blood and enters the tissues.

Haemoglobin saturation, that is the combination of oxygen with haemoglobin to form oxy-haemoglobin in the red blood cells, is almost 100 per cent at the lungs. However, as the acidity in the blood increases towards the tissues (lower pH), caused by increased levels of carbon dioxide or lactic acid, the partial pressure of oxygen decreases. This causes oxygen to be released (dissociated) from the haemoglobin and released to the tissue.

This is known as **oxygen dissociation** (see Figure 3.66). As levels of carbon dioxide increase, pH lowers even more, thus allowing the oxygen to unload even quicker (Bohr effect). Only during very heavy exercise do blood carbon dioxide, oxygen and pH values change very much from their normal values. Measurement of the relative amounts of oxygen between arterial blood and venous blood (**arterio-venous difference**) indicate the efficiency of the uptake of oxygen at the muscle during exercise. At rest only about 25 per cent of oxygen consumed is actually used, whilst during intense activity this increases to approximately 80 per cent.

The effect of asthma on athletic performance is to restrict the passage of air through the bronchiole pathways and this can therefore inhibit performance. Use of steroid-based inhalers can relieve the restriction.

It is thought that after a period of training the brain 'learns' to match the rate of respiration with the intensity of the exercise. Well-trained individuals will therefore match their respiratory rates subconsciously to their physical exertions more efficiently than untrained individuals.

Adaptation of the CVR systems

As the intensity of exercise increases, it requires larger amounts of energy in the active working muscles. This necessitates the delivery of increased amounts of oxy-gen to the muscle. This demand is met via increased ventilation and through the blood. It is possible, in severe exercise, for 100 litres of air and 25 litres of blood to be 'exchanged' per minute. These are increases of roughly twelve and five times the respective resting requirements. As discussed on pages 191–92, the cardio-vascular and respiratory (CVR) systems are involved in these exchanges. In its quest for homeostatic balance, the body shows two kinds of responses to exercise:

- immediate, short-term responses that only last for the duration of the activity and the recovery itself
- longer-term adaptations (chronic effects) that are achieved after a period of exercise and training.

Building speed and endurance through continuous, Fartlek and interval training not only has effects on the musculo-skeletal system. It also accounts for differences before and after a training period in terms of the CVR systems:

- at rest
- during exercise (aerobic and anaerobic)
- in recovery.

The benefits of the long-term structural and functional adaptations to the CVR systems at rest, brought about by training, are as follows:

- **cardiac hypertrophy** occurs – the heart increases in size; endurance athletes develop larger chambers (particularly the left ventricle), whilst power athletes increase the thickness of the left ventricular wall. This affects the relative volume of the heart: the amount of blood that can pass through it relative to its overall size (the absolute heat volume) – see Figure 3.67.
- as a result of this hypertrophy, stroke volume increases; larger chambers and thicker walls mean improved extensibility and contractility – a greater blood volume is ejected each beat
- since the cardiac output required at rest is constant, increases in stroke

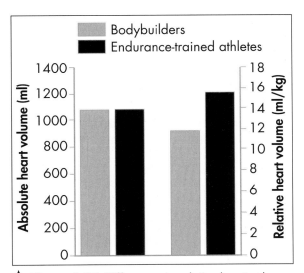

▲ **Figure 3.67** *Differences in relative heart volumes of élite bodybuilders and highly trained endurance athletes*

volume are accompanied by corresponding decreases in heart rate – known as **bradycardia** – with the resting heart rate below 60bpm; this is an indication of high fitness

- there is increased blood volume and haemoglobin – training stimulates increased plasma and red blood cell volumes, thus improving the effectiveness of O_2 delivery and waste removal
- blood pressure, particularly in those who previously had had high levels, reduces towards normal
- there are slight increases in all lung volumes as respiratory muscles become stronger and enhance an individual's pulmonary diffusion capacity
- there is increased capillarisation (blood flow) at the muscles.

Training effects

Training effects during *sub-maximal aerobic (steady state) exercise* compared to the period before training (at similar levels of exercise) are exhibited as follows:

- heart rate at a given level of exercise decreases – cardiac output remains fairly stable (due to cardiac hypertrophy or enlargement). Increases in stroke volume and lower heart rate lowers the overall exercise heart rate

- oxygen consumption (VO_2) decreases due to increased physiological and bio-mechanical efficiency – the body has to work less hard to do the same activity
- blood flow to muscles decreases as muscles extract more O_2 increasingly effectively from the blood
- the strengthening of the muscles involved in respiration improves lung function and assists in diffusion of blood via the pulmonary artery
- aerobic capacity increases as a result of the above effects.

Training effects during *maximal anaerobic exercise* compared to the period before training (at similar levels of exercise) are exhibited as follows:

- VO_2 max increases due to increased cardiac output and more efficient oxygen extraction from blood at the working muscles
- increases in cardiac output – as training reduces the maximal heart rate, increases in cardiac output are caused by increased stroke volume.

Recovery rates improve due to:

- enhanced cardiac, vascular and respiratory systems; increased capillarisation at muscle sites means that oxygen, nutrients (including glucose) are supplied more effectively to the muscles and waste products are removed
- blood flow to the skin improves, enhancing sweat production and the cooling of the body.

Regular endurance activities such as distance running can increase the blood plasma volume, making the blood more dilute. Blood tests on trained athletes indicate relatively lower platelet and red/white cell counts compared to untrained individuals. However, platelet and cell counts in endurance athletes should still remain within a normal range. If this is not the case, and blood cell counts are extremely low, it is likely that this is caused by a medical condition. An enlarged spleen is a common cause.

Table 3.3 *A comparison of cardio-vascular and respiratory factors affected by continuous training*

	Before training	After training	Élite athlete
HR at rest (bpm)	72	58	36
Vol. of blood leaving the heart (cm^3)	64	89	128
Max. vol. of blood leaving the heart (cm^3)	120	140	200
Heart vol. (cm^3)	750	850	1200
Breaths per min. (rest)	14	12	12
Max. no. of breaths per min. (rest)	40	45	55
Lung vol. (litres)	5.8	5.8	7.0
Resting vol. of O_2 absorbed by blood/min. in cm^3/kg of body mass	3.6	3.8	4.1
Max. vol. of O_2 absorbed by blood/min in cm^3/kg of body mass	40	50	77
Resting level of lactic acid in the blood in mg/$100cm^3$ of blood	20	20	20
Maximum tolerated level of lactic acid in the blood in mg/$100cm^3$ of blood	110	125	185

The overall effect of training cardio-vascular and respiratory systems is that there is more efficient delivery of oxygen to the working muscles, thus enhancing performance leading to better performance on aerobic tasks. CVR training effects are best developed by continuous, circuit and interval training methods.

Table 3.3 provides some indicative data on CVR factors affected by training.

Acclimatisation and altitude

Attempting endurance events in a hot and humid climate places the body under extreme stress. In order to perform under these conditions, the body must undergo **acclimatisation to heat**. Individuals will need to increase skin-blood flow to enable heat to be lost from conduction, convection and radiation. Thus, sweat rate may double from one litre per hour in normal temperate conditions to two litres per hour or more. In extreme heat conditions, the rate of heat loss may be 20 times that of normal conditions. Salt will be conserved far better, although such a high sweat rate clearly may lead to dehydration. At this extreme, sweating exceeds the digestive system's capacity to absorb water. An athlete can only attempt to remain hydrated by continually taking small amounts of water during activity and replacing lost fluids at the end of activity.

To acclimatise, an athlete should train in conditions that encourage the raising of core body temperature by more than 10°C for more than an hour. This is the temperature at which the body will begin to sweat freely. Heat adaptation can be encouraged by:

- training in a sauna
- training in extra layers of clothes
- wearing plastic bags during training.

Approximately 90 per cent acclimatisation can be achieved in this way within 10 days of such training.

At heights of about 1000m and above training produces **altitude training effects.** The reduced oxygen concentration (hypoxia) has the following effects as the body's homeostatic response tries to compensate for the relative lack of oxygen in the air:

- increased depth of breathing (tidal volume) and/or increased respiratory frequency

- levels of the critical enzymes of the aerobic system rise
- the number of red blood cells (haematocrit) increases
- haemoglobin concentration increases
- initial increases in heart rate return to normal after a few days.

It takes about 2–3 weeks for all these changes to fully manifest themselves. When an athlete moves back down towards sea level, they can perform at an advantage until the process of homeostasis reverts and they return to the previous physiological condition. Although there are clear benefits to altitude training, these are sometimes outweighed by the inability to train at high intensity, and by the possibility of mild altitude sickness. The current theory is that it is best to live and do low-intensity training at altitude, and travel down to lower altitudes for high-intensity training.

Altitude training will not be of benefit to the strength or power athlete. It is of most use to the endurance athlete. Those athletes born and living at altitude are at most advantage when competing at altitude. The longer-term adaptations they demonstrate are a result of their living conditions. Some athletes are now taking the opportunity to live in specially designed living facilities that mimic altitude conditions but are found at sea level. Thus they can live 'at altitude' but train in normal conditions.

Erythropoietin (EPO)

Erythropoietin (EPO) is a naturally occurring hormone produced by the kidneys, which stimulates the production of red blood cells in the body, such as occurs when training at altitude. Illegal use of the artificially manufactured recombinant EPO (RhEPO) mimics the effects of training at altitude, without the associated difficulties. However, this type of **blood doping** is a cause of much concern as the increase in haemaglobin causes the blood to become more viscous, slowing down circulation.

5. Measurement and evaluation of fitness components

The collation of physiological data regarding an individual's physical performance capabilities enables coaches and trainers to plan effective programmes that can maximize your opportunities for success. Measurement and evaluation by means of fitness testing engages both coach and sportsperson in setting specific fitness goals. These may be new performance targets or revisions made in the light of illness or injury (rehabilitation). **Fitness testing** is therefore a way of gathering information or monitoring components of fitness.

The setting for fitness testing

The modern élite sportsperson has the full back-up of expert physiologists at accredited testing facilities. Here the accuracy of results are rigidly enforced and analysed to assess performance. In the UK these testing

▲ **Figure 3.68** Fitness testing is a way of gathering information or monitoring components of fitness

TASK

Complete an investigation into your own physiological adaptation after a period of CVR training. This could include results from fitness tests and discussion of the types of exercise and training undertaken, with explanation for the changes that have/have not taken place.

facilities must meet stringent criteria laid down by Sport England. They must also be accredited by the British Association of Sport and Exercise Science (BASES) as part of a co-ordinated preparation programme for the élite athlete.

Field-based tests, outside the sports science laboratory, are clearly the most accessible and less costly approach to fitness testing. The range of tests available for A level Physical Education reflects this.

However, as a result, you need to be aware of how to gain the most effective and realistic results from such tests. Every test has an element of error, but the tester must minimise this. Laboratory tests reduce error but can lack specificity. So, it can be argued that as long as field tests are administered effectively, they provide a better measure of performance in a sports setting.

Other sports-specific performance tests may also be undertaken in various conditions that reflect the changing environments a sportsperson may have to perform in. Thus, performance itself may be assessed in the context of a range of environmental factors.

Testing in a performance situation, outside the confines of a sports testing facility, offers measurement in a realistic sporting environment. However, because of the nature of sporting competition this obviously restricts and limits the acquisition of accurate data.

The wider use of fitness testing

Fitness testing can also be used to educate and inform the public. Fitness, health and wellness centres use testing to inform participants of progress. It is also used to gain attention for their programmes by marketing successful gains in client fitness through publicity campaigns.

Testing of particular social groups by interested bodies such as the Health Education Authority (HEA) can indicate areas of public concern regarding the general health and fitness of these groups.

Fitness testing has also been used to identify talent in addition to supporting an individual's fitness development. In the early 1970s, the Soviet Union did not have a successful 100m sprinter who could challenge the world élite at that time. A search was undertaken amongst the Soviet Army to find someone suitable. The search (backed up by testing) produced a young captain, Valerie Borzov, who subsequently went on to compete successfully as an Olympic sprinter.

Similarly, in 1989, the Australian Institute of Sport in Canberra, identified 16 year-old Megan Still within their specially designed talent identification 'Sports Search' programme as a potential Olympic rower. In the Barcelona Olympics of 1992 she successfully competed in the final of the single sculls.

Reasons for testing

The following summary of reasons for testing is adapted from Wilkinson and Moore (1995):

- to highlight component strengths and weaknesses
- to evaluate training programmes as a benchmark for competition
- to measure performance after a return from injury or rest
- to assist in goal setting and encourage adherence to training
- to determine health status
- to determine the fitness demands of an activity
- to determine components that may limit performance
- to assist in overall profiling and to contribute to talent identification
- to provide feedback for performers.

Issues in testing

Determining the current physiological capacity of an individual enables a whole remit of performance measures to be undertaken on behalf of the sportsperson. Regular and controlled testing that follows published and recognised **test protocols** can indicate to the individual the current level of physiological performance to an agreed set of standards. Whilst measurement to these standards (norms) is useful, the key element for the élite individual is the monitoring of performance to enable structured measurable and progressive training programmes to be developed. Following the SMARTER principles of goal setting (see page 167), the coach or trainer can plan fitness and training programmes.

Physiological research studies can identify the essential characteristics needed for élite performance. However, they cannot assess *all* the qualities required to become a winner. Fitness testing is just one facet of assessing the likelihood of an individual becoming a champion performer.

Prior to any testing, an individual's current state of health and fitness should be assessed by means of a **Physical Activity Readiness Questionnaire (PARQ)**. Also the person being tested should give **prior consent** for tests to be undertaken.

KEY SKILLS

Using information technology, design and produce a PARQ for use within the group that would meet the criteria for Key Skills IT Level 3.

Test specificity

Test specificity means that the chosen test must be designed to assess an individual's fitness for the activity in question. For example, as Wilmore and Costill (1994) point out, subjects that followed a 10–week swim training programme showed an 11–18 per cent improvement in a swimming endurance test, but no improvement in treadmill endurance. It would therefore be of little use to reflect on treadmill data as an indication of fitness for swimmers.

Test validity

Do fitness tests always measure the characteristic that they are supposed to? **Test validity** considers the objective nature of testing. Since most fitness tests measure more than one thing and are affected by a range of factors, it is essential that, as far as possible, testing adheres to correct procedures or test protocols and are objective (Figure 3.69).

Test objectivity

An objective test must ensure that the key factors that may influence or distort results are taken into account (**test objectivity**).

Human error and opinion must not be allowed to influence testing. The agreed specific test protocol will have attempted to eliminate the elements which may produce inaccurate data. These include:

- use of efficient and accurate recording equipment
- adherence to the scoring methodology as laid down in the protocol
- elimination of external motivating elements (peers, crowd)
- controlled warm up
- choice and use of an appropriate test surface that is the same one used each re-test
- re-tests under the same conditions (same time of day, place, temperature etc.).

Test reliability

Test reliability considers whether or not a range of internal and external factors can influence the results. Can consistent results be achieved? If tests are not 100 per cent reliable, what influences will cause variation in our results?

Table 3.4 *Variations in heart rate response to running at 14kph on a treadmill with environmental alterations*

Environmental factor	Heart rate – rest (bpm)	Heart rate – exercise (bpm)
Temperature (50% humidity)		
21°C (70°F)	60	165
35°C (95°F)	70	190
Humidity (21°C)		
50%	60	165
90%	65	175
Noise level (21°C, 50% humidity)		
low	60	165
high	70	165
Food intake (21°C, 50% humidity)		
Small meal 3hr before exercising	60	165
Large meal 3hr before exercising	70	175

Wilmore and Costill, 1994

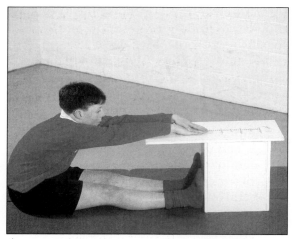

▲ **Figure 3.69** *Sit and reach: what are the validity issues in this test?*

A range of factors can affect test performance. These include:

- environmental factors such as weather, temperature, humidity, noise level (Table 3.4)
- personal factors or biological variance (health, diet, motivation/mood)
- prior test knowledge/experience
- test conditions – surface
- diurnal factors – time (Table 3.5)
- is the same tester used – are results the same if different testers are used?

The most reliable results are demonstrated with participants who completely understand the test procedures; have rehearsed

Table 3.5 *An example of diurnal variations in heart rate at rest and during various levels of exercise*

Time of day	2 am	6 am	10 am	2 pm	6 pm	10 pm
Condition	Heart rate (beats per minute)					
Resting	65	69	73	74	72	69
Light exercise	100	103	109	109	105	104
Moderate exercise	130	131	138	139	135	134
Maximal exercise	179	179	183	184	181	181
Recovery	118	122	129	128	128	125

Original data: Reilly and Brooks, 1990

Wilmore and Costill, 1994

or practised any difficult aspects of the test; have been prepared for the test in accordance with consistent guidelines (rest, food/water intake, warm up) and are aware and ready to be tested. Accuracy of testing can therefore be assisted by:

1 fully preparing the individual to be tested
2 comprehensively organising the test
3 paying close attention to the protocol of the test procedure.

Fitness measures with age
As we get older, some fitness tests are more appropriate and indeed safer than others. **Fitness measures with age** describes the need to select tests that are appropriate to use in consideration of a person's age.

Fitness tests
Regular laboratory or non-laboratory based fitness tests require careful monitoring to ensure validity and reliability are maintained. Non-laboratory tests form the basis of this level of study, although an appreciation of laboratory-based testing is useful. Correct protocols must be observed for tests using procedures identified in currently available texts. Measurement is made of both physical (health-related) and skill–related (motor) components.

Components of testing
Physical fitness components (see page 203) are those which allow us to perform everyday tasks without undue stress. In performance terms, these components (as with the skill components) vary in their importance according to the sport or activity concerned. Each component of physical fitness can be measured by using appropriate tests.

- **Strength** testing requires measurement using own body weight as a resistance or hand or back dynamometers to give measurement of the force generated within muscles. One repetition maximum (1R-M) can also be used.
- **Speed** can be measured using the 30m running test.
- **Power** can be measured using a specialised jump meter. Otherwise a standing broad jump or vertical

(Sergeant) jump measurement will suffice.

- **Local muscular (anaerobic) endurance** may be tested by performing chin-ups or abdominal curls in a set period of time.
- Anaerobic endurance may be assessed by means of the running based anaerobic test (RAST).
- **Cardio-vascular (aerobic) endurance** (VO_2 max.) can be assessed by means of a range of tests including the NCF multistage fitness test, the Queen's College Step Test or the Harvard Step Test.
- The sit and reach test or the shoulder reach test measure **flexibility** in the specified areas of practical assessment in Unit 2 (see page 100).

Skill-related components can be measured by a combination of tests which can be more subjective, without objective scoring/ results systems to measure performance against. **Co-ordination** and **balance** can both be assessed in variety of ways. Co-ordination may be judged by means of a double ball bounce or juggling. The stork/beam balance or wobble board can be used to test balance in either a static or dynamic (moving) situation. Measurement of **reaction time** can be made simply using a 'Kwik-Stik' or using a ruler drop test. **Agility** can be measured using the Illinois Agility Run.

Body composition can be estimated in a number of ways:

- the use of skin-fold callipers
- Magnetic Resonance Imagery (MRI)
- Bio-electrical Impedance Analysis (BIA).

Bio-electrical Impedance Analysis is the estimation of body fat percentage by the passing of safe (low) electrical currents through the body. It is based upon the principle that fat impedes the flow of electric current whereas fat-free (hydrated) mass is a good conductor of electricity. Commonly used tests of the various components of fitness are summarised in Table 3.6.

Table 3.6 Commonly used fitness performance tests with identified components

Fitness component	Fitness test
Strength	1 repetition max. (1 R-M)
	10 repetition max. (10 R-M)
Speed	30m sprint (running start)
	60m sprint
Power	Vertical jump (Sergeant jump)
	Standing broad jump
Local muscular endurance	Abdominal curl test
	Press-ups
Anaerobic endurance	Repeated sprints
	RAST
Cardiovascular aerobic endurance	Chester Step Test
	Harvard Step Test
	Cooper run
	NCF multistage shuttletest
Flexibility	Sit and reach
	Shoulder reach
Co-ordination	Double ball bounce
	Juggling
Balance	Stork/beam balance
	Wobble board
Reaction time	Ruler drop
	'Kwik-Stik'
Agility	Illinois Agility Run
Body composition	Skin-fold callipers
	MRI
	BIA

TASK

Perform a range of tests and produce a performance profile for your sport, matching the required components with your own results.

These results could then be discussed by your group in order to develop a training programme that will enable physiological improvements to be made.

▲ **Figure 3.70** *Active recovery – a change is as good as a rest!*

6. Planning of fitness and training programmes

Exercise and training programmes are about preparing the body so it is able to tolerate the changes that occur during the stimulus or stress of exercise. Someone who is trained can perform exercise at levels that do not easily cause fatigue and at more intense levels of exercise with reduced stress levels on the body.

Exercise is a positive stress stimulus when it allows the body to adapt and become healthy and stronger. It can, however, be a negative stimulus when performed incorrectly or if it causes injury or sickness. This can happen by **over-training.** The dynamic nature of homeostasis (see page 162) is demonstrated as the body adapts itself to the disruption of exercise in an attempt to maintain a constant physiological equilibrium or environment.

Training principles

The overload principle describes the need to impose workloads in training that make the body do more than it normally does at rest. As the body adapts and shows physiological improvements, additional training workloads can be undertaken.

Progressive overload

Progressive overload is a gradual increase in workload that leads to physical adaptation according to the intensity, duration and type of training undertaken. As previously discussed, the training stimulus describes the process of disrupting homeostasis by exercise and training.

Recovery

Gains in fitness are produced not only in training. Only during the subsequent rest intervals prior to the next training session will the benefits be demonstrated. Rest and **recovery** can take several forms. Aerobic runs or cross-training activities such as cycling can allow the body rest if they are not too demanding and different from the normal high intensity training activities (Figure 3.70). Such work should be performed at a level well below normal training and competition activity.

The use of a heart rate monitor allows you to consider variations in resting heart

▲ **Figure 3.71** *Practising on the beach!*

rate that may indicate insufficient recovery from a previous training session or competition, or even the onset of illness. Similarly, such monitors may allow you to regulate the training load to a set percentage of maximum capacity. This can prevent the unnecessary overload of an already stressed body (see 'Over-training'). Rest must be a key feature of any training programme.

Specificity

As already discussed on page 201, the design of exercise and training programmes must be specific to the sport or activity to be undertaken (Figure 3.71). **Specificity** means that not only must training be sports-specific (i.e. relevant to the demands of that sport) but the relevant components of fitness must be trained appropriately and at the relevant time of the competitive season. For example, basic training or general aerobic-based training underpins pre-season training for most team sports. Quite often intensive skill-related work is needed so that 're-learning' can take place as fitness and strength levels improve. In basketball, a player who can jump higher after training needs to adjust jump-shooting technique to allow for release at a greater height than before.

Reversibility and moderation

Reversibility concerns the effects of de-training. If you take too long to rest or recover between exercise bouts or sessions, the physiological adaptations you have gained will be lost. This is because the homeostatic mechanism readjusts the body's systems to the decreased demands being placed upon it. This is also called regression.

Through **moderation** of training, the training and recovery periods are balanced to allow the body sufficient time for recovery without losing the benefits of training.

TASK

Using a range of fitness training texts and information from other sources, report on the recommended programmes specific to your chosen sport. Produce a word-processed summary sheet.

Over-training

Long periods of intense training with poor and/or little recovery will lead to conditions of over-training or burn-out. Physiological indicators of over-training may appear as:

- increased resting heart rate
- rapid unexplained weight loss
- prolonged loss of appetite
- excessive muscle fatigue or soreness
- susceptibility to injury
- frequent colds, infections, allergic reactions
- sleep disturbances
- lack of motivation to train.

FITT principles

The acronym **FITT (frequency, intensity, time** (or **duration**), **type)** embodies the basic principles of fitness training. How often, how hard, for how long and what type of training is appropriate or required by the individual to perform more effectively? The many texts on training recommend a range of programmes for the components of fitness based on these principles.

Continuous training

A practical example of continuous training includes long slow distance running (LSD). By establishing **target training zones** (see below), an individual can exercise or train at the most relevant intensity. By varying these training zones from day to day, not only are you allowing recovery from more intensive runs, but also challenging your body to improve.

Target training zones

Target training zones were first presented by the Finnish physiologist Karvonen (Figure 3.72). They are based on **Karvonen's principle** of working at a given percentage of maximum heart rate in relation to an individual's age. The basic formula for calculating maximum heart rate (HR) is:

$$\text{max. HR} = 220 - \text{age}$$

The heart rate calculated using this formula is then used to estimate the heart rate percentage training load for the individual. The American College of Sports Medicine (ACSM) recommends a range of intensities of exercise for healthy adults:

- 30–49% of heart rate maximum for light intensity
- 50–69% for moderate intensity
- 70–84% for hard intensity
- >85% for high intensity

The ACSM figures above are lower than when first published in 1978. This is to account for the distinction now being made between health and fitness. The quantity and quality of exercise needed for an adult to gain health-related benefits differs from that which may be recommended to improve sports specific fitness.

Calculation of heart rate training zones, which takes into account individual differences in resting heart rate, would be as follows:

- find your maximum heart rate by subtracting your age from 220 (for men) and 226 (for women)
- multiply by the appropriate percentage training zone (max HR × 0.7 for 70%)
- add your resting heart rate which will give you your 70% level
- repeat this for the other heart rate training zones

There are different physiological gains to be made with each training zone. An understanding of how you will benefit is essential in planning training. Further understanding of exercise and energy systems is required to appreciate fully the physiological benefits (see Unit 6A, page 373). However, the following guidelines are useful:

- light intensity activity (30–49% HR max) is aerobic, 'energy efficient' and also useful as a recovery zone
- moderate intensity (50–69%) activity trains the CVR systems, improving aerobic capacity, has fat burning capacity and helps develop muscle strength
- hard intensity (70–84%) activity develops the anaerobic threshold and through correct training enables the onset of blood lactate (OBLA) to be delayed. Speed and power are improved with this level of exercise
- high intensity activity – beyond 85% – is only possible for a short period of time. A high level of fitness is required to train at this level. By training fast twitch fibres at high intensity level, speed is enhanced.

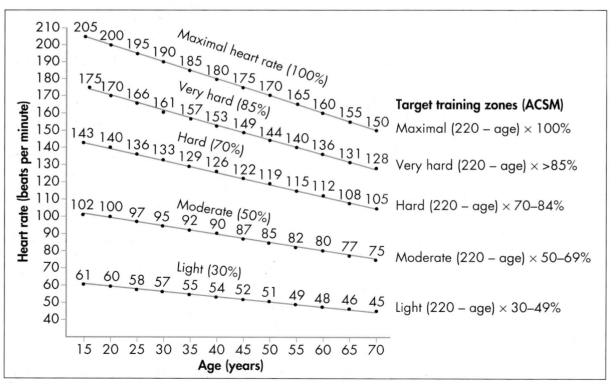

▲ **Figure 3.72** *Recommended target heart rate training zones (American College of Sports Medicine)*

Components of fitness

Designing and implementing exercise, training or conditioning programmes requires knowledge of the different components of fitness that will specifically improve performance in a particular sport.

Strength

Strength is the ability of a muscle or group of muscles to exert a maximum force during a single maximal contraction. Resistance training – pushing or pulling against a load – builds strength over a period of time. However, the role of strength varies in different activities and sports. A variety or different qualities of strength are required in a range of sporting activities (Table 3.7).

Maximum strength involves the production of high forces during a given movement of unlimited length. This strength quality is common to all others and is the foundation of any strength training.

Explosive (dynamic) strength involves the production of high forces in a minimal amount of time. **Reactive strength** involves high force production where the active muscles first stretch then contact.

Sustained strength involves the ability to maintain maximal forces over several repeated contractions or throughout a single contraction of long duration (static strength).

Strength endurance involves the ability to sustain this high force over several minutes of continuous activity.

Speed

Speed can be defined as the capacity to move either limbs or the whole body at the greatest possible velocity. Speed can be described as any one or a combination of the following:

- **maximum speed**
- **elastic strength (power)**
- **speed endurance.**

Running speed can also be expressed as:

stride length × stride frequency

Thus athletes with longer limbs tend to have an advantage mechanically. Flexibility and correct warm up will also enhance stride length and frequency. Correct development of muscular strength, power, strength endurance and running technique will further enable improvement of speed.

Speed is measured in metres per second or as the time taken to complete a task. Speed is the key factor in explosive sports and relies on anaerobic energy pathways.

Power

Power is defined as:

strength × speed

Power to weight ratio describes strength relative to an individual's body weight. For

Table 3.7 *Range of strength qualities for different activities/sports*

Maximum strength e.g. power lifting, wrestling	**Explosive strength** e.g. kicking a football **Reactive strength** e.g. impact of running
Sustained strength e.g. repeated pushing in rugby maul	**Strength endurance** e.g. road cycling, triathlon, marathon

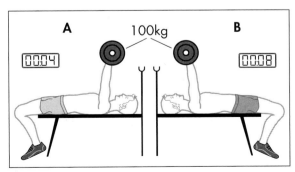

▲ **Figure 3.73** *Athlete A has twice the power of Athlete B because he can bench press 100kg in half the time.*

example, a weightlifter could lift a considerable weight above his head – much greater than anything a gymnast could lift. However, the gymnast could put a weightlifter to shame in a chin-up competition.

If the weightlifter had the same relative strength as the gymnast it is estimated that he could lift 3 to 4 times the world record for the clean and jerk!

Local muscular endurance

Local muscular endurance accounts for the ability of the individual to exercise muscle groups and repeat movements without fatigue.

Cardio-vascular endurance

Cardio-vascular endurance (**aerobic endurance**) is required for aerobic or endurance sports and is concerned with the ability of the CVR systems to supply oxygen and other nutrients to the working muscles (see page 196).

Anaerobic endurance

Anaerobic endurance is the length of time that we can exercise at high intensity whilst tolerating increasing levels of lactic acid in our muscles.

The **anaerobic threshold** (also known as the point of deflection – POD) is the point at which lactic acid build-up begins to restrict muscular performance. This is measured in terms of lactic acid content in the blood. Resting levels of lactic acid are around 0.5–1.0mmol/l. Élite endurance runners can sustain levels as high as 4–8mmol/l for up to one hour, whilst élite power athletes can sustain levels of 25mmol/l for very short periods of time. The generally identified threshold (the point at which lactic acid accumulation starts to inhibit the working muscles) is around 4mmol/l.

Calculation of the anaerobic threshold by collection of blood lactic samples to estimate the onset of blood lactate (OBLA) uses sophisticated scientific apparatus in a laboratory environment. Laboratory analysis of the anaerobic threshold involves increasing the level of intensity of exercise (usually on a treadmill), and measuring the blood lactic acid level, work output and heart rate at each level. By determining the heart rate or work output at which blood lactic acid levels begin to rise and accumulate, an individual's anaerobic threshold can be established.

It is possible to estimate the anaerobic threshold without such equipment, for example using the running–based anaerobic test (RAST).

Other components of fitness

The ability to change or alter direction as quickly as possible without losing control is described as **agility**. This is essential in team games.

Co-ordination considers the individual's ability to perform tasks by moving under control, quickly, accurately and effectively.

In the fitness contest, **balance** is the ability to maintain body mass over the base of support whilst either remaining still (static) or moving (dynamic).

Reaction time is the time it takes for a person to initiate a muscular response to a given signal or stimulus.

Flexibility is described as increasing the length and flexibility of the soft tissues, especially muscles and tendons, but also the ligaments, nerves and skin by stretching.

Mobility considers the range of motion (ROM) at a joint.

Body composition

This describes the relative percentage of muscle, fat and bone within the body's make-up. **Body composition** has two basic components:

1 body fat (essential fat) or accumulated adipose tissue fat (storage fat)
2 lean body mass or the fat-free mass, including the mass of other tissues such as muscle, bone and skin.

Body composition analysis is a suitable tool for the assessment of a person's fitness. The simplest method of measurement is self-evaluation by means of measurement of skin-folds.

Body mass index (BMI) is calculated as follows:

$$\frac{weight}{height^2}$$

So, for example:

$$\frac{90\text{kg}}{1.86\text{cm}^2} = \frac{90\text{kg}}{3.4596\text{cm}} = \text{BMI of } 26.01$$

According to the Department of Health, if the resultant value is greater than 30, then the subject is obese.

Women have, on average, around 25 per cent and men around 15 per cent body fat ratio. A trained female may reduce this to as little as 18 per cent whilst a male can reduce this to 5 per cent.

An individual's body fat percentage (body fat ratio) can have a variety of effects for the individual sportsperson. For many sports excess body fat is clearly a disadvantage as this excess (dead) weight creates an extra load and therefore a mechanical disadvantage. Jockeys, who often need to keep themselves underweight, may have a body fat ratio as little as 5 per cent.

However, for some, body fat can be an advantage. In high contact sports, such as rugby, fat adds protection to the bruising physical encounters. A forward may have a body fat ratio of around 15 per cent. Fat also provides buoyancy in aquatic activities and has value as an energy store in endurance activities. Ultimately, the body composition of an individual should be appropriate for optimal performance in the activity to be undertaken.

TASK

Identifying the components of fitness required for your selected sport and suggest reasons for your choices.

Methods of training

The Edexcel PE specification for Unit 3 requires you to consider continuous and interval training methods with regard to developing the musculo-skeletal system and the cardio-vascular and respiratory systems. Obviously, a combination of training methods has an effect on a range of body systems, but specific training methods should be adopted to focus on the main component of fitness to be conditioned.

The American College of Sports Medicine (ACSM) recommend intensities for resistance-type exercise that can be found on pages 205–206.

Interval training

In **interval training**, the exercise period is punctuated by a period of rest. **Circuit training** and stage circuits are both frequently used forms of interval training.

Interval training is based on the idea that the variables of training are manipulated to provide stimulus for a range of body systems and energy systems to be stressed. ('Stress' here is the physiological term meaning overload or a body or energy system.) These variables include:

- speed or intensity of the exercise period
- the amount of time taken on each exercise
- duration of the interval (rest) period
- the number of repetitions of an exercise
- the number of sets in the training session
- the type of exercise or activity undertaken.

Sprint training is an explosive form of interval training that develops whole body or limb speed. There are several ways an individual can 'sprint train'. **Hollow sprints** are punctuated by a lowering of speed i.e. sprint/jog/sprint/jog etc. over set distances. **Repetition sprints** are undertaken over a set distance in a set time with a set recovery, e.g. 10 × 100m in 14.5 seconds with 45 seconds' recovery. **Acceleration sprints** are based on increasing sprinting speed over a set distance, e.g. 50m at half speed, next 25m at three-quarter speed, final 25m at full speed. **Resistance sprint training** involves running with some form of resistance provided. This may be in the form of running parachutes, heavy motor tyres or even running in sand.

Fartlek

Fartlek (Swedish for 'speed-play') developed in the 1930s as a means of providing variety on training runs of a duration of over 40 minutes. Fartlek offers freedom from consideration of time and distance where the individual can run whatever distance and speed they wish, varying the intensity, and occasionally running at high intensity levels.

Plyometrics

Plyometrics is based upon the need for those sports requires power (strength and speed combined) to develop specific training methods which enhance these components effectively. Bounding, jumping and hopping have long been used to improve explosive movements.

Plyometrics describes the rapid and excessive eccentric contractions of muscles as such exercises are performed. By following a concentric contraction quickly with an eccentric contraction, the forces generated dramatically increase and the movement is more powerful. Much of the energy required to stretch a muscle is lost as heat, but some of it is stored by the muscle and can be used immediately in a subsequent contraction (stretch shortening cycle).

Plyometric exercises must be specific to the requirements of the sport. Exercises such as low hurdle jumps and low drop jumps develop stretch (elastic) strength, whilst standing long jumps, and high hurdle jumps develop concentric strength and high drop jumps develop eccentric strength.

Lower and upper body exercises include:

- bounding/hopping exercise – over-sized striding (bounding) gives extra time in the air followed by one-legged hopping
- drop jumping exercise – the individual drops (not jumps) to the ground from a set height (pre-stretch) and then immediately jumps (concentric contraction), with the exercise being more effective the less time feet are in contact with the ground on landing. The height of drop should be between 30–80cm, with greater height placing greater loading on the drop. This is a form of high impact plyometrics
- medicine ball plyometric training, using a variety of ball weights, can help to develop explosive movements in both the lower and upper body.

Extreme forces are placed on the musculo-skeletal system by plyometric training. It is therefore important that individuals are sufficiently free from any injury and have good strength and endurance before undertaking this form of training.

Continuous training

Any form of training in which the individual exercises in a steady aerobic way can be described as **continuous training**. **Long slow distance (LSD) training** places the emphasis on distance rather than speed. The individual rarely exceeds a training load of 60 per cent to 80 per cent of maximum heart rate and distance ranges from between 15 and 30 miles a day. It is used by those who want to improve endurance for health reasons, or for general endurance conditioning either during the competition phase or off-season to maintain condition.

LSD provides a means of endurance training for the development of general stamina and places less strain on the cardio-vascular and respiratory conditions than more intensive forms of training. It is therefore a form of exercise that is suitable for older people, although it should be noted that extreme distances can place strain on musculo-skeletal structures.

Skill training

Skill training develops the sports-specific components of fitness. It combines the movements of the sport with the training of the components required for that action. Skill circuits can introduce a competitive edge to training that brings variety and motivation to sessions.

TASK

Design a skills circuit for a sport of your choice identifying the specific skills to be developed and detailing the equipment required for the circuit to take place.

Individual differences

Even when sportspeople train as hard as one another, there are clear differences in performance. Some people seem to be faster, some show more endurance, others are stronger. This is because we are not all equal – there are individual differences between us all.

Our anatomy and physiology is basically the same, but the small differences that exist between each individual and the way that we train can combine to make a huge difference in the sporting arena. Understanding the fundamentals of human anatomy and how we exercise and train can have a significant impact on our performance.

In terms of exercise and training, individual differences may be explained as measures of physical performance comparing **trained and untrained** individuals, **males and females** and having regard for **age**. A range of notable physiological differences may be exhibited across rest, exercise and during recovery. (See Figure 3.74.)

People of a similar age can exhibit maximum heart rates which vary by as much as −/+10 beats. Maximum heart rates also vary between gender – females tend to have higher resting heart rates, therefore allowance needs to be made for a decrease in maximum heart rate. This is also the case with age. The heart rate decreases about 10 beats for every 10 years. Thus, when calculating heart rate training zones, it is clear that these figures are only estimations.

Trained sportspeople and untrained (sedentary) individuals demonstrate a range of physiological performance differences. These differences have previously been identified by comparing the effects of training (before and after a period of training).

The anaerobic threshold (see page 205) of an average, untrained person is about 60–70 per cent of maximum heart rate. Well-trained élite endurance athletes can have an anaerobic threshold heart rate as high as 90 per cent of maximum capacity.

While aerobic capacity (VO_2 max) indicates endurance capacity, it is not always possible to determine the finishing order of an endurance race by VO_2 max values alone. An individual can still improve running times after reaching their VO_2 max peak. Wilmore and Costill (1994) estimated that most marathon runners complete the race at between 75 and 80 per cent of their VO_2 max. More successful marathon run-

ners will be able to race at a percentage higher than 80% of their VO_2 max – in fact, nearer to the 90 per cent mark previously stated. It would therefore appear that both VO_2 max and the percentage of VO_2 max that an individual is able to maintain are the crucial factors in performance.

The anaerobic threshold is the point at which exercise has increased to such an intensity that energy can no longer be supplied aerobically and must be supplied by the anaerobic energy systems (see Unit 6A, pages 379–84).

This occurs when ventilation cannot match the demand for oxygen by working muscles. As exercise intensity increases to maximum, ventilation will, at some point, increase without a corresponding increase in oxygen consumption. During steady-state exercise, ventilation will match the energy demands of the exercise. The point

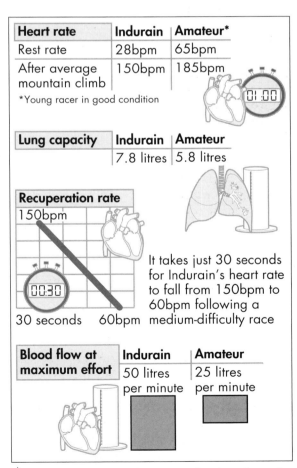

Heart rate	Indurain	Amateur*
Rest rate	28bpm	65bpm
After average mountain climb	150bpm	185bpm

*Young racer in good condition

Lung capacity	Indurain	Amateur
	7.8 litres	5.8 litres

Recuperation rate
150bpm
30 seconds   60bpm

It takes just 30 seconds for Indurain's heart rate to fall from 150bpm to 60bpm following a medium-difficulty race

Blood flow at maximum effort	Indurain	Amateur
	50 litres per minute	25 litres per minute

▲ **Figure 3.74** Miguel Indurain: the physiology of a supreme athlete at which ventilation increases but oxygen consumption is no longer sufficient to meet the oxygen requirements of the muscles is known as the ventilatory breakpoint. Ventilatory breakpoint indicates a respiratory response to increasing levels of carbon dioxide in the blood. At this point the body starts to provide energy anaerobically.

The ability to delay this move to anaerobic energy production relies on the ability of the body to supply oxygen sufficiently. Differences in the fitness of the CVR structures, combined with the development of the musculo-skeletal structures, can account for the greater performance of some individuals over others. The anaerobic threshold can be expressed in terms of the percentage of VO_2 max at which it occurs. Thus an anaerobic threshold of 60 per cent of VO_2 max would indicate a greater performance potential for the same VO_2 max than an anaerobic threshold of 45 per cent VO_2 max. A higher percentage of VO_2 max indicates that an individual can work at higher aerobic levels of exercise before having to rely on the limiting anaerobic energy systems.

Women athletes

Today women are performing and competing at increasingly higher levels than ever before. In virtually every competitive sport women have demonstrated dramatic improvements relative to their male counterparts.

That female performances are rapidly catching up to males' is particularly evident in endurance events such as the marathon. Until 1984, women were not even allowed to compete in the Olympic marathon due to the mistaken belief that a woman's body could not sustain the physiological demands being placed upon it.

Current research indicates that, in fact, female physiology may actually be better suited than male physiology to endurance-orientated events. Essentially, women are also running faster in events where the efficiency of fuel storage and the use of energy is paramount. An approximation of such improvements is given in Table 3.8.

Puberty

At puberty, the secretion of hormones promotes the development of male and female characteristics. In females, physiological changes that occur at puberty include:

- development of sexual characteristics
- physiological and anatomical changes associated with pregnancy/childbirth, such as pelvic tilt/adjustment, broadening of hips
- start of the menstrual cycle
- early growth spurt of bones that does not last as long as that of males (males grow longer for longer!)
- increased water content/retention

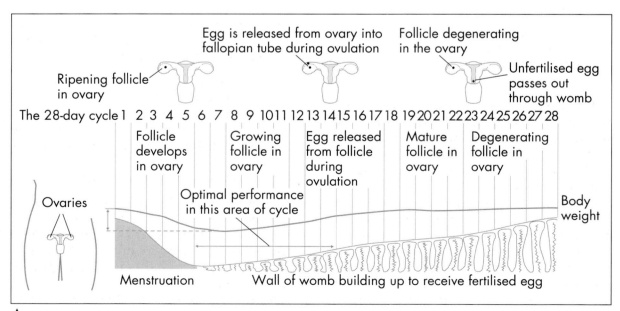

▲ **Figure 3.75** Menstruation and the time of optimal performance

Table 3.8 *1500m average speed records (km/h and mph)*

	1920	1997
Male	23.5	26.0
	14.6	16.2
Female	17.0	23.5
	10.6	14.6

- decreased sebaceous gland secretion (reducing possibility of acne)
- increases in fatty tissue on thighs and hips.

In terms of strength related to the size of the cross-sectional area of only muscle tissue, men and women are largely equal, except for the fact that women possess a higher fat content and men possess higher testosterone levels. These factors combine to give men a higher cross-sectional area.

At, and after, puberty, the hypothalamus stimulates the process by which the female hormones, oestrogen and progesterone, are released. These hormones stimulate the female reproductive system and initiate menstruation. This is the cycle of changes that occurs in the tissue lining of a woman's womb. It culminates approximately every 28 days when the blood-enriched lining of the womb is released as the menstrual flow (Figure 3.75). Menstruation places the female athlete under additional stress.

During menstruation sportswomen may be affected by:

- changes in strength–weight ratio
- femur to tibia alignment
- metabolic changes
- iron deficiency due to loss of blood.

Some research suggests that sportswomen may need to take certain drugs to adjust the menstrual cycle to optimise performance at the key time in the menstrual cycle. However, the long-term effects on the female body of doing this has not been fully studied.

Special focus in recent years has been on the so-called 'female triad'. This is the unhealthy combination of disorders associated with disordered diet (anorexia nervosa and bulimia nervosa); amenorrhea (abnormal absence of menstruation); and osteoporosis (loss of protein from the bone matrix resulting in porosity or brittleness of bone). Young athletes appear to be most at risk. A combination of excessive dieting, poor nutrition (including iron deficiency and salt imbalance) and other such factors have direct implications for the wellbeing of female athletes.

Any exercise undertaken during pregnancy must take into consideration that pregnancy itself places strain on the female body. However, studies have shown that exercise places no undue strain on the foetus by either depriving it of oxygen or causing distress. The latter has been determined by studies undertaken to assess the foetal heartbeat whilst mothers-to-be were exercising.

General practitioners give advice to those who wish to exercise through pregnancy by issuing the following general guidelines through the British Medical Association (BMA):

- avoid exhaustive exercise
- aerobic exercise is advised
- avoid exercise in heat
- drink plenty of fluids
- use regular not intermittent exercise
- decrease levels near the birth (last three months)
- beware of the danger signs.

Clearly, the individual needs are assessed by the woman's doctor, but there is no suggestion that a well-structured exercise programme during pregnancy is not reasonable and safe to pursue within the given guidelines.

For males, puberty sees the increasing activity of the male hormone, testosterone, responsible for the development of:

- male sexual characteristics
- male emotional profile
- increased synthesis and deposition of protein in skeletal muscle allowing greater gains in strength during puberty than in females
- maturation of the long bones.

In both males and females, the largest gains in flexibility are estimated to occur between the ages of seven and twelve (**pre-adolescence**). As a child grows, they develop better co-ordination and agility due to development of the nervous system.

From birth through to **adolescence** there is a steady increase in muscle mass that is mirrored with increases in weight. The acceleration in muscle mass in boys occurs at puberty due to increasing testosterone levels. Differences between boys and girls are only accounted for here by the male hormone levels and the increasing levels of oestrogen in girls promoting body fat deposits. Fat cells form and fatty deposits accumulate from the early development of the foetus.

Evidence suggests that the number of fat cells becomes constant during the adolescence. Since fat cells can increase in size at any age it is thought that by keeping the total fat content of the body low during this period of time the number of fat cells can be minimised, reducing the risk of extreme obesity in later life.

The degree of fat accumulation with growth and **ageing** is dependent on the diet and exercise habits of the individual. While hereditary status cannot be changed, diet and exercise can be manipulated to decrease fat stores and improve muscle mass. At birth, body weight is around 12–14 per cent fat. This reaches around 15 and 25 per cent respectively at maturity in males and females.

Care needs to be taken when planning programmes of training for young sportspeople, particularly pre-adolescents. Moderation of some aspects of training is required to avoid placing relatively immature physical structures, such as developing bones, under undue stress.

In adolescence, the body will respond to dedicated and intense training during puberty. A well-planned resistance training programme, using the correct techniques that have been modified or adjusted to the individual persons is considered safe. Specific guidelines or rules are suggested to prevent injury. Growth spurts at puberty require modifications to resistance training programmes. The spine and joints should not be placed under undue strain since the forces compact on both the spinal column and the joint bony structures which are more pliable during growth spurts. Similarly, plyometrics and ballistic exercises are not recommended. The volume of any weight should be closely monitored. The use of heavy resistance exercises with weights for younger individuals should be avoided.

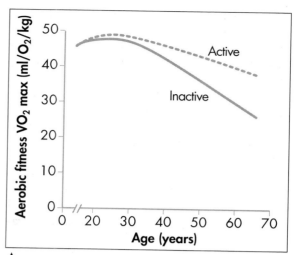

▲ **Figure 3.76** *Age and aerobic fitness: an active lifestyle minimises the fitness decline normally associated with age*

Ageing and fitness

After about 20 years of age, the ageing process begins to affect flexibility. In **adult** life, older people can minimize the fitness decline normally associated with ageing if an active lifestyle is maintained (Figure 3.76). Fitness components do deteriorate as people grow older, but a degree of this deterioration arises from the fact that adults, for a whole range of reasons, exercise less as they get older and become increasingly inactive and sedentary.

Older people who do not maintain an active lifestyle may see greater deterioration in the following aspects than those continuing to maintain regular fitness patterns in their lifestyle:

- loss of flexibility and mobility – ageing of connective tissues makes soft tissue more resistant to stretching
- muscular hydration decreases, resulting in the decline of nutrient delivery and the loss of joint lubrication.

Older individuals should avoid high intensity, short burst exercise, such as sprinting. Exercise such as this places undue strain on key physiological structures, putting the wellbeing of the individual at risk. Suitable exercise, including strength training, stretching and movement-related activities, along with diet and hormones, can maintain and improve the condition of the bones and joints.

Decreases in lean body weight (decreased muscle mass) and reduced mineral content of bones are due in part to lower levels of physical activity in older age. Similarly, increased dietary intake and reduced levels of exercise do not allow the mobilisation or usage of fat stores in the body.

Studies of older individuals have shown that strength in regularly used muscle groups declines very slowly. Exercise also promotes bone growth in this age group which is increasingly affected by osteoporosis (bone thinning). It also offers potential benefits to the cardio-vascular and respiratory (CVR) systems.

Isometric exercises should be avoided by the older age group. This is due to the unusually large increases in blood pressure associated with isometric contractions, which could cause serious cardio-vascular complications. Older people should progress slowly in the early stages of their exercise programme to reduce the potential for stiffness and soreness. Stretching and flexibility exercises are of particular importance to alleviate joint and muscular problems, which develop more frequently later in life.

Avoiding stereotypical images of the older population, Smith and Gilligan (1987) classified this generation in the following way:

- *athletic old* >55 years with good fitness
- *young old* >55 years with moderate fitness
- *old old* >75 years with very low fitness.

This approach seems to be a sensible one when designing exercise programmes. Obviously the degree of activity needs to be tailored to the individual but some general guidelines are appropriate here.

Those in the *athletic old* group may indeed be able to cope with modified activities that are relevant for an average young adult. Those in the *young old* category should exercise large muscle groups at low intensity levels. Activities such as swimming, walking and cycling are advisable.

The *old old* require activities that demand the appropriate low level of cardio-respira-tory fitness that they possess. Activities are done sitting or standing with support.

Performance-related planning
Periodisation

Periodisation is the concept of dividing the training programme into periods or blocks. It is therefore a way of organising an individual's exercise and training. Each block or period is designed to prepare a specific component of performance. Periodised training programmes consist of **microcycles** and **mesocycles**.

A microcycle is a specially designed training block of 7–21 days aimed at preparing a specific component of fitness or performance to meet the goals of the longer mesocycle and **macrocycle** training blocks. There is daily and weekly variation in the frequency/volume (type of exercise/amount of exercise in terms of repetitions/sets, distance and duration), and intensity (load, force, weight lifted and speed).

The mesocycle is an intermediate training block made up of a number of microcycles. It is designed to meet the objectives of the larger macrocycle. Mesocycles last 1–4 months.

A macrocycle can be described as a long-term training block (12 months – 4 years). It is used to develop a major fitness or overall (long-term) performance goal.

These periods of training may include a speed development period, a strength training period, a skill development period or a recovery period. For the competitive sportsperson this is linked with the need to peak for performance at key events or competitions.

TASK

Devise and implement a training or exercise programme for a sport or activity of your choice, incorporating the main topics in this section.

You may decide to focus on specific aspects of your own performance by producing an individual performance profile identifying areas for development.

Records should be kept showing test results and their application to the design of the programme. This could then be added to your Individual Performance Portfolio (IPP).

Key words and phrases

1. Introduction

• Homeostasis   • Exercise stimulus or stress   • Recovery

2. Immediate effects of exercise – a practical introduction

• Fight or flight   • Skills practice   • Static stretching   • Ballistic stretching
• Active stretches   • SEAM   • Passive stretches   • Dynamic   • Stretch reflex
• PNF   • Golgi tendon organs (Gtos)   • Muscle spindles   • Myotatic
• Inverse stretch reflex   • Reciprocal innervation   • Range of motion (ROM)
• Mobility   • Physical Activity Readiness Questionnaire (PARQ)   •SMARTER
• Physiological changes   • Anticipatory effects   • Heart rate
• Depth and rate of ventilation   • Blood flow patterns   • Aerobic capacity
• Anaerobically   • Heat generation

3. Musculo-skeletal structures in action

• Gross musculo-skeletal structures   • Connective tissues   • Skeletal muscle
• Smooth muscle   • Cardiac muscle   • Fascia   • Endomysium   • Fasciculi
• Perimysium   • Epimysium   • Parallel   • Strap-like   • Fusiform   • Pennate
• Unipennate   • Bipennate   • Convergent   • Circular   • Muscle size
• Hypertrophy   • Muscle length   • Muscle fibre type   • Slow twitch   • Fast twitch
• Muscle fibre type proportions   • Suitability   • Effects of training fibre type
• Bone types   • Cartilage types   • Fibrous   • Hyaline   • Elastic   • Posture
• Muscle tone   • Postural defects   • Effects of exercise
• Short-term responses   • Long-term adaptations   • Muscle fatigue
• Static flexibility   • Dynamic flexibility   • Resistance training
• Hypo-kinetic disorders   • Muscular contraction   • Isotonic muscle action
• Concentric   • Prime mover   • Agonist   • Eccentric   • Antagonist
• Isotonic muscle contraction   • Isokinetic   • Fixators   • Synergists   • Kinesiology
• Immovable/fibrous joints   • Slightly movable/cartilaginous joints
• Freely movable/synovial joints   • Anterior and posterior cruciate ligaments
• Fibular collateral ligament   • Medial collateral ligament   • Menisci
• Medial and lateral menisci   • Synovial fluid/capsule   • Bursae   • Proprioception

4. The circulatory, vascular and respiratory (CVR) systems in action

• Cardiac cycle   • Cardiac diastole   • Cardiac systole   • Negative feedback control
• Cardiac output   • Stroke volume   • Vascular shunting   • Vasomotor centre
• Blood pressure   • Systolic pressure   • Diastolic pressure   • Blood plasma volume
• Red blood cell (RBC) count   • Haemoglobin   • Haematocrit   • Myoglobin
• Mitochondria   • Venous return   • Starling's Law   • Ventilatory control
• Respiratory volumes   • Tidal   • Inspiratory reserve   • Expiratory reserve
• Residual volume   • Capacities   • Partial pressure   • External respiration
• Internal respiration   • Oxygen dissociation   • Arterio-venous difference
• Cardiac hypertrophy   • Bradycardia   • Acclimatisation to heat
• Altitude training effects   • Erythropoietin (EPO)   • Recombinant EPO (RhEPO)
• Blood doping

5. Measurement and evaluation of fitness components

- Fitness testing • Test protocols • Physical Activity Readiness Questionnaire (PARQ)
- Prior consent • Test specificity • Test validity • Test objectivity
- Test reliability • Fitness measures with age • Strength • Speed • Power
- Local muscular (anaerobic) endurance • Cardio-vascular (aerobic) endurance
- Flexibility • Co-ordination • Balance • Reaction time • Agility
- Body composition

6. Planning of fitness and training programmes

- Over-training • Progressive overload • Recovery • Specificity • Reversibility
- Moderation • FITT (frequency, intensity, time (duration), type)
- Target training zones • Strength • Karvonen's principles • Strength
- Maximum strength • Explosive (dynamic) strength • Reactive strength
- Sustained strength • Strength endurance • Speed • Maximum speed
- Elastic strength (power) • Speed endurance • Running speed • Power
- Local muscular endurance • Cardio-vascular endurance • Anaerobic endurance
- Anaerobic threshold • Agility • Co-ordination • Balance • Reaction time
- Flexibility • Mobility • Body composition • Interval training • Circuit training
- Sprint training • Hollow sprints • Repetition sprints • Acceleration sprints
- Resistance sprint training • Fartlek • Plyometrics • Continuous training
- Long slow distance (LSD) training • Skill training • Trained and untrained
- Males and females • Age • Pre-adolescence • Adolescence
- Ageing • Adult • Periodisation • Microcycles • Mesocycles • Macrocycle

REVIEW QUESTIONS

1 Explain the components of a properly constructed warm up and give three physiological reasons for warming up.

2 What does the term 'homeostasis' mean?

3 Explain the acronyms SEAM and SMARTER.

4 Describe the benefits of increasing muscle temperature on muscular performance.

5 Explain the term 'stretch reflex'.

6 Explain the main characteristics of skeletal muscle when stimulated by the nervous system to initiate movement.

7 Give examples of hypo-kinetic musculo-skeletal disorders.

8 Give an explanation of how the anatomical structures of the knee protect and support this joint in sport.

9 Describe the movements of the hip in terms of the muscles that act on this area and the movement patterns allowed.

10 Explain the relationship between cardiac output, heart rate and stroke volume. Give figures to support your explanation.

11 Give examples of how heart rates can vary between individuals as a result of individual differences.

12 Describe possible long-term adaptations of the circulatory, vascular and respiratory systems with training.

13 For a sport of your choice, state the dominant components of fitness that are required for success and give examples of the types of training that could be used to develop these components.

14 Explain what is meant by test specificity and give an example for a sport of your choice.

Texts used in the writing of this section

- Bangsbo, J. *Fitness Training in Football – A Scientific Approach*, HO+Storm, Bagsvaerd, 1994
- Crisfield, P., *Measuring Performance – A Guide to Field-based Fitness Testing*, NCF, 1995
- Dick, F., *Sports Training Principles*, 3rd edition, A & C Black, 1997
- Foss, M. & Keteyian, S., *Fox's Physiological Basis for Sport and Exercise*, Brown & Benchmark, 1998
- Marieb, E., *Human Anatomy and Physiology*, Benjamin/Cummings, 1989
- McArdle, W., Katch, F. & Katch, F., *Exercise Physiology*, 3rd edition, Lea and Febiger, 1991
- NCF, *Fitness Practicals – A Teaching Guide*, NCF, 1993
- Sharkey, B. J., *Fitness and Health*, 4th edition, Human Kinetics, 1997
- Smith, E. & Gilligan, C., 'Effects of Inactivity and Exercise on Bone', in *The Physician and Sports Medicine*, 15 (11), pp. 91–102, 1987
- Wilmore, J. & Costill, D., *Physiology of Sport and Exercise*, Human Kinetics, 1994

Texts used in the writing of this section

- Davis, D., Kimmet, T. & Auty, M., *Physical Education – Theory and Practice*, Macmillan, 1996
- Thompson, F., *Manual of Structural Kinesiology*, 12th edition, Mosby, 1989
- Wirhed, R., *Athletic Ability and the Anatomy of Motion*, Wolfe Medical, 1992

Unit 4

Global trends in international sport

Introduction to Unit 4

In Unit 1A you focused initially on historical and more current sporting developments in the UK and also considered the place of sport in society in the wider European context. In Unit 1B, using the Olympic Games as a case study, several issues concerning sport in a global perspective were introduced and considered.

Unit 4 develops this global perspective. Section A offers a range of cultures for examination. You must choose ONE for in-depth study and examination with knowledge of a second providing a basis for comparison.

The structural analysis in this Unit is similar to Unit 1 so that you should be familiar with the range of issues/institutions under review. Such issues as gender, racism, commercialisation occur in the global as well as the national and European contexts. You will be required to study these and other aspects of sport and recreation from the historical and contemporary point of view of the culture(s) of your choice. The emphasis is on specific elements within countries rather than the countries themselves. This will be reflected in the nature of questions, which will require you to use examples in support of your answers.

In Unit 4B, issues such as national identity and the pursuit of excellence encourage you to develop an overview of these phenomena and their significance in the global context, rather than in specific national contexts. This element of the Unit requires a synoptic approach to such issues so that scientific influences should be included in your considerations and in the framing of your answers.

The areas of emphasis will also include those topics studied under Unit 1 but will require you to develop a broader picture of how such issues impact upon a global sporting network.

The Unit will be assessed by means of a one and a quarter hour written paper requiring you to answer TWO questions.

One question will be from your chosen culture in Section A and will require you to provide evidence of your knowledge of sporting systems and trends that may be highlighted in the context of international sport.

The second question will be based on your work in Section B of the Unit. It will examine synoptically your knowledge of issues which affect the social basis of sport but which may be founded in other fields. You will therefore be expected to show that you have understood the scientific content in other Units in order to satisfy the requirements of this question.

Section A(1): World cultures: North America

1. Historical and cultural background

North American life and its values have grown out of **colonisation** and continued with **immigration**, the opening up of new frontiers to the west, **industrialization**, and, most recently, the growth of '**mass consumerism**'. This last phase also includes the growth of mass transport, mass media, mass production and – perhaps most significantly – mass entertainment.

The mainstream social values that go with each phase of development have all contributed to what is known as 'the American way of life'. The English colonists, though sent packing in the War of Independence, left behind the embryo of today's system of education and traces of a class system now perpetuated by meritocratic rather than aristocratic values. A two-party system of government owes much to the English 'Mother of parliaments' although it is now in federal form. The present-day legal system in the USA contains many features of the legal system of its former colonial masters.

The heritage of the slave trade and the treatment of the North American Indian both contribute to the cultural 'stacking' or ranking according to ethnicity, which still carries on today. Ironically, subsequent immigration policies have helped both cultural and economic activity develop across a broad perspective, but at the same time have maintained a strict 'pecking order' socially and politically.

In seventeenth and eighteenth-century colonial America, just as in Britain, 'play' was often disapproved of once adulthood was reached. Religious constraint saw to it that energy was directed towards productive and purposeful activity rather than what was seen as pointless recreation. The reforming social influences, including those of rationalised recreation were also significant. By the time the industrialisation of the late nineteenth and early twentieth centuries had created the wealth that spawned mass consumerism, recreational activity could be enjoyed without attracting disapproval. At the same time this new industrial wealth was significant in the redefining of a class system that was no longer based entirely on status at birth alone but on whether or not such advantage and wealth was put to work economically.

Mainstream social values

Such slogans as 'winner takes all' and 'there ain't no prizes for second' perhaps most aptly reflect the American attitude today to almost every aspect of life – including sport. A strong belief in the capitalist ethic and the pursuit of wealth inevitably produces both winners and losers. This is seen very clearly in a society which is made up of those who appear to possess everything in the material sense but a rather greater number of 'have nots' than you might expect in the world's richest economy.

'Nice guys win nuthin' is another very revealing epithet. Whilst being an over-generalisation in many respects, it says a lot about the competitive approach to business which also finds its way into the culture of the sports field – or is it the other way round?

In the 1960s, the writings of Veblen (1899), a nineteenth-century economist, were reproduced as being appropriate for the time. They included the comment that:

> ... *one of the redeeming factors in sports was that its predatory character might easily be translated into the self-assertiveness required for modern life.*
> Veblen, *The Theory of the Leisure Class*

At the end of the nineteenth century, this view would have been very much at odds with that held in Britain and Europe, where sport was still seen as part of a 'moralizing' process.

For many disadvantaged or minority groups in the US, sporting achievement has become one way of climbing the ladder of social acceptability. It is also a means of acquiring a lifestyle that would otherwise be unattainable. The **'glass ceiling'** operates just a little less brutally in sport than in business, particularly in the last thirty years or so. Since then increased access to college education via sports scholarships has become for many the passport to a better life.

TASK

Describe how and why the 'glass ceiling' is more likely to be broken in a society with a 'winner takes all' ethic than might be the case in other multi-cultural environments.

Ethics present in North American sport

There are three ethical viewpoints in North American sport:

The Lombardian ethic

Vince Lombardi was an American football coach of the 1950s. His attitude to winning was particularly ruthless, and at the time very controversial. His 'win-at-all-costs' approach has been adopted by many professional sports teams and individuals and to some people the **Lombardian ethic** goes against the previously held ideals of sportsmanship.

The radical ethic

The **radical ethic** states that winning is important but not at all costs. There is value in the means by which victory is achieved and in the development of the performer, either as an individual or as a member of a group. This is a re-statement of the early 'participation' ethic, a product of the Christian/European cultures of the early immigrants, where the value gained from participation alone was considered a full justification for physical activity.

The counter-culture ethic

The **counter-culture ethic** says that the process (or experience) is all that matters. The notion of competition beyond its essential process is derided as 'self-posturing' and flag-waving. Winning is irrelevant other than

▲ *Figure 4.1* *The great outdoors and the wilderness trail: the American pioneer spirit found its way to the sport and recreation*

as a reflection of the quality of effort. The notion of challenge is acceptable but only as a means of personal and cultural enrichment, rather than the establishment of 'heroes' and the servicing of egos. The 'new games' concept of the mid 1970s was an attempt to establish the principle of participation as the prime motivation for games with outcome relevant only as an acknowledgement of achievement. Everyone could be a winner, simply by taking part.

To summarise:

- **Lombardian ethic:** Outcome is valued above the means of achievement
- **Radical ethic:** Both outcome and process are equally valued, without the former being achieved at the expense of the latter
- **Counter-culture ethic:** The process or experience is valued more highly than the outcome.

The 'frontier spirit' in sport

There have always been frontiers in American life. The taming of the Wild West; the crossing of the Rockies and survival in harsh environments (Figure 4.1).

The courageous **pioneer spirit** of the early settlers has found its way on to the sports field, in names like 'Redskins' and 'Forty-niners'. It is also lived out in the camping-hunting-fishing philosophy which is seen in many middle-class American father–son relationships.

American summer camps, often set in environments in 'the great outdoors', are an attempt to pass on these values to American youth preparing them for the rigours of adult life. Sporting heroes are often seen as gladiators defending their communities against the invaders from outside – until, that is, the team owner decides to move the team headquarters elsewhere!

Environmental and topographical factors

The sheer scale of the land mass that makes up North America is advantageous both economically and in terms of recreational activity. The country's diversity of raw materials has allowed self-sufficiency in both primary industries, such as agriculture or coal mining, and secondary industries, those based on the manufacture of goods from these raw materials. This in turn has been enhanced by more recent technological developments.

North America is made up of all kinds of terrain from the almost polar regions of the north, through cool and temperate belts to the tropical conditions of the Florida swamps. The extensive coastlines in both the east and west support a range of marine and coastal activity that is both recreational and economic. Generally speaking, the warm climate in the south allows people to spend more time out of doors and the economy tends to be agrarian. It is therefore not surprising to find that lifestyles, as well as work and survival skills, are reflected in the hunting, fishing and equestrian activities which form a major part of recreational activities.

In the north, where the economy is much more orientated towards heavy industry and the climate is rather harsher, recreational activities tend to be more institutionalised and reliant upon 'created environments' than in the south.

The views of the '**gun lobby**', who support the possession of guns and believe in the right to self-defence, are remnants of the early pioneer days, when a man had to defend himself against all-comers and took pride in being prepared to do so.

2. Physical education and sport in high schools and colleges/universities

Historical development of physical education

Following the pattern in Europe, early American schools virtually ignored the physical side of their students' well-being. Curricula were strictly classical and it was not until the early nineteenth century that physical exercise – often in the form of **gymnastics** – began to be considered seriously as an aspect of education (Figure 4.2).

Swanson and Spears (1995) quote the Round Hill School in Northampton, Massachusetts, as an early example of the adoption of the 'European school' of physical education where gymnastics was held in high esteem. Charles Beck, a German immigrant, was appointed in 1825 as instructor in Latin and gymnastics at about the same time that P. H. Clias and Carl Vöelker had brought German gymnastics to Britain (see Unit 1a, page 20). Boys were also taught to ride, skate and swim as well as play baseball and football.

In 1825, the Female Monitorial School in Boston also introduced formal German gymnastics, as well as marching, running, jumping and weightlifting. Catherine Beecher's 30-minute daily programme of light exercises became known as **calisthenics**.

▲ *Figure 4.2* *The beginnings of physical education in the US – F. L. Jahn's Treatise on Gymnastics was translated by Beck at Northwood College in 1828*

TASK

What common influences led to gymnastics play a leading part in physical education in both the USA and the UK?

▲ **Figure 4.3** *German gymnastics in the United States in the late 1880s*

Three young German men, Leiber and Follen at Harvard University and Beck at the Boston Gymnasium, are credited with bringing gymnastics to the US around the time it also arrived in Britain (Figure 4.3).

By 1885, public (state) school provision had begun to expand, particularly in the heavily populated and industrialised north and increased throughout the country prior to World War I. The trend at about this time was a decline in the interest in gymnastics and a growing interest in games (Figure 4.4).

In 1889 the Boston Normal School of Gymnastics began to advance the cause of **Swedish gymnastics** over the previously established German system. Again, this was similar to the situation in the UK at that time. In 1885 Madame Österberg opened her college in the UK to train young lady teachers of gymnastics utilising the Swedish System.

Women began to play sports, including basketball (Figure 4.5) and football (soccer). Just as in Europe, there was fearsome opposition from many of those in power who held conventional views. By the end of the first decade of the twentieth century, sports had

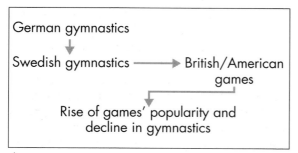

German gymnastics
↓
Swedish gymnastics ⟶ British/American games
⟶ Rise of games' popularity and decline in gymnastics

▲ **Figure 4.4** *Gymnastics declined in favour of British then American games*

▲ **Figure 4.5** *Women's basketball at Smith College, Massachusetts: women began playing in 1891, the same year as men.*

continued to increase in popularity and the high school athlete and the college sports star were beginning to make an appearance in the American education system.

Sport in high schools

Today these trends continue in high schools. Sport has to some extent ousted physical education in terms of provision, funding and staffing. Many high school games take place in front of large crowds, deriving considerable revenue and kudos for their establishment.

Many school principals appear to view physical education programmes as expendable, and local district boards seem to agree with them. There is, of course, considerable variation between high schools. Whilst it is undoubtedly true that many PE programmes have been dropped, there are some areas where physical education still has a high value in its own right.

Whereas in the past sport came within physical education departments, in American high schools today it has its own department: the **Athletic department**. Coaches instead of teachers are employed, with the clear intention of creating a successful athletic programme – in other words, winning teams. Some teachers do work in both capacities, and are paid extra to do so, but this is by no means the norm.

In many cases the athletic director has over-all charge of both physical education and sport (Figure 4.6) and will appoint head coaches to each varsity sport (high school) who are quite often paid far more than teachers.

Coaches must be members of the faculty teaching staff but this is often simply a mat-ter of teaching a minimum number of class-es in order to satisfy regulations. Coaches are also required to hold an approved coaching qualification, recognised in the State where they work. This also applies to teachers, even if they are qualified teachers of physical education.

Sport in American high schools is driven by the culture within which it exists – name-ly one of winners. Schools derive much kudos from success and capable students build a scholarship-winning profile. In high-er education (see below), college athletic departments create the sports stars of tomorrow; physical education has in many cases been renamed 'Kinesiology' or 'Movement' in an attempt to redefine it with an educational rather than an athletic focus.

Sport in higher education

Inter-collegiate sport had become reason-ably well established by the mid-1880s. The first of these was rowing, and competition between Harvard, Yale, Brown and Trinity Colleges was evident from the 1860s onwards. Oxford University visited Harvard in 1869, apparently triggering an interest in the sport in a wide number of colleges. Rowing reached its peak in the mid-1870s,

by which time inter-collegiate competition had also expanded to include baseball, football and track and field athletics.

The **AAU (Amateur Athletic Union),** which for many years was to rule collegiate sport with a rod of iron, was formed in 1888. It differed from sports' governing authorities in the United Kingdom in that it held a wide brief covering many sports. Alongside this, the rather awkwardly enti-tled Inter-Collegiate Athletic Association of the United States was formed in 1905 but later became the National Collegiate Athletic Association (NCAA). Individual sports governing bodies took over from the AAU in 1971.

In the twentieth century, sport became firmly established within the US collegiate system, with inter-collegiate games and championships such as the Rose-Bowl in football having prominent places on the sporting calendar. The *New York Times* reported in 1937 that 20 million people had watched college football games that year. NCAA basketball was inaugurated in 1939 and, along with football, is a central pillar of collegiate sport.

Today, after many scandals and accusa-tions of illegal payments, falsification of exam scores and other inducements to stu-dent athletes, college sport is run in divi-sions, with the number of scholarships (see below) and players strictly limited, accord-ing to status. Top division colleges are allowed a greater number of scholarships than others, but this status can be removed if illegal activities in recruitment or man-agement are proven. The NCAA report for 1998 shows that the average 'spend' for top division colleges in football alone was a staggering four and a quarter million dol-lars per institution.

The bridge between collegiate and pro-fessional sport is the **draft system** which, together with salary capping, ensures that teams are not simply able to buy their way to success. In the draft system, teams in each of the major professional sports are ranked at the end of each season, as are the outstanding college players likely to arouse the interest of professional clubs. The low-est-ranked club has first choice of the high-

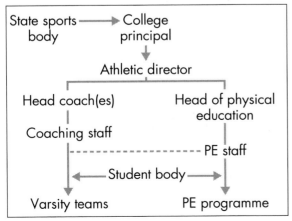

▲ *Figure 4.6* *The simplified structure of sport/PE in American high schools*

est-ranked player so that, theoretically at least, some form of parity is maintained.

Clubs are allowed to 'trade their drafts', so, if a quarterback is allocated to a club that already possesses strength in that position, they may negotiate an exchange with another club that has been allocated a player they *would* like (Figure 4.7).

Salary capping works by limiting the salary bill for a whole playing staff, so that one player's lucrative contract may well deny the rest of the team a reasonable salary. In fact this is no great deterrent, as many players also have lucrative media contracts negotiated as part of their 'package' (and these are not subject to capping). For example, Michael Jordan, now retired from basketball, currently still earns over $850,000 per week purely from 'other interests'.

The sports scholarship system

The **scholarship** system is the means of entry to higher education for an increasing number of young Americans. Scholarships exist in a number of subject areas but those awarded to sportsmen and women attract by far the greatest attention. In the days of pure amateur sport, opponents of this system likened it to simply paying sportsmen so that they were able to dedicate themselves to sport in the same way that a professional would. This therefore meant that most American 'amateur' athletes were not eligible for such competition.

Such views, whilst not unusual, never had much influence, and in recent years the practice has become much more widespread. Broadened access for black students in particular is particularly evident from the details given in Figure 4.8. The fact that more basketball scholarships go to black students is indicative of a 'cultural adoption' of the game by the black population. Theories of **'white flight'**, whereby white students simply move on to other things, are also indicative of the fact that for many black students college scholarships are their only way into a better life.

The advent of professional sport – particularly in Olympic competition – has meant that the scholarship system is now, in effect, part of a huge system of excellence that has developed with virtually no central funding. At one time, many college admissions were 'suspect', with scholarships being awarded to those with little or no academic merit. This became both a

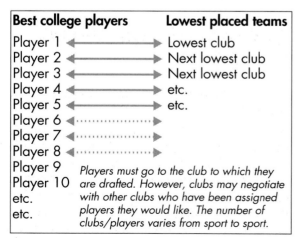

Best college players	Lowest placed teams
Player 1	Lowest club
Player 2	Next lowest club
Player 3	Next lowest club
Player 4	etc.
Player 5	etc.
Player 6	
Player 7	
Player 8	
Player 9	*Players must go to the club to which they*
Player 10	*are drafted. However, clubs may negotiate*
etc.	*with other clubs who have been assigned*
etc.	*players they would like. The number of clubs/players varies from sport to sport.*

▲ *Figure 4.7* The 'draft pick': most prominent in football and basketball

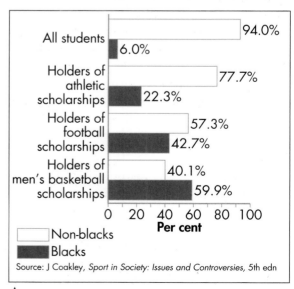

Source: J Coakley, *Sport in Society: Issues and Controversies*, 5th edn

▲ *Figure 4.8* Percentage of sports scholarships in US colleges: 1991

▲ **Figure 4.9** *Women's basketball*

major criticism and a major concern. In the early 1990s, new ground rules established clear guidelines for college entry. Consequently, entries to basketball scholarships in particular declined as coaches were forced to ensure all awards were given on genuine academic grounds.

In the UK, the 'cult of the coach' is seen as one of the less commendable aspects of American sport, both at high school and college levels. On the 'plus' side, there seems to be little interference (at least officially) with developing sportsmen – and now women – from professional influences. No athlete can be approached by professional clubs prior to their year of graduation, a rather different situation from the UK in, for example, soccer. In baseball, however, it is not unusual for young players to decline college careers in order to sign for professional clubs.

Women and collegiate sport
The Association for Intercollegiate Athletics for Women (AIAW) was formed in 1971 and

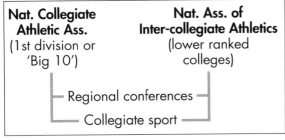

Nat. Collegiate Athletic Ass. (1st division or 'Big 10')	Nat. Ass. of Inter-collegiate Athletics (lower ranked colleges)
Regional conferences	
Collegiate sport	

▲ **Figure 4.10** *Collegiate sport: a simplified* structure

by 1980 the NCAA had taken on board the notion of women's athletics. The AIAW was subsequently disbanded in 1983, having served its purpose.

One of the most visible of collegiate sports for women is basketball (Figure 4.9), which in the 1970s and 1980s was perhaps the first team sport to grow significantly out of the Civil Rights Act of 1964 (which allowed black people equal rights in education and access to sports teams). Subsequently, **Title 1X** (sexual equality) amendments of 1972 laid down rights of access to sport for women and girls on an equal basis to men.

The number of women's athletic scholarships increased significantly following the defeat of the then AIAW in 1971 in a court case. This was brought about because it denied access to a tennis tournament to a group of female students. The students had received financial assistance with their studies in the form of scholarships, which until that point were not recognised by the AIAW. Although a women's organisation, the AIAW would not support what they saw as 'professionalism' in women's sport. The organisation was forced to change its rules, thus paving the way for women to receive the same scholarship assistance as men. College sport is now organised into regional 'conferences' under the auspices of the National Athletic Collegiate Association (NCAA) representing the leading colleges and the National Association of Inter-collegiate Athletics (NAICA) for the others (Figure 4.10).

3. Professional (élite) sport

The history of professional sport
Baseball and boxing were 'the people's sports' in the United States, long before football and basketball became professional. Horse-racing and golf were also established quite early as professional sports, with neither of them featuring prominently at collegiate level. Baseball was established well before the end of the nineteenth century, with the first **World Series** being played in 1903.

Baseball and boxing

A distinct parallel with the later split over broken time in rugby in Britain (see page 36) occurred in 1869. The Cincinnati Red Stockings baseball team openly became professional as a result of the 'no compensation' policy of the National Association of Baseball Players (NAPB). The NABP refused to allow players to be paid for lost (or 'broken') time from work. Unlike the response of the RFU in England some twenty-five years or so later, it was faced with a situation where clubs unanimously declared themselves professional. The NABP was therefore forced to accommodate professional clubs within its ranks the following year. A succession of short-lived organisations sprang up but, essentially, by the mid-1880s, agreements were in place which became the model not only for professional baseball but for other sports as well.

Clearly, the roots of both baseball and boxing lay in the masses who populated the eastern and central states. Baseball was popular at the grass-roots level, rather like soccer in the UK. Boxing existed on the one hand as the 'noble art of self-defence', much as it did in England, and was firmly entrenched as a middle class 'manly' pursuit. However, to many young men from poor backgrounds, it also became the passport to a better life.

'Gentleman Jim Corbett', John L. Sullivan, Bob Fitzimmons and Jack Johnson were successful boxers who became folk heroes in the last decades of the nineteenth century and the early years of the twentieth. Somewhat later, 'Babe' Ruth and Jo Dimaggio occupied roughly equivalent spots in the hearts of baseball fans.

Football and basketball

Professional football and basketball did not really emerge until the mid-1930s and were distinct from baseball in that their roots were firmly established within collegiate sport.

Football had begun in the 1890s but the American Professional Football Association was not formed until 1920 with eleven clubs. Within a very short time this became the National Football League (NFL). Big city clubs have always dominated the game, as in basketball. An early success in professional sport was the American Basketball League, founded in 1925 but soon discontinued. Its successor, the National Basketball League, was formed in 1938 and later became the National Basketball Association (NBA).

Structure of professional sport

Professional sport in the US today still has at its centre baseball (perhaps still the most popular) basketball and football. Ice hockey is popular in the northern states but modern technology now allows franchises (team headquarters) to be moved to such places as Texas and California, where, historically, there are no connections other than financial ones.

Most team sports are organised into conferences (as in college sport) or leagues, with American and National usually being the first word of their title. This structure occurs in all three major sports and in ice hockey too. The strangely-named World Series in both basketball and baseball reflects, on the one hand, a wish that this were really the case; on the other, the influence of marketing 'hype', intent on con-

▲ **Figure 4.11** *The structure of American professional sport*

vincing TV audiences that their own sports really are world class (Figure 4.11).

The college system (see page 226) with its scholarships and high profile image serves as a proving ground for would-be professional sportsmen and women who want to make a career in professional sport. Basketball and football are the major benefactors of the system. However, track and field athletics, which have always had a high profile within collegiate sport, now also have a 'legitimate' professional outlet for those college stars who rise to the top. Athletics has not traditionally had a great following beyond the level of collegiate track and field but interest is now growing as potential earnings in that sport slowly rise to meet those of the stars in the more established professional sports.

Commercial nature of professional sport

Hand in hand with the rise of professional sport has grown an increasing level of **commercial interest** and investment. Professional athletes are used in every way imaginable to market products for an increasingly global market, and earnings derived from such involvement often outstrip already huge sporting salaries.

The presentation of American team sports has been designed with business in mind. Short, sharp bursts of activity are followed by a break during team changes, conferences with coaches and change of innings, etc. This allows breaks to be filled with short commercial 'hits' from sponsors. American sport has grown up with commercial interests featuring strongly, and contrasts with the continuous play that typifies team games in the UK.

The media and professional sport

The media, particularly television, has enhanced the earning potential of sportsmen and women in two ways:

- the income derived by clubs/franchises from the sale of TV rights has allowed for considerable increases in salaries
- the role of sports stars as 'advertising bill-boards' has allowed valuable contracts to be secured, both in sports-related and other products.

Rather more questionable is the degree to which – in return for their huge investment – media companies (e.g. Rupert Murdoch with Foxtel) seek to gain control, not only of sporting events, but of clubs and their governing bodies. Media companies now own a considerable number of America's leading sports teams/franchises. This issue is also raised in Units 1a (page 47) and 1b (page 71) in respect of both European and global sporting events. This has instigated much debate as to the ownership of sport.

The status of professional sport

Without doubt, the status of professional sport in North America generally has never been more firmly established. This is because it now serves not only sporting interests but commercial ones as well. Basketball, football, baseball and, of course, ice hockey are served up to a huge market, with ice hockey's Stanley Cup rivalling both World Series and the **Superbowl** in popularity.

Sports stars are fêted wherever they go and as **role models** they have a huge influence on young people's tastes – in both sporting and wider markets. The status of sport and its 'mega-stars' is now such that they can influence considerably the spending habits of millions of people outside the immediate sporting culture of the nation. The great interest people have in sport means that it provides a market-place for a huge range of goods and services – far wider than the market immediately connected to sport. This market has an enormous influence on a global scale.

4. Recreational sport (mass participation)

Sport in North American society

An artist accompanying one of the early seventeenth century voyages to America painted the indigenous people of Virginia fishing and dancing. Another source also described:

... a game with a ball of a strange resilient material which bounced, a ball game in which players 'carried in their hands two wooden spoons, curiously carved, not unlike our large iron spoons'.
Cullin, *Games of the North American Indians*

Clearly, there was **indigenous sport** in the new lands discovered by the first settlers, and the development of today's sports and pastimes in America has had contributions from the following groups:

- Native Americans
- colonists
- European settlers.

Each has brought aspects of their own culture to bear upon the sports and pastimes of the people who followed. Sadly, the native influence was heavily suppressed until relatively recently. However, lacrosse has survived. Under its native name of baggattaway, it was both a popular game and a highly significant ritual. Its modern name is believed to be a derivation of the term 'La croix' and betrays French influence at the time of colonisation. Evidence of various football-type games has been discovered, as well as games of 'hoop and spear' and 'shinny' (or shinty) which would appear to have been very similar to the Scottish game of Camanchd.

From the early colonists came the European versions of hunting and game sports, whilst those few members of the aristocracy who emigrated to America took with them the pastimes of hawking, court tennis, and what would appear to be some evidence of early forms of cricket. The common people took with them their village games of football and stoolball – its various forms still fuelling arguments today about the origins of modern baseball. Foot races, fights and games of the tavern also found their way across the Atlantic.

Many of the colonists and settlers had the same religious **work ethic** as their European cousins. This served both to foster games which grew out of work and to constrain any activity which was considered to be 'misspent and pleasurable'.

European (largely Protestant) influences became the dominant culture, so that prior to the nineteenth century it would have been difficult to differentiate between American and European recreations. It was the development of heavy industrialisation in the northern states towards the end of that century that gave rise to the sports we now recognise as American: large centres of population made mass audience sport possible.

Community participation

It was the acceptance of play as a healthy, respectable activity that heralded today's community-wide involvement in sports. As in the UK, the Young Men's Christian Association (YMCA), public parks and playgrounds all played their part, particularly in the north, in provision and opportunity for those least able to provide their own. Scout troops, boys' clubs and many church related organisations also contributed in this respect.

Interestingly, attempts in New Jersey in the 1970s to have girls banned from **'Little league'** competition were defeated in court – a decision which had a great impact on the number of opportunities for girls in the arena of sporting opportunity.

On account of this and other moves towards equal opportunities, it is generally held that the concept of 'sport for all' has been a reality in America since the 1970s. However, this is not necessarily the case. The 1970s saw the enactment of legislation which removed any substance to arguments for exclusion on the grounds of sex or race. However, the federal nature of administration means that only Title 1X (see page 227) legislation carries federal funding and this largely relates to opportunities within the field of education.

States are required to make provision for all with opportunities to attend **summer camps,** for example. However, there are inadequacies in this and federal funding which often means that deprived urban communities remain deprived – in both the recreational and wider social sense. Much of the provision relies on private rather than public funding.

Junior sport

Programmes such as 'Little league baseball' (begun in 1939) and 'Pee-wee' and 'midget' hockey grew up in the 1940s and 50s, as did the Universities Athletic Union's programme of age-related sports. The All-American Girls

▲ Figure 4.12 *America's parks service: a structural model*

Baseball League was formed in 1943. One criticism of these innovations is that they did not serve the needs of the children involved but of adults, keen to ensure new generations of American sports stars. An article written in 1975 commented that:

> *the degree to which children's sports became organised mirrored an often proclaimed American characteristic of being overly regimented, businesslike and competitive.*
>
> Berryman, Jack, W., *From Cradle to the Playing Field*

Whilst watching TV is a passive pastime, sports coverage on TV is likely to spur parents to encourage their children to participate in it. Increased coverage of a growing range of sporting activities may also be an inducement to the great American public to 'give it a go'.

National parks, alternative and wilderness sports

The early **national parks** were created out of the sites of former battlefields or from areas of remote wilderness and so were relatively easy to acquire for the nation. The National Parks Service was created in 1916 during Woodrow Wilson's time as president.

Until the 1920s, all but one of the national parks were in the west, simply because most of the land was federally owned. Since then the service has expanded considerably and includes much of America's natural

scenery, **wilderness areas** and historic monuments. State and local parks are administered separately by appropriate state or municipal authorities (Figure 4.12).

For most Americans, the combination of cars and a wilderness which is easily accessible has proved irresistible. Backpacking, hunting, fishing and camping trips are some of the alternative wilderness sports that were part of recreational life for most of the twentieth century. Television continues to create an awareness of this natural environment just as cars and mass transport systems have created access (Figure 4.13).

In the 1970s there was also a reaction against the highly commercialised, 'staged' mainstream sporting events. This was fuelled in some respects by the hippie movement of the 1960s and the disillusionment of many of the younger generation with America's involvement in the war in Vietnam. There was a 'return to nature' and also an emergence of new 'wilderness sports'.

Mountain biking and a range of **extreme sports** are now very popular and figure prominently on American TV.

TASK

America's national and state parks (Figure 4.12) show an unusual level of centralised administration. Can you explain why this is the case and how the structure compares with that of national parks in the UK?

▲ Figure 4.13 *There was a huge increase in alternative and wilderness sports from the mid-1970s onwards*

Section A(2): New world cultures: Australia, New Zealand and South Africa

1. Historical and cultural background

The mainstream social values in Australia, New Zealand and South Africa are very similar. This is hardly surprising considering their common **historical and cultural influences** and the continuing relationships that exist through the Commonwealth of Nations. A clear difference exists, however, in the treatment and status of the indigenous populations of each country. The Aborigine tribes of Australia were almost wiped out as a result of indiscriminate slaughter on the part of the new white colonists. Many thousands also died as a result of contracting disease brought in by the new settlers, against which they had no natural defences.

Native indigenous population – cultures and sports

Australia

The first recorded game of Australian Rules football is said to have taken place in 1858 between Scotch College and Melbourne Grammar School. However, it was not until the 1980s that a truly 'national' competition developed. Aborigine players took part in Australian Rules football as early as the 1880s but their involvement has been exceptional in the context of the broader sporting picture. Instances of **discrimination** against many Aborigine sportsmen who were clearly superior to their white counterparts are only just beginning to emerge.

Because of the suppression of the native populations, many indigenous sports and recreations have been lost. Sepaktakraw, an early football game of Malaysian/Aboriginal origin, for example, resurfaced in the Arrafura Games in Australia's Northern Territories only as recently as 1974.

Richard Holt in his *Sport and the British* (1995) suggested that:

> *sport played a major role in the transmission of imperial and national ideas ... manly exercise slowly came to be a kind of common language superficially obscuring divisions of ethnicity, religion, and economic interest.*

New Zealand

In New Zealand, the Maori, a fearless and warlike race (unlike Australia's Aborigine population), withstood all attempts to make them subservient to British colonial rule. As a result, the **Treaty of Waitangi** (Te Tiriti O Waitangi) gave the Maori people continued access to their ancient lands. The treaty was signed on 6 February 1840 by Captain William Hobson, several English residents and approximately 45 Maori chiefs. It lays the foundation for the way Maori and other New Zealanders share responsibility for their country. It is generally considered to be the founding document of the nation of New Zealand.

This is very different from the treatment of the indigenous populations in Australia and South Africa at the hands of their new colonial masters. Maori women obtained the vote in 1893, whereas full voting rights were not given to all Aborigines in Australia until 1967.

TASK

Why was it that the Maori tribes in New Zealand fared much better at the hands of their new colonial masters than Australia's Aborigines?

232

However, the predominant sports and recreations in all three countries have been those of the colonial masters rather than the native populations – even though Maori contribution to New Zealand rugby has been significant and in stark contrast to the situation in Australia.

South Africa

The plight of the native populations in South Africa is well documented from the earliest colonial times. The subsequent policy of **apartheid** kept that country out of most international sport between 1960 and 1992, when it was dismantled.

Colonial historical development and the development of new identities and values

In each of the countries under review in this section, the colonial infrastructure included the most influential **cultural institutions**, including sport and education. Sport was an aspect of the 'cultural power' through which the British Empire imposed and maintained itself rather more easily than would have been possible by using military force.

In New Zealand, Maori tribal elders became part of a middle-class establishment that embraced rugby wholeheartedly with the first tour to the British Isles taking place in 1888. This touring party consisted entirely of New Zealand-born players (many of them Maoris). It played 107 games during

▲ *Figure 4.14* A Picture Post *sketch of New Zealand's first goal in international rugby*

the tour, which also took in Australia on its way home (Figure 4.14).

In terms of sport and recreation, the influential groups in all three cultures embraced the English or British pattern of team games and worthwhile individual pursuits, as suitable vehicles for purposeful educational and recreational improvement.

New identities and values

Whilst these countries wished to remain, initially at least, within the embrace of the 'mother country' (i.e. Britain), the establishment of separate identities within the family of the Commonwealth was obviously important. The sports field provided clear opportunities for this and the adoption of team names such as **Kiwis** (New Zealand) and **Springboks** (South Africa) provided a clear national identity within the acceptable context of sporting challenge.

Sport as a vehicle for nation-building

The British colonies were all 'young countries' and the establishment of a sense of national identity whilst remaining loyal to Britain was important. By playing the games of their colonial masters, these new communities were able to demonstrate both loyalty and a sense of *espirit de corps* (group loyalty and identity) at the same time.

The concept of the **test match**, now a term used for many international sporting contests, grew out of the need for these expatriate communities, now living together in a foreign land, to prove themselves against their so-called superiors. National pride and self-esteem were considerably enhanced by victory in such contests. This was more evident in team games (particularly cricket and rugby football) as they also embodied the elements of strategy and cohesion that were important in the developing culture of new countries. Australia's current slogan 'All Golds' refers to the coincidence that the country's playing colours and the colour of the winning medals at most major Games are both gold. In many respects, such 'test' matches might be regarded as having been early forms of truly global sport.

State and federal policies in relation to games and sports

All three countries have recognised the value of sports and games but there are clear differences in the way this has been done.

Australia

Australia has developed its policies along a federalised two-tier structure with policy implementation occurring at Commonwealth and State levels. Policies of inclusion with regard to the Aborigine population seem to have been rather less than effective.

New Zealand

Whilst it would be untrue to claim that there are no disagreements about minority inclusion in New Zealand, for the most part its indigenous Maori population have consistently been included in policy-making and have made significant contributions to that country's sporting endeavours. This is particularly so in rugby.

South Africa

In the case of South Africa, it is only very recently that policy-making and implementation have even begun to embrace the needs of (and provision for) its native populations. South Africa has always seen sport as an expression of its identity but unfortunately until very recently policy-making extended only as far as the white minority.

Political factors

The political background against which sporting development must be measured is seen most clearly in the case of South Africa. Cecil Rhodes, who was governor of Cape Colony between 1890 and 1896, patronisingly referred to South Africa's natives as children, just emerging from barbarism. Rather more sinister was the typical Afrikaner view of blacks expressed some forty years later by Alfred Hoernlé:

> If we civilise the native and let him acquire skill, if we let him enter the learned professions, we cannot in the end refuse him political equality; if we grant him political equality, we cannot deny him social equality; if we grant him social equality, we cannot in the end avoid race mixture.
>
> In Douglas Booth, *The Race Game*

Such attitudes were certainly not unknown in Australia in the mid-twentieth century nor indeed in New Zealand. However, as mentioned before, in New Zealand official policy at least acknowledged the rights of its indigenous minorities and to a large degree catered for them in policy implementation.

The fact that South Africa's policy of **racial segregation** was subject to international condemnation was due to the fact that:

- it had a name – apartheid – and was pursued vehemently by sections of the white minority
- unlike Australia and New Zealand, South Africa's native populations represented a massive majority of the population who were visibly oppressed by a tiny white minority.

Perhaps more than in any other case, the apartheid issues in South Africa made the rest of the world realise that politics and sport are not in fact mutually exclusive. The idea of politically motivated exclusion of a country from competition on the basis of racial discrimination on the sports field has made governments aware that such action can force political change. It must also be remembered that South Africa's isolation also included a wide array of import and export embargoes which placed the country's economy under great strain.

The situation in South Africa and the changes there brought about by sporting sanctions challenges the view that sport exists in some kind of vacuum and should not be tainted by the unpleasant things of life. The connection between the two was seen again in the period leading up to the Olympic Games in Sydney in 2000. Australia's treatment of its native population came under extreme scrutiny and once again global exposure of the problem became the necessary catalyst in the process of change.

Sport as an instrument of unity

Following his country's victory in the 1995 Rugby World Cup, President Mandela clearly stated that he saw sport as an instrument which could unite South Africans both politically and socially (Figure 4.15). In

Australia, the sometimes fierce differences between members of its Commonwealth of States seem to disappear when the green and gold colours of Australia appear on the sports field.

The use of sport as an instrument for nation-building is not new. However, it is perhaps now more acceptable than when it was used for purely political motives by the Eastern bloc countries in the 1960s, 70s and 80s.

In South Africa, the African National Congress (ANC) has quite clearly appropriated sport as part of its nationalising process (Booth, 1998). All three governments of the countries under review in this section acknowledge the value of sports in establishing a national pride and identity by moving towards increasingly centralised administrations and funding of sport at both élite and community levels.

TASK

Write a short account of the difference in the use of sport for political purposes in present-day South Africa and its use by the former Soviet and Eastern bloc powers.

Environmental factors

All three countries have large areas of natural beauty and wildlife and have developed policies to ensure minimal impact in respect of intrusion in such areas.

▲ **Figure 4.15** *President Mandela congratulates Peinar: the beginning of a new age?*

Australia has particular difficulties with regard to its most famous natural attraction, the Great Barrier Reef. It has to be safe-guarded against pollution and destruction of its varied species of coral. There may also be environmental/land use issues as a result of Aboriginal land claims currently being processed.

With its new social and political order, South Africa has much to do in order to develop policies that address the exploitation of natural assets and open spaces by a privileged minority.

Globally, the growth of sport has generated a need for newer, bigger and better stadia. This raises the question of how these and other sporting facilities impact upon the environment. Organisations such as the International Olympic Committee (IOC) now have policies in place requiring national organising committees to address this question appropriately as a condition of being awarded the Games.

Topography

Australia has by far the largest land mass of the three countries, although much of it is uninhabitable and unusable for most sporting and recreational purposes (Table 4.1). In all cases, however, the terrain available and climate offer a wide choice of setting for most sporting activities.

New Zealand is the smallest of the three countries with a land area similar to that of the UK. With a population of only just under 4 million people its sporting achievements on the international stage are remarkable. In comparison, Australia has a population of just over 18 million and South Africa is the most heavily populated with a little over 43 million people.

In this post-apartheid period, South Africa now clearly has the potential in terms of its population base to produce excel-

Table 4.1 *Land area and population of Australia, New Zealand and South Africa*

Country	Land area (sq km)	Population
Australia	7.6 million	18.3 million
New Zealand	0.3 million	3.9 million
South Africa	1.2 million	43.3 million

lence in a whole range of sports. However, there is much work to be done first in broadening access and opportunity under a newly formed sporting administration.

2. Physical education and sport in high schools and colleges/universities

Physical education today in all three countries under review has developed from the same **colonial influences** that shaped nineteenth-century sport and most other areas of life. Early British colonists responsible for the development of education were nearly always educated themselves in an English public school or, at very least, in one of the many independent or grammar schools which were modelled on them. As a result, many of their educational principles found their way into the New World.

Sport and PE in high schools including sport education

New Zealand

In New Zealand, Health and Physical Education is compulsory for all students up to the age of 15 (Year 10). The programme is centred upon the Maori word **'hauora'** (sense of well-being) and reflects the country's native culture in both language and content. Many of the key terms are expressed in the Maori language as well as in English.

There are eight stages of learning within seven key areas. These are:

- mental health
- sexuality education
- food and nutrition
- body care and physical safety
- physical activity
- sport studies
- outdoor education.

Sport studies is not simply a programme of sporting activities but involves such topics as sportsmanship and the place of sport in society. The teaching guidelines state that participation in competitive school sport is not a substitute for this programme.

Australia

In Australia, the State of Victoria led the way with its own **Physical and Sport Education programme (PASE)**. This was soon followed by the federally funded **Sport Education in Physical Education Programmes (SEPEP)**. There is a clear indication here that the notion of sportsmanship, which appears to be under serious threat in the big money world of professional sport, is at last being seriously addressed by educators.

South Africa

An early influence on the development of physical education in South Africa was **Ernst Franz Jokl**, a German who emigrated to South Africa in 1933, where he also qualified as a medical practitioner. Sometimes referred to as the 'Father of Physical Education in South Africa', Jokl was also a pioneer in exercise physiology and in sports medicine.

Following his appointment at Stellenbosch University in 1936, he left for Johannesburg the following year. There he founded the first Physical Education Department in a South African University and was also instrumental in the formation of the **National Advisory Council on Physical Education**. He compiled the first 'Syllabus for South African Schools' in 1940. This was based initially on the British system but this was later influenced by the Danish gymnastics of Neils Bukh.

Programmes of physical education in South Africa have therefore developed largely in the white community and in the country's private schools. Missionary schools that were inclined to teach physical education adopted such procedures as facilities would permit. The key issue at present is the plight of the schools in the township areas where policies for the provision of PE exist but in many cases have yet to be implemented. This is often because of the huge deficiencies in facilities rather than a lack of willingness on the part of the authorities. Reports as recent as 1999 highlight the fact that many schools still have no textbooks.

High rates of truancy and delinquent behaviour also present major problems. Examination papers are tampered with and prior notice of questions devalues the worth of examinations in many cases. Whilst this may have little relevance to the implementation of physical education policy, it puts many of the problems relating to a broadening of access into some sort of perspective.

Extra curricular sport in high schools and in higher education

Australian school sport

Australian school sport originated in private and grammar schools as a result of the country's colonial past. Currently the governing body of school sport is the **Australian School Sports Council (ASSC),** based in Canberra. It is staffed by representatives of the various state sport organisations (SSOs) and decides policies, structures, age-group rules, etc. which apply to national school sporting activities. Unlike the UK, these representatives are less likely to be teachers and will probably be employed full-time in this capacity within their own state. The ASSC also has a remit to work closely with the **Active Australia** programme.

Each state has a Department of School Sport (or equivalent) and its officials administer school sport in each state. Victoria has ten full-time officers employed in this capacity. They organise and administer a whole range of sporting activities at both primary and secondary level.

School sporting associations (primary and secondary) are run by teachers, who work closely with state officials. Schools are normally affiliated to the appropriate senior body for a particular sport. There is usually a close association with federally run and funded programmes such as Active Australia which have their grass-roots bases in both local community groups and schools. Some schools sports associations are merged in that primary and secondary sections join together where such a situation helps them to function – in remote areas, for example.

New Zealand school sport

In New Zealand, school sport has long played a significant part as an extension of physical education programmes and as preparation for sporting and recreational life after school. As in many countries influenced by British colonial values, sport began in the country's private education system. Ryan (1999) comments that the curriculum of New Zealand secondary schools prior to 1914 – particularly sport and specifically cricket – was aimed at:

> producing superior specimens capable of serving New Zealand and the wider British Empire in a military or domestic capacity.

This was almost certainly true of both Australia and South Africa as well. Schools in New Zealand (and elsewhere) adopted the trappings of 'Englishness', including school magazines, the house system and school uniforms.

Institutions such as Wellington College and Christ's College, Christchurch, which established cricket by the early 1860s, used that game rather than rugby to promote such values. Rugby played its part in the international sphere – enjoying rather more success globally than cricket.

Currently school sport is run by the **New Zealand Secondary Schools Sports Council (NZSSSC).** This was set up in 1992 in response to the wishes of secondary school principals who preferred an organised approach designed to minimise disruption to other school activities. The Council regulates the sports that are offered and when events can take place. It is elected by all Regional Principals' Associations and has the power to co-opt two members. This regional structure also helps promote the aims of initiatives such as 'Sportfit' with the Council's regional directors also acting in a promotional capacity, encouraging New Zealand's youngsters to become and stay active.

South Africa

As in other nations, the development of sporting patterns in South African schools owed much to its colonial roots. The singular difference in the case of South Africa is the clear historial and cultural divide between the white minority and the hugely disadvantaged black majority, who until recently could not benefit from such patterns of development.

▲ **Figure 4.16** *Sportsfield, Khabazela Secondary School, KwaZulu, 1991*

▲ **Figure 4.17** *Sportsfield and facilities at St John's Private School, Johannesburg, 1991*

Without in any way trivialising the clear discrimination suffered by many of Australia's indigenous population – and there are many parallels in terms of social exclusion and land rights issues – the stark reality of the huge scale of South Africa's discriminatory policies prior to the dismantling of apartheid is poignantly reflected in Figures 4.16 and 4.17.

Currently school sport in South Africa is run under the auspices of the **United School Sports Association of South Africa (USSASA)**, which was formed in 1994 out of the South African Primary Schools Sports Association and several other schools sport bodies. These largely consisted of groups of white high schools who had previously affiliated through the

sports governing bodies to the National Sports Congress This was a multi-racial body which had been so successful in the early 1990s in bringing to a halt rebel sports tours of South Africa. This amalgamation of school sports bodies included suggestions that white schools should share their facilities with nearby black schools but, according to Booth (1998), this presupposed that all white schools had an abundance of facilities – apparently not the case!

Such disadvantage covered (and still covers) the whole social/political spectrum, not only sport.

Missionary schools and, more recently, the programmes sponsored by **SANGALA (South African National Games and Leisure Activities)** to develop sporting opportunity in the hard-pressed township communities, are simply the beginning of a long process of access and provision that will take years to put in place with any real effectiveness.

TASK

Why is it that effective PE and school sports programmes for all appears to be less widespread in South Africa than in New Zealand or Australia?

University sport

Universities in all three countries are affiliated to FISU (International Federation of University Sport).

In Australia all thirty-seven universities belong to Australian University Sport which organises over forty sports. There is an annual University Games and participation in both the World University Games and championships in several other sports.

University sport in both South Africa and New Zealand is organised in a similar way with national championships and participation in major Universiades. The most recent development occurred with the formation of the South African Student Sports Union (SASSU) in 1994. Six different bodies had formerly run university sport with the exclusively white South African University Sports Council being the most powerful. SASSU has since been granted full membership of both FISU and the Confederation of University and College Sports Associations of Africa (CUCSA).

3. Professional (élite) sport

Historical background

The history of professional sport in all three countries has some parallels, with the same colonial roots and similar patterns of development.

Horse-racing in New Zealand, Australia and South Africa has developed as a professional rather than amateur sport, in much the same way as in the UK. Football, whilst popular, has never really become the 'sport of the people' other than in South Africa. Here, however, the followers and participants of football were mainly black and disenfranchised. It was rugby, therefore, the game of the ruling élite, which even as an amateur game generated income and influence for both players and ruling body alike.

Rugby league is played in all three countries but has only developed real strength in Australia's New South Wales. All three have regularly toured Britain and France, however, South Africa's participation has been curtailed as a result of its government's apartheid policies.

Australian Rules football centred in Victoria is an example of the development of an indigenous game, fashioned out of the games of the 'colonial masters' but as a direct challenge to their control. This is similar to development of American sports in the USA, to some extent a reac-

tion against the sports of the English, who had been banished back across the Atlantic. It might well be that in the future in South Africa rugby league is adopted by many blacks as part of a symbolic rejection of the rugby that was for so long the game of their white masters (Figure 4.18).

In all three countries, cricket began as the sport of middle-class gentlemen but it has always been played by all who could muster a bat, a ball and some passably flat land – grass often being a luxury. Cricket differed only in where and by whom it was played, and in both South Africa and Australia there is a history of exclusion on the grounds of social/racial class. This characteristic is not peculiar to New World cultures, as a study of social class and sports clubs in the UK shows (see Unit 1, page 31).

Structure of professional sport

Generally, as in the UK, most sports began as amateur pastimes and became (overtly or otherwise) professional with the passage of time, growing opportunism and the broadening of tolerance. Most early professional sports had their own governing bodies that were operating outside the more mainstream amateur organisations which had the power and influence.

South Africa's leading professional sport, in terms of the number of participants, is soccer. As long ago as 1948, the South African Football Association met the South African Amateur Football Association in a game designed to be the beginning of the integration of the sport. In 1951, the South African Indian Football Association also became involved but it was not until 1983 that the multi-racial South African Soccer Federation (SASF) was formed.

White clubs formed the first professional league, the National Soccer League, with SASF clubs forming their own professional league (The South African Soccer Federation Professional League) in the same year. Initially the white clubs had better organisation and much easier access to capital for development purposes but the SASF-PL had by far the greater number of players. Ironically, both organisations now have their headquarters at the First

▲ **Figure 4.18** Boys in a township play with a rugby league ball: will this become the 'people's rugby'?

National Bank Stadium in Soweto (known as 'Soccer City').

Rugby remains popular in Capetown and Port Elizabeth but soccer is by far the most popular sport amongst black South Africans, especially in urban areas (Figure 4.19).

A major structural change, which is also reflected in the UK, took place with the increasing acceptance of professionalism and the growing interest of governments in sport for social, economic and political reasons (see also page 241). The development of policies of excellence and general acceptance of professionalism means that the governing bodies of such sports are now part of the mainstream rather than on the fringe.

In Australia, the former Victorian Football Association ('Aussie Rules') has become the Australian Football Association (AFL) because of its efforts to popularise the game nationwide through television. Aussie Rules is now accepted as a mainstream sport with students able to obtain scholarships to centrally funded programmes of excellence.

In New Zealand and South Africa, as well as in Australia, rugby, for many years the subject of allegations of under-the-counter payments and 'boot money', now also has a central position in the professionally orientated sporting establishment.

Commercialism of professional sport

In all three countries, the role of television has been crucial in broadening such acceptance. It has also provided an invaluable source of income and is useful to those commercial interests that see the sporting public as a potential market. Satellite TV, particularly the American channels, has been a huge catalyst in this respect and has also generated public interest in sports such as basketball and baseball, particularly in Australia.

The professional sportsman (and increasingly woman) in all three countries now has a status rivalling that of pop stars and movie stars. They attract huge fees for advertising and commercial ventures and are used as role models for aspiring youngsters.

The media and the status of professional sport

In both Australia and New Zealand, the role of the media and its influence on sport is similar to many other countries in the free world. It is used as a promotional tool and it can build and destroy careers and/or reputations.

Issues such as those of gender and ethnicity are aired more freely now than in earlier decades (Figure 4.20). Any unscrupulous under-the-table activities are exposed ruthlessly.

In any culture, the free press highlights the role of today's professional sportsmen and women and proffers them as role models for its young people. The status of professional sport is accepted as 'desirable with reservations'. Recent exposés of match-fix-

▲ **Figure 4.19** For millions of blacks these are South Africa's sporting heroes

▲ **Figure 4.20** Kathy Freeman: a young woman who has provided headlines as sporting heroine, gender role model and ethnic icon

ing, drug-taking and bribery are a reminder that there are pressures associated with sporting stardom.

In South Africa the process of change is perhaps one of the most prominent issues that affect sport. Before apartheid was dismantled the establishment press always lauded and promoted the country's sports stars as 'Afrikaner' heroes – white and of European origin. Now things are changing and the media generally is learning to present coverage differently – minus the racial segregation and ethnic purity attitudes of former times. Professionalism is upon this growing culture almost before it can walk.

In all three countries, the growing influences of professionalism and commercialism provide their media with both headline fodder and business opportunity. In the end (particularly in the case of South Africa) it may become a welcome nation-building tool.

National institutes of sport and sport academies

Australia

The search for sporting excellence began in Australia after its dismal performance in the 1976 Olympic Games at Montreal. The **Australian Institute of Sport** (AIS) was set up by the federal government in 1981 to provide the expertise and the back-up necessary to produce champions. It was soon realised that a broader base of participation was needed at grass-roots level and in 1989 the control of sport at all levels was passed into the hands of the newly formed **Australian Sports Commission** (ASC).

The ASC is the Australian government's sporting arm. It controls policy and funding for all aspects of sport but devolves the responsibility for programmes of excellence to the AIS.

State institutes of sport

All of Australia's states and territories have their own sports institutes, which exist independently of the federal structure and which are funded independently of it. Their job is to develop excellence in sport at state level.

As with the ASC and the AIS, which are funded jointly by the federal government and private/corporate sponsorship, the state

▲ *Figure 4.21* *Australia: a structure for sporting excellence*

institutes of sport are funded by state governments and local/state sponsorship, including state lotteries. For practical reasons, state and national sport institutes often share the same sites, although each functions as an independent entity. AIS sites do not have authority over the running of state institutes but there is co-operation between the two organisations (Figure 4.21).

Each state sports institute has a policy developed by its own administration providing programmes of excellence in activities considered as being key sports within that state.

TASK

Australia established the AIS in 1981 but the ASC was not formed until 1989. Explain the different roles of these organisations and suggest (with hindsight) why it might have been better if the ASC had been formed first.

New Zealand

The principal provider of funding and services to New Zealand sport is the **New Zealand Sports Foundation** (NZSF). It is a private organisation although its funding comes from government via the **Hillary Commission** (see below and Figure 4.22). Its philosophy is simply the pursuit of excellence. Its mission statement actually reads:

> ... *to assist athletes to succeed at international level and, by so doing, bring credit to themselves, their sport and New Zealand.*

The New Zealand Sports Foundation was created in 1978 and had limited success.

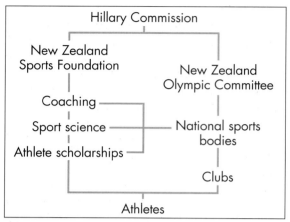

▲ **Figure 4.22** *New Zealand sport: a structure for excellence*

However, the awarding of the 2000 Olympic Games to (relatively) nearby Sydney acted as a spur and the funding and profile of the NZSF has been considerably increased since then.

The Hillary Commission

The Hillary Commission for Sport, Fitness and Leisure was established by an Act of Parliament in 1987. Its broad title indicates that its role includes more than just sports excellence, although as the government's arm of sport it does bring influence to that arena. The Commission and the NZSF together perform much the same twin role as the ASC and the AIS in Australia (see page 241).

South Africa

Roberts (1990) predicted that in order for a national sports policy to be effective, national reconstruction and then development would have to take place within a policy framework. She also said that short-term programmes of action would be necessary as a foundation for the longer term. Within four years – albeit at the end of a very long road – Nelson Mandela was standing alongside Francois Peinar, the South African captain, holding aloft the Rugby World Cup.

The Department of Sport and Recreation had overall responsibility for sports policy and for the provision and delivery of sport and recreation until 1988. Then it and the National Sports Council were merged to form the **South African Sports Commission** (**SASC**). Its responsibilities include:

- the promotion of sport and recreation through the **National Sports Council**

(**NSC**), the **National Olympic Committee of South Africa** (**NOCSA**) and the national federations
- recreation policy, with the most important agent being the **South African National Recreation Council** (**SAN-REC**) (see page 244)
- funding the above-mentioned agencies
- the upgrading of facilities for national and international events.

A special programme has been set up for the development of life skills. It is intended to provide assistance to top athletes in dealing with success or failure. It includes media skills, financial management, interpersonal skills and mental training. This life skills programme is administered by the Department of Sport and Recreation.

Another special high-performance sport programme in South Africa promotes high-performance sport.

It focuses on the following:

- raising the profile of South African sport
- assisting in greater success for individuals, and South African teams
- promoting broader representation and entering into meaningful government level agreements with other countries.

In order to do this, 'sports ambassadors' are identified. These are high-profile athletes who are chosen to convey a message of nation-building to all South Africans.

The Department of Sport and Recreation also set itself the following targets which have been assumed by the SASC:

- to increase levels of participation in sport and recreation activities

▲ **Figure 4.23** *South African sport: a structure for excellence*

- to raise sport's profile in the face of conflicting priorities
- to maximise the probability of success in major events
- to place sport and recreation in the forefront of efforts to reduce crime levels.

In November 1998, the **South African Sports Commission Act** was approved, whereby the National Sports Council and the Department of Sport and Recreation were merged to form the South African Sports Commission. This body is responsible to the Minister of Sport.

Each provincial Department of Sport and Recreation will be represented on the Commission, which respects the autonomy of sport and recreational organisations, and acts in an advisory capacity to the Minister. It also co-ordinates the provision of facilities and community centres in disadvantaged areas, in consultation with the relevant authorities (Figure 4.23).

The 1998 Act required specific development in respect of previously disadvantaged communities. This aspect was further highlighted in the **National Sport and Recreation Act**, also introduced in 1998, which provides for the promotion and development of sport and recreation, and initiatives that address imbalances of equity and democracy. The SASC and other agencies at national and provincial level are required to work towards drastic improvements in these areas.

The South African Institute for Drugs-free Sport Act was approved by Parliament in 1997. The institute is managed by a board of directors appointed by the Minister of Sport and Recreation in October 1997. Its main objectives are to promote drugs-free participation in sport and the development of a national strategy to counter doping in sport.

4. Recreational sport (mass participation)

Role of sporting participation in New World cultures

Each of the cultures under review here have strong traditions of sports participation as part of a healthy outdoor life.

Australia

In Australia, although the predominantly white population have a reputation for surf, sea and sand recreation, its minority Aboriginal population have largely been denied access to such pursuits. Currently, questions over land rights and the return of ancient lands to the native population are key to the future of self-determination in the broad cultural sense – including that of recreation (Figure 4.24).

As part of an increasingly common pattern, Australian government involvement in recreational programmes is delivered through the ASC and its Active Australia programme. This programme, which is an extension of the former Aussie Sport initiative, has as its slogan 'From Six to Sixty', a clear message that everyone should be actively involved in recreation of some kind.

New Zealand

Policies of inclusion have traditionally been part of sports provision in New Zealand, with access and participation for its Maori people written into constitutional rights.

The Hillary Commission is central to all government-sponsored activity and its programmes include Sportfit and Push Play, both designed to encourage the broadest participation in either sport or recreation. The slogan '30 minutes' is designed to remind people that this is all that is needed as a minimum level of activity for a healthy life.

Programmes such as Young People First, supported by the Hillary Commission's **Community Sport Fund,** offer funding to

▲ **Figure 4.24** The 'average' white Australian's recreation ground: the beach!

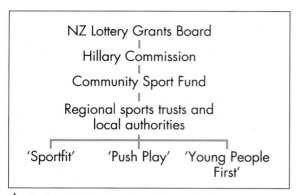

▲ **Figure 4.25** *Community sport funding in New Zealand*

sports clubs and other organisations who promote active leisure. This fund is managed at grass-roots level by local authorities who ensure that, in particular, youth sport programmes are better supported than is often the case. This is particularly effective in rural areas where population levels might not normally justify an adequate level of funding. The New Zealand Lottery Grants Board funds all of the Hillary Commission's programmes (Figure 4.25).

The fitness industry in New Zealand runs a programme called Fitness New Zealand. This includes a self-monitoring scheme to ensure fair and ethical practice and a programme of awareness designed to make everyone in New Zealand aware of the whereabouts of their nearest gymnasium or fitness centre.

South Africa

In South Africa, until recently opportunites have been largely limited to the white minority group. However, recent post-apartheid reforms include proposals to redress this situation (see 'Community participation' below).

The South African National Games and Leisure Activities (SANGALA) programme is the result of co-operation between SANREC and the Department of Sport and Recreation. It was launched in February 1996 to involve all South Africans in healthy recreational activities in the nation-building process.

The country's provincial governments are responsible for policy development within the context of the national sport and recreation. They also work in partnership with the provincial sports federations.

The SANGALA project consists of:

- Community SANGALA – targeted at the broad community, without any differentiation in age or status
- Training SANGALA – specialises in the training of community recreation leaders
- Corporate SANGALA – aimed at middle and senior management in both the private and public sectors
- Senior SANGALA – encourages physical activity among senior citizens
- Street SANGALA – a life skills project for homeless children.

The Movers-in-Action projects are aimed at three- to six-year olds, providing them with recreational activities to develop small and large motor skills.

Community participation

Australia

All Australia's states and territories have departments of Aboriginal affairs. These include programmes of recreational activity designed to incorporate Aboriginal culture. This is very much an 'outreach policy' with officers employed to go out into Aborigine communities and implement policies of inclusion. Unfortunately, these policies do not seem to be very successful. Aborigines are still regarded as 'social outcasts' by many white Australians and even those who have achieved sporting fame have not always found that this leads to broader social acceptability.

Sport is part of the way of life for most Australians, although this includes beach activities and spectator sports. The **Moneghetti Report** into the level of activity amongst Australian School children in 1993 revealed a surprisingly low level of participation at levels that would be beneficial to health and well-being. The subsequent Aussie Sport and Active Australia programmes recognised a need to raise the level of involvement of all Australians and attempted to do so by using local communities as a base for a whole range of recreational activities.

New Zealand

Community participation in physical recreation in New Zealand has traditionally been founded in the farmstead and the healthy outdoor life. Rugby, cricket and, to a lesser degree, athletics form the mainstays of sporting and community life. Changes have occurred in that women and girls are now readily included in many activities. The development of city life has caused alarm, however, as general levels of sporting activity have declined.

Push Play and Sportfit programmes and the slogan '30 minutes' (see page 243) have been promoted by the Hillary Commission in the same way as Active Australia is promoted by the ASC.

South Africa

The situation is quite different in South Africa, where post-apartheid reforms have seen major infrastructural changes. Those cultural groups formerly excluded from access to recreation in South Africa represent a huge majority. They are therefore more likely to gain from reforms than might be the case in Australia where Aborigines represent (approximately) only six per cent of the population.

In South Africa where football (soccer) is the sport of the masses, far more people play the game than rugby and the same is also true of cricket. That the white minority groups have better facilities and far greater representation on national teams has long been an issue. It is now likely that in time such imbalances will be redressed.

An initiative known as the **RecRehab** project rehabilitates youth and women in prisons. The project started at a youth rehabilitation centre in KwaZulu-Natal and is now firmly established in some fifteen prisons nationwide.

A white paper called 'Sports Information in South Africa' was produced in 1995 by the **Department of Recreation and Sport (DSR)**. It outlines the government's intentions in terms of policy and is summarised below. Only time will tell whether these intentions materialise into actions.

1 Identification of stakeholders in sport and agreement of roles between the State and sports management, to ensure efficiency in the delivery of sport.
2 Creation of basic, multi-purpose facilities in disadvantaged areas.
3 Upgrading sports administrators' level of expertise from club level upwards through the development of volunteer corps training and staff teaching.
4 Promotion of health consciousness via theme campaigns aimed at specific interest groups.
5 Identification of talent, especially via mass participation programmes.
6 Investments in the preparation of sportspeople for competition via the establishment of sports support services, i.e. sports information, technological support, drug testing, and the establishment of a central élite sports academy and provincial grass-roots academies.
7 Institution of appropriate affirmative action controls aimed at redressing racial, gender and demographic imbalances, as well as narrowing the gap between able-bodied and less able sportspersons.

SANREC

The South African National Recreation Council (SANREC) came into being in 1997 and is responsible for developing community recreational programmes, facilities and training and research. It has a network of nine **Provincial Recreation Committees (PRORECS)** which administer its programmes within each province.

The task facing South Africa's politicians and administrators is huge. Quite clearly it will take some time before the benefits of new policies will have an effect on the daily lives of millions of South Africans.

National parks

New Zealand

New Zealand has fourteen national parks under the control of the Department of Conservation and managed by the staff of the departmental minister. There are key policies with regard to the management of recreation and conservation, which enable wide use of these areas, but within guidelines. The policy of including Maori rights and culture within such a framework ensures that any likely impact upon sensitive areas is negotiated with Maori representatives. This requirement is written into the more recent additions to the Treaty of Waitangi (see page 232) which ensures that Maori rights are not violated

Australia

In Australia the numerous national (state) parks are administered by the state in which they lie. Little allowance is made in their management for the cultural associations which might be held by their native inhabitants.

The only natural area in Australia which comes under a federal remit is the **Great Barrier Reef Marine Park (GBRMP)**. This is both funded and protected by federal law. Australia does, however, have in place policies of low impact habitation governing the use of and residence in areas of natural beauty.

South Africa

South Africa has 53 national parks or protected areas, including the world famous **Kruger National Park**. Traditionally, these areas have been the preserve of the privileged white minority but have also been used to attract foreign tourists and their currency. Present policies centre on conservation as opposed to recreation. They have traditionally made little allowance for the rights and cultures of those largely nomadic native groups whom history has dispossessed.

Adventure and wilderness sports

Areas such as national parks are prime targets for those groups interested in the promotion and development of wilderness and extreme sports. Issues arising out of this use are likely to centre on levels of impact and potential damage to delicately balanced environments. There will also be a need for effective policies and controls to avert potential confrontations between sports enthusiasts and environmental groups. As always, such issues are likely to be a balance between the need for conservation and the right to recreation.

Of these countries, South Africa alone has to address issues of wildlife conservation. Both Australia and New Zealand have wildlife species to protect but neither has the big game population under threat from trophy hunters or poachers, nor the attendant problems of adequately resourcing measures to combat this type of undesirable activity.

Section A(3): Developing cultures: with reference to Argentina and Kenya

1. Historical and cultural background

Argentina

Europeans first occupied Argentina in the early sixteenth century and the Spanish went on to establish a permanent colony on the site of the present Buenos Aires. Formal declaration of independence from Spain was made on 9 July 1816 and, after periods of civil strife in 1853 Argentina established limited national unity and adopted a constitution.

Conservative elements dominated politics until 1916, when their traditional rivals, the Radicals, won control of the government through a democratic election. The Radicals attempted to open opportunities for the expanding middle class until 1930, when a military coup returned the Conservatives to power.

A further constitution was adopted in 1949 but a lack of consensus caused its failure. It was not until the **Law of Basic Consensus** (1993) and the subsequent reforms of 1994 were passed that Argentina finally acquired an acceptable and recognisable democratic political structure. Even so, it is still the opinion of many that there is an unacceptably high degree of military influence in both day-to-day and long-term politics.

The country has 23 provinces and the population is largely white with approximately 15 per cent **mestizos**. These are people of mixed European/native descent and 'Amerindians' (native Indians).

During the early twentieth century, British investment figured largely in the construction of railways and ports and utilised an influx of European labour.

Kenya

Early western explorers became interested in East Africa in the second half of the nineteenth century when Britain and France were attempting to control the trade routes to India and Asia.

German missionaries were the first to venture into Kenya's interior. In 1857 two Britons, Richard Burton and John Speke, began their search for the source of the Nile. This was followed some years later by Livingstone's 20-year sojourn in Africa on the same quest. Henry Stanley's search for Livingstone is legendary and he returned to Africa after Livingstone's death to complete his exploratory work.

The first British missionaries arrived in Kampala in 1871 and gleaned sufficient local knowledge to enable the discovery of the shortest trade route to the coast. By the late 1880s, that part of Africa now known as Kenya was pretty well charted by a succession of British, American, French and German explorers.

The development of trade with the major European powers and the opening of trade routes were significant in the exploitation of the region. Most of the major towns grew up along the developing railway, built for the purpose of transporting goods.

By the early twentieth century, a small number of European settlers had been enticed in to Kenya. An increasing number of civil servants were posted there to administer the protectorate and, later, colony. Kenya's wildlife was an attraction to largely white big game hunters and explorers. British culture became the norm in influential circles until the uprising by the Mao-Mao in the 1950s. This was a secret, anti-European terrorist movement and symbolised native discontent. Large-scale reforms were put in place as a result of the unrest. Subsequently the Lancaster Agreement brought colonial life to an end and Kenya gained independence in 1963.

As in many other parts of the world, British (and European) influences shaped many areas of life in Kenya, including education. **Missionary schools** formed the backbone of early education. As elsewhere, games, drill and physical training was largely an extension of the Arnoldian philosophies which had been very influential in Britain, the 'mother country'.

Native indigenous population

Argentina

About 85 per cent of Argentina's population is of European origin and the country has relatively few mestizos (native Indians) – unlike most other Latin American countries (see 'Culture and sport' below).

Kenya

The indigenous population of Kenya has been broadened over centuries and now includes the following major tribal groups:

- hunter/gatherers (the oldest population group)
- Cushites
- Nilotes
- Bantus
- others (including Arab, Asian, European and Swahili).

Only Nairobi (1.4 million) and Mombasa (1.0 million) are significantly large population centres and only around 25 per cent of the country's population live in an urban setting.

Culture and sport

Argentina

It is likely that English or British influence in the development of sport in Argentina began with the arrival of a Scottish doctor, **Andrew Dick**, in Buenos Aires in 1807. He organised foot races as a healthy form of recreation. British influence in athletics continued until the formation of the Asociación Nacional de Ejercicios Físicos and several other Argentine athletic clubs just after the beginning of the twentieth century.

Early games of cricket were also played, largely by British ex-patriots. The Buenos Aires Cricket Club was formed in 1858 and the Argentine Cricket Association nearly forty years later, in 1897. Football was being played by 1867 and the British community figured significantly with **Thomas Hogg** and **William Heald** captaining respective sides on the Buenos Aires Cricket Club pitch.

Gymnastics, however, did not take hold until the mid-1940s, developing very differently from Europe and North America. Hockey became popular in the early years of the twentieth century, with the first team coming from members of San Martín Athletic Club, in 1905. In 1923 five clubs formed an association for the advancement of ladies hockey which had expanded to fifteen teams in two divisions.

British influence was again evident in the establishment of that most Argentinian of sports – **polo.** The first recorded match took place in 1874 in the grounds of an estancia (estate or ranch) some 130 kilometres from Buenos Aires between teams named 'City' and 'Scotland'. King George V (then the Duke of York) is reputed to have watched polo games there in 1881 (although he would have been only sixteen at the time). The first polo club was founded the following year, as was the River Plate Polo Association. This organisation merged with the Argentine Polo Federation in 1923 to form the Argentine Polo Association. Rowing began in 1856–5, and as in cricket, the names of James Hogg and William Heald figure prominently.

Like polo and soccer, rugby is a game which is becoming increasingly associated with Argentina. The first known game was played in 1873 between 'Banks' and 'City', suggesting a distinct middle-class connection, as was the case in England at that time. Although championships have been contested since 1899, it was not until 1951 that the River Plate Rugby Union became the Argentine Rugby Union, indicating that until then the game had been centred largely around Buenos Aires.

Although basketball has been played here since the late 1920s, it was never really popular until the 1950s. Again, the highest level of activity seems to have been in Buenos Aires.

It is significant that more than one-third of the population lived (and continues to live) in or around Buenos Aires, as is the fact that almost 85 per cent of the population live in urban areas. Once provision is accelerated, it is relatively easy to provide for closely grouped communities such as Buenos Aires, as opposed to largely rural and sparsely scattered ones.

The other important cities of Cordoba, the river port of Rosario La Plata and the capital of Buenos Aires Province; Mar del Plata, San Miguel de Tucuman, Salta and Mendoza collectively contain the vast majority of Argentina's population. This means that any improvement in sports provision in this small number of major population centres will be far more effective than in countries with a largely rural/remote population.

TASK

Unlike Kenya, Argentina was never a British colony. Can you explain why it was that many of Argentina's sports and recreations still developed along the same lines as those of countries that were British colonies?

Kenya

There is a wide variety of sports played in Kenya. This fact is often overshadowed by the publicity and attention given to the country's long-distance runners who have won countless medals at Olympic, Commonwealth and other major championships.

Kenya's cricketers now compete in the World Cup tournament and beat the highly rated West Indies in 1996. Kenya was invited to host the International Cricket Council (ICC) knockout tournament, the biggest cricket tournament to be held on East African soil, in October 2000.

Although soccer is very popular, basketball is probably Kenya's fastest-growing sport. There is now a two-division National League and the men's and women's teams are ranked amongst the top African nations. Kenyan basketball players are amongst

those being offered sports scholarships at American universities, and a small number are now playing professional basketball in countries such as Canada, South Africa and India. Many of the sport's teams are based upon institutions such as banks and commercial organisations including railway and bus companies.

Rugby is also growing in popularity, and the annual Safari and Paris–Dakar rally motoring events draw both enthusiasts and tourists to Kenya each year.

The seeds of most of the country's sports today were sown by the **early colonists** and many of the activities date from just after the beginning of the twentieth century. Prior to that time and even today in more remote areas, tribal activity formed the basis of movement-associated recreations.

Boys played games such as 'whipping' (an activity associated with cattle-herding), fighting games and other boisterous activities that prepared them for life as adult males. There seem to have been very few ball games, with the exception of *adhula*, a form of hockey, played largely in the west of the country. Girls' activities mirrored the roles of adult females, for whom dancing was the most common recreational outlet. This was also the case for males, for whom physical prowess and a masculine beauty was crucial to attaining high rank and social status.

Such practices were frowned upon by the colonial 'incomers' and the institutionalised sports of Victorian England that were considered 'fit for natives' became required activity for both children and adults. This did not, of course, extend to the full range of recreations of Victorian England, some of which were considered inappropriate for the 'native class' of people. Kenya's first golf club – The Royal Nairobi – was formed in 1906 and, as its title implies, was very much a gentlemen's club in the colonial mould. Sadly, this pattern is still the predominant one with the recently built Windsor Golf and Country Club catering largely for European ex-patriots and the lucrative tourist market.

Kenya has over 30 golf courses, 6 of which are within a few miles of Nairobi.

Most facilities, however, are beyond the reach, both socially and economically, of most of the country's native population.

Tourist literature highlights that many courses are at an altitude of more than 1500 metres (5000 feet), enticing golfers by saying that such conditions are likely to add ten per cent to the distance the ball may be hit.

There is little doubt that sports ventures, along with Kenya's wildlife and natural scenery, are amongst the assets exploited to the full in the country's quest to gain some economic viability. There is sadly a great gulf between the lifestyle and recreational pursuits of those who, for example, live in Nairobi's plusher suburbs, and the vast majority of the city's population who live in the sewerless ramshackle shanty towns around it.

The emergence of a host of middle- and long-distance runners in the 1970s is an important quite recent development. The attention gained by athletes such as Kipchoge ('Kip') Keino (Figure 4.26) and Naftali Temu amongst others, signalled Kenya's arrival into world sport. Kenya also hosted the 4th African Games in the city of Nairobi in 1987.

Colonial historical development

Argentina

Between 1850 and 1940, more than 6.6 million Europeans settled in the country. **Immigrants** came largely from Spain and Italy, but significant numbers were also from France, Britain, Germany, Russia, Poland, and Syria. The popularity of **pelota** is clearly attributable to immigrant (Basque) groups, but the influence of British immigrants was of major significance across a wide range of sports.

European immigration is still officially encouraged and this continued influx has had a continued 'colonising' influence upon Argentina's culture and, most importantly, its sports. (See 'Culture and sport' on page 248.)

Kenya

Kenya was important to colonising European countries largely because of its position on trade routes to the coast.

▲ *Figure 4.26* 'Kip' Keino, the first in a long line of Kenyan athletes to achieve international fame

Colonisation by Britain not only brought British sports into the country, but also left an administrative framework in place once independence had been granted in 1963. (See below.) The imposition of an alien culture upon a tribal one had considerable drawbacks and ancient infrastructures, although much subdued, have never really disappeared. Much of the country's current difficulties, both cultural and economic, centre upon the resistance of the 'old' to the 'new', even though the old colonial masters are now gone.

State policies in relation to games and sports

State policies

It was not until the first period of the government of **Juan Peron** (1945–55) that Argentina adopted the notion of sport as a nation-building tool. The Peronist administration was noted for its strong support of Argentine sport but on a domestic rather than a wider level. Sport had lapsed in popularity in the war years between the late-1930s and mid-1940s. Peron personally promoted sporting activity as a way of rebuilding national pride that followed this unsettled period.

More recently, following the Federation of 1993–94, policies are being enacted to bring Argentina up to date with many other countries in recognising that political, social and economic motives can be served through the provision of sport at all levels.

Kenya

Until the 1960s, Kenya's sporting policies reflected the needs of the colonisers rather than its indigenous population. Following independence, the emergence of the country's excellence in running has allowed some investment in sporting infrastructure, although, in comparison with other cultures, this is minimal.

Sport in Kenya today is run from the office of the Vice President and **Ministry of Home Affairs, Heritage and Sports,** which has a huge brief that includes prisons, the probation and vocational services and approved schools; national archives, public records, the national library service and national museums and monuments; development and co-ordination of sports and social welfare and services.

The development and co-ordination of sports is just one of an extensive list of responsibilities. Even though the work of this government department is shared by three Assistant Ministers, it would seem to reflect Kenya's lack of the economic resources necessary to support a more sophisticated infrastructure.

The **Kenyan National Olympic Committee (NOCK)** is an entirely independent organisation that is completely separate from government control. Its purpose is to promote Olympism in Kenya as well as amateur sport. Rather unusually in today's world, it claims to resist all political, religious or commercial pressure. The Kenya National Olympic Association and the country's Amateur Athletic Association were both founded in 1952.

Sport as foreign policy

Sport is an aspect of the foreign policy of both Argentina and Kenya. It brings attention and interest to each country in a broader economic field as a result of sporting successes or exports.

Argentine horsemen have travelled the equestrian world for decades bringing both sporting and economic benefits as a result, as have polo teams for which the country is renowned. Whilst they bring kudos to Argentina, both activities are directly beneficial to only a small section of the Argentine community.

Currently, Argentine soccer players live and work all over the world and earn vast sums (as do some of the country's leading coaches), bringing benefit to a broader social group.

In Kenya, the same might be said of the many middle-distance runners who raise the profile of their country worldwide, attracting both interest and foreign currency on their travels.

Nation building

As well as the economic benefits derived from the success of their sportsmen and women at home and abroad, sport is instrumental in the development of national pride and identity in both countries.

Argentina is in the process of rebuilding a national image after the war with the British in the Falklands in 1982, and the ensuing political unrest. It now has a democratically elected government, allowing for sporting pressure groups to lobby on behalf of the development of sport in the country, and on behalf of its talented sportsmen and women.

In the case of Kenya, its distance runners have provided a model for success based on natural talent and low-level facility provision. This has now extended to soccer and Kenya's success in the African Nations Cup is broadening the range of role models and has become a source of national pride.

TASK

Research the number of Olympic medals won by sportsmen/women from Argentina and Kenya in the last thirty years.

a Which country has won the most medals?

b Which country has won medals in the greatest number of different sports?

Environmental and topographical factors

National parks

Argentina

Argentina has eleven major areas designated as national parks, stretching from the sub-tropical rainforests in the north to the almost Arctic coast of Tierra del Fuego in

Table 4.2 *Land area/population of Argentina and Kenya*

Country	Land area (sq km)	Population
Argentina	2.8 million	36.3 million
Kenya	0.6 million	28.1 million

the south. The country has a long-standing tradition of protecting such areas. As well as national parks there are a number of provincial or state parks.

National parks include the Bosques Petrificados, which is a large petrified forest, and Los Glaciares National Park, which is a UN 'biosphere' site of mountain peaks and huge glaciers. A small number of these areas have been developed commercially, encouraging tourism and recreations such as fishing and hiking.

Aconcagua Provincial Park contains Mount Aconcagua, the highest mountain peak in the western hemisphere. Many climbers have died attempting to reach its summit.

Kenya

Kenya's national parks are both wildlife and botanical sanctuaries and have been set aside for the purposes of:

- conservation and education
- recreational enjoyment by Kenyans and overseas visitors.

In comparison to Argentina's national parks, the **Masai Mara National Park** in Kenya is much more widely known. It is but one of forty-three such areas, amounting to a considerable proportion of the country's land mass (Figure 4.27).

The National Parks' legislation and infrastructure was created in 1945 under the British colonial administration. Following the country's independence in 1963 it was

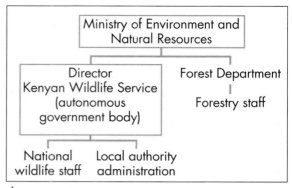

▲ **Figure 4.28** *Management structure of Kenya's national parks and reserves*

merged with the Game Department to form the National Parks Service under the Wildlife Conservation and Management Act of 1976.

Kenya clearly recognises the environmental value of these areas and its economic importance in terms of tourism. The service now has semi-independent status, deriving its income partly from central funding but largely from tourism and related activities.

Four of Kenya's reserves are given the status of biosphere reserve where general recreational activity is not allowed. However, many do permit and encourage activities such as swimming, sailing, water-ski-ing and fishing, with the exception of marine national parks where such activities are also prohibited.

Biosphere reserves are protected environments containing unique landforms and systems of land use. There are 271 such reserves worldwide.

National reserves are administered by the appropriate local authority but are staffed by national parks staff. Nature and forest reserves come under the direct control of and are staffed by the Ministry of Environment and Natural Reserves (Figure 4.28).

2. Physical education and sport in high schools and colleges/universities

Historical development of physical education

Argentina

Early forms of physical education devel-

▲ **Figure 4.27** *Kenya's Masai Mara National Park: a magnet for tourists and a major source of foreign currency*

oped in Argentina within the private sector at institutions such as St Hilda's College. Canon Stephenson founded the school as St George's College in 1912 and the first headmistress of its girls' section, Miss Mabel Holland, was brought in from Cricklewood, London. The college was re-named St Hilda's in 1927 and today is a mixed boarding school.

It was probably **Alexander Watson Hutton** who made the best known contribution to school sport and physical education. He introduced 'English' models of games, drill and physical training at St Andrews Scottish School in 1882, and two years later at his own school, the Buenos Aires English High School. In the second establishment, he opened a gymnasium and a tennis court and founded the school's Alumni Football Club which dominated the club championships in Argentina for several years. As in many other corners of the world, the English model (both academic and athletic) was to form the foundation of an education system in a far-off land (Figure 4.29).

Kenya

Formal education in Kenya has much in common with other former colonies being the result of missionary involvement from the middle of the nineteenth century. The main aim of such innovation was of course evangelism – the spreading of the Christian message – but schools also became the means by which skilled labour was trained for work on white settlers' farms and, for a fortunate few, work as clerical staff in the colonial administration.

▲ **Figure 4.29** A massed drill display in the 1950s illustrates the strength of the European influence on Argentine physical education

Physical education in its muscular Christian form (see page 15) was a useful adjunct to work in the classroom. However, education in the colonial period was different for various ethnic groups, with separate schools and curricula for those of European origin. European schools had far superior resources, including playing fields and sometimes gymnasia, as to a lesser degree did the Asian and Arab schools, which were also administered separately.

Since independence such differences have become less clearly defined, but there are still a number of exclusive private schools.

School sport

Argentina

The private schools in the Buenos Aires province (not to be confused with the city) play their sport under the auspices of an organisation called the **Asociación Deportiva Estudjantil** (ADE). Further evidence of Englishness is apparent in such schools in the house system, where students are grouped in teams or 'houses' each with its own identity, as the basis of sporting and other endeavours. This is designed to foster a sense of identity and team spirit. Other large centres have similar such organisations but for private schools only.

In state schools, the situation is very much left to each province. The Buenos Aires province provides a structure of sports competitions for its state school children but this is organised by the provincial department of education and not the schools themselves. Buenos Aires province is apparently the only one to have such a structure in place. Elsewhere school sport in Argentina is run by the local senior sports clubs. This, however, would seem to be a rather *ad hoc* arrangement with no central infrastructure. Children play in junior teams representing their clubs rather than their schools, mirroring to some degree the pattern that is prevalent in many European countries – if rather less well organised.

Kenya

Schools in Kenya are administered through 55 regions. This structure is reflected in the nature of sporting competition with district championships, largely in European sports such as soccer, cricket and netball. Some hockey is played but this tends to be much stronger in the private schools, which generally have far better facilities than those that are government/parent run.

To some extent the poor range and extent of activity is explained by the relatively recent huge upsurge in the number of government schools, and also by the fact that a large percentage of the school population is in small rural schools, well away from large centres of population. In many respects this is almost the exact opposite of the situation in Argentina.

The most successful aspect of school sport in Kenya so far has been the National Schools Athletics Championships, which were initiated in 1967 and have continued since then. Kenya's athletes are known around the world and most are a product of the close relationship between school and senior athletics administrations. Soccer and basketball (largely outdoors) are also well established, as is girls' netball. However, athletics, with its long-term financial assistance from Coca-Cola, is able to fund schools' activity in a way that has not yet been possible in other cases.

Ironically, for many Kenyans their time at school, however basically provided for, represents the high point of their sporting involvement. While provision (in government schools) is typically less than what would be termed adequate in Western Europe, involvement in soccer and athletics for boys is common, as is involvement in netball for girls. Such opportunity, however basic, does not feature in the lives of many Kenyan adults.

Physical education in high schools

Argentina

The **National Institute of Physical Education** was created in 1985 during the presidency of Raul Alfonsin and has been based in Buenos Aires since the beginning of 1994. It was charged with the task of co-ordinating scientific, psychological, sociological and political aspects of life into physical education. It also had to assess the suit-

ability of those applying for courses to become physical educators.

Documentation associated with the above developments identifies that children should:

> *... learn to relate to their own bodies and their movement as part of the formation of complete people.*

The body is seen as central in communication and expression, and its movement as essential components in the development of knowledge and of the world.

The common contents of physical education programmes are centred around four learning blocks:

- Block 1: The body and its movements utilising gymnastics as the main medium of learning
- Block 2: Bodily health and well-being in the world around us and the acquisition of simple and complex skills
- Block 3: Motor games and the use of 'play' to integrate personality and expression and develop motor skills. To gradually move towards the playing and understanding of normal adult games with appropriate rules
- Block 4: Applied learning – the application of knowledge of their own bodies, abilities and motor skills to both spontaneous and regulated games. Hygienic habits and consideration for their own bodies and those of others. The care and conservation of the surroundings.

The above is a scant resumé of a very detailed programme which, however well intentioned, is being implemented against a background of very poor levels of attendance in secondary education. (sixty per cent). Contrastingly, attendance at primary level is almost 100 per cent and at least ensures that the initial levels of the programme will be widely delivered.

Current reforms

The establishment of a **democracy** in Argentina in 1984 led to the federalisation of education in 1993, including higher education, with provincial regions funding 20 per cent of the overall cost.

Current reforms have been instrumental in restructuring the seven forms of primary education and five forms of secondary education into this new federal system. Education is now available at three years of age but compulsory from six with ten years of compulsory schooling thereafter.

Although compulsory education only applies to students up to the age of fourteen, the federal programme of **General Basic Education (EGB)** has, as a common component, one year of initial education and nine years of primary and secondary education for students up to the age of sixteen. Provision for physical education has been included as part of this EGB. Figure 4.30 illustrates this federal model. The Common Basic Contents are adapted at provincial level and again locally by each individual school – within agreed constraints.

There is some inconsistency here as government figures show that although the attendance levels for primary education are high this cannot be said for the secondary sector. Attendance here has increased from approximately 44 per cent in 1980 to just under 60 per cent in 1998.

Students are allowed to leave school early to take jobs but many find that appointments are often short-term and they simply become unemployed. Implications for physical education here are that programmes in the secondary sector are delivered to far fewer students than is desirable. Unemployment is high (approximately 20 per cent). Once having left school many young people are reluctant to complete their EGB programme, making entry to tertiary (intermediate) education very difficult.

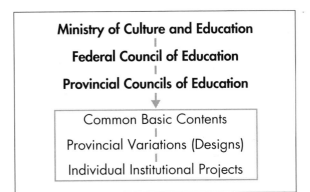

▲ Figure 4.30 Education in Argentina: a federal model with provincial and local variants

Kenya

Great strides have been made in education provision since independence in 1963. Then there were only 151 secondary schools, providing for approximately 30,000 students. Today there are almost 3,000 such schools educating well over half a million students of which just over 40 per cent are girls. Such figures are, at first glance, quite impressive but such expansion in the face of a very poor economy has caused some difficulties.

Physical education in Kenya's government schools is poorly taught and poorly funded. In some parts of the country the educational system is either barely adequate or in some isolated cases, almost non-existent. Within this context physical education takes a poor second place and where it does exist, teacher-led sessions of drill and group displays are often part of the staple diet.

Provision for physical education rests very much on the shoulders of parents. Although the Kenya government builds schools and pays teachers' salaries, building maintenance costs and the provision of sports and PE equipment are borne locally by parents. This is a reflection of the economic situation in that country with revenue to its exchequer quite unable to extend to all the 'ideal' provisions it might like to embrace.

Official policy requires that physical education is taught in all the country's state schools. However, this is not widely practised due, in many cases, to lack of either facilities or adequately qualified teachers. In a country where famine and drought impact hugely on both lifestyle and policy implementation, this is perhaps hardly surprising. It is not unknown for up to 20 per cent of schoolchildren to drop out from school as a result of these factors and the inability to pay fees which are levied by the government, even in its own schools. In the case of individual schools, the efforts of parents are often crucial in material provision for subjects such as physical education.

University sport

Both Argentina and Kenya are affiliated to FISA, the world student sport organisation

– Argentina through the Conito Tecnico del Deporte Universitario Argentino and Kenya through the Kenya University Sports Association. In neither case does the place of university sport approach anything like the sophisticated and highly commercialised system in place in the USA. Although in the case of Argentina the number of university places has grown enormously since the reforms of 1993 and 1994, in both countries university sport is considered still the province of a small élite.

3. Professional (élite) sport

History of professional sport

The Basque game of pelota was one of the first Argentinian sports to acquire professional status and several forms of the game have been played since 1830. At various times since then its popularity has almost rivalled that of football. The latter began in 1867 with a friendly kickabout at a Buenos Aires cricket club and became the country's leading sport. It was, however, the Scotsman, Alexander Watson Hutton, who is credited with the real expansion of the game in the years following his arrival in Buenos Aires in 1882 (see page 253).

The first Argentine championship in football was held in 1891 and by 1901 some twenty clubs were affiliated to the Argentine Association Football League. The first professional championship was not held until 1931, by which time over 130 clubs fielding over 700 teams were playing regular fixtures. Despite slow growth in the thirty or forty years following its introduction into Argentina, football is now massively popular and Argentine teams have for some years been regarded as amongst the best in the world.

Professional sport has arrived in Kenya much more recently and currently includes athletics, basketball, cricket, rugby and soccer. Prior to independence in 1963, the amateur sporting principles of the colonial class were applied. It is only since then, and the subsequent expansion of professional sport globally, that Kenya has begun to flex its muscles in this area of sporting endeavour.

The structure of professional sport

Argentina

The **Comite Olimpico Argentino (COA)** was founded in 1927 and has traditionally looked after the selection of and provision for Argentina's Olympic athletes. Even local Argentinian opinion regarded this as a fascist organisation with a noticeably large military presence on its committees. It must, however, be acknowledged that since the end of the Galtieri regime in 1982 this military influence has been considerably reduced.

As its name suggests, the **Confed-eración Atletica de Deportes (CAD)** was a confederation of the major sports organisations in Argentina that organised and fostered the development of high performance sports generally. This and the COA were amalgamated during the period of the Peron administration (1945–55) to form the CAD-COA (a combination of the two titles), which covered the two aspects of high-performance sport.

It was not until 1989 that the **Secretaria de Deportes de la Nación** (National Secretariat of Sport) was created. This organisation is responsible directly to the national president. In theory its aim is to co-ordinate every effort to foster community, educational, high performance (including professional) and Olympic sport. In practice, it concentrates on the awarding of scholarships to gifted athletes and organises Olympic preparation and selection.

Kenya

In Kenya, the Ministry of Home Affairs, Heritage and Sports has sole responsibility for any government involvement in sport. As mentioned on page 251, however, its huge range of responsibilities prevents little more than cursory attention being paid to what in other countries is far more extensively funded. The governing bodies of individual sports rely on income from limited but increasing commercial involvement. Although both soccer and basketball are highly popular, only Kenya's athletes are a financial success on the global stage.

Sport at national level is organised by the **Kenya National Sports Council (KNSC).**

This supervises more than 30 individual sporting associations and the government has posted sports officers to all provinces and districts to develop sports programmes. The morality of such expenditure is questionable. In a country where drought and famine are major problems is it ethical to invest huge sums of money in building the magnificent ultra-modern Moi International Sports Centre (named after the country's president and built with aid from China), and the Nyayo National Stadium?

The commercial nature of professional sport

In both Argentina and Kenya, the commercial appeal of professional sport is broadening rapidly. Kenyan running has brought the world's attention to a hitherto relatively unknown sporting nation. The country is now broadening the scope of its sporting ambitions and venturing into the worlds of international cricket and soccer. As with most forms of professional sport, particularly at the élite level, this generates commercial activity.

Similarly, the attention that has traditionally followed Argentina's soccer stars is now also being given to its rugby players, both domestically and on the world stage. Much of the increase in commercial activity, whether it is sponsorship, advertising or soaring wage levels, is directly attributable to the growth and acceptance of professional sport (Figure 4.31).

Both countries benefit considerably from the connection between business and sport, stimulating, as it does, further commercial markets both sporting and non-sporting. In Kenya, the growth of professional soccer is particularly significant. Many people believe that this has almost displaced that country's athletes as its leading sporting earner of foreign currency. The role of the media is also of considerable importance here, providing both a platform for the creation of superstars and role-models and a marketplace for associated wares and commercial services.

Role of armed forces as sports nurseries

Both Argentina and Kenya have a history of military involvement in sport. In Argentina this extended to the military having almost complete control in addition to it providing favourable conditions for training and competition. Under the recent reforms this influence has been considerably reduced. With some exceptions, military influence no longer affects the country's sporting policies and selection procedures.

In Kenya, service in the army or as a police officer is still considered to be an advantage for sportsmen and women who wish to compete globally. However, in both countries the relatively recent broad development of professional sport has altered the situation. Individuals can now reasonably hope to become financially independent of this type of patronage and as a result such influence is now on the decline.

Disproportionate selectivity in sports played

Disproportionate selectivity is a device used by poorer (emerging) nations in order to focus very limited resources on a very small number of sports. This is done so that success is more likely to be achieved than if these very limited resources were spread thinly across a wider range of activities. The number of sports played relates to the sporting opportunity available to the population as a whole. Argentina has a record of broad sporting participation going back in some cases for well over a century.

It has an international (if still somewhat élitist) reputation for its show jumpers and polo players which goes back at least fifty years. Its soccer players have maintained a high profile since their appearance in the first World Cup competition in 1950.

▲ **Figure 4.31** Argentine rugby: professionalism has brought media attention and money

▲ **Figure 4.32** *Gabriel Batistuta: he earns far more in Europe than he could in Argentia*

There is some similarity to Kenya in that at one time a broad base of sporting opportunity did not exist amongst the whole population – and to some extent that remains the case. Argentine teams, however élitist in some cases, have graced the international stage in many sports for many years.

Kenya is a relative newcomer to the international sporting stage, with the exploits of Kipchoge Keino in middle-distance running in the early 1970s ensuring its place in world sport. Only recently has Kenya also become noticed in connection with international basketball and soccer and, to a lesser extent, cricket.

Move to West of players and coaches

In the case of both countries, players and coaches have moved to Europe in order to further their careers and maximise their earning potential.

Kenyan athletes come to Europe (and North America) to compete on the lucrative road-running circuit and also in Grand Prix meetings in the summer where large sums in both appearance and prize money can be earned. Basketball players are moving to

the USA on athletic scholarships and some are now playing professional basketball in Europe.

Argentinian footballers and coaches have a healthy professional scene in their own country but the 'real money' is in Europe. Players such as Gabriel Batistuta (F.C. Roma) and Diego Simeone (Inter Milan) can earn several times more abroad than they can at home (Figure 4.32)

TASK

Why is it that countries such as Kenya and other 'emergent' sporting nations appear to participate (well) in only a very small number of sports?

4. Recreational sport (mass participation)

Sporting participation in developing cultures

Argentina

The major period during which public programmes of recreation were put into place in Argentina was during the first Peronist period (1945–55) (see page 250). These programmes, however, were not maintained by succeeding administrations. It was not until the 1970s and early 1980s that there were further attempts to put into place programmes of public recreation. One example, known as the **Playas Programme**, involved community sports leaders working in the centre of urban communities (*playas* or civic squares). Such programmes were amongst the few publicly funded initiatives at that time but it did not come to fruition before public finances were used to conduct war with Britain in the Falkland Islands in 1982. Sporting initiatives are now being reconsidered but as yet there are few signs of implementation.

The potential benefits of mass participation in sport and/or recreation in terms of health, social integration and control and national defence are now widely accepted.

The Secretaria de Deportes de la Nacion (see page 256) is responsible for the development of such policies. As in many other relatively poor countries, however, the cost of implementation is often a stumbling block. The disadvantaged groups who suffer as a result of the lack of policy implementation include native Indian groups, the disabled, women and the native people of the provinces outside the urban areas known as 'cabicates negras' (black little heads). These people do not generally play sport due to lack of provision outside the main centres of population.

Kenya

The situation is much the same in Kenya where there is little provision outside main urban centres. The vast majority of the population lives outside Nairobi and the few other urbanised areas which puts them beyond the reach of the limited provision that is available. The major difference between the two countries in this respect is that a far greater proportion of the Argentine population is urban than is the case in Kenya.

The government-funded district sports officers work in all areas with the brief of developing sports programmes. But this is clearly with the intention of discovering talent as opposed to stimulating mass participation. In Kenya it seems to be that professional sport has to grow first in order to provide both the impetus and funding needed to develop and implement broader policies for all. As in many other cultures, it might well be soccer that is the means of access for many.

Section A(4): Asian cultures

1. Historical and cultural background

Societal values and sport

In most Asian countries there is a cultural mix of eastern and western philosophies. These have been shaped by events in history and, to a significant degree, by British and European colonial and trading practices. The former Indian colony, now partitioned into India, Bangladesh and Pakistan, has retained much of its indigenous culture whilst absorbing much that was British into its administrative infrastructure and education systems.

In the sporting context, these countries have retained a love of hockey and have also adopted cricket with great passion.

In Hong Kong and Singapore, rugby is played with much enthusiasm, as is cricket. These are all influenced by trading/colonial ties stretching back in some cases for centuries. At the same time, traditional activities have continued in Asian countries. In many ways this reflects the mixture of ancient and more recent practices in the broader sphere of business and commercial life. Even Japan, proud as it is of its cultural heritage, has succumbed to baseball, volleyball and to rugby. More recently, it has adopted soccer as has much of the rest of the world. This transportation of 'soccer culture' has been due largely to the modern medium of satellite television rather than influences of the colonial or historical kind.

Cricket and the British Empire

The historical association of the **British Empire** and much of the Asian sub-continent has meant that cricket has been a central plank in the development of recreation and sport. In colonial times those in senior positions (almost certainly English or British) would have played the game and the junior civil servants native to the many parts of Asia under colonial rule would also

▲ *Figure 4.33* Kumar Sri Ranjitsinji: prince of Indian cricketers

have played it (Figure 4.33).

Of nearly forty clubs currently playing in India's Ranji Trophy competition, first held in 1934, only a small number have been formed since the end of the Raj period in 1947. The oldest, simply known as Services, began in 1919 as part of the Army Sport Control Board. This was formed by the War Office in England after the end of World War I to encourage soldiers stationed throughout the Empire (in this case in India) to maintain fitness levels.

It is also important to consider the relationship of (often) ancient cultures and modern sporting philosophies. Clement (1985), writing about the potential for sports success in Asia as a whole, made the comment that:

> *... sport as a whole has little or no meaning for most Indians. The very notion of foot racing or indeed any other sport which demands intensive training, is alien to the country's way of life.*

In the west there is sometimes a misguided assumption that the world's cultural perspective is a western one. In many cases, however, it is simply an imposition on the culture of others.

India has many ancient sports. Many of these are still practised today in the regions in which they are traditional activities. Kabbadi is one of the few games that has developed a general appeal to modern day audiences, particularly to young people.

China

Mainland China provides a most interesting example of the diffusion of English/British sporting and recreational practices which lasted until the middle of the twentieth century. This was followed by an utter rejection of them in the period leading up to and following the establishment of the communist regime of the People's Republic of China in 1949.

Until the middle of the nineteenth century, the Chinese government forbade trade with foreign countries. The Opium Wars of the early 1840s saw Britain force access to some Chinese ports for trade and Hong Kong was ceded to Britain until its recent return in 1997.

A desire for health and long life and a liking of recreation and entertainment had long been part of the ancient traditional Chinese culture. In the hundred years or so between the Opium Wars and the mid-twentieth century, these traditional activities continued to be promoted as folk sports and in public schools and the military.

Activities included various forms of physical improvement such as martial arts, games and yangsheng – the art of keeping fit. As in other cultures, these activities developed out of military skills (Figure 4.34).

With increased contact with the west, the Chinese military also increasingly adopted western-style weapons and systems of drill and training. This spread into the nation's schools before being replaced in the 1920s by German gymnastics, track and field athletics and western ball games.

The Christian message

Along with British trade in the nineteenth century came Christianity in the form of missionary and British schools and organisations such as the **YMCA** and **YWCA**. Knuttgen (1990) records that by 1916 over 7,000 church schools, churches and cathedrals had been built in China. He also notes that the first ever western-style 'sports meeting' (track and field athletics) was held at St John's College, Shanghai, in 1890. The North China Games were held on eighteen occasions between 1913 and 1934, with the YMCA playing a major organising role.

Even though full British colonisation of China did not actually occur, the 'colonial model' was applied there as it was wherever British interests gained a trading or business foothold. An example of this is also found in Argentina (see page 247).

State and federal policies in relation to games and sports

China

The administration of sport in mainland China nowadays is very much under the centralised control of the communist state. It is reminiscent of the former Soviet and

▲ *Figure 4.34* Wushu: the ancient art of sword fighting

Eastern bloc systems. In other Asian countries, where control might be considerably less 'directed' than in the strictly centralised system of the Chinese state, certain conclusions may still be drawn from the way in which responsibility for sport-related policies is delegated.

Pakistan

In Pakistan, for example, the **Pakistan Sports Board (PSB)** was established in 1962 under the direct control of the Ministry of Education.

The functions of the PSB include:

- promotion and development of standards of national fitness as well as competition to an international level
- control and regulation of sports
- assisting national games and sports organisations in the execution of their programmes of activity
- encouraging the training and coaching of sportsmen at all levels
- encouraging and promoting the development of sport in Pakistan including developing a sports consciousness and broader participation
- constructing and maintaining stadia, gymnasia, training and coaching centres, squash courts and other areas
- consulting with the Pakistan Olympic Association
- approving awards and scholarships in the field of sport.

In 1977 the administrative control of the PSB was transferred to the newly created Ministry of Sport, Culture and Tourism, which controls policy through its executive committee. With this arrangement, there are obvious indications that policy direc-

tion is influenced by government. The PSB is under the direct control of a government ministry unlike, for example, in the UK where UK Sport and its associated organisations are independent autonomous bodies.

There are currently 39 national sports federations affiliated to the PSB, each of which is responsible for the promotion and development of its respective sport. Their funding depends upon the PSB, which in its turn, is funded by the Ministry of Sport, Culture and Tourism (Figure 4.35).

The sports given official support by the PSB include some that are not performed at Olympic level. This indicates how activities in one culture may not be given the same priority in others:

- athletics
- badminton
- basketball
- billiards/snooker
- body-building
- boxing
- bridge
- chess
- cricket
- cycling
- football
- golf
- gymnastics
- hockey
- kabbaddi
- polo
- rowing
- squash
- swimming
- table tennis.

India

In India the move towards formal centralised provision for sport did not occur until 1984, when the **Sports Authority of India (SAI)** was formed as a result of a government resolution (Figure 4.36).

In 1987, the Society for National Institutes of Physical Education and Sports (SNIPES) was amalgamated with the various bodies responsible for academic studies into sport and the training of coaches and PE teachers. They are now all under the authority of the SAI. There are six regional centres of excellence – at Bangalore, Gandhinagar, Calcutta,

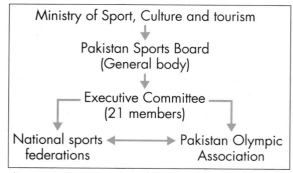

▲ **Figure 4.35** Pakistan: a structure for excellence

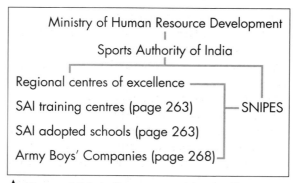

▲ **Figure 4.36** India: a structure for excellence

Chandigarh, Delhi and Imphal – and one sub-centre at Guwahati, with sports science/medicine facilities at Delhi, Patiala, Bangalore and Calcutta.

The SAI is managed by a governing body, under the chairmanship of the Minister of Human Resource Development. It is financed by the Indian government on a 'meet the deficit' basis.

The SAI runs several initiatives for the promotion of sport, including:

- All India rural sports tournaments
- Promotion of Sports among women
- Sports festivals and scholarship schemes
- Regional/area 'games'
- National Sports Talent Contest (NSTC)
- National Coaching Scheme (for 8–17 year-olds)

Of particular interest in the above structure are:

- **SAI training centres**
- **SAI adopted schools.**

SAI training centres

The SAI training centres, of which there are 40 spread all over India, also offer sports training with residential accommodation, and education in all cases. Altogether, fifteen sports disciplines are covered in these centres, with three or four disciplines offered at each one of them. Collectively they make provision for the following activities:

- archery
- basketball
- football
- hockey
- table tennis
- wrestling
- athletics
- boxing
- gymnastics
- judo
- volley ball
- badminton
- cycling
- handball
- swimming
- weight-lifting

These centres combined with the regional centres of excellence provide a sophisticated network of support which, at least theoretically, appears to be more elaborate than the structure currently being put into place in the UK. Candidates for places at the training centres are assessed on the basis of current performance or future potential and are all between the ages of fourteen and twenty. However, it should be noted that the number of sports provided for is far less extensive than in more prosperous countries.

TASK

Both India and Pakistan have invested heavily in the development of systems of excellence when there is obviously need for high levels of investment in other areas of sports.

a Why do you think this is?

b Should young children be sent away from home in order to prepare them for sporting excellence? Explain your views.

Adopted schools

In the light of the recent development of sports colleges in the UK, this initiative is particularly interesting, if not controversial. Adopted schools are those considered by SAI to have considerable expertise and talent already available. They must have a good academic record and extensive facilities, which if they are selected for 'adopted' status, are further enhanced with grant aid from the SAI.

Candidates for places at these schools are those already identified as having potential and must be under fourteen years old. They may be sent to any participating school where full accommodation and education is provided. In 2000 there were 29 such schools, with just over 1000 trainees in place. In harness with the **Army Boys' Sports Company** scheme (see page 268), the adopted schools programme ensures that potential talent will not escape the net.

Sport as a foreign policy

In the case of all three countries so far mentioned, there is overt involvement of government in the promotion and development of sport. There are normally two major reasons for this:

- a genuine wish to improve the lifestyle and health of the population and an acceptance that centralised provision and promotion is the most expedient way of doing this
- a realisation that, in the lucrative world of professional sport, there is also an economic return on any investment.

The world of sport offers an ideal opportunity for contacts to be extended and alliances sought and cemented outside the political arena. The hosting of major games such as the **Asian Games** (see page 269) and the newly established **Afro-Asian Games** provides further opportunities for such contact. At the same time sporting facilities that can be put into wider community use afterwards are built or improved.

India, Pakistan, Bangladesh and even China may all in different ways be regarded as emergent or developing nations. Each recognises the value of sport in developing a national identity that is acceptable both to their own population and to other countries. This **nation-building aspect** of sporting involvement and success is often viewed as justification for what otherwise might be seen as frivolous spending on programmes to foster a sporting élite rather than cater for the rest of the population.

Political factors

In China it is almost impossible to separate politics and sport. Under the slogan, 'Promote physical culture and build up the people's health', the People's Republic (founded in 1949) used the **State Physical Culture and Sports Commission** and the **All-China Athletic Federation** (1952) to develop programmes in schools, factories and rural communes. Their aim was to drive home the message that health was essential to the nation's well-being.

The Cultural Revolution (1966–70) brought a re-emphasis on military aspects of physical education, which had disappeared from school programmes in favour of western-style games and gymnastics in the 1920s. Similarly, the awarding of individual prizes was discontinued in favour of collective awards for endeavour.

Some time ago one writer made the comment that:

The People's Republic of China has a definite idea what her commitment to physical culture is. A utilitarian, practical motivation underlies this commitment where sport is used to 'serve the people' and in this culture 'the people are the state'.

Semotiuk (1974)

Although some years have passed since this was said, it would generally seem to hold true today.

TASK

a Why do you think China has been so reluctant to open its doors to the rest of the world in both the political and sporting sense?

b Can your group generate arguments 'for' and 'against' China's position in both respects?

2. Physical education and sport in high schools and colleges/universities

Development of physical education

The history of physical education in Asian cultures has been influenced by four factors:

- indigenous historical influences
- external historical influences
- more recent global influences
- economic constraint.

Asian cultures include some of the oldest in the world. The ancient cultures of China and Japan are probably the best known generally. Increasing exposure to outside influences, particularly in the form of colonisation and trade, has meant that European culture has made a significant impact, even upon the most closed of these societies. More recently, the development of global communication has made 'closed frontier' policies more difficult to sustain. In reality, even China is finding it difficult to maintain a closed-door policy in the age of satellite television broadcasting and the growth of internet communication.

The Chinese model

Physical education in China is mandatory for all pupils in state schools. The curriculum is highly structured and includes an emphasis on formal gymnastics and western-style games; it also covers the development of gross motor skills and a small component allowing older students to select specific study areas from the syllabus. PE classes play an important role in identifying.

Other activities

Curriculum PE activity is supported by spare-time activities. In line with custom outside school, these are morning exercises and exercises during class breaks, followed by further exercise after school (Figure 4.37).

Sport in the form of various contests takes place both after school and during the school holidays. Knuttgen (1990) suggested that at the time he was writing there were approximately 360,000 physical education teachers working in schools in China.

Pupils in all Chinese schools study wushu, in both its martial art and free exercise forms (see Figure 4.34 on page 261).

The 'collective' cultures (cultures with one class or 'classless') of China, Japan and North and South Korea have always acknowledged the value of physical culture, both in education and in the wider social sphere. Japan has had the economic means to transpose such values into its education system, whereas China and Korea have done so as part of their centralised system of government.

In Japan, PE in schools is administered by the physical education division, which is one of the four divisions of the **Physical Education Bureau** (Figure 4.38).

India and Pakistan

India and Pakistan are somewhat different from China and the other south-east Asian countries reviewed here. High population levels and a poor economy have prevented full implementation of an education system for all. This clearly has implications for programmes of physical education (Figure 4.39).

Attitudes

Attitudes to physical education are a reflection of the factors listed on page 264 and those referred to in Figure 4.40. In China and Japan, for example, a high value has always been placed on physical culture. All that has changed over the centuries is the nature of such programmes. Modern activities have replaced, or exist alongside, the more traditional ones and a centralised political influence gives them a high priority.

In Bangladesh, India and Pakistan, there is a traditionally lower cultural valuation of sport than in countries like China and Japan. Traditionally, physical exercise is not valued as part of the way of life as, for example, in China. There are also genuine difficulties in financing even a basic system of education. This means that, with the exception of the relatively small private and endowed sectors of education, enthusiasm for such programmes at government level has been a relatively recent development.

Such policy development that has taken place often seems to confuse the development of programmes of physical education with programmes of sports excellence. This can be clearly seen in the initiatives emanating from both the Pakistan Sports Board and the Sport Authority of India.

Sport in high schools including extra-curricular sport

India

School sport in India has been run by the department of Youth Affairs and Sport since

▲ *Figure 4.37* *Mass exercises are part of the physical education programme for all Chinese pupils*

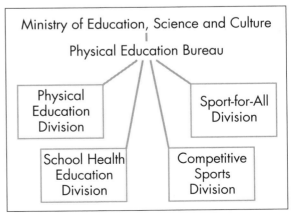

▲ *Figure 4.38* *Japan: the administrative structure of health, physical and sport education in schools*

Full implementation:	
China North Korea	'Collective policy' as part of centralist philosophy
Japan	State-funded by healthy 'capitalist' economy
Low implementation:	
India Pakistan Bangladesh	Poor economies and very high population levels constrain implementation of education policy (including physical education)

▲ *Figure 4.39* *Asian countries: the implementation of physical education for all is controlled by political/economic criteria*

1986 and is highly selective in terms of the range of activities offered. With the exception of athletics, which is commonly included, each district identifies four disciplines in which there are to be local championships. These are chosen on the basis of their local popularity. District and state championships are then held in each sport.

State championships take the form of inter-state tournaments, organised by the **School Games Federation of India (SGFI)**. Financial assistance is given in respect of organisational and travel costs. Other competitions, organised on a free basis, are not subject to financial assistance although some state governments do help in this respect.

An unusual aspect of these competitions is that there is prize money awarded to winning teams at national level that may be added to by the government of the winner's home state at its discretion!

There is little provision for physical education in this structure, other than the fact that the competitions fall under the heading of that subject. However, it must be remembered that in some Asian countries the battle for full and broad educational provision, let alone provision for PE, has yet to be won. In India, for example, the aim is still to attain five years of primary education for all by the year 2007 and eight years of elementary (basic secondary) schooling by 2010. In this context, any progress in sport/physical education must be seen in this context.

China

In China school sport provision is quite different. Future athletes are cultivated in the nation's **secondary sports schools** and **schools of sport and physical culture**. These are part of mainstream education and attendance is reserved for gifted performers. Students may be sent to national team squads from the age of fifteen and those going on the sport and physical culture schools who are not sent to provincial or national squads are trained as teachers of physical education. This heavily centralised system is very like the one operated by the former USSR. As with the Soviet system, this is the subject of much criticism both in terms of its political function and allegedly questionable methods of achieving success.

Sport in higher education

University sport in Asian countries is variable and depends on individual cultural setting. The majority of Asian countries have some level of international contact and FISU (see page 238) includes the following amongst its membership:

- Bangladesh Inter-University Sport Board
- Federation of University Sport of China
- Japanese University Sport Board
- Korean University Sport Board
- Pakistan University Sport Board
- Sport Association of Indian Universities.

In some cultures, university sport along with most other sporting activity is part of a wider political structure. China is the most obvious example. Here, university sport, along with military and worker sports is highly organised and success in championships at local, regional and national level are highly coveted.

In India, hockey is by far the most popular sport with over 120 universities participating in the national championships each year.

TASK

Write a short account of why you think that Japan and the People's Republic of China, which are political opposites, seem to have a common belief in the value of programmes of physical education.

3. Professional (élite) sport

The history of professional sport in Asia is relatively short in comparison with elsewhere.

The Japanese involvement with baseball began towards the end of the nineteenth century, with a professional game emerging in the 1930s. Japan's feudal lords had initially viewed the game as a martial sport and this was instrumental in its acceptance. It is now the most popular sport in Japan and is rivalled only by the growing interest in football, with volleyball also exceedingly popular.

There is little interest in professional sport in China, although its slow emergence into the wider world commercially has seen the growth of a professional baseball league. This is sponsored by an American marketing company keen to exploit the huge market that could grow out of continued interest (Figure 4.40).

In India, Pakistan and Bangladesh, the spread of professional cricket, along with that of soccer, has been the most significant, with the exploits of such athletes as India's P. T. Usher being a rare occurrence in the world of track and field athletics: even more so because she is female.

The commercial nature of professional sport

Professional sport is, by definition, commercial. In the case of Asian countries generally, the recent growth of professional sport is a reflection of increased global exposure and the availability of foreign interests to invest capital in such developments.

Not surprisingly Japan, with its sophisticated market economy, is particularly receptive to associated developments in the field of professional sport. Because it is involved with media and communications technology, an association with the developing global market-place for sport based on such technology is also hardly coincidental. In contrast, China has made little economic use of its sporting infrastructures for economic purposes and the potential economic value of sport has instead been realised in the bolstering of its political image at home – and rather less successfully abroad.

▲ **Figure 4.40** China now has a professional basketball league

The same political aims have been at the heart of Korean efforts to be seen as a sporting nation. However, when it hosted the Summer Olympics in 1988, its politically driven and closed economy was exposed to the possibilities presented by the global free market. Football, boxing, basketball and volleyball have large followings and the development of professional badminton has provided Koreans with a specific focus in terms of sporting success. Although the communist North now effectively runs both North and South Korea, the wholesale embracing of capitalism in industry and technology has provided a sound platform for further expansion in the field of professional sport.

The role of company teams

The involvement of company teams in high-level sport across Asia is a particular feature of the region. As in the UK many decades ago, the **workplace** is a central feature in many people's lives (see also page 270). It provides a convenient catalyst for those who are keen to participate in sport. In this way the large industrial/commercial/technological conglomerates that are still part of the Asian economy find that they are also part of the country's sporting as well as industrial infrastructure. Going back a century or more, such involvement was fairly typical in the UK, with Arsenal F.C. being made up of workers at the Royal Arsenal and even Manchester United starting life as the railway workers of Newton Heath.

Transport companies and business houses, as well as factories, commonly field teams in the top flight of Asian sport. It may well be that in time they will transform themselves into independent clubs, as has been the case in the UK and in other parts of Europe. In China, such teams are part of a huge centrally-run organisation but elsewhere in Asia they are part of both amateur and professional sports leagues.

The role of the media and the status of professional sport

In India, the *Sportstar* magazine is in its 23rd year of publication and *Tribune India* and the *Bangalore Age* newspapers cover sport and feature sports advertising. Asian TV companies increasingly cover sport and the availability of satellite television has heightened the awareness of professional sport, both in terms of its popularity and its potential as a tool of the market-place.

The Indian national television network (Doordarshan) is one of the largest TV organisations in the world. It operates 21 channels through its network of 1090 transmitters. It puts out nearly 1400 hours of programmes every week including sport and reaches almost 90 per cent of the country's population of 950 million people. With such exposure it is difficult to imagine that professional sport will not continue to grow, with its stars and associated businesses reaping a rich reward.

In south-east Asia, Japan's highly developed economy has utilised media technology to sell sporting commodities for some time. The rising status of professional sport globally has encouraged such countries as Korea to develop its own media infrastructure along capitalist lines. South Korea's KBTV-1 channel broadcasts both domestic and international sport, as does its satellite channel Satellite TV-2. Even China has an eight-channel TV network and a satellite channel broadcasting sport.

Role of armed forces as sports nurseries

The role of the military as a nursery for sporting talent is evident in the Army Boys' Sports Company scheme in India. Here, the army works with the Sports Authority of India to develop talent in a range of sports.

Boys' Companies (formerly units that trained boys for military service) in the Indian army had been disbanded. It was then realised that the facilities and infrastructure necessary to identify and nurture young sporting talent were already in place. The Boys' Company scheme was launched in 1992 and there are presently 16 boys' sports companies providing places for approximately 700 trainees between 8 and 17 years of age. All boys receive full accommodation and a full-time education together with a guaranteed career in the army. Interestingly, but not surprisingly, there is no mention of similar provision for girls!

Selection is based on talent identification tests used in SAI training centre schemes (see page 263) and after three years boys who do not continue to perform well are 'weeded out'.

The cost of this scheme is shared by the army and the SAI and includes competition exposure at both domestic and international levels.

China is an example of a country where there is obvious miliary involvement in sport. Here it is used as an expression of the importance attached to physical culture and discipline. The army team is known as 'August 1st' commemorating the date of the formation of the Chinese People's Liberation Army. It makes specialist provision for over 30 sports. There are army championships in all these activities, with many military personnel being included in full national squads.

TASK

In a short written answer explain why you think that the armed forces in several Asian countries are still used to nurture talent.

The Asian Games

The Asian Games is important both as an expression of cultural identity and a platform for Asian athletes to perform internationally but still within an Asian context. It was also part of an agreement between Asian leaders to work towards harmony and unity amongst Asians (Figure 4.41).

The first Games was held in 1951 in New Delhi with newly independent countries such as Korea, India, the Philippines and Indonesia finding an early sporting outlet for an expression of this new freedom.

The first celebration of the Games involved 600 athletes and officials from 11 countries and lasted for 8 days, whilst the 13th Games, held in Hiroshima in 1998 attracted over 700 athletes and officials and lasted for 15 days. Kazakshtan and Uzbekistan, formerly part of the Soviet Union, entered for the first time in 1998 and were ranked fourth and tenth respectively in the medal rankings. Not surprisingly, China has topped the medal rankings for the last four consecutive Games.

4. Recreational sport (mass participation)

In Japan and China in particular, the role of sport and exercise as part of a healthy lifestyle is interwoven into the culture of both countries. The type of sport that people participate in is a mix of the traditional and modern.

Mass sport in Japan has a definite Olympic flavour. The Japanese National Olympic Committee and the **Japanese Amateur Sports Association (JASA)** organise a whole range of activities for all sections of the community. These include the **Junior Sports Club**, the **National Sports Festival** and the new National Sport and Leisure Festival.

The Junior Sports Club was founded in 1962 as a means of generating interest prior

to the 1964 Olympiad in Tokyo. Today it has more than 1.5 million members. There are nine branches throughout Japan and sports meetings are organised at a local level. In July each year a major national event is held lasting for one week. This includes tournaments for children and adolescents and is an efficient and effective way of detecting promising youngsters.

The National Sports Festival, founded in 1946, is a year-long affair taking place in each of three seasons. This is the largest event in Japan with athletes from all 47 prefectures taking part. The programme takes the form of summer, autumn and winter Games and covers over forty sports, each during its appropriate season. These Games are like mini-Olympics and are held in a different prefecture each year. Entry is open to all and almost half of the activities include categories for those over 40, women over 35, those over 20 and children of primary school age. There are usually between 15,000 and 20,000 entries each year.

The Olympiads held in Tokyo (1964) and Sapporo (1972) fostered an Olympic spirit that has transmitted itself into the daily lives of ordinary Japanese people. Perhaps this is something of the essence of de Coubertin's dream.

In Korea, as well, enthusiasm for sport is fostered amongst the very young, with intramural sporting competition (competition within a school) being a major feature of early school life. Success at this level brings entry to the **Children's Games** each spring and the **National Games** each August. The possibility of participating in serious competition appears to be a contrast to the sociable Junior Sports Club competitions in Japan. The situation in China is also different. A rather more overtly political approach to the role of mass sport is reflected in the viewpoint that whilst people are important: so is the state.

Mass participation, social control, integration, health and defence

The benefits of mass participation in sport and exercise are increasingly accepted across Asian cultures. In China, Japan and Korea, the concept of **collective exercise**

▲ *Figure 4.41* The Asian Games are intended to promote harmony and unity

▲▼ **Figure 4.42** *When both civil and religious law forbid public association women can suffer discrimination*

(everyone taking exercise together) has been part of pastoral and spiritual life for as long as history has been recorded. Workplace sport and physical exercise form part of the daily routine of countless workers. Such activity is as much part of their culture as the philosophies on which they are based.

Wushu exists in several forms in China. This ancient form of sword-fighting is also a series of exercises designed to aid breathing, relaxation and develop a sense of inner calm. Other activities such as qigong, taijiquan and wuqinxi all have military forms but are also exercise/relaxation techniques. In Japan and elsewhere, most of the martial art forms also have associated exercises which have a place in the national culture.

Sport and/or exercise in the workplace is much more common in the collective cultures of China, Japan and Korea and its traditional roots have played a major part in its continued acceptance. In some places, western-style exercises have found their way into exercise regimes. It is unlikely that such initiatives, where everyone exercises together, would ever find their way into the

European workplace, unless of course they happen to be Asian-owned companies!

China particularly has an extremely sophisticated workplace sports structure, which includes teams from trade organisations, railways, water and power industries and government workers' associations.

Sport-for-All policies, workplace sport and the concept of mass recreation generally have been utilised by governments to impart a sense of belonging and purpose which is both health-giving and also promotes a political message.

India and Pakistan have now grasped this ideal and current initiatives through the

TASK

a What is the difference between workplace exercise and the role of company teams in Asian sport?

b Could workplace exercise ever become popular in the UK?

c Why do company teams no longer figure in high-level sport in the UK?

Pakistan Sport Board and the Sports Authority of India seem to underline this development, possibly at the expense of more urgently needed social provision.

Religious constraints: women and Islamic states

The Islamic religion forbids men and women to mix socially and/or recreationally. This practice, in an increasingly secular wider world, is currently the source of much debate and controversy. It also gives rise to many associated social issues. For Islamic women this obviously affects their ability to participate in sport. It is also an issue of politics and gender.

The difficulty is compounded by the fact that in Islamic states religious and state authority are one and the same. Sportswomen from these states cannot, therefore, go against **religious authority** without also flouting civil law, and penalties for this are very severe, sometimes incurring the death sentence. For example, in the case of the North American Olympic champion Hassiba Boulmerka, there was great concern after she had won the 1500m gold medal in Barcelona that her life would be at risk because she had competed in front of men showing her bare legs and shoulders (Figure 4.42).

Many women from Asian or Islamic countries face great difficulties before they can enjoy the freedom to compete openly. This raises a major question for the organisers of global events such as the Olympic Games. It has been suggested that countries not allowing equal op portunity (in this case to both sexes) should have their invitation to the Games withdrawn. There is concern, however, that this might exacerbate rather than resolve the dilemma.

TASK

Discuss the issue of Islamic women and sport.

a How do you think such problems might be resolved:

  i at a local level

  ii at a global level?

b What action should be taken by global Games organisers over this issue?

Key words and phrases

SECTION A(1): WORLD CULTURES: NORTH AMERICA

1. Historical and cultural background

- Colonisation
- Immigration
- Industrialisation
- Mass consumerism
- Glass ceiling
- Lombardian ethic
- Radical ethic
- Counter-culture ethic
- Pioneer spirit
- Gun lobby

2. Physical education and sport in high schools and colleges/universities

- Gymnastics
- Calisthenics
- Swedish gymnastics
- Athletic department
- AAU (Amateur Athletic Union)
- Draft system
- Scholarships
- White flight
- Title 1X

3. Professional (élite) sport

- World Series
- Commercial interest
- Superbowl
- Role models

4. Recreational sport (mass participation)

- Indigenous sport
- Work ethic
- Little league
- Summer camps
- National parks
- Wilderness areas
- Extreme sports

SECTION A(2): NEW WORLD CULTURES: AUSTRALIA, NEW ZEALAND AND SOUTH AFRICA

1. Historical and cultural background

- Historical and cultural influences
- Discrimination
- Treaty of Waitangi
- Apartheid
- Cultural institutions
- Kiwis
- Springboks
- Test match
- Racial segregation

2. Physical education and sport in high schools and colleges/universities

- Colonial influences
- Hauora
- Physical and Sport Education programme (PASE)
- Sport Education in Physical Education Programmes (SEPEP)
- Ernst Franz Jokl
- National Advisory Council on Physical Education
- Australian School Sports Council (ASSC) • Active Australia
- New Zealand Secondary Schools Sports Council (NZSSSC)
- United School Sports Association of South Africa (USSASA)
- SANGALA (South African National Games and Leisure Activities)

3. Professional (élite) sport

- Australian Institute of Sport (AIS) • Australian Sports Commission (ASC)
- New Zealand Sports Foundation (NZSF) • Hillary Commission
- South African Sports Commission (SASC) • National Sports Council (NSC)
- National Olympic Commission of South Africa (NOCSA)
- South African National Recreation Council (SANREC)
- South African Sports Commission Act • National Sport and Recreation Act

4. Recreational sport (mass participation)

- Community Sport Fund • Moneghetti Report • RecRehab
- Department of Recreation and Sport (DSR)
- Provincial Recreation Committees (PRORECS)
- Great Barrier Reef Marine Park (GBRMP) • Kruger National Park

SECTION A(3): DEVELOPING CULTURES: WITH REFERENCE TO ARGENTINA AND KENYA

Historical and cultural background

- Law of Basic Consensus • Mestizos • Missionary schools • Andrew Dick
- Thomas Hogg • William Heald • Polo • Early colonists • Immigrants
- Pelota • Juan Peron • Ministry of Home Affairs, Heritage and Sports
- Kenyan National Olympic Committee (NOCK) • Masai Mara National Park

2. Physical education and sport in high schools and colleges/universities

- Alexander Watson Hutton • Asociación Deportiva Estudjantil (ADE)
- National Institute of Physical Education • Democracy
- General Basic Education (EGB)

3. Professional (élite) sport

- Comite Olimpico Argentino (COA) • Confederación Atletica de Deportes (CAD)
- Secretaria de Deportes de la Nación • Kenya National Sports Council (KNSC)

4. Recreational sport (mass participation)

- Playas Programme

SECTION A(4): ASIAN CULTURES

1. Historical and cultural background

- British Empire • YMCA • YWCA • Pakistan Sports Board (PSB)
- Sports Authority of India (SAI) • SAI training centres • SAI adopted schools
- Army Boys' Sports Company • Asian Games • Afro-Asian Games
- National-building aspect • State Physical Culture and Sports Commission
- All-China Athletic Federation

2. Physical education and sport in high schools and colleges/universities

- Physical Education Bureau • School Games Federation of India (SGFI)
- Secondary sports schools • Schools of sport and physical culture

3. Professional (élite) sport

- Workplace

4. Recreational sport (mass participation)

- Japanese Amateur Sports Association (JASA) • Junior Sports Club
- National Sports Festival • Children's Games • National Games
- Collective exercise • Religious authority

REVIEW QUESTIONS

1 What were the four phases of development that influenced social values in America?

2 Explain what is meant by the terms:
 • Lombardian ethic
 • Radical ethic
 • counter-culture ethic.

3 The frontier or pioneer spirit is said to be part of the American recreational culture. How does the American national park system cater for this aspect of recreational life?

4 Explain why there has been a decline in physical education in American high schools.

5 Explain what is meant by the terms 'white flight', 'glass ceiling' and 'stacking'.

6 In what way has Title 1X legislation improved provision for the participation of girls and women in sport and physical education in the USA?

7 How has the American system of athletic scholarships helped to broaden opportunities for black sportsmen and women?

8 'Little league' competitions are simply adult 'toys' – discuss.

9 What does the term 'common historical and cultural influences' refer to in connection with sport in Australia, New Zealand and South Africa?

10 What is the origin of the term 'test match'?

11 How would you differentiate between the roles of the ASC and the AIS in sport and recreation in Australia?

12 What is the 'Community Sport Fund' in New Zealand and how is it administered?

13 When South Africa won the Rugby World Cup in 1995 President Mandela described sport as a 'tool for nation building'. To what extent do you consider this to be true?

14 Why do you think there is, as yet, a lack of clear direction in a structure for PE and school sport in South Africa?

15 Why is New Zealand still the only country of the three New World cultures under review which does not have a reputation for discriminating against its ethnic population?

16 What part do SANGALA and SANREC play in the development of community sport programmes in South Africa?

17 Active Australia is a government-sponsored programme of mass participation in sport. What is the name of its counterpart in New Zealand?

18 What is the significance of the 'law of basic consensus' for the people of Argentina?

19 What specific contribution did Andrew Dick, Thomas Hogg and William Heald make to Argentinian sport?

20 Why has British/European influence been so significant in the nature of Argentine sport?

21 Kenyan athletes have had much success. As a result of this how is the 'nation-building' ethic being applied to the broadening of sporting excellence?

22 How are levels of urban population likely to affect the implementation of physical education programmes in poorer countries?

23 Why do physical education programmes in Argentina not reach their maximum intended target group?

24 Why do Kenya's leading athletes increasingly tend to live abroad?

25 How might the development of professional sport in Asian countries eventually help broaden sporting and recreational provision for the mass of the population?

26 China was never colonised by Britain. How therefore did British influence have such an impact on sport there?

REVIEW QUESTIONS (Continued)

27 Which aspects of traditional Chinese culture are still reflected in today's physical activities?

28 Both the Pakistan Sport Board and the Sports Authority of India have invested heavily in programmes of excellence. How does this differ from the programmes in place in China? To what degree is such investment justified in the face of overwhelming poverty in both countries?

29 In India, the Army Boys' Companies and the adopted schools scheme provide opportunities for young people to become sports stars. Are such schemes for very young people justifiable?

30 Why has professional sport in Japan developed earlier and more extensively than in most other Asian countries?

31 The development of sport on a global basis involves activity which is largely of western/European origin. How does this make the development of sporting infrastructures in Asian countries more difficult than might otherwise be the case?

32 How can the development of such sporting festivals as the Asian Games, the African Games and the Afro-Asian Games help in the above respect?

Texts used in the writing of this section

❑ Alabarces, P., (University of Buenos Aires) *Argentine National Identity and Football: 'The Creole English' Adventures of a Scot in the River Plate*, A paper delivered to the Annual Conference of the British Society of Sports History, Chelsea College, April 1999

❑ Anon., 'Japan: A History of Sport', in *Olympic Review*, 1990, No. 275–276, pp. 426–30

❑ Bale, J. and Sang, J. *Kenyan Running*, Frank Cass, 1996

❑ Berryman, J. W., 'From Cradle to Playing Field' in *Journal of Sport History*, No. 1975

❑ Booth, D., *The Race Game: Sport and Politics in South Africa*, Frank Cass, 1998

❑ Bose, M., *A History of Indian Cricket*, André Deutsch, 1990

❑ Cashman, R., *Paradise of Sport*, Oxford University Press, 1995

❑ Clement, R., 'Asia, Rich in Unrealised Potential', in *Olympic Review*, 1985, No. 213, pp. 401–04

❑ Coakley, J., *Sport in Society: Issues and Controversies*, 5th edition, Mosby, 1994

❑ Cullin, *Games of the North American Indians*, New York Dover, 1975

❑ Figler, S. K., *Sport and Play in American Life*, Saunders College Publishing, 1981

❑ Hardman, K. & Marshall, J., *Worldwide Survey of the State and Status of Physical Education*, University of Manchester, 1998

❑ Holt, R., *Sport and the British*, Clarendon Press, 1995

❑ Knuttgen, H. et al., *Sport in China*, Human Kinetics, 1990

❑ Lumpkin, A., *Physical Education and Sport: A Contemporary Introduction*, 3rd edition, Mosby, 1994

❑ Mahlmann, P., 'The role of sport in the process of modernisation: the Kenya case' in *Journal of East Africa Development*, 1992, pp. 120–31

❑ Morales, F., 'Physical Education and Its Prospects in South America', in, *Olympic Review*, 1986, No. 227, pp. 529–32

❑ Mosely, A., Cashman, R. *et.al. Sporting Immigrants*, Walla Walla Press (ASC Australia) 1997

❑ Nauright, J., *Sport, Cultures and Identities in South Africa*, Leicester University Press, 1997

- Roberts, C. (ed.), *Challenges Facing South African Sport*, Township Publishing Co-operative, Cape Town, 1990
- Roberts, C. (ed.), *Against the Grain: Women and Sport in South Africa*, Township Publishing Co-operative, Cape Town, 1992
- Roberts, C. (ed.), *Reconstruction of South African Sport*, National and Olympic Sports Congress, East London, S.A., 1992
- Ryan, G., 'Cricket and the Moral Curriculum of the New Zealand Elite Secondary Schools c.1860–1920', in *The Sport Historian*, 19 (2), British Society of Sports History, November 1999
- Semotiuk, D., (University of Western Ontario) 'Some Historical Interpretations of Physical Culture in the People's Republic of China', in *North American Society for Sport History. Proceedings & Newsletter*, 1974, pp. 12–13
- S.I.P.A., *Synthesis of Argentine Sport*, Argentine Publications International Service, 1952
- Swanson, R. A. & Spears, B., *History of Sport and Physical Education in the United States*, 4th edition, WCB McGraw-Hill, 1995
- Vamplew, W. & Adair, D., *Sport in Australian History*, Oxford University Press, 1997
- Vamplew, W. & Stoddart, B. (eds.), *Sport in Australia*, Cambridge University Press, 1994
- Van der Merwe, F., 'Ernst Franz Jokl as the Father of Physical Education in South Africa', in *North American Society for Sport History. Proceedings & Newsletter*, 1990, p. 81

Suggested further reading

- Cashman, R., *Paradise of Sport*, Oxford University Press, 1995
- Knuttgen, H., et al. *Sport in China*, Human Kinetics, 1990
- Morales, F., 'Physical Education and Its Prospects in South America', in *Olympic Review*, 1986, No. 227, pp. 529–32
- Nauright, J., *Sport, Cultures and Identities in South Africa*, Leicester University Press, 1997
- Roberts, C. (ed.), *Reconstruction of South African Sport*, National and Olympic Sports Congress, East London, S.A., 1992
- Swanson, R. A. & Spears, B., *History of Sport and Physical Education in the United States*, 4th edition, WCB McGraw-Hill, 1995
- Vamplew, W. & Stoddart, B. (eds.) *Sport in Australia*, Cambridge University Press, 1994

Section B: A synoptic analysis of trends in international sport through global games

1. Sport as a show of national identity

The benefits of sporting success

The benefits of sporting success may manifest themselves both within and beyond a country, and for a variety of reasons. They might include the totally spontaneous – such as the 'feel good factor' referred to by many politicians following England's extended participation in the 'Euro 96' football championships held in the UK. They may be material – in the sense of increased economic activity arising from success; or the benefits may be social – as in the general upsurge of patriotic pride resulting from the performance of the England team.

Programmes designed to produce successful athletes may also have any of these types of benefit as part of their intended purpose. In today's material world, with the growth of professional sport and the importance of marketing to maximise benefits, the production of excellence can have a host of spin-offs. These range from tourism and increased attendance at major fixtures to increased levels of commercial activity and employment in sporting and non-sporting goods and services.

The old adage 'everyone likes a winner' is not lost on those (in both the private and public sectors) who mastermind success in sport as a platform for success on a much broader social and/or economic front.

If success also has the added effect of encouraging broader participation in sport, then there are also likely to be **health benefits**.

Sport used as a shop window

Health benefits were claimed to be a major priority in the policies of mass participation adopted by the Eastern bloc regimes of the 1960s, 70s and 80s. Behind the public façade of wholesome recreation for all were rather more sinister agendas, reminiscent of Adolph Hitler's 'youth movement' and the Nazi party's subsequent attempts to take over the Olympic movement in the Games of 1936 in the cause of National Socialism.

These **political overtones** were also manifest in the later East German, Soviet and Cuban use of major sporting occasions to parade their political doctrines to the rest of the world. This still occurs in China where the national identity is promoted in the workplace and the school room and fostered by élitist programmes of excellence, as suspect in some cases as those of the former Soviet bloc.

The transformation of amateur sports into professional ones has clearly stimulated many governments into embracing sport as a tool of national promotion. In both the ideological and the commercial sense, the sporting **'shop window'** now provides a truly global medium through which national interests may be promoted. Many governments (including the UK) are now adopting a much more proactive attitude to the development of sporting infrastructures.

In many respects it is the loss of amateur status which has allowed sport and its participants to be regarded (as in the European Court rulings in the Bosman Case – see page 39) as professional workers carrying out their trade. The establishment of this precedent has also allowed governments to adopt a much more 'hands on' approach to

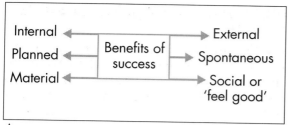

▲ **Figure 4.45** *Benefits of success*

the organisation and financing of sport. This was not possible in the days of (largely) private amateur sporting bodies that rejected any possibility of government 'interference'.

A more honest form of competition

The development and wider acceptance of professional sport has allowed many formerly 'unacceptable' practices, such as state support for programmes of excellence, to be publicly proclaimed. These are now (ironically) part of the 'array of goods' in the shop window of many countries.

France was one of the first to give state aid to sport in the 1960s. Since then a steady stream of Sport Boards, Sports Commissions and Academies of Excellence have also joined France's Institut Nationale du Sport et Education Physicale (**INSEP**), as countries vie with one another not just in competition but also in the degree of sophistication employed in their preparation for competition.

The use of sport as a shop window in the purely political/ideological sense still persists in those countries (such as Cuba and China – see page 264) where political doctrine of collectivism is still seen as more important than individual freedom. For much of the rest of the world, however, the involvement of governments in sport, whilst acknowledging the notion of a national sporting image, also embraces a desire to maximize success in much broader terms.

The American government, clearly alarmed at what it saw as the unfair advantage of centrally-funded Soviet and Eastern bloc Olympic teams, began to support financially the efforts of its own Olympic committee in order to 'level the playing field'. Ironically, America's own system of athletic scholarships had faced the same criticism for decades.

Government influence and policy in sport

The growth of major Games and sport at the global level has caused governments to rethink former policies, whereby limited financial assistance was provided only at times of major events. At one time little further involvement was sought and would almost certainly have been rejected by the then largely amateur Olympic and sports bodies. Ironically, it was the need to compete effectively against communist countries that subsidised sport heavily that left the 'amateur countries' with little choice but to accept (and even lobby for) government help.

Accentuating the positive

The benefits of sporting success do not just include rewards for those who compete (Figure 4.45). Major international events bring visitors, media attention and a global audience. The interest and scrutiny of outsiders drawn to sports events may extend beyond sport and sports-related products. Therefore, any investment of public money in sporting infrastructures and related areas can often be justified as an extension of investment in the global market-place.

The National Indoor Arena in Birmingham has hosted several major international sporting events. The infrastructure of hotels and other facilities alongside it and the National Convention Centre have jointly produced major improvements in the centre of Birmingham. Visitors are attracted to both venues and investment enhances the surrounding environment for everyone.

Investment in sporting excellence can often produce technologies and commodities that are exportable in addition to being both saleable and beneficial to the domestic consumer. Health clubs and spas now have modern technology at their disposal which until recently was only available in élite human performance laboratories. The growth of interest in health and fitness generally can have health/cost benefits which are both economically desirable as well as morale boosting. Success on the sports field also often serves as an inspiration to the general population to participate and can also provide a filip to national pride.

GOVERNMENT INFLUENCE	
Direct/centralised	e.g. China, Cuba, France
Indirect influence	e.g. Through indirect funding such as national lotteries
Limited influence	e.g. Finland – where funding is provided for grass-roots sport and Olympic teams
Minimal influence	e.g. USA – funding only for Olympic teams

▲ ***Figure 4.46*** *Type of state funding for sport*

Levels of government funding are often now considerable (Figure 4.46). Centralised economies such as those in China and Cuba fund on an 'as needed' basis, whilst France's policy, developed in the 1960s, provides direct centralised funding without the same constraining degree of centralised control. At the other end of the spectrum lies the United States of America, where federal funding is provided only for its Olympic teams.

In the case of Australia, funding is provided from the federal purse but is matched by money from private sponsorship, e.g. banks and businesses. In the UK, the government is at pains to point out that it is UK Sport and the four sports councils of England, Scotland, Wales and Northern Ireland that control policies of excellence, and that funding for such ventures comes largely from **lottery income** and not from the government. It was the Lotteries Act which made this possible as the result of government legislation. There is also a view that lottery income as just another form of (back-door) taxation.

TASK

Hold a discussion within your group on the topic of government funding of sport. Consider the advantages and disadvantages of such involvement:

- to the sporting fraternity
- to the nation generally.

Motivation and pride in one's country

For the individual sportsperson, the motivation to compete and the pride in achievement is purely personal. Sports psychologists tend to refer to such motivation as being derived from internal or external sources (intrinsic and extrinsic), whilst freely acknowledging that no two individuals are exactly the same.

It is more difficult to be precise when referring to motivation within a group or team, and more so in the case of a sport's governing body, a national government, or indeed, a whole nation. It seems clear that pride in the performance of an individual or of a team can extend beyond the competitor(s) and immediate support group and is often assumed by a whole nation.

The motivation for individuals or groups who are members of minority causes, for example, can be both personal and group-orientated. Any success on the international stage can bring personal pride; it may also confer pride and esteem onto the group associated with the performer(s). The processes of **access** and **integration** may be considerably enhanced as the wider community also takes pride in any such success.

Government motivation

The motivation for governments is based on what rewards success might bring for the nation as a whole. Governments will also often make what political mileage they can out of any success – both in terms of domestic points-scoring and enhanced international image. It would be difficult for governments in free economies to take absolute control over sporting policy – at least overtly. The creation of what are effectively government sporting arms, such as the ASC in Australia and UK Sport in the UK, allows governments to control indirectly the purse-strings whilst officially distancing themselves from apparent control.

Systematic approach to preparation for political/national success

The means by which nations now prepare their young people for international sporting success have become far more highly structured and sophisticated than before.

Until relatively recently, the ethic of amateurism (see Unit 1) restrained all but the most politically-driven countries from resorting to what have been termed the 'excesses of professionalism'. Roger Bannister, in preparation for the first four-minute mile in 1954, simply climbed over the local park railings twice a week after studying as a medical student by day, and jogged around its paths for half an hour or so in the dark. Many of his earlier Victorian counterparts frowned on the idea of training as an altogether ungentlemanly way of carrying on. To prepare for a contest in any specialised way was almost regarded as cheating!

Sport – particularly international sport – has moved on from the time when it was simply a recreational pursuit of a privileged few. Losing didn't matter and the manner of losing often attracted more praise than winning. Sport in those early days was an entirely personal thing. If it gave pleasure to others that was very nice but the fact that sport was also entertaining was entirely incidental.

The process of change

The remarkable change in the definition of sport and the context in which it now takes place did not occur overnight. Neither did the involvement of governments in sporting infrastructures nor the programmes of excellence which they directly or indirectly sponsor.

The Berlin Olympiad of 1936 was probably the first occasion when a government (in this case Hitler's) made open attempts to use the Games for its own political ends (Figure 4.47). Of greater relevance here was the vast investment in terms of money and direct interference in the arena of sport by Hitler's government. Most of the free world was appalled at this brazen attempt to hijack sport for political ends but, as history has since shown, it was perhaps a sign of things to come. Training camps, the selection of athletes on the basis of physical type and specialised training programmes were all used – with unlimited funding – in order to ensure their success. Although in Hitler's case his plan did not work, it may well have provided a 'prototype' that would be used far more successfully by others at a later time.

▲ **Figure 4.47** *The Berlin Olympics were used by Hitler to promote a non-sporting agenda and the Nazi Party*

The Iron Curtain countries

The social and political history of the immediate post-war period from 1945 is relevant here in that it spawned the Cold War. This was the name given to the antagonism between the free states in the west – such as USA and Britain – and the communist bloc of countries led by the USSR. The border between the countries of the east and west was known as the Iron Curtain.

The symbolic relevance in sporting terms of the Iron Curtain was that what went on behind it was easy to conceal. Thankfully, the Soviet sports schools and the system in East Germany run by secret police called the Stazi are no more. However, until the fall of communism (at least of the Soviet variety) in the early 1990s, the Eastern bloc countries led the world in sport. This was as a direct result of their centrally-funded systems of excellence which were based on both sound scientific research and more than just a little deviance!

The free world learned that a systematic approach to excellence could pay huge dividends. Unfortunately at that time the system that sought to achieve excellence did so by encouraging athletes to take drugs and enforcing pregnancies and abortions – all in the name of sport. Only conjecture can tell what might have happened to international sport if the political system which supported such abuses had survived; and only the future will reveal whether the remnants of such practices which still do survive will be dealt with effectively – or even be detected.

Coming clean?

The end of the Cold War, the ensuing growth of professional sport and the more open involvement of governments in sport has given rise to what might be termed as a third generation of systematic approaches to excellence. Such involvement is now seen to be politically and socially acceptable. However, in some less wealthy countries it is rather more difficult to justify on either economic or moral grounds when funds are much needed for other projects. Nevertheless, millions of dollars are now invested in sports programmes around the world, in the hope that the returns justify such investment – which is not quite the same as saying that the ends justify the means!

Use of global games for protest

Inevitably success attracts a great deal of attention. Such attention is not always welcome – particularly if it spoils the general enjoyment of the party.

Global Games have been used for **protest** (both systematic and non-systematic) on several occasions. One of the most memorable instances is that of the Black Power salute at the Mexico Olympics in 1968 (see page 68), although there have been others, with far greater implications for the future of global sport (see Unit1B: 'Political uses of the Olympics').

Even as long ago as 1908, at the Games in London, there was a protest by the Americans over the actions of the largely British officials. Matthews (1980) recalled that:

> *The Americans, among others, felt that some of the decisions, practices, and rulings of the British officials were less than impartial. The number of protests and the amount of animosity generated by this situation during the London Games of 1908 are astounding.*

Whilst this protest was about the Games themselves, it may well have provided food for thought for others wanting to draw attention to their cause. As the Games grew in stature, they increasingly attracted the attention of governments and the media, ensuring the protests would be heard.

Unit 1B suggests that the major forms of protest in the case of the Olympics (as in most other global Games) are:

- non-systematic
- systematic.

Global Games can also be used for propaganda – see Unit 4A and, in the case of the Olympics, Unit 1B.

Non-systematic protest

Non systematic protest includes those such as the Black Power salute by Lee Evans and Tommy Smith and by John Carlos following his victory in the 400 metres. Almost forgotten, and certainly hardly reported, was the protest at the same Games by the Czech gymnast **Vera Caslavska** at the invasion of her country by the Soviet Union. These isolated protests were viewed largely as an unacceptably overt political use of the Olympic victory podium. With hindsight, such a view might not be the predominant one today.

The mayhem caused by Arab terrorists at the Munich Games of 1972, in which eleven people were killed, was widely reported – and in graphic detail – as the full horror of the events unfolded. There was also coverage of the terrorist bomb attack at the Atlanta games of 1996.

There was protest over the inclusion of Zola Budd in the British team for the Los Angeles Games of 1984. Many felt that the young woman was simply using her dual nationality to get around South Africa's exclusion from the Olympic movement. Many felt this view was vindicated when she returned to that country fairly soon afterwards.

Systematic protest

A rather more systematic (or organised) approach to protest is seen in the cases of the **boycott** by the African nations of the Montreal Games in 1976; the mass boycott of the Moscow Games in 1980 and the 'tit-for-tat' boycott by the Soviet bloc countries of the 1984 Games in Los Angeles (see 'Power of the boycott' on page 282).

Protest extended beyond the Olympics, although many of the issues involved were the same. **Apartheid** was one such issue. New Zealand's continued relationship with South Africa in rugby and cricket led to

▲ *Figure 4.48* Anti-apartheid protestors at work: disruption was a necessary aspect of effective protest

Was Avery Brundage right to castigate the efforts of those athletes who chose the Mexico Games of 1968 as a vehicle for their political grievances? Present a short written answer, justifying your views.

protests by anti-apartheid groups in both countries, as well as in the UK during the New Zealand rugby tour.

The view of the contemporary media was largely hostile to these protests; the general view was that sport and politics should be kept separate (Figure 4.48). Young (1988) writing on the views of *The Australian* (often vociferous on issues that threaten Australians with deprivation of their beloved sports) was overwhelmingly against such actions.

With the benefit of hindsight and the unfolding of events in South Africa in the 1990s, it is unlikely that such views would now be in the majority. Opinions clearly changed since Avery Brundage, President of the IOC from 1952 until 1972, said that:

> *athletic contests could never be held hostage to cries of human rights violations.*
>
> Quoted in McQuilkin, 1992

This expressed the widely-held view of those times. Brundage's references to members of the Black Power movement as 'misguided young men' and 'a little ungrateful' (McQuilkin) now seem as absurd as his views on amateurism (see Unit 1B, page 63).

Power of the boycott

Boycotts – the shutting out or exclusion of someone or a nation – are by definition protests, but protests do not necessarily involve boycotts. Protests often include individuals or smaller groups, whereas for boycotts to be effective and sway opinion they must mobilise a considerable number of people and create effective and noticeable impact.

In the 1970s and 1980s, the actions of the former Soviet Union and the apartheid policy of the then South African government were at the heart of the boycott activity. Taking into consideration the subsequent downfall of both political systems, it is likely that these sporting boycotts went some way to change opinions. Governments should perhaps take note that professional sport is a much more 'political animal' than its amateur counterpart.

Apartheid and the old South Africa

South Africa's policy of apartheid split the sporting world for almost thirty years: largely because the sporting community considered itself apart from politics. The racist doctrine of the *Broederbond* and *Afrikaner* purity, which discriminated against non-whites, had pervaded South African society from its foundation as a secret society in 1918 until the end of apartheid under the government of F. W. de Clerk in 1992.

In many respects, the Olympic community was quicker to take action against racism by excluding South Africa than the governments of many of its member nations. It took almost thirty years for politicians to take such actions as they deemed 'appropriate' as a stand against discriminatory practices. In the final analysis, it might be said that it was really the power of the boycott that forced change upon a reluctant South African government.

The old South Africa had made privilege the backbone of its sport selection process, thus excluding all who were not of its own kind. Although non-whites are in the majority in South Africa, they are poor and under-privileged and so were not treated equally. Perhaps more effectively than in any other instance, its demise has sent a message to the world that racial discrimination will not be tolerated in sport and that professional sport is big enough to exercise its own **political influence** when necessary.

'Ping-pong' diplomacy

The term **'ping-pong' diplomacy** was born out of America's involvement with the People's Republic of China prior to the Olympic Games of 1976. Following many years of China's non-involvement in global Games (the IOC regarded non-communist Taiwan as the true representative of the Chinese people), a group of American table-tennis players visited mainland China, thus signalling the USA's acceptance of a return to normal sporting contact for the Communist Republic. This was supported by a further visit from a USA swimming team, much against the wishes of the international swimming body (FINA). Richard Nixon, who was US President at the time, was criticised by many for sending table-tennis players to China instead of diplomats. The term now tends to be used when sporting contact is used to clear a path for politicians. Again this underlines the power and influence of sport, both on and off the field.

International sport as a focus for nationality

For an increasing number of countries, the success of its teams and individuals on the sports field has become part of an expression of nationality. This in itself is a powerful reason for remaining 'included' amongst the world's sporting fraternity. Those countries who persist with policies of persecution and discrimination do so at their own peril. In many respects sport has become a more powerful influence than the diplomat, or even the threat of military intervention. The expression sporting nationalism is a welcome change from more belligerent and destructive forms of nationalism to which people have resorted throughout history. To claim that sport is a substitute for war is a little over-simplistic and certainly naïve. However, as governments realise that the economic and other benefits to be gained from sporting success are also socially cohesive, the trend towards the development of a sporting identity alongside a political one will continue.

TASK

Is the pursuit of a national sporting identity justifiable in the case of governments presiding over social deprivation in their own country? Explain your views.

2. The pursuit of global excellence

Systems of nurturing sports talent

Reference has been made previously to various sporting initiatives that aim to foster and develop sporting talent. These systems often reflect the political philosophies of their country of origin.

These philosophies are reflected in the style of a country's administration. These range from the highly **centralised** and controlled system in China to the largely **de-centralised** and devolved free-market system of the USA. It is therefore not surprising that the way in which sporting talent is nurtured also reflects the political environment in which it occurs (Figure 4.49).

Provision and opportunity

In any culture there are a range of government policies which influence the provision and opportunity afforded to its population. The implementation of such policies depends on whether provision is to be on an ad hoc basis (although this is in fact very unusual), or whether it is highly structured and directed towards specific aims. Provision may be publicly or privately funded, or in some cases (as in Australia) a mixture of both. Usually the areas of recreation, physical education and sport are the typical conduits of such policies, irrespec-

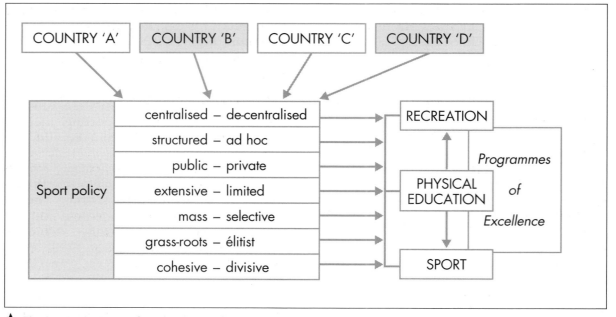

▲ **Figure 4.49** *Areas of government policy, level/manner of implementation and major areas of delivery*

tive of political persuasion, as they are often central to talent identification and policy implementation.

In both France and Australia, attendance at either of the respective national sporting academies is funded by **scholarships**. These cover the cost of training, coaching, etc. as well as the cost of residence. This is also the case in India, either at SAI approved centres, adopted schools or Boys' Company Sport Units attached to army units (see page 268).

In the latter case, the term 'nurturing' may well be used guardedly, particularly when young athletes are sent away from home to follow overly demanding training regimes. In some cases even parents are guilty of using their children to foster their own ambitions.

The nurturing of talent implies a caring environment and, clearly, this is not always the case. In France, Australia and New Zealand, no young athletes below school-leaving age have extended periods away from home. Nor is this the case in America, save for the much vaunted but also often maligned summer camps, which some young people enjoy and others hate. However, in China, India, Korea and Cuba, it is not uncommon for children to spend years away from home with only occasional breaks from sometimes particularly harsh surroundings.

Some sports, particularly ice skating, gymnastics and swimming, have traditionally required their future stars to train hard when very young. This is often to the detriment of their physical and psychological well-being in both the short and longer term. In your examination, **synoptic** questions may well require you to consider this aspect of talent preparation in terms of its desirability and/or justification.

Similarities and differences between countries and the factors that affect this

Although the pursuit of excellence in sport may be a common goal, the financial means available for it, and therefore the degree of sophistication, varies considerably from country to country. Other variables that also influence the nature of programmes of excellence are:

- wealth
- population levels/types/distribution
- political philosophy/dogma
- centralised/de-centralised administration (often linked with political philosophy)
- historical/cultural association with sport

- land area/physical topography
- global/political relationships with other countries.

The differences/similarities reflected in the above are to a large degree self-evident. There are some aspects which are not subject to change, for example land area or physical size, whilst others such as political philosophy can be subject to fluctuation. Population levels may also change over an extended period but this is unlikely to affect the age distribution in a way that will be influential in the short or medium term.

The USA, France and Australia are all (relatively speaking) wealthy democracies. However, the way in which they fund their programmes for excellence is different in each case and reflects the political and cultural philosophies of each.

The East German model

The former East German model of 'early talent identification', sports schools, high level coaching and advanced scientific support is now being widely copied throughout the world. Former East German coaches have been employed (notably in China and Australia but also elsewhere) in an attempt to recreate the 'East German machine' of yesteryear (Figure 4.50). Unfortunately the rather more sinister associations and accompanying accusations of malpractice still linger and (particularly in the case of China) continue to cause much disquiet amongst sporting nations.

It should, however, be acknowledged that many acceptable aspects of the East German system have been taken up widely. In particular, the **sports academy** or institute.

The use of academies and sports schools

These two terms refer to quite different types of establishment. Sports academy is usually applied to those establishments with the primary aim of developing performance at and to the highest level – largely with promising and/or established athletes. Attendance at such institutions is often but not always residential and is usually for a specified period – often for six or twelve months.

The term **sports school** has quite different implications. It tends to be associated with children, often as young as seven or eight years old, being sent away to a residential facility which also provides a full-time education. There are many question marks over the desirability of this practice, particularly because of the bad reputation of the sports schools of the former East German and Soviet regimes. In both China and India sports schools are now common and have some association with military influence in sport in those countries.

This raises the long-held concern of whether it is desirable to rob young people of a normal childhood and adolescence in order to produce the sports stars of tomorrow.

▲ *Figure 4.50* Athletes training at Australia's AIS in Canberra: such facilities are now in place in many other countries, following the East German model

TASK

In some countries many young people, driven either by personal ambition or a wish to please others, allow themselves to be sent to a strange environment in the quest for sporting success.

a Is it time that such practices were seriously questioned and possibly stopped?

b How and by what authority would such censure by applied, and what problems would you foresee in its effective implementation?

Funding of élite athletes

The funding of élite sportsmen and women varies, as does the range of systems that sponsor them. At one extreme are the college athletic scholarships of the United States, funded from the benevolence of free-market entrepreneurs; at the other are the state-funded systems of China and Cuba. In between lie a variety of 'funding mixtures' which will depend on the social and political communities in which athletes reside.

Scholarships

The term 'sports scholarship' also covers a whole range of variants. This can mean attendance at a university, funded on the basis of sporting or athletic ability; in return, commitment to the college or university athletic programme is expected. It can also mean that a (much smaller) sum of money has been awarded to a promising athlete, to be used in approved ways, such as in the defrayment of travelling and training expenses.

In India funding awarded is shared either by the government education department and the SAI or in the case of military units, by the military and the SAI. This, in effect, amounts to direct government funding.

Types of funding

In Australia, although funding for such places comes from the ASC, 50 per cent of it is raised from private sources and/or **lottery funding**. In Australia and France, the 'second layer' of excellence provision in state institutes of sport or regional INSEPs is largely non-residential. Awards cover the cost of tuition/coaching and daily travel costs. In France this second layer exists in the form of regional INSEPs and in Australia the sports academies which operate in each of its federal states (see page 241).

In India sports schools or colleges are effectively funded by central government (see above). Contrastingly, in Australia, sports schools attached to state-run schools are funded privately by parents and local business sponsorship. In America, high schools (nominally not sports schools) receive funding from the huge attendance at inter-scholastic sports competitions.

These fund both athletic programmes and often much of the rest of the school.

In the UK, schools that specialise in sport, such as Millfield in England and Gordonstoun in Scotland, are run very much as many other private schools, with parents paying fees in order to send their children there. There are, however, in both cases private scholarships available to allow talented children to gain access which might otherwise not be possible.

Funding sports stars?

Some consideration must also be given to existing sports stars. For them the funding situation varies quite considerably.

Professional soccer has had to rely very little on funding from outside its own structure. Professional clubs in most countries where soccer is a major sport fund their own programmes of excellence and potential élite performers normally receive financial assistance from the club with whom they are associated. Established performers in individual sports are often funded when part of a team but not when they compete or train as individuals.

In the USA, **federal funding** is available for Olympic preparation programmes. However, when athletes travel to Europe for Grand Prix athletics meeting, for example, they do so either at their own expense or at the invitation of the meeting promoter. Top-level athletes in many countries are also expected to pay the salaries of their own coaches/trainers, except when they are

▲ **Figure 4.51** Élite funding is generally for up-and-coming performers who are representing their country

included as part of an international or Olympic team.

Élite athlete funding is generally intended to fund the efforts of performers in reaching international standard in their sport and not to fund those who are already wealthy as a result of their sporting success (Figure 4.51).

Funded institutions

The type of institution which receives such funding will vary from one country to another. There are, however, some common systems in place. The precise nature of an institution will reflect its intended purpose and the philosophies of sporting excellence

Table 4.3 The funding of élite athletes

	Purpose	Funding
National Sports Institute	Residential – an extended period	Direct or indirect state funding
	Short/occasional courses for specific purpose	Privately funded, sponsorship, or small bursary
Regional Sports Institute	Usually non-residential but for an extended period	Direct or indirect state funding
	Short/occasional courses for specific purpose	Privately funded, sponsorship, or small bursary
State-run sports school	Residential for extended period – often involving young children	Funding nominally 'shared' but effectively state funding
Sports school run in normal state schools	Usually non-residential with the exception of some private schools	Fees if residential, state or parental funding if day schools
Communist countries	Sports schools, physical culture institutes, national squads: often residential, extended period – all ages	Almost always total state funding
USA	No specific purpose; sports academies or sports schools	Atheletic scholarship or privately funded college place

of the country it serves. Table 4.3 gives the most common range of alternatives.

The appliance of sports science through different training regimes

In looking at global sport and global Games synoptically, you should be aware of issues that may normally be considered to be outside the socio-cultural perspective.

The appliance of science in the context of training regimes, skill acquisition and motor performance and the psychological well-being of the performer are all areas which come within the remit of the synoptic viewpoint (see Unit 3). The academic/scientific aspects of those areas are dealt with by specialists in those fields. However, the implications of their application form part of the overview of sport addressed by synoptic questions.

We now know, for example, that in the teaching or training of very young people gross motor skills should be well established and at the appropriate stage of development. To attempt to teach/coach more advanced skills may well impede both further progress and the transfer of skill to other sports. Such practices that do not take this knowledge into account are still quite common. Training regimes which rely on this approach are questionable in just the same way as those that are inappropriate for either the situation, the technical requirements of an event or the particular group of subjects in question. (See 'Individual differences' in Unit 3 page 210 and page 299 of Unit 4B.)

Winning, or how you win?

The question about whether the **outcome** or the **process** is the major consideration in sport introduces the question of morality into the appliance of science. The East German and Soviet regimes ignored the morality of process, considering 'outcome' to be all that mattered – in other words, the means justified the ends, even if this was to the long-term detriment of the performer.

Clearly, in addressing global sport, the practices of some scientists need to be questioned in terms of their effectiveness and also of their morality.

The role of drugs and medicine in global sport

The moral aspects discussed above also apply to the area of drugs and medicine (Figure 4.52).

The purely scientific aspects of these contentious areas are the domain of the pharmacist, the chemist and the doctor. However, there are two distinct moral arguments which are the subject of much wider debate:

- When used openly in competition, at what point does the taking of drugs and medication put the notion of fair competition into question?
- Is it right that performance-enhancing substances should be considered unacceptable? If scientific training regimes can be used to enhance performance, is the use of pharmacological substances not simply an extension of this?

Medicine or morals?

The 'moral' question of whether it is acceptable to use a substance that is primarily intended to relieve genuine medical discomfort is easily answered. On that basis such medication should clearly be allowed. If, however, it may also give one competitor clear advantage over others then the rules clearly forbid it.

The problem for the scientist, sports physician and administrator is: How do we frame rules to ensure that they are not flouted? Is the answer to allow no medication at all?

The issues surrounding performance-enhancing drugs are clear-cut. It would be naïve to believe that there are no cheats in sport and that all banned substances can be easily detected. Sadly, neither is the case and nor (realistically) is it ever likely to be.

The consequence of this state of affairs is the never-ending battle between the sports administrators and their official laboratories on the one hand and the back-street chemists and their willing clients on the other.

Finally, you should also consider the morality of those (including at least one leading British athletics coach) who support the view that adult athletes should be free to take such substances if they wish – on the basis that all athletes would be free to make the same decision. Clearly if such freedom were made legal for athletes, it would also apply to society at large, with possibly disastrous consequences. If the argument applies only to substances that are not otherwise illegal but still enhance performance artificially, then presumably we would still be faced with the problem of those who would still be tempted to take substances that are or were banned?

TASK

a What is your view on the taking of medical substances in sport? Remember that not all substances are taken in order to cheat.

b Within your group, debate the proposal that athletes should be free to take what they like providing it is freely available.

Geographical and cultural differences

Geographical factors have influences upon recreational and sporting patterns, particularly in extreme instances. Where there are no coastlines and few rivers, watersports are unlikely to be developed, just as mountainous regions will be less likely to have a history of recreations that need large areas of flat land. These limitations are also likely to influence the way a people expresses its cultural identity.

A **primitive** or **emergent** culture is far more likely to develop patterns of recreation that both tradition and topography can support rather than adopt those that are beyond its reach. More advanced (and

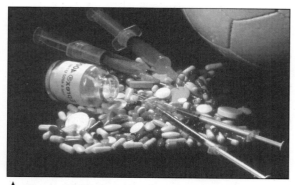

▲ **Figure 4.52** Drugs and medicines: essential medication or a convenient excuse?

wealthy) cultures are more easily able to use modern technology to create sporting and recreational environments. Often investment in a sport is made to satisfy demand from a small élite rather than for mass programmes of recreation (Table 4.4). Most of the golf courses in Kenya, for example, have been built to bolster its tourist trade rather than to facilitate recreation for the mass of the country's population (see page 249).

Table 4.3 *Types of sport and recreation in different cultures*

Type of sport, recreation and culture	
Primitive cultures	Simple, naturally available activities
Emergent cultures	As above but with some 'targeted' investment and technology
Advanced cultures	Full range of naturally occurring and technologically enhanced activities

This pattern can be seen when sport is used as a nation-building tool (see Unit 4A). Poorer countries utilise a small number of **low-tech** sports as a relatively inexpensive means of gaining international recognition and attracting both interest and investment from elsewhere. A limited number of hi-tech (often élitist) sports are developed in order to earn foreign currency from tourists and cater for those indigenous groups who possess the means to use them.

Land area, communications, transport systems and demographic spread can also make the implementation of recreational policies easier or more difficult, irrespective of political or cultural influences.

Culture
Cultural influences on sport and recreational patterns are reflected in the nature of activities normally found within a particular society. Cultural analysis can often explain why it is that some activities are found in one part of the world but not in another. Some cultures do not lend themselves to sports that involve, for example,

heavy, seemingly violent, physical contact. In India, despite the colonial influences that popularised rugby elsewhere, the game has not been adopted with the same level of enthusiasm, although cricket has.

The degree to which women and girls have traditionally been involved in physical recreation has influenced current opportunities for them. Many cultures where there is no overriding objection to female participation have now adopted policies of inclusion. Where religious objections exist, women may not be able to take part. (See Units 4A, page 270 and 4B, page 300.)

3. Deviance and cheating in global games

Reasons and methods
The reason why anyone cheats is to gain unfair advantage, although some have argued, particularly in more recent times, that it is simply to 'level the playing field' and allow them to compete against others who cheat.

In a global context, the notion of cheating can be rather more difficult to define than in the case of any specific culture. **Cultural values** and codes of behaviour vary, so that which is seen as cheating in one part of the world may not be regarded quite so harshly in another. There are also cases where athletes are required by the regime in which they live to undertake programmes designed to cheat or give an unfair advantage, and against which they may not have complete freedom to object. An example of this is the case of Petra Schneider, the former East German swimmer, who deprived Britain's Sharon Davies of a gold medal in the Moscow Games of 1980 (see Unit 1B, page 87). There may still be cases where athletes have reason to be fearful for themselves or their families of a **deviant regime** against which they have little or no redress. The stories emanating from the former East Germany suggest that such fears are not without substance.

The reasons for cheating in such cases are not a question of individual choice.

They are associated with the perceived benefits that a particular (usually political) culture may derive from international sporting success.

The increasing commercialisation of global sport and its effect on deviance

There are two issues here. One is the undeniable upsurge of commercial interest and involvement in sport. The second centres upon how, if at all, the growth of this commercial interest has given rise to deviant behaviour.

Sport: the growing business

Increasing commercial interest is relatively easy to demonstrate. The American sportswear company Nike, for example, currently sells its products through some 20,000 retail outlets in the USA alone and in count-

▲ **Figure 4.53** *Sports stars earn a fortune just by wearing a hat: is there a temptation to forsake traditional sporting values?*

less others in some 110 countries around the world. During the year that ended in February 2000 the company's net income rose by 27 per cent to $453.1 million out of a turnover of over $6 billion (Figure 4.53).

Clearly Nike is just one company specialising in a sports-related field. There are others from hamburger chains to electronics giants who all use a relationship with sport in order to give themselves a more acceptable image, broaden their appeal to consumers – and, of course, to maximise their profit margins. At the beginning of the twenty-first century, McDonalds, the American hamburger chain, ran a huge advertising campaign declaring itself to be fully supportive of that most 'English' of sports – soccer. It had also done so prior to the World Cup competition in 1998!

Sponsorship and advertising, as well as the personal endorsement of goods and services by leading sports stars, are the major means by which commercial interests market their wares in an ever growing global market-place. The rapid growth of a **communications technology** capable of taking these messages and creating markets around the world has also had a major influence both in market growth and levels of commercial involvement.

A club entering the English premier league in soccer can anticipate additional income of at least £10 million from **television income** plus other commercial benefits. Manchester United, for example, now earns far more money from sales of replica kits, etc. than it takes through the turnstiles at matches. In many other sports also, it is now the income derived from a range of other 'involvements' rather than purely from paying supporters that secures a club's financial viability.

Growing business – growing deviance?

We are reminded almost daily that business practice often includes a certain amount of deviant behaviour. This can range from 'fiddling' petrol money and other day-to-day expenses by an individual, to large-scale corporate fraud or mis-representation designed to dupe would-be clients into buying goods or services that they either do not really need or are clearly inappropriate for them.

As sport is now big business, it is hardly surprising that to some extent such practices have also permeated its once almost entirely honourable 'amateur' principles. To be surprised that this is sometimes the case is in many respects simply naive. If business practices are imported into the sporting arena it is almost inevitable that this will also involve at least some **dubious practices**.

Recently there have been highly publicised allegations of bribery in football and of match fixing in cricket. Some of these indicated the alleged possibility of an individual's personal gain – but all suggested that there were rather larger business interests behind the scenes.

With sport now part of the global market-place it also becomes susceptible to the deviant practices and behaviour that are to be found there. As indicated above, some of these influences show in the deviant behaviour of individuals, whilst others are more apparent in the commercial sense. The use of agents by many sports performers in contract negotiations, whilst not deviant, is clearly a reflection of hard-headed business rather than sporting motivation.

Sporting ethics – their rise and fall

Such motivations also influence what have been referred to as sporting ethics. To some extent this has been unavoidable, with huge material rewards replacing, or at least competing with, those of an entirely intrinsic nature, such as personal satisfaction.

It might also be considered that sporting ethics, like many other areas of life, are simply a reflection of the values held by society at large, and as such they are subject to change or re-interpretation. Clearly, the Victorian schoolmaster who took the view that to **lose honourably** was by far preferable to **winning dishonourably** would find rather fewer allies today than would have been the case even thirty years ago.

In Victorian times, the ethics of sporting behaviour were being redefined by a controlling **middle class** for whom such values were an essential aspect of their own **morality** (see Unit 1A, page 14). The dilemma today is therefore set in the context of whether such values should remain sacred in a world that has totally changed, or whether sporting ethics should now be subject to drastic re-interpretation.

If we opt for change, we must consider if the values and moralities of the business and wider world should be reflected in sporting moralities; or whether (and for what reasons) sport should set itself apart from such associations. Should the shirt-pulling in even the most prestigious of soccer tournaments simply become accepted, or do the laws of business consider a focus on such trivial transgressions as the last kick of an ageing dinosaur? Is the football star who holds out for the best deal he can get simply being sensible in the market-place, or insulting all those fans who struggle to pay the entrance fees which will escalate as a result?

History tells us that sport is older than the Victorian morality that shaped its values until relatively recently. Perhaps the forces that influence sport today are simply a reversion to those that prevailed before such intervention?

TASK

What does this apparent redefining of sporting ethics tell us about the traditional middle-class control of sporting values?

Drug abuse

The use of illegal substances, along with the biased behaviour of some officials and violent behaviour both on and off the pitch, can all be seen as the result of increased emphasis on winning rather than simply taking part. Some of these activities can be attributed to the heat of the moment, but there are also some individuals and groups who have premeditated intentions to flout or bend the rules to their own advantage.

In the case of drug-taking, there is little doubt that nearly all cases are pre-meditated. They are also perpetrated with the sole intention of gaining unfair advantage.

Although there is debate surrounding this topic (see page 289), the present rules are quite clear and people found to be in breach of them have little to offer in their own defence. Or have they?

Recent cases have highlighted errors in testing procedures as well as instances where it is claimed that illegal substances have been created naturally in an athlete's own body. It is therefore becoming increasingly difficult for sports governing bodies to frame effective legislation in this sphere. It is even more difficult to apply such legislation in situations where scientific knowledge is being updated more quickly than legislation.

Whilst this situation continues, it presents a threat to fair-minded sportsmen and women; it also provides opportunities for those with an intention to cheat to do so with impunity.

Bias

Biased behaviour on the part of sports fans is – within reasonable limits – an acceptable part of supporting one's team or individual sportsperson. The cheering of the home team and the booing of the away team is, for many, part of the banter of the crowd and accepted as fairly normal behaviour. However, when such behaviour and racial and other personal remarks are targeted at particular individuals, it is generally regarded as reprehensible. The perpetrators of such behaviour – very often small minorities themselves – are as offensive to sports-lovers as they are in the wider social sphere. Whilst the **bias** of the crowd in supporting their team is acceptable, the nasty cynicism of the bigot has no more place in the sports stadium than it does anywhere else.

The biased behaviour of officials is, on the other hand, always unacceptable. Care must be taken to differentiate between behaviour that is intentionally biased and that which is perhaps the result of genuine error, or simply a differing point of view. **Inconsistencies** in the decisions of football referees or cricket umpires have long been the subject of allegations of biased behaviour, but they are very difficult to prove. Replaying contentious points on video (officially or otherwise) enables some decisions to be seen as clearly erroneous. Whether such decisions were made intentionally is very difficult to prove – however obvious they may appear. There are growing calls for the wider use of video replay facilities in dealing with difficult or 'questionable' decisions. This is partly to make the task of officials easier but there is also concern that not all decisions are always made honestly.

In answering synoptic questions in the examination you may also wish to consider such possibilities as the bribing of officials and bias due to nationalistic/racist partiality.

TASK

In your group, debate the motion that 'If players simply abided by the decisions of officials in the true spirit of sportsmanship, there would be no need for video replay evidence to be used in sport'.

Violence

One area where video evidence has been useful is in the identification and subsequent arrest of those guilty of violence in and around sports stadia. Violence is now less frequent in the UK than it was twenty or so years ago but seems to have moved on to the international stage instead. The sophisticated policing mechanisms that have been put in place in the UK now have to be replicated on a European and possibly a global scale.

It is the sport of the **mass culture** that is often associated with this type of deviance. Football appears to be the main focus for such

▲ *Figure 4.54* Violence at football matches appears to have shifted from the domestic to the European scene

behaviour in Europe, although cricket matches in Asia and baseball fixtures in the USA are not entirely free from violence among spectators (Figure 4.54 and Table 4.5).

Table 4.5 *Violence in sport*

Violence in the UK	Declining due to effective policing and targeting of resources
Violence in Europe	Currently a growing problem and requiring 'sharing' of intelligence and resources
Violence in the global context	Becoming evident in global events in Europe and in Asia

It seems that as the global sporting stage expands, violence seeks out new arenas and seems to be particularly associated with sports that have a mass following.

On the field

Violence on the sports field can also be either pre-meditated or spontaneous. Whilst neither is excusable, the latter is more understandable than the former. Once again, such behaviour is often associated with football, but rugby players can also come to blows on the field, sometimes causing quite serious injury. In the USA it is not unknown for a whole team of players to invade the stands to retrieve of a stolen baseball cap. And the provision of 'additional entertainment' in the form of mass fisticuffs is sometimes a feature of Australian rules football.

▲ ***Figure 4.55*** *Some eruptions are spontaneous but does that excuse them?*

Many of these occurrences are spontaneous and are attributed to over-reaction or mistimed tackles. However, there are also those individuals who go into the game with a **preconceived intention** to rile the opposition or target an individual known to have a very quick temper. 'Sledging' in cricket is where the fielding side goads and teases the batsman in order to break his concentration. Opposing players undermine his confidence and may even provoke him to threaten or physically assault a bowler or member of the fielding side.

Just who is behaving badly is often difficult to determine and will vary in each case. However, some professional players, even though they should be above such behaviour, seem to be no less likely to have deviant intentions or capable of violent retaliation than many ordinary people. It is likely that both intent and response are also heightened by the **pressure** of the situation and the **rewards** which come from success.

In global sport, administrators and governing bodies have a difficult task when framing rules and disciplinary codes which take account of cultural differences, impartially and effectively. For example, some cultures are referred to as being 'hot-blooded' or 'hot-tempered' and their behaviour may be quite fiery; and what is acceptable in the physical rough and tumble of the English premier league may not be so to players from another culture.

Role of international sports bodies in combating cheating

At an international level, appropriate legislation and punishment to combat cheating has a much broader dimension than when considered in the purely domestic sense. Consensus is difficult to achieve across a range of cultures, and effective monitoring and implementation on a global scale is fraught with rather more problems than at national level.

Sport has also been unable to stay out of the political arena. Administrators sometimes have to contend with the rantings of politicians on contentious issues. An example of this was the intervention of Cuba's President Castro following the disqualification of Javier Sotomayor from the high jump competition in the Pan-American Games of 1999. The high jumper was found to have taken massive doses of cocaine but Castro insisted that this was a plot by the host country (USA) to discredit his administration.

In global games a further layer of administration often complicates matters. Where many sports are involved, as in the Olympic or Commonwealth Games, then the IOC or the Commonwealth Games Committee are the respective bodies responsible. This requires very close liaison with a range of international governing bodies, each of which has responsibility for the running of their own particular sport. With the Olympics, the IOC has its own testing laboratories, as do some of the sports governing bodies. The IOC insists on dealing with transgressions of its rules but then requires individual sports governing bodies to support it, or rule on its behalf. In individual sports such as athletics, its world championships are organised and administered by the sport's own governing body, the **IAAF**. This means that only one body is responsible and it is quite straightforward for the IAAF to deal with it. This is rather different from the scenario at the major multi-sport global games.

Sport was once run by largely amateur officials whose middle-class morality and sense of fair play made the rules. Today, sports administrators working globally have to accommodate a range of moralities. They must also contend with largely professional performers, political influence, commercial and media interests and (increasingly) with common law.

The agendas of all these interested parties are often based on quite different mores and a range of motivations. This leaves sports administrators – some of whom also have agendas of their own – with a very difficult task indeed.

4. Commercialisation and media in global sport

Amateurs and professionals – the development of 'open sports'

The clear distinction that once existed between amateur and professional sport has now almost disappeared – certainly at the élite level of performance. In any brief account of this change, there are certain key points that are relevant to an understanding of how it occurred.

Sport is no longer just the preserve of middle-class gentlemen. Increasingly it includes wider aspects of culture, class and gender. Along with this broadening of **access**, sport has also been required to accommodate a wider interpretation of its role in an increasingly global society. For example, business and commercial interests have created a sports-related marketplace. The success of developments such as Jack Kramer's professional tennis 'circus' of the 1960s and the Kerry Packer cricket rebellion of the 1980s forced sporting establishments to concede that such commercial ventures could not be ignored.

Sports governing bodies and tournament promoters have been forced to accept that the distinction between amateurs and professionals cannot be maintained at the élite level. As sporting opportunity becomes available to a wider section of the community, it has become inevitable that those wishing to make a professional living from their sporting talents will follow any breakaway groups in order to do so.

The All-England tennis tournament at Wimbledon was forced to go 'open' in 1968 and allow professional players to compete. This was because top performers boycotted the event and the organisers wanted to avoid the threat of an alternative tournament taking place that would have attracted the world's best players. English cricket

TASK

Discuss the concept of a world sports governing body. Would this concept work?

a Frame your ideas into a model showing how responsibility would be apportioned. Explained how the global control concept would be accommodated.

b List the potential advantages and disadvantages of this type of body.

abolished the distinction between 'gentlemen' and 'players' (amateurs and professionals) in 1966. By the 1970s the football authorities in England saw little point in continuing to distinguish between amateur and professional players.

Some sports held out for some time, with British rugby (union) becoming a professional game only relatively recently. Gymnastics in the UK has become a professional sport following changes to the sporting infrastructure and the availability of lottery funding. The major spectator sports were the first to be forced to address such changes.

There were two major influences in this process of change. First, as opportunity for participation broadened it was inevitable that more participants would take up sport professionally. Second, there was an increasing **resentment** on the part of élite performers because businesses and governing bodies were profiting from the heightened levels of commercial interest in sport. The performers themselves, however, were still expected to have a full-time job, train, and travel around the world in return for a free tracksuit and a daily 'pocket-money' allowance.

Some sports (boxing and golf, for example) still do have amateur championships for those who wish to consider themselves as such. However, for many younger performers, this is merely a step on the ladder to success in professional sport.

Role of TV and the 'Americanisation' of global games

As the global community becomes more and more a reality, American sport and culture continues to influence developments beyond its own setting. Americanisation is not new – there were baseball tours to the UK and Europe as early as 1870, and lacrosse was adopted by English girls' schools at the end of the nineteenth century following visits from touring groups including North American Indians. Later, at the time of World War I and more particularly World War II, the American military left a legacy of baseball and basketball in its embryo state all over Europe and south-east Asia. This was in addition to other aspects of American culture such as fast-food, popular literature, a televi-

sion culture and of course, the ten-pin bowling alley (Figure 4.56).

This assimilation of American culture was underpinned by the endless stream of Hollywood movies, advertising and popular music. This was, to some extent, a reversal of the diffusion of English and European culture which had found its way to America during preceding centuries.

More recently the dynamic relationship between business and sport in the USA has become a feature in Europe and globally. Using the medium of television, both terrestrial and satellite, American sports leagues are televised regularly. Global initiatives also include the incorporation of baseball, basketball and American football into both European and other cultures.

This development has highlighted two dynamics that occur simultaneously. One is a limited **cultural assimilation** of both sports and their media formats. The other is a measure of **cultural resistance** that makes people reject the most unacceptable aspects of this imported culture.

The transplantation of basketball and baseball has been particularly successful in parts of Asia and Australia. Although there are both British and European leagues in these sports and in American football, they have yet to mount a real challenge to more traditional forms of sport in the UK. The reverse, of course, also applies!

Television has been particularly influential as a marketing agency for both sport and associated commercial enterprise. The

▲ **Figure 4.56** Bowling alleys thrived in the UK in the immediate post-war period. They have recently regained some of their former popularity

professionalisation of sport has made it more accessible and receptive to commercial influences. Television, both satellite and digital, can now offer a breadth of coverage that maximises potential audience figures as well as providing a range of activities with which potential sponsors and advertisers can identify.

Sponsorship and sports as commodities

Sponsorship is perhaps the most familiar aspect of commercial activity in sport. It is difficult not to notice the sponsor's name on the shirt of a favourite football star or test cricketer. Competitors' numbers in major games and Grand Prix athletics events are always prominently displayed, so that the sponsor's name above or below it catches the attention of spectators and figure prominently in any television close-ups. Strategically placed advertising boards at most sporting events carry the event sponsor's name; match programmes, courtesy cars and other vehicles ensure that no one is left in any doubt as to the identity and the area of business activity of the event sponsor (Figure 4.57).

Sponsorship brings much needed finance to events, competitions, leagues, development programmes and individuals. In return, the sponsor receives agreed advertising priority, assistance with marketing promotions and, in some cases, a

▲ *Figure 4.57* Sponsorship is about exposure and association with 'acceptable' activity

degree of influence over the way an event is staged and/or its timing.

Sponsorship or control?

How much influence a sponsor is allowed to exert will reflect the level of financial support they inject, or the ability of the sport/event to survive without such investment. English county cricket, for example, could not survive nowadays in its present form if it were to rely on gate receipts alone. In fact it is the huge income from televised test cricket, international one-day matches and major domestic competitions, that is shared amongst the cricketing counties, that makes the game viable at senior level.

In this respect alone, sport at an élite level has become a commodity which can often attract huge television audiences far in excess of the capacity of any single stadium. It is this audience which sponsors and advertisers see as their potential market, and which allows many sports to command enormous amounts of funding from these sponsors. In many respects the wheel has almost turned full circle. The most marketable sports are now able to induce potential sponsors to compete against one another – they will pay huge sums to become sponsors and so gain access to vast untapped markets or be in a position to maintain existing ones.

There are those who do not agree with the marketing of sport in this way and they point to the potential loss of control by sports of their own destinies. Sports in some countries are now regarded as **franchises** to be bought and sold as business commodities, with little regard for the close associations built up over decades with the town or place of origin of a particular club. Purists recoil in horror at English county cricket teams appearing in the new coloured strip of sponsors (often referred to as pyjamas) instead of traditional whites. Others applaud such developments on the basis that the game 'has to move with the times'. There is an argument that if one ventures into the market-place then the commodities put on view must be marketable. Whether in such cases the commodities in question retain their **integrity** remains the subject of intense debate.

▲ *Figure 4.58* *'Bloodsucker' or negotiating genius? Eric Hall has made fortunes for many of the sports stars he represents.*

TASK

The growth of sponsorship will eventually lead to commercial identities replacing traditional club or team identities for sports fans.

a Discuss the above statement in your group.

b Write a short argument EITHER in support of OR against sponsorship in sport and present your thoughts to the rest of your group.

The rise of the sports star: the agent and the promoter

Sports stars

There have always been sports stars, fêted in their immediate communities and sometimes beyond them. There have always been *professional* sports stars, some of whom have managed to make a lucrative living from their chosen profession; and there have always been those who have either not quite 'made it' or who have never earned the rewards they aspired to.

The rise of the modern-day sports star implies more than just achievement and making a living – even a comfortable living. Today's sports stars can earn vast fortunes very quickly and quite often from a multitude of sources.

Roy Keene's reputed £85,000 per week at Manchester United fades into relative insignificance when set against Michael Jordan's $850,000 per week as a retired sports star. Global exposure elevates the a country's stars into internationally-known figures. Such

exposure also means that their potential as marketing icons further enhances both likely earnings and fame. Most professional footballers in the better English premier league clubs, for example, will be multi-millionaires in less than five years.

Agents

Such earning potential is now maximised by **agents** acting on behalf of performers. They are also aware that their own income depends on their bargaining ability (Figure 4.58). Quite often, an agent negotiating on a player's behalf can de-personalise discussions and obtain far better contractual terms than a player might on his or her own behalf.

Bloodsucker, parasite or negotiating genius just about covers the range of commonly-held opinions about agents. But authors, actors and other professionals have used their services for generations: why should sportsmen and women be any different?

The promoter

In boxing and athletics in particular, it is the **promoter** who has enabled the stars of these sports to amass considerable personal wealth. The promoters in boxing are part of the folklore of the sport. They are often the key figures in multi-million dollar deals put together in negotiations with managers, lawyers, media companies and boxing authorities (Figure 4.59).

There is, however, much controversy surrounding the promotion of the sport. Allegations of fight fixing, the careful selection of 'easy' opponents and out and out fraud are not uncommon. Some promoters

▲ *Figure 4.59* *Don King, the American boxing promoter: a history of alleged 'shady deals' has caused considerable damage to the reputation of professional boxing*

manage to manipulate boxing authorities and fighters to a degree that prompts the question: just who is in charge?

People outside the sport find it incredible that there are often several versions of a world championship title at each weight, with an equivalent number of organisations claiming to be *the* boxing authority. Professional boxing, especially at heavyweight, is now far removed from the traditional concept of sport. A history of shady deals has caused considerable damage to the reputation of professional boxing. Consequently its credibility as a sport is questioned by many.

Concerning other sports, perhaps the newest breed of promoters are those currently developing athletics competitions such as the European Grand Prix circuit. They are also instrumental in bolstering the income of track and field stars, negotiating appearance money and prize money for the most well-known and successful performers.

At the moment, Grand Prix events take place only in Europe. Although attempts are being made to institute their equivalent in the USA, this has not so far been successful. Ironically, whilst track stars at Olympic level receive high acclaim in the USA, track and field athletics in general makes little other impact there beyond the level of the college track team. Success in American sport is inescapably bound up with the accumulation of personal wealth from it. Traditionally this has not been the case in track and field athletics except in a comparatively small number of cases. If the promoter has his way and the number of track millionaires in the US begins to expand considerably, the ensuing battle for popularity between track and baseball will be very interesting.

The 'win ethic' versus the recreational ethic

There are those who still feel that Vince Lombardi (see Units 1A, page 47 and 4A, page 222) has a lot to answer for! It is clear, however, that the '**win ethic**' has been part of American sporting philosophy for much longer than fifty years. Paradoxically, in the UK and Europe where the '**recreational ethic**' has been uppermost, there now seems to be a revaluation of this sporting philosophy. Since the growth of commercial involvement in sport, there is a requirement for winning to be valued above simply taking part.

Financial reward can only be achieved by winning, whether in team or individual sports. It is therefore entirely logical that in élite (professional sport) the joy of participation alone is insufficient to ensure success.

Nevertheless, there is a vast difference between wanting to win and the dubious way in which some people do so. A 'win-at-all-costs' ethic even in professional sport where the stakes are high is difficult to justify within an acceptable sporting philosophy (Figure 4.60).

Professional sport demands that winning is a top priority – commercial support for 'also-rans' would be very difficult to come by in a harsh business world. However, the concept of recreation, fair play and sportsmanship is not dead, and millions enjoy their sport in competitive and recreational form without losing sight of that philosophy. Nor is there any reason to suppose that for professional sportsmen and women the only aspect of their sporting lives they enjoy is the income they derive from it.

If the essence of sport is not only in competition but also in the *nature* of competition then a 'win-at-all-costs' ethic has no place in sport in the accepted (traditional) meaning of the word.

When considering this idea, it is worth remembering that an 'ethical' concept of

▲ *Figure 4.60* Does the fact that sport is now largely professional mean that this is OK?

sport is much more easily afforded by the relatively comfortable middle-class culture that spawned it.

The culture of professional sport is essentially that of the 'hungry fighter' who makes sport his profession because it provides a means of satisfying material and psychological needs. He is not espousing a philosophy or even a particular culture. However enjoyable and worthwhile, it is simply a means to an end that hopefully will include a degree of otherwise unattainable material wealth. Perhaps a recreational ethic – at least in élite sport – is a luxury its modern exponents simply cannot afford?

TASK

Should 'win-at-all-costs' mean just that? As a coach how would you support such a philosophy?

The relationship between international competition and friendship

An individual basis

Friendship between individuals – even the closest rivals – is one of the bonuses of participating in sport. Some of the strongest lifelong friendships are formed between former team-mates or opponents.

Internationally, such friendships are invaluable in breaking down **cultural barriers**. Many sportsmen and women now spend much of their time training and/or competing in cultures other than their own and the social bonds formed in such circumstances quite often transcend differences which may exist between governments. These relationships may also involve members of media and broadcasting teams, sponsors and others who frequent the global sports arena. In some sports it is quite

TASK

To what degree – if at all – is it reasonable to expect sporting contact between nations to play a part in solving problems that are purely political?

common for players (such as in cricket and football) to spend extended periods in other countries, thereby aiding **cultural exchange** and the development of greater understanding and tolerance.

A group basis

Much of the above also applies to groups, particularly in the case of touring teams and tournaments, which run for extended periods. Like individuals, groups can facilitate exchanges of views, expertise and experiences in both the sporting and non-sporting sense.

Inward investment in poorer countries is crucial to their development and the involvement of business groups in the spreading of capital into such areas is of considerable importance. With the increased involvement of many governments in sport and visits abroad by ministers in a semi-official capacity to global sporting events, there are now opportunities for both sporting and political issues to be aired in a less formal atmosphere than at a summit meeting or official (political) visit. Whilst getting more business is obviously the major motive for a company seeking to expand its markets, it is nevertheless advantageous to commercial interests to foster the growth of friendships by providing the means by which politicians and others can exchange views out of the glare of the media's spotlight.

Both individual and group friendships are a good base for friendship between nations. Cultural diversity, whilst it can enrich the lives of those who are able to embrace it, can also present formidable obstacles to **integration**. The concept of respecting such differences without necessarily understanding or agreeing with them can only come from a greater level of interchange both socially and politically.

Sportsmen and women and those others associated with sport at a global or international level are uniquely privileged in this respect. However, it is not reasonable to expect them to negotiate with tyrannical regimes when their respective governments cannot or will not do so. Organisations such as the IOC compromise by ignoring difficult issues unless external pressure (as exerted by many countries in the case of South Africa's apartheid laws) leaves them no alternative but to take action.

It is now accepted that sporting excellence is only achieved through programmes of mass participation at grass-roots level. It may well be that friendship between nations can only be achieved when individuals, groups, commerce and the media have broken down at least some of the barriers created by governments.

5. Opportunity in global games

Individual differences

Opportunity in sport is influenced by constraint and there are several factors that must be considered.

In terms of athletic capability, a person's **physiological**, **psychological** and/or **biomechanical** make-up will determine whether or not they can maximise opportunity. It is possible that individuals whose physical make-up would normally restrict the likelihood of athletic success might, by sheer determination, still out-perform others who are physically better equipped than they are.

Fortunately, the rich variety of sporting activities practised at élite level does not favour any one particular physical type; so that the shot-putter, the basketball star and the diminutive gymnast or marathon runner have all been able to use their particular physical characteristics in the most appropriate sporting context.

Those whose physiological make-up includes a predisposition to long distance or endurance events can utilise that capability; whilst the athlete built for short explosive activity can excel in sprinting and other anaerobic events. Gymnasts typically have comparatively short (biomechanical) levers that allow them to maintain mechanically efficient control over the extremes of their body. Basketball players, on the other hand, use their much longer levers in reaching and jumping to compete in a sport which takes place way over the heads (literally) of most of us.

▲ **Figure 4.61** *Sport provides opportunity for all physical types*

In the history of sport, globalisation and wide-ranging influences of different cultures is relatively recent. It means that global games now comprise activities requiring very diverse physical characteristics and settings. This mix of activities ensures that sporting opportunity is open to a whole range of people of all physical and psychological types (Figure 4.61).

The influence of race, gender and religion

Opportunity can also be constrained by issues of **race**, **gender** and/or **religion**. These can seriously restrict access and **opportunity** in sport at all levels (see Units 1A and 1B.

Race

Some ethnic minority groups are discriminated against and this restricts opportunity both at local and global levels. Where racial groups are also predisposed to certain body types, there may be a positive or negative impact upon opportunity, in the sense that some body types/racial groups are thought to be more (or less) suited to particular types of activity.

In the case of Kenyan distance runners, for example, it was thought for some time that it was the lifestyle of certain tribal groups (at altitude) that gave them a particular advantage in such events. New research is now steering towards the view that there are certain tribal groups who possess certain physical qualities that would predispose them to excel in such events anyway. Traditionally the ability of Kenyan runners is attributed to their living at altitude and to their running considerable distances (e.g. to school) each day. Some Kenyan runners have recently been reported as saying that they did not run vast number of miles to school – in fact one said he walked 200 metres down the road!

It is not yet possible to make definitive statements on such matters but indications are that certain physical types occur in certain parts of the world.

Gender

The increase in the number of women participants in most sports may lead you to believe that gender issues are no longer a factor in limiting opportunity. However, in some cultures, it is still not accepted that women should compete in sports events for a range of reasons. Many African men still do not like the idea of their women leaving home to run in international competition, or indeed to run at all. Some do so reluctantly; the pill sweetened no doubt by the thought of the prize money that may be brought back home.

There are issues surrounding women who wish to participate in any sport that is physically aggressive and therefore considered 'inappropriate', such as boxing or playing rugby. Disapproval is usually by men but sometimes by other women as well.

Religion

Possibly the most contentious area in sport is that of women wishing to compete when it goes against the teachings of their religion (see pages 270–71). This usually manifests itself in two ways:

- Performance on Sunday, the Christian day of rest, is disapproved of by certain religious groups – this issue can also affect men. Additionally, some western religions take a dim view of women being seen in public clad in brief athletic kit.

- In the Islamic world, women are not only forbidden to take part in sport publicly but also from attending any outside activity where both sexes are involved. This is especially difficult in fundamentalist Muslim countries, where religious and state authority are one and the same. Many women who have decided to fight against such views do so in fear of their lives.

In this last respect, there is a particularly difficult dilemma facing global sports bodies. Some commentators call for male competitors from those countries preventing female competitors from free and open access to competition to be excluded as well. However, this also contravenes another principle – that of access to those of all religious persuasions.

How do governing bodies deal with religious views that discriminate against women? This presents a challenge and is an instance of rules having been formed within a European concept of free opportunity that does not take into consideration quite different views held in other parts of the world.

TASK

a Discrimination against minority groups within a culture that allows other groups free access to sport, as with apartheid, is clearly indefensible. What is your view on the discrimination against part of a cultural group (e.g. women) by their own culture?

b Would you agree with the view that where such constraints are part of cultural or religious beliefs they should not be subject to outside interference?

Olympic and other ideals

Major-General Richard Leathes, writing in the *Olympic Review* (1984), reminds us of a short statement of De Coubertin's aims for the Olympic movement:

The aims of the Olympic movement are to promote the development of those fine physical and moral qualities which are the basis of amateur sport and to bring together the athletes of the world in a great quadrennial festival of sports; thereby creating international respect and goodwill and thus helping to construct a better and more peaceful world.

The first part of this short statement has not transported well into the world that exists some 110 years since it was made in 1890. If we ignore the obvious social divide that existed between De Coubertin and the mass of those who would populate his 'better and more peaceful world', we are still left with '… fine physical and **moral qualities** …' and '… amateur sport …' to be translated into twenty-first century terms rather than those of the nineteenth.

The Olympic movement undoubtedly helps to develop physical qualities, as De Coubertin envisaged. There is some doubt, however, as to whether his ideals are still upheld regarding the moral qualities of amateur sport in the context of élite Olympic sport today.

The arrival of sporting professionals into the Olympic arena that was formerly purely for amateurs, has been justified with an agreement on the part of competitors to respect the **spirit of Olympic competition** for the duration of the games. Many might consider this to be something of a 'fudge'. The moral qualities of amateur sport are not just about the Olympic movement and, in today's multi-cultural world and differing philosophies, it would probably be difficult to frame any definition that would not be so broad as to be meaningless.

The second part of De Coubertin's statement transports from the nineteenth to the twenty-first century rather more easily. Few would disagree that 'a better and more peaceful world' is still a most laudable aim.

The 'ideal' of 'sportsmanship'
Sportsmanship had (and still has) a much broader application than in the purely Olympic context. It is probably subject to more questioning in today's sporting world than any other of its more traditional terms. These traditional interpretations embody such qualities as chivalry, honour and integrity, and a sporting demeanour that is as honest in its intention as in its application.

Quite simply sportsmen and women were expected to have a genuine desire to play within rules rather than to their limits. Notions of **gamesmanship** and the professional foul were unacceptable. Where the major test of a sportsman was not only how well but also how honourably he played the game, such terminology as 'the professional foul' was unnecessary. It is, in the opinion of many, professionalism that has brought the morality of the market-place into sport and devalued the true meaning of sportsmanship.

Respect for one's opponent(s)
The baiting and taunting of opponents has traditionally been frowned upon in most sporting circles. It shows no respect for the valiant (if sometimes woefully inadequate) attempts by another to test his or her ability in fair competition. This requires courage, particularly when facing an opponent whose reputation may be formidable. It should be respected for what it is – a courageous act.

Today's sporting mercenaries, however, are intent on winning – some at all costs. For many performers, the unsettling of an opponent is a device they are prepared to employ in their pursuit of victory. Clearly, the morality of sport has changed, as has that of the world in which it exists. How much of what goes on, though, does so because sports administrators 'fudge' such issues rather than address them?

Should the batsman walk?
This is a highly contentious issue, which also includes the wider issue of the questioning of officials' decisions. It is increasingly the subject of discussion in a world of video replays and post-match analyses.

Cries of 'get some specs ref' and 'that umpire must have been blind at birth' have sounded around sports grounds since the birth of mass spectator sport. With some exceptions, the almost abrupt refusal by some players to accept officials' decisions is a relatively recent phenomenon.

The right of the batsman to stand his ground is fairly easy to defend. If he is playing the game according to the rules, it is the umpire's decision whether or not he is out – not his own. If he feels he has nicked the ball and 'walks' or begins to leave the pitch – without waiting for a decision – you could say he is just as guilty of taking matters into his own hands as another batsman who waits for a decision and then refuses to accept it.

TASK

In a cricket match, the batsman edges the ball to first slip who catches it cleanly. The batsman 'walks', without waiting for the umpire's decision.

This is traditionally the honourable way to behave in cricket but is the batsman in fact being 'unsporting' in not waiting for the umpire's decision? Discuss.

The traditional 'ideal' of sportsmanship expected a player to play within rules and this also applied to the decisions made by officials. It was not a question of whether the decision was correct – simply that it had been made! This is not so easy to accept where it can now be clearly shown that the decision was made in error in a video reply, for example, nor when the integrity of some officials seems no longer to be beyond reproach (Figure 4.62).

This raises the question of whether **sporting ideals** are now redundant. Or does it simply mean that nineteenth-century ideals are outdated and cannot be transported successfully into another era?

▲ **Figure 4.62** It seems that official decisions are now subject to review, replay and consultation.

Sport as a vehicle to break discrimination

South Africa's apartheid laws were dismantled in 1992, following years of political, economic and sporting sanctions. This sends a clear message to other governments that they must consider carefully the consequences of their actions in the sphere of human rights – or does it? There are several points here to consider.

Sport was one of the tools used by governments and sporting organisations to bring about this change. However, it took nearly *thirty years* for a whole raft of **sanctions** to take effect. Although the desired effect was eventually achieved, it was only done as a result of an accumulation of pressures – including the sporting isolation of South Africa.

It is understandable that the notion of sport as a discrimination-breaking tool has a certain appeal. Headlines with this message are perhaps more 'attention-grabbing' than less emotive topics. Sport, especially global sport, is big news in most cultures. Any use that can be made of its popularity in such circumstances is obviously advantageous.

However, we must remember that up until the 1980s some governments (and many sports bodies) were insisting that sports and politics were totally separate entities. This has now been shown not to be the case.

Also of considerable importance is the changing nature of sport during the last thirty years or so. When South Africa was expelled from the Olympic movement and cricket and rugby tours were also suspended, cricket was the only one of those sports that could be considered professional. In the interim, global sport has not only turned to professionalism but has become associated with commercial and business markets to a degree that was probably not foreseen in the mid-1960s.

Consequently, the loss to South Africa was not just in terms of sporting involvement. It also lost out on the inward investment and foreign earnings that were becoming associated with sport. Sporting sanctions had therefore become economic sanctions. This made sporting isolation doubly effective – eventually. Although sport is influential in such matters, it is only concerted pressure across a much broader front that is really effective.

Ethnic games and counter-cultures

The increasing globalisation of sport and the growing level of professionalisation has in turn brought greater exposure of some **ethnic games** and activities. There has also been the development of a number of **counter-cultures** (see Unit 4A, page 222).

The sport of kabbadi, for example, is now televised to Asian communities around the world. This is as a result of both its popularity within a specific cultural group and the group's increasing mobility. This mobility has broadened the game's exposure and may well subsequently enhance its popularity amongst other cultural groups.

Beach volleyball, a derivative of the more well-known indoor game, is specifically associated with the beach sub-cultures of Australia and the west coast of the USA. Its inclusion in the Olympic Games reflects this growing popularity. It forces us to recognise that all sports at some time in the past were in fact 'ethnic' games until their appeal broadened into mainstream adoption.

The opportunities afforded by globalisation may well bring other sports to the fore which up to now have not been widely known but which, with increased exposure, may quite possibly become popular in other cultures.

Some of these alternative cultures, founded in the recreational ethic, have themselves created sports. These include skateboarding, snowboarding, mountain-biking, diverse forms of ski-ing and other extreme sports which themselves have become 'professional' and are creating their own heroes and sporting icons.

TASK

The number of sports included in global games such as the Olympics continues to grow. Winter sports were recognized as a separate entity many years ago.

a Is there now a case for further dividing the Olympics into smaller units, such as team sports, winter sports etc.?

b How would you suggest this might best be done?

Professional sport does not meet with universal approval and reasons for this have been discussed earlier in this section. There are those who object to the money it attracts and the idols it creates. Such people often also claim that the value of sport or recreation should be in participation and personal enrichment rather than extrinsic reward.

Issues of stacking, centrality and myths

Also central to the question of access to the increased opportunities that come with the globalisation of sport are the constraints that some cultures place upon certain minority groups. This often takes the form of resistance by a dominant group to the granting of access to others. In Australia, the Aboriginal minority, for example, is still highly marginalised. Despite the success of a few notable exceptions such as Kathy Freeman, many others do not have the opportunity to realise their potential in the same way. Such restrictions often reflect the intention of a dominant or central culture to ensure that opportunity is granted to its own kind rather than 'outsiders'.

Similarly, the concept of **stacking**, or social ranking, centres upon the dominant culture selecting other cultures to whom it grants approval. In the old South Africa, for example, the former white-dominated administration practised discrimination against all other groups in order to preserve its own (minority) values and culture. Within this discriminatory system there was an order of discrimination – blacks were treated differently from coloureds, for example, and were stacked at the bottom of the social pile.

This is in evidence today in Australia and in the USA, where stacking affects a number of minority cultures, who gain a degree of acceptance according to the desires of the dominant (white European) culture. Often the indigenous (native) populations find themselves at the bottom of the pile. In almost every case, the dominant culture is of white European origin.

The implications of stacking for opportunity in sport is fairly obvious, whether at global or national level. The lengths to which some dominant (often white) groups have gone to ensure the continued exclusion of minority groups have given rise to myths. These are only now slowly being disproved as a result of a growing body of well-constructed research.

The often-repeated belief that 'black men can't swim' is a good example – so effective that even today it is considered to be fact by many involved in sport. There is, of course, no denying that there are some physical types that are not 'at home' in the water – and some of those physical types may be found among black sections of the world's population. To perpetrate the belief that no black person can swim well is however just as ridiculous as maintaining that all white people can!

There is an interesting reversal of this assigning of physical qualities to certain racial groups. It involves some research that is now beginning to accumulate evidence to suggest that many non-white racial groups may in fact possess innate sporting abilities that white racial groups do not. Stereotypical phrases such as 'white men can't jump' are being supported by performances in athletics that might seem to indicate that white men can't sprint either.

The term **white flight** has been coined precisely because of this phenomenon. The disappearance, for example, of white sprinters on the global sporting stage is underlined by the slow emergence of the black quarterback in American football (Figure 4.63). The position of quarterback, as the 'mastermind of the attack', has traditionally been filled by a white player, to reinforce the perceived superiority of the

▲ **Figure 4.63** The black quarterback in American football: for many a sign that white superiorty is waning

white race over other racial groups who might make up the rest of the team. As suggested in Unit 4A (page 226), one of the ironies of 'white flight' is that it reflects the fact that generally speaking, whites do have somewhere, or something else, to turn to.

It is perhaps worth noting that since the first modern Olympic Games in 1896 American athletes have won well over half of the medals available in the 100m sprint – by far the majority of these were won by black athletes.

Under the global spotlight
One of the outcomes of the development of global sport, and the sophisticated communications technology that supports it, is that discrimination is harder to hide and just as difficult to justify. Many governments may well be forced to re-think their approaches to such problems, simply because the threat of sporting isolation, together with other potential sanctions, can be very costly. This is not the ideal way in which such issues as discrimination should be resolved but for those who suffer as a result the means by which such constraints are removed are less important than the end result.

The critics of professional sport and its marriage to communication and business should acknowledge that it is no bad thing if the tyrants of the world themselves feel themselves under pressure as a result of such developments.

Many businesses now not only support sport through sponsorship, advertising and other means, but by doing so they also indirectly support deviant regimes. Perhaps they could express their disapproval of discriminatory cultures by refusing to support events in which such countries fielded teams or individual competitors?

The world is now increasingly referred to as the '**global village**'. This is because it is becoming easier to communicate freely thanks to modern satellite technology and supersonic flight. Such improvements have brought new challenges to sport and created new possibilities and opportunities. It seems indefensible that there are still sections of this global village that are discriminated against. It is even less justifiable that those who perpetuate such constraint are allowed to do so with impunity.

TASK

Many workplaces now have to conform to 'quota' figures in their workforce to include a percentage of ethnic minorities. Discuss the suggestion that this should also apply to large multi-sport teams travelling to major games.

This would clearly be unworkable in individual sports but what about in an Olympic team of maybe over 100 competitors?

Key words and phrases

1. Sport as a show of national identity
- Health benefits
- Political overtones
- Shop window
- INSEP
- Lottery income
- Access
- Integration
- Protest
- Vera Caslavska
- Boycott
- Apartheid
- Political influence

2. The pursuit of global excellence
- Centralised
- De-centralised
- Scholarships
- Synoptic
- Sports academy
- Sports school
- Lottery funding
- Federal funding
- Outcome
- Process
- Primitive
- Emergent
- Low-tech

3. Deviance and cheating in global games
- Cultural values
- Deviant regime
- Communications technology
- Television income
- Dubious practices
- Lose honourably
- Winning dishonourably
- Middle class
- Morality
- Bias
- Inconsistencies
- Mass culture
- Preconceived intention
- Pressure
- Rewards

4. Commercialisation and media in global sport
- Access
- Resentment
- Cultural assimilation
- Cultural resistance
- Television
- Sponsorship
- Franchises
- Integrity
- Agents
- Promoter
- Win ethic
- Recreational ethic
- Cultural barriers
- Cultural exchange
- Integration

5. Opportunity in global games
- Physiological
- Psychological
- Bio-mechanical
- Race
- Gender
- Religion
- Opportunity
- Moral qualities
- Spirit of Olympic competition
- Sportsmanship
- Gamesmanship
- Sanctions
- Ethnic games
- Counter-cultures
- Stacking
- 'White flight'
- Global village

REVIEW QUESTIONS

1 What are the benefits of sporting success other than those which quite clearly accrue to successful competitors?

2 What is meant by the term 'shop window' as it applies to sport? How has this changed since the demise of the Soviet bloc countries and the growth of professional sport?

3 How has the nature of government involvement in sport changed in the last twenty years? What are the reasons for this?

4 How does the funding of élite sport differ in the case of a communist country such as China and a free-market country such as the USA?

5 Differentiate between the terms 'outcome' and 'process' in the context of the aims of programmes of sports excellence.

6 As a sports administrator, how would you deal with the question of the performer who cannot compete without medication but in doing so gains an unfair advantage over other athletes? Assume that there is no alternative medication.

7 What is meant by the term 'low-tech sports' and why is their adoption so evident in emergent cultures?

8 Deviance and cheating in sport can be perpetrated by individuals or by larger groups or institutions. Can you give an example of each of these?

9 Should traditional sporting values remain sacrosanct in a world that appears increasingly prepared to disregard them?

10 Why has violence at sports grounds in the UK apparently declined whilst it appears to be on the increase elsewhere in Europe?

11 Why is it more difficult to combat cheating in multi-sports games such as the Olympics than in individual sports?

12 What is meant by the terms 'cultural assimilation' and 'cultural resistance'?

13 Why is it that many professional sports could not survive without sponsorship?

14 What is meant by the terms 'win ethic' and 'recreational ethic'?

15 What is meant by the term 'gamesmanship'?

16 Is sporting isolation alone sufficient to break discriminatory practices?

17 What is meant by the terms 'stacking' and 'white flight'?

Texts used in the writing of this section

- Guttmann, A., *The Olympics: A History of the Modern Games*, University of Illinois Press, 1992
- Horne, Tomlinson, and Whannel, *An Introduction to the Sociological and Cultural Analysis of Sport*, E&FN Spon, 1999
- Jennings, A., *The New Lords of the Rings*, Simon & Schuster, 1996
- Leathes, R., 'The Olympic Aims, 1985', in *Olympic Review*, 1984, No. 205, pp. 863–9
- Maguire, J., *Global Sport: Identities, Societies, Civilisations*, Polity Press, (Blackwell), 1999
- Matthews, G., 'The Controversial Olympic Games of 1908, as viewed by *The New York Times* and *The Times* of London', in *Journal of Sport History*, Vol. 7, No. 2, 1980, pp. 40–52
- Mayall, D. & Cronin, M., *Sporting Nationalisms (Identity, Ethnicity, Immigration and Assimilation)*, Sport in the Global Society Series, Frank Cass, 1998

❏ McQuilkin, S. A., 'Fanning the Flames: Avery Brundage, the USOC, and the 1968 Black Power Revolt', in *The North American Society for Sport History, Proceedings & Newsletter*, 1992, p.140

❏ Senn, A. E., *Power, Politics and the Olympic Games*, Human Kinetics, 1999

❏ Young, M., 'The Melbourne Press and the 1980 Moscow Olympic Boycott Controversy', in *Sporting Traditions*, 1988, Vol. 4, No. 2, pp. 184–200

Suggested further reading

❏ Guttmann, A., *The Olympics: A History of the Modern Games*, University of Illinois Press, 1992

❏ Jennings, A., *The New Lords of the Rings*, Simon & Schuster, 1996

❏ Maguire, J., *Global Sport: Identities, Societies, Civilisations*, Polity Press, (Blackwell), 1999

❏ Senn, A. E., *Power, Politics and the Olympic Games*, Human Kinetics, 199

Unit 5
Refining performance

Introduction to Unit 5

This introduction will enable you to meet the requirements of Unit 5 by further extending your knowledge and understanding of practical performance through three Unit sections. This will provide you with the knowledge of:

- how to **refine** your own performance
- an understanding of how to complete the assessment assignments
- the extended processes of examination that you will be required to complete.

Occasionally reference is made to work you have covered in other Units – or in the case of Unit 6, work that you have yet to do. This is purely a reminder that the summative nature of A2 examinations will in some cases require a thorough grasp of the content of *all* Units. This is particularly the case with Units 4B and 6C, which will be examined synoptically.

Unit 5 provides you with the opportunity to refine your knowledge, skills and understanding of practical activities. Building on the enhancement of performance achieved in Unit 2, you will further acquire and apply knowledge and evaluate your own performance and that of others. Leading on from the experiences you gained from the Advanced Subsidiary course, you will again be given the opportunity to follow your own particular study route in one section.

In Section A, the experiences gained through practical activity will enable you to acquire, apply and evaluate the knowledge required of **factors affecting performance** to a range of practical activities. In Section B you are required to construct and perform a **Personal Exercise Plan**. For Section C, you have the option of selecting either a practical pathway for assessment in one activity only, or you can undertake a piece of investigative research.

When worked through together, Sections A, B and C of Unit 5 will give you the opportunity to demonstrate a *progression* from the Advanced Subsidiary course. From both a theoretical and practical standpoint you will be able to display the knowledge and understanding needed for the refinement of a performance.

Throughout Unit 5 you should build on and use all the experiences gained from Units 1 and 3 of the Advanced Subsidiary course but more importantly those from Unit 2. Reference will be made to these at various points throughout this Unit.

Unit weighting

The weighting for Unit 5 forms 15 per cent of the Advanced Level course. The total contribution of practical Units 2 and 5 is 35 per cent of the final Advanced Level award. The individual sections are weighted as follows:

- Section A: Factors affecting performance – 5 per cent
- Section B: Personal Exercise Plan – 5 per cent
- Section C: Option A: Practical performance or Option B: Investigative study – 5 per cent

Key Skills

The development of Unit 5 continues to provide you with a variety of opportunities to develop your Key Skills. While you will focus in particular on communication, application of number and information communications technology, the Unit will require you to show greater independent learning and improved performance. This will extend your ability to work with others and provide some opportunities for problem solving.

The level of knowledge and understanding gained from this Unit, and the experiences of Unit 2, is intended to prepare you for your examination and assessment requirements at the end of the course. But it will also prepare you for study in Further and Higher Education and, additionally, give you the confidence to be physically active in adulthood.

Developing your Individual Performance Portfolio (IPP)

You will already be familiar with the Individual Performance Portfolio (IPP), which you developed for Unit 2. In Unit 5 there is a requirement to continue and further extend this personal document. By the end of Unit 2, the IPP should contain a record of the experiences that you have gained and it should reflect the progression you were able to make in your practical performances, the knowledge and understanding of skill acquisition and the ability to analyse a performance. The additional understanding of the local and national provision of an activity will also be included. You may also have been able to obtain external awards in coaching and refereeing/officiating and these should be in your portfolio (Figure 5.1).

The development of your IPP requires you now to collate evidence of your knowledge, understanding and practical experiences gained from three sections of Unit 5. For Sections A and B you will produce two major pieces of written coursework. For Section A you complete an evaluative assignment on improving performance by looking at the factors affecting performance in your chosen activities. The second piece for Section B reflects your ability to plan, perform, record and evaluate a Personal Exercise Plan.

In addition, you will be able to record the progress you have made in refining your own practical performance. If you choose Option A of Section C, you will need to collate as much evidence as possible which will reflect on the standard of the performances you have been able to produce. You will still be assessed in structured practices and competitive situations but also in your performance of specific skills in isolation. **Playing records, performance records**, **match analysis** and **observation assessments** can all form part

▲ **Figure 5.1** *The IPP will reflect your considerable achievements*

of your portfolio. You must remember to record any formal assessment made of you by your centre, in particular if these are of 'seasonal' activities such as athletics, tennis or cricket. If you undertake Section C: Option B you will carry out an investigative study, which will also be contained in your IPP.

All the work presented in your IPP will be submitted for moderation by an external examiner towards the end of the completion of Unit 5. This is normally by the end of April in the year of the final award.

It should be noted that the IPP itself is not directly assessed and does not therefore contribute to your final award. It is the evidence of the work you have completed in Unit 5 that is contained in the IPP that forms the assessment of the Unit. You should not, however, underestimate the importance of the final quality of presentation of your IPP. As a document detailing two years' practical experiences and assessed components, it is evidence of your abilities and levels of attainment. As such it will be a useful document to present at interviews and it will reflect considerable achievements.

KEY SKILLS

The presentation of your IPP may satisfy the requirements of Level 3 in both Information Communications Technology and Communication. If, in addition, you undertake the investigative study, this may also meet the requirements in 'Application of number'.

Unit overview

Section A: Factors affecting performance

This section requires you to further extend your ability to link theoretical knowledge to practical activity as in Section A of Unit 2. Your centre will select a minimum of three activities with at least one from each of the specified category groups of team games, racket games and individual activities. These activities offer you a variety of practical experiences. From these and the supplementary knowledge derived from associated study, you will gain a knowledge and understanding of coaching, physiological and psychological factors that affect a performance. You will focus on specific techniques in order to refine your performance.

This section is worth 5 per cent of your Advanced Level award.

Section B: Personal Exercise Plan

Section B of Unit 5 requires you to plan, perform, record and evaluate a Personal Exercise Plan (PEP). You will use your knowledge and understanding gained from Unit 3, and in particular Section C of Unit 2 where you may draw upon the work undertaken in the analysis of performance, to form the basis of the PEP. For the PEP you will complete a programme of exercise training of your choice (Figure 5.3).

This section is worth 5 per cent of your Advanced Level award.

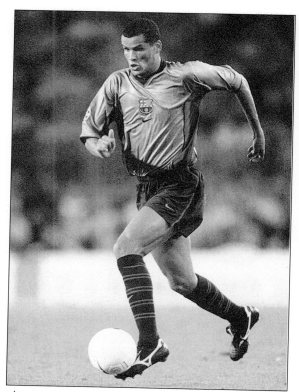

▲ **Figure 5.4** *The choice of practical activity for assessment will be yours*

▲ **Figure 5.2** *Performances require preparation*

Section C: Option A: Practical performance or Option B: Investigative study

For Section C you will *either* select one activity for practical assessment or carry out an investigative study.

With Option A, you will be required to demonstrate specific techniques in isolation as well and perform in structured practices and competitive situations. The choice of activity will be yours (Figure 5.4). It can be one already offered for assessment in the Advanced Subsidiary course. It must be taken from the activities category list contained in the full specification document.

You may instead decide to undertake an investigative study of 2500 words into a practically related topic (Option B). You will need to set and then test a **hypothesis** and draw conclusions from this. In order to do this, you will be required to set up research, review related literature and collate empirical data (Figure 5.5). Further details of this investigative study can be found in the Unit exemplification provided by Edexcel.

▲ **Figure 5.3** *For the PEP you will complete a programme of exercise training*

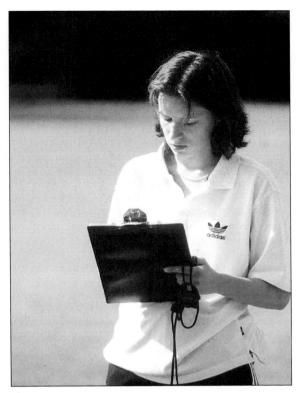

▲ *Figure 5.5* You may decide to undertake an investigative study

This section is worth 5 per cent of your Advanced Level award.

Key features of Unit 5

The following key features summarise the content and direction of study of this Unit:

- the continued development of an IPP reflecting your refined knowledge, skills and understanding of practical performance. Contained within the IPP will be:
- an evaluative assignment of 1500 words on improving performance, based on a topic of study from the list of factors affecting performance
- the construction and performance of a Personal Exercise Programme
- the refinement of your performance in one practical activity *or* the undertaking of an investigative study.

The rest of this Unit explores and outlines the subject knowledge of each section and details the examination and assessment procedures

relevant to each. This should help you to maximise your examination grades.

It is important for you to draw upon all the experiences you gained from your Advanced Subsidiary course. By aiming to refine your knowledge, skills and understanding of practical activity, you will be able to provide the necessary practical examples to answer questions set for Units 4 and 6. In particular, you will be required to provide a wider level of applied knowledge and understanding to complete the synoptic questions for those Units.

In Unit 5 it is acceptable to undertake activities that by their very nature will need to be conducted off-site. As with such choices in Unit 2, there is a requirement for your centre to be responsible for your development and to make known the requirements of examination to the instructor or coach taking you. Your centre will be required to make the final judgement on your attainment in the practical performance of any activity conducted off-site. You will need to include a record of these and **video evidence** of any training, competition or related experiences that you have undertaken for your activity. These are submitted in your IPP for moderation by an external examiner.

Unit 5 will be viewed as your *practical coursework* option.

> **Unit 5 Examination A2:**
> **Weighting of 15%**

> ## Key words and phrases
>
> - **Refine**
> - **Factors affecting performance**
> - **Personal Exercise Plan (PEP)**
> - **Playing records**
> - **Performance records**
> - **Match analysis**
> - **Observation assessments**
> - **Hypothesis**
> - **Video evidence**

Section A: Factors affecting performance

1. Introduction

The purpose of this section is to provide you with a variety of experiences from which you will be able to refine your practical performance. This will enable you to develop a **holistic** approach to the acquisition of knowledge and establish a level of understanding of a variety of factors that can affect, shape and determine a practical performance. The focus of knowledge is on physiological, psychological and coaching topics. The development of your skills of **analysis**, **organisation** and **evaluation** of your own performance, as well as that of others, is a central theme of this section. Your experiences in Unit 2 will have prepared you in some way for this.

The use of simple techniques involved in the analysis of performance, aided by your experiences in preparing for your practical assessments, will be of value to you here. Some students will also have begun to coach others and organise training sessions. This personal development will reflect your wider appreciation of a sporting performance and reference to this can be made in your **IPP**.

The delivery of the content of Section A is very much dependent on each individual centre. The selection of which three practical activities to use as a medium for delivery will be dependent on the sporting expertise of each centre, the facilities available and the activity choices of candidates. You are advised to be open-minded – look upon this section as providing you with the experiences, knowledge and understanding to answer fully the synoptic examination papers related to Units 4 and 6 as well as complete the specific written assignment required for this section.

2. Evaluation techniques for skill, positional and match analysis

A central theme of Unit 2 Section C was the development of the knowledge and understanding of how to analyse a performance. Analysis of performance is built up through the systematic appraisal of the technical components that underpin the production of skill, along with the tactical awareness to improve positional play and the ability of a performer to analyse a match or performance.

What is evaluation?

Evaluation is the end-point of the interpretation of information within the context of the overall coaching plan.

NCF, 1999

Evaluation is concerned with formulating **judgements** and it is therefore the opinion of an observer. Knowledge and experience help provide the frame of reference from which a judgement can be made. However, in order to extend this process further, there are various methods of analysis that can be used for evaluation purposes:

- systematic questioning of players
- player profiles – techniques, skills, tactics and physical attributes
- statistical match analysis sheets – phases of play, application of principles of play, tactics, games plans, decision making
- notation – patterns of play, technical errors and achievements, work/rest intervals
- video – slow motion replays, different angles, instant/permanent feedback
- bio-mechanics – kinetic and kinematics.

Evaluations are, nevertheless, still subject to personal opinion. They tend to **qualitative** in nature, and you need to be aware of the desire to make *objective* rather than *subjective* evaluations. An evaluation becomes more secure if it is based on valid and reliable information gained through detailed observation and defined analysis with **quantitative** data.

The use of video as a means of recording performances is worthwhile. Video offers, in some circumstances, almost immediate feedback and enables slow motion and freeze-frame technology to be used. This will enhance your own observation skills by giving you time to study a performance. It is also an examination requirement for you to video performances of activities conducted off-site. In addition, it is a safety net for all performers when they are moderated as a recording of standards achieved during the course can accompany a live performance.

The nature of some sports means that they are more amenable to evaluation than others. Modern soccer and rugby matches are now full of evaluations based on, for example, the time a team has possession of the ball, shots on and off target, scrums won and lost and now individual player statistics.

Sports based on empirical measurement, such as swimming and athletics, make full use of evaluations for technical, physiological and performance purposes. Cricket has for

TASK

Look at the recent scorecard given in Figure 5.6 below and the soccer analysis in Figure 5.7 and see what evaluations you can make from the information given.

Wanderers scoreboard

in Johannesburg   England won toss

South Africa

	Balls	Mins	4s	6s
H H Gibbs c Knight b Gough	**8**	22	17	1	0
N D McKenzie b Caddick	**4**	28	18	0	0
J H Kallis b Gough	**0**	1	1	0	0
W J Cronje c Knight b Mullally	**56**	133	113	4	1
J N Rhodes c Hick b Caddick	**5**	9	8	1	0
S M Pollock c White b Caddick	**0**	4	5	0	0
M V Boucher c Hick b Alleyne	**36**	89	59	3	0
L Klusener c Hussain b Gough	**10**	36	25	0	0
P C Strydom c Maddy b Caddick	**3**	13	9	0	0
S Elworthy not out	**8**	15	7	1	0
H S Williams run out (Gough)	**7**	11	9	0	0
Extras (lb5, w6, nb1)	**12**				
Total (45 overs, 186 mins)	**149**				

Fall of wickets: 1–14 (Gibbs, 5.4 ov), 2–14 (Kallis 5.5) 3–14 (McKenzie, 6.1), 4–21 (Rhodes, 8.1), 5–21 (Pollock, 8.6), 6–95 (Boucher, 32.2), 7–129 (Cronje, 39.3), 8–132 (Klusener, 41.2), 9–134 (Strydom, 42.3), 10–149 (Williams, 44.6).

Bowling: Caddick 9–1–19–4; Gough 9–2–18–3 (4w); Mullally 9–3–22–1 (2w); White 7–0–38–0 (1nb); Ealham 5–0–24–0; Alleyne 6–0–23–1.

Umpires: R E Koertzen & D L Orchard.

▲ **Figure 5.6** An analysis of a cricket innings, Daily Telegraph, 14 February 2000

Georgia v England, Tblisi, Sat. 9 November 1996

	Sher'ham	Ferdinand	Wright	Ince	Beckham	Gascoigne	Batty	Campbell	Adams	Hinchcliffe	Southgate	Seaman
Time on Pitch	90	81	9	90	90	90	90	90	90	90	90	90
Goals												
Inside Box	1	1										
Goal Att.												
On Target			1			1						
Near Miss					3							
Throw-ins												
Given Away	1			1	1	3	2	3	2	4	4	
Own Player				1	5	1		2		6	3	
Opposition					1			1				
Passes												
Short	30	30	1	34	29	65	73	35	33	31	19	
Long	1		1				5	1	4		7	
Failed Short	8	14	1	6	4	8	4	4	1	5	3	
Failed Long	2			3	2	4	1	1	3		6	
Tackles												
Won	1	2		2	2	1	6	3	3	2	2	
Lost				1	3	5	1			1	1	
Interceptions				2	4	4	8	7	7	4	5	1
Clearance				4	1	1	1	8	10	2	7	2
Blocked								3				
Dribbling												
Retained						2		2	1		1	
Ball Lost			1				4					
Run Over 15 Yards		1		1			3	3			1	
Free Kicks												
Foul	2	2		2	3	1		1	1			
Offside	1				2							
Yell. Card						1						

▲ **Figure 5.7** Soccer match analysis, Observer, 10 November 1996

centuries prided itself on statistical analysis – overs bowled, runs scored etc.

This aspect of 'Factors affecting performance' demands that you further extend these elements to include a more detailed depth of knowledge of the three aspects of skill, position and an overall match/performance. It is not possible within the scope of this text to explore how these relate to all the activities contained in the full specification. Instead you will find here some examples from the categories of team games, racket games and individual activities.

By looking at these examples, it is possible to form broad evaluation techniques which can be applied generally. You will need to formulate evaluation programmes based on your own playing knowledge and experiences and the direct help given to you by your teachers.

Evaluation of skills

This aspect of evaluation requires you to draw together your work in Section A and Section C: Option A of Unit 5 where you will be seeking to refine your practical performance.

If you choose to do Option B, the investigative study, for Section C of Unit 5, the experience of taking part in practical activities for Section A will provide you with opportunities to develop the ability to conduct an evaluation of skills, positional and match analysis.

Part of the examination requirement is that you are assessed in your performance of skills *in isolation*. Building on knowledge you obtained through the 'Analysis of performance' in Unit 2, you will appreciate that skills can be broken down into their technical components. As a result, this will enable you, as an observer as well as a performer, to make judgements and comparisons from which an evaluation of the overall skill is possible.

The NCF (1999) called this the **sequential method** of analysis. You will need to develop a technical understanding of how the fundamental skills are performed in your activity.

Using the example of swimming, the individual strokes can be analysed by observing the whole body action and then broken down into 'leg action', 'arm action', 'breathing', 'timing' and the overall efficiency of the stroke. In the case of the leg action in front crawl, the observer may pose the general question, 'is the swimmer performing a recognised technique?'. From this, the following more specific questions can be asked:

1 Is the leg kick initiated from the hip?
2 Does the leg kick balance the stroke?
3 Are the feet flexible and plantar flexed?
4 Does the leg kick provide propulsion?

By means of observation you will be able to give a simple yes/no answer to these questions and subsequently form a judgement on

▲ *Figure 5.8* Through the process of evaluation you should be able to tell what the performer is doing correctly and incorrectly and make recommendations

the swimmer's leg action. These judgements allow for a qualitative evaluation to be made from which you will be able to make recommendations on what changes, if any, need to be made (Figure 5.8).

Some evaluations will make use of scales, that is a range of marks that allow for more exact or detailed judgements. In tennis you may wish to make an overall evaluation of a particular stroke. By identifying the stroke and applying a scale of 1–7, for example, you will be able to make an evaluation of that stroke. You will also be able to make a comparison of that particular stroke to other strokes and to other parts of a player's game.

A tennis player may need the following qualities in order to play successfully:

- co-ordination, dexterity (quick reactions, timing and control)
- athleticism (speed, agility, nimbleness)
- anticipation
- competitiveness
- racket skills (full technique, flair, improvisation).

Each of these qualities can be evaluated by applying a simple scale of 1–7:

1	2	3	4	5	6	7
POOR.................AVERAGE................. HIGH						

Therefore, a player can be judged to possess a high level (6/7) of ability in, say, competitiveness but only a below average (2/3) level of anticipation. From such judgements training programmes, targets for improvement and practice sessions can be organised.

If you studied PE at GCSE level you will be familiar with this type of process from your assessments by using a scale of 1–10. Your assessments for both the Advanced Subsidiary course and the Advanced Level course are made by forming judgements about a performance and then by applying the evaluation to a range of descriptive criteria on a scale of 1–15.

Remember the whole process of evaluation is carried out in order to assess a skill, position or a match performance. We are all able to make simple statements that a performer is good or bad at a particular sport. What you will be required to develop is a more thorough and objective framework from which objective evaluations can be made.

Once you have become familiar with the examination requirements for your practical activities you will know how specifically the skills assessments in isolation are to be made. By working on the technical proficiency of the performance of these skills you will clearly develop the ability to go through the process of self-evaluation.

Evaluation of position

The process of evaluating a performer's positional ability is similar to that of the evaluation of skills. This aspect builds on the tactical knowledge and experiences you will already have from playing and performing.

You may find this process very easy to do. For instance in rugby union, all players are required to be dynamic and possess power, strength, agility and mobility which can be judged and then evaluated against a self-constructed set of criteria.

In addition to the above qualities, the RFU (1999) suggest that all players should have the following attributes:

- handling skills – passing, catching, falling, picking up and winning the 50/50 ball (Figure 5.9)
- contact skills – the ability to retain or win the ball, to stay on your feet, to put body between man and ball, to tackle effectively
- running skills – to run on the right lines, to punch, have evasive skills, be effective in penetration, have acceleration and have pace
- support skills – as a ball carrier can the player find support? Does the support come from deep/have depth? Does the player make intelligent decisions in supporting the ball carrier?
- decision making – do the player's decisions improve the team's situation?

With a little adaptation, you will be able to apply these evaluation questions to a whole variety of invasion games and formulate additional ones as appropriate. Try to devise a scale to make a judgement on these questions.

In considering the **positional requirements** of your own activity, or the demands of activities such as dance or gymnastics, you may be able to further evaluate an individual performer. In rugby, each player has specific positional requirements based on the broad player attributes listed on the previous page. When playing on the wing, for example, the

▲ *Figure 5.9* *Common rugby skills – catching passing and tackling*

position requires a player to demonstrate handling skills, running skills, the ability to kick, tackle and make decisions.

More specifically, with regard to handling skills, three evaluation questions are posed:

1 Can the player receive a ball from both left and right?
2 Can they keep the ball alive?
3 Are they safe under the high ball?

In this instance evaluation of performances are made by applying the following four criteria to the simple questions above:

- always
- usually
- sometimes
- never.

TASK

Think back to your last performance and draw up a list of the positional requirements you needed for it. Then make an honest evaluation of these by applying the four criteria above. How well did you do?

Evaluation of a position may not always be based on technical or tactical requirements. All performers must be effective in their position from both a physiological and psychological standpoint. In soccer, for example, you do not see many goalkeepers in the Premier League under 6ft in height; midfield players, by virtue of their position, are required to run further than strikes or defenders. What type of character would you need to be to handle the pressure of test match cricket or perform in gymnastics when your every movement is being judged?

The Football Association has identified the following attributes in the assessment or evaluation of a player:

- size – is the player of slight, athletic or of powerful physique?
- speed – does the player have quick feet explosive bursts and pure pace?
- technique – what is the player's touch/timing, accuracy in passing, neatness and balance like?
- playing qualities – what is the player like under pressure? Has he stamina and a good work rate? Is he determined and brave? Is he mentally alert?

You may be aware of the now famous Ajax soccer system called 'TIPS'. These characteristics evaluate a potential player or player in four ways, based on:

- **Technique**
- **Intelligence**
- **Personality**
- **Speed**.

You will certainly have an opinion of how good a performer you are, and an opinion of the abilities of your peers and professional players. The key question with any evaluation should be whether or not it is based on secure, valid and reliable data: or purely personal opinion (Figure 5.10).

Practical assessment
Remember that as part of your practical asssessment in Section C of this Unit an evaluation will be made of your ability to perform skills with a good technique, a judgement of your decision making, an assessment of your 'fitness for purpose' and your application to practise and competition – the complete performer!

In summary, six aspects of a performance can be used to form the basis of your positional

▲ **Figure 5.10** What makes this player the best in the world in his position?

evaluations and the beginnings of a performance development programme:

- decision making and tactical awareness
- fitness levels per desired component
- level of skill/technique
- co-operation and teamwork
- concentration when performing
- ability to dominate when in a given 'position'.

For the specialist playing positions such as goalkeeper, evaluation of performance should be based on their effectiveness as an individual without ignoring their overall contribution to the team effort. In soccer you may base the evaluation of a goalkeeper on the following:

- Is the goalkeeper's starting position correct?
- Do they move into and then down the line of 'goal to ball'?
- Is the correct 'set' being carried out?
- How do they perform specific techniques?
- Do they have the ability to cope with secondary chances?
- How good is the quality of distribution?
- How well do they organise a defence?

From these check points you are able to establish secure judgements by quantitative methods in order to make an objective evaluation.

Evaluation of a match

In many activities, the need to evaluate the overall performance of a team can be more important than the evaluation of individual performers within that team.

For individual activities and racket games, the competitive performance lends itself more readily to analysis and objective evaluation. We all have an opinion of just how good a team is when performing in a competitive match. Larger teams can be broken down into units such as defence, scrum or midfield. From this point individual players are easier to evaluate as their positional responsibilities are identified.

The way these units and individual players contribute to the whole performance can then be evaluated. The term 'match' is usually applied to competitive team games that involve a great diversity of tactics, player units and a combination of playing systems and player responsibilities. The focus of this part of the Unit will be to develop some ideas and methods for the evaluation of team games in a match situation.

Brackenridge and Alderson (1985) highlight the connection between coaching and the ability to observe and then evaluate:

Coaching is a deliberate act of intervention in sport with the intention of improving performance. The process of match analysis is to evaluate performance in order to inform the coaching process.

In team games the simplest way to begin to evaluate a performance or match is to apply the common **principles of play**. Initially evaluation can be based on two key areas that are determined by who has possession of the ball. These are:

- attacking as a unit
- defending as a unit.

For invasion games such as netball, hockey and basketball, these principles of play also allow for evaluation of positional responsibilities. A clear picture emerges of the level of skill employed in order to play effectively within a competitive situation. These games have elements in common and therefore some evaluations can be based on a generic form of analysis. Essentially we are concerned with finding a solution to a problem and defining the requirements of players both on and off the ball.

The match evaluation cycle (Figure 5.11) places the process of evaluation in a continuing cycle to improve a performance. The use of modern technology, notation and other methods are only purposeful if they improve or, in our terminology, refine a performance. Figure 5.13 shows the principles of play and their components. Here analysis questioning has been related to ball possession in attack and defence. In attack there are three key components – possession, progression and the end product/scoring – to apply to a match evaluation. In defence, two key components need consideration – individual responsibilities and the team unit.

Traditionally, the principles of play in soccer have centred on ball possession as the major influence.

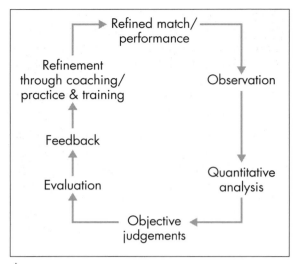

▲ **Figure 5.11** *Match evaluation cycle*

▲ **Figure 5.12** *Organisation, teamwork and tactics*

Attack	Defence
penetration	depth
improvisation	delay
width	concentration
depth	balance
mobility	control

When attacking as a unit in soccer, for example, the team must focus on keeping possession of the ball. When evaluating attacking play, you can base your judgements on:

- a team's ability to create space and move defenders from good to bad defending positions
- the decision making shown by players
- the quality of technique employed by players and their ability to improvise
- the level of support play
- the end product of possession, penetration and goal attempts.

When considering defence, evaluate the performance by focusing on the speed and position from which possession is regained and judge:

- whether defenders or the defensive unit pressurise the ball/players
- the degree of support play shown
- the quality of recovery runs
- how compact the defence is as a unit
- whether the defending side communicates with one another
- whether the defence has depth, balance and if they can delay an attack(er).

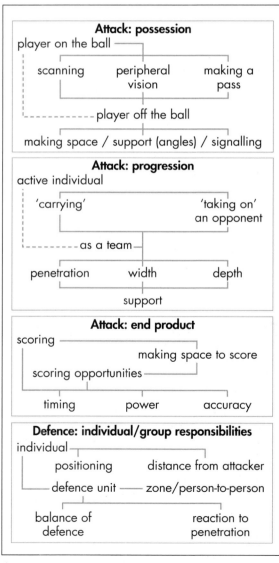

▲ **Figure 5.13** *Principles of play and components*

Invasion games – evaluation extension

The whole process of evaluating both attacking and defensive play for invasion games allows for six more key questions to be formulated. These questions also take account of both tactical solutions and the requirements of players both on and off the ball to be made. Knowledge of these requirements, helping define positional attributes and technical components, provide a sound basis for the process of evaluating of a performance.

The next stage in the development of a match evaluation is to introduce **notation**.

Notation is used to provide quantitative data on a performance or match by focusing on patterns of play, technical achievements and errors. Unit contributions (e.g. 'attack' or 'defence') and duration/intensity of work and rest intervals can also be recorded. Such analyses have been part of American sport for decades and can provide statistical evidence of player workrate and their overall or specific contribution to a game or competition.

Notation sheets are relatively easy to produce providing you have been able to identify the core components of a successful performance within the competitive match or performance situation.

The notation sheet for badminton (Figure 5.15) can be used to record information about a performer and from this information tactics and strategies can be decided for

▲ *Figure 5.14* Do great teams just have the best players?

future matches. This may appear complicated and you might need to practise recording before you can make full use of notation.

Figures 5.15 and 5.16 are examples of analysis sheets used in badminton and in soccer. Use them, or make up your own, as a basis for your own analysis of a football or cricket match; or, if you prefer, another sport of your choice.

The aim of this aspect of Section A is to further develop the knowledge and understanding of practical activities through the process of evaluation. By understanding the core techniques fundamental to the execution of skills and by formulating the requirements of players and performers, supplemented by the ability to analyse a match or performance as a whole, you will be able to further refine your own playing performance.

TASK

Try applying these six key questions to your activity chosen from the list of team games and offer tactical solutions.

a In possession/attacking:
  i   How can we keep possession?
  ii How can we invade the territory?
  iii How can we score?

b In defence/seeking possession:
  i   How can we regain posssession?
  ii How can we stop/delay the opposition invading our territory?
  iii How can we stop the opposition scoring?

TASK

Using one of your own activities or one from the categories list, devise a notation sheet to record the next match/performance you observe. Discuss with your centre tutors what to include, based on what you need to find out.

	s = serve		* = in net
	sl = slash		sm = smash
	d = drop		c = clear
	l = lift		d = block
	n = net return in front court		wh = whip out
	h = hit down in front court		bh = backhand
	fh = forehand		m = miss
	w = weak		o = hit
	f = fail to return		

	A	B	A	B	A	B	A	B	A	B
A0–O	s	c	d	n	l	m	b			
B0–O		s	l	c	d	n	l	c	d	n
A0–O	s	c								
A1–O	s	c								
A2–O	s	b	h	m						
B0–1	etc.									

A0, A1, B0, B1 = players
B0–1 = score at that point in the game

▲ **Figure 5.15** Badminton notation sheet (NCF, 1999)

		1st half	2nd half	Total
Date............... Team A v Team B				
Entries into the attacking third	A			
	B			
Regained possessions in attacking third	A			
	B			
Effective crosses	A			
	B			
Non-effective crosses	A			
	B			
Achieving set plays in attacking third	A			
	B			
Strikes at goal but off target	A			
	B			
Strikes on target	A			
	B			
Goals	A			
	B			

▲ **Figure 5.16** Match analysis sheet for Association Football

3. Principles of coaching

A **principle** can be defined as a fundamental truth or a general law. As a student of physical education you will need to understand the principles by which you will be able to coach and subsequently refine not only your own performance but also that of others'.

> **coaching**: giving technical information in an organised manner to improve and develop a practical performance by individuals or groups. The coach aims to motivate and teach athletes by moulding theoretical and practical training

Martens (1997) identified five key areas of focus for coaches. You should understand and be able to apply knowledge of these key areas to refining your practical performance. The five key areas are:

- coaching objectives
- coaching styles
- evaluating and developing your communication skills
- principles of reinforcement
- understanding motivation.

Coaching objectives

A major consideration in any practical performance environment is the objectives of the athlete and coach. The term 'athlete' means any performer in a practical activity. Martens makes the distinction between the need to be successful in competitive situations balanced against the objectives of the physical, social and psychological development of an athlete. In addition, you will be fully aware of the need for practical refinement to be fun and enjoyable in order to create a positive learning environment.

Through the various practical activities you choose from the three categories contained in the Edexcel specification, you will gain some of the experience and skills needed by a coach. You will also become aware of the wider benefits of improved fitness and a healthy lifestyle on the individual. The coach is in a position to instil **moral values** and **ethical values** both within and outside the sporting arena without detracting from improving performance standards (Figure 5.17).

Coaching styles

The style of coaching that you adopt will be related to your coaching objectives. There is a requirement for you to learn how to deliver

▲ *Figure 5.17* *Ben Johnson's disqualification for drug use raised the ethical question: 'Is it acceptable to win at all costs?'*

technical information and motivate an athlete through the coaching style that you use. This will link into the more common theme of teaching styles and although there is debate on the differences between 'coaching' and 'teaching' it is not of crucial importance here. The style you adopt will depend on the particular circumstances under which you coach.

Woods (1998) identifies four main styles of coaching. The knowledge of each will help develop your ability to coach others and yourself. The four styles are:

- **command style**
- **reciprocal style**
- **problem-solving style**
- **guided discovery**.

You will note that there is a marked resemblance between these coaching styles and some of those in the model of teaching styles by Mosston and Ashworth in Unit 2 on pages 108–109.

TASK

What are the real benefits that you have obtained from being a successful performer?

(It may be that the list is full of non-sports specific benefits, such as leadership qualities, character development and self-confidence.)

Command style

The command style (Figure 5.18) is one of direct instruction and places the coach in the position of a dictator. This allows for little personal development of the performer and no real opportunity for self-discovery. Giving instructions in an authoritarian way has its place in potentially dangerous situations and when coaching large groups. However, it is not suitable for refining a performance and in complex situations, or ones where the level of perception demanded is high.

Reciprocal style

The reciprocal style requires the learner to participate in the process of learning. This will allow learners to take some responsibility for their own development as well as increasing self-confidence. It will also enable feedback to be more immediate and, crucially, movements can be analysed as an aid to refining a performance. However, without close monitoring, incorrect techniques can be learned. The performer may also lack the communication and analysis skills that this style demands.

Problem-solving style

The problem-solving style asks the learner to solve a problem set by the teacher or coach. More suited to the skilled performer or groups, this style allows for a wider appreciation of tactical considerations. It also develops perception and the ability to make decisions in competitive situations. It is difficult to gauge the extent of learning in this style and benefits may be limited if the performers do not feel confident about expressing themselves.

▲ *Figure 5.18* *The command style of coaching: 'Do as I say and do not dare think'*

▲ *Figure 5.19* *Is coaching just passing on your experiences?*

Guided discovery

The final coaching style is that of discovery, or, more appropriately, guided discovery as there will be some direction to the learning process. The learner is given freedom by the teacher, or coach, to explore a variety of potential options that facilitates a refinement in performance through creativity. This has great benefit in particular to dancers and in outdoor activities. This style does, however, have its disadvantages and is not so effective when working with large groups. It can also be very time-consuming.

Developing your communication skills

The ability of a coach to communicate to athletes is paramount in refining a performance. Martens (1997) has identified three dimensions for communication:

- the sending and receiving of messages
- verbal and non-verbal messages
- the content and emotion within a message.

As you work through this part of Section 5A, there will be opportunities for you to gain experience as a coach. This will develop your ability to send and receive messages. The term 'messages' means the relaying of infor-

mation. It has been suggested that as much as 70 per cent of communication in the sports environment can be non-verbal.

Building on the skills that you developed for the 'Analysis of performance' in Unit 2 (see pages 146–153), it will be apparent that in both *enhancing* and now *refining* a performance communication is vital. The giving of technical detail, the sending and receiving of messages to provide motivation, and the use of technology all provide the platform from which a performance can be improved.

Video footage and analysis by observation will be of continued benefit to you and further detail of how this can be used is given later in this Unit (see page 340). As you work through this Unit, you will be given the opportunity to coach and therefore aid the refinement of the performances of others as well as your own. You should aim to coach in a friendly and positive manner, showing empathy with the performer and creating a positive learning environment.

The process of communication

It has been suggested that there are six steps in the process of communication. These steps begin with developing your thoughts and ideas as a coach, which are then sent as messages to the performer. These messages can

▲ **Figure 5.20** *Are you getting your message across?*

be either verbal or non-verbal forms of general body language and gestures that are then received by the performer. The messages have then to be interpreted before the performer can make any response to them.

If you wish to be persuasive as a communicator, Woods (1998) believes that the model for success is based on four related factors. A knowledge and understanding of these may help you with this part of the Unit (Figure 5.20).

1 The source of the message – the status and credibility of the person giving the message is crucial. You are much more likely to believe what you are being told if the person delivering the message to you is respected and has your attention.

2 Transmitting the message – the message itself and how it is presented depends on clear instruction and, if needed, appropriate demonstrations. Knowing what to say is worthless unless you have the ability to transmit the message in such a way that it can be understood. Messages should be high in information and be consistent. It has been estimated that even when attentive we only take in 20 per cent of what is being said!

3 Receptiveness to the message – recipients must be willing to accept what they are being told: this reflects their attitude and receptiveness to learning. Communication in all its forms should serve to motivate and build positive relationships between the coach and the performer.

4 The situation and context of the message – this often determines the impact that the message has. If the context in which it is given is formal it may be seen as judgmental or evaluative. If informally given it can lack substance and/or credibility.

Developing your communication skills and gaining the self-confidence to help others is a feature of Unit 5. It is not a condition of the course that you become a recognized coach in your chosen activity. However, your own performance will improve as the depth of your activity knowledge and the exchange of ideas, the understanding of technical detail and tactical awareness develops in order to refine performances.

Principles of reinforcement

Any performer requires **reinforcement**, a form of feedback, to develop in their activity. By definition, reinforcement seeks to build on the positive aspects of a performance and to eliminate the negative aspects. In reality, reinforcement can be anything that increases the probability of an athlete repeating a skill, movement or overall performance. There are four ways in which you as a coach may seek to reinforce a performance:

- external reinforcement
- internal reinforcement
- positive reinforcement
- negative reinforcement.

As you develop a range of coaching experiences you will be able to use reinforcement to refine and therefore shape a performance. As a performer you will also experience reinforcement at first hand. The four types of reinforcement should be used as appropriate and will be affected by the particular environment, activity, individual(s) and expectations that you are working with.

External reinforcement

External reinforcement occurs through the actions of another person. We often seek social approval and praise following our performances and the reaction of 'significant others' can be more important than the opinion of a coach, the media or spectators. The use of

▲ **Figure 5.21** *Hard work brings its own rewards, which in turn help to reinforce a sporting performance*

tangible rewards such as medals and trophies also serve to reinforce a performance (Figure 5.21).

Internal reinforcement

Internal reinforcement can often outweigh other forms of reinforcement. The performer's own feelings of pride and satisfaction in knowing that they have played or performed well have a strong affect on a sporting performance. For most of you the knowledge of your own progress and attainment through the course and the rewards that this will bring to you is a strong incentive to develop your performance.

Positive reinforcement

From a psychological point of view all performers need to given positive reinforcement that they have done well. They need to be told that they have performed to their highest possible standard, or beyond, and that they have progressed in the quality of such a performance. The link between the repetition of a performance and the use of appropriate desired rewards is stronger if the reinforcement occurs as closely as possible to a response. This is particularly so in young or novice athletes. Rewards need to be used sparingly and tie in with the goals set for and by a performer.

Negative reinforcement

Sometimes it is necessary to use negative reinforcement in order to remove an undesirable response, distractions or bad habits. Punishments for poor performances can work on occasions but may also turn an athlete off

performing rather than encourage future performances that match desired goals.

It is worth remembering that all performances are built on a mixture of rewards and punishments. Fear of failure should not overtake the challenge of competition. Rewards should be made for the performance not the outcome as such and reflect the effort put into a performance. Rewards should also reflect social skills, self-control and sportsmanship.

Understanding motivation

The need to be motivated and eager to practise and compete is often taken for granted. Whilst working through Unit 2 there may have been times when you felt that you could not be bothered or had lost interest in the work being undertaken. The topic of motivation will be covered in more detail in Unit 6. However, a brief explanation here of motivation and its place in coaching will reinforce its value in helping to achieve desired goals. Motivation can be defined as:

> *... the internal state which tends to direct a person's behaviour towards a goal.*

> Kent, 1994

or, more simply:

> *... motivation has been seen as having two aspects: it is what drives us to do things ... and it makes us do particular things.*

> Woods, 1998

In effect, motivation *energises* us and *directs* our behaviour.

As a coach and as a performer, you will now be aware of the division between **intrinsic and extrinsic motivation**. Performers may become motivated intrinsically by personal ambition, by the drive to have fun and to feel worthy. While the need to gain extrinsic rewards can at times overtake personal drive, this is perhaps based more on the likely response to you becoming a winner than winning itself.

Martens (1997) has identified fun and enjoyment as being far more important in the motivation of performers than anything else. Making training as well as competition enjoyable is a key principle to success in sport.

Motivation has two main dimensions – those of *intensity* and *direction*. Intensity is concerned with arousal, that is the level of effort being given to reach certain goals, or the movement towards a particular goal.

When you have studied intrinsic and extrinsic rewards in Unit 6, you will have developed an understanding of the difference between those performers who need to achieve and those who need to avoid failure. You will also be able to distinguish between performers motivated by a desire to reach their own goals and those who take part simply to win. Given the competitive nature of sport, however, and the dedication needed to succeed, it is unlikely that there are too many performers at the highest level who do not also enjoy their activity.

Motivating performers can be made easier if the following key principles are observed and then applied to refining a performance:

- winning may be important but must not be seen as the only form of success. Success is exceeding your own goals and not necessarily surpassing the performance of others
- winning has to be placed into perspective
- rewarding effort and not just outcomes motivates all performers
- motivation is greatest if achieved through a performer feeling a sense of worth for what they been able to do rather than what they may achieve
- emphasise the greater value of intrinsic rewards above extrinsic ones
- motivate through avoiding giving constant instructions or evaluating a performer
- motivation through fear will only last a short time.

4. Coaching individuals, groups and/or teams in a skill, drill or practice

When working with individuals, groups and teams it is possible to apply certain principles to the methods of coaching used in order to further refine skills, drills and practices.

Essentially, you will be concerned with how you as both a coach and a performer can develop learning situations in order to

acquire skills more effectively. Woods (1998) views the following four factors are being central to this process:

- the purpose of teaching
- the skills which are taught
- the abilities and motivation of the learners
- the resources available – time, space, equipment.

As you will have seen from Unit 2, the purpose of practice is the pursuit of perfection. Whilst the adage 'practice makes perfect' should not be taken literally, it is the case that by *purposeful* practice performances can be refined and will become permanent.

Baddeley and Longman (1978) found that typists who practised more than others did not perform any better than the others, the implication being that if you practise too much you will become bored, de-motivated and generally stale. This is more widely called a **plateau** where a performance either remains static or even deteriorates.

The quality of any practice, therefore, becomes far more important than the sheer quantity that a performer undertakes. Practice can be classified in two ways: first, the method of practice reflecting how a skill can be broken down in order to be learned and, second, the type of practice to then be used.

Methods of practice

The methods of practice employed by a coach are determined by the type of skill that is to be learned. Some skills lend themselves to be broken down into smaller units, technical components or subroutines more readily than others.

Continuous skills, such as swimming and cycling, are an example of this. Gestalt theory saw learning as being more effective if the skill is experienced as a whole.

The two methods that are commonly used by teachers and coaches are the **whole method** for such skills as catching (Figure 5.22) and the **whole-part-whole method** of skill learning. The tennis serve or the triple jump are typical examples of this (see pages 109–110).

There are occasions when only certain parts of a skill should be learned until fully mastered. This is best used where the skill is

▲ **Figure 5.22** *Catching a basketball is a skill that is learned as a whole*

complex or lengthy, as in hurdling or a gymnastic routine. In addition to the part method, you will already have experienced the need to learn the parts of a skill in isolation and then 'chain' or progressively put them together. As someone now involved with the coaching of learners, the selection of coaching style is dependent upon the ability of the learner and the type of skill to be learned.

Types of practice

The coach must also be aware of the types of practice that enable learning to take place. There are three common forms:

- **massed practice**
- **distributed practice**
- **variable practice.**

Massed practice allows for continuous activity and multi-repetition of a skill or combination of skills. This extends into the concept of **drilling**, or, as it is sometimes known, 'grooving', although this type of practice is more accurately termed 'fixed' practice. Constant repetition has many benefits in that unit skills such as a rugby lineout and set back player moves are practised in their entirety so that they become habitual. The clear drawbacks are boredom, players becoming devoid of improvisation or flair, and fatigue.

Distributed practice helps to overcome the failings of massed practice in that it provides opportunities for rest in between work sessions when feedback or recovery activities can be undertaken.

Variable practice is a mixture of both types and again its use depends on the type of sub-

ject being coached, their ability and the time available for practice.

Demonstrations

A coach can improve the performance of individuals, groups and teams by also using clear and effective demonstrations. This is based on the principle that we learn most quickly by copying the actions of others. Bandura's 'social learning theory' (1977) concerned the process of attention, retention, motor production and motivation as used by a coach in order to communicate the knowledge and understanding necessary to refine a performance.

Guidance

In addition to good, appropriate and well presented demonstrations, a coach can also use many forms of guidance (see page 111). You will already have come across some or all of the following:

- **visual guidance** – charts, coaching diagrams, technical pictures
- **verbal guidance** – instructions, advice and the technical detail that should be delivered in short spells, be relevant and of a clear manner
- **manual/mechanical guidance** – to build confidence and enable the performer to develop a **kinaesthetic awareness** of a skill or movement.

By kinaesthetic awareness, we mean the ability of a performer to perceive a movement through the proprioceptors – the state of contraction of muscles, and the position of the limbs and the body in space.

5. Organisation of learning environments to refine performance

The organisation of practice and learning environments provides the platform from which a coach is able to refine and extend the performance of an athlete. The purpose of this aspect of Section A is to provide you with some insight into the wider role of a coach. This knowledge may help you to best organise your own practice and coaching sessions and benefit not only your own performance but also that of others.

The need to plan, organise and control practice sessions has been considered by Davies (1989) as central to the coaching process. He remarks:

Planning, organising and controlling practice sessions occupies a major portion of coaching time.

Formatting the learning environment

There are clear guidelines to help format the learning environment. These reflect the time, space and equipment available to a coach as well as revisiting the role of a coach in the development of a performance. The guidelines given by Davies focus on the following key areas:

- context of practice – practice sessions need to be conducted in an area as close in size to the real game and simulate the real competitive environment
- type of practice – distributed practice has been found to be most effective in the learning of skills. Sessions should be long enough to enable learning to take place but not evoke boredom and fatigue. The inclusion of tactical awareness and perception training is also of benefit in placing a skill in the context of the competitive performance
- performer participation – keeping all performers involved in sessions is vital. Those not performing can undertake

▲ *Figure 5.23* *There's more to coaching than just 'being in charge'!*

analysis and player evaluation work
- performer stimulation – players need to be stimulated by challenging and testing practice. Practices need to offer reward and satisfy a performer in their own right.

Key features of practice sessions

Concerning the organisation of practice sessions by a coach, Davies (1989) identifies the following four key features:

- coaching material
- organisation of time
- organisation of facilities and equipment
- organisation of the performers.

Coaching material

The coaching material for each session must be correct in terms of theoretical detail. It must include an understanding of the appropriate physiological, psychological, technical and tactical components for an activity.

Time

This is often regarded as the single most determinant factor in refining a performance. Coaches are always remarking that 'if only they had more time with their players, then ...'.

Whilst this may hold some truth, time spent with a performer needs to be related to their short-, medium- and long-term goals. Allied to this there must be a realistic agreement on the potential for performance and the level of competition available. Time in individual sessions may be restricted, with added feedback sessions and goal setting removed to a time away from the main learning environment. However, this in itself is a part of the 'learning environment'.

Facilities and equipment

To be totally effective, coaches need to be able to utilise efficiently the facilities and other resources at their disposal. Health and safety issues must always be a high priority and the correct equipment should be used at all times. For practice to be effective it must 'mirror' the competitive situation as far as possible.

While specific skill refinement will only be achieved in practice sessions, outlined both in this Unit and in Unit 2, you will now be building a wider view of a performance. This will include physiological, psychological and

▲ **Figure 5.24** Do indoor facilities really prepare you for the real thing?

sports-specific components. Therefore, the use of all resources that contribute to developing the performance both in part and as a whole should be utilised (Figure 5.24).

Climbers now have the opportunity to practise skills in an indoor environment so that attention to detail, away from possible extremes of climate and real risk, is now possible much nearer to home.

The performer

Perhaps the most important consideration for the effective refinement of performance is the performer. Adding a sense of worth and purpose to the performer's efforts must then be placed into the context of 'reality'. The organisation of an environment that is conducive to learning requires that practices incorporate competition: a practice that lacks reality lacks credibility.

6. Attitudes and strategies for changing attitudes

Triandis (1971) defines attitudes as:

> . . . ideas charged with emotion (positive and negative) which predisposes a class of actions to a particular social situation.

We learn our attitudes from direct experience and from other people. You will be able to understand this fully from your own experiences as a player, spectator or as someone involved in coaching.

We all have particular attitudes for specific situations or as part of our general psychological make-up, or personality. Attitudes are displayed towards people, places and concepts and these can be called '**attitude objects**' (Webster, 1996). You will have your own attitude towards sporting activities, sports ethics, fair play in professional sport, drug abuse and so on. Attitudes are not measured equally and the intensity, or strength, of an attitude conveys an emotional component.

Triadic model

Woods (1998) uses the established analysis of attitudes as incorporating three parts:

- ideas or cognitions
- emotions or effects
- actions or behaviour.

The cognitive component is the thinking part of an opinion, based on information and knowledge which helps form a belief. The affective component is an emotional response to an 'attitude object' representing likes and dislikes. The third component defines how a person intends to behave towards an 'attitude object'.

These three parts, called the ABC of attitude, are the affective, behavioural and cognitive components to an attitude. They form what is known as the **triadic model**.

As a student of physical education, you will be concerned with the way in which a performer's attitude affects their behaviour. Honeybourne et al. (1996) has provided a typical example of how this relates in practice:

> *Your attitude to fitness training could be made up of the belief that fitness training will keep you fit and will enhance your body image – this is the cognitive element of your attitude. You enjoy fitness training and you have fun being with others who are training with you – this is the affective element of your attitude. You go to fitness training twice a week – this is the behavioural element of your attitude.*

Positive and negative attitudes

Attitudes may be viewed in two simple forms – positive and negative. There is a third category of neutral attitudes which, while not of concern at present, is evident in sporting situations.

Positive attitudes reflect an admiration and liking for a particular activity or event. Negative attitudes reflect more on unpleasant experiences or failures which then condition the way we view similar situations. For example, a young player at school may be injured taking part in a sport such as rugby. This has the effect of creating a negative attitude not only towards rugby but other forms of contact sports. Conversely, a player who gains rewards from playing, avoids injury and develops a high level of self-esteem from being involved, engenders a positive attitude. There is some evidence to suggest that attitudes are learned rather than being innate. The question here is, given the existence of a particular attitude within the sporting environment, how can such an attitude be changed?

Changing attitudes – strategies

The need to change a person's attitude invariably means from a negative to a positive one.

Most sports participants, coaches and spectators have positive attitudes although aggression and racism are two negative attitudes found within the sporting environment. Such attitudes are often deep-rooted and associated with wider social issues. An understanding of the following strategies and the experience of applying them to practical activities will help you to develop an appreciation of how important having a positive attitude is in a sports context. The methods given below are just a starting point and further research will be useful if you select this topic for your written assignment.

▲ *Figure 5.25* *Attitudes do not always predict behaviour*

Persuasion

Persuasion by oral and physical communication is effective if delivered by a significant and influential person, using an appropriate message that has meaning and credibility. The willingness of the recipient to 'hear' the message being given and the context in which it is delivered also need to be taken into account.

Cognitive dissonance

According to Festinger's (1957) theory of **cognitive dissonance**, individuals know certain things – **cognitions** – about their own attitudes, thoughts and beliefs in relation to their own behaviour and surroundings. In order to create a feeling of *consonance* – positive or good attitudes – the three elements of the triadic model (see page 330) must be consistent with one another.

To alter an attitude, an individual must experience two or more opposing beliefs. This causes *dissonance*, or disharmony, in the mind and the person becomes uncomfortable and so changes their attitude to become comfortable again with one belief dominating. The cognitive component can be changed by allowing an individual to experience new situations that will promote positive feelings. The behavioural component can be changed by altering the circumstances in which an attitude object is perceived. By using punishments and/or rewards the behavioural component can be changed as an attitude object becomes more popular.

Role models

Favourable role models and stereotypical images can be used to build positive rather than negative attitudes towards specific situations. By presenting objective arguments rather than subjective opinion, individuals can be 'persuaded' into a set of beliefs. Our attitudes, therefore, evolve as we experience different sporting situations.

7. Group dynamics: cohesion, loafing and group productivity

Sports psychologists regard the way in which individuals behave when in a group as an important area of study. This largely covers the influence that a group has on an individual that results in a change in their behaviour.

This interactive process is concerned with shifting patterns of tension, with conflict, adjustments and the building of cohesion within a group situation. The **dynamics** of a group affect the way in which leadership and dominant sub-group patterns emerge.

This influences why people exhibit certain behaviour patterns and the way that within the group specific attitudes among individuals are altered both in the short term and in the long term. Changes in attitude may be temporary or permanent. Groups build and foster conformity and create cohesion patterns (Figure 5.26).

According to Shaw (1976) the definition of a group is:

. . . two or more people interacting with one another in such a manner that each person influences and is influenced by each other person.

The application of the word 'dynamics' to a group implies that within a group and between groups there is a force, or pressure, that serves to shape and direct behaviour. Woods (1998) sees one of the defining features of a group as that of its

. . . members having common beliefs, usually unspoken, about what is acceptable and unacceptable, how things are done . . .

Groups in sport are usually seen in the form of a team – the playing team or the management team. The crowd is often referred to as a team of supporters. Although a team has both interaction and common goals, a large group of spectators should not be regarded as a 'group' in this context.

Section A will require you to draw upon your existing experiences of working in and being part of a group to understand how and why people work together. By using these experiences in practical activities, you will develop an understanding of the concepts of **cohesion**, **loafing** and **group productivity** in an applied form.

TASK

Think of your own involvement in sport. List the reasons why you are attracted to take part in a particular activity.

Cohesion

Cohesion, or 'sticking together', is a common term associated with the concept of group dynamics and is a two-way process. Individuals are attracted to a group through common motivation and value the relationships within the group. As a result, there is some resistance to any breaking up of the group. Groups have 'norms', which are the often unspoken value beliefs that attract individuals to a group.

In addition to the rewards of playing, you may take part in an activity for the image, beliefs and social setting in which that activity

▲ **Figure 5.26** *The England Rugby squad – an example of group cohesion*

functions. The 'club' atmosphere and comradeship in rugby, the social mixing of a hockey club or the friendship among track and field athletes are examples of this, and are termed 'social cohesion'. 'Task cohesion' refers to a group with shared formal goals who are normally 'successful' as a group competitively.

Carron (1980) defined a cohesive group as having the following characteristics:

- a collective identity
- a sense of shared purpose
- structured patterns of communication.

Using these three characteristics as the basis for group stability, it is possible to improve and enhance group cohesion by employing strategies that focus on these three characteristics and maximise their influence and effects. How can you build a better collective identity, enhance a shared sense of purpose and develop communication within a group? One material way is reflected in the numerous clubhouses and pavilions to be found in almost every town and village in the UK (Figure 5.27).

Loafing and group productivity

To answer the above questions, two additional areas of study related to this part of Section A can be considered. First, although a group may be seen as a productive unit, one of the consequences of working within a group has been identified by Ringlemann (1974) as 'social loafing'.

According to Ringlemann, when an individual is working within a group their own per-

▲ **Figure 5.28** *Social loafing – an individual's decline in effort may go unnoticed!*

formance will decrease. Using the example of the tug-o'-war, he noted that a group of eight did not pull eight times harder than a solo puller. Latane (1979) placed this decline in effort as a result of an individual suffering motivational losses within a group. That is, you may be able to hide within the overall team performance with your reduction in effort going unnoticed (Figure 5.28).

The other area to consider is the process of group productivity as put forward by Steiner. For Steiner, the potential for any group to perform is a result of their 'potential productivity' minus 'losses due to faulty processes'. That is, losses due to poor form, reduced motivation and a lack of teamwork. In order for a group to perform to their highest level of performance, methods and strategies need to be employed which not only further group productivity but also help reduce the potential effect of social loafing. Subsequently, the result will be to foster greater cohesion and develop positive group dynamics.

Methods and strategies

- Practice sessions need to involve all members and be fun in order to build a sense of collective worth. Enjoyment helps increase motivation.
- Bonding exercises, such as training camps, can draw players together and help break down sub-groups which alienate others to the detriment of the whole group.
- By stressing the importance of all individuals to the success and productivity of the group, by outlining their roles and responsibilities, all players will not only appreciate their own worth but also the value of their fellow performers. This can be enhanced by the effective use of rewards.

▲ **Figure 5.27** *The building of such facilities expresses shared goals as well as serving a functional purpose*

- Within a team, natural combinations of players form into effective units, e.g. the forwards in rugby union. By building upon the importance of these units and the players within the unit, they become an essential ingredient in the success of the whole team. Other players start to rely on them to carry out their functions.
- Group goals and shared targets should be stressed above those of any one individual. The group is always more important than one individual player.
- Social activities build friendships and establish personal identities within the group. Sports tours and social functions are often more important to older players than how they actually perform.
- By keeping individual statistics and through constructing player profiles, players will know that they are part of the group and their contributions are noted.
- Team meetings and group discussions led by the coach and captain help develop the feeling that all players have a contribution to make to the group.
- Place difficult players or newcomers with a 'mentor'. An older and well-respected member of a group who places the value of the group above personal feelings will help deliver the message of group identity and worth.

▲ **Figure 5.29** Group dynamics: interaction within the group and the influence over other groups

- Increase the value of the intrinsic rewards obtained through group productivity and cohesion above personal extrinsic rewards. It is a common feature for teams playing in major championships to run a 'players pool' for everyone's benefit.

8. Techniques for enhancing performance: stress management techniques and goal setting

All popular sport now seems to be accompanied by the term 'stress'. This is evident at school or college level through to professional performers and is now a common theme for the media. Webster (1996) defines stress as a:

stimulus resulting in arousal or a response to a situation.

What is stress?

Stress is commonly seen as being caused by circumstances and beliefs such as frustration, competition importance, climatic conditions and concerns over a performer's ability. The term **stressor** is applied to the demands that begin the stress process. The demands placed upon us in the sports arena can become threatening – when they do, the greater the likelihood of arousal and anxiety and impaired sports performance. The stressors that may be perceived as threats to the sports performer are:

- threats to self-esteem
- causes of personal harm
- creation of uncertainty or fear of the unknown
- creation of frustration
- creation of pressure.

For Woods (1998) there is a clear relationship between the three key components of arousal, anxiety and stress and the resulting effect on an individual's behaviour. Although there is a distinction between arousal, anxiety and stress, all three components are interconnected and together form the overall **stress process**.

▲ *Figure 5.30* *Stress release – Pearce lets go!*

The stress process can cause a performer to produce an impaired performance, display aggression or conversely produce an improvement in performance (Figure 5.30). Stress can therefore be both a positive and a negative factor in the performance achieved by an individual. While stress may help a performance, we normally view the build-up of stress as a factor that has a negative effect on a performance. For this topic in Section A you are required to have a limited working knowledge of the stress process. More importantly, you must display an understanding of how to cope with and overcome the negative influence of stress.

According to Woods, the stress process is the result of an athlete's perception of the demands of a situation. This causes an increase in arousal levels. As a consequence a performance is either impaired (Figure 5.31) through an increase in anxiety and negative thoughts – **distress**; or enhanced through increased motivation and energy – **eustress**.

Arousal is the state of alertness and anticipation that prepares the body for action. Anxiety is viewed as a vague form of fear and apprehension that is caused by arousal. As such it is a negative emotional state. Stress, or distress as it is correctly termed, can be

viewed as a whole process occurring when a performer sees themselves as unable to meet the demands of a situation.

Lazarus and Folkman (1984) have also defined stress as:

> ... *a pattern of negative physiological states and psychological responses occurring in situations where people perceive threats to their well being which they may be unable to meet.*

As a performer you will be able to feel the effect of stress through the physiological and emotional responses that it brings. These include the physiological signs of increased muscle tension, higher respiratory frequency, increased heart rate and perspiration. Emotionally you will feel apprehension, fear and produce negative thoughts, all of which can lead to poor concentration, aggressive behaviour and so on.

Managing stress and goal setting

The techniques that can be used to manage stress and develop the strategy of **goal setting** to aid a performance can be classified into two groups:

- **somatic techniques** which relate to the body
- **cognitive techniques** which relate to the mind.

▲ *Figure 5.31* *You need to control stress to prevent it impairing your performance*

Somatic techniques

As you have seen on the previous page, the human body responds physiologically to arousal because you become anxious over a particular situation. Control of these physiological responses can be achieved by the following techniques:

- *biofeedback* – by using physiological measuring equipment to help achieve the objective of controlling physiological responses. For example, by hearing your own heart beat you can think of slowing it down
- *breathing* – reducing your breathing rate by taking slower and larger breaths helps reduce arousal. Taking deep breaths and then letting the air out slowly can also reduce muscle tension. Counting controlled exhalations may also help to relax the body. This is a simple and quick method that can be used in all situations
- *relaxation* – by using progressive muscular relaxation (PMR), muscle tension can be reduced. This involves the systematic contraction and relaxation of muscles working from one end of the body to the other, or from one side to another. In addition, meditation and hypnotism can be used.

Cognitive techniques

The desire to reduce worries and eliminate negative thoughts is an essential part of a sportsperson's preparation for both training and competition. Cognitive techniques involve the following:

- *goal setting* – this is the setting of future performance targets. By moving an athlete's focus away from the source of stress to something realistic and achievable, stress can be reduced
- *performance-related goals* – these need to replace goals centred on the outcome of a performance, such as success only being measured by winning. Goals need to be set both in the short-, medium- and long-term, while offering a challenge. Goals that give immediate and specific attainment appear to be more effective. Short-term goals can be set for a day or week, while long-term goals can be set for periods of a month, a year or longer

- *goals related to past performance* – these need to be based on past performances. They can be written down, must be flexible, should be reviewed and can include effort. All goals should be related to the overall aim of a performance
- *measurable goals* – they have to be measurable and used as small achievable steps for sustained success
- *mental rehearsal* – imagery techniques can be used by visualising relaxing situations. This can be a form of practice based on internal feelings of a movement with external imagery of thinking and imagining the sporting environment. Creating a mental picture of a movement helps capture an emotional feeling. Sounds can also be heard – the correct movement is accompanied by a certain sound
- *key points* – it is important to focus on the key points and visualise the performance and the way skills should be performed. A performer should think of only what will be successfully completed and not ponder on the things that could go wrong
- *self-talk* – by perceiving arousal as a positive factor, the performer can use it as a positive attribute. By constantly repeating a set phrase or a method of performance, an athlete is able to focus attention on to the performance rather than negative factors
- *self-confidence* – this is a major factor in any sporting performance. By using the other techniques mentioned above, a performer can be convinced of their value and potential for success. Success should be defined as not simply a matter of winning. The confidence to perform to your potential is nurtured by an inner belief in being able to reach the competition, or performance, fully focused and with all negative thoughts removed.

9. Physiological, psychological and/or biomechanical applications to improve performance

Any sports performance is built on the relationship and interdependency that exists between physiological, psychological and bio-mechanical elements.

Ergogenic aids

An **ergogenic aid** can be simply defined as any factor that improves an athletic performance beyond normal expectations. As such they provide the focus for this part of Section A.

Ergogenic aids can be classified into the five categories below, thus rejecting the common belief that they are only concerned with pharmacological agents. These five categories bring together a necessary understanding of the physiological, psychological and bio-mechanical aspects of the Edexcel specification. The nature of this topic, therefore, requires you to draw together the specific knowledge and understanding obtained from Units 3 and 6 to the refinement of a performance.

The five categories of ergogenic aids are:

- **pharmacological aids**
- **physiological aids**
- **nutritional aids**
- **mechanical aids**
- **psychological aids.**

Pharmacological aids – agents and drugs to promote performance enhancement.

Physiological aids – natural substances such as creatine and colostrum. Recent developments include the use of herbal medicine, physiotherapy, sports massage and acupuncture. A knowledge of such matters is of specific interest to sportsmen and women who are usually particularly keen to utilise 'erogenic aids' in an effort to hasten recovery rates.

Nutritional aids – these can be put into three groups: *macronutrients* including the effects of such practices as carbohydrate loading; *micronutrients* such as antioxidants and the use of an additional group of substances or *supplements* such as creatine, caffeine and bicarbonate of soda. The knowledge and general effect of how a good and well-balanced appropriate 'sports diet' aids performances.

Mechanical aids – these include modern sports equipment, clothing, footwear, rackets, timing equipment and training aids.

Psychological aids – these include the established methods of goal setting, imagery techniques and mental rehearsal. Developing

▲ *Figure 5.32 Modern technology in sport – but the performer still needs physiological, psychological and bio-mechanical input*

a positive approach to training and learning how to focus and concentrate during competition are also important.

It is not within the scope of this text to fully explore the detailed subject knowledge of ergogenic aids. However, by providing you with a broad outline of the subject content, you will have a knowledge base from which you can research further. You will then be able to complete the assessment requirement of this Section if you choose this area for your written evaluative assignment.

The use of ergogenic aids has always been an area for debate. Many sports coaches and performers feel that, despite all the advantages that they may bring, there is still no substitute for traditional practice and training (Figure 5.32).

10. Tactics, strategies, perception and decision making appropriate to refining performance

The requirement here is to focus on the further development of your earlier work in this section and apply your knowledge and understanding gained from Unit 2 and, if applicable, Unit 6. Some of the questions that can emerge from this section aim to place theoretical knowledge into a practical setting. For instance, how will a player react if he becomes over-aroused or is being tactically outplayed? This focus will help prepare you for the practical assessment requirements in the one activity if you chose Option A Section C.

For those undertaking an investigative study in Section C: Option B, the further development of practical experiences will enable you to give appropriate sports examples in the written examination. If appropriate, it will also provide you with further knowledge and understanding required for the completion of the written assignment for this section.

The assessment of your chosen practical activity will be based on a similar pattern to Unit 2; that is, an assessment of your attainment in structured practices, competitive situations and the performance of skills in isolation. In Unit 5, this will also include the competitive situation. The criteria for performance assessment also make clear reference to the specific ability of the performer to exhibit tactical awareness, use strategies and display both perception and decision making in their performance.

In order to develop a refined competitive performance you will need to have an applied knowledge and understanding of these content areas for your chosen practical activity and in some part for the other activities that you have experienced.

Tactics and strategies

A knowledge of tactics and strategies – that is, playing systems, positional and performance requirements, and the ability to adjust them as conditions require – must not be underestimated.

In a team game, this will involve playing systems and specific unit integration into an overall performance (Figure 5.33). In cricket, for example, players should start to show a knowledge of how to use a wicket to their advantage. In field games, they will need to know how to use the weather or pitch conditions and their own playing abilities to best effect. They may also have the knowledge and understanding of how to overcome an opposition player by exploiting their weaknesses and limiting the effects of their playing strengths.

In individual activities, there is often less scope for the application of tactics and strategies. However, in competition, the performer

▲ **Figure 5.33** In a team game such as rugby, playing systems will be incorporated into an overall performance

needs to be focused to perform to a predetermined plan of action that can be altered or adjusted to best exploit a change in circumstances. Awareness of this requirement should be evident in your knowledge and understanding of the activity concerned.

Perception and decision making

As an individual performer, you must develop an understanding of how perception and decision making affect your ability to perform. In addition, you will be required to develop both anticipation and reaction times.

In tennis, for example, the decision-making process is

... based upon perception which in turn involves an identification and interpretation of the playing situation.

Dent, 1994

Decision making is preceded by perception and anticipation. A player requires a knowledge and understanding of the inter-relationship between several performance variables if decision making is to be effective. These include:

- environment
- state of the match
- characteristics of the incoming ball
- court position of both players
- your opponent's characteristics
- your characteristics.

It should now be possible for you to adapt this simple model to your own activity and from this starting point develop further understanding of your performance requirements. One of the ways this can be achieved is to develop a 'scenario bank' of situations and then play them out under the formal competitive situation.

Mental rehearsal and goal setting also have a part to play in this development. Practice, like competition, should be dynamic and force players to make decisions under pressure.

In analysing passing and receiving in soccer, Royce (1994) found that in order to be successful in passing, a player needed to develop a refined ability to 'scan'. This meant the ability to read the game unfolding in front of him and interpret the movements of both his own team and the opposition.

For Royce 'understanding chaos' was a vital part of a player's ability to make decisions. Inexperienced players fail to spot the opportunities to pass, or perhaps retain possession for too long. They may select the wrong pass at the wrong time.

In endeavouring to refine your own performance, some measurement of your development in the areas of perception and decision-

making is a core requirement. You should therefore seek every opportunity to widen your knowledge and understanding of these two most important perceptive components. Practice within the competitive situation (Figure 5.34) is especially important within the context of this Unit.

11. Extension of the use of feedback, teaching styles and practices in refining performance

Building on your own knowledge and understanding gained from Unit 2, you will be required to further consider the applied effects of feedback; how the use of different teaching styles aids learning, and why the organisation of practices affects the development of a performance.

Feedback is the receiving and giving of sensory information concerning both positive and negative outcomes of a performance. Feedback, as you will be aware from Unit 2 (see pages 111–12), can be both intrinsic (occurring during a performance or movement) and extrinsic, which is post-performance. The use of feedback helps you to construct two bodies of knowledge that will be used to further refine your own performances. These are the **knowledge of performance (KP)** and the **knowledge of results (KR)**.

The knowledge of a performance involves the technical information about how a performance should feel using kinaesthetic information. Revisit your research and understanding from earlier in the section to refresh your memory on the evaluation of a performance. This will give you another opportunity to refine the technical accuracy of a performance, and detail through methods of statistical and notation-keeping, an objective basis from which to prepare for assessment.

The knowledge obtained from the results (or outcome) of a performance will enable you to make judgements on how to refine specific movement patterns or an overall performance.

The quality and technical detail of feedback in Unit 5 needs to be higher than in Unit 2. It must also reflect a higher level of accuracy in analysis. You should now be utilising a variety

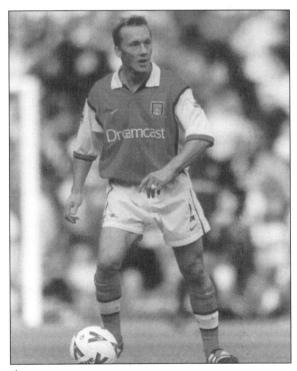

▲ *Figure 5.34* *Do I dribble, pass or shoot? – improved decision making is most important in refining performance*

of means in order to obtain the detailed knowledge required including video, notation and observation (Figure 5.35).

Feedback will help to motivate you in your efforts to refine a performance; it should be used to reinforce the strengths in a performance and eliminate the weaknesses. By applying the specific forms of feedback as outlined in Unit 2, you will need to be aware of which types of feedback are more effective for you, personally, and how these can aid the progress of other performers.

The teaching or coaching styles used to refine a performance were discussed in both Unit 2 and earlier in this Unit. In addition, your work in the classroom will also have heightened your awareness that the presentation of information allied to a variety of learning strategies can affect your development.

The teaching styles covered in Section 2A range from the 'command' style at one end of the spectrum to a 'problem-solving' style at the other. You will be required to draw upon this knowledge and understanding and apply it to a variety of practical situations. You will already have covered much of this work earlier in this section, but it may be worth going back over this so that you are able to take some responsibility for your own performance development.

By being aware of the strengths and weaknesses of each particular style, you will be able to refine your own performance.

The use of practice to refine a performance is an integral requirement of this Unit. Your assessment in structured practices will be based on the application and progress made by you as a result of the coaching and training that you have received. This will be a judgement of the technical, tactical and perceptual requirements of your activity.

By understanding the advantages and disadvantages of the types of practice conditions and methods of practice available, you will be able to devise your own practice sessions and those of others. You should now be able, for example, to explain the difference between massed and distributed practice, whole versus part methods of learning and in general how best to develop a performance technically, tactically and perceptually.

From this base, both decision-making and performance levels become refined as you prepare for your final assessments. For those undertaking the investigative study for Section 5C, this aspect will provide you with further practical experiences and a suitable written assignment topic.

12. Implication of resource and technical developments on refining and advancing performance

The requirement for you to refine your practical performance throughout Unit 5 can be aided by both resource and technical developments.

For some practical activities, technology lends itself more readily to the building of a performance. The use of modern hydraulic 'scrum machines' in rugby is now commonplace, as is the use of bowling machines in cricket. Technology has provided the means of playing on artificial surfaces, and synthetic athletics tracks are now the norm in modern sports complexes (Figure 5.36).

For this part of Section A, it is envisaged that your centre will provide you with the opportunity to experience some of the technological and other resources that aid the refinement of a performance. Some students may already have made full use of them and as a result may be able to list the benefits this has brought to their own performances.

▲ *Figure 5.35* *You should now be utilising a variety of means to obtain feedback*

▲ **Figure 5.36** *Since the development of artificial surfaces, playing on a muddy grass field now seems unthinkable*

Technical and resource development in sport

The following list suggests ways in which you can experience some of the technical and resource developments in sport. Where possible, you should do as many of these as you can as part of your course:

1 Experience the use of an artificial 'astro' hockey surface and compare playing on it to traditional grass.
2 Play against a bowling machine to refine batting techniques in cricket.
3 Play a racket sport with a modern racket and then use an old one. Find an old cricket bat. How does that feel compared to a new design?
4 Find an old pair of playing boots (Figure 5.37) or training shoes and compare them to a modern up-to-date pair. Which do you prefer and why? Is it just a question of being fashionable?

▲ **Figure 5.37** *How would YOU like to have to play in these?*

5 Clothing is now the subject of technical developments. Try swimming in an old woollen swimsuit. What are the new materials available and how do they help the performer?
6 How has the use of modern cardio-vascular training equipment aided performances? Can you access the use of step climbers or treadmills for training purposes and experience their effect?
7 Modern sport now makes full use of technical devices for more accurate playing and refereeing performances. Video analysis and individual player profiles spotlight strengths and weaknesses. Do you consider these have improved a sport or created unwanted controversy?
8 Can you make a list of those technical developments which affect your own chosen activity, or a list for those experienced as part of this Section; and explain how these have advanced and refined performances?

13. Preparation for competition, training routines, game plans, training systems and developments

The final part of Section 5A requires you to study further how you can prepare for competition, develop training routines, **game plans** and training systems to refine your practical performance.

This will enable you to draw together almost all of the content of this section and that of Units 2 and 3. Clearly, you should now regard yourself as an experienced performer, able to take responsibility for developing your own performances.

In order to do this, you will need to liaise with your centre staff or club coach to devise how best you can use all the knowledge and understanding gained from studying PE at A level. Although there is no synoptic element in Unit 5, it is important from a practical standpoint that you develop the concept of tying together the tactical, physical and technical aspects of your own performance through the process of mental preparation.

You should use this aspect to work individually, or in small groups, as a final preparation for examination in structured practices, competitive situations and in the performance of skills in isolation.

Devising a plan of action

By devising a plan of action with specific goals, training routines and game plans appropriate to your activity, you will aim to fully maximise your potential. It is clearly recommended that your centre makes judgements of your abilities as part of an ongoing assessment programme.

The need to video performances and cater for those playing seasonal activities such as tennis mean that you will have an opportunity to confirm a mark or improve upon it.

> **game plan**: a plan of action to bring about success in a game; sets out how to attack or defend in certain ways, how to use set plays as appropriate, how to overcome an opponent's strengths and exploit their weaknesses. Ensures the effective use of tactics and strategies

When preparing for competition you should take into account the following factors:

- The specific objective of the competition. Is it to achieve a personal best, to win a particular match or to beat a particular rival?
- The competition in relation to previous performances. Are you expected to win, reach a set target or consolidate previous achievements?
- Can you devise a game plan, tactics and strategies to cope with the competition and the quality of the opposition?
- Are you and, if appropriate, your team psychologically prepared to compete? Are you focused, do you have clear goals and have you mentally rehearsed key aspects of your performance?
- Have you prepared contingency plans in the event of the context and circumstances of the competition changing?
- Do you have the correct equipment? Are there legal requirements to be met?
- Are you able to undertake an appropriate pre-competition routine, devised to prepare you psychologically?

▲ **Figure 5.38** Do you warm up and then cool down correctly for your activity?

- Do you warm up and then cool down correctly for your activity (Figure 5.38)?
- Has your training prepared you physiologically for your competition?
- Do you know what is expected from you in competitions? Is this realistic?

How will I be assessed?

Section 5A requires you to write an evaluative assignment on improving performance by developing an area from the content of 'Factors affecting performance'.

This will take the form of an extended essay of no more than 1500–2000 words. The choice of which topic to select and its specific nature is left to your discretion, after discussion with your centre, and assumes an ability to draw together factors that affect a performance. Central to the study will be your ability to relate the factors affecting performance to those influencing an improvement in performance.

For those candidates undertaking the practical assessment in Section C of Unit 5, the assignment should be related to your chosen practical activity. For those students undertaking Option B, the investigative study route, it will be based on an activity chosen from the activities category list contained in the full Edexcel specification.

Marking

Your assignment is assessed and marked out of 45, made up of the following criteria headings:

- Introduction and planning of the areas to be investigated – 5 marks

- Review of related topics and literature – 15 marks
- Discussion/conclusions – 15 marks
- Appraisal of the study and the implications for improvement in performance – 10 marks

Your centre should provide you with a detailed breakdown of the assessment criteria from the main specification document. The assignment in Section A has a weighting of 5 per cent of the final Advanced Level award.

The assignment will be internally assessed by your centre and contained in your IPP for moderation by an external examiner.

Example titles

The following assignment titles are suggested as an indication of the type of areas of study you could undertake. The study may require you to carry out a small-scale research activity in order to provide data for discussion and evaluation.

- Strategies for changing attitudes in hockey
- The use of different methods of feedback to improve techniques in trampolining
- Goal-setting techniques for swimmers
- Different training programmes for specific positions among rugby union players.

KEY SKILLS

The completion of the assignment for this section also provides an opportunity for you to obtain Level 3 accreditation in the Key Skills of Communication, Information Communications Technology, and if appropriate, the Application of Number.

Key words and phrases

1. Introduction
- Holistic • Analysis • Organisation • Evaluation • IPP

2. Evaluation techniques for skill, positional and match analysis
- Judgements • Qualitative • Quantitative • Sequential method
- Positional requirements • Principles of play • Notation

3. Principles of coaching
- Principle • Moral values • Ethical values • Command style • Reciprocal style
- Problem-solving style • Guided discovery • Reinforcement

4. Coaching individuals, groups and/or teams in a skill, drill or practice
- Plateau • Whole method • Whole-part-whole method • Massed practice
- Distributed practice • Variable practice • Drilling • Visual guidance
- Verbal guidance • Manual/mechanical guidance • Kinaesthetic awareness

5. Organisation of learning environments to refine performance
(There are no key words and phrases in this sub-section.)

6. Attitudes and strategies for changing attitudes
- Attitude objects • Triadic model • Cognitive dissonance • Cognition

7. Group dynamics
- Dynamics • Cohesion • Loafing • Group productivity

8. Techniques for enhancing performance

- Stressor   • Stress process   • Distress   • Eustress   • Goal setting
- Somatic techniques   • Cognitive techniques   • Mental rehearsal

9. Physiological, psychological and/or bio-mechanical applications to improve performance

- Ergogenic aid   • Pharmacological aids   • Physiological aids   • Nutritional aids
- Mechanical aids   • Psychological aids

10. Tactics, strategies, perception and decision making appropriate to refining performance.

(There are no key words and phrases in this sub-section.)

11. Extension of the use of feedback, teaching styles and practices in refining performance

- Feedback   • Knowledge of performance (KP)   • Knowledge of results (KR)

12. Implication of resource and technical developments on refining and advancing performance

(There are no key words and phrases in this sub-section.)

13. Preparation for competition, training routines, game plans, raining systems and developments

- Game plans

REVIEW QUESTIONS

1 Outline the principles of coaching and discuss their importance in the refinement of a performance.

2 What do you understand by the term 'notation'? Extend your answer by devising a notation system for an activity of your choice.

3 How could you evaluate a skill?

4 What methods and strategies can be used to change an athlete's attitude?

5 Define 'social cohesion' and explain why group productivity can overcome individual weaknesses.

6 How can stress be managed?

7 What purposes do goal setting and mental rehearsal serve?

8 Explain what you understand by a 'game plan'. Expand your answer with an example from an activity with which you are familiar.

9 How can a coach use feedback to refine a performance?

10 What factors must be taken into account when planning a 'Personal Exercise Plan'?

11 Using examples from the three activities studied as part of Unit 5 Section A, describe the value of technical developments in refining a performance.

12 What variables may affect a performer's decision making?

Texts used in the writing of this section

❏ Baddeley, A. & Longman, D. J. A., 'The Influence of Length and Frequence of Training Session on the Range of Learning', in Woods, B., *Applying Psychology to Sport*, 'Ergonomic' pp. 627–35, Hodder & Stoughton, 1978

❏ Bandura, A., *Social Learning Theory*, Prentice Hall, 1977

❏ Carron, A. V., *Social Psychology of Sport*, Mouvement Publications, 1980

❏ Davies, D., *Psychological Factors in Competitive Sport*, Falmer Press, 1989

❏ Festinger, L. A., *A Theory of Cognitive Dissonance*, Harper and Row, New York, 1957

❏ Honeybourne, J., *et al., Physical Education and Sport*, Stanley Thornes Ltd., 1996

❏ Latane, B., *et al.*, 'Many Hands Make Light Work', *Journal of Personality*, 1979

❏ Lazarus, & Folkman, *Stress Appraisal and Coping*, Springer, New York, 1984

❏ Martens, R., *Succesful Coaching*, American Sports Education Program, 1997

❏ NCF, *Observation, Analysis and Video*, NCF, 1999

❏ Ringlemann, A., 'The Ringlemann Effect', in Ingham, A. G., *Journal of Experimental Psychology*, 1974

❏ Royce, J., 'How Do You Coach Decision-making?', *Coaching Focus*, No, 26, National Coaching Foundation, Summer 1994

❏ Shaw, M. E., (1976), unattributed reference in Wesson, K., *et al., Sport and P.E.*, p. 469

❏ Triandis, A., *Impersonal Behaviour*, Brooks/Cole, 1977

❏ Webster, S., *Sports Psychology*, Jan Roscoe Publications, 1996

❏ Woods, B., *Applying Psychology to Sport*, Hodder & Stoughton, 1998

Section B: Personal Exercise Plan

1. Introduction

The requirement for this section of Unit 5 provides you with the opportunity to undertake a Personal Exercise Plan (PEP). The PEP will allow you to apply your knowledge and understanding gained from Units 2, 3 and 5 (and later from Unit 6) to the planning, performing and evaluation of a fitness and training programme of your own choice. You are advised not to under-estimate the importance of this part of Unit 5 as it carries a 5 per cent weighting towards your final course award.

The PEP will be based on your chosen practical activity offered for assessment in Section C: Option A. For those candidates undertaking Option B, the investigative study, your PEP must be related to one of the activities contained in the full specification document.

During your assessments in a competitive situation, a judgement will be made on your level of 'fitness for purpose'. This aspect of the criteria requires your centre to make an assessment of your ability to participate from a physiological standpoint. That is, to judge whether you have the necessary fitness components to take part in and influence a competitive situation in your chosen practical activity. The PEP has the specific intention, therefore, of improving an aspect of your 'fitness for purpose'. This will enable you to identify and then enhance an aspect of fitness that directly underpins a successful performance.

Units 3 and 6 and your PEP

As part of your studies in the Advanced Subsidiary course you will have completed Unit 3 'Exercise and training'. That Unit provided you with the knowledge and understanding of applied physiology and how the individual responds to and adapts through exercise. Inherent in that Unit was the ability for you to relate the appropriate knowledge gained from the Unit to your own practical performances.

You will also have been able to take part in and experience a number of physical fitness tests that will have helped you evaluate your own physical condition. This will provide you with an essential understanding of the planning of fitness and training programmes and how to conduct an appropriate warm up and cool down.

By extending the practical assignment through the content contained in Unit 6 'The scientific principles of exercise and performance', you will be able to relate the content of that Unit to the different types of training that a performer may undergo. You will also be required to understand the subsequent effects that the correct preparation, practice and training will have on a performer when preparing for competition.

The following key content areas of Units 3 and 6 will be relevant to the conduct of your PEP:

- warm up and cool down
- the measurement and evaluation of fitness components
- planning of fitness and training programmes
- energy systems and the energy continuum.

2. Your Personal Exercise Plan

The timescale

Given the requirement for you to draw upon the knowledge and understanding gained from Unit 3 of the Advanced Subsidiary course, you should be able to begin planning your PEP as early as possible. It is envisaged that you will be able to start the process at the beginning of the first term of the Advanced Subsidiary course. However, you may be able to begin planning your PEP at the end of the first year after the completion of the summer examinations.

Having outlined the aim of your PEP and identified the methods of training to be used, you will need to spend a reasonable period of time researching the exact format of your PEP. As you will also need to draw upon the content of Unit 6, you may not be able to

▲ **Figure 5.39** *A programme of eight weeks will bring recognisable gains*

complete this part of the planning process until the end of your first term of the Advanced course.

There is some debate amongst exercise physiologists and sports coaches over the length of time that a training programme should take. Clearly, this will depend on the aims of the programme and the potential for improvement.

For the purposes of successful completion of the PEP, it is recommended that a minimum of 6 weeks and a maximum of 12 weeks should be spent undertaking the programme.

Contrary to popular belief, prior training does not hasten the rate of improvement nor increase the training benefits gained from subsequent training programmes. Fox (1989) recommends that the **frequency of training** should be from three to five sessions per week and that a programme of eight weeks will bring recognisable gains (Figure 5.39).

The actual performance of your PEP is left to your own discretion and it is recommended that you begin the period of PEP workload no later than January of the final year of examination. You must leave adequate time to complete the recording of your PEP and write the evaluation. This must normally be finished by the end of April in the year of the final award.

The knowledge and understanding derived from the course will combine with your own playing experiences to form the base from which you will be able to undertake the PEP.

It is a requirement of the examination that all candidates take responsibility for the **planning**, **performing**, **recording** and **evaluation** of their PEP under the direction of their own centre staff.

It is possible for you to perform the PEP off site and with additional guidance from a qualified instructor, providing you are monitored by your centre. They will also be responsible for all assessments. Those candidates already performing at a relatively high level of competition may already be familiar with the concept of a PEP.

How do I construct my PEP?

As a result of analysis and evaluation, you will have been able to identify the core fitness components that are required for the activity you have selected. From these you will be able to devise your programme. Your centre should support you in identifying the most **appropriate component of fitness** that you will select for your PEP and how you can improve it. It is recommended that you identify *one* key component for your PEP rather than a number. It is also acceptable for a student to formulate a PEP based on a programme of rehabilitation following an injury or illness. This, by its very nature, may involve more than one component of fitness but the concept of the PEP remains the same.

It is not recommended that you identify a component of fitness such as agility or balance as the main focus for your PEP. These skill-related components have limited specific training opportunities and are significantly harder to measure accurately in relation to their contribution to an activity.

The process of constructing and completing your PEP is best understood by relating it to the way in which the PEP will be assessed. Whilst at this point a detailed description of the assessment process is not necessary, an understanding of how you will be assessed can be used as the starting point.

Assessment of your PEP

Your PEP will be assessed by applying descriptive criteria to the following four key areas:
- planning
- performing
- reporting
- evaluating.

You will be required to show evidence that you have not only planned and performed the PEP, but also made a report and provided an evaluation of it.

You will need to be realistic in devising your PEP and set attainable goals. In order for you to successfully complete your PEP, the following factors need to be considered carefully:

- How long will I have to carry out the PEP?
- What facilities are available for me to use?
- Will I be able to gain qualified help when I need it?
- Will I be able to keep to the planned programme and remain motivated?
- What forms of ongoing assessment do I need to undertake?
- What type of records do I need to keep?

Beginning the process of planning

Your own playing experiences will give you a very good understanding of the activity chosen for your PEP.

In addition the requirements of Unit 2 to carry out an analysis of performance will have enabled you to identify the individual components that combine to produce an enhanced performance. By being able to identify strengths and weaknesses in a performance and have a knowledge and understanding of planning, practices and training, you will already be able to plan to some extent how to improve a component of fitness.

Components of fitness

During your studies in Unit 2 you will have gained an understanding of the components of fitness that combine to form part of the core physiological make-up of an athlete. To some extent these components are found in all athletic performances, regardless of the specific discipline. An understanding of the part that they play in a successful performance is central to the PEP. These components should be familiar to you and include:

- static, explosive and dynamic strength
- speed
- cardio-vascular endurance
- local muscular endurance

▲ *Figure 5.40* Which components of fitness does the skier need to improve to be more successful?

- dynamic and static flexibility
- gross, static and dynamic balance
- gross, hand-eye and eye-foot co-ordination
- agility
- reaction time
- power, visual activity and tracking.

In order to decide which component to use in your PEP, you may wish to undertake a series of tests to provide you with the data from which you are able to make an informed judgement.

For instance, you may have identified that speed, cardio-vascular endurance and flexibility are the core components of your activity. You will now need to undertake some simple testing and then use the information gained to assess which component could be enhanced and as a result make an impact on your overall aim of refining a performance.

Tests that may be used include heart rates, specific muscle/muscle group strength tests, flexibility measures, timed runs, local muscle endurance timed tests and established tests for cardio-vascular endurance such as the multi-stage fitness test. It is important to consider the implications of your testing and their suitability for your PEP.

By tracing the path of a typical PEP through a 'case study', you will gain an appreciation of the processes and procedures involved in completing a PEP.

PEP: A case study

A performer has identified that he has been unable to compete as competitively as he would have liked in rugby while progressing through the age groups and levels of performance. The person has been able to test his static and dynamic strength through a number of simple tests that have identified a weakness in upper body strength. As a result the player wishes to focus his PEP on developing greater upper body strength in the shoulder joints and arms while maintaining joint flexibility.

The performer must now carry out a small amount of research to provide answers to the following questions, which draw upon the relevant content of Units 2, 3 and 5 and also Unit 6:

- How do the principles of training affect my programme?

- What types of training will best suit the aims of my PEP?

- When will I need to test and measure my progress?

- Which tests should I use and are these tests valid?

- What frequency, intensity and time do I need to train for?

- What facilities and resources are appropriate for an effective training programme?

- What would be a suitable warm up and cool down programme for me to undertake?

Once these questions have been researched the answers will leave the performer in a position to plan his PEP along the following lines:

- The performer must begin his PEP with a record of the starting point in the component(s) identified for training and the specific aims and goals that are hoped for.

- The performer will be able to apply the training principles of overload specificity and progression to a series of strength training exercises.

- The programme will make use of recognised weight training exercises using fixed weight systems and free weights.

- An initial assessment will be made of strength in a number of selected muscles/muscle groups by carrying out a maximum repetition, e.g. in the deltoids, biceps, pectorals.

- Measurements will also be made of shoulder flexibility.

- These tests will be repeated every two weeks and the results recorded.

- The programme will require the student to train three times per week for approximately one hour's duration per session and at a high intensity in order to promote an increase in muscle strength. A sensible training schedule not only contains an appropriate exertion phase but also sufficient time for recuperation.

- The programme will be for ten weeks' duration.

- Access to a weights room with suitable weight stations and with appropriate supervision is necessary.

- The programme will be based on using heavy weight combinations at 90 per cent of maximum lift in 3 sets of 5-8 repetitions.

- The warm up should specifically prepare the muscles, the joints and the cartilage for training. This can be achieved through light jogging, using lower weights and higher repetitions on the specific exercise being used, stretching exercises and some mental preparation to focus the mind.

The programme will require the performer to record his attendance for each session and obtain **verification** of the testing undertaken. This may take the form of a training diary or logbook, which can be filled in as progress is made.

How will I be assessed?

Once you have completed your final training sessions and carried out the appropriate testing and measurement of the progress that you have made relevant to the aims of your PEP, a final written assignment of 1500 words will be presented to the staff at your centre.

For this you will be able to use ICT and include any graphs, charts or schedules that you have constructed. The complete PEP document will be assessed by your centre using an established set of criteria. This is centred upon planning, performing, reporting and evaluation.

KEY SKILLS

The nature of the PEP document quite clearly lends itself to submission for Key Skills competency Level 3 in all three fields identified by the Edexcel specification: Communication, Information Communications Technology and Application of Number.

Planning – 5 marks

In order to be awarded the maximum marks available for the planning of your PEP, you will be required to show a clear understanding of how to devise and plan an exercise programme based on specific aims, and make use of the appropriate recognised testing methods.

You must apply the principles of training to good effect and be able to draw upon the theoretical knowledge of Unit 3 (and later, Unit 6) to good effect. As a result of the successful completion of the PEP, you will be able to discuss the programme with your centre staff and an examiner. It is important that your PEP does not simply become an 'exercise' to be completed as easily as possible. Your research and testing on components of fitness will be invaluable for your further work in Section C of this Unit, irrespective of whether you have chosen to do Option A or B.

Performing – 25 marks

This aspect of your PEP carries the greatest number of marks and reflects upon your ability to sustain the programme you have devised. Not only will you be expected to follow the timescale of the plan and attend sessions of training, you will also be judged on your ability to successfully perform an appropriate warm up and cool down. This should be detailed in your PEP. You will also need to have worked safely and at times without direct supervision. Your ability to remain motivated and offer support to others will be taken into account.

Recording the programme – 5 marks

This aspect will carry a maximum of 5 marks based on the scope of your PEP. A more detailed PEP which reflects a wider appreciation of the related principles of training and additional information which further demonstrates the depth of your knowledge and understanding of a PEP is taken into account. This extended knowledge can include current topics and issues relating to personal fitness. You must be accurate and consistent in recording your progress, any tests and measurements and give a clear account of all the work that you have undertaken.

Evaluating the programme – 10 marks

The PEP will allow you to demonstrate a clear knowledge and understanding of how to evaluate an exercise programme and incorporate the reasons for doing this. You will need to assess the success or failure of your programme and show reasons for the outcomes in relation to your original aims. You will be expected to take this knowledge and use it to devise future programmes. Your ability to discuss your evaluation with your centre staff, or an examiner, will be taken into account.

```
PEP ASSSESSMENT = /45
```

Your assessed PEP will be contained in your IPP and submitted to an examiner for moderation.

Key words and phrases

- **Frequency of training**   • **Planning**   • **Performing**   • **Recording**   • **Evaluation**
- **Appropriate component of fitness**   • **Verification**

REVIEW QUESTIONS

1 How will you decide the activity on which your PEP is to be based?

2 What is meant by the term 'fitness for purpose'?

3 What is the relevance of the contents of Unit 3 'Exercise and training' and Unit 6 'The scientific principles of exercise and performance' for your work on your PEP?

4 What are the minimum and maximum periods of time over which your PEP should be based?

5 What are the four areas of assessment against which your PEP will be measured?

6 What is a 'component of fitness'?

7 List *six* different components of fitness.

8 How will you decide which component of fitness on which to base your PEP?

9 Produce, on a single sheet of paper, an outline plan of the main contents of your PEP.

Section C: Option A: Practical performance

1. Introduction

For this section you will offer one practical activity for assessment. This will be the culmination of all your studies and practical work in order to refine a performance.

The choice of activity can be based on your achievements during the Advanced Subsidiary course and it can come from the categories of team games, racket games and individual activities listed in the activity group table. The central focus of this Unit is that you continue with one of your selected activities from the Advanced Subsidiary course in order to refine a performance and demonstrate specific techniques in isolation (Figure 5.41).

The format for assessment of this option will be familiar to you and follows the same format as that carried out in Unit 2.

You will be judged on your ability to perform in three areas of assessment: in

▲ **Figure 5.42** *A refined performance comes with experience and maturity*

structured practices and competitive situations and in the performance of skills in isolation. The nature of the assessment criteria and the concept of refining a performance is based on your continuing development of performance over the two-year cycle of the full course.

The timescale for the completion of your practical work for Section 5C: Option A means that the process of assessment will have to begin at the start of the course. A final judgement, however, will not be made until almost the end of the spring term in the final year of your Advanced award.

At this point it is worth reiterating that any performance quite clearly requires a foundation of productive practice and appropriate competition. The combination of these elements in a planned and programmed way and the technical improvement in the performance of skill in a developing **skill repertoire** are central to your obtaining a higher mark award (Figure 5.42).

▲ **Figure 5.41** *For this section you must demonstrate specific techniques*

2. Developing a performance from Advanced Subsidiary to Advanced Level

The progress that you will have made during the course will be measured by applying an upgraded set of **performance criteria**. The demands made of you will now focus on the ways in which you are able to demonstrate a refinement in performances in the three areas of assessment.

> Do not forget about your IPP. You are advised to keep this updated with all your practical experiences in addition to your formal assessment assignments.

The content of Section A of this Unit will have provided you with a clear understanding of how a performance can be evaluated and how the correct use of practice promotes a refinement in performance. Your knowledge gained from Unit 3 (and what you will learn from Unit 6) in the development of a PEP should also be used to help raise your performance levels. It is important that you also continue to keep as detailed records as possible of your performances and training sessions in your IPP as this will reflect what you have been able to achieve.

Evidence of improvement

An improved performance at Advanced Level will be identified by a number of observed refinements. For individual activities there should be clear progression in your performances by the more challenging activity requirements. The performance will also be of a higher quality and skill standard (Figure 5.43). For team and racket games, the following changes in performances are expected of an Advanced Level candidate:

- *polished technique* – you will be able to perform the underlying techniques more accurately and consistently thereby producing skills to a more refined level. Your level of technical proficiency will be significantly improved
- *greater consistency* – in racket games you will be able to play an increasing number of strokes more consistently on your weaker side
- *increased perception and decision-making capability* – the level of your perceptual skills will provide a base for improved decision making and a greater awareness of the requirements of your activity will be evident
- *tactical awareness* – tactically, and through the use of advanced strategies, you will be able to take part in and influence an appropriate competitive situation more effectively
- *accuracy of skills under pressure* – when asked to perform skills in isolation, and when they are subjected to increasing pressure, your level of technical accuracy remains
- *composure, creativity and confidence* – when performing competitively you will be able to keep your composure, show creativity and play with confidence.

▲ **Figure 5.43** *At Advanced Level, improvement should be readily apparent*

> 'polished technique'
>
> consistency
>
> perception & decision making
>
> tactical awareness
>
> better skills under pressure
>
> composure, creativity & confidence

▲ **Figure 5.44** *Evidence of improvement*

▲ *Figure 5.45* *Even international stars need to train effectively and play consistently*

Structured practices

The demands now placed upon you in your **structured practices** will reflect an improved ability to perform skills at a higher level and under an increased degree of pressure. An expanding skill repertoire will enable you to concentrate on the correct tactics and strategies to employ and you will be expected to show a mature application to the purpose of refining your performance.

Due to the diversity of practical options, you may have completed your structured practices away from your examination centre. This is acceptable although your centre will still be responsible for carrying out an assessment on you by applying the appropriate examination board criteria.

Competitive situations

There is a continued requirement for you to perform in **competitive situations** at the highest possible level open to you. The resulting level of performance achieved in your structured practices will be to produce a refined competitive performance.

It is important for you now to draw together the physiological, psychological and technical knowledge and understanding that you have obtained throughout the course to refine a competitive performance. The focus of your development will be to ensure that you are able to consistently apply a high level of technique to competition.

You must also be able to play effectively in more than one position if required. You are strongly recommended to take every opportunity to compete in a formal setting. If you are selected to represent your area, district or region, you will see your final practical marks adjusted accordingly to reflect such attainment.

> **Remember** – competition can bring out the best in some performers!

Tactical awareness

The ability to perform effectively is significantly improved by the level of tactical awareness possessed by a performer. Section A of this Unit will have given you some indication of the need to show both positional and game understanding. Your preparation to play must include a broader understanding of this aspect of a performance. As the level of your competitive experiences increases, the ability to improvise and dominate opponents will be a part of your refined performance.

Fitness for purpose

The experience of completing a Personal Exercise Plan will have given you a clear insight into the core components of fitness that are crucial to your ability to take part in competition successfully. A developed 'fitness for purpose' will be taken into account when assessments in your competitive performances are made.

Skills in isolation

The challenge of performing skills in isolation will be a natural extension of your work carried out in structured practice. The Edexcel specification details a number of **compulsory skills** that a candidate must undertake and the opportunity to select a skill from the given options list. You will be required to perform four compulsory skills and a single option choice. For some individual activities, there may be a slight change in this format to allow for the unique nature of these activities to be assessed in relation to the demands that they place on the candidate.

The assessment of these skills will focus on the technical detail and proficiency required

▲ *Figure 5.46* Technical merit deserves reward

by them and the degree to which they remain consistent under applied pressure. In all cases the exact requirements of this aspect of the coursework are given in the full Edexcel specification document.

There are however certain **generic characteristics** relevant to the skills performed in team games and in racket games. You will be aware of these from your work in Unit 2. Essentially they centre on movement control, technical accuracy and the timing of the movement patterns (Figure 5.46).

The refinement of a skill can be developed by the physiological improvements that have occurred during the course. This should be taken into account when planning your PEP.

How will I be assessed?

Candidates completing the Advanced Level course must produce a higher level of performance than for AS Level in order to gain comparable marks. You must not expect to be given the same or a similar mark as awarded for the Advanced Subsidiary Level if no improvement or refinement in a performance. The demands of many of the individual activities require evidence of a clear progression in the technical level of skills produced in your attainment during the second year course.

The process of assessment of your practical activity will follow a similar pattern to that at the end of Unit 2. You will be required to demonstrate a standard of performance over the period of the course in structured practices, competitive situations and, additionally, in performing skills in isolation. It will help you to revisit the detailed assessment procedures outlined in the chapter covering Unit 2 assessment of practical activities on pages 134–136. The **progression of performance** required for Unit 5 is indicated below:

- isolated skills
- structured practice
- competitive situation.

These three areas will be judged against the appropriate set of assessment criteria. The highest mark you are able to obtain for each part of the course is 15. The criteria give details of those elements that will determine your progress in refining a performance.

Separate criteria exist for the two activity categories of team and racket activities, whilst individual activities have their own unique assessment criteria. Performances are placed into 'bands' as in keeping with your assessment at AS Level and are used to judge and distinguish between performances.

Advanced Level assessment overview

The total mark possible for Option A is 45 and represents 5 per cent of your Advanced Level award. The mark of 45 consists of:

- isolated skills   = 15 marks total
- structured practices   = 15 marks total
- competitive situation = 15 marks total

Total mark available   = 45
(section weighting of 5 per cent)

The total weighting of Unit 5 is a 15 per cent contribution towards your final Advanced Level award.

Section C: Option B: Investigative study

1. Introduction

The investigative study represents 5 per cent of the marks of the A Level and is a written assessment of up to 2500 words on a performance-related area. The study will require you to test a hypothesis and draw conclusions from this. Unlike the research project (Unit 2B: Option B), the investigative study must include **empirical research**. This requires that you collect your own data and analyse the findings.

The task

In the process of carrying out the study you should:

- identify an area of investigation suitable for a small-scale enquiry
- locate and review relevant literature and documentation (including the integration of knowledge from other Units)
- select appropriate methods of investigation
- use appropriate techniques of investigation, data collection and analysis
- interpret and draw meaningful conclusions from the collected data
- organise and present findings in a coherent manner.

2. Identify an area of investigation suitable for a small-scale enquiry

For many, the investigative study will follow on directly from the research project conducted in the first year. There are three advantages to this:

1 The process of identifying the research problem is made easier as the problem should come directly out of the appraisal section of the research project.
2 The bulk of the research required for the review of literature will already have been completed.

> **RESEARCH TIP**
>
> A research diary should be used from the start of the investigative study right up to the end. Your diary should include:
>
> - planning dates and deadlines
> - a log of progress and problems
> - a compendium of references
> - sources of guidance.

3 A good knowledge of the research area will have been cultivated already.

If you did not conduct a research project for the AS part of the course, however, it would be advisable to begin this process for the investigative study during the summer term or summer holidays at the end of the first year. The stages involved in the investigative study are identified in the research process diagram (Figure 5.46).

Your strengths and interests

The first stage involves reflecting on your own areas of expertise, whether performing, coaching or spectating. You must then match these with your strengths and interests from the A Level specification.

Preliminary identification of the research area

This stage involves refining your broad area of interest to a particular aspect of the A Level specification. For example, you may be a keen club athlete interested in pursuing a study related to athletics. Using a variety of PE textbooks or the A Level specification itself, you could further refine this area of interest to the exercise and training aspects of athletics, and, more specifically, to the principles of training.

Further discussion with your tutor or friends might direct your investigation towards ways in which different warm-up procedures affect performance in the 100-metres sprint.

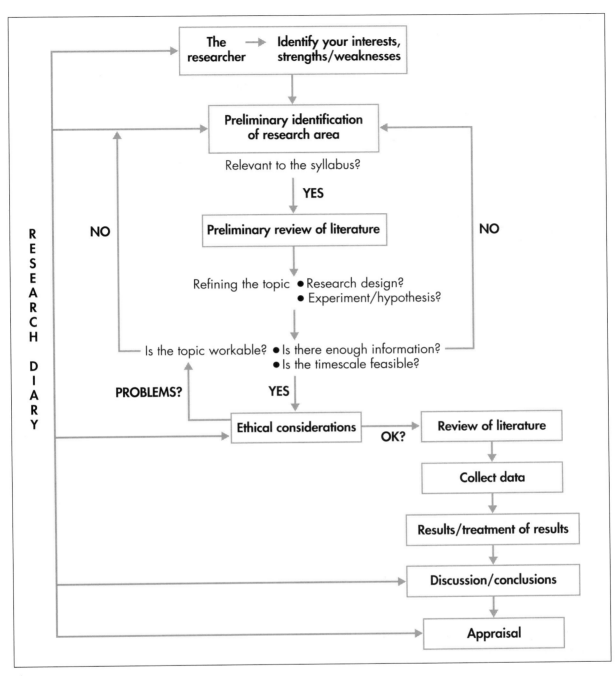

▲ *Figure 5.47* The research process

Preliminary review of literature

A library search is required at this point in order to refine a particular area of study and to investigate its feasibility.

It is essential to find out whether there are sufficient resources in your school/college library to enable you to carry out the study. If there is insufficient material, you will need to select another research topic or investigate other sources of information that may be available locally. If there is a lot of research material available, it will be necessary either to be selective in its use or to further refine the subject matter of your research topic.

Defining the research area

The next process is to define the research area and to decide how you will carry out your research (the research method).

Using the previous example, a research question might be:

Is performance in the 100-metres sprint affected by different warm-up procedures?

In order to answer this, the research methodology could involve a **field experiment**, comparing the 100-metres times of a group which undergoes two different warm-up procedures (a **repeated measures design**).

Information highlighting the common approaches to research can be found on pages 359–60.

At this point you should have:

- decided on your research question
- ascertained that there are sufficient resources to work from
- decided on a research design which is manageable and feasible within the allotted timescale.

You now need to address potential ethical considerations.

Ethical considerations

The problems involving an investigative study of this kind were identified in Unit 2B (see pages 141–42). It would be beneficial to re-read this section and consider the pitfalls that might apply to your proposed investigation.

Examples of suitable areas for study

The examples below are meant to act as a starting point and guide rather than offer a definitive list:

- **Exercise and training aspects**
  i) *A comparative study of the flexibility levels of two selected populations e.g. dancers and rugby players.* ▶

  ii) *A comparison between plyometrics and weight training as a means of developing strength.*

- **Psychological aspects**
  i) *An investigation into the transferability of skills between two activities e.g. squash and badminton or diving and trampolining.*

  ii) *A comparison of the differences in reaction times between two specific groups e.g. introverts and extroverts.*

- **Social aspects**
  Research problems in this area can prove too complex for a study of this size. Therefore it might be advisable to adopt a more qualitative approach, such as a case study which makes a comparison between the sporting opportunities available in a state funded and a privately funded school.

- **Bio-mechanical aspects**
  An investigation into the relationship between height and power production in a tennis serve.

3. Locate and review relevant literature and documentation

The review of literature aims to synthesise all of the information relevant to the research problem. It helps to set the scene for the specific investigation. On a practical level, this involves researching all relevant information from a variety of sources. You will need to be imaginative and thorough when doing this.

Sources of information include books, journals, newspapers, video, CD-ROMs and the Internet. More information about each of these areas was provided in Unit 2B on page 142.

The review of literature should follow the format below.

1 A broad introduction to the research area, including definitions of any relevant technical terms. The research topic should then be introduced and related to the research area.

2 A synthesis of the information is provided from a variety of sources relevant to the research topic.

3 The research problem should be placed in the context of the information reviewed and the aims of the study should be evident.

4 Finally, If the research involves descriptive or experimental methods, the **hypotheses** related to the problem need to be stated.

When writing the review of literature it should be presented in clear, fluent prose and there should be a logical progression from the background research to the statement of the aims and hypotheses (if relevant).

4. Select appropriate methods of investigation

Types of research

The information below is a brief introductory overview of the various research methods you could use to provide a general introduction to a broad area. For more details about each method you should refer to the suggested further reading at the end of this section.

Qualitative research

Qualitative research aims to understand an experience or phenomenon from the viewpoint of the participants. The researcher therefore tries to build up a picture of the phenomenon through direct interaction with the key players.

The range of methods utilised in this type of research include:

- open-ended questionnaires
- interviews
- direct observation of participants in their natural setting.

Qualitative research would be a good choice for students who already have inside knowledge or access to a particular group or sports team. For example, a case study incorporating interviews and/or observation could be used to compare the leadership styles adopted by a gymnastics coach and a hockey coach.

Quantitative research

Quantitative research tries to break down sporting phenomena into quantifiable units (variables). These variables can be characteristics of various groups, for example, age, weight, size, or sporting characteristics such as performance, injury, psychological or sociological attributes.

Quantitative research aims to quantify the relationships between the different variables. For example, an experimental design might investigate whether an audience affects the accuracy of a tennis serve, or whether there is a transfer of learning effect between a squash forehand and a badminton forehand.

Quantitative research aims to find the causes of events in order to predict what will happen in the future. This type of research involves precise measurement and statistical analysis and the data tends to be numerical. Quantitative research methods can be descriptive or experimental.

Descriptive methods

With **descriptive methods** no attempt is made to change behaviour or conditions. They are fact-finding studies with the aim of establishing how the facts relate to the problem under investigation.

Fact-finding methods include:

a **correlational analysis** – this aims to measure the degree in which two phenomena are related. For example, a study might investigate whether there is a relationship between muscle size and strength.

b **surveys** – these are usually used to obtain information from relatively large numbers of people in order to gain a broad overview of a situation. Survey approaches can incorporate:

- interviews
- observation
- content analysis.

Experimental methods

Experimental methods manipulate treatments in order to make things happen, i.e. cause and effect. The research follows a distinct format:

a developing the problem
b formulating a hypothesis
c gathering the data
d analysing the results.

Developing the problem involves the identification of the dependent and the independent variables. For example, a researcher wishes to investigate the effect of different warm-up procedures on sprint performance in the 100-metres. The **independent variable** is that which the researcher would be manipulating, e.g. the type of warm-up procedure. The **dependent variable** would be sprint performance because it is dependent upon the way the researcher manipulates the independent variable.

Hypotheses

The *research hypothesis* is a statement about what the researcher intends to prove or disprove.

The *experimental hypothesis*, on the other hand, is a statement about the predicted outcome of an experiment. In the example above, the experimental hypothesis would be:

'It is proposed that different warm-up procedures will have an effect on sprint performance in the 100-metres.'

The above is a two-tailed hypothesis since it does not state whether the outcome will increase or decrease performance. A one-tailed hypothesis would predict the outcome.

A null hypothesis is a statement of 'no difference', or 'no relationship' between the variables under investigation. Again, using the above example, the null hypothesis would be:

'There is no difference in sprint performance in the 100-metres as a result of different warm-up procedures.'

The experimental hypothesis, therefore, predicts that the independent variable will affect the dependent variable.

Essentially the aim of the experimental method is to produce data which can be statistically analysed in order to disprove the null hypothesis so that the experimental hypothesis can be accepted. It is important, therefore, when designing the experiment to make sure that the hypothesis is testable.

It is clear by now that there are a variety of ways in which to conduct your research. In many cases the nature of the question dictates the research method.

5. Use appropriate techniques of investigation, data collection and analysis

Whichever method of research you choose you must make reference to **reliability**, **internal validity** and **external validity**.

Reliability refers to the repeatability of the results. That is, if the procedure of the experiment or research were to be carried out again, would the results be the same?

Internal validity refers to whether the experiment or research measures what it is supposed to. External validity refers to the extent to which the results can be generalised to the real world.

RESEARCH TIP

You have a greater chance of creating a procedure that is both reliable and valid if a pilot study is carried out beforehand.

Experimental design

The following is a brief overview of the main experimental designs that you could follow when conducting experimental research.

Repeated measures design

This design involves the same group being subjected to different treatments. For example, the experiment might investigate how the intensity of a stimulus affects reaction time. Therefore, one group of people could be subjected to a light stimulus of low intensity, followed by light stimulus of high intensity.

Matched pairs design

Matched pairs design involves the researcher matching every subject in one group with a subject in another group. The two groups then undergo different treatments.

Independent measures design

This design involves using different subjects in each of the experimental conditions.

Related and unrelated designs

A **related design** is one in which the results presented in one treatment are related to the results in another treatment. In this sense, repeated measures and matched pairs are also related designs. The **independent measures design** is an **unrelated design** since the comparison of results is between two groups of subjects whose scores are unrelated.

Results analysis

Once you have decided on your experimental design (if an experiment is carried out) and collected your data, you need to **present** and **analyse** the information.

Depending on the type of research design, the nature of the data obtained could be either qualitative or quantitative (see page 359). For example, the data obtained from interviews and questionnaires would be qualitative if a lot of open-ended questions were asked, or quantitative if tick-boxes were employed and numerical data generated.

The results need to be organised in a way that is clear and presents the findings in a logical flow. This is best achieved using **descriptive statistics**, which provide a means of summarising sets of raw data. This could involve the use of measures of central tendency, the mean, median and mode or measures of dispersion, the range and standard deviation. To make things more clear, you could use bar charts, pie charts, histograms and frequency polygons.

Inferential statistics are used in quantitative research since they enable the researcher to draw conclusions about the wider population from which a particular sample is drawn. Inferential statistics help to determine whether the results of your research were due to chance. If an experiment is carried out, the statistics will indicate whether the differences predicted by the experimental hypothesis (see page 360) are significant, or whether the researcher should accept the null hypothesis that such differences were due to chance factors.

Unfortunately there is no single statistical test that enables you to find this out. In order to decide which test is appropriate, refer to the list of texts for statistical reference at the end of this section.

The type of test you use depends on:

- the design of the experiment, i.e. repeated measures, matched pairs, independent measures or correlation analysis
- the type of data you collected, i.e. nominal, ordinal, interval or ratio.

Types of data

Nominal data can be the product of counting. For example, you might count the number of people who watched a hockey match: 30 males, 50 females.

Ordinal data (also known as ranked data) is presented in a particular order, e.g. the positions at the end of a 100-metre race: Greene first, Bailey second, etc.

Both interval and ratio data are derived from the use of measuring instruments, therefore the intervals between each value along the scale are consistent across the entire scale.

The difference between ratio and interval data is that ratio has a logical zero point, whereas for interval data the zero point can be arbitrary. Temperature is a good example of interval measurement: $0°C$ does not mean that there is no temperature at this point! Ratio data can be collected by using measuring tapes, stop watches or scales.

These types of data measurement provide more information than just the order. For example, if Greene came first in 10.0 seconds and Bailey was second in 10.1 seconds it is clear that the difference between first and second place is 0.1 seconds.

KEY SKILLS

If your study involves the collection of a large data set (over 50 items), the appropriate use of both descriptive and inferential statistics should provide the necessary evidence to satisfy the criteria for Key Skills Level 3 Application of Number.

6. Interpret and draw meaningful conclusions from collected data

At this point you will have collected your data and decided on the most appropriate descriptive and inferential statistics. The next stage is to examine and evaluate the findings of your study.

For experimental research you need to discuss how the results relate to your hypothesis and aims. You must also relate your findings to the research in the review of literature section. For example, did the findings support the studies mentioned earlier? If the alternative hypothesis was rejected or if your results are in disagreement with previous research, you should account for this critically.

When analysing qualitative information, the researcher must make reference to internal validity, i.e. the extent to which the results can be attributed to the act of conducting the research; and external validity, i.e. how well the results can be generalised to the wider population or to the real world.

Conclusions

This is a brief synopsis of the outcome of your study. The conclusions should comment on the overall findings and their relevance to the theories or information presented in the review of literature.

7. Organise and present findings in a coherent manner

The length of your investigative study should be up to 2500 words submitted on A4 paper.

The layout of the study

Introduction and planning

The purpose of this section is to introduce the reader to the topic being studied in a way which creates an interest in the study.

First, the topic should be introduced followed by its relevance to the candidate. The introduction should then focus on the nature of the research question itself, providing a clear coherent plan which states how the investigation is to be carried out. If the investigation uses experimental methods, the reader should be able to identify the dependent and independent variables and the controls.

Review of literature

The review of literature aims to synthesise all the information relating to the research problem. It is usual, after the review of literature, to formulate the hypotheses. Studies involving an experiment will need to state an experimental hypothesis, while studies involving descriptive methods of research must state a research hypothesis.

Research methods

This section should explain the conduct of the study. As a general rule the method should be detailed enough for someone else to reproduce the study and it should include:

- subjects: how many, how they were chosen, e.g. age, gender and sampling procedures used
- apparatus/materials
- procedures: an account of exactly how the experiment was conducted.

Results

Results should be shown in a way that can be clearly understood by the reader. If an experiment was conducted, a suitable statistical analysis needs to be carried out and included.

Discussion/conclusions

The first section should focus on what the results actually mean. If an experiment was conducted, reference should be made to the way in which the results compare to the hypothesis at the beginning of the study.

The second section should explain how the results support or refute the research presented in the review of literature section.

Appraisal

The researcher analyses any difficulties encountered in the study and suggests how they might be addressed if the study were to be repeated. They should also comment on the validity and reliability of the research design and, if any wider implications are raised, they should be stated here. The section should conclude by suggesting possible directions for future research.

Bibliography

See the notes on pages 144–45 in Unit 2, Section B.

You will find the following texts useful for statistical reference:

❏ Coolican, H., *Introduction to Research Methods and Statistics in Psychology*, Hodder and Stoughton, 1995

❏ Heyes, S. *et al.*, *Starting Statistics in Psychology and Education*, Weidenfield & Nicholson, 1986

❏ Thomas, J. & Nelson, J., *Research Methods in Physical Activity*, Human Kinetics, 1996

Appendices

Information that interrupts the flow of the study should be included in the appendices, e.g. raw data, instructions or calculations. Your research diary should also be included in this section.

Note that the research checklist given on the next page is, as its title implies, intended to assist you in the planning and checking of research procedures in the investigative study. It may be photocopied freely and/or adapted following discussions with your teacher.

KEY SKILLS

The research process of the investigative study not only provides numerous opportunities to use information communications technology. It also represents a good example of a 'substantial activity' required to satisfy the evidence for Key Skills Level 3 Information Communications Technology. Remember, you must provide evidence of each stage of the process, showing how each page/graph/table was created.

REVIEW QUESTIONS

1 What is meant by the term 'refining a performance'?

2 What is meant by the term 'skill repertoire'?

3 What are the three main areas in which your performance in Unit 5 will be assessed?

4 Under 'Evidence of improvement', 'composure, creativity and confidence' are given as measurable criteria. What other criteria might be used to measure improvement?

5 What is meant by the term 'generic characteristics' in relation to team games?

Key words and phrases

Option A: Practical performance

1. Introduction

- Skill repertoire

2. Developing a performance from Advanced Subsidiary to Advanced Level

- Performance criteria
- Structured practices
- Competitive situations
- Compulsory skills
- Generic characteristics
- Progression of performance

Option B: Investigative study

1. Introduction

- Empirical research
- Research diary

2. Identify an area of investigation suitable for a small-scale enquiry

- Field experiment
- Repeated measures design

3. Locate and review relevant literature and documentation

- Hypotheses

4. Select appropriate methods of investigation

- Descriptive methods
- Correlational analysis
- Surveys
- Experimental methods
- Independent variable
- Dependent variable

5. Use appropriate techniques of investigation, data collection and analysis

- Reliability
- Internal validity
- External validity
- Matched pairs design
- Related design
- Independent samples design
- Unrelated design
- Present
- Analyse
- Descriptive statistics
- Inferential statistics

6. Interpret and draw meaningful conclusions from collected data

(There are no key words and phrases in this sub-section.)

7. Organise and present findings in a coherent manner

(There are no key words and phrases in this sub-section.)

INVESTIGATIVE STUDY CHECKLIST

NO ✗   **YES ✓**

Presentation
☐ Is the study the right length? (up to 2500 words)   ☐
☐ Has the spelling and grammar been checked?   ☐

Title
☐ Does the title reflect the nature of the study?   ☐
☐ Is it succinct? Not too short, and not too long?   ☐

Introduction and planning
☐ Is the general area of the study stated?   ☐
☐ Are the reasons for studying the topic given?   ☐
☐ Is the introduction clear?   ☐
☐ Has a detailed plan been included?   ☐

Review of literature
☐ Are all the sources acknowledged?   ☐
☐ Was a wide range of resources consulted?   ☐
☐ Are all the sources relevant to the study?   ☐
   If an experiment is going to be conducted:
☐   Is the hypothesis precisely stated?   ☐
☐   Is the null hypothesis stated?   ☐

Research methods
☐ Is this section divided into the relevant sub-sections: ☐
   subjects/apparatus/materials/procedure?
☐ Are reasons for the research methods given?   ☐
☐ Has the number of participants been stated?   ☐
☐ Has the population of participants been stated?   ☐
☐ Have details been given of apparatus and materials?   ☐
☐ Are the standardised instructions included?   ☐
☐ Is the procedure clear?   ☐
☐ Have ethical considerations been taken into account?   ☐

Results
☐ Is the data presented in a clear, logical manner?   ☐
☐ Have appropriate graphs/charts been used?   ☐
☐ Have the appropriate inferential statistics been used?   ☐
☐ Is the significance level stated?   ☐
☐ Have the results been related to the hypotheses?   ☐

Discussion/conclusions
☐ Have the findings been related to the hypotheses?   ☐
☐ Have the findings been related to the review of literature?   ☐
☐ Is the style clear and coherent?   ☐

Appraisal
☐ Are limitations of the study given?   ☐
☐ Are suggestions made regarding future research?   ☐
☐ Are wider implications of the study addressed?   ☐

Bibliography
☐ Are all the sources acknowledged?   ☐
☐ Was the Harvard system used?   ☐

Appendices
☐ Is the raw data and other related information included?   ☐
☐ Is the research diary included?   ☐

Texts used in the writing of this section

- Boulton-Hawker Films Ltd., *Ergogenic Aids*, 1999
- Cardwell, M., Clark, L. & Melrum, C., *Psychology for A level*, Harper Collins, Publishers Ltd., 1996
- Coolican, H., *Introduction to Research Methods and Statistics in Psychology*, Hodder & Stoughton, 1995
- Dent, P., 'Decision Making in Racket Sports', in *Coaching Focus*, National Coaching Foundation, No. 26, Summer 1994
- Dick, F., *Sports Training Principles*, 2nd Edition, A. & C. Black, 1992
- *Gestalt Theory* Taken from a review of gestalt theory in Woods, B., *Applying Psychology to Sport*, Hodder & Soughton, 1998
- Green, J., D'Oliveira, M., *Open Guides to Psychology*, Open University Press, 1990
- Harre, D., *Principles of Sports Training*, Sportverlag, Berlin, 1992
- Hay, J. & Reid, J., *Anatomy, Mechanics and Human Motion*, Prentice Hall, 1988
- Kent, M., *The Oxford Dictionary of Sports Science and Medicine*, Oxford University Press, 1994
- NCF 'Coaching Focus' Periodicals: *Analysis of An Athlete*, No. 15, Autumn 1990 *Assessment of Performance*, No. 30, Winter 1995/96 *Focus on Peaking for Competition*, No. 18, Winter 1991 *Focus on Perception and Decision Making*, No. 26, Summer 1994 *Focus on Performer Assessment*, No. 29, Summer 1995 *The Athlete's Mind – The Last Frontier?* No. 4, Autumn 1986

Suggested further reading

- Fox, E., *The Physiological Basis for Exercise and Sport*, Brown and Benchmark, 1989
- Heyes, S., et al., *Starting Statistics in Psychology and Education*, Weidenfield & Nicholson, 1986
- Martens, R., *Successful Coaching*, American Sports Education Program, 1997
- NCF 'Coaching Focus' Periodicals: *Assessment of Performance*, No. 30, Winter 1995/96 *Focus on Peaking for Competition*, No. 18, Winter 1991 *Focus on Perception and Decision-Making*, No. 26, Summer 1994 *Focus on Performer Assessment*, No. 29, Summer 1995
- Woods, B., *Applying Psychology to Sport*, Hodder & Stoughton, 1998

Unit 6

Scientific principles of exercise and performance

Introduction to Unit 6

This Unit adds to the work you will have done in Unit 3: Exercise and training. This work will be extended in Section A, which looks at energy systems for sport and recreation. This section of the Unit is compulsory and with Unit 3 consists of a through grounding in the preparation for sports activity at all levels and for all ages.

The second part of the Unit (Section B) provides you with an opportunity to study either sports psychology or sports mechanics. Either of these two options will provide a broader base of study and will allow you to specialise in a particular field, in addition to providing insight into a wider area of scientific study. This will be particularly useful when engaging the final (compulsory) part of the Unit, the synoptic analysis of scientific principles in the development of performance.

This synoptic part of the Unit is designed to encourage you to engage in matters relating to globally focused scientific issues in sport but will also require you to draw upon your knowledge of social issues in Units 1 and 4 and how they influence or are influenced by scientific issues and advances in the global sporting environment.

There is a clear link between your work in this Unit, that of Unit 3 and the requirement of your Personal Exercise Plan that will be part of your IPP portfolio.

There is a clear 'holistic' component to this Unit that should allow you to develop knowledge that is not only academically testing but also practically useful at a personal level as well as a preparation for further study at a higher level.

It should be clearly understood that although the emphasis in this Unit is scientific there will be a requirement to address and engage issues in the social sphere, as previously mentioned.

It is also suggested that a practical 'hands on' approach should be part of your study programme.

The Unit will be examined by means of a one and three-quarter hour paper from which you will be required to answer *three* questions. One question must be from Section A: Exercise and energy systems and one further question must betaken from Section C: A synoptic analysis of scientific principles in the development of performance.

One additional question must be answered from *either*:

* Section Bi: Sports mechanics *or*
* Section Bii Sports psychology.

In the last instance, obviously, you are advised to answer a question only from the optional Unit you have been studying.

Section A: Exercise and energy systems

1. Introduction to basic chemistry for sports science

Before embarking on the study of exercise and energy systems, it is essential to have a basic grasp of some fundamental chemistry. This will help in understanding the body's chemical processes.

All living and non-living things are composed of **matter**, which exists in solid, liquid or gaseous states. Matter is anything that occupies space and has a mass. **Energy** is less tangible. It has no mass, takes up no space and can be measured by its effect on matter. It is defined as the capacity to do work, or put mass into motion.

Matter

All matter is composed of **elements** and the periodic table gives a complete list of known elements. Twenty-six elements occur in the human body with carbon (C), oxygen (O), hydrogen (H) and nitrogen (N) making up about 96 per cent of its mass. Each element is made up of **atoms**; the smallest atoms (H) are less than 0.00000001cm in diameter and the largest only 5 times larger. If 50 million of the largest atoms were placed end to end, they would measure approximately 2.5cm.

An atom consists of **neutrons**, **protons** and **electrons**. The negatively charged electrons (e^-) orbit the nucleus which is made up of positively charged protons (p^+) and uncharged neutrons.

The planetary model shown in Figure 6.1 is a simplistic view of the structure of atoms but is a useful tool for understanding chemical reactions. Note that a hydrogen atom has only one proton as its nucleus; there is therefore no separate neutron shown.

Atomic structure

The atomic number of an atom is equal to the number of protons it has, e.g. H=1, C=6. The mass number is the total number of protons

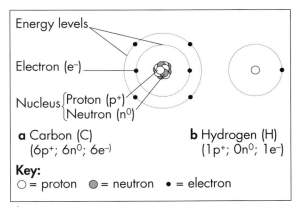

▲ **Figure 6.1** The structure of carbon atom and a hydrogen atom

and neutrons, e.g. H=1, C=12 (H does not have any neutrons). The atom is electrically neutral because the number of protons always equals the number of electrons. Atoms of one element may have different mass numbers because they have different numbers of neutrons. These are called **isotopes**. For example, C may have 6, 7 or 8 neutrons and thus form ^{12}C, ^{13}C and ^{14}C. When investigating metabolism, isotopes may be used to 'tag' molecules so that the path of chemical changes can be monitored. Atoms of different elements are composed of different numbers of protons, neutrons and electrons. When atoms combine with or break apart from others, a chemical reaction occurs. *Electron interactions are the basis of all chemical reactions*.

Electrons are in shells (energy levels) which surround the nucleus and the number of electrons in each shell conforms to a set of rules. The first shell may contain up to 2 electrons, the second 8 and the third 18 (*but* this shell is in balance at 8). Isolated atoms are always looking to fill their outer shell to remain stable. They therefore chemically react or **bond** with others to achieve this. When two or more atoms share electrons after a chemical reaction, the resulting combination is called a **molecule**. A **compound** contains atoms of two or more different elements.

Bonding

When an atom loses or gains an electron then its electrical neutrality is lost. The acquisition of an electron results in a negatively charged particle, whilst the loss of one means the charge is positive. A particle with a negative or positive charge is called an **ion** (e.g. Na^+ or Cl^-). A compound that splits into positive and negative ions in solution is called an **electrolyte** because the solution can conduct an electrical current. When Na^+ combines with Cl^- then this **ionic bond** results in sodium chloride (NaCl) or table salt (Figure 6.2).

Covalent bonding occurs where up to three atoms combine to share up to three pairs of electrons to form single, double or triple covalent bonds (Figure 6.3).

The **hydrogen bond** occurs where two other atoms (usually oxygen or nitrogen) associate with a hydrogen atom. These are weak bonds and cannot form molecules but

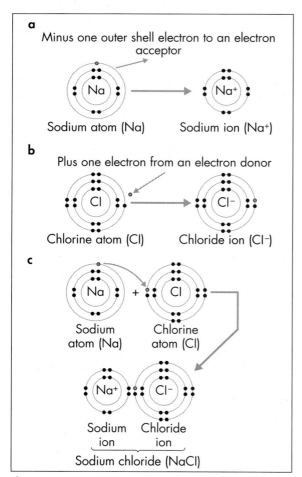

a

Minus one outer shell electron to an electron acceptor

Sodium atom (Na)   Sodium ion (Na^+)

b

Plus one electron from an electron donor

Chlorine atom (Cl)   Chloride ion (Cl^-)

c

Sodium   Chlorine
atom (Na) atom (Cl)

Na^+ Cl^-

Sodium   Chloride
ion   ion

Sodium chloride (NaCl)

▲ **Figure 6.2** Ionic bonds – sodium chloride (NaCl)

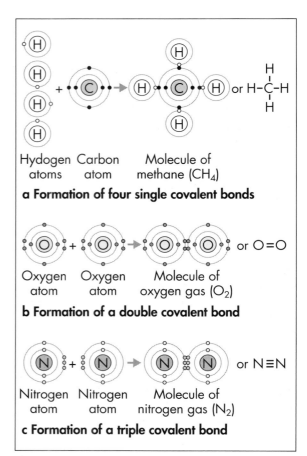

Hydogen   Carbon   Molecule of
atoms   atom   methane (CH_4)

a Formation of four single covalent bonds

Oxygen   Oxygen   Molecule of
atom   atom   oxygen gas (O_2)   or O=O

b Formation of a double covalent bond

Nitrogen   Nitrogen   Molecule of
atom   atom   nitrogen gas (N_2)   or N≡N

c Formation of a triple covalent bond

▲ **Figure 6.3** Covalent bonds

do provide useful links between molecules (e.g. water molecules). The sum of all these chemical reactions in an organism is referred to as the **metabolism**.

Chemical reactions

In chemical reactions, the breaking of bonds requires energy and the forming of bonds releases energy. Reactions releasing energy are termed **exothermic** and those requiring energy are **endothermic**. Most chemical reactions can be categorised as either: **synthesis** or **decomposition** (Figure 6.4), or **exchange** or **redox** reactions.

Synthesis (or **anabolic** reaction) occurs where atoms, molecules or ions combine to form new larger molecules:

$$A + B \rightarrow AB$$

Decomposition or **catabolic** reaction is when the chemical is broken down into smaller molecules or its constituent atoms:

$$AB \rightarrow A + B$$

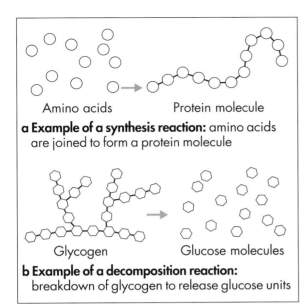

Amino acids   Protein molecule

a Example of a synthesis reaction: amino acids are joined to form a protein molecule

Glycogen   Glucose molecules

b Example of a decomposition reaction: breakdown of glycogen to release glucose units

▲ *Figure 6.4* *Examples of synthesis and decomposition reactions*

Exchange reactions involve both synthesis and decomposition. In an exchange reaction, parts of the reactant molecules change partners to produce a new product:

$$AB + C \rightarrow AC + B \text{ and } AB + CD \rightarrow AD + CB$$

Redox reactions involve oxidation and reduction. They may be viewed as a combination of decomposition and exchange reactions. The reactant losing electrons is referred to as the electron donor and is then **oxidised**. The reactant (called the electron acceptor) is **reduced** as it takes up the transferred electrons. The equation for glucose metabolism is:

$$C_6H_{12}O_6 + 6O_2 \rightarrow 6CO_2 + 6H_2O + ATP$$

glucose   oxygen   carbon   water
                               dioxide

Glucose is oxidised to carbon dioxide as it loses hydrogen atoms, and oxygen is reduced to water as it accepts the hydrogen atoms. Many chemical reactions are reversible when the product of a reaction can revert to the original reactants. The breakdown and reformation of **adenosine triphosphate** (ATP) shows this:

$$ATP \leftrightarrow ADP + P_1 + energy$$

The rate of chemical reactions can be controlled by increasing the temperature or

pressure. Our body needs to maintain a constant temperature so we have catalysts that increase the rate of reactions without becoming chemically changed or part of the product. These catalysts are called **enzymes**.

Compounds

Most of the chemicals in our bodies exist in the form of compounds, which can be divided into two categories:

- **organic** – these always contain carbon such as carbohydrates, lipids and protein
- **inorganic** – these are small and lack carbon and often contain ionic bonds (e.g. salts, many acids and bases and water).

Acids

Acids are substances that release H^+ and a **base** accepts H^+ (a H^+ may also be called a proton). The more hydrogen ions contained in a solution, the more acidic it is. The greater the concentration of hydroxyl ions (OH^-) the more alkaline the solution becomes. The concentration of H^+ is measured in **pH** units. The pH scale runs from 0–14 with 7 being neutral. A solution with a pH below 7 is acidic and above 7 alkaline.

Our body must maintain balanced quantities of acids and bases for normal functioning. If we get a rise or fall in pH then our body uses **buffers** to control the level of H^+. A good example is the carbonic acid (bicarbonate system) that controls the pH of blood.

Response to rise in pH
$$H_2CO_3 \xrightarrow{} HCO_3^- + H^+$$
$$\xleftarrow{}$$
Response to drop in pH

This brief review of the basic chemical terms may help you to understand the biochemistry involved in the energy systems.

2. Energy concepts for exercise physiology

Energy concepts

Energy can be defined as the capacity to perform work. This however ignores the many biological functions that depend on the production and utilisation of energy. All energy on earth comes from the sun. Plants use this light energy to form carbohydrates, fats and proteins. Animals (including humans) eat the plants and other animals and their muscle fibres convert the **chemical energy** from these sources into **kinetic (mechanical) energy** in order to perform movement or for storage as **potential energy**.

Figure 6.5 shows a variety of different forms of energy, and how they relate to each other. An important principle to note is that energy in its various forms is neither created nor destroyed. Instead it is transformed from one type to another. This is the first law of thermodynamics.

Measurement of energy

The measurement of energy expenditure, work and power has many applications in sports science. For example, a coach may need to know the energy requirements of playing a hockey match in order to plan training and dietary programmes for team members.

A fitness consultant who is prescribing a weight loss programme for their client will

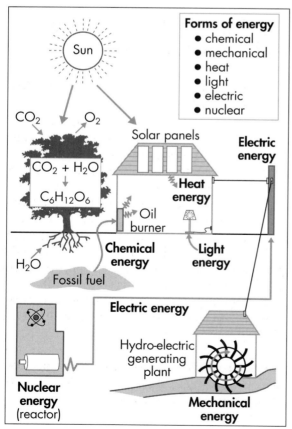

▲ *Figure 6.5* The relationships between different forms of energy

need to know the energy requirements of exercising at particular intensities to ensure success of their exercise regime. Energy requirements for living over a 24-hour period are also useful.

Metabolic rate
The **basal metabolic rate** (**BMR**) is the energy required for essential physiological functioning after 8 hours sleep and 12 hours fasting. The BMR may vary between 1200 and 2400kcal or kilocalories per day. It decreases approximately by 2 per cent and 3 per cent per decade in men and women respectively. Women have a smaller BMR due to their lower fat-free mass. To find total metabolic rate, we must add the energy requirements of physical activity. The average total metabolic rate of an individual engaged in normal daily activities is between 1800 and 3000kcal. An active sportsman/woman who is training hard may require 5000–7000kcal.

Units of measurement
An ongoing problem in sports science is the failure to standardise measurement units. Energy is measured in **calories**: 1000 calories = 1 kilocalorie (kcal) and **joules**: 1000 joules = 1 kilojoule (kJ). Food labels give the energy content in both forms and we can see from Figure 6.6 that 1 cal = 4.184 joules.

A calorie is defined as the amount of heat energy needed to raise the temperature of 1g of water through 1°C.

Work
To measure physical activity we need to calculate work done. **Work** is the product of force multiplied by distance and can be measured in calories or joules. Force (in the case of weight) is calculated by multiplying the mass by acceleration due to gravity (98.1 ms/^{2}). Force is measured in Newtons (N). So if, for

NUTRITIONAL INFORMATION		
TYPICAL VALUES	**Per 100ml**	**Per tablespoon (15ml)**
Energy	1205kJ/288kcal	181kJ/43kcal
Protein	1.7g	0.25g
Carbohydrate	9.0g	1.35g
Fat	27.0g	4.05g

▲ *Figure 6.6* Example of a food label showing kilocalories and kilojoules

example, if you lift a 5kg weight through a vertical distance of 2m, the work performed is calculated as follows:

force × distance

work = 5 kg × 2m
     = 10 kgm

To convert kilograms-metres (kgm) to joules you multiply by 9.81, so 10 kgm in the above example is equal to 98.1 joules.

TASK

Margaria Step Test

This test involves running up a flight of stairs two at a time.

a Measure the distance between the 8th and 12th stair (4th and 6th step) and measure the time it takes between these two points.

b Weigh yourself before the test and use the data collected to work out the power output.

Use the calculations above and below to help you.

Power

Power is the work performed per unit of time and measured in Watts.

$$\text{power} = \frac{\text{work}}{\text{time}} \quad \text{Watts (W)} = \frac{\text{joules}}{\text{seconds}}$$

The concept of power is important since it describes the rate at which work is being performed. The term power often describes the intensity of the exercise. Let us use an example of stepping up and down on a bench at a specified rate. If a 70kg man steps up and down on a 50cm bench for 10 minutes at a rate of 30 steps per minute, then the amount of work performed during this task can be computed as follows:

force = mass × acceleration
       = 70kg × 9.81m
         686.7N
work   = force × distance
         686.7N × 150m
       = 103,005 joules

The power can be calculated as:

$$\frac{103,005 \text{ joules}}{600 \text{ seconds}} = 171.7 \text{ Watts}$$

TASK

The estimated BMR for males is that 1kg of body weight burns 1kcal per hour. For females, the figure is 0.9kcal per hour.

For example:

70kg male = 70kg × 1kcal × 24hrs
          = 1680kcal

Using these estimates, weigh yourself and work out your own BMR.

Oxygen utilisation

All energy-releasing reactions in the body ultimately depend on the utilisation of oxygen. It is estimated that 5kcal of heat energy is produced for every litre of oxygen consumed. So if we can measure a person's oxygen uptake during exercise, it is possible to obtain an indirect estimate of energy expenditure. To do this, you would need a gas analyser to measure oxygen consumption directly. Such equipment may be found in physiology laboratories and high-quality fitness testing centres.

3. Molecular muscle cell structures

Motor units and motor neural firing patterns

The nervous system provides the body with its own internal wiring system through which electrical impulses can be sent and received. For our muscles to contract they must first receive an electrical impulse. The nervous system carrying these impulses is divided into the **central nervous system (CNS)** and **peripheral nervous system (PNS)** (Figure 6.7). The PNS can be further divided into the **sensory** portion, which contains afferent fibres that transmit impulses *to* the CNS; and the **motor** portion, which conducts nerve impulses along efferent fibres *away* from the CNS.

The functional unit of the nervous system is the neurone. The **motor neurone** that conducts impulses towards muscles can be divided into three regions:

- cell body
- dendrites
- axon.

Structure of the motor unit

Figure 6.8 shows the structure of the motor unit. The **cell body** contains the nucleus, which is the centre of operation for the neurone. The **dendrites** conduct electrical impulses towards the cell body. The **axon** (nerve fibre) carries the electrical messages away from the cell body to another neurone or effector organ such as muscle. Axons can vary in length from a few millimetres to a metre. They branch at the end into axon terminals whose tips are dilated into tiny bulbs called synaptic knobs.

The large nerve fibres innervating skeletal muscle are covered with an insulating layer of Schwann cells that contain a fatty substance called myelin. This **myelin sheath** is not continuous but exhibits gaps along the length of the nerve fibre known as **nodes of Ranvier**. These gaps allow rapid conduction of

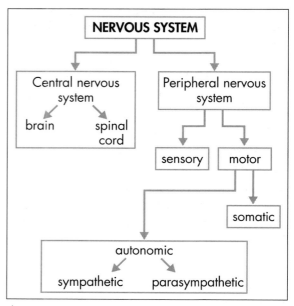

▲ **Figure 6.7** Anatomical divisions of the nervous system

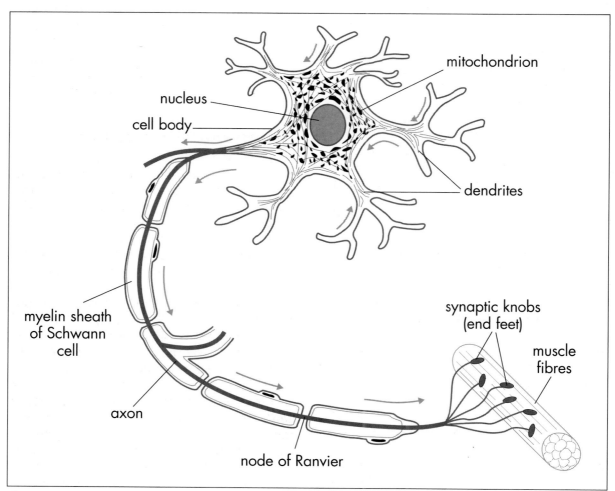

▲ **Figure 6.8** Motor unit = motor neurone plus muscle fibres

impulses along the length of the axon as they jump from one node to the next (saltatory conduction).

The velocity of nerve impulse transmission in large myelinated fibres can approach 120 metres per second (more than 250 miles per hour), 5 to 50 times faster than in unmyelinated fibres.

Propagation of a nerve impulse

Neurones are considered excitable tissue for their ability to conduct an electrical signal. This is initiated via a stimulus that causes a change in the resting electrical charge on each side of the nerve cell membrane.

At rest, neurones, like all cells, have a negative charge on the inside of the cell compared to the outside. This negative charge is known as the resting membrane potential and the neurone is said to be **polarised**. For an impulse to travel along the neurone, this resting potential has to be changed (shown in Figure 6.9).

This change in the resting electrical charge is known as **depolarisation**. It is caused by the stimulus allowing an influx of Na^+ (positively charged sodium ions) into the inside of the neurone, thus reversing the electrical charge so that the inside becomes positively charged compared to the exterior. If this depolarisation, which is measured in millvolts (mV), reaches a threshold (from –70mV to –55–50mV) then an **action potential** is reached and the impulse will travel down the neurone.

The **impulse** will travel the length of the axon without a decrease in voltage. There must therefore be a minimum depolarisation of 15–20mV to initiate the action potential (impulse). If this minimum depolarisation is not reached no impulse will be propagated. This is referred to as the **'all or none' law** and before another impulse (action potential) can be initiated the resting membrane potential must be returned.

This **repolarisation** is accomplished by K^+ (positively charged potassium ions) flowing from the inside to the outside of the cell membrane so that the inside is negatively charged compared to the outside again and another impulse may be propagated.

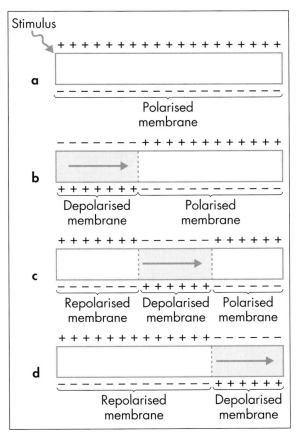

▲ **Figure 6.9** Propagation of a nerve impulse

Neuromuscular junctions

Neurones communicate with other neurones at junctions called **synapses** (sites of impulse transmission). These functions rely on neurotransmitters to carry the impulse across the small gap (20–30 nanometres) so that the propagation can continue. A motor neurone communicates with a muscle fibre at a site known as the **neuromuscular junction** (Figure 6.10).

The neurotransmitter secreted by the synaptic vesicles in the synaptic knob of motor neurones is called **acetylcholine**. This allows depolarisation of the motor end plate portion of the sarcolemma of the muscle cell. The motor neurone and the muscle fibres that it innervates are referred to as a **motor unit**. The amount of fibres that a neurone innervates is related to the muscle's particular movement function. For example, neurones may control fewer than ten muscle fibres of the eye muscles for fine complex movements. A motor neurone may innervate

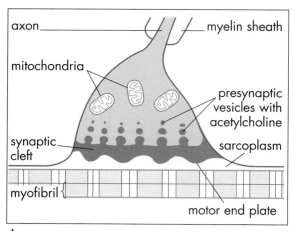

axon
myelin sheath
mitochondria
presynaptic vesicles with acetylcholine
synaptic cleft
sarcoplasm
myofibril
motor end plate

▲ *Figure 6.10* Neuromuscular junction

as many as 3000 fibres of the large muscles involved in gross movements, such as the rectus femoris.

As stated earlier, a stimulus must be strong enough to reach the threshold to initiate an action potential (impulse). This 'all or none' law can be extended to the firing of the muscle fibres in a motor unit. The impulse travels along the motor neurone to the muscle fibres at a constant voltage and thus stimulates a contraction. There is no such thing as a strong or weak contraction from a motor unit. Either the impulse is strong enough to elicit a contraction or it is not. Therefore all the fibres in the motor unit contract or none at all ('all or none').

Controlling strength

This raises the question of how we can control the strength of our contractions and the length of time for which they are held. To do this the body/brain increases the number of motor units being recruited by a particular muscle. If only a few motor units are recruited then the contraction will be weak but if all are activated then a considerable force can be generated. Another way of increasing the force of contraction is to increase the frequency of impulses so that the muscle fibres being activated do not have time to relax.

This wave upon wave of impulses is known as **wave summation**. If all the motor units of a particular muscle are recruited at once then the force of contraction will be great, but only for a short time. To increase the length of time of contraction, the motor units are recruited

in a synchronised way so that a kind of rotation system is evoked to allow certain units to relax when others are contracting. This spacing of the recruitment of motor units is termed **spatial summation**.

Muscle cell (fibre) structure

When we think of muscles, we tend to think of each muscle as a single unit with a particular name. But we have seen that muscle fibres and motor neurones make up motor units, which in turn make up whole muscles. We need to look in more detail at how the muscles are put together.

If you were to dissect a whole muscle (Figure 6.11) you would first cut through a layer of connective tissue encapsulating the whole muscle. This is called the **epimysium**. With a cross-section of the muscle you can see bundles of fibres referred to as **fasciculi** surrounded by a further layer of connective tissue called the **perimysium**.

With the use of a microscopic enlargement we can see that each fibre in a particular fasciculus is surrounded by its own sheath called the **endomysium**. This acts as insulation for each muscle fibre. This is also shown in Figure 6.11.

Muscle fibres range from 10–80 micrometres in diameter but may be more than 35cm long. There are many structures that are common to all cells that are also found in the muscle cell as well as some that are unique. The cell membrane surrounding the muscle fibre is called the **sarcolemma**. Beneath the sarcolemma is the muscle cell cytoplasm called the **sarcoplasm**.

The sarcoplasm contains glycogen, fats and important organelles called the **mitochondria**. This is the powerhouse of the cell. Their function will be discussed in more detail in Energy systems and the energy continuum on pages 379–91.

The muscle cell also has its own network of tubules and membranous channels that crisscross throughout the cell much like the underground system of a major city. The membranous channels are called the **sarcoplasmic recticulum** and are an important site for storing calcium ions involved in muscular contraction. The **transverse tubules** extend inwards from the sarcolemma through the muscle cell. They allow the impulses received by the

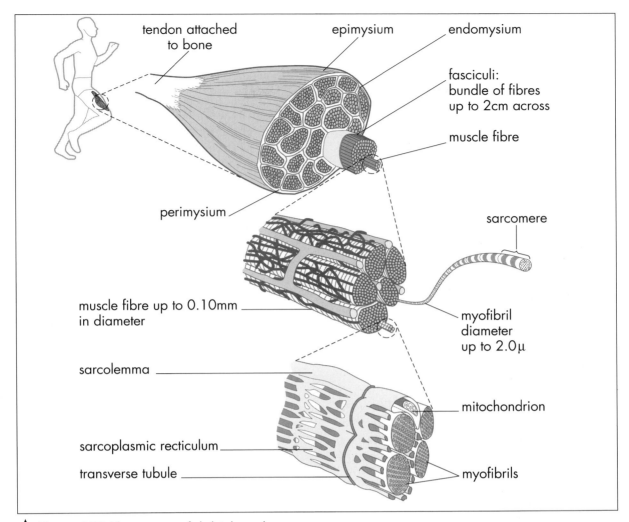

▲ **Figure 6.11** *The structure of skeletal muscle*

muscle cell sarcolemma (motor end plate) to be transmitted rapidly to individual **myofibrils**.

Each muscle fibre contains several hundred to several thousand myofibrils. These myofibrils are rod-like structures that run the entire length of the muscle fibre. Myofibrils contain the contractile proteins involved in muscle contraction: **myosin**, **actin**, **troponin**, **tropomyosin**.

The myofibrils can be further divided into distinct segments called **sarcomeres**, which are separated by sheets of protein called the Z-line. The sarcomere is the functional unit of the muscle cell and it is this segment that we will look at in detail to understand how our muscles contract.

Figure 6.12 shows that under a microscope skeletal muscle is striped or striated. This is due to the myosin (thick protein filaments)

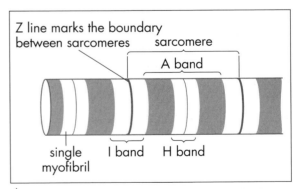

▲ **Figure 6.12** *Microscopic view of a myofibril*

and actin (thin protein filaments) overlapping and giving distinct bands. The lighter area is known as the I band (only actin filaments are seen) and the A band is dark where both myosin and actin overlap.

The Z-line bisects the I band and attaches to the sarcolemma to give the structure stability. The H band is in the middle of the A band and is the section where you only see myosin filaments. The sliding of actin over myosin and the consequent reduction of the distance between Z-lines is thought to be the way in which muscles shorten and hold tension.

Sliding filament theory

Muscular contraction is a complex process but it can be broken down step by step (Figure 6.13).

Stage 1

An impulse arrives at the neuromuscular junction and causes the release of acetylcholine. This causes depolarisation of the motor end plate on the sarcolemma of the muscle cell. This depolarisation is transmitted down the transverse tubules into the muscle fibres causing calcium ions (Ca^+) to be released from the sarcoplasmic recticulum.

Stage II

The Ca^+ bind to the troponin-tropomyosin complex, which surrounds the active sites on the actin filament. This reveals the active binding sites and enables the myosin heads to attach to the actin to form a **cross bridge**.

Stage III

The myosin cross bridge is then energised by the breakdown of adenosine triphosphate (ATP). The enzyme **ATPase** catalyses the breakdown of ATP. The energy given to the myosin enables it to pull the actin inwards and thus shorten the muscle. This happens to every single sarcomere along the myofibril and in all the myofibrils of the muscle cell that is being innervated. The pulling of the actin by the myosin is known as the **power stroke**.

Stage IV

Myosin detaches from the actin when an ATP molecule binds to its head. Then ATP is broken down again and Stage III can be repeated. The contraction cycle can be repeated as long as Ca^+ are available.

Stage V

When the impulse stops, the contraction cycle is broken, the Ca^+ are pumped back into the sarcoplasmic recticulum, the actin moves back out and the muscle returns to its relaxed length.

This five-stage model enables us to see the step-by-step activities of muscle contraction. It

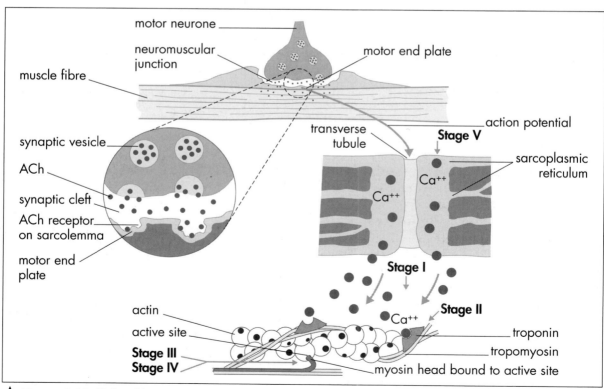

▲ **Figure 6.13** Sliding filament theory

must be noted that a single power stroke of all the cross bridges in a muscle results in a shortening of only about 1 per cent. Since contracting muscles may shorten up to 35 per cent of their resting length then each myosin cross bridge must attach and detach many times during a single contraction. It is thought that only half of the myosin heads are actively exerting a force at the same time whilst the rest are seeking their next binding site. This alternate use of the myosin cross bridge is referred to as the **ratchet mechanism**.

As we have seen, ATP is essential for muscle contraction. We now need to look at ATP, its role in energy production and how we may resynthesise this essential molecule.

TASK

In a group devise your own role-play to mimic propogation of a nerve impulse and sliding filament theory. You will need to make posters of the major components of the muscle cell.

Divide the process into the five stages outlined in the text and get people to play the roles of ATP, actin, myosin, sarcoplasmic recticulum, energy, Na^+, K^+ and decide how you are going to represent Ca^+ and H^+.

Use the text to put together a list of all the substances involved and identify the part they play in each stage of the process.

4. Energy systems and the energy continuum

ATP in energy production

The foods that we eat are primarily composed of carbon, hydrogen, oxygen and in the case of protein, nitrogen. The bonds in these foods are relatively weak and thus give little energy when broken. Therefore food is not used directly for providing energy. The energy stored in the food molecule bonds are chemically released and then stored in the form of a high energy molecule called adenosine triphosphate (ATP).

When energy is required to perform exercise, it is supplied from the breakdown of ATP

to adenosine diphosphate (ADP) and a free phosphate. This is the only substance the body can use and is often referred to as our 'energy currency' as it powers all forms of biological reactions.

$$ATP \xrightarrow{\text{ATPase}} ADP + P_1 + energy$$

The enzyme ATPase catalyses ATP breakdown. This stimulates the release of the high energy phosphate bond making energy available to do work (Figure 6.14).

This breakdown of ATP releases energy and is said to be an exothermic reaction. The body only has a limited store of about 85g ATP and would use this up very quickly if it did not have ways of resynthesising (remaking) it. This requires an endothermic reaction, one that needs energy to remake ATP.

$$energy + ADP + P_1 \rightarrow ATP$$

Many of the chemical reactions occurring in the body are linked, with those energy-*generating* reactions being coupled with energy-*requiring* reactions. These are referred to as 'coupled reactions'.

The resynthesis of ATP is achieved through the energy systems.

Energy systems

There are three systems that produce energy to resynthesise ATP:

- ATP–PC
- lactic acid
- aerobic.

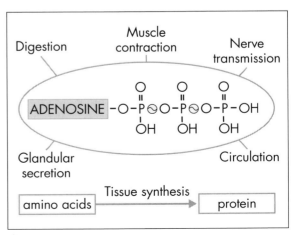

▲ *Figure 6.14* Universal energy currency

They all operate at the same time but the duration and intensity of exercise will determine which system predominantly provides the energy.

ATP–PC (phosphocreatine) system/alatic anaerobic system

Phosphocreatine (**PC**) is another high-energy bonded molecule found in the muscle sarcoplasm. The splitting of the bond between the phosphate and creatine caused by the breakdown of ATP liberates a large amount of energy to resynthesise some of it (Figure 6.15).

This breakdown of PC is catalysed by the enzyme **creatine kinase**, which responds to rising levels of ADP. We have about 120g of creatine in our body, 95 per cent of which is found in muscle. PC gives an immediate source of energy to resynthesise ATP at a high rate. The system lasts for 8–10 seconds before the PC is depleted. Try timing yourself over 100m with stop-watches placed at 10-metre intervals. You will find that you slow down after about 50 metres as you begin to run short of phosphocreatine. If you have to sprint flat out in a game of football, it is the PC that will provide the source of energy.

This system does not require oxygen and is thus anaerobic. Longer periods of exercise require you to lower the intensity and obtain your energy to resynthesise ATP from another source.

Lactic acid system/anaerobic glycolysis

The second metabolic pathway capable of releasing energy to resynthesise ATP without the involvement of O_2 is called **anaerobic glycolysis**. This involves a series of ten chemical reactions that break down carbohydrates in the form of glucose or **glycogen** to **pyruvic acid** or lactic acid. These chemical reactions release enough energy to resynthesise two ATP molecules. Glycogen is the synthesised form of glucose (glucose molecules joined together) and is an efficient way of storing our carbohydrate in our muscle and liver.

The chemical reactions referred to as glycolysis are regulated by various enzymes and take place in the muscle sarcoplasm (Figure 6.16). The most important of these is **phosphofructokinase** (**PFK**).

Glycolysis results in pyruvic acid being formed from glucose or glycogen. Hydrogens are a by-product of glycolysis and need to be removed. This is because a build-up of hydrogen ions (H^+) will make the muscle cell acidic and interfere with its functioning. Carrier molecules called **nicotinamide adenine dinucleotide** (**NAD$^+$**) remove the H^+. The NAD^+ are reduced to NADH and deposit the hydrogens at the **electron transport chain** (**ETC**) to be combined with oxygen.

If there is not sufficient oxygen then the NADH cannot offload the H^+ and they begin to build up in the cell. To prevent this rise in acidity, pyruvic acid accepts H^+ and this process forms **lactic acid**. Researchers have recently advanced other factors contributing to lactic acid formation and many believe that adrenaline rising during intense exercise will increase the rate of glycolysis. In this way H^+

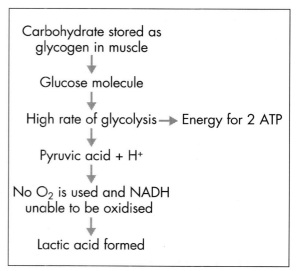

Carbohydrate stored as glycogen in muscle
↓
Glucose molecule
↓
High rate of glycolysis → Energy for 2 ATP
↓
Pyruvic acid + H$^+$
↓
No O_2 is used and NADH unable to be oxidised
↓
Lactic acid formed

▲ **Figure 6.16** Lactic acid system/anaerobic glycosis

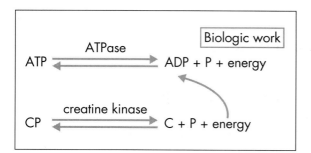

ATPase
ATP ⇄ ADP + P + energy |Biologic work|

creatine kinase
CP ⇄ C + P + energy

▲ **Figure 6.15** Energy from phosphocreatine breakdown

will increase and lactic acid will form. However, all agree that the NADH must be oxidised to NAD to stop intracellular H^+ increasing and the acidity rising in the muscle cell.

Once lactic acid is formed it dissociates into lactate and H^+. Some of the lactate diffuses into the blood and takes the H^+ with it as a mechanism for reducing the H^+ concentration in the muscle cell. We measure the lactate in blood to assess the rate of production within the muscle cell. The normal pH of the muscle cell is 7.1 but this may fall to 6.5 as H^+ increase. At 6.5 enzymes such as PFK are inhibited.

The increase in H^+ is thought to interfere with the binding of Ca^+ to the troponin-tropomyosin complex so muscle contraction is affected. The low pH also stimulates free nerve endings in the muscle, resulting in the perception of pain. You can relate these feelings to running a 400-m race. You will 'feel the burn' at about 300m and begin to 'tie up' in the last 80–50m as muscle contraction is affected and enzyme action is inhibited. Judging your pace/intensity is the key to success and stopping the build-up of lactate and H^+.

Aerobic system

The **aerobic system** provides the largest amount of energy for resynthesising ATP but at the lowest intensity. It is called aerobic because oxygen is an integral part, breaking foods down to CO_2 and H_2O. At the onset of exercise the body struggles to deliver O_2 quickly enough to muscles and the complex reactions involved in the aerobic system take a couple of minutes to activate. We therefore rely on anaerobic systems to supply energy in the first few minutes of exercise. The aerobic system may be broken down into three phases as illustrated in Figure 6.17. These are:

- glycolysis
- **Kreb's cycle**
- electron transport chain.

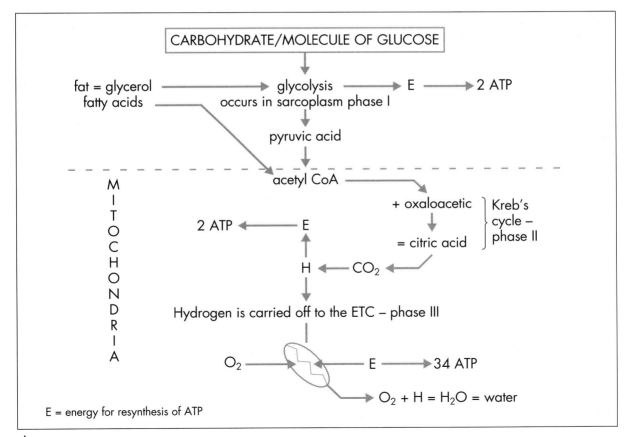

▲ **Figure 6.17** Aerobic system

TASK

a Use the information on calculating the amount of work completed to measure energy output on stepping up and down on a bench.

You will need to weigh yourself, measure the height of the bench and use a metronome to set the stepping rate per minute. Try different times (5, 10, 15 minutes) and stepping rates (30, 40, 50 steps per minute). Note down how your body feels at the different intensities. You should be able to use your knowledge on energy systems, recovery and fatigue to give physiological reasons for your responses.

b Run a 400m-race and describe the energy systems that you use. Explain why you slow down near the end of the race.

Phase I – glycolysis

Glycolysis occurs in exactly the same way as it does in the lactic acid system (see page 380), breaking down our carbohydrate (glucose or glycogen). The only difference is that the NAD^+ carrier molecules can cope with the hydrogens being produced and thus there is no need for the pyruvic acid to help buffer the H^+ and form lactic acid.

As previously mentioned, this all occurs in the muscle sarcoplasm. Enough energy is released to resynthesise two ATP molecules.

As the rate of glycolysis does not produce too many hydrogens, the pyruvic acid is able to continue to be broken down in the mitochondria. The hydrogens are carried to the electron transport chain in the mitochondria to combine with oxygen to form H_2O.

Phase II – Kreb's cycle

As pyruvic acid enters the mitochondria it is converted to **acetyl coenzyme A,** a two carbon compound. Once formed acetyl CoA enters Kreb's cycle (also known as the citric acid cycle) and combined with oxaloacetic acid (a four carbon compound) to form the six carbon compound, citric acid (hence the alternative name of the cycle). Citric acid undergoes a series of chemical reactions that produce enough energy to resynthesise two ATP.

The by-products of these chemical reactions are CO_2 (which is transported to and exhaled by the lungs), and hydrogens. Again, the carrier molecule NAD^+ and another carrier, **flavin adenine dinucleotide (FAD)**, transport the hydrogens to the electron transport chain.

The main functions of Kreb's cycle are removing the hydrogens (reducing NAD^+ and FAD to NADH and $FADH_2$) and forming two ATP. The cyclical nature of the process is shown by the fact that **oxaloacetic acid** is the end product and it is ready again to combine with acetyl CoA to start the whole process again.

Phase III – electron transport chain

The hydrogens carried as NADH and $FADH_2$ are transported to the inner membranes in the mitochondria (Figure 6.18).

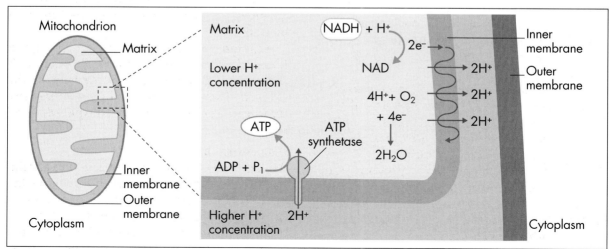

▲ **Figure 6.18** Electron transport chain in the mitochondria

Here the NADH and $FADH_2$ are oxidised and the hydrogens split into electrons and protons. (Hydrogen has one electron and one proton.)

The electrons are passed through a series of reduction and oxidation (redox) reactions (see page 370), which release energy to resynthesise ATP. These redox reactions cause the protons (H^+) to be pumped across the inner membrane into the space between the inner and outer membrane of the mitochondria. This creates an imbalance with excess H^+ in this outer chamber compared with the inside of the mitochondrial matrix.

The accumulation of H^+ is a potential source of energy. As it diffuses back across the inner membrane energy is produced to resynthesise ATP. The final reaction is hydrogen combining with oxygen to form water (H_2O). All these reactions produce enough energy to resynthesise 34 ATP.

The total energy yielded from one molecule of glucose resynthesises 38 ATP molecules. As long as the intensity of exercise is low, the aerobic systems can work for several hours.

We have only considered carbohydrate as a food fuel source but there is a limited amount stored in our body. An average 70kg man may have 400g of carbohydrate stored, yielding approximately 7040kJ (1676kcal) of energy. The energy cost of running a marathon is 12,000kJ so an alternative energy source must be used. This is fat.

Fat/lipid metabolism

We store 95 per cent of our fat as **triglyceride** in our adipose tissue. We also store small amounts in our muscle and liver. When required as an energy source the triglyceride is broken down into glycerol and **free fatty acids** (**FFA**) by the process lipolysis. This is catalysed by the enzyme lipase.

These substances are then released into circulation and it is the FFA that can be utilised by skeletal muscle. When entering the muscle, the process of **beta oxidation** breaks down the FFA molecules into acetyl CoA, which can then progress through Kreb's cycle and the electron transport chain (see Figure 6.17). The FFA molecules are made up of a chain of carbon atoms that can be broken down into the two carbon acetyl CoA.

Let us look at the rather abundant palmitic acid, a 16-carbon FFA. This can make eight molecules of acetyl CoA and thus has the ability to provide us with lots of energy for resynthesising ATP. If the 70kg man in the previous example had a body composition of 15 per cent fat then he would have 10.5kg of fat. This would provide him with 388,500kJ of energy (enough energy for about 30 marathons). It is obvious that he cannot run 30 marathons back to back so what is restricting the use of fat?

It is essential that oxaloacetic acid is present in Kreb's cycle for acetyl CoA to combine with. Oxaloacetic acid comes from carbohydrate breakdown and so if we run short of glycogen or glucose then it affects our ability to oxidise fat as a fuel. It is often said that 'fat burns in a carbohydrate flame'.

Protein metabolism

Only in situations of extreme exhaustion, sustained prolonged exercise or starvation does the body metabolise protein as an energy source. It is this basic unit, the amino acid, which is converted to acetyl CoA. Protein can provide 5–10 per cent of energy requirements during prolonged exercise and may be relied on more as glycogen stores are depleted.

Mode of energy regeneration

Although we have looked at the three energy systems as distinct entities here, this is not the case. Providing energy for the resynthesis of ATP involves all the systems operating *at once*. At rest we still need energy to function and this is provided mostly by our aerobic system. When we begin to exercise, the demands for energy increase – by as much as 120 times in all-out sprinting.

Anaerobic sources can supply energy at four times the rate of aerobic sources. It is therefore the duration and intensity of the exercise that governs which of the energy systems can resynthesise ATP at the required rate.

Continuum

We may view the energy systems as a continuum, with exercise at high intensity lasting 8–10 seconds requiring the PC system to provide a majority of the energy. As duration increases intensity of supply decreases and we use the lactic acid system. The point at which lactic acid builds up so it interferes with muscle functioning occurs between 30 seconds and 3 minutes depending on the intensity of exercise and fitness of the athlete.

This point has demanded a lot of attention by researchers and is often measured as the lactic acid or anaerobic threshold, or **onset of blood lactate accumulation (OBLA)**. It appears in untrained subjects between 50% and 60% of VO_2 max and trained athletes at 65% and 80% of VO_2 max.

The 400-metre race is a classic example of deriving energy from the lactic acid system. Table 6.1 illustrates the estimated energy contribution from anaerobic and aerobic sources in athletic events using world records (as from 1 January 2000) as a guide to duration.

Table 6.1 shows that as duration of exercise exceeds three minutes, a majority of energy comes from the aerobic system. We know that we use both carbohydrate and fat as a food fuel during aerobic exercise but the relative contribution of both during exercise is important, especially if we are giving someone a weight-reduction programme.

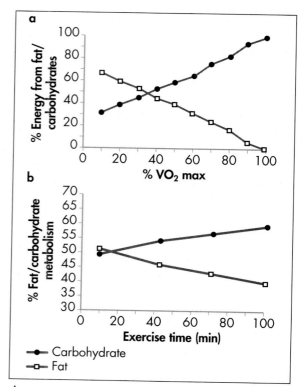

▲ **Figure 6.19** Intensity and duration of exercise and fuel source

Table 6.1 Approximate contribution of anaerobic and aerobic energy sources to total energy production in different athletic events

Distance	Time (h:m:s)	% Anaerobic	% Aerobic
100m	9.79	90	10
400m	43.18	70	30
800m	1:41.11	40	60
1500m	3:26.0	20	80
5000m	12:39.36	5	95
10000m	26:22.75	3	97
42.2km	2:05:42	1	99

Duration and intensity of exercise

Duration and intensity of exercise play a major role in the type of food substance that we use. Figure 6.19 shows that fats are the primary food source during low intensity (less than 30% in VO_2 max) and contribute a majority of the energy in exercise lasting longer than 40 minutes. This is due to the fact that at high intensity workloads lactate is produced which inhibits fat metabolism and fast-twitch muscle fibres are recruited which contain few mitochondrial and lipolytic enzymes (enzymes responsible for fat breakdown).

As duration increases and intensity is lowered the lipases become more active as levels of adrenaline, nor-adrenaline and glucagon rise.

Slow-twitch fibres are also recruited which will metabolise fat. Lipolysis is a slow process and an increase in fat metabolism occurs only after several minutes of exercise. Studies have shown that fat metabolism can only supply ATP at a rate sufficient to maintain exercise at an intensity of 60% VO_2 max. Higher intensities will require carbohydrate to be utilised. From these findings we now recommend exercise at intensities of 50–60% VO_2 max (66%–74% maximum heart rate) for at least 20 minutes, three times a week for cardiovascular improvements in health and loss of weight (as long as you do not take in more kilocalories than you expend).

Fatigue

Fatigue can be defined as an inability to maintain power output during repeated muscle contractions. Decrements in muscle performance are usually associated with feelings of tiredness. It is obvious that the feelings of fatigue associated with a 400-metre race differ from those of a marathon. We also feel tired at the end of the day but this has little to do with lack of ATP. The causes of fatigue vary and are associated with the duration and intensity of exercise.

There may have been times when you have felt that you cannot go on any longer in a race or a sprint in a game, but with a coach/teacher/parent giving verbal encouragement you have managed to find that little bit extra in reserve. This situation has been tested in the laboratory and researchers have concluded that the central nervous system (CNS) may play a role in **central fatigue**. They say that individuals may have a psychological limit and have shown reduction in fatigue when the CNS has been stimulated. This stimulation and increase in motivation is said to recruit more motor units and thus delay fatigue.

Peripheral fatigue

Much of the research has concentrated on **peripheral fatigue**. Depletion in sources of energy and inhibition of muscle contraction, due to metabolites, has been shown to cause peripheral fatigue.

'I had no energy; I felt drained' is a common complaint of fatigued sportsmen and women so it is obvious that the study of energy systems is important. Fatigue may be viewed as a simple imbalance between ATP requirements of a muscle and its ability to resynthesise ATP. Immediate demand for energy in maximal events lasting 8–10 seconds comes from phosphocreatine breakdown. This depletion of PC reduces the intensity of ATP resynthesis and thus the muscle reduces the power output (see page 380). This is shown by the fact that athletes slow down after 50–60 metres of a 100-metre race. It has also been shown that rises in P_1 following PC and ATP breakdown interferes with the cross bridge formation in muscle cells. The athlete at the end of 100 metres also starts to build up lactic acid (Figure 6.20).

Activities lasting longer than ten seconds but still requiring an intense supply of energy rely on anaerobic glycolysis to resynthesise ATP. As indicated on pages 380–81, lactic acid dissociates into lactate and H^+ and it is the latter that causes an increase in acidity in the cell. The build-up of H^+ is thought to interfere with Ca^+ binding to the troponin-tropomyosin and thus preventing cross bridge formation in muscle. This results in reduced power. This increase in

▲ **Figure 6.20** *Lactic acid accumulates – even after short duration events*

acidity also interferes with the action of enzymes. PFK (see page 380) is particularly affected, which slows down glycolysis and therefore reduces ATP resynthesis resulting in fatigue. A pH of 6.4 stops glycogen breakdown altogether and thus ATP is soon depleted which leads to exhaustion. The decrease in pH also affects the free nerve endings and so there is a sensation of pain (the burning sensation).

TASK

Use a grip dynamometer to find out the maximum grip strength of a group of students. Divide the subjects into three groups and follow three separate protocols:

Group 1 – perform a maximum grip every 10 seconds for 5 minutes.

Group 2 – perform a maximum grip every 30 seconds for 5 minutes.

Group 3 – perform a maximum grip every 60 seconds for 5 minutes.

Each grip should last about 2 seconds.

Record all your data and present it on a graph. Average out the group scores and present your own individual results.

You can work out the fatigue index as a percentage: final grip mark divided by maximum grip and multiplied by 100. For example:

20kg = final grip   50kg = max grip
20/50 × 100 = 40% fatigue index

Explain the processes causing fatigue in each group.

The limited carbohydrate stores (glycogen and glucose) are used in both anaerobic and aerobic energy systems. Again, duration and intensity of exercise will determine the balance between the two sources used. Blood glucose plays a major role in exercise of low intensity and long duration whereas glycogen is predominantly the source at high intensities. This is because of the recruitment of fast-twitch muscle fibres. During the first hour of exercise most of the carbohydrate metabolised is in the form of glycogen.

When levels of glycogen decrease then blood glucose becomes increasingly important. Glycogen levels dropping over time will lead to fatigue. The liver will break down its glycogen to form glucose to keep blood glucose levels up.

However, if the uptake of glucose by muscles exceeds the output of the liver, blood glucose levels will drop (hypoglycemia), the muscles will soon deplete their glycogen reserves and exhaustion will occur. This may be one of the reasons for 'hitting the wall' in a marathon (Figure 6.21).

▲ **Figure 6.21** *Energy depletion is often evident during events of long duration such as a marathon*

With diminishing glycogen stores, fat is increasingly used as a fuel source. It is important to remember that although we have large reserves of fat, the intermediates of Kreb's cycle (for example, oxaloacetic acid) must also be available to combine with the acetyl CoA. Many of these intermediates are derived from carbohydrate so when glycogen stores are depleted, fat metabolism is also inhibited, causing fatigue.

Fluid loss/dehydration

Adequate **hydration** is essential when avoiding fatigue. Sixty per cent of a typical young male and fifty per cent of a young female body is made up of water. It is essential for carrying red blood cells in plasma, transporting nutrients and waste products, maintenance of blood pressure and controlling body temperature.

During exercise, water is primarily lost in the form of sweat. Although aerobic energy production results in the formation of water, sweating during an hour of exercise can result in losing ten times the amount that is produced.

It is estimated that distance runners will be forced to slow their pace by 2 per cent for every 1 per cent of body weight lost through dehydration. If the loss reaches 4–5 per cent of body weight then capacity for prolonged aerobic effort is reduced by 20–30 per cent. A reduction in plasma volume and thus a reduction in blood flow to the muscles and skin causes fatigue. Heart rate and body temperature rise and heat cramps, heat exhaustion and ultimately heat stroke may occur if fluid is not taken in. A marathon runner may reduce hydration levels by 6–10 per cent in a race despite efforts to take in fluid (Figure 6.22).

In addition to water, electrolytes such as sodium, chloride, potassium, magnesium and calcium are also lost in sweat. These electrolytes are needed for normal functioning of nerve tissue, enzyme and hormone action. Reductions in the levels of these will obviously cause fatigue.

Recovery process

Oxygen debt

You now realise, upon finishing a short sprint, that you obtained your energy for this activity from anaerobic sources. Why then should you be breathing so heavily? Your

▲ *Figure 6.22* Fluid intake is crucial in avoiding fatigue

body must be demanding oxygen. Historically, the term **oxygen debt** was used to refer to this excess oxygen uptake above rest after exercise. In 1922, the British physiologist A. V. Hill first used the term oxygen deficit and he proposed that it was repayment for the **oxygen deficit** incurred at the start of exercise (Figure 6.23).

This **oxygen deficit** is defined as the difference between oxygen consumed during exercise and the amount that would have been consumed had aerobic metabolism been reached immediately. In the 1930s, researchers in the United States divided the oxygen debt into a fast component and a slow component. The reasons for this were that the *rapid component* represented the oxygen required to replenish ATP and PC stores, whilst the *slow component* was the oxygen required to convert lactic acid to glucose in the liver.

At the time it was thought that by looking at O_2 debt, they could estimate the amount of anaerobic activity taking place. Recent research has shown that this is an over-simplification and that **excess post-exercise oxygen consumption** (EPOC), which is a replacement term for O_2 debt, is used for several additional functions during recovery (Figure 6.24).

Breathing and heart rates are elevated after exercise to help remove CO_2 and will require energy from aerobic metabolism (oxygen). Elevated body temperature increases metabolic rate and breathing rates, which will require excess oxygen. Also, after intense exercise, levels of the hormones adrenaline and nor-adrenaline are elevated which result in increased oxygen consumption. All these factors contribute to EPOC.

It is vitally important that a coach/athlete should know how long it takes to recover after different types of exercise. With this information, they can plan duration of rest intervals during training. ATP and PC stores

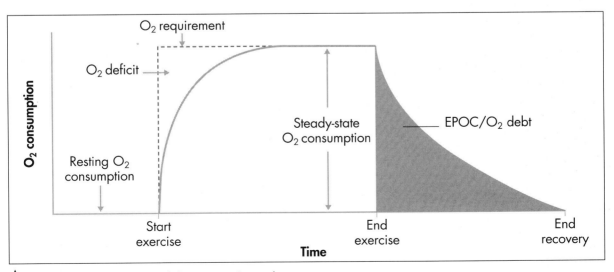

▲ *Figure 6.23* Oxygen need during exercise and recovery

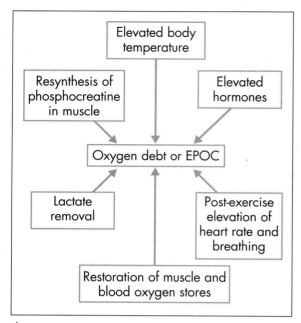

▲ Figure 6.24 Factors that contribute to EPOC

are replenished quickly in line with the classical view of the fast component.

- 50 per cent of PC is restored within 30 seconds of recovery
- 75 per cent restoration takes about 60 seconds
- full replenishment three minutes
- within these first few minutes haemoglobin and myoglobin stores of oxygen are also restored.

We have already seen how lactic acid contributes to fatigue. The body makes several attempts to stop the build up of H^+ by combining with NAD^+. To stop the rise in acidity, the body also has buffers that accept H^+. These buffers include proteins, haemoglobin, bicarbonate and phosphocreatine. We know that a dramatic fall in pH can result in cell damage and even cell death so maintaining the acid-base balance is essential. If exercise intensity is too great and the NADH cannot be reduced and the buffers cannot cope with the amount of H^+, acidity rises and fatigue sets in.

Lactic acid and recovery

It is essential to remove lactic acid but we must not view it as a waste product. Research has shown that the majority of lactic acid is oxidised during recovery. This means that lac-

tic acid is converted back to pyruvic acid and used as an energy substrate by the heart and other muscle tissue. Investigations have shown that the heart can derive almost 50 per cent of its energy from lactic acid during prolonged intense exercise.

This shows that the recovery process is complicated and may be occurring as we exercise. Although this is a difficult concept to grasp, lactic acid build-up may be seen as a balance between production and removal.
It is estimated that:

- 70 per cent of lactic acid produced during exercise is oxidised
- 20 per cent is converted to glucose through the Cori cycle in the liver
- 10 per cent is converted to protein.

It takes about an hour to remove lactic acid from our system when cooling down with gentle exercise. It is estimated that 50 per cent is removed in the first 15 minutes. This time can be doubled if no exercise is taken and highlights the importance of gentle physical activity in the cooling-down process.

Glycogen and recovery

Glycogen stores can be depleted after a heavy training session. However, an adequate high carbohydrate meal (preferably within one hour of exercise) will replenish them. Problems may arise when strenuous exercise of a long duration is repeated on successive days. A state of fatigue known as 'staleness' may set in due to a reduction in glycogen stores (Figure 6.25).

An experiment showed running 10 miles (16.1km) a day on three successive days nearly depleted glycogen stores in the thigh muscles. This was conducted on a diet of 45 per cent carbohydrate. When this diet was increased to 70 per cent CHO, no glycogen depletion occurred. It may take at least 24 hours to restore muscle glycogen levels after prolonged exhaustive exercise such as a marathon. This highlights the need for adequate nutrition and hydration, before, during and after exercise.

Nutrition

High performance in physical activity is achieved by a careful dietary balance of essential nutrients. These include carbohydrates,

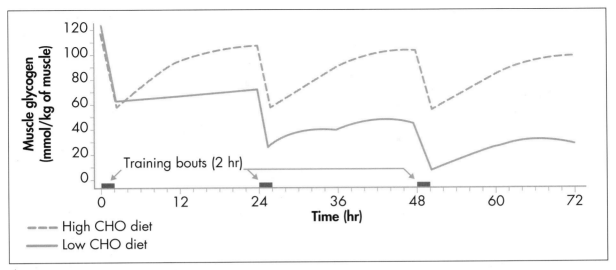

▲ **Figure 6.25** *Glycogen depletion*

fat, protein, vitamins, minerals and water – the six nutrient classes. The nutritional advice for good health is to have a diet consisting of:

- 60 per cent carbohydrate
- 30 per cent fat
- 10 per cent protein.

Carbohydrates

Sportsmen and women may need a higher percentage of carbohydrates (not sugar) to optimise performance (Figure 6.26). Traditionally, it was thought that if you cut back carbohydrate intake a week before a competition and trained hard, then loaded your diet with CHO for three days before competing, you could increase your glycogen stores. This **carbo-loading** had the desired effect, though athletes found that training and sleep patterns suffered and they felt very tired.

Currently, the view on carbo-loading is that athletes are advised to eat a diet high in CHO – nearer 70 per cent. Sportsmen and women whose diets consist of 7–10 grams of carbohydrate per kilogram of body weight (7–10g/kg) have been shown to increase glycogen stores and delay fatigue in endurance events.

Those athletes taking part in prolonged events can also benefit from ingesting a solution containing 4–8 per cent carbohydrate. It has been shown that an athlete can lose between one and two litres of fluid per hour from sweating when exercising hard in a hot environment. Hydration is essential (see page 386) and, in exercise lasting longer than

▲ **Figure 6.26** *Sources of carbohydrate*

an hour, 600–1200ml of fluid (containing 4–8 per cent CHO) should be consumed. Thirst is a poor indicator of dehydration and athletes should be encouraged to drink little and often. An easy way to measure fluid loss is to weigh a subject before and after exercise. 500g lost in weight means 500ml of water lost and in need of replenishing.

Protein

The **reference nutrient intake (RDI)** for protein in the diet is 0.8g/kg/day. Athletes who take part in heavy endurance exercise may require 1.2–1.4 g/kg/day. Those involved in strength training and looking to increase muscle mass may need between 1.2–1.7 g/kg/day. Is it necessary then to take

▲ *Figure 6.27* *Visible animal fat is saturated fat*

protein supplements? It appears not, in that most western diets average 1.5g/kg/day (88 per cent more than the RNI). There may be some dangers associated with taking in too much protein as the kidneys are put under pressure to excrete the excess.

Fat

As with protein, the average western diet contains too much fat (Figure 6.27). We know that this can lead to cardiovascular diseases. However, some fat is essential as it functions as our main energy source while at rest. Fat also supports vital organs and insulates the body. It is an essential component of cell membranes and steroid hormones in the body are produced from cholesterol. Therefore we need fat to contribute 30 per cent of our diet with less than 10 per cent saturated (e.g. visible animal fat).

Vitamins and minerals

Vitamin supplementation is unnecessary for the athlete on a balanced diet. Mineral supplementation may be needed if the athletes have a poor diet. Iron deficiency and associated anaemia (reduced haemoglobin levels) are a problem for athletes who are not taking in the required amount of iron. This should be 10mg/day for an adult male and 15mg/day for a female. The major source of iron deficiency is an inadequate diet. Also athletes destroy more red blood cells when exercising and women lose blood at menstruation. To correct this, athletes should be encouraged to eat fish, meats and fresh green vegetables. Some athletes with low calorific intake may require iron supplementation.

Salt (NaCl) intake is too high in many western diets and is associated with hypertension. Although athletes can lose NaCl through sweating, the average intake of salt of 12.5g/day will usually cover this loss. Only in events lasting more than three hours should salt be added to drink (0.5–0.7g/litre of fluid). This helps palatability, replacement of electrolytes and promotes fluid and CHO absorption.

TASK

Food diary

To do this, you must note down and weigh everything you eat and drink for either one day, three days or a week, depending on how detailed your analysis is to be. Most food packets will give you nutritional information. You may also need to calculate values for food which does not have packaging with dietary information. A book from the library on nutrition may be helpful.

In terms of feasibility, it may be easier to give a different person the task for each day of a week. Some accuracy will be lost here but it will be interesting to arrive at a 'notional group figure'.

Record the total amounts of fat, CHO and protein each person takes in and see how close your group comes to the recommended intake of 60 per cent CHO, 30 per cent fat and 10 per cent protein. Note that:

- 1g CHO = 4kcal
- 1g fat = 9kcal
- 1g protein = 4kcal.

Estimate the total energy intake and calculate an average daily figure.

Ergogenic aids

When world records and gold medals can be won or lost within a fraction of a second, it's no wonder that all types of sportsmen and women are looking for that special something to give them the edge over their competitors.

Many turn to **ergogenic aids**, which are work-producing substances, or phenomena, believed to increase performance. The variety of ergogenic aids is immense and includes nutrients, drugs, hypnosis, blood doping, oxygen breathing, warm-up, music and bio-mechanical aids. It is impossible to cover all these in this limited space and only those of recent interest, highlighting the dangers of many pharmacological agents, will be dealt with here.

A well-known ergogenic aid is the warm-up, used to increase blood supply to the muscles and raise the body temperature. Some athletes use nutritional practices such as carbo-loading (see page 389). Another popular supplement that is readily available is creatine (an amino acid). Sportsmen and women ingest extra creatine in the hope that they will increase their PC stores. They also hope that they can last longer in events requiring all out effort.

Research shows 4 × 5g doses of creatine per day for five days increases muscle PC stores, particularly in athletes whose PC levels are low. Higher work output during repeated bouts of high intensity exercise has also been recorded, as well as a lowering of recovery time. The side effects that have been noted are weight gain and water retention in some athletes.

There appear to be no dangers with **creatine supplementation** as long as the recommended dosages are followed. However, there is no information on the long-term effects. We know that the body can produce its own creatine but this capability is suppressed if supplements are taken. Meat and fish are plentiful sources, but if you already have the maximum level of creatine in your body any additional intake will simply be excreted.

Anabolic steroids and **human growth hormone (HGH)** were developed to stimulate protein synthesis and tissue growth. Athletes began to discover the possible advantages of muscle growth and increased strength following ingestion of these pharmacological agents. The abuse of these drugs has been shown to have dangerous side effects:

- excess HGH has been associated with diabetes, heart and bone disease
- steroid abuse has caused genital abnormalities, changes in sexual characteristics for men and women, heart disease, liver disease and an increase in aggressive behaviour ('roid rage').

Amphetamines and **caffeine** are drugs that stimulate your central nervous system. They result in an increase in arousal, decrease in reaction time, a sense of increased energy, decreased sense of fatigue and enhanced fat utilisation. With amphetamines there is also a redistribution of blood to muscles. Amphetamines may:

- be very dangerous and addictive
- cause elevated HR (heart rate), increased blood pressure, cardiac arhythmia (irregular heartbeat), extreme nervousness, anxiety, insomnia and aggressive behaviour
- cause death; there have been cases of athletes who have taken amphetamines and pushed themselves beyond their physiological limits.

Caffeine is also addictive, produces nervousness, insomnia and tremors. As a diuretic it can lead to dehydration when exercising in hot environments.

It is known that elevated H^+ causes a rise in acidity and fatigue. Our principle buffer is bicarbonate so researchers have investigated ways of enhancing our stores of bicarbonate. They have found that ingesting 0.3g/kg of bicarbonate mixed with a litre of water has improved performance in high intensity exercise lasting one to ten minutes. Again, there are dangers as high levels of **bicarbonate** can cause diarrhoea, vomiting and cramps.

▲ **Figure 6.28** Athletes take creatine supplements like this one in the hope of increasing PC stores

5. Physiological responses and adaptations of the energy systems

This last section brings together the knowledge you have gained so far on muscle cell structure, energy production, recovery and fuel sources and links them to different types of exercise.

Immediate changes to the energy systems during exercise are referred to as **responses to exercise**. Long-term, permanent changes from training are **adaptations to exercise**. Sportsmen and women want to know that their training is beneficial. To get this information they need knowledge of training principles, energy systems and fitness tests. They can monitor their training programmes and test results and record this information in a diary or IPP. With the knowledge of the physiological responses and adaptations that occur they can set out specific plans for future exercise training.

Responses to high intensity exercise

- ATP stores are depleted within about two seconds.
- Rising ADP level stimulates PC breakdown.
- PC stores are depleted within 8–10 seconds and anaerobic glycolysis reaches a maximal rate after 5 seconds.
- Anaerobic glycolysis produces lactic acid (lactate and H^+). Submaximal high intensity exercise can last up to 4–5 minutes in this system.
- If the intensity of exercise is too great for the individual (50–60% VO_2 max for the untrained, 65–80% VO_2 max for the trained) then lactic acid will reach the point where it interferes with muscle contraction, inhibits enzyme action (especially PFK) and affects the free nerve endings causing pain. This point is referred to as the lactic acid (lactate) threshold or anaerobic threshold. Another term used when the level of lactic acid reaches 4 millimoles per litre is the onset of blood lactate accumulation (OBLA) (Figure 6.29).
- Fatigue sets in when ATP resynthesis can-

not match ATP demand and power output falls.
- High intensity training, especially exercise involving eccentric muscle contraction (e.g. plyometrics), can result in muscle soreness within 24–48 hours. This is referred to as **delayed onset muscle soreness** (DOMS). It is thought to arise from damage to the Z-lines and sarcolemma in the muscle cell. This causes the leakage of Ca^+, which activates enzymes, which in turn break down the muscle proteins. To mend these proteins the body has an inflammatory response which causes the pain.

Adaptations to high intensity exercise

- Strength training can lead to **hypertrophy** of muscle fibres.
- There is an increase in the rate of glycolysis due to the increased level of the enzymes. More lactic acid can be produced.
- There is an increase in phosphocreatine and glycogen content in muscle.
- Eight weeks of anaerobic training has shown an increase in muscle buffering

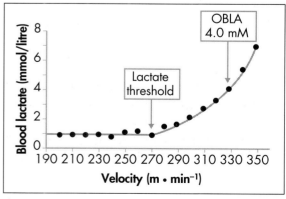

▲ *Figure 6.29* Blood lactate levels rise as a result of high intensity exercise

capacity by 12–50%. This means that the trained athlete can cope with higher levels of lactate because the H^+ are being buffered.

Responses to aerobic exercise

- Anaerobic systems provide energy in the first few minutes of exercise.
- Once a steady state has been reached CHO and fat are metabolised to provide energy through the aerobic system.
- CHO stores alone could fuel about 80 minutes of aerobic exercise before becoming depleted.
- The intensity and duration of exercise determines the source of fuel used. The higher the intensity, the greater the reliance on CHO. Fat metabolism cannot supply ATP at a rate sufficient to maintain exercise intensities above 60% VO_2 max.
- During prolonged aerobic exercise there is a gradual shift from carbohydrate to fat as an energy source.
- As intensity and duration of exercise increase, the muscle glycogen stores become depleted. The body then relies on liver glycogen stores to provide the fuel source.
- As CHO stores are depleted there is a greater reliance on fat as a fuel.
- 'Fat burns in a carbohydrate flame' so glycogen depletion will affect fat metabolism.
- Fatigue arises as muscle and liver stores become depleted and fat metabolism cannot provide the intensity of energy required.

Adaptations to aerobic exercise

- There are increases in the capillary density in muscle.
- Increases in number and size of mitochondria occur.
- There are increases in the number of oxidative enzymes and thus an increase in the activity of Kreb's cycle.
- Stores of glycogen, triglyceride and myoglobin in muscles are all increased.

- During exercise there is an increased ability to metabolise fat as a fuel and a fall in lactate production.
- These metabolic adaptations supplement the increase in blood volume, stroke volume and cardiac output.
- The better utilisation of oxygen by muscles enhances the arterio-venous oxygen difference.
- There is an increased ability to work at a higher percentage of VO_2 max without reaching the lactate threshold.

TASK

a Analyse a game of your choice (football, hockey etc.) and estimate the relative contribution of the three energy systems in your chosen game. Give specific reasons for your analysis.

You may require stop-watches to measure the time taken for walking, jogging and sprinting. You should devise your own sheet to help analyse the different aspects of the game, e.g. distance travelled, number of sprints, time taken, number of jogs, time spent walking. There may be a number of other categories that you wish to introduce or you may want to focus on a particular position.

b How will this information influence your training plan?

Understanding your IPP

1 Give physiological reasons for the adaptations that have taken place due to your training.
2 How has your knowledge of energy systems, recovery, fatigue and nutrition affected your training plan?
3 Give specific physiological reasons for changes to intensity and duration of the exercises you have undertaken.

Key words and phrases

1. Introduction to basic chemistry for sports science

- Matter • Energy • Elements • Atoms • Neutrons • Protons • Electrons
- Isotopes • Bond • Molecule • Compound • Ion • Electrolyte • Ionic bond
- Covalent bonding • Hydrogen bond • Metabolism • Exothermic • Endothermic
- Synthesis • Decomposition • Exchange • Redox • Anabolic • Catabolic
- Oxidised • Reduced • Adenosine triphosphate (ATP) • Enzymes • Organic
- Inorganic • Acids • Base • pH • Buffers

2. Energy concepts for exercise physiology

- Chemical energy • Kinetic (mechanical) energy • Potential energy
- Basal metabolic rate (BMR) • Calories • Joules • Work • Power

3. Molecular muscle cell structure

- Central nervous system (CNS) • Peripheral nervous system (PNS) • Sensory
- Motor • Motor neurone • Myelin sheath • Nodes of Ranvier • Polarised
- Depolarisation • Action potential • Impulse • 'All or none' law • Repolarisation
- Synapses • Neuromuscular junction • Acetylcholine • Motor unit
- Wave summation • Spatial summation • Epimysium • Fasciculi • Perimysium
- Endomysium • Sarcolemma • Sarcoplasm • Mitochondria
- Sarcoplasmic recticulum • Transverse tubules • Myofibrils • Myosin • Actin
- Troponin • Tropomyosin • Sarcomeres • Cross bridge • ATPase
- Power stroke • Ratchet mechanism

4. Energy systems and the energy continuum

- Phosphocreatine (PC) • Creatine kinase • Anaerobic glycolysis • Glycogen
- Pyruvic acid • Phosphofrucktokinase (PFK)
- Nicotinamide adenine dinucleotide (NAD^+) • Electron transport chain (ETC)
- Lactic acid • Aerobic system • Kreb's cycle • Acetyl coenzyme A (acetyl CoA)
- Flavin adenine dinucleotide (FAD) • Oxaloacetic acid • Triglyceride
- Free fatty acids (FFA) • Beta oxidation • Onset of blood lactate accumulation (OBLA)
- Central fatigue • Peripheral fatigue • Hydration • Oxygen debt • Oxygen deficit
- Excess post-exercise oxygen consumption (EPOC) • Carbo-loading
- Recommended daily allowance (RDA) • Ergogenic aids • Creative supplementation
- Anabolic steroids • Human growth hormone (HGH) • Amphetamines • Caffine
- Bicarbonate

5. Physiological responses and adaptations of the energy systems

- Responses to exercise • Adaptations to exercise
- Delayed onset muscle soreness (DOMS)

REVIEW QUESTIONS

1 Define what is meant by the term 'energy'.

2 Describe the stages of the sliding filament theory of muscle contraction.

3 How is a nerve impulse propagated?

4 Draw a diagram of a motor unit.

5 Describe the predominant energy system used to resynthesise ATP in the following athletic activities:
- shot putt
- high jump
- 400 metres
- 1500 metres
- 5000 metres
- marathon.

6 Draw diagrams to represent the processes involved in the three major energy systems.

7 What is meant by the term 'fat burns in a carbohydrate flame'?

8 State the type, frequency, intensity and duration of exercise that you would recommend for weight loss. Give physiological reasons for your exercise programme.

9 Explain the reasons for fatigue in the following events:
- 100 metres
- 400 metres
- marathon.

10 What happens in the process of recovery from these events?

11 What nutritional advice would you give to a sportsman or woman who was training five days per week?

12 How do the energy systems respond to different forms of exercise?

13 How do the energy systems adapt to different forms of exercise?

Texts used in the writing of this section

❑ Clegg, C. A., *Exercise Physiology and Functional Anatomy*, Feltham Press, 1995
❑ Hargreaves, M., *Exercise Metabolism*, Human Kinetics, 1995
❑ Marieb, E. N., *Human Anatomy and Physiology*, 4th edition, Benjamin Cummings, 1999
❑ Maughan, R., Gleeson, M. & Greenhaff, P. L., *Biochemistry of Exercise and Training*, Oxford University Press, 1997
❑ McArdle, W. D., Katch, F. I. & Katch V. L., *Essentials of Exercise Physiology*, Lea and Febiger, 1994
❑ Powers, S. K. & Howley, E. T., *Exercise Physiology – Theory and Application to Fitness and Performance*, WCB McGraw Hill, 1998
❑ Robergs, R. A. & Roberts, S. O., *Exercise Physiology – Exercise, Performance and Clinical Applications*, Mosby, 1997
❑ Tortora, G. J. & Grabowski, S. R., *Principles of Anatomy and Physiology*, 8th edition, Harper Collins, 1996
❑ Weltman, A., 'The Blood Lactate Response to Exercise', *Current Issues in Exercise Science*, Monograph No. 4, Human Kinetics, 1995
❑ Wilmore, J. H. & Costill, D. L., *Physiology of Sport and Exercise*, 2nd edition, Human Kinetics, 1999

Suggested further reading

❑ Clegg, C. A., *Exercise Physiology and Functional Anatomy*, Feltham Press, 1995
❑ Marieb, E. N., *Human Anatomy and Physiology*, 4th Edn. Benjamin Cummings, 1999
❑ Powers, S. K. & Howley, E. T., *Exercise Physiology – Theory and Application to Fitness and Performance*, WCB McGraw Hill, 1998
❑ Wilmore, J. H. & Costill, D. L., *Physiology of Sport and Exercise*, 2nd edition, Human Kinetics, 1999

Section B: Option A: Sports mechanics

1. Fundamental qualities of motion

Matter, time and space

Matter is anything with mass. From GCSE Science you will know that it can be solid, liquid or gas. However, in the study of PE we are mainly concerned with solid matter, whether it be a solid human being or a solid object such as a hockey ball or discus.

Throughout the text, matter will be referred to as a body or an object with mass and is measured in kilograms (kg). **Time** is the measurement used to describe how long a certain event has lasted for and is measured in seconds (s). **Space** describes the amount of room or an area that an object covers. Linear space is measured in metres (m). It is important that all calculations are based on the above units (known as SI units) with any necessary conversions being completed before the calculation.

Motion

The term **motion** is used to describe the change of **position** of an object. To be able to accurately analyse motion, you need to describe the position and the time taken between its different positions.

The position of a body will tell us exactly where it is in space in relation to a fixed point and is usually described graphically.

In Figure 6.30, the swimmer has started at position A and is moving 10 metres from the start to position B.

In Figure 6.31, the hockey player is just inside the 'D' and is therefore 14 metres from

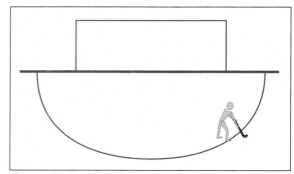
▲ **Figure 6.31** *The goalpost is a fixed point from which you can work out the position of the player*

the goal line directly in line with the right-hand goalpost.

An orienteer or mountain walker can be more specific about their position with a grid reference. In Figure 6.32, for example, the co-ordinates of the walker are 446245.

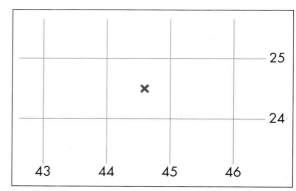
▲ **Figure 6.32** *The coordinates on the map are the fixed point*

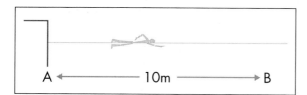
▲ **Figure 6.30** *A swimmer starts at position A and moves to position B*

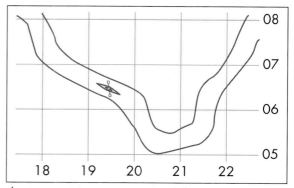
▲ **Figure 6.33** *Canoeing the Ardeche*

▲ **Figure 6.34** *On the rugby field*

TASK

Describe the positions shown in Figures 6.33 and 6.34.

The **distance** that the body has moved describes the actual ground covered. So an athlete who runs a 1500-metre race will have covered a distance of 1500 metres. The javelin in Figure 6.35 has covered a distance of 68.72 metres.

It is important to understand that 'distance' describes the total ground covered, irrespective of the pathway taken. **Displacement** measures the ground covered from position A to position B over the shortest possible route, that is 'as the crow flies'. For example, an athlete who has run the 400-metre race as in Figure 6.36 will have covered a distance of 400-metres but will have a displacement of zero as the start and finish are in the same position.

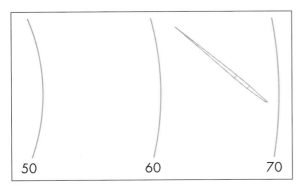

▲ **Figure 6.35** *The javelin has covered a distance of 68.72 metres*

▲ **Figure 6.36** *400m – the road to nowhere*

▲ **Figure 6.37** *This could be three hours' running for a displacement of three miles!*

The marathon runner will have covered a distance of 42,156 metres (26.2 miles) but his displacement may only be, for example, 4827 metres (three miles) due east (Figure 6.37). Direction is important as displacement is a **vector** quantity (see page 399).

To summarise, the distance covered in moving from A to B in Figure 6.38 will vary, depending upon the route taken, but displacement from A to B will not change.

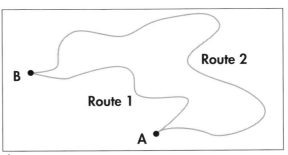

▲ **Figure 6.38** *Two routes: different distances, same displacement*

2. Analysis of linear speed, velocity and acceleration

Linear motion

Linear motion refers to the change in position of an object in a straight line. To understand this better we need to consider three factors:

- the **speed** of this motion – how fast it is moving?
- the **velocity** of this motion – the rate of change in displacement
- the **acceleration** – the rate of change in velocity.

Speed

To calculate the speed of an object, divide the distance travelled by the time taken. Figure 6.39 helps you remember this. For example, Paddy swims 100 metres in 60 seconds:

$$\text{speed} = \frac{\text{distance travelled}}{\text{time taken}}$$

$$s = \frac{d}{t}$$

$$s = \frac{100\text{m}}{60\text{s}}$$

$$s = 1.67\text{m/s}$$

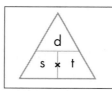

▲ **Figure 6.39** The sdt formula triangle

This is described as an **average speed** as it is highly unlikely that Paddy swims at the same speed throughout the race.

By plotting a graph of distance against time, it is easy to observe the change in motion (Figure 6.40).

Imagine you have just run 3000 metres in a time of 12 minutes. What would your average speed be?

$$s = ?$$

$$d = 3000\text{m}$$

$$t = 12 \text{ minutes} = 12 \times 60 = 720\text{s}$$

$$s = \frac{d}{t} = \frac{3000\text{m}}{720\text{s}} = 4.17\text{m/s}$$

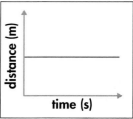
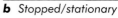

a Steady speed   *b Stopped/stationary*

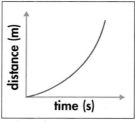
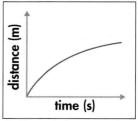

c Speeding up   *d Slowing down*

▲ **Figure 6.40** Changes of motion shown on a graph of distance against time

TASK

Figure 6.41 below is a graph of speed against time for a race. Describe what is happening at positions A, B and C, giving possible reasons for your answer.

Figure 6.42 on the next page is a graph showing distance against time for the same race.

Both graphs show that although the average speed for this race was 4.17m/s, the actual speed varied tremendously throughout the race. Speed is a **scalar** quantity, which means it has only size or **magnitude** value and does not tell us anything about the direction in which the body has travelled.

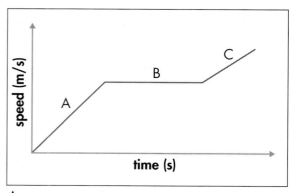

▲ **Figure 6.41** Speed against time

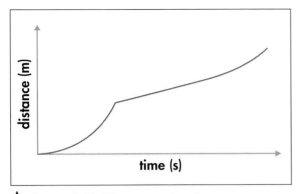

▲ **Figure 6.42** *Distance against time*

▲ **Figure 6.43** *200-metre run*

Velocity

Velocity is speed in a particular direction. It is defined as follows:

$$\text{velocity} = \frac{\text{displacement}}{\text{time taken}}$$

In this instance you need to think of displacement as a distance in a certain direction. If an athlete runs one way, a positive velocity will occur. If the athlete then runs in the opposite direction a negative value will result.

This is illustrated in Figure 6.43. An athlete runs 200 metres in a time of 25 seconds.

The athlete's speed would therefore be:

$$s = \frac{d}{t} = \frac{200m}{25s} = 8m/s$$

The athlete's displacement would be 200 metres and therefore velocity would be:

$$v = \frac{\text{displacement}}{\text{time taken}} = \frac{200m}{25s} = 8m/s$$

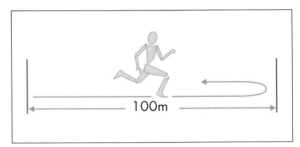

▲ **Figure 6.44** *100m forward and 100m back*

TASK

Set up the experiment as shown in Figure 6.45, with each student at a cone and in possession of a stop-watch.

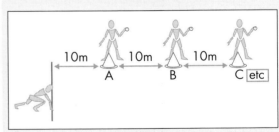

▲ **Figure 6.45** *Ten cones, ten stop-watches and one runner*

The runner runs 100m as fast as possible. All timekeepers start their watches on the gun and stop it as the athlete passes their cone. (Alternatively, you could use a video with onscreen timing facilities which will provide far more accurate results.)

a Record your results in a table like the one on the next page: ▶

TASK

If the athlete ran the same 200m as shown in Figure 6.44, i.e. 100m forward and 100m back, work out speed, displacement and velocity.

As velocity takes into consideration the direction of travel as well as the distance it is described as a vector quantity, because it has both magnitude and direction.

Position	Distance (m)	Time (s)	Time for section(s)
0	0	0	0
A	10	1.6	1.6
B	20	3.1	1.5
C	30	4.4	1.3
D	40 etc.		

b Describe the motion of the runner from one point to the next, e.g. 0 to A = acceleration, A to B = acceleration, etc.

c Plot your results on a graph of distance against time. Do not join your points in a straight line but sketch curves or lines which best reflect the motion of the runner.

d Work out the average speed for each 10m section of the run and plot a graph of speed against time. As the student has run in a straight line, velocity will be equal to speed since distance and displacement have the same value in this instance.

Another way of calculating velocity is to use your graph of distance against time. The gradient of the slope can be used to calculate velocity. (Figure 6.46).

$$velocity = gradient\ of\ slope$$

$$= \frac{change\ in\ 'y'\ value}{change\ in\ 'x'\ value}$$

$$= \frac{5}{15} = 0.33 m/s^2$$

Acceleration

This describes the rate of change of velocity and can be defined as:

$$acceleration = \frac{change\ in\ velocity}{time\ taken}$$

$$a = \frac{final\ velocity - initial\ velocity}{time\ taken}$$

$$a = \frac{v-u}{t}$$

TASK

a Using your results from the 100m sprint develop a spreadsheet containing the times for each 10m section.

b Insert formulae that will calculate results for the following column headings:

'Average speed for 10m section' and 'Acceleration over each 10m section'.

If the student slows down during the run, you should give a negative value.

3. Force

Force is the term used to describe the pushing or pulling effect of an action exerted on an object, usually altering its state of motion.

Forces that act on the body can be external, originating outside the body, or internal, originating within the body.

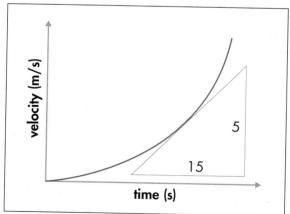

▲ **Figure 6.46** Distance against time for 100m run

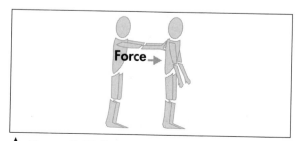

▲ **Figure 6.47** Force = movement

Force can have a number of effects on a body. If enough force is applied to a stationary object, it will begin to move (Figure 6.47).
If a moving object has a force applied in the same direction as travel, it will cause the object to speed up/accelerate (Figure 6.48).

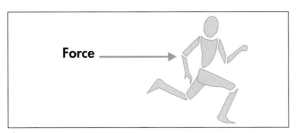

▲ **Figure 6.48** *Force = acceleration*

If a moving object has a force applied in the opposite direction to travel, it will cause the object to slow down or decelerate (Figure 6.49).

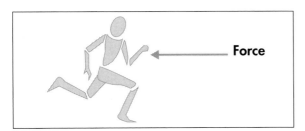

▲ **Figure 6.49** *Force = deceleration*

If an object has a force applied from a different direction, it will cause the object to change direction (Figure 6.50)

▲ **Figure 6.50** *Force = change of direction*

Force also produces three types of movement:

1 **Deformative** movement. This is when the shape of the object is changed (Figure 6.51).

▲ **Figure 6.51** *Ouch!*

2 **Translational** movement. This is when the position of the object is changed (Figure 6.52).

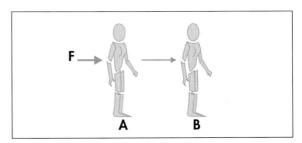

▲ **Figure 6.52** *The position changes from A to B*

3 **Rotational** movement. This is when the object is rotated (Figure 6.53).

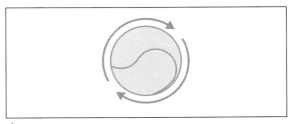

▲ **Figure 6.53** *Rotational movement*

There are many sporting examples where applying force can result in all three types of movement at once.

The tennis serve 'squashes' the ball on contact (deformative), sends the ball forward (translational) and puts spin on the ball (rotational).

Force has direction and magnitude so it is a vector quantity. In diagrams, the magnitude of the force will be proportional to the length of the line drawn. The direction in which the force is being applied will be represented by the direction of the arrowhead as shown in Figures 6.54 and 6.55.

The direction of a force is of great significance to the outcome, especially in a sporting context. Often there will be more than one force being applied at any given time.

The overall effect of these forces is known as the **net** or **resultant force**. In Figure 6.54, two equal forces are acting in opposite directions, producing a resultant force of zero. Therefore, there is no movement, despite a lot of force and effort from both teams. In this illustration the resultant force = zero, therefore there is no movement despite a lot of force and effort from both teams!

However, even a small resultant force will result in movement, so if one team can apply just a little more force than the other, they will be able to move the scrum forwards (Figure 6.55). The greater the resultant force, the greater the acceleration will be.

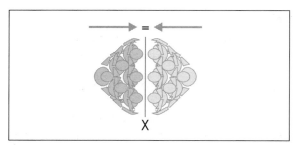

▲ **Figure 6.54** Evenly matched scrum

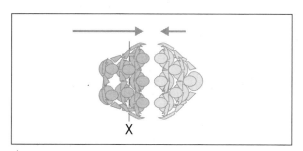

▲ **Figure 6.55** The effect of an extra player

TASK

Describe the motion of A in illustrations i, ii and iii below, discussing direction and speed.

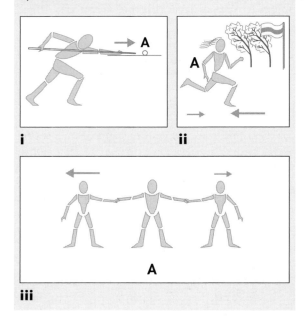

i

ii

iii

As previously mentioned, many forces can act upon an object at one time and in many directions. Therefore, the resultant force will determine the effect. When two forces act at the same time, the **parallelogram rule** is applied to work out the resultant force (Figure 6.56).

In Figure 6.56, two forces, f1 and f2, act at the same time. By extending the lines from the forces to form a parallelogram, the resultant force (R) can be found by drawing a diagonal line across the parallelogram.

Where two forces act at 90°, we can simply use Pythagoras' theorem (Figure 6.57), in which the square of the hypotenuse is equal

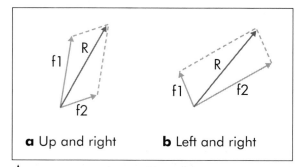

a Up and right   **b** Left and right

▲ **Figure 6.56** The parallelogram rule

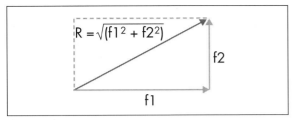

▲ **Figure 6.57** *Pythagorus' theorem can be used to find R when two forces act at 90°*

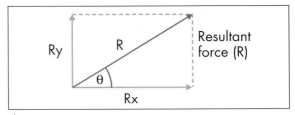

▲ **Figure 6.60** *Resolving a vector*

to the sum of the squares of the other two sides.

If enough dimensions are known, simple trigonometry equations can be used to find the missing ones. (Refer to physics textbooks for formulae.)

When more than two forces act at the same time, as in Figure 6.58, the forces need to be continuously paired until the resultant force is found. The pairs can be taken in any order and will still produce the same result.

You could begin by combining A and B to get F. Then add F to C to get G. Add G to D to calculate resultant force.

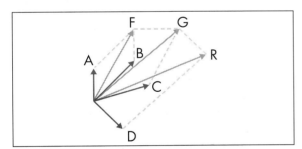

▲ **Figure 6.58** *Four into one*

TASK

Work out the resultant force in each of the actions in Figure 6.59. Show your working.

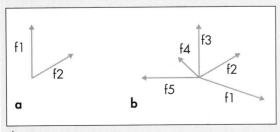

▲ **Figure 6.59** *Which way will it move?*

Forces can also be **resolved** into components. This is when the resultant action is broken down into a vertical and horizontal component. To resolve a vector (Figure 6.60), the resultant force becomes the diagonal of a rectangle and produces a rectangle with the vertical (Ry) and horizontal (Rx) sides becoming the resolved components.

Once again, if enough of the figures are known, trigonometry can be used to calculate the missing ones using the following formulae:

$$Rx = Rcos\theta$$
$$Ry = Rsin\theta$$

and

$$Tan\theta = \frac{Ry}{Rx}$$

$$\theta = tan^{-1}\frac{Ry}{Rx}$$

Impulse

Force **impulse** is defined as the change in **momentum** of an object. Therefore:

impulse = (change in) momentum

Impulse is measured in kilogram metres per second (kg m/s). As velocity is involved in the equation, impulse is a vector quantity. On a graph of force against time (Figure 6.61), the shaded area represents the impulse.

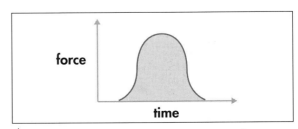

▲ **Figure 6.61** *Force against time = impulse*

Examples of impulse include kicking a ball, hitting a golf ball, a tennis serve, playing a shot in snooker or putting the shot. All of these actions produce acceleration. This means the object moves in a forward direction with increasing velocity.

The contact time between the player and the object in these examples of impulse force is very small. Therefore **follow through** will increase the contact time (Figure 6.62), increase the impulse and consequently increase the change of momentum of the struck object, sending it further and quicker.

A tennis ball has a mass of approximately 0.07kg. The player serves the ball producing a force of 980 Newtons. The time of contact between racket and ball is 0.005 seconds. The resulting velocity of the ball would be:

$$v = f \times \frac{t}{m}$$
$$= 980N \times \frac{0.005s}{0.07kg} = 70m/s$$

If, by following through, the player can increase the contact time to 0.007 seconds the velocity of the ball would increase:

$$v = f \times \frac{t}{m}$$
$$= 980N \times \frac{0.007s}{0.07kg} = 98m/s$$

Therefore, even a slight increase in contact time caused by a good follow through will greatly increase the velocity with which the ball travels, making it more difficult to return.

This notion is also important in impact activities. If a fielder in cricket catches a fast moving ball and the contact time between his hands and the ball is short, there is a sudden change in momentum so catching it hurts! If the fielder increases the contact time by moving hands with the ball to catch it, the decrease in velocity over a longer time reduces the force and makes it all less painful. (Fig. 6.63)

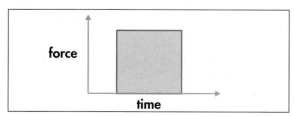

▲ **Figure 6.62** Increased contact time (follow through) = increased (constant) impulse

TASK

Using any hitting implement and a ball, hit the ball as hard as you can but stop your swing on contact. Repeat this 10 times and record the distance the ball travelled. Work out the average distance.

Repeat the same exercise with the same implement and ball, but concentrate on the follow through. Again, repeat 10 times and record the average distance.

Discuss your results.

Internal force

Internal force is where the body uses muscle force to help overcome or increase external forces. The effect of the muscle contraction is dependent upon several factors:

- if the body is in contact with the ground
- the size and structure of the body parts involved.

For a body part to move, the muscles must work in conjunction with the skeletal system as a series of levers.

The way the lever works will depend on its 'order' or class (**order of lever**), but all consist of a fulcrum (pivot point), load (resistance) and effort (force).

▲ **Figure 6.63** Moving hands with the ball reduces the force

First class of lever

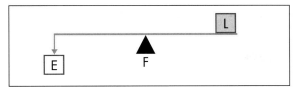

▲ **Figure 6.64** *First class lever*

This is a very efficient lever where a little effort can lift a large load (Figure 6.64). The fulcrum (F) lies between the effort (E) and the load (L). This is rare in the human body but one example is the head nodding (Figure 6.65).

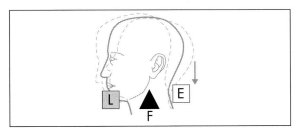

▲ **Figure 6.65** *Nodding the head uses a first class lever*

Second class of lever

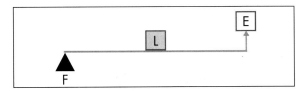

▲ **Figure 6.66** *Second class lever*

Here the load lies between the fulcrum and the effort (Figure 6.66). An example in the human body is the effort of the Achilles tendon lifting the load of the athlete at the ankle joint with the toes being the fulcrum (Figure 6.67).

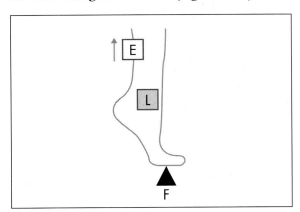

▲ **Figure 6.67** *The Achilles tendon is an example of a second class lever*

Third class of lever

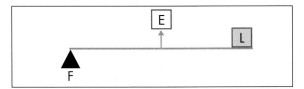

▲ **Figure 6.68** *Third class lever*

Here the load and the fulcrum are at opposite ends of the lever, with the effort lying somewhere in between (Figure 6.68). This type of lever is very common in the human body, with a clear example being the biceps action on the elbow joint (Figure 6.69).

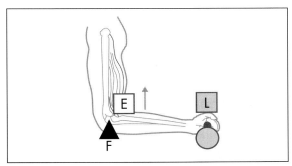

▲ **Figure 6.69** *Bending the elbow joint uses a third class lever*

The effect of this lever system is to:

- increase the load that can be moved
- increase the velocity at which a body moves.

With third class levers, the effort is always greater than the load as the load is further from the fulcrum than the effort.

TASK

Work out what kind of lever is being used in each of the following actions and draw simple diagrams to show load, fulcrum and effort.

- using a screwdriver to lift the lid off a tin of varnish
- performing a biceps curl
- rowing a boat
- lifting a wheelbarrow full of compost.

Newton's Third Law of motion

When a muscle contracts, Newton's Third Law (see page 408) concerning reaction still applies: the force on the origin of the muscle (the static end) is equal and opposite to the force on the insertion of the muscle (closest to the joint that moves). This means that the origin and insertion are pulled towards each other as the muscle contracts (Figure 6.70).

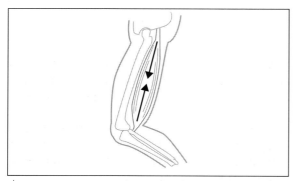

▲ **Figure 6.70** *Equal forces in opposite directions*

To calculate the **moment of force** produced, measure the distance from the load to the pivot point. This is then multiplied by the weight of the load moved (Figure 6.71). For example, when performing a bicep curl with a 10kg mass, the following moment of force is produced.

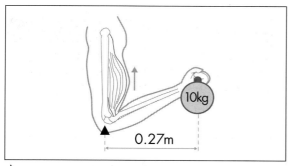

▲ **Figure 6.71** *Calculating the moment of force*

The moment of force = force × distance to the fulcrum, so that:

> moment of force =
> 100 Newtons (10kg × 10) × 0.27m (dist)
> (0.27m) =
> 27N/m (Newton/metres)

NB The distance must be measured at right angles to the force.

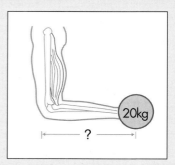
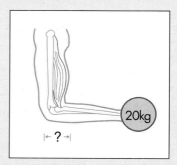
Angle of pull

The angle of pull greatly affects the efficiency of the muscular contraction. This is the angle between the insertion of the muscle in relation the position of the joint (Figure 6.7).

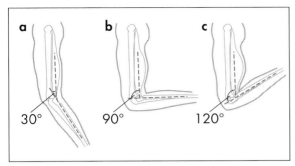

▲ **Figure 6.72** *A muscle is most effective with an angle of pull of 90°*

4. Planes and axes of rotation

Divers, trampolinists and gymnasts all perform twisting and somersaulting moves in their routines. This involves **rotation** around one of three theoretical axes of rotation: **longitudinal**, **lateral** and **dorso-ventral**.

Longitudinal rotation takes place around the *vertical* plane and allows the body to twist or spin (Figure 6.73).

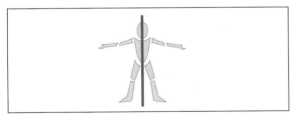

▲ **Figure 6.73** *Longitudinal axis*

Lateral rotation takes place around the *horizontal* plane of the body and allows the body to tumble and somersault (Figure 6.74).

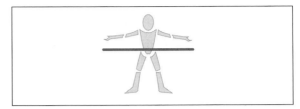

▲ **Figure 6.74** *Lateral axis*

Imagine that a pole has been thrust through your body from side to side across your middle. What sort of movements could you perform?

Dorso-ventral rotation takes place around the *frontal* plane during actions such as a cartwheel in gymnastics or half-turntable in trampolining (Figure 6.75).

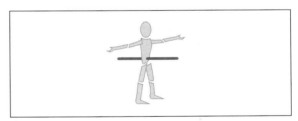

▲ **Figure 6.75** *Dorso-ventral axis*

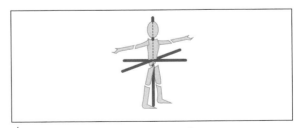

▲ **Figure 6.76** *The three axes of rotation*

All three axes of rotation pass through the body's centre of mass and are at right angles to each other (Figure 6.76).

5. Gravity

Gravity causes a force that pulls everything towards the centre of the earth. This means that it always acts in a downward direction and what goes up … must come down!

The amount of pull effected by gravity is dependent upon the mass of the object (how much matter it has) and the gravitational field strength. On earth this is approximately 10 Newtons per kilogram. The resulting force is described as the **weight** of the object.

weight (in Newtons) =
mass(m) × gravitational field strength (mg)
(kg)   (Newtons per kg)
(where mg is the product of mass × gravitational field strength)

So an athlete with a mass of 70kg will exert a downward force of 700N. A 4kg shot will exert a downward force of 40N (Figure 6.77).

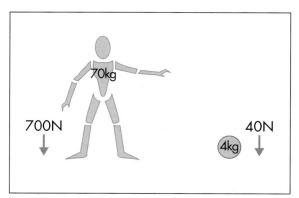

▲ *Figure 6.77* The effects of gravity

Newton's laws of motions

Many scientists have studied the notion of gravity. In a sporting context it is **Newton's laws of motion** that we must be concerned with when we look at force and its effects.

Newton's First Law

This states that an object will continue in its state of rest or uniform motion in a straight line unless a force acts upon it. This means that, for example, an athlete or the shot will remain stationary until a force is exerted upon them (Figure 6.78).

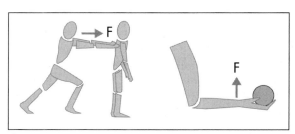

▲ *Figure 6.78* No force = stationary; force = movement

As Newton stated, an object may also travel at a constant speed in a straight line if there is no resultant force to change it. Therefore, for an athlete to be running at a constant speed, the resultant force must be zero (Figure 6.79).

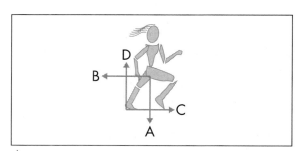

▲ *Figure 6.79* If an athlete runs at a constant speed, the resultant force must equal zero

Weight also becomes the predominant force acting on matter moving through the air. Little else will have any effect on its flight path or

▲ **Figure 6.80** 'Oomph'! The athlete feels the force of hitting the ground

velocity once it has left the thrower's hand, for example, or the athlete has left the ground. Once in flight, they will be 'pulled' downwards by gravity. Remember Newton's law: 'an object will continue in a straight line unless acted upon'; the next force to act upon such objects will be the force of hitting the ground (Figure 6.80)!

Newton's Second Law
This states that the acceleration (moving forwards) of an object is directly proportional to the force acting upon it and can be defined as:

$$acceleration = \frac{force}{mass}$$

Therefore, for an object with a constant mass (nearly everything involved in a sporting context) to have a change in acceleration, the force acting upon it will have to change and the greater the net force, the greater the acceleration.

A stationary athlete at the start of a race responds to the gun and moves forward (accelerates). Therefore, the resultant force must be greater than zero and in a forward direction (Figure 6.81).

▲ **Figure 6.81** Go!

TASK

a Find the mass of one member of your class.

b Time them sprinting off the blocks over 10 metres.

c Calculate their acceleration over the 10 metres.

$$speed = \frac{distance}{time}$$

$$acceleration = \frac{final\ speed - initial\ speed}{time}$$

$$final\ speed = average\ speed \times 2$$

d Calculate the initial driving force of the runner (force = mass x acceleration).

e Repeat this exercise 10 times and give reasons for differences in results.

The driving force that the athlete exerts results from **friction** (the grip on the ground). Therefore, better grip should result in greater force and greater acceleration.

If an athlete changes direction but maintains the same speed (i.e. swerves), their velocity changes due to the change in direction. Therefore, the player accelerates in the direction of the force (in this case friction from the ground) (Figure 6.82).

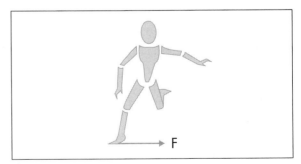

▲ **Figure 6.82** Friction helps swerve

Newton's Third Law
This law states that for every action there is an equal and opposite reaction. This can be demonstrated by asking: Why, if an athlete exerts a downward force of 700N due to gravity, does the ground not move?

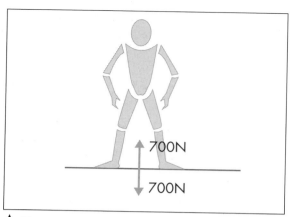

▲ **Figure 6.83** *Normal reaction force*

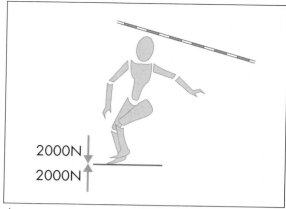

▲ **Figure 6.85** *Push off*

The ground actually exerts an equal and opposite force of its own, 700N upwards. This force is at right angles to the ground and is known as **normal reaction force** (Figure 6.83).

All actions have equal and opposite reactions. So, for example, the gymnast who is hanging stationary on the parallel bars exerts a downward force of 540N. The bars exert an upward force of 540N on her hands and so the gymnast and the bars remain stationary (Figure 6.84).

This same law of reaction also applies to impact sports such as football. So, when the player strikes the ball with a certain force forwards, the ball will exert an equal and opposite force backwards on the foot (Figure 6.86).

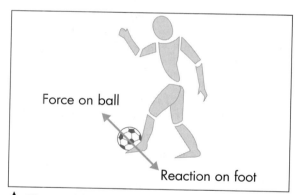

▲ **Figure 6.86** *The ball reacts with an equal and opposite force backwards on the foot*

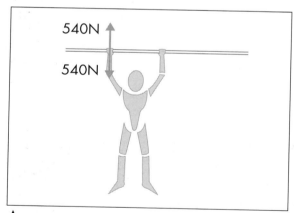

▲ **Figure 6.84** *All actions have equal and opposite reactions*

6. Principles related to the stability of the body

Centre of gravity

The **centre of gravity** of an object or a person is defined as the point at which weight is acting on the object. In uniform objects such as a hockey ball or a shot, the centre of gravity would also be the geographical centre. However, for something like the human body, which is constantly changing shape, the centre of gravity also continually changes (Figure 6.87).

A high jumper pushes down on the ground with a force of 2000N. The ground therefore pushes back with an upward force of 2000N. The jumper is pushed up and the ground is pushed down. However, you only really notice the jumper moving up as the ground has such a huge mass (Figure 6.85).

If you place a ruler on your index finger with your palm facing upwards and adjust the ruler's position until it balances on your

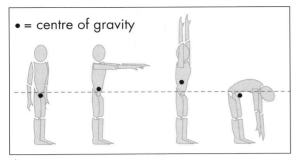

▲ **Figure 6.87** *Changes in shape alter the centre of gravity*

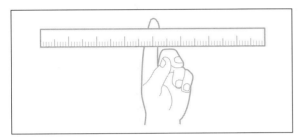

▲ **Figure 6.88** *The centre of mass is at the same point as the centre of gravity*

finger, this will be the centre of gravity of the ruler (Figure 6.88). Because the ruler is a symmetrical object of constant density, its centre of gravity will also be its mid-point.

Centre of mass

As this concept also works in weightless situations, it cannot be dependent upon gravity and this point is therefore more often referred to as the **centre of mass (CoM)**. The centre of mass of an object has a very similar definition to that of the centre of gravity. It is the point at which mass is concentrated: the 'balance' point. If an object is suspended in mid-air by its centre of mass it will remain in a balanced position (Figure 6.89).

A body or other object suspended from any other point will hang so that the centre of mass lies vertically below the point of suspension (Figure 6.90).

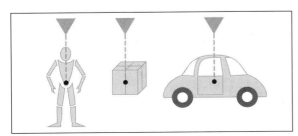

▲ **Figure 6.89** *A balancing act*

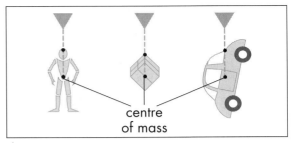

▲ **Figure 6.90** *Centre of mass in line below the point of suspension*

Equilibrium

A gymnast in a handstand position, or a footballer ready to kick the ball, are still in a balanced position but would be quite easy to push over. This is known as **unstable equilibrium** (Figure 6.91).

Neutral equilibrium is where the object pushed simply adopts a new balanced position and this relates to the concept of **stability**. Most sporting activities are done in a balanced position which requires the centre of mass to be above the **base of support** to make them stable. If the centre of mass is outside the base of support, then the athlete becomes unstable.

Some athletes are difficult to push over and would usually return to their original position (Figure 6.92). This is known as **stable equilibrium** and is difficult to alter. Stability depends upon the position of the CoM and the size of the base of support (Figures 6.93 and 6.94).

▲ **Figure 6.91** *Balanced but unstable*

CoM directly over large base of support.

▲ *Figure 6.92* *Difficult to knock over*

CoM directly over small base of support.

▲ *Figure 6.93* *Balanced but easy to knock over*

CoM outside base.

▲ *Figure 6.94* *About to fall off!*

TASK

Adopt the following positions:

a press-up position

b headstand

c handstand

d stork stand

e on all fours

Get a friend to gently push you whilst in each position. Rank each position in order of stability, explaining why each is stable or unstable.

Overbalancing

Occasionally, an athlete will deliberately become 'off balance' to help their performance. The sprinter or the swimmer at the start of a race will push their centre of mass right to the edge of their base of support. On the gun, they literally fall forward with loss of balance before regaining a stable position as in Figure 6.95.

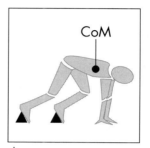
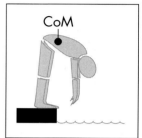

▲ *Figure 6.95* *On the edge*

A change in movement of the body will result in a change of the centre of mass.

In all three examples in Figure 6.96, you can see that the centre of mass follows a parabola. The shape of the body may change greatly and a skilful performer will use his knowledge of this to help raise or lower the CoM. For example, the high jumper arches his

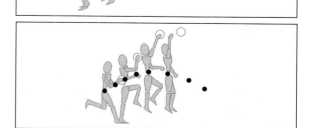

▲ *Figure 6.96* *The path of the centre of mass*

back as he goes over the bar and his centre of mass actually now passes underneath the bar (Figure 6.97).

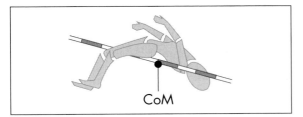

▲ **Figure 6.97** *Arching back to change the CoM*

The long jumper pikes her legs to make her heels land where her centre of mass should land (Figure 6.98).

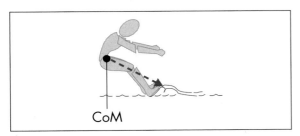

▲ **Figure 6.98** *Piked landing*

The basketball player lowers his free hand and leg at the top of a jump to lower the centre of mass (Figure 6.99).

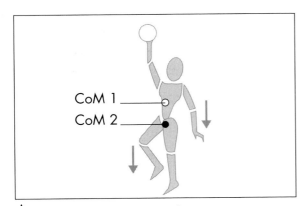

▲ **Figure 6.99** *A higher reach*

Friction

Friction also plays a very important role in stability. Friction always opposes the movement of an object and occurs when one object slides over another. Although friction has a

'nuisance' factor in that it tends to slow things down, without it, walking, running and jumping would be impossible.

Friction becomes particularly important for stability when turning or swerving (see page 409). It also provides a centripetal (or inward) force that helps the athlete 'grip' the ground (Figure 6.100).

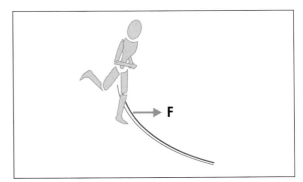

▲ **Figure 6.100** *Friction is particularly important when turning or swerving*

Friction will alter with changes in surface and changes in footwear/tyres etc. If, whilst swerving, a football player steps in a particularly muddy patch, friction is reduced and the footballer slips. If a cyclist suddenly hits some wet leaves whilst turning a corner, the wheels lose grip and the bike goes out of control.

TASK

Discuss the forces acting upon the two athletes in Figures 6.101 and 6.102 on the next page – and the movement that will occur as a result.

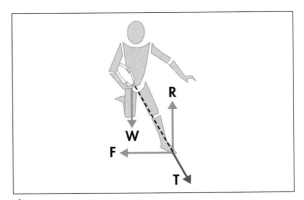

▲ **Figure 6.101** *A rugby player swerving*

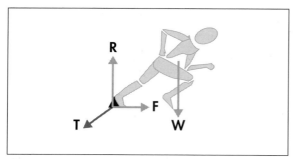

▲ **Figure 6.102** *Driving out of the blocks (F = Friction; W = Weight; R = Reaction; T = Thrust)*

TASK

a Using a number of sporting examples, discuss the positive and negative aspects of friction.

b Perform a number of 50m sprints over a variety of surfaces and wearing a variety of footwear. Time these runs and discuss the effects of friction on your performance.

Influence of external forces

The direction of the resultant force in relation to the centre of mass will determine the type of motion that occurs. If the force passes through the body's centre of mass, the body will have translational movement in the direction of the resultant force.

When an athlete is involved in a jumping action, the line of action of force in relation to the centre of mass will determine the flight path. For example, as a basketball player drives straight upwards, the resultant force acts through the CoM so there is no rotation (Figure 6.103).

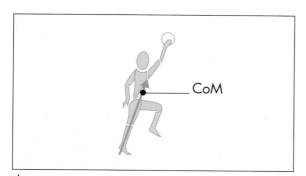

▲ **Figure 6.103** *Resultant force passes through the centre of mass*

If, however, the resultant force does not pass through the centre of mass, the body will have translational and rotational movement. For example, when a high jumper pushes off the ground, the force acts to one side of the centre of mass, causing rotation in the air (Figure 6.104).

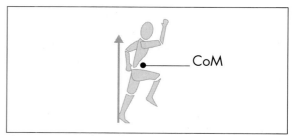

▲ **Figure 6.104** *Resultant force does not pass through the centre of mass*

A long jumper at take-off has the resultant force lying behind the centre of mass. This means that there will be some forward rotation. However, the athlete is able to counteract this forward rotation by changing the shape of the body. The most common methods of cancelling rotation are the hitch-kick or the hang technique (Figure 6.105).

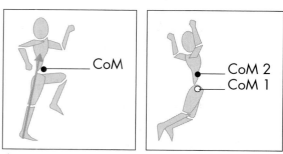

▲ **Figure 6.105** *Take-off (left) and the hang technique (right)*

7. Momentum

Momentum simply describes how difficult or easy it is to stop an object moving. An object with a large momentum will require a large force to stop it, whereas an object with less momentum will require less force to bring it to a stop.

In the case of linear motion (in a straight line), momentum can be defined as

momentum (kgm/s) = mass (kg) × velocity (m/s)

As velocity is a vector, momentum is a vector. It has magnitude and direction, and is related to Newton's Second Law of Motion (see page 409).

In a sport, mass tends to remain constant whether it be a person or an object. Therefore, to increase momentum, it is necessary to increase velocity: that is, there must be acceleration.

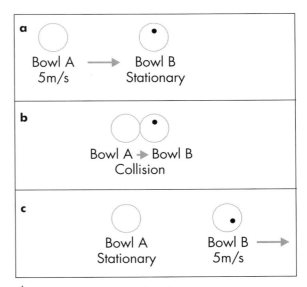

▲ **Figure 6.106** *Transfer of momentum*

In Figure 6.106, there are no external forces acting as neither bowl touches anything else during the collision and therefore the momentum of Bowl A is transferred to the Bowl B.

TASK

a Find the mass of each group member.

b Time each other sprinting over 20m.

c Discuss the resulting momentum with reference to mass and velocity.

d Why do people with the same mass have different momentum?

e Why do some 'heavier' students still have the same momentum as 'lighter' students?

f In rounders, the ball is bowled at a velocity of 20m/s and the batter sends the ball back out with a velocity of 30m/s. The ball has a mass of 0.07kg and the contact time between bat and ball is 0.015s.

   i Calculate the momentum of the ball:

     • whilst it is being bowled

     • after the hit.

   ii Calculate the change in momentum.

   Remember the batter sends the ball back in the direction it came from and it will therefore have a negative velocity value.

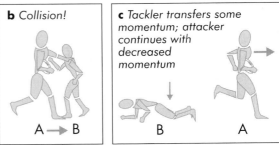
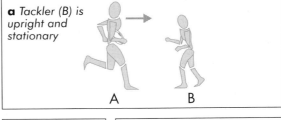

▲ **Figure 6.107** *Momentum is transferred through the handoff*

The momentum of one body will always be transferred to a second body during a collision. This is referred to as **conservation of momentum**. As long as there are no external forces acting on the objects during the collision, momentum will be conserved.

As the tackler starts upright in Figure 6.107, there are no other external forces acting during the collision of the two rugby players. Momentum is therefore transferred through the handoff, knocking the tackler over and allowing the attacker to run on with only a slightly decreased momentum. If the tackler was to lean into the attacker, an external force from the ground would then be acting, making it harder to knock the tackler over.

In both examples, the total momentum is the same immediately before and immediately after the collision.

A + B before collision = A + B after collision

This transfer of momentum is also important in striking and fielding games. A batter has to decide whether to use a light bat and swing with a large velocity or a bat with a bigger mass and swing with a lower velocity.

TASK

Using a variety of bats with different masses but the same ball each time, experiment to find which bat you can hit the ball furthest with. This will be the ball to which you have transferred the most momentum.

8. Air resistance and fluid friction

Fluid friction and **air resistance** are forces acting against moving objects and they slow them down. This acts in direct opposition to the moving object and the amount of force will depend on the size, shape and speed of the object. For example, a large light ball thrown at great speed will encounter more air resistance than a small hard ball thrown gently. A Great Dane doing the doggie paddle will encounter more drag than a Daschund!

The law of resistance states that:

Resistance increases proportionately with the square of the body's velocity.

This means that the faster an object moves, the more resistance it will encounter.

The resistance experienced by swimmers, runners, cyclists and motor racing drivers is often referred to as **drag force**. The amount of drag will depend greatly on the shape of the object and the way in which the fluid or air flows past it. If the object allows it to flow smoothly, it will create less friction than an object that 'disturbs' the flow (Figures 6.108 and 6.109).

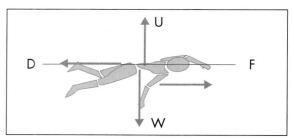

▲ *Figure 6.108* Swimmers experience resistance known as drag force (U = Up thrust from the water; W = Weight; D = Drag; F = Force from the swimmer)

If the swimmer in Figure 6.108 can be more streamlined by lying flat in the water, less drag will be experienced.

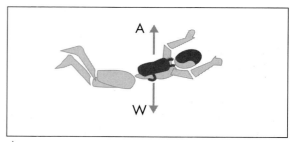

▲ *Figure 6.109* Skydivers are also affected by drag force (A = Air resistance; W = Weight)

Whilst free falling, the skydiver in Figure 6.10a will be pulled down by gravity. As the velocity of the fall increases, so will the opposing force of air resistance. On opening the parachute, air resistance will increase enormously, equalling the force of gravity, and the diver will continue to fall at a steady speed, until hitting the ground.

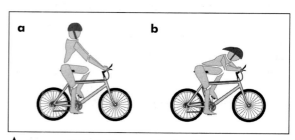

▲ *Figure 6.110* The crouched cyclist is creating less drag

Both cyclists in Figure 6.110 have the same mass, body shape and velocity.

The cyclist in (**a**) is upright and wearing an old-style helmet. The one in (**b**) is crouched and wearing a streamlined helmet. He therefore allows the air to flow past more smoothly, creating less drag.

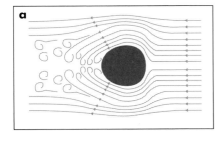

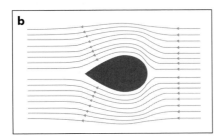

▲ *Figure 6.111* *Airflow around the old helmet (top) and the new one (below)*

In Figure 6.111, the airflow around the old helmet (**a**) is disturbed, creating a large amount of drag. The airflow in (**b**) is smoother, resulting in little resistance.

The concept of fluid friction and air resistance is also important to objects in flight. The flight path of a shot is unlikely to change, regardless of how it is thrown, as it is smooth and spherical and therefore air resistance is negligible. However, a discus thrown incorrectly greatly increases the amount of air resistance experienced, slowing it down more quickly resulting in less distance.

Lift forces interact with objects in flight and are caused by the aerodynamic shape of the object. Air passes both over and under the object (Figure 6.112). If the object has a curved top and a smoother bottom, the air will have further to travel over the top than the bottom. For effective streamlining the two airflows need to reach the back of the object

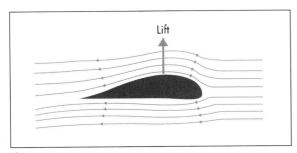

▲ *Figure 6.112* *Airflow and lift*

TASK

a Throw a javelin as far as you can.

b Repeat the throw but add a lump of modelling clay or plasticine to the front tip.

▲ **i** *Changing mass*

c Repeat the throw again but this time add a cardboard 'collar' to the javelin.

▲ **ii** *Changing 'frontage'*

d Repeat again, this time with thin strips of crepe paper around the javelin.

▲ **iii** *Changing shape*

e Describe how and why the distance thrown is affected in each case.

f Record the results of the distances thrown for each javelin in **a**, **b**, **c** and **d** above. Use the data to produce a database.

g Write up a report to account for the differing distances thrown. Present this report to your group using visual aids. Be prepared to answer any questions that may be asked.

at the same time, with the air above flowing faster. This means that there will be less pressure above the object than below it and the object will therefore 'lift'. The greater the speed of the object, the greater the pressure difference, and therefore the greater the lift. This is often referred to as the **Bernoulli effect**.

Magnus effect

When spin is applied to an object, this is known as the **Magnus effect**.

If a ball is thrown with no spin, air flows smoothly over its surface and resistance is therefore low. If spin is applied, airflow, pressure and the ball's flight path are affected. Spin is applied in order to change the flight path and deceive an opponent. Applying topspin decreases the distance covered (Figure 6.113) whilst backspin has the reverse effect (Figure 6.114) and may cause the ball to lift.

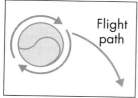

▲ **Figure 6.113**
Topspin

▲ **Figure 6.114**
Backspin

As a result of applying sidespin, the ball will veer either to the right or left (Figure 6.115).

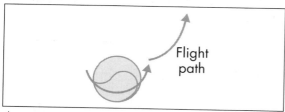

▲ **Figure 6.115** *Sidespin*

Look again at topspin to understand why the flight path changes (Figure 6.116).

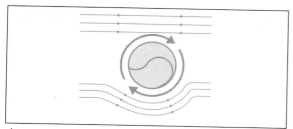

▲ **Figure 6.116** *Topspin: why does the flight path change?*

The airflow over the top of the ball will be in the opposite direction to the spin and will therefore be slowed down by surface friction (high pressure). The airflow beneath the ball will be in the same direction as the spin and will therefore experience less surface friction and will not be slowed down as much (low pressure). The difference in speed of airflow

results in a pressure difference. This causes the flight path of the ball to be changed and the ball swerves in the direction of the spin applied (in this case downward).

TASK

a Describe what happens during backspin, hook and slice. Give examples from table tennis, golf and football, stating why various types of spin might be applied.

b Throw the following three projectiles:
   • a shot
   • a badminton shuttle
   • a tennis ball with backspin.

   Ensure that similar conditions apply for each throw.

   i Measure the distance each has travelled.

   ii Observe the flight path of each object.

   iii Sketch a graph showing flight path and distance of each projectile.

   iv Account for your results, discussing the forces acting upon the projectiles and the effect they have on the distance thrown.

9. Angular motion

Moment of inertia

Inertia is the amount of force required to move a certain mass in a straight line. The **moment of inertia** is a comparable concept but relates to rotational movement.

The terms used for linear and angular motion differ slightly:

Linear motion	Angular motion
• object moves in straight line	• object spins about an axis
• acceleration (m/s²)	• angular acceleration (rads/s²)
• force	• moment of force

The further away a mass is from the axis of rotation, and the more spread out the mass is, the greater the moment of inertia and therefore the greater moment of force required to get it moving (or to stop it moving).

TASK

a Sit on a swivel chair with your arms folded.

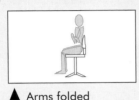

▲ Arms folded

b Get a partner to spin you as quickly as possible.

c Repeat the exercise adopting the following positions:

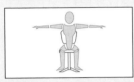

▲ Arms outstretched

▲ Arms above head

▲ Legs and arms outstretched

▲ Lying flat across the chair

d Discuss the effect that body shape had on the rate of spin and give reasons for your answer.

e Repeat the above exercise:

  i with arms outstretched – then folded.
  ii with arms folded – then outstretched.

f What effect did moving your arms in or out have on the rate of spin?

The moment of inertia is defined as:

moment of inertia (MI) =
mass × rotational radius²

(for all body parts)
(distance from axis of rotation)

and is written as:

$$MI = \Sigma(m \times r^2)$$
(with the unit of measurement being kgm²)

For an average person standing in an upright position, assume that I has a value of 1kgm² (Figure 6.117).

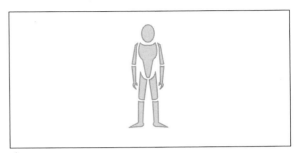

▲ *Figure 6.117* I = 1kgm²

The moment of inertia will be *increased* for rotation around the longitudinal axis as more body parts move away from that axis (Figure 6.118).

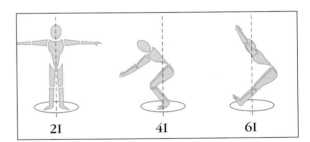

▲ **Figure 6.118** MI is increased

MI can also be *decreased* by extending the arms above the head (Figure 6.119).

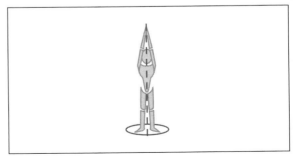

▲ *Figure 6.119* MI is decreased

For forward and backward rotation, the moment of inertia can also be varied by changing body position (Figure 6.120). Again, assume that the straight position has a value of 1.

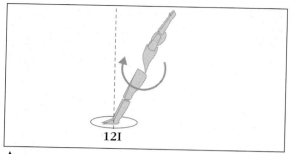

▲ **Figure 6.120** *MI can be varied by forward and backward rotation*

By tucking or piking (Figure 6.121), the moment of inertia can be decreased as the distribution of mass moves closer to the axis of rotation.

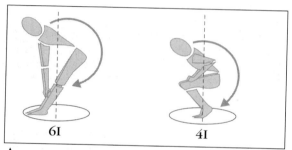

▲ **Figure 6.121** *Distribution of mass moves closer to the axis*

This concept is very useful in a number of sports where the athlete can control the rate of spin by adjusting body shape.

▲ **Figure 6.122** *By tucking the diver increases the rate of spin*

▲ **Figure 6.123** *Controlling a turn in skiing*

A trampolinist in an open position will have a large MI and therefore will spin slowly. By tucking, the trampolinist decreases MI and therefore increases the rate of spin (Figure 6.122).

In Figure 6.123, the skier starts a turn crouched low with a high moment of inertia then pushes up to actually turn. This halves his moment of inertia, increasing the rate of the turn.

However, the laws of moment of inertia do not need to involve the whole body. For example, in sprinting the leg rotates around the hip joint. If a sprinter kicks heels as close to the bottom as possible, the distance from the axis of rotation, and therefore the radius, will be small. This means that the leg will have only a small moment of inertia and will require only a small moment of force to swing it forward again. This is therefore an efficient style of sprinting.

Angular velocity

Angular velocity is the rate of turning or spinning and is defined as:

$$\text{angular velocity} = \frac{\text{angle turned (radians)}}{\text{time taken to turn}}$$

Angular momentum is defined as:

angular velocity × moment of inertia

Therefore, if the moment of inertia increases, angular velocity decreases and vice versa,

▲▼ **Figure 6.124** *Diver in straight position (left) and in tucked position (right)*

as long as the object is not influenced by another force. A diver in an open position, for example, has a large MI and low velocity, but, by tucking, MI decreases and velocity increases (Figure 6.124).

In field events such as discus and hammer, the athlete attempts to transfer as much momentum to the object as possible. A good athlete will spin with a high velocity and low moment of inertia.

Point of release

The next important factor in determining how far the object will go is the **point of release**.

The hammer moves in a circular motion as the athlete spins round. This means that the

force needed to keep the hammer following a circular path is directed to the centre of the circle – the athlete (Figure 6.125).

Once the hammer is released, the pull force is also released and the hammer flies off at a tangent to the circular path along which it was rotating.

If the object is released too early during the spin, it flies off in completely the wrong direction, travelling behind the thrower, crashing into the cage or not making the designated landing area. If it is released too late, the discus or hammer again either flies into the cage or lands outside the landing area (Figure 6.126).

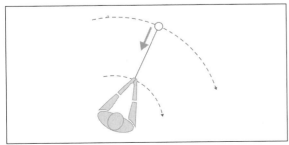

▲ **Figure 6.125** *The force needed to keep the hammer on a circular path is directed inwards*

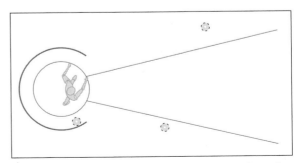

▲ **Figure 6.126** *Release too late or too early and the discus or hammer either falls outside the landing sector or crashes into the cage.*

TASK

a Using a hammer or discus, work out the optimum release point by releasing the object at varying times in the spin. (Try to keep force and angle of release constant.)

b Using Figure 6.127, describe the motion of the diver with reference to the moment of inertia, angular velocity and angular momentum.

KEY SKILLS

Moment of inertia

Deliver a short seminar on this section. Your delivery should include the use of video, photographs and transparencies. You should also produce revision notes for your fellow students.

Be prepared to answer questions.

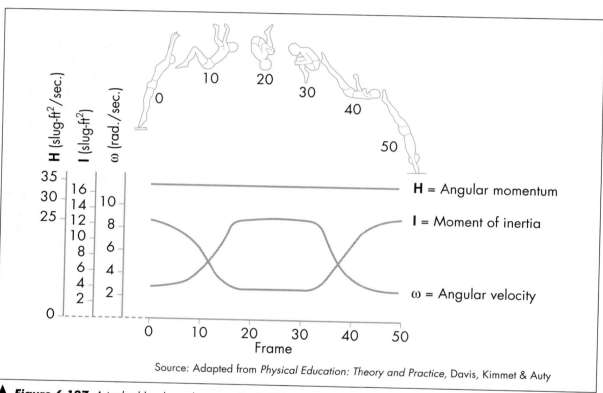

Source: Adapted from *Physical Education: Theory and Practice*, Davis, Kimmet & Auty

▲ **Figure 6.127** *A tucked backward one-and-a-half dive*

Section B: Option B: Sports psychology

1. Introduction to Option B

Section B: Option B builds on some of the themes investigated in Unit 2 Section A: Acquiring skill. You should by now be aware of individual differences in performers, both in terms of personality, learning, development and performance. This option investigates the social influences on performance and the effect of the sporting environment. It also investigates the effect of anxiety on performance and methods for managing it.

You will need to be aware of the psychological concepts, but, more importantly, you will need to apply them in the sporting context. The exam questions will ask you to apply knowledge, so a purely theoretical approach is not sufficient.

It has now become obvious to most people involved in sport that success is more than just the result of physical development. The psychological element is now seen to be one of the many factors that can make the difference between winning and losing. At the top level, performers are of very similar physical abilities and have very similar levels of fitness. It appears that those who win are not only the best physically, but also those who are best able to deal with the performance situation.

In the past, psychology and sport have failed to work together. Scully and Kremer (1994) recognised the lack of real knowledge in the area and identified the need for detailed investigation into the psychology of performance. In recent years this has happened. In fact the Americans have used psychologists for years and, in the 1976 Olympics, the American team appointed psychologists to advise performers. This is now the norm rather than the exception.

Psychologists can help performers in sport and physical education by improving:

- concentration – helping performers/ learners to concentrate on the task in hand, focusing on the activity rather than the surroundings

- self-belief/confidence – often self-belief is a key to success. Psychologists can help performers/learners gain confidence in their ability to perform and to win
- coping strategies – performers need to learn how to cope with a variety of situations if they are to reach their potential and psychologists can help.

The psychology of sport has become an institutionalised discipline within sports science ... It is now possible to say that sports psychology has emerged as a distinctive sub-discipline and as a member of the sports sciences ... Sports psychology has now become a profession in many countries.

Gill, 1986

Much of the work on sports psychology is based in traditional psychology, showing direct applications of existing theories. But more recently specialists have been concerned with this approach and have attempted to generate theories which are directly associated with sport, for example, Alderman, 1984, Dishman, 1983 and Martens, 1980.

2. Learning theories

When looking at the way we develop skills in Unit 2A, we recognised the many factors influencing the learning process. As we learn, we move through three distinct phases: cognitive, associative and autonomous. In this Unit, it is vital to understand in more detail how learning takes place.

As with many psychological issues, there are a number of different schools of thought. These can be divided into two main categories:

- **associationists**
- **cognitivists**.

In simple terms, associationists view learning as the linking of particular stimuli with particular responses, whereas cognitivists see it as more of a function of the brain, where we learn through developing understanding.

Associationist perspectives

Edward Thorndike (1932), the forerunner in the development of associationist theories, recognised that there are a number of factors influencing the linking of a stimulus and a response (S–R). **Thorndike's Laws**, which were formulated in the early twentieth century, are still accepted and used today (see below).

Thorndike's Laws

Law of exercise
A bond between a stimulus and a response will become stronger if it is repeated.

Law of effect
A response will be repeated if a 'satisfier' follows it, a response will not be repeated if an 'annoyer' follows it.

Law of readiness
Learning can only take place if the learner is physically and mentally mature enough.

Another major influence on the development of association theories was Clark Hull (1943), who saw learning as needs, drives and incentives. His **drive theory** views learning to be a result of, in particular, *inhibition*. Hull suggests that a performer will perform worse at the end of a session than in the middle, but even the end of the session will be better than the end of the previous one.

Pavlov

This associationist approach to learning is also referred to as a connectionist approach as it is based on the linking of stimuli with responses (S–R). Ivan Pavlov (1849–1936) developed his theory of **classical conditioning** whilst working on the responses of dogs. He discovered that dogs that salivated when given food could be taught/conditioned to salivate at the sound of a bell. Thus the dogs were conditioned to respond to a stimuli completely unrelated to the response.

Pavlov's experiments showed how it is possible to develop an association between a

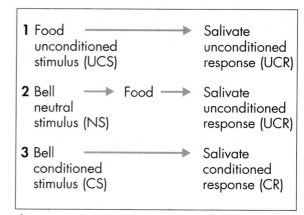

▲ **Figure 6.128** *Pavlov's theory of classical conditioning*

stimulus and a completely unrelated response (Figure 6.128).

The dogs had learnt to associate the bell (neutral stimulus) with food and had been conditioned to salivate at the sound of a bell. If the reward of food is not given with the sound of the bell, the conditioned response is quickly extinguished.

Pavlov also found that if the response did stop, and he then tried to re-condition the dogs to salivate at the sound of the bell, the response was learned more quickly than it had been initially.

TASK

What is the implication of the dogs learning more quickly the second time around?

Pavlov's theories, although relating to instinct responses, are relevant to sport. This is not just because his research was taken further by Skinner (see below), but also because the connecting of a particular response with a stimulus can also benefit sporting performance.

An example where this approach may be used is in psychological preparation. A player may be taught to associate walking out on to the pitch with switching into 'the zone'. This will need to be a gradual process where the conditioned stimulus is introduced alongside the original unconditioned stimulus to get the performer into the zone.

▲ **Figure 6.129** *Switching into 'the zone'*

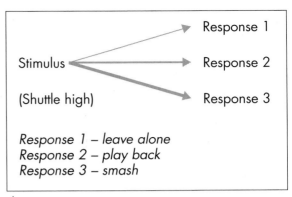

▲ **Figure 6.130** *Skinner's theory of operant conditioning as related to badminton*

TASK

Give other examples where a player may be conditioned to respond to a stimulus completely unrelated to the response.

TASK

Why, if Skinner's conclusions are correct, don't teachers/coaches use more punishment when teaching/coaching?

Skinner

Skinner (1938), who investigated the linking of stimuli with learned responses under the conscious control of the performer, took on the work of Pavlov. He developed the theory of **operant conditioning** (Figure 6.130).

Operant conditioning involves the moulding of behaviour through the actions taken following a response.

Skinner initially investigated the way a reward could mould the behaviour of a pigeon. He found that the pigeon could be made to turn in circles if it was given food each time it turned, or if it was given a programme of reinforcement. The pigeon learned to associate the action of turning with food. In his later experiments, Skinner used rats to investigate the influence of rewards, punishment and negative reinforcement (the taking away of the reward or the punishment).

Skinner found that positive reinforcement (the giving of a reward) led to the action being repeated (a strengthening of the **stimulus–response (S–R) bond**). No reward led to the action not being repeated (a weakening of the S–R bond) and negative reinforcement, in removing or not initiating any reward, also led to the action not being repeated (also weakening of the S–R bond). In his experiments, he found that reward and punishment both led to faster learning than negative reinforcement, or inaction.

The relevance of operant conditioning is more obvious than classical conditioning as it relates to the linking of a stimulus with a particular learned response. In other words, the required response can be encouraged by rewarding it each time it is performed and an incorrect response can be discouraged if it is followed either by no reward or a punishment.

TASK

a Use Figure 6.130 to show how you would ensure that the learner smashes when in the same position again.

b Why and how is Response 1 discouraged more than Response 2?

In your explanation, give specific examples of what you would use to strengthen and weaken the S–R bond.

In conclusion, associationist approaches can be an efficient method of teaching/learning. For generations, parents have been using this approach, rewarding children with pocket money and punishing them when they misbehave. In sport, this method lends itself to a parts method of information processing (see page 116), with each part being learnt through an association and skills-based approach to the teaching of sporting activities.

It is important to consider *motivation* when using this approach. Punishment can de-motivate if it is used too much and at the wrong time with some individuals. Others it will motivate and spur on to improve further.

Cognitivist perspectives

Cognitive theories of learning recognise learning as more than just a process of association. They see it as more of a holistic experience, with performances requiring an understanding of the situation and the performer and then selecting the most appropriate action.

The Gestalt school

The **Gestalt** school of thought (founded around 1910 in Germany) initially proposed the notion of insight or intuition as a means of learning. They suggested that in the initial stages of learning, trial and error learning allows a person to slowly organise and reorganise information and then suddenly a solution is reached. This has been referred to as the EUREKA effect (from the Greek, meaning 'I've found it!'). This is often evident in sport where a child appears to not understand or cannot perform one day and then the next they grasp the concepts and can perform the skill.

Koffka, Koehler and Lewin were three cognitivists who believed in the Gestaltists' dictum 'the whole is more important than the sum of the parts'. In other words, they suggested that learning through insight and understanding would lead to greater understanding and performance than learning all of the separate parts. They suggested that *the why* and *the how* need to be understood, not just the programmed response put forward by the connectionists.

Learning using the Gestalt theory requires a whole approach, where a problem is set and the learner then develops his or her own solution. Köehler (1925) investigated this way of learning with chimpanzees. He recognised that in contrast to associationist/S–R approaches, where trial and error would be used until a correct solution is reinforced, learning takes place following an analysis of the problem and the formation of a solution.

That solution can then be instantly repeated rather than having to be conditioned. An example of this might be when we work out for ourselves how to programme a video recorder; we can then programme it again because we understand the concepts involved and not just the actions. The same is true in sport; someone who understands the concepts of batting is likely to perform better than someone who is programmed to play particular shots.

TASK

Plan a lesson to develop a racket game using a Gestaltist approach.

a How would this differ from an associationist approach?

b Which one of Mosston and Ashworth's teaching styles (page 108) is most appropriate for use with the Gestalt approach?

Koehler's conclusions followed observations of his chimpanzees using a combination of sticks to reach food through the bars of the cage or the use of crates to stand on to reach food. The chimps analysed the situation and then formed a solution that they then used again. The Gestalt approach would suggest that to learn to perform in sport, we must develop a clear understanding of the requirements, and then work out a solution if we are to perform the skills correctly and in the correct circumstances.

Harlow and Gagné

Obviously cognitivists and associationists are at opposite ends of the theoretical continuum. Some theorists have attempted to bring together the two schools and to show a link. Harlow (1949) suggests that they are both part of a continuous learning process. He investigated the hierarchical nature of learning (that each element of learning builds on the next), through the setting of tasks for monkeys. He found that monkeys could develop the ability to differentiate between objects, and that if the monkeys built up skills gradually, complex tasks could be completed successfully. Although this work has been shown to have a limited effect on the learning of physical skills as opposed to cognitive skills, the notion that similar skills can be developed through a gradual process is true.

Gagné (1970) furthered this view, identifying eight varieties of learning, ranging from the simple, involving connection, to the complex, involving insight. He also suggests that learning is hierarchical with the learning of simple tasks and abilities being required for performance at the next level (Figure 6.131).

It is clear that learning is an extremely complex process involving many different approaches and concepts. As we saw in Unit 2 Acquiring skill, there are various ways of teaching and learning depending on the situation. We need to identify how an individual learns, what the requirements of the task are, and then ensure that the best learning environment is provided.

TASK

a Using your knowledge of Mosston and Ashworth's spectrum of teaching styles on page 108, discuss the different styles and how they might be linked to the different stages put forward by Gagné.

b What are the implications of Gagné's suggestion – that we learn simple tasks initially through conditioning and gradually develop our learning abilities – to the teaching of PE in primary and secondary schools?

---

1 Signal learning
Establishment of a simple connection (classical conditioning)

2 Stimulus–response learning
Connecting a learned response with a stimulus (operant conditioning)

3 Chaining
(Must have achieved **1+2**)
The connecting of two or more S–R bonds

4 Verbal association
The learning of verbal chains

5 Discrimination learning
(Must have achieved **3+4**)
Responding differently to different stimuli; being able to distinguish minor differences

6 Concept learning
(Must have achieved **5**)
The learning of common responses which differ in physical characteristics

7 Concept learning
(Must have achieved **6**)
The learning of rule concepts or a chain of concepts (if A then B etc.)

8 Problem-solving
(Must have achieved **7**)
Involves understanding, linking and insight (Gestalt approach)

▲ **Figure 6.131** Gagné's hierarchy of learning

3. Personality

As with all areas of psychology, sports psychology is concerned with issues of individuality. It is our **personalities** which make us different and which lead us to behave in different ways. Much of the research has attempted to identify a particular sporting personality or personalities that suit one sport and not another.

Griffiths (1927) concluded that although there is not a specific sporting personality there are a number of identifiable common characteristics: ruggedness, courage, intelligence, exuberance, buoyancy, emotional adjustment, optimism, conscientiousness, alertness, loyalty and respect for authority. Ogilvie (1968) continued this work and developed the Athletic Motivation Inventory (AMI) to identify the characteristics.

TASK

Discuss whether you can identify a personality type common to all sports performers; or if there are certain personalities who play certain sports.

The various theories differ in their interpretation and understanding of personality and its development, and there is much debate concerning individuality. How is it that two people with completely different personalities can do the same job? What makes them behave the way they do?

One useful analysis of what personality is was put forward by Hollander (1971). He describes personality as:

The sum of the individual's characteristics which make him unique.

This definition is the basis of a widely held view that sees personality as unique to the individual. There are, however, differences of opinion as to changes in personality over time and where those differences come from.

Hollander (1971) saw the structure of personality as having three layers (Figure 6.132).

- The psychological core – the key to the personality, being made up of the basic attitudes and values which remain relatively constant and which influence responses
- The middle layer – 'the typical response' is the way in which the person will tend to respond in any given situation, based on the psychological core, as the response will be closely linked to the attitudes and values, e.g. if a player believes in good sportsmanship, they will call the ball out in a game of tennis or admit to the ball hitting their feet in hockey
- The outer layer – 'the role-related behaviours' will be influenced by the situation the individual is in. As the situation varies massively, so will this aspect of behaviour.

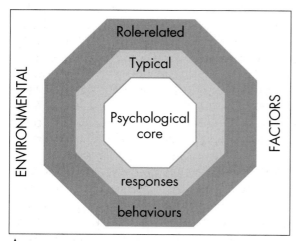

▲ **Figure 6.132** *Hollander's theory of personality*

Role-related behaviour might bear no resemblance to the psychological core as the pressures of the environment may be stronger than the core.

The different theories of personality include **psychoanalytic**, **interactionalist** and **humanistic** perspectives which are discussed below.

Psychoanalytic perspectives

Sigmund Freud (1856–1939), the father of psychoanalytic theory, saw personality as instincts driving us to behave in particular ways. These instincts are innate, that is they are inherited from our parents, and achievement of the drive leads to satisfaction. The instincts fit into two opposing categories: death instincts and life instincts (Figure 6.133).

The psychoanalytic perspective suggests that our behaviour and our personality are outside our conscious control. We do things not to gain rewards, e.g. a medal or a team place, but to satisfy some form of a drive.

Freud suggested that there are three components to the mind: the *id*, the *ego* and the *superego*.

Id

This is the basic biological determinant in our behaviour and includes food, love and, the most important, sex. These may appear to have similarities with the characteristics identified in trait theories (see page 446). However, Freud suggests that these are over-written by social and emotional learned behaviours.

Ego

The ego ensures that we behave in a way that won't damage us. It is a control or protection measure. It is what we have learned to be and the ego is seen to be our self. We tend to see ourselves in terms of our ego as it is the window through which we present ourselves.

Death instincts	destructive and dangerous, e.g. aggression
Life instincts	positive and creative, e.g. empathy

▲ **Figure 6.133** *Life and death instincts*

Superego

The superego is said to include our ideal self, how we would like to be and is based on an image of our parents. This tends to be our moral control. 'I should not retaliate in a game because that is not the ideal way to behave.' Unfortunately, suggests Freud, this area of our mind leads to conflict and guilt and thus controls impulses.

Interactionalist perspectives

The interactionalist theories of learning view personality as just one element that influences how we behave. This is similar to the work of Hollander. Interactionalists see our behaviour (B) as being a function (f) of both our personality (P) and the environment (e) in which we exist:

$$B = f(Pe)$$

B = behaviour
P = personality
e = environment

This approach suggests that we behave in a way governed by our core personality, but act in a way to suit the situation in which we find ourselves. This appears a sensible approach, allowing for the different ways we behave in different situations.

We don't behave in the same way with our friends as we do with our grandparents, for example. We will behave differently when selected to play in a county sports team than we would if simply kicking a ball around with friends in the local park (Figure 6.134).

▲ *Figure 6.134* We behave differently in different situations

TASK

Discuss why we don't always behave in the same way in all situations. Give examples of occasions when you have behaved differently in sporting situations. Why did you behave as you did?

Humanistic perspectives

The humanistic approach sees the person as a whole *person – not just a mind that thinks, but a body that feels and has its own language, and a spirit that aspires beyond what can be seen, heard and touched.*

Humanists are seen as the third element in psychology, and are different from the psychoanalytic and interactionalist perspectives, concentrating on the whole self. Rogers (1957) suggests that the human personality is made up of many elements, all combining to make us what we are.

Another way to characterise humanistic psychology is through its emphasis on the self. Thus, constructs like: **self-concept**, self-esteem and self-image are part of the humanist vocabulary.

Rogers suggests that our personality is made up of three key components, which create our self-concept and develop our feelings of worth:

- academic
- social
- physical.

Later, Fox (1988) saw our self-concept as the picture we have of ourselves which then leads us to behave in particular ways. With the addition of 'attitudes' as the fourth component, these key areas constitute a combination of overall feelings and image that make up 'the self' (Figure 6.135).

The physical 'self' is of most interest to us in the sporting context, and can be seen as being both appearance and skill-based.

This and other humanistic approaches suggest that all of our experiences throughout life combine to make us what we are. If we feel we have a big nose, or that we are no good at football, this will influence our self-concept and ultimately our personality.

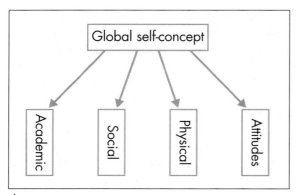

▲ **Figure 6.135** *Our self-concept is made up of four key areas*

Rogers suggested that we have an ideal self – how we would like to be. The further away from the ideal we feel we are, the more conflict there is likely to be.

The influence of PE and sport on the self-concept is important and can be seen to link with Bandura's theory of **self-efficacy**. There appears to be a circular relationship, in that success in sport will lead to positive feedback. This in turn gives a boost to self-esteem, which then motivates us to perform and thus improves performance still further (see page 435).

> ## TASK
> Give examples of how sport has helped develop your self-confidence.
>
> How has this changed you as a person?

Nature versus nurture

One debate that occurs repeatedly is that of *nature versus nurture*. That is, are we what we are because of birth (inherited factors), or do we develop into the individuals we are through a social process (upbringing and experiences)?

> ## TASK
> From your experience, do you think we are born with a particular personality or is it shaped by our experiences?

Trait theories of personality

Those psychologists who believe we are born with a particular personality that will remain throughout our lives are known as **trait theorists**. They think that we are born with certain characteristics that are inherited from our parents and that these will not change.

This traditional perspective has dominated psychological thinking for more than 50 years. It has the benefit of being simple to measure and understand and at a basic level can be used to explain what makes us all different. It suggests that our personality is made up of a number of traits or characteristics that combine to form our behaviour. Most research has centred on several common traits. Cattell identified 16 key traits.

Eysenck regards personality as being primarily an inborn phenomenon. To him, it is more like eye colour or height than something that is learned. He has proposed a scheme with three dimensions:

- neurotic vs. stable
- extroverted vs. introverted
- stupid vs. intelligent.

He has created a test to measure individuals on those three dimensions.

Norman's 'Big Five' personality traits are similar to Eysenck's. They are:

- neuroticism
- extroversion
- openness
- agreeableness
- conscientiousness.

4. The performer in action: Theories and applications

One of the most important roles of the sports psychologist is to motivate the performer to gain optimum performance.

Achievement motivation

Individuals are motivated by different factors. When we are presented with choices, our decision will be influenced by our motivation. Atkinson (1974) recognised that some of us want to be challenged and are motivated by the need to achieve (nAch). These people will want to take the difficult option, as they want to see if they can do it. Others need to avoid failure (naF). These people will take the easy option as they are afraid of failure and don't want to be seen to fail. For example, if there are three options to climb on a climbing wall, one easy, one medium and one hard, a person with a high nAch will attempt the difficult route. If they succeed, they have achieved a difficult task; if they fail, it does not matter as they at least took a chance. The opposite is true for someone with a high naF; they would select the easy route to ensure success. They would be worried that if they chose a more difficult route, they would be seen to be a failure.

Figure 6.136 shows that nAch and naF tend to be inversely proportional to each other, although there are some performers who seem to have both high nAch and naF or low nAch and naF. In other words, if a performer has high nAch they will have low naF and vice versa.

Achievement motivation + personality

The **achievement motivation** of an individual is often related to their personality. In sport, someone with extrovert tendencies is likely to have high nAch as they want to be seen and will therefore take the difficult option. On the other hand, an introvert will take the easy option in the hope that they will not fail and will not be noticed.

In the earlier discussions of personality (page 427), we considered whether there was a particular sporting type. In team sports, it seems there is a need for a combination of different types of achievement motivation. In

general, those motivated to avoid failure do well in defensive areas and those motivated to achieve are more suited to attacking positions. Thus those defending will not take risks – 'if in doubt, kick it out' – and those attacking who need to be creative will take risks – 'shoot on sight'.

TASK

Give examples of top level performers who demonstrate either a high need to achieve or who are motivated to avoid failure.

What makes you think they are high nAch or high naF?

Situational factors

Although slightly simplistic, Atkinson's suggestions relating to choice and motivation are well supported within sports psychology and have been expanded. Atkinson identified that there were situational factors that govern our decisions, that is, the probability of success and the rewards available for success (Figure 6.137). If the task is difficult, there is a low probability of success but a high value to the success. For example, a school level tennis player who plays the Wimbledon champion will have high value from winning but a low probability, whereas a good performer playing a weak opponent is likely to win, but will get little satisfaction from the result.

Roberts (1974) suggests that this means that individuals with high failure avoidance

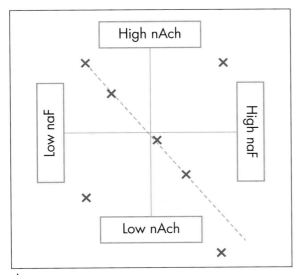
▲ **Figure 6.136** Achievement motivation

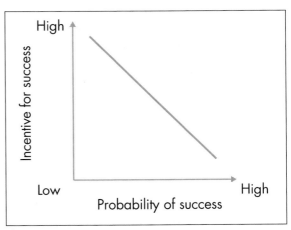
▲ **Figure 6.137** Situational factors

will not only select the easy option, but also the very difficult option. and that high achievers select areas with difficulty, but also some possibility of success as they require the rewards that go with success.

TASK

Roberts suggests that some people may take the very easy or very hard option. Why might they do this?

The relationship between the likelihood of success and the potential rewards is usually written as a formula:

$$nAch = (Ms–Maf) \times (Ps \times (1–Ps))$$

nAch: Need to achieve
Ms: Motive for success
Maf: Motive to avoid failure
Ps: Probability of success
1–Ps: Incentive value of success

In other words, our need to achieve is the difference between the motives for success and failure multiplied by the product of the probability of success and its incentive value.

Various tests have been designed to recognise levels of nAch and naF. As with many psychological measures, these have been by questionnaire, observation and experiment. Carron (1981) and others have devised questionnaire-based approaches. The problem with any such approach is that they rely on the honesty and accuracy of answers if the results are to be valid and reliable.

A rather more effective method of assessing nAch and naF is to use experiments. It is important that those being tested are not aware of the reason for the test and that various different situations are used to avoid sport-specific bias.

The attitude questionnaire and the achievement motivation test in the Tasks below illustrate the theories of Atkinson et al. These theories have been augmented by further work on achievement goal orientation (Covington, 1984), where two levels of achievement goals have been identified.

TASK

Attitude questionnaire

		Agree ⟷ Disagree
1	Winning in sport is essential	1 2 3 4 5 6
2	I would rather play someone I find it difficult to beat	1 2 3 4 5 6
3	I enjoy a challenge	1 2 3 4 5 6
4	I enjoy close games	1 2 3 4 5 6
5	I don't worry about the result	1 2 3 4 5 6
6	I make mistakes under pressure	6 5 4 3 2 1

The subjects of this questionnaire should be unaware of its purpose. Ask them to give a score for each of the statements above. A low score represents *high nAch*, whereas a high score gives a *high naF*.

TASK

Achievement motivation test: basketball

1 Give each candidate ten shots from the free throw line and record the scores.
2 Give each candidate ten further shots from anywhere, recording where they shot from and if they scored.
3 Score the second set of shots as follows:
   • 1 point if nearer
   • 2 points if from free throw line
   • 3 points if further away.
   It is important that the candidates are not aware of what the experiment is testing and that they are told they must count the number of shots scored.
4 Calculate the total score for the second set of ten shots.
5 Give each candidate their results:
   10–15pts: low risk taker
   16–24pts: average
   25–30pts: high risk taker

The taking of risks should correlate with the need to achieve. Remember to discuss the results with the candidates, explaining what you did and why you did it.

You could attempt this experiment in a range of situations to ensure there is no influence of ability/skill on the results and to ensure validity and reliability.

The achievement motivation test has a more practical application than the attitude questionnaire and can easily be re-designed to test a whole range of sports skills.

Mastery goals

Mastery goals are appropriate for students who are motivated by incremental targets leading to improvement, where the goals are set to be challenging but achievable.

Goals set by a performer should be SMART:

S – specific, easily understood and concise

M – measurable: progress can be seen

A – attainable: set within possible levels

R – realistic: set at sensible levels, not too hard and not too easy

T – time-bonded: the goal(s) should be set within a specific time framework.

Failure avoidance goals

Failure avoidance goals may be used by students who are motivated not to fail. They set targets they can achieve, and so leave their self-image intact. If they do fail, they tend to blame other or external factors, for example, 'I hate football, that's why I don't play for the school team.'

The risk to a performer of being a 'failure avoider' is that by setting themselves easy targets they won't improve their skills. Eventually, when faced with an unavoidable situation, they may then fail later on. In this case they may become what Covington refers to as **failure acceptors**. This can be a problem for coaches/teachers who then need to take action to develop a more positive approach.

Although Covington and others have modified the theories of achievement motivation, there still remains the basic premise put forward by Atkinson – that some individuals want to be tested, and others want to remain in a 'comfort zone' where success is virtually guaranteed without fear of challenge.

TASK

Why would a coach prefer to work with a mastery-orientated learner rather than a failure-avoiding learner?

Attribution theory

A major weapon in the sports psychologists' armoury is an approach based on the work of Weiner (1979). Weiner identified a number of factors as being responsible for sporting performance. He then devised a self-report framework by which a performer/coach can create an attributional profile that can then be used to motivate and improve performance. One strong argument in favour of Weiner's **attribution theory** is his discovery that one major difference between high and low achievers is the way in which they develop attributions about success and failure.

TASK

Following a game/match, write down a list of the factors you feel were responsible for the result, e.g. you played well/badly, poor referee etc.

Weiner carried out a similar exercise to the task above with a large sample. He then grouped the wide range of factors discovered into four 'constructs' or areas of attribution, and these four into two further dimensions.

The four constructs identified were:

- ability – how good the performer is or how well they can cope with the task
- effort – the amount of effort put into the task, both physically and mentally
- task difficulty – how hard the activity was to perform, either in terms of tariff (difficulty) or the ability of the opposition
- luck – the bounce of the ball, the decisions of the referee etc.

TASK

Using your list from the previous task, divide your factors into these four constructs.

The two dimensions into which these four constructs were then divided he called *locus of causality/control* and *stability*. In simple terms, these relate to the extent to which the performer controls the construct and the extent to which the construct is the same from week to week, or game to game.

Weiner did not claim these to be the only factors, but that the majority of other influences could be catered for in this model (Figure 6.138).

This figure can be used to analyse the reasons for success and failure, with performers giving a STEN (score out of ten) for the amount they feel each factor was responsible for the result.

The results of the attribution process, either from a team as a whole, or from an individual, can be used to gain a valuable insight into the psychological state of the performer. The scores can give indications of:

- performance satisfaction
- performance expectancy
- learned helplessness.

Performance satisfaction

Use of this approach allows us to identify whether success leads to **performance satisfaction** and failure to dissatisfaction. This can then be used to identify the areas of satisfaction/dissatisfaction and to pinpoint those

needing attention. It is important that the learner identifies problem areas if they are to apply themselves fully to their improvement.

Weiner (1974) recognised that successful performers/teams are more likely to attribute success to internal and stable factors. In this way they gain satisfaction from the feeling that the success is due to themselves and that it is likely to happen again in the future as it is stable.

He suggests that this should be encouraged as it helps with motivation, and also that less successful teams should be encouraged to attribute failure to external and unstable factors as this allows the blame to be placed away from the individual and allows for the situation to change next time.

If a team who are having a losing season can be persuaded that their failure so far is due to bad luck rather than inept performance, this perception might lead them to believe that their luck might change the next time they play. If failure is also attributed to lack of effort, a determination to address this shortcoming may well succeed in producing rather better performances in the future.

Performance expectancy

Attribution can be seen as both a retrospective tool, analysing what happened, but also as a predictor of future performance (**performance expectancy**). If we continually recognise the same factors as being responsible for success or failure, that can then become 'a self-fulfilling prophecy'. For example, if I identify that 'I expect to win because my ability is good and I try hard', I therefore tend to play well, try hard and usually win. This kind of attitude is often referred to as 'positive mental attitude' or the 'power of positive thinking'. It is a result of previous experience as well as **attributional retraining**.

Learned helplessness

Similar to performance expectancy, some performers learn to attribute failure to internal and stable factors (**learned helplessness**). Again this can become a self-fulfilling prophecy.

A performer may feel that they have lost the last three matches because of a poor second serve and that the others in the tennis league are far better at this. This leads to the player entering the next game expecting to serve badly and anticipating that the opponent will

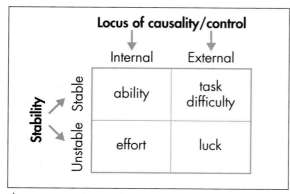

▲ *Figure 6.138* *Weiner's attribution model*

be ready to punish this weakness. This attitude is reflected in the performance and the player has virtually lost the match before they begin. In this situation a coach needs to break the cycle. The player needs to develop confidence and begin to expect to win. This is strongly linked with Bandura's theory of **self-efficacy** (see below).

TASK

Discuss how you would change a performer from a position of learned helplessness to one where they have a positive mental attitude.

Uses of attribution

A coach or psychologist can use the attribution process to develop understanding and motivation in the performer. By identifying the reasons for a performance, the performer can be encouraged to improve (Figure 6.139).

Confidence

Attribution can be used to give the performer confidence: 'You won because you are good and you try hard.' This shows the performer that it is perfectly likely that success may be repeated.

Effort

A performer who attributes failure to a lack of effort can be made to realise that if they try harder they can win.

Pressure reduction

Many top level performers use prior attribution or attributional retraining before competing to take the pressure off themselves. Athletes will often publicly announce that they are injured but will do their best, or a Grand Prix driver will say at the start of the season that his car is not good enough to win. Thus if the athlete or the driver wins, they are given greater positive feedback because they did so against the odds. If they don't win then it was the fault of the car, or the injury, leaving them exonerated in their own eyes and, hopefully, in the eyes of others.

Motivation

One of the best ways to use the attribution approach is to gain greater effort in training. A coach who can instil correct attribution into his performers can make them realise what needs improving and how hard they need to work even when they are winning and playing well.

Self-efficacy

Self-efficacy is defined as the:

level of confidence in the likelihood of achieving a goal.

Coolican, 1996

Earlier, Bandura (1977) described it as:

Self-confidence in any given situation.

Self-confidence is essential if a performer is to achieve at the highest level of their capability. The development of a positive mental attitude will enable the achievement of a self-fulfilling prophecy of success.

Many psychologists have investigated and written about self-confidence. These include Weinberg (1995), who suggests that when we are confident, we remain calm, concentrate, set challenging goals, try harder, take more risks and persevere.

Performers need to be aware of the benefits of feeling confident, but also the risks of over-confidence which can lead to a lack of effort, excessive risk-taking and even a lack of concentration.

▲ *Figure 6.139* Attribution theory

Give examples of performers who show high levels of confidence that have led to success, and examples where over-confidence has caused problems.

Of the many theories of self-confidence, that of Bandura seems to be the most widely accepted. He identified four key factors in the development of self-efficacy and our expectations of future success. These four are essential if the performer is to expect and achieve their best. They are:

- performance accomplishments
- vicarious experiences
- verbal persuasion
- emotional arousal.

Each of these factors will influence efficacy expectations and ultimately, performance (see Figure 6.140).

Performance accomplishments

This is the level of success previously experienced by the performer. High levels of success will allow the individual to feel confident and to expect future success. For the teacher this is an essential element. Learners require success, but do not always experience it, so it is important that what is meant by success is set at an appropriate level. To an able performer, this may be winning a game; to a less able performer, just hitting the ball may be appropriate. The coach/teacher must provide suitable opportunities for success if the learner/performer is to grow in confidence.

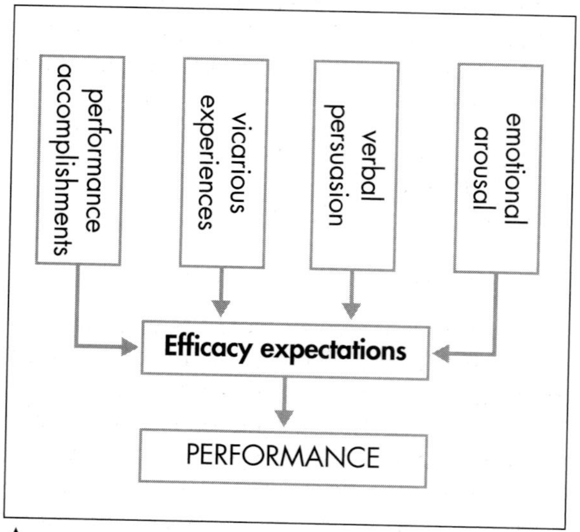

TASK

Give examples of different types of success and how they can add to confidence.

Vicarious experiences

Vicarious experiences or modelling refers to observing others perform (see also page 438). If we see someone else succeed, then we feel that we can succeed as well (especially if the other person is of a similar standard to ourselves). For example, if we are in a high jump competition and the jumper before us clears the height, we will feel confident that we can too.

TASK

a Give examples of vicarious experiences you have had that have given you the confidence to perform.

b Are there any occasions when vicarious experiences lead to a decline in efficacy?

Verbal persuasion

This concerns the role of the coach and significant others in ensuring that the performer believes they can succeed. The coach can instil confidence through discussion and persuasion. For verbal persuasion to influence efficacy, the message must be believable and from a respected source. If not, the message will be ignored and have no effect on confidence.

Emotional arousal

This refers to the motivational components of performance. If we feel under-aroused, we will lack confidence, knowing that we are not in the right frame of mind to perform. Again, the coach/teacher has a key role to play in ensuring optimum arousal levels.

▲ *Figure 6.140* Bandura's self-efficacy model

TASK

a Discuss the kinds of phrases a coach might use to motivate a performer.

b Why does a coach's team talk not always ensure the ideal levels of arousal?

Knowledge of Bandura's theory of self-efficacy shows the influences on confidence, whilst theorists such as Weinberg (1995) suggest ways in which confidence may be developed. They consider that mental and physical preparation are key to the ideal confidence levels (Figure 6.141).

Self-motivation

We are motivated to take part in sport by a number of factors. Cratty (1989) suggests that these factors include: a desire to achieve a sense of mastery, a wish for status, friendship, challenge or excitement.

Gross (1992) described motivation as the 'why of behaviour'. Coaches and teachers constantly attempt to give the performer the why. However, it is also vital that the performer is self-motivated (Figure 6.142).

As discussed in Unit 2A on page 121, the place of motivation in learning is central. This is also true in performance in general – if a performer is to be at their best, they must know what motivates them.

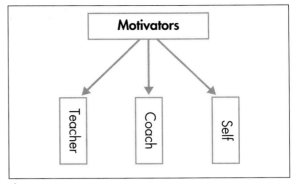

▲ *Figure 6.142* Who motivates a performer?

The motivation to participate and to succeed may come from within the performer (intrinsic) or from outside (extrinsic). In this section we are concerned with the motivation from within, or **self-motivation**. As Bidell (1984) suggested, this ultimately is the most important motivation if we are to continue to succeed.

Self-motivation is the internal drive to succeed. It is the performer's intention to achieve their best, for personal satisfaction and happiness. It is not the desire to succeed for outside rewards, such as money or fame. Psychologists have investigated the need for self-motivation and how performers' focus can be moved away from the extrinsic to the intrinsic. In a study of rugby players by Spence in 1999, it was found that the drive for success was developed through a combination of common team drives and individual satisfaction drives. Players all have common team goals – winning, succeeding etc. – whilst different players have their own personal motivation factors which can be identified. These include:

- personal achievement
- challenge
- achieving ambition
- fitness
- contribution to the whole.

It is important to note that people may be motivated by a variety of different factors. An inventory of motivational factors will include intrinsic and extrinsic aspects. A coach or psychologist should help players to identify what motivates them to ensure that they all perform to their best and do not allow their efforts to slip.

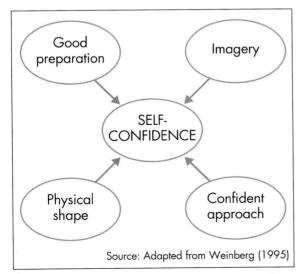

▲ *Figure 6.141* Developing confidence: mental and physical preparation are essential

Observational learning

The concept that we learn through watching others and model our behaviour on them is clear. We see children mimicking adults and developing their skills and personalities. Bandura (1969), in his theory of social, **observational or vicarious learning**, bridges the gap between the traditional behaviourism and cognitive approaches.

He suggests that there are four key factors that influence observational learning as shown in Figure 6.143:

- attention
- retention
- motivation
- reproduction.

Attention

We must pay attention to what we see. If we are concentrating on something, then we are more likely to copy it later. For example, if you are watching one of your sporting heroes, you are more likely to pay attention to what they are doing than someone you do not like.

Retention

If the learner is to model the actions through observation, the information must be retained (remembered).

Therefore the information must be memorable; that is, it must stand out or be unusual. That is why children often learn better when they see something outstanding or when they see something different. For example, the 'Cruyff turn' in football was copied by millions who saw it on television as it had not been seen before (Figure 6.144).

Motivation

The individual must be motivated to copy the action being demonstrated. If they do not want to copy the act they will not, and so observational learning will not take place.

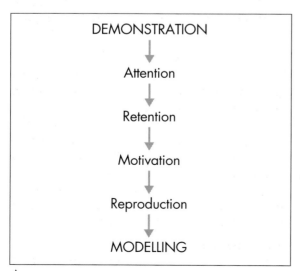

DEMONSTRATION

↓

Attention

↓

Retention

↓

Motivation

↓

Reproduction

↓

MODELLING

▲ **Figure 6.143** Observational learning

▲ **Figure 6.144** Johan Cruyff was famous for his turns, seen on TV and copied by millions

Reproduction

The action or behaviour observed then needs to be reproduced or copied. This may require experimentation and practice, with the original observation having to be repeated.

There are two major aspects of Bandura's work that are important for the teacher and coach to consider:

- skill development
- behavioural influences.

Skill development

Teachers and coaches can improve skill development through attention to the four factors identified by Bandura. If they make demonstrations memorable, easily understandable and they motivate the performers, the actions are likely to be copied.

Behavioural influences

Top level performers who become role models are watched by millions who will then learn vicariously from them. It is vital that they set good examples for those watching. Conversely, observational learning can also be seen to be one cause of **aggression** (see below).

TASK

Observe children playing football in the park. What do they do when they score a goal? Explain how their actions have been learned.

Observational learning was also linked to conditioning theories when Bandura *et al.*, (1963) demonstrated that children spontaneously imitate adult behaviour and then adjust their imitations, depending on whether the modelling is rewarded or punished. This is important as it demonstrates observational learning takes place whether rewarded or not, but that if it is to continue, it needs reinforcing.

TASK

Discuss why this aspect of Bandura's work is important for a coach/teacher.

---

5. The performer in action: Aggression

Definitions

The term aggression is used in many different ways to describe a huge range of actions. In general terms, these range from a strong but fair tackle to a fight in a football game. It is important, therefore, to understand what is meant by aggression and the different forms it can take.

Baron (1977) believed it to be:

Any behaviour directed at the goal of harming or injuring another being who is motivated to avoid such treatment.

Baron is suggesting here that a key element is the intent to harm. This may be physical or mental, but the harm is intentional.

Lloyd *et al.* (1984) regarded aggression in terms of being a socially undesirable act.

Baron in his work identified that aggressive acts take different forms and can be divided into three categories:

- **hostile/reactive aggression**
- **instrumental aggression**
- **assertive behaviour.**

Hostile/reactive aggression

Acts falling into this category reflect Baron's original definition, in that the main intention is to cause harm. A player who retaliates to a previous occurrence is showing reactive aggression – they are reacting and are intending to cause injury to the opponent. This form of aggression is outside the rules of the game and is often punished with a penalty or a punishment in sport.

Instrumental aggression

This second form of aggression involves an aggressive act where the intention is to win and to cause harm, even if the harm is psychological. The intention may be to win the ball with a firm tackle or to 'soften-up' a batsman by bowling a bouncer. It is often difficult to legislate against this form of aggression as it often falls within the rules of the game, as the main aim is to win in spite of the fact that there is still the intention to harm.

Assertive behaviour

It can be argued that assertion is not really a form of aggression as it falls within the rules of the game and there is no intention to harm. Assertive behaviour in sport is the use of legitimate force to win, not to harm. A hard tackle in rugby or a drive through a group of players in basketball is assertive but not aggressive as the aim is to get the ball or score a basket rather than to hurt the other players.

TASK

Categorise the following examples into the three forms of aggression:

- a football player tripping an opponent as they are about to shoot into an open goal
- a tennis player abusing an umpire after a close call
- a boxer knocking out his opponent
- a badminton player smashing directly at an opponent.

A number of theories have been developed to explain why we are aggressive. Most of these relate in particular to hostile aggression, but also to some degree to instrumental aggression. They also do not just concern aggression in sport.

TASK

Give examples of occasions when you have been aggressive in sport.

- What caused the aggression?
- What type of aggression was it?

Instinct theory

The **instinct theory** of aggression is based on the work of Sigmund Freud (1933). He held the view that aggression is an instinct that we all have and that we are born with. It is a *death instinct* (see page 428) which generates a subconscious self-destructive force (*thanatos*). This instinct, Freud suggests, manifests itself in different ways, one of which is in acts of aggression. Research by Freud and Lorenz et al. (1966) suggest that, as in animals, we are biologically determined to act aggressively in an attempt to become dominant. Lorenz puts forward the idea that aggressive energy builds up and needs to be released.

It has been suggested that sport can play a central role in a civilised world for the release of this aggressive energy.

TASK

Give examples how sport can release aggressive energy.

Social learning theory

Leakey and Lewin (1977), Bandura (1969) and other advocates of **social learning theory** believe that there is much more to aggression than the purely biological. They suggest that whatever aggression we are born with is culturally over-ridden. To them aggression is based on modelling; that is, we learn from watching and mimicking others and our behaviour relates to our experiences.

Bandura in his experiments with Bobo dolls found that children who observed aggressive acts were more likely to show aggression than those who didn't. As discussed on page 438, key elements in observational learning are: what we see, who we see doing it and also how our actions are then reinforced.

TASK

What are the implications of the influence of the social learning theories of aggression for sports administrators, players and the media?

Frustration/aggression hypothesis

Many aggressive acts in sport appear to be the result of frustration – whether over performance, a referee's decision or the score. The **frustration/aggression hypothesis** was formulated following the work of Dollard (1939). This hypothesis suggests that when an aim or a goal (a need) is frustrated, then aggression results. This theory is related to the instinct theories in that it suggests that when we are frustrated in fulfilling a need, the pent-up frustration and aggression are released through aggressive acts. However, with instinct theory, aggression itself is the goal, whereas with the frustration/aggression theory, aggression is the result (Figures 6.145 and 6.146).

As illustrated in Figure 6.146, the more a performer becomes frustrated, the more likely they are to become aggressive.

One further theory that relates to the impact of frustration, but also shows the influence of arousal, is **Berkowitz's aggressive cue theory** (1969). Berkowitz sees frustration leading to an increase in arousal, which can then, depending on the situation, lead to aggression or not. He suggests that if there are aggressive cues such as guns or bats, or the sport itself is aggressive – rugby, boxing, etc. – or you are in a situation where you have been aggressive before, you are more likely to be aggressive than if those cues do not exist.

Causes of aggression

Research into aggression in sport has highlighted a number of causes. Once these have been identified, possible solutions can be suggested.

The score

Aggressive acts tend to be more common in games where the score is close, possibly due

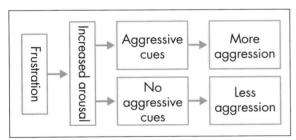

▲ **Figure 6.145** *Dollard's frustration/aggression cues*

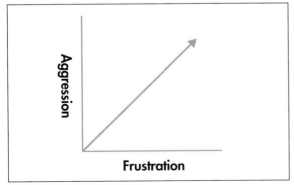

▲ **Figure 6.146** *Frustration/aggression hypothesis*

to over-arousal. However, at the higher levels, aggression occurs less in close games because of the implications of giving away a penalty or being sent off.

Playing venue

There is some evidence that there is more aggression from away teams than home teams. This is possibly due to the pressure and relates to **social facilitation**.

The time of the game

Aggressive acts seem to occur more towards the end of the game than at the beginning, possibly due to frustration and tiredness leading to a loss of control.

The result

The frustration/aggression hypothesis (see page 440) predicts that we are more likely to see aggressive acts from the losing team than the one winning.

Perceptions of intent

This cause links with Baron's definition of reactive aggression (see page 439) in that the belief that an opponent has done something to you intentionally will lead you to retaliate (Redeemer and Shields, 1986).

Social facilitation

Zajonk (1965) investigated the influence of the presence of others on our actions (see page 443). He identified that we all react differently to the presence of others when we perform. A crowd can have a negative influence on both performance and performers, as the latter can become over-aroused and thus lose control.

Teaching/coaching

Social learning theory (see page 440) identifies that what we see and experience will influence how we behave. Thus if a teacher or coach shows aggressive tendencies and does not punish aggressive acts, then the performer is likely to develop more aggressive tendencies.

The rules of the game

Sports that encourage physical contact and require assertion are more likely to experience aggressive acts. The reasons for aggression in these activities and the forms it takes will vary and this can be explained from all theoretical perspectives.

Psychological state

The influence of the performer's psychological state on performance has been widely investigated, looking in particular at the influence of arousal levels on performance (see page 446).

Ways to eliminate aggression

There are ways in which the number and severity of aggressive acts in sport, both on and off the pitch, can be reduced. Depending on the reason for the aggression, and the theories to which you subscribe, different actions can be taken.

Reducing football hooliganism

In 1984 the British government put forward a proposal to reduce football hooliganism (Figure 6.147). The plan involved all supporters carrying an identity card. However, the authorities realised that much of the aggression was occurring away from the ground. Other proposals for reducing aggression amongst spectators have included: alcohol bans, a change of image, closed circuit television, severe penalties for those involved and education of the fans to make them realise the implications of their actions (Goldstein, 1983).

On-field aggression

Moves to reduce on-field aggression are based around the causes and the theoretical basis of the aggression. Leith (1991) suggested:

- providing positive, non-aggressive role models
- severe penalties for those involved in aggressive acts

- rewards for those not reacting aggressively
- the use of psychologists to help performers to deal with over-arousal and frustration
- the reduction in media coverage of aggression (so violence is not glamorised)
- penalties for coaches whose players are involved in violence.

TASK

Hopefully the above methods for reducing aggression are going to be successful.

a For each point, explain the theoretical basis of the measure.

b What are the problems associated with the implementation of these measures?

c What else could players, coaches and administrators do to ensure that future sports participants are assertive rather than aggressive?

6. The sporting environment

The focus has been on the individual throughout this unit, and the factors identified that influence the psychological state of the performer. This section looks at the *situation* in which the sportsman/woman is performing and what influences the quality of the performance (Figure 6.148).

▲ *Figure 6.147* Football hooligans – a heightened state of arousal?

▲ *Figure 6.148* The situation influences the quality of performance

Social facilitation

Social facilitation was investigated by Zajonk in 1965, following initial work by Triplett (1898). It recognises the influence the presence of others has on performance. Zajonk's research was more productive than earlier work, thanks to his careful categorisation of those who are present during a sporting performance (Figure 6.149).

He grouped the audiences into *passive* and *interactive others*. He recognised that, on the whole, interactive others are those who have more of an influence on the performer than those who are passive. There has been some research to suggest that passive others can lead to anxiety in the performer when the others are significant to the performer; and if the performer feels that their performance is being assessed (see below). However, the majority of research relates to the major impact of an interactive audience upon a performer.

The real influence of social facilitation exists when the performer is in front of passive observers. Interactive others can directly influence the performance – this may be competitors who physically interfere with performance and supporters who actively attempt to disturb the concentration of the performer. Passive others, it has been found, can effect a change in performance standards.

Zajonk found that there was a clear difference between performing alone and in front of an audience. Some performers clearly improved whilst the performance of others deteriorated.

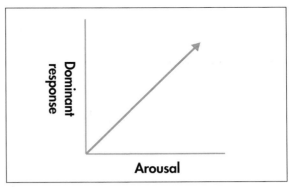

▲ **Figure 6.150** *Drive theory*

Zajonk also investigated the different influences and discovered that, depending on the stage of learning and the ability of the performer, the results differed. This phenomenon he called **drive theory**.

Drive theory suggests that the higher the level of arousal, the more the *dominant response* occurs. In other words, a performer who is in the early stages of learning or is of low ability will perform worse when pressure is perceived (for example, in front of an audience); whereas an able performer who is performing a skill they have learnt well will improve in similar circumstances (Figure 6.150). The dominant response is dictated by practice and experience and reflects the level of performance likely to be maintained under pressure. A beginner is more likely to have a lower level of dominant response than an experienced, well-practised performer.

The social facilitation effect occurs when others are passively observing due to what Cottrell (1968) calls **evaluation apprehension** – the worry that those watching are assessing the quality of performance.

Homefield advantage/disadvantage

Courneya and Carron (1992) recognised differences in the performances and the behaviour of teams and performers when playing at home compared with away games. As discussed on page 441, players tend be more aggressive when playing in front of an away crowd (**homefield advantage/disadvantage**).

Most of the research in this area has taken place in America where there are often very

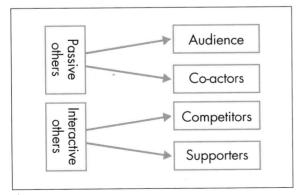

▲ **Figure 6.149** *Others present during a performance – note that 'co-actors' are team-mates and coaches, etc.*

few away fans at matches, due to the distances to travel. This research has found that between 55 per cent and 65 per cent of games are won by home teams, a significant figure. Other general examples include:

- 1992 Barcelona Olympics – Spain won many more medals than they had in the past
- 1995 Rugby World Cup – South Africa won at home despite New Zealand being the big favourites
- 1998 Football World Cup – France won on home soil.

These examples seem to be replicated in many world and Olympic competitions.

Varca (1980) recognised that the crowd can lead to increased arousal of the performers. He also found that there was an increase in dysfunctional behaviour amongst away teams. The changes in performance recognised at home and away games can be linked to inverted-U hypothesis (page 445), catastrophe (page 445), aggression (pages 439–41) and social facilitation theories (page 443), all of which identify how the presence of different 'others' can influence arousal and ultimately performance.

TASK

a Discuss the reasons you think teams win more at home than away.

b Obtain records of results of a team over a season. Is there a pattern?

Leadership

In Unit 2A, we investigated leaders in sport and theories relating to **leadership** including Fiedler's theory of task/person orientation and Chelladurai's theory of leadership components (see page 115). Aspects of styles of leadership were also introduced, as well as their effectiveness. In this section, these are revisited and the influence leadership has on performance further investigated.

Many sports involve elements of teamwork, including the role of the leader, who is a key element in developing team cohesion and consequently maximising the potential of the team's performance. As is identified in the Ringleman Effect (Gill, 1986), the more elements that exist in a team, the more difficult it is to co-ordinate its actions, both strategically and psychologically, and the more likely it is that some people in the team will not pull their weight (e.g. social loafing – see page 333).

TASK

a Organise a three/four/five/six-legged race, with a pair, a three, a four and a five strapped together.
  - Who wins?
  - Why?

b Carry out the same race again. This time allocate a leader who is to plan a strategy for movement.
  - Was the result the same?
  - Were the teams more efficient this time?

If there is a leader, whether prescribed, emergent, autocratic, democratic or whatever, the team has more potential for success. If the leader is efficient, there are likely to be fewer faulty teamwork processes, more efficient teamwork and less social loafing.

7. Anxiety in sport

One of the key roles of sports psychologists is to help performers deal with the pressures of competition. A great deal of research, both in traditional psychology and in sports psychology, has investigated what **anxiety** is, how it affects performance and how it can be used productively.

Levitt (1980) defines anxiety as:

The subjective feeling of apprehension and heightened psychological arousal (feelings) often associated with fears, worries and doubts (thoughts).

Anxiety is closely linked to the terms **stress** and arousal. Stress is seen as the psychological reaction to a stressor such as an important game, and arousal as the physiological response to the stressor. Thus stress and arousal occur as physiological and psychological responses to anxiety.

Inverted-U hypothesis

Traditionally anxiety and its effects have been seen as one-dimensional; that is, that anxiety has one form and that the relationship with performance is linear. The **inverted-U hypothesis** (Yerkes/Dodson and Jones/Hardy) is one such theory.

The inverted-U hypothesis, although superseded by recent research, is still widely quoted. It states that as the level of arousal increases, so does the level of performance until a point is reached where any higher levels of arousal will lead to a decline in performance (Figure 6.151). It suggests that different individuals and different activities require different arousal levels to achieve optimum performance. An extrovert will require and cope with higher levels of arousal than an introvert, and gross motor skills require a higher level of arousal than fine motor skills.

TASK

a Using the graph in Figure 6.151 explain how anxiety can influence performance.

b Produce a similar graph to show you and a partner in the same sport. Explain the different shapes.

Cognitive and somatic anxiety

More recent analysis of the influence of arousal on performance involves a **multi-dimensional approach** (McGrath, 1970). This challenges the inverted-U theory that there is an optimal arousal level and does not see the relationship between anxiety and performance as being linear.

McGrath recognises the difference between **cognitive anxiety** and **somatic anxiety**, and that a somatic response is based on physiological arousal – an increase in adrenaline, an increase in heart rate, etc. Cognitive anxiety is recognised as the psychological response, such as worry about performance, an inability to concentrate, a loss of attention and the fear of failure.

The theory then draws the following conclusions:

- There is a negative linear relationship between cognitive anxiety and performance – the more we worry, the worse we perform.
- The relationship between somatic anxiety and performance resembles an inverted-U.
- Somatic anxiety should decline once we begin performing.
- Cognitive anxiety may remain high during performance, especially if we worry about failing.
- Cognitive anxiety remains relatively constant over time, although somatic anxiety varies greatly, especially prior to competition.

Catastrophe theory

Another multi-dimensional approach, the **catastrophe theory** (Hardy and Fazey 1987) is now the most widely used approach to anxiety in sport. The catastrophe theory recognises a non-linear relationship between anxiety and performance. It acknowledges that mistakes lead to anxiety which leads to more mistakes and so on, and that a small increase in arousal can often lead to a dramatic or *catastrophic* decline in performance. For example, a place kicker in rugby who misses a kick in front of the posts will then kick and play badly. No matter what he does, he cannot get back to the previous performance levels, even if the arousal is then returned to its previous levels. This approach sees the relationship as three-dimensional.

Figure 6.152 shows what happens to performance when the three factors are taken into account. Performance is shown by the height of the performance surface on the

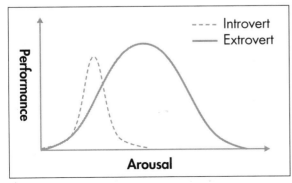

▲ *Figure 6.151* Inverted-U theory

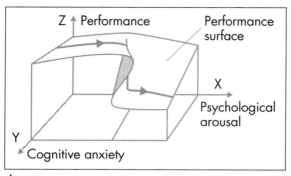

▲ **Figure 6.152** *Anxiety, performance and arousal*

Z-axis, psychological arousal (somatic anxiety) on the X-axis, known as the *normal factor*, and cognitive anxiety on the Y-axis, known as the *splitting factor*.

The important factor is the level of cognitive anxiety (the Y-axis). As it increases, it has a catastrophic effect on performance. This shows the central role played by thought in increasing anxiety and influencing performance.

In simple terms, what catastrophe theory is saying is that performance will increase as anxiety increases, but that at some stage, when we worry about performance (cognitive anxiety) our performance will suffer rapidly and that we will not be able to return to our previous performance levels even if the cognitive anxiety is reduced.

Reversal theory

One more way of thinking about anxiety is in terms of **reversal theory** (Apter 1989, Kerr 1990). This approach stresses the subjective nature of arousal, i.e. different interpretations of it. In other words, we all have different preferred levels of arousal at which we wish to operate. For example, some people enjoy playing a non-competitive game of tennis whilst others find the lack of competition tedious or boring (Figure 6.153). Some people find high-pressure important sporting events exciting and challenging whilst others find them distressing.

Kerr describes those who prefer low anxiety situations and find high-pressure situations anxiety provoking, as being in a state of *telic dominance*. Those who enjoy high arousal and find low-pressure situations boring are said to be in a state of *paratelic dominance*.

Reversal theory suggests that in some situations we rapidly change – we *reverse* from one state to the other. Thus we may feel high levels of anxiety just before an important match, but *reverse* into a feeling of excitement and enjoyment once we start.

At the same time as Kerr's research, and of importance in the measurement of anxiety in sport, Martens developed the Competitive State Anxiety Test. This research tool, a questionnaire-based approach, is used widely in sports psychology to identify the specific response of performers to the competitive situation.

Trait/state anxiety

Spielberger (1971) suggested that there are two different types of anxiety:

- trait anxiety
- state anxiety.

Trait anxiety

As discussed in this Unit on page 430, a trait is a predisposition to behave in a particular way in a particular situation: a personality characteristic. Trait anxiety is a characteristic of our personality. It is a relatively stable element; it is our general anxiety level. It is our tendency to view situations and aspects of life as stressful.

State anxiety

State anxiety is our response to any particular situation. It varies from situation to situation and will depend on our interpretation of the stressfulness of the situation. For example, some will find bungee jumping stressful whilst others view it as enjoyable.

▲ **Figure 6.153** *Tennis at the local park: stimulating for some – seemingly pointless for others*

The implications of research into anxiety in sport

There are implications – both positive and negative – of research into anxiety for the coach or sports psychologist. These are:

- Anxiety can have both positive and negative effects on performance. It can lead to a raising of performance levels, but it can also have a detrimental effect.
- All players are different and require their own special preparation; not just the traditional team 'psyche up'.
- Players need to be introduced to relaxation techniques for use when in situations they perceive as stressful.
- Players need to be taught to ignore pressure and forget any mistakes, thus avoiding increases in cognitive anxiety. This will involve focusing and achieving 'the zone'.
- Players need to be able to identify when anxiety levels are increasing in order to avoid the catastrophe occurrence and to take avoidance action.

Coaches must identify what level of trait anxiety a performer has, as well as identifying specific situations which lead to state anxiety. Traditionally there has been an assumption that in order to prepare sports performers to reach their optimum, they must practise and perfect the required skills, train hard physically to gain optimum fitness levels and, in team sports, work on teamwork.

Research into the effects of arousal on performance confirms what many psychologists have believed for years. Psychological preparation and strategies are the missing elements in the performance portfolio of many sports performers. Success at the top level is dependent on the ability to deal with the pressure of competition and being able to use such situations to gain a positive advantage and reach the highest possible levels of performance.

Sports performers and coaches must be aware of the different forms of anxiety. They need to be able to recognise when the performer is showing signs of somatic anxiety and what level is good for performance, and at what stage performance suffers.

They must also understand the catastrophic effects of cognitive anxiety and devise strategies that help performers to maintain the optimum level by not worrying when mistakes are made, and by channelling their attention to block out any negative and stressful occurrences.

TASK

a Using examples from a variety of sports, explain why performers in different positions need different psychological preparation.

b Identify the symptoms and feelings a performer may experience when anxiety levels are increasing. Consider both somatic and cognitive anxiety.

TASK

Organise the following experiment. It can be modified and used with a range of theories outlined in this Unit.

- Select between 10 and 20 candidates picked at random.
- Ask 5 to shoot 20 times from the free throw line when alone in the sports hall and to record the score.
- Ask 5 to shoot with you watching.
- Ask 5 to shoot with the other candidates watching in silence.
- Ask 5 to shoot with the other candidates watching and encouraging/shouting at the shooter.
- Rotate the groups so they shoot in all four situations.
- Present the data gathered in graphical form.
- Produce a word-processed report of findings, method, results and conclusions.

Key words and phrases

Option A: Sports mechanics

1. Fundamental qualities of motion
• Matter • Time • Space • Motion • Position • Distance • Displacement
• Vector

2. Analysis of linear speed, velocity and acceleration
• Linear motion • Speed • Velocity • Acceleration • Average speed • Scalar
• Magnitude

3. Force
• Force • Deformative • Translational • Rotational • Net or resultant force
• Parallelogram rule • Resolved • Impulse • Momentum • Follow through
• Internal force • Order of lever

4. Planes and axes of rotation
• Rotation • Longitudinal • Lateral • Dorso-ventral

5. Gravity
• Gravity • Weight • Newton's laws of motion • Friction • Normal reaction force

6. Principles related to the stability of the body
• Centre of gravity • Centre of mass (CoM) • Unstable equilibrium
• Neutral equilibrium • Stability • Base of support • Stable equilibrium
• Friction

7. Momentum
• Momentum • Conservation of momentum

8. Air resistance and fluid friction
• Fluid friction • Air resistance • Drag force • Lift forces • Bernoulli effect
• Magnus effect

9. Angular motion
• Moment of inertia • Angular velocity • Angular momentum • Point of release

Option B: Sports psychology

1. Introduction to Option B
(There are no key words and phrases in this sub-section.)

2. Learning theories
• Associationists • Cognitivists • Thorndike's Laws • Drive theory
• Classical conditioning • Operant conditioning • Stimulus–response (S–R) bond
• Gestalt

3. Personality
• Personalities • Psychoanalytic • Interactionalist • Humanistic • Self-concept
• Self-efficacy • Trait theorists

4. The performer in action: Theories and applications

- Achievement motivation • Mastery goals • Failure avoidance goals
- Failure acceptors • Attribution theory • Performance satisfaction
- Performance expectancy • Attributional retraining • Learned helplessness
- Self-motivation • Observational or vicarious learning • Aggression

5. The performer in action: Aggression

- Hostile/reactive aggression • Instrumental aggression • Assertive behaviour
- Instinct theory • Social learning theory • Frustration/aggression hypothesis
- Berkowitz's aggressive cue theory • Social facilitation

6. The sporting environment

- Drive theory • Evaluation apprehension • Homefield advantage/disadvantage
- Leadership

7. Anxiety in sport

- Anxiety • Stress • Inverted-U hypothesis • Multi-dimensional approach
- Cognitive anxiety • Somatic anxiety • Catastrophe theory • Reversal theory
- Trait anxiety • State anxiety

REVIEW QUESTIONS

1 Discuss the difference between displacement and distance. (You must use words such as vector, scalar, magnitude and direction.)

2 Describe the effects that force can have on an object.

3 The parallelogram rule is often used to work out the resultant force when two forces act at the same time. Describe a situation when two forces act at the same time. Draw a diagram to display this, and explain how the parallelogram rule works.

4 Give a sporting example of the use of 'follow through' and explain how this will increase impulse.

5 If momentum = mass x velocity, calculate how much faster a rugby player with a mass of 70kg has to run to have the same momentum as a 90kg player running at a velocity of 6m/s.

6 Explain how changing body shape can affect moment of inertia. Give examples from three different sports where the athlete changes body shape to control the rate of rotation.

7 Using examples from sport, discuss how mass, shape and velocity affect the amount of air resistance experienced.

8 State Newton's three laws of motion, using a sporting example to highlight each one.

9 Describe a sporting example of when a person may wish a to raise their centre of mass, and b to lower their centre of mass. Explain why it is beneficial to do so.

10 a Sketch a graph of distance against time for the following train journey:

Edinburgh	07:20	0km
Carlisle	10:13	165km
Oxenholme	10:57	752km
Birmingham	13:21	2448km
Oxford	14:51	1088km
Southampton	16:20	1072km

10 b Calculate the average speed for each section of the journey. Which was the fastest leg and which was the slowest?

REVIEW QUESTIONS (continued)

11 How does catastrophe theory differ from the traditional inverted-U approach to anxiety and performance?

12 How can operant conditioning be used to ensure a performer always responds with the correct action in a given sport. Give examples.

13 What is the difference between negative reinforcement, positive reinforcement and punishment?

14 What is the Gestalt approach to learning? How does it relate to different teaching approaches?

15 What are the three layers of personality outlined by Hollander and how do they influence behaviour?

16 How do the three approaches – psychoanalytic, humanistic and interactionalist perspectives of personality – differ?

17 What are personality traits, and what traits are common to sports performers?

18 What are the problems associated with personality assessment?

19 How do motives differ when performing in sport?

20 What are the causes of aggression in sport?

21 How can the occurrences of aggression in sport be reduced?

22 How does the presence of an audience or a crowd influence the levels of performance?

23 What difference can a good leader make in a team sport?

24 What is the difference between trait and state anxiety?

25 How are arousal, anxiety and stress related?

26 How does anxiety influence performance? Is it always positive or negative?

27 Why is the catastrophe theory now seen as more accurate than the inverted-U in showing the influence of anxiety on sporting performance?

Texts used in the writing of this section

❑ Alderman, R.B., *Psychological Behaviour in Sport*, Philadelphia, London, 1974

❑ Apter, M.J, *Reversal Theory: Motivation, Emotion and Personality*, Routledge, 1989

❑ Atkinson, J.W., *A Theory of Achivement Motivation*, Robert E. Krieger Pub. Co., 1974

❑ Bandura, A., *Social Learning Theory*, Prentice Hall, 1977

❑ Bandura, A., et al., *Social Learning and Personality Development*, Holt Rincheart & Winston Inc., 1963

❑ Baron, R.S., *Human Aggression*, Plenum, 1977

❑ Berkowitz, L., *Aggression: A Social Psychological Analysis*, McGraw-Hill, 1969

❑ Biddle, S., *European Perspectives on Exercise and Sport Psychology*, Human Kinetics, 1995

❑ Carron, A.V., *Social Psychology of Sport: An Environmental Approach*, Mouvement Publications, 1981

❑ Coolican, H., *Applied Psychology*, Hodder & Stoughton, 1996

❑ Coolican, H., *Research Methods and Statistics in Psychology*, Hodder & Stoughton, 1999

❑ Cottrell, N.B., *Performance in the Presence of Other Human Beings*, Allyn & Bacon, 1968

❑ Cox, R., *Sport Psychology: Concepts and Applications*, Brown, 1933

❑ Cratty, B.J., *Social Psychology in Athletics*, Prentice Hall, 1989

❑ Davis, D., Kimmet, T. & Auty, M., *Physical Education: Theory and Practice*, Macmillan, 1998

❑ Dollard, *Frustration and Aggression*, Yale University Press, 1939

❑ Fox, K.R., *The Physical Self: From Motivation to Well Being*, Human Kinetics, 1977

- Fullick, P., *Physics,* Heinemann, 1994
- Gagné, R.M., *Learning and Individual Differences: A Symposium,* Merrill, 1967
- Gill, D., *Psychological Dynamics of Sport,* Human Kinetics, 1986
- Gross, R., *Psychology: The Science of Mind and Behaviour,* Hodder & Stoughton, 1996
- Hardy, L. & Fazey, J., 'The Inverted-U Hypothesis: A Catastrophe for Sport Psychology?', in *British Association of Sports Sciences, monograph no. 1,* NCF, 1987
- Haskey, *Sports Science,* Hodder & Stoughton, 1981
- Hayes, N., *Foundations of Psychology,* Routledge, 1994
- Hollander, E., *Principles and Methods of Social Psychology,* Oxford University Press, New York, 1971
- Jones, J. & Hardy, L., *Stress and Sport: Experiences of Some Elite Performers,* John Wiley, 1990
- Jung, C., *Psychological Types,* Routledge, 1989
- Leakey, R. & Lewin, R., *Origins: What New Discoveries Reveal About the Emergence of Our Species,* MacDonald & Janes, 1978
- Leith, L., 'Choking in Sport', in *International Journal of Sports Psychology, no. 19,* pp.59–64, 1988
- Levitt, E., *The Psychology of Anxiety,* 2nd edition, L. Erlbaum Associates, New Jersey, 1980
- Lloyd, P., et al., *Introduction to Psychology: An Integrated Approach,* Fontana, 1984
- Lorenz, K., et al., *Studies in Animal and Human Behaviour,* Methuen, 1966
- Maglennon, K., *Practical Psychology,* Collins, 1993
- Martens, R., *Sport Competition Anxiety Test,* Human Kinetics, 1980
- McGrath, J.E., *Groups: Interaction and Performance,* Prentice Hall, 1970
- Roberts, G.C., *Learning Experiences in Sport Psychology,* Human Kinetics, 1986
- Rogers, C., *On Becoming a Person: A Therapist's View of Psychotherapy,* Constable, London, 1967
- Scully, D. & Kramer, J., *Psychology in Sport,* Taylor & Francis, 1994
- Singer, R., Murphy, M. & Tennant, L., *Handbook of Research on Sport Psychology,* Macmillan, 1993
- Speilberger, C.D., *Anxiety and Behaviour,* Academic Press, 1971
- Weinberg, R.S., *Foundations of Sport and Exercise Psychology,* Human Kinetics, 1995
- Wirhed, R., *Athletic Ability and the Anatomy of Motion,* Wolfe, 1984
- Yerkes & Dodson, 'The Relation of Strength of Stimulus to Rapidity of Habit Formation', in *The Journal of Neurological Psychology,* 1908
- Zajonc, R.B., 'Social Facilitation', in *Science, no. 149,* pp.269–274, 1965

Suggested further reading

- Coolican, H., *Applied Psychology,* Hodder & Stoughton, 1996
- Cox, R., *Sport Psychology: Concepts and Applications,* Brown, 1933
- Davis, D., Kimmet, T. & Auty, M., *Physical Education: Theory and Practice,* Macmillan, 1998
- Wirhed, R., *Athletic Ability and the Anatomy of Motion,* 2nd edition, Mosby, 1997
- Woods, B., *Applying Psychology to Sport,* Hodder & Stoughton, 1998
- Video: *Biomechanics: The Sports Science Series,* University of Western Australia, 1988

Section C: A synoptic analysis of scientific principles in the development of performance

1. Introduction

Synoptic analysis involves the interpretation and exploration of the underlying concepts and themes within the broad sphere of physical activity. In practice, this means reviewing your previous study in *all* units. Although the emphasis in this section of Unit 6 will be on the scientific principles, the social factors that influence performance will also be considered.

The content of this section is based on the summative concepts that unite the different elements of the specification. Therefore, when answering examination questions, you will need to demonstrate an understanding of the connections between disparate aspects of the specification.

Each part of Unit 6C aims to provide you with a framework for the analysis of each concept. It is important to understand that each part presents merely an overview of the information from other Units. Each part does not aim to present a definitive review of all the aspects related to each concept. Synoptic questions also offer you the chance to include relevant information from your own training experience. In order to gain a fuller understanding of specific areas mentioned in this section, you will need to refer back to earlier sections of the book where the relevant concepts are dealt with in greater detail.

KEY SKILLS

Using one of the main themes of this Unit as a focus, make a synoptic presentation to your group followed by group discussion. The records of this process together with records of the sources consulted provides a means of satisfying components 3.1 and 3.2 of Key Skills Level 3 Communication.

2. Individual differences

Individuals differ in their physiological and psychological make-up. One of the enduring arguments in physical education and sport is the extent to which these factors are a product of **nature** or **nurture**. Factors which are innate include functional flexibility, the proportions of muscle fibre types (type 1, type 2a and 2b), reaction time, hand-eye co-ordination, personality traits, VO_2 max and anaerobic capacity. Although all of these can be improved by training, basic capability is determined by the genetic blueprint inherited from our parents.

However, it is the nurturing environment that determines the extent to which a person can fulfil their genetic potential. Environmental factors include reinforcement, nutrition, facilities, training, coaching and time.

Figure 6.154 shows the relationship between heredity and training.

Sporting superstars like Michael Jordan or Marian Jones are fortunate to have inherited the **physiological**, **psychological** and

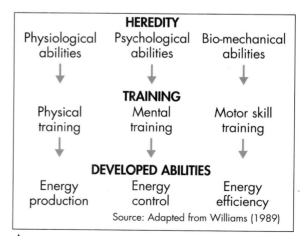

▲ *Figure 6.154* *The relationship between heredity and training*

▲ **Figure 6.155** *Marian Jones has inherited the characteristics needed to excel in her chosen sport with a nurturing environment to support her*

bio-mechanical characteristics necessary to excel in their chosen sport. They are equally fortunate to have been supported by social structures that have enabled these characteristics to flourish.

Issues relating to access and opportunity

Unit 1 looked at the social influences in sport and participation. At the most basic level, the requirements for sports participation are **time**, **space** and **freedom**.

The extent to which these factors operate is influenced by the wider social networks in which they exist. Unit 1 identified a framework integrating the cultural setting – primitive, emergent or advanced – with constraints which were either contrived or naturally occurring.

The provision of resources for sport in any society is a result of the interdependence of the economic, political and cultural influences operating at any one time.

Ultimately, it is this relationship which has a significant influence upon participation in physical activity.

Generally, in modern industrialised nations, the groups commonly denied access and opportunity to sport are restricted on the basis of:

- age
- class
- disability
- education
- ethnicity
- gender
- poverty.

Age issues

Units 1 and 4 reviewed the role of sport in different cultures. These Units highlighted the fact that high level sporting performance is often a product of strict training regimes from an early age.

If you have been involved in coaching or teaching children, you will be aware of the fact that a young performer has different needs from older performers. In general, outside of developmental considerations, younger children:

- are less tolerant of exercise
- are not able to concentrate for long periods
- are not able to make a lot of decisions
- can have difficulty understanding complex language
- have different emotional needs.

TASK

Identify the issues related to the training of young élite athletes.

Remember your answer must include reference to physiological, psychological and social factors.

A number of **physiological changes** accompany the ageing process. These include a reduction in muscle mass, which in turn causes a reduction in strength and movement speed.

Strength tends to peak between 20–30 years and then decreases. Reaction time also decreases with age. Further reductions occur in heart rate, stroke volume, joint flexibility and VO_2 max. Older individuals who do not train or exercise regularly experience greater deterioration compared to those who follow regular exercise patterns.

Active participation in sport tends to diminish relative to age. However, this trend appears to be less prevalent in societies with a healthy outdoor ethic such as Australia and the USA. In the USA, the National Senior Sports Organisation (NSSO) actively promotes participation in sports by older age groups.

In the UK, it may be low esteem that accounts for less involvement in sport by older people. The absence of role models, together with lack of access to recreational and sporting facilities, has also hindered participation.

However, attitudes are changing. This is largely as a consequence of a greater percentage of the population being over 55 years of age. This population shift should also facilitate an increased exposure of veterans' events in the media.

Class issues

In the UK the influence of social class as a constraint to access is less marked than was the case in the past. This trend is also seen in Europe and globally. However, there are cultures where the place you live or social class you were born into still greatly affect the opportunity you have to take part in sport.

In Argentina, the *'cabecitas negras'* (black little heads – or people of the provinces) have been largely denied access to sport since the demise of the Peronist Government in 1955. In India and other areas of the Asian sub-continent, class (or caste) influences the lives of whole sub-cultures, including their access to recreation and sport.

The widening global horizons of sport means that such situations – largely seen as 'domestic issues' – will be exposed to scrutiny by a broader cultural morality and called into question. The advent of global games may well serve to emancipate many whose cultural and/or political exclusion has attracted little attention before.

Disability issues

The USA and Australia have active policies to encourage disabled athletes to participate in sport, such as the Aussie Able programme and the Adaptive Sporting Programs in the USA.

In the UK, despite a high proportion of the population having a disability (one fifth of the adult population in 1987) and the existence of organisations such as the British Sports Association for the Disabled, discrimination still exists and equal opportunities in sport are still denied.

Education issues

Many cultures now embrace education as a means whereby inequalities can or should be addressed. In many cultures, broad access to academic education is now the norm and the association with physical/recreational education is well established. The use of physical education as a means to identify excellence is an issue that concerns many.

In the USA, the diverse paths of two apparently similar sub-cultures is causing great concern, particularly in the secondary or high school sector. Here the demise of physical education seems to be gathering momentum in some areas. The diverse cultural canvas which is the basis of Unit 4B requires that you pay particular attention to this feature within your own 'chosen culture'. You will be required to assess whether or not the educational process (PE) is being devalued by emphasis on athletic outcome (sports programmes).

Ethnicity issues

Societies in some countries in Europe, such as the UK and France, are becoming increasingly multi-cultural as a result of immigration, e.g. Afro-Caribbeans and Asians into the UK and Algerians into France.

However, there is still **discrimination** in sport and in wider society and it tends to be linked to social class and stereotyping. These, in turn, are linked to the order in which the new migrant groups enter the host country. Even in the USA, the best documented multi-cultural society, economic power still tends to be in the hands of the White Anglo Saxon Protestants (**WASPs**) (see Unit 1A, page 33).

Ironically, in many countries (including the United States), the native indigenous populations now find themselves in very lowly positions on both the social and economic ladder. Examples of this occur in Argentina, Australia and South Africa (see Unit 4B).

Stacking and **centrality** have become issues in football and rugby in the UK, operating in a similar fashion to American football, baseball and basketball in the USA. These phenomena are linked to cultural values and racial stereotyping.

Gender issues

The European Commission reports that gender issues represent the largest proportion of cases brought to its attention through its law courts by disadvantaged groups or individuals. The European Charter for Sport (1975 and 1992) recognised the right of such groups or individuals to have a forum for their grievances, where no opportunity existed (or could be accessed) within their own environment. Unit 4B addresses sport within the global games context where such grievances are not always so readily or easily dealt with.

At a global level, a vast range of cultural values have to be taken into account. This places an onus of responsibility upon international bodies (such as the IOC). In many ways this is beyond their mandate. How should the IOC and other global organisations tackle what are seen as clear breaches of human rights when they occur within a culture where they are perfectly acceptable? Are sanctions appropriate – or should enlightenment and conciliation be the approach? How does one enlighten those who consider themselves to be already enlightened?

Physiological differences

A more in-depth study of physiological differences between male and female sports performers can be found in Unit 3 on pages 212–14. Generally, females have two-thirds of the strength of males. This difference is greater, however, when comparing upper to lower body strength because males have higher testosterone levels, which increase muscle hypertrophy. On the other hand, women are more flexible and seem to metabolise fat more efficiently than men. The fact that (generally speaking) women compete against women and men against men would seem to solve this problem. However, such variations also occur within both sexes; within cultural groups and between ethnic groups.

Typically, the Japanese rugby player will never match his European counterpart in jumping in the lineout. Can such differences be addressed – or should they? Do we want a completely level playing field – or is the acceptance of such disparities part of the challenge of sport? Again, the growth of the global perspective highlights such differences, which at a domestic level can be much more easily accommodated. The Kenyans and other African nations have identified sub-cultural or tribal groups with a physiological pre-disposition to distance running. Will the growth of global sport heighten the processes of 'selection' for which notorious 'regimes' have been brought down?

Effects of training

The issues surrounding developmental changes and training are covered in Unit 3. Though current research suggests that training has similar effects on both sexes, as already stated, muscle hypertrophy is not as pronounced in females due to lower levels of testosterone.

There is also the 'moral question' relating to the narrow line between training and cheating. How far can one go in preparing for competition before the methods used become unacceptable? For example, is blood replacement thorough preparation or unfair practice?

Cultural differences

Cultures often vary in their attitudes to gender and sport. For example, the frontier spirit in the USA and Australia has enabled sportswomen to become more prominent in those countries than in the older, more established, cultures of western Europe.

Strong feminist movements in the USA and Australia have also enabled legislation to be introduced which has helped to develop equal opportunities between the sexes, for example, **Title IX** in the USA. However, in both these countries male sport still dominates in the media and as a profession.

In the UK, more men participate in sport than women, although involvement by women is increasing. Access to sport for women is closely linked to socio-economic variables, such as class, and historical gender stereotypes do still exist. Professional sport, sports administration and coaching continue to be dominated by men.

In the global arena, the image and power of female athletes are growing. There are now more women competitors than ever in more events at the Summer and Winter Olympic Games (see page 74), and the

1999 Women's World Cup Football Final took place in front of a global TV audience of one billion and a live audience of more than 80,000 people.

Poverty issues

In the older established societies such as the UK, the concept of social class emerged out of historically determined cultural traditions and access to sporting activity was, and to some degree still is, closely linked to class.

In the USA, where the European class system is not as evident, social division tends to be based on wealth. Professional sport, therefore, has been seen as an 'avenue of escape from the ghetto' and poverty for the lower socio-economic groups.

At the other end of the scale, certain élite sports, such as polo, cannot be enjoyed by the masses because of the considerable wealth needed to take part.

Differences between untrained individuals and the trained athlete

Physiological differences

The effects of exercise on the body were identified in Unit 3. Following a training period of at least ten weeks, the body undergoes various long-term physiological adaptations.

These will vary according to the type of training, its intensity and the physiological make-up of the person(s) undertaking the training.

Adaptations resulting from *aerobic* training include:

- increase in the size and strength of the heart (hypertrophy of the myocardium)
- increases in stroke volume and maximum cardiac output
- bradycardia (slowing down of the heartbeat)
- changes in skeletal muscle such as an increase in the size and number of mitochondria, increased capillarisation, increased enzyme activity involved in energy production, increased energy stores
- increase in blood volume and less lactic acid production during sub-maximal exercise

- the respiratory muscles become more efficient
- increases in maximum minute ventilation.

Overall benefits of aerobic training include:

- a 5–15% increase in VO_2 max
- an increase in the body's capacity to utilise fats
- a reduction in blood pressure and a reduction in the build-up of fatty deposits, which in turn reduces the risk of coronary heart disease.

Adaptations as a result of *anaerobic* training include:

- muscle hypertrophy, particularly type 2a and 2b fibres
- increase in stores of ATP, CP and glycogen
- increased enzyme activity improving the efficiency of the ATP-PC and lactic acid systems
- increased tolerance to high levels of lactic acid and a more efficient removal system during recovery
- a delay in the thresholds of the ATP-PC and lactic acid systems, which means that the trained performer is able to generate more ATP and work at a high intensity rate for a longer period of time.

Psychological differences

Long-term training assumes that the performer has become skilled. Sharp (1992) suggests that as a result of training athletes will have become skilled in three main areas:

- **cognitive domain** – knowing the vital aspects of their sport,
- **psychomotor domain** – being able to produce successful movements
- **affective domain** – acquiring a number of psychological skills in order to adapt to the sporting environment.

The latter could include coping with high arousal and showing a good mental attitude.

In relation to the Acquiring skill section of Unit 2 (see page 102), trained (and therefore skilled) performers will be able to:

- achieve goals consistently
- execute movements which are efficient and economic

- perform movements which look aesthetically pleasing
- be able to analyse a situation and initiate the most appropriate response.

In order to achieve the above, the trained performer will have enhanced their innate abilities through practice. They will have developed their gross motor abilities such as strength, flexibility and speed, as well as perceptual abilities such as hand-eye co-ordination and reaction time.

Enhanced information-processing capabilities will have heightened levels of perception in trained performers. They will also have developed an increased ability to selectively attend to relevant cues, such as the ball toss or the racket action of an opponent in tennis. In addition, they will be able to disregard irrelevant ones, such as crowd movement or noise.

The trained performer will also to be able to draw on past experiences from long-term memory (see page 118), which will enable them to anticipate and thereby respond more effectively to a specific situation. In this last respect, it is also likely that appropriate skill selection will be assisted by referral to a bank of schemas developed through experience, with such schemas being adjusted or fine-tuned to specific situations.

As a result of training, appropriate responses are more likely to be automatic, allowing time for tactical considerations, ploys and disguises to conceal intentions. These will mean that more attention can be paid to peripheral (e.g. positional) cues which may be missed by a beginner.

Feedback

A trained performer will be able to interpret **feedback** to identify and correct their own errors more effectively. A more developed kinaesthetic sense will enable them to identify how a movement feels and be able to compare that feeling with previous experiences (see page 111).

Transfer

The skilled performer will be able to adapt or **transfer** their knowledge, skills and movements to new situations more effectively.

Differences in relation to sports psychology

The following areas could be considered when comparing a trained athlete to an untrained individual:

- **personality** – whilst research is inconclusive, common characteristics of sportspersons include ruggedness, courage, intelligence, exuberance, buoyancy, emotional adjustment, optimism, alertness, loyalty, conscientiousness, and respect for authority
- cognitive strategies – trained performers are better able than untrained performers to use cognitive strategies such as **imagery**, **mental rehearsal** and **positive self-talk** to cope with high levels of **anxiety** and **stress**
- **attribution** – trained performers are more likely to attribute success to internal and stable factors, while attributing failure to external and unstable factors.

Mechanical differences

The extent to which individuals differ regarding **size**, **body composition** and **body mass** has a profound affect on their ability to perform well in different activities.

▲ **Figure 6.156** *Body composition and size can have a significant influence on performance!*

For example, long arms (providing long levers) might be an advantage in throwing events such as the discus. Body height gives an advantage in activities such as basketball and the high jump, whilst shorter arm and leg length might be an advantage in gymnastics and weight-lifting (Figure 6.156).

Generally, the trained athlete will also possess the physical attributes necessary to generate high force production. However, they will also have learned how to generate efficient movement more effectively.

3. Short-term preparation

Short-term preparation refers to the processes involved prior to performance or competition. It represents the **competition phase** of the **periodised year**. This section will also focus on pre-match or event preparation.

Training during this last phase of the cycle can involve physiological, psychological, mechanical and biomechanical components.

Physiological considerations

The areas covered below are expanded in Unit 3.

Acclimatisation

Improved transport and communications have enabled sports events to be staged on a global scale and venues for such events can vary considerably. This has serious implications for athletes and teams who must travel to each venue and adapt to a new environment once they are there. This can include adjusting to different temperatures, weather conditions and time zones.

There are special considerations necessary for events taking place in very hot or very cold climates. In hot climates, it is important to take fluid loss into account and make provision for it. Also, clothing must be designed to maximise heat loss. In cold climates, athletes need additional or special clothing to reduce heat loss and maintain core body temperature. This is critically important.

Athletes can aid the **acclimatisation** process by simulating such extreme condi-tions as part of their training before they leave their own country. This might include steps such as wearing additional clothing or training in a sauna.

Acclimatisation is particularly important for events taking place at high altitude and especially for aerobic/endurance events. Altitude acclimatisation involves 2–3 weeks' training in the high altitude environment. The body adapts by increasing its red blood cell count and, therefore, haemoglobin concentration, which enables more oxygen to be transported around the body.

Nutrition

Controlling and monitoring the athlete's **nutrition** in the long and short term is important in order to ensure:

- energy stores are at a maximum level
- the optimum weight for performance is achieved and maintained
- sufficient quantities of minerals, vitamins and water are consumed for optimum performance
- pre-game or competition food intake sufficiently satisfies the demands of the event.

On the day of competition, performers need to ensure that they have sufficient supplies of energy. This can be achieved by a meal high in glycogen, taken 3–4 hours before the event. During competition, consuming drinks or snacks high in glucose can top up stores. One week prior to competition, **carbohydrate loading** can be used to increase glycogen stores to higher than normal levels (see page 389). This is a useful technique for endurance activities, where carbohydrates are used as the main fuel source. Additionally, athletes must ensure that fluid intake is adjusted appropriately, both prior to and during the event.

Warm up

The **warm up** usually involves a gross motor activity/light cardiovascular exercise. This is followed by a series of general and sports-specific **flexibility exercises** and finally a series of skill-related drills. Flexibility exercises can include **static**, **passive**, **ballistic** and **PNF** stretches (see Unit 3, page 164).

The physiological effects of carrying out a warm-up include:

- increased blood flow, enabling oxygen to be transported to the muscles
- increased circulation due to decreased vascular resistance
- increased muscle temperature, facilitating cellular reactions
- increased temperature reducing muscle viscosity and enabling smoother muscle contractions
- increased range of motion
- increased speed of nerve impulses
- increased cardio-vascular response to the demands of sudden exercise.

Performance-related planning

The physiological aspect of short-term preparation and training concentrates on maintaining conditioning levels achieved during the pre-season phase. For most sports this stage of **performance related planning** concentrates on skill development and making preparation for the next competition.

Psychological factors

In any top sporting event there are a number of athletes who possess the necessary skills and physiological capabilities to win. It is widely recognised that, increasingly, it is psychological factors prior to and during the event which make the difference between winning and losing. Such factors involved in the short-term preparation of athletes include those in Figure 6.157.

Motivation

The task of motivating different individuals to perform well and succeed is a complex process. It is an important aspect of short-term preparation. For more details concerning the areas covered below, refer to Unit 5A and Unit 6B: Option B.

Motivation can be described as the 'why of behaviour' (Gross, 1992).

An individual's behaviour in any situation is the result of interaction between their personality characteristics, attitudes, needs, abilities, expectations and the demands of the situation. Personality characteristics include the degree to which an athlete is motivated by his/her own achievement (**achievement motivation**).

It is generally agreed that **intrinsic motivation** and **extrinsic motivation** need to be combined to achieve optimum motivation.

Examples of intrinsic motives include participation for fun, pleasure or enjoyment. Extrinsic motives include participation for money, awards or trophies.

The relationship between intrinsic and extrinsic motivation has generated a great deal of research in sports psychology (see page 437).

In practice, a great number of professional sports teams and event managers use extrinsic rewards prior to an event in an attempt to improve performance. This may take the form of win bonuses or the offering of gold bars for world records in athletics.

However, Deci's (1985) **cognitive evaluation theory** summarises the complex relationship between athlete and coach. He states that in order to increase an athlete's intrinsic motivation, the coach should aim to provide the athlete with a sense of control over their behaviour and generate a feeling of accomplishment. Deci further summarises that if the athlete feels 'manipulated' or pushed around by others, they may perceive potential extrinsic rewards as being responsible for this and intrinsic motivation will be reduced. The more an athlete feels that their actions are a result of self-determination, personal competence and a result of their own motives and goals, the greater the degree of intrinsic motivation.

Developing a positive mental attitude

This involves being confident and displaying a **positive mental attitude** to the event.

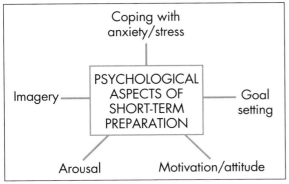

▲ *Figure 6.157* The psychological aspects of short-term preparation

In relation to self-confidence in specific situations, Bandura (1977) referred to the term self-efficacy (see Unit 6B, pages 435–37). He identified four key factors in the development of **self-efficacy**:

- performance accomplishments
- vicarious experiences
- verbal persuasion
- emotional arousal.

Goal setting

Prior to an event, **goal setting** can increase motivation levels and confidence. The goals set could be outcome goals, process-orientated goals or performance goals.

Imagery

Imagery can also be used to help concentration, develop confidence and rehearse movement patterns immediately prior to competition.

Arousal

Coaches try to ensure that athletes are at their optimum level of **arousal** before a competition. In order to achieve this, the type of activity, the skill level required and the personality of the performer need to be considered (see Unit 6B: Option B, page 436). For example, a contact sport, such as rugby, requires a relatively high level of arousal for successful performance, compared to snooker.

Coping with anxiety and stress

Participation in global games and some other international competitions involves athletes living in a hotel or sports village for extended periods of time. In the preparation prior to the event, the manager or coach can reduce an early build-up of **cognitive anxiety** through behavioural engineering. This means avoiding situations that cause stress and anxiety, and could involve arriving close to the start of the event. However, this in itself might create anxiety. It is common, therefore, for teams or individuals to live in a hotel or complex, in quiet tranquil surroundings, away from the media spotlight. Individuals respond differently to such situations and debates that often centre upon the fact that some

team members miss opening ceremonies whilst others attend, often ignore such differences.

Prior to competition, performers need to be able to manage stress responses in order to reduce anxiety. Various methods can be employed to reduce **somatic anxiety** (body) and cognitive anxiety (mind).

For example, relaxation methods such as **self-directed relaxation** and **progressive relaxation training** can be employed. **Self-talk** can combat cognitive anxiety and increase concentration levels, whilst imagery can improve concentration for the task in hand and build confidence and a positive mental attitude. It is also a means of reducing anxiety.

Team preparation

Wherever possible, élite sports teams try to meet together for a few days (or weeks if the event is global) prior to performance. The purpose of this is threefold:

- it helps build both 'task' and 'social' **cohesion** and enables each player to identify their own role within the team
- it helps the team to understand the group norms and gives individuals time to adjust their behaviour appropriately so that it fits in with these norms
- co-operation and co-ordination problems can be reduced as the team undergoes training and practice relevant to the task.

These processes can also help reduce **social loafing**.

Mechanical aspects of short-term preparation

These factors include the sporting environment itself, and performance considerations related to the opposition.

Environmental considerations

- The playing or performance surface – in some activities **friction** needs to be increased in order to produce good performance. This can mean the wearing of spikes in athletics or applying chalk to the hands in gymnastics. In other activities, friction needs to be minimised in order to produce good performance: for example, skiers applying wax to their skis.

- **Fluid forces** – by wearing a hat and shaving all body surfaces, the swimmer can reduce drag due to fluid friction.
- **Air resistance** – this needs to be taken into account in activities played outside. In windy conditions the server in tennis will need to reduce the height of the ball toss or the golfer might hit their drive with a lower trajectory.

Equipment and sportswear

The selection of appropriate **equipment** and **sportswear** can play an important part in short-term preparation. In addition to the correct footwear (mentioned above), hi-tech fabrics can also be used to help conserve or dissipate heat according to the environment. The adoption of suitable padding, taping or protective headgear is also vital for injury prevention.

Adaptations to technique

Prior to performance athletes may need to consider **adaptations to technique** to counter their opponents' strengths and weaknesses (see Unit 6B, Sports Mechanics, page 415). For example, in rugby a smaller player has a greater chance of tackling a larger player if a wider base of support is created (thereby creating a lower centre of mass). Alternatively, a low tackle around the legs has a greater chance of moving the centre of mass of a larger player.

In basketball and netball, players can increase pivoting speed by keeping their arms and legs closer to the centre of their body so that angular velocity is increased whilst the moment of inertia is decreased.

In tennis, a player needs to analyse their opponent's backswing in order to be able to predict the flight path of the ball. Topspin will cause the ball to loop in the air whereas slice will flatten the flight path and keep the ball low.

Social factors influencing short-term preparation

The motivation of athletes through intrinsic and extrinsic rewards is still evident in top level sport. However, the balance seems to be shifting between those sports that receive media coverage and have become fully professional and those that do not. The commercialisation of sport means that so-called intrinsic motives are being increasingly called into question.

As explained in Unit 1A, many popular team sports such as football, rugby and hockey developed from localised versions of mob games. These popular recreations were replaced by more rational forms of sport as a result of industrialisation and the growth of a new middle-class morality. Despite a national administrative structure, the emerging professional sports teams and clubs still had a keen sense of local identity and generated pride in the community they served. Over many years, a strong and **passionate** fan base developed.

On a national level, sport also generates strong feelings of **national pride** and **morale**. This sense is further reinforced by the singing of national anthems, and the use of team colours and ceremonies at the start of international matches.

Success on a European and world stage can also generate a 'feel-good factor' within the country. This was evident in England during the Euro 96 football tournament (Figure 6.158). National success not only boosts national pride and morale but it can also be advantageous to the economy, help reduce the crime rate and encourage mass participation in sport.

The power of sport to unite people in a common cause has not been ignored by political leaders. Success in competitive sport can be used by newly emerging nations as a means of establishing their **national identity** on the world stage, as

▲ **Figure 6.158** *Pride and passion!*

well as developing a sense of **national unity**. Australia and Kenya are a good example of the former and the new South Africa the latter.

Asian countries such as India and Pakistan have also realised this and have been developing national sports policies for some time. An advantage of using sport to gain international status is that the new world system of sporting excellence doesn't have to correspond to the old system based on trade and political power. For example, Brazil and Argentina are amongst the world's top football nations and receive the respect and media attention that such a position attracts.

Emerging countries wishing to join the world order of sport make careful choices about the sport in which they will commit their resources. Kenya chose middle- and long-distance running since it involved abilities that were already present in some sections of its population.

With the revival of the Olympic Games in 1896, sport became an avenue for government involvement. The concept of a host nation and use of national anthems and flags at the opening and medal ceremonies, and the fact that the athletes eventually represented their countries rather than themselves, all helped to reinforce national pride.

Ironically for a movement that was meant to be free from political involvement, history has shown that many governments have not been reluctant to use the Games as a political weapon. Unit 1B shows how the Games have been used in this way, including Hitler's exploitation of the 1936 Olympics in Munich to promote Aryan supremacy.

TASK

Discuss the advantages and disadvantages of direct government involvement in sport.

4. Long-term preparation

This section is concerned with the long-term processes that need to be considered in the preparation of athletes. This represents the preparation phase of the periodised year.

As with short-term preparation, long-term preparation can involve physiological, psychological, mechanical, and biomechanical components.

Physiological considerations

Figure 6.159 illustrates the physiological components in long-term preparation.

Assessment of relevant fitness levels

In order to design and implement a long-term training programme for a particular activity, it is necessary to determine the components of fitness that will improve performance in that activity.

As discussed in Unit 3, these can include:

- **physical fitness components**
  - strength
  - speed
  - power
  - local muscular endurance
  - cardio-vascular endurance
  - anaerobic endurance
- **skill-related components**
  - agility
  - co-ordination
  - balance
  - reaction time
  - flexibility
  - body composition.

Fitness testing

Once the relevant fitness components have been identified, the athlete's performance capabilities in these areas need to be assessed to determine the structure of the fitness training programme. The specific tests and issues regarding **fitness testing** are provided in Unit 3.

Training principles

The **training principles** of **progressive overload**, **specificity**, **reversibility**, **moderation**, and application of the **FITT principles** ensure that any training programme is relevant, effective, sensible and safe.

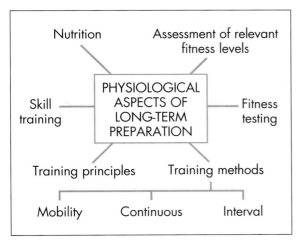

▲ **Figure 6.159** *The physiological aspects of long-term preparation*

Once the coach/trainer has identified the relevant components of fitness, assessed the athlete's fitness levels and identified the principles that govern the training, they must then determine which will be the best **training methods**.

Training methods

Training can involve **continuous**, **interval** and **mobility** methods. These methods are considered in depth in Unit 3.

Continuous methods stress the aerobic system and include running, cycling, swimming and rowing. Optimum improvement can be achieved by ensuring training takes place at the correct intensity (see **target training zones** in Unit 3).

Interval methods can stress both the aerobic and anaerobic systems. The activities involved in interval training are shown in Figure 6.160.

Mobility training can involve static, active, passive, ballistic and PNF stretches.

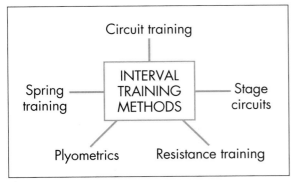

▲ **Figure 6.160** *Methods of interval training*

Skill training

Skill training must also be incorporated into long-term preparation in the form of circuits or drills to develop the sports specific components of fitness. This aspect is expanded further on pages 470–74.

Psychological factors

Motivation

Unit 6B: Option B highlighted the fact that we are motivated to take part in sport as a result of the interaction of a number of factors. These can be both intrinsic and extrinsic. The coach and teacher play an important part in maintaining and developing motivation over a period of time, but it is also vital that the performer is **self-motivated**.

Goal setting

Long-term goal setting is important in order to direct attention, regulate effort at any one time and maintain effort over a long period. Goal setting also plays an important part in dealing with success and coping with failure. Failures, however, can be used as a part of the learning process required in order to achieve **long-term goals**.

Long-term goals need to be set in combination with short-term goals and should comply with the **SMART principles** (see Unit 3: Option B, page 167).

Arousal levels and the control of stress and anxiety

Learning the technique of developing optimal arousal levels and controlling stress and anxiety responses requires long-term practice. These should be an integral part of the overall training programme.

Self-confidence

Self-confidence can be developed from a combination of the following: good preparation, imagery, a confident approach, and physical shape.

Mechanical aspects of long-term preparation

Bio-mechanical analysis is used in the long-term preparation of athletes to improve movement technique, improve or adapt equipment and to reduce the chances of injury.

Improving technique

Students choosing Option A of Unit 6B should be able to cite numerous examples of the way in which bio-mechanical analysis can lead to new techniques and a resulting improvement in performance.

A good example is provided in athletics by the development of the flight technique in the long jump. A bio-mechanical analysis of the jump reveals that the athlete's centre of mass during flight follows the path of any other projectile, i.e. a parabola. Therefore, the speed, angle and height of take-off govern the flight distance.

Since speed is by far the most important of these parameters, the athlete's training should include a high volume of sprint work. It should also include practice in approaching the take-off board at the fastest possible speed. A 'stuttered' run-up will result in deceleration and loss of speed at take-off.

During flight the body has constant angular momentum and the athlete's body tends to rotate forward as a consequence of the rotation imparted on the run-up.

There are two specific techniques that have been developed to counter this forward rotation and place the jumper in the optimum landing position. These are the hang (Figure 6.161) and the hitch-kick (Figure 6.162).

The hang technique increases the athlete's moment of inertia about their transverse axis, thereby decreasing their angular velocity. The hitch-kick technique involves a running action in the air. The resulting action of the arms and the legs causes a reaction and transfer of angular momentum and the trunk to rotate backwards.

▲ **Figure 6.162** *The hitch-kick technique*

Other examples of the advantages gained by using bio-mechanical analysis include the following (see also Unit 6A).

- Footballers/tennis players use the magnus effect to impart spin on the ball causing it to curve in its flight path.
- The sprinter transfers angular and linear momentum to other parts of the body in an attempt to improve their speed out of the blocks. The throwing action of the arms forward and a strong driving action of the lead leg help to transfer momentum to the whole body for faster movement. This is also evident in the high jump or lay-up in basketball, when the athlete swings their arms upwards at take-off.
- In both the discus and hammer events, athletes try to spin with a high velocity before release in an attempt to transfer as much momentum as possible on to the implement.

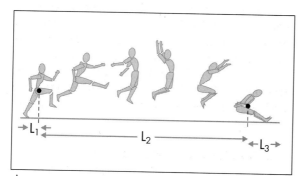

▲ **Figure 6.161** *The hang technique*

TASK

Using examples from your own practical experience, explain how bio-mechanical analysis has improved technique.

Improving equipment

The use of high-tech equipment in the long-term preparation of athletes is expanded on pages 466–69).

Reducing injury

Bio-mechanical analysis can play an important part in the **reduction of injury**.

Injuries can often occur as a result of incorrect technique. For example, in the high jump, incorrect foot placement can lead to patellar tendonitus, or a fibular stress fracture. In cycling, incorrect handlebar or saddle height can cause thoracic or lumbar spine injuries. Tendonitus at the elbow is common in racket players as a result of excessive wrist action in the follow-through for the backhand shot.

Alternatively, injuries can occur due to anatomical or functional abnormalities. For example, sportspeople who suffer from lower leg abnormalities such as bowed legs (genu varum), knocked knees (genu valgum) or differences in leg length often experience knee pain. These conditions can be treated in the first two instances by orthotic inserts, which are placed in the shoes. In the last example treatment involves building up the sports shoe on the foot of the shorter leg.

Long-term preparation: support roles and finance

The pursuit of excellence in sport in order to develop a sense of national identity and pride, as well as to create political platforms, has been identified on pages 461–62. This section presents an overview of the administration of excellence, i.e. the various strategies required to produce élite athletes.

Up until the 1970s, nations tended to develop their own strategies and mechanisms for identifying, developing and supporting élite athletes. The resulting structures were a product of the historical, geographical, political and socio-economic determinants at work in that country.

However, following the Olympic success of the Soviet Union and the German Democratic Republic in the 1960s, 70s and 80s, governments wishing to improve sporting performance (including emerging sporting nations such as Australia) have tended to copy the aspects of the model developed by these two countries.

The requisites for the development of excellence are given below.

Support roles and finance

Unit 1A reviewed the historical development of élite sport (see pages 35–41). It highlighted the fact that in the United Kingdom the nurture of talent has tended to be rather 'hit and miss'. The divide between amateurism and professionalism in sport delayed the adoption of a coherent, scientific and centralised approach that was evident in other cultures.

The decentralised approach has led to the emergence of a number of agencies providing supporting roles and finance (see Unit 1A, pages 42–44). These include:

- **Sport England** – through its 'More Medals' policy this has the responsibility of co-ordinating the development of excellence. It receives its funding from the Department of Culture, Media and Sport and through the National Lottery Fund
- **UK Sport** – this has the responsibility of overseeing the UK Sports Institute
- various sports **governing bodies**
- **Sports Aid**
- **British Olympic Association (BOA)**
- **National Coaching Foundation (NCF)**
- **schools' sports associations**
- sports clubs
- schools.

Administration of élite athlete preparation

Until recently, the development of excellence in the UK rested with the schools, clubs and national governing bodies of sport. Since 1997, however, a new streamlined structure for excellence has been in operation (see Unit 1A, pages 42–43).

The new **United Kingdom Sports Institute (UKSI)** aims to provide facilities and a support network for the country's best athletes.

Academies/training camps

Unit 1 (pages 42–43) described the training camps and sports schools in the UK.

The longstanding National Sports Centres at Lilleshall, Bisham Abbey, Plas-y-Brenin, Crystal Palace and Holme Pierrepoint, and the National Cycling Centre at Manchester, are now part of the framework of centres linked to the UKSI.

In addition, most of the top professional clubs in football, cricket and rugby have academies or centres of excellence, providing high level coaching and facilities. There are also private schools such as Millfield that specialise in sport and a growing number of designated sports colleges.

Cultural variations
USA
Sport in the USA is characterised by its lack of centralised administration. Commercial sponsorship from the private sector and the media have a big influence on the organisation of sport there.

Athletics (high level sport) is developed within the educational system. The main professional sports (baseball, basketball and gridiron football), in addition to a wide range of other sports, are all nurtured through high status programmes at high schools and colleges.

The collegiate scholarship system allows for extensive training and coaching. Most colleges are able to offer these excellence programmes because of earned income from their sports teams in the form of TV rights and gate receipts. The 'draft system' facilitates top college players entering the professional ranks.

Australia
In comparison to the UK, Australia spends nearly twice as much of its gross domestic product (GDP) in the preparation of its élite athletes.

The Australian Sports Commission (ASC) co-ordinates a pyramid system involving a range of programmes, such as Active Australia and Sportstart, to promote sport for all.

Talent identification programmes such as Sportsearch identify talented 11–15 year olds through an array of fitness tests. A computer programme then matches these individuals to their ideal sport.

Talented performers are fed through the system into the Australian Institute of Sport (AIS). This is funded by the federal government and caters for nearly 600 athletes on scholarships in twenty different sports. This approach is supported in each state by a system of state-funded sports institutes, which co-ordinate programmes of excellence on a non-residential basis.

France
In France, more than 3500 athletes are state-funded, either at the Institut National de Sports et Education Physicale (INSEP) in Paris, or at one of the regional INSEPS which provide facilities for non-resident students.

India
In India, residential schooling and even specialised 'boy's units' in the Army are being added to the array of initiatives which are part of the quest for sporting excellence (see Unit 4, page 268).

TASK

Talent identification in the UK is a rather 'hit and miss' affair compared to, say, Australia.

Discuss the strengths and weaknesses of the British system with reference to its physiological, psychological and socio-cultural aspects.

5. Technology in sport

The last few years have witnessed a sharp rise in performance levels (Table 6.1).

In many activities, such rises in performance levels are a direct result of improved training methods, which have increased both in intensity and volume. Additionally, modern training is based on the most up-to-date scientific advancements including diet, technique and mental preparation.

Table 6.1 Men's and women's 100-metre world record times

Year	Men	Year	Women
1912	10.60	1913	13.10
1921	10.40	1928	12.00
1930	10.30	1936	11.50
1936	10.20	1955	11.30
1956	10.10	1972	11.07
1960	10.00	1973	10.80
1968	09.99	1988	10.49
1968	09.95		
1983	09.93		
1988	09.92		
1991	09.86		
1994	09.85		
1996	09.84		
1999	09.79		

▲ **Figure 6.163** Improved technology can transform sporting techniques and performances

Application of modern technology

Ergogenic aids

Unit 5A identified the role of **ergogenic aids** in the improvement of athletic performance (see page 339). An ergogenic aid is any factor that improves athletic performance beyond normal expectations.

The application of modern technology has played an integral part in the development of ergogenic aids in particular, and the refinement and advancement of sporting performance in general.

For example, in sports such as the pole-vault, advances in performance have clearly gone hand-in-hand with technological improvements. In the 1800s vaulting poles were made out of wood (ash, spruce or oak) and by the 1900 Olympic Games competitors were using bamboo. In 1939 aluminium was introduced, but the rigidity of the pole meant that the 15-foot barrier could not be broken. The introduction of the fibre-glass pole in 1948 resulted in the subsequent raising of the world record to over 20 feet (Figure 6.163).

Clearly some sporting activities are more reliant on technological advances than others – yachting, motor racing and cycling being good examples of this (Figures 6.163 and 6.164).

▲ **Figure 6.164** Human endeavour matched by advanced technology

TASK

a Using the data supplied in Table 6.1 on page 467, produce a graph showing the improvement in times at 100m for both men and women.

b With reference to physiological, psychological, mechanical and socio-cultural aspects of the specification, suggest reasons for the improvements in performance.

This section will also review the way modern technology has been applied to:

- **training analysis**
- **training enhancement**
- **performance evaluation**.

The application of technology in **injury prevention** and **rehabilitation** is covered on pages 474–76.

Technology in training analysis

Computers now play an important part in training analysis. Most of the techniques below are dependent on computers to assess the mass of data that is produced. Computers also play a key part in producing and creating **simulations**.

Technology in training analysis is intended to determine what the athlete's body is doing, internally and externally. **Internal monitoring** can involve measuring the performer's heart rate, blood lactate level, haematocrit and brain telemetry. **External monitoring** includes a number of techniques:

- **video analysis** can be used to measure technique and body segment parameters. Two and three dimensional video and cinematography can also be employed
- **pressure measurement** (properly known as dynamometry) is used to measure the forces produced during movement. **Force platforms** are utilised to measure the contact forces between the performer and the ground, whilst **accelerometers** are used to measure acceleration

- **electromyography** is the study of muscle activity as it contracts
- **stroboscopy** is a modern photographic technique used to study movement
- **electrogoniometry** gives information about the angles of the joint as part of the total movement pattern.

Technology in training enhancement

Improved technology has not only significantly influenced the techniques adopted by élite and recreational performers; it has also had an impact on the equipment used and the training environment.

For example, wind tunnel testing has been instrumental in improving the aerodynamics of both the equipment and the performer (Figure 6.165).

The training environment

The training environment has undergone radical change at all levels over the last few decades. Increasingly, facilities are being designed so they are not affected by the weather or climate. In competition, too, advances have also included better provision for mass spectator events in stadia that incorporate retractable roofs, air conditioning and artificial heating. Other sports benefit from astro-turf pitches, artificial tracks, artificial ski slopes and indoor tennis courts.

▲ **Figure 6.165** Improved streamlining helps to reduce drag

In swimming, modern pools minimise wave interference and provide greater grip for kick-turns off the walls. The use of **flume tanks** has provided invaluable information regarding stroke technique, oxygen consumption and velocity.

Success at the élite level can depend upon having the best equipment available. If an athlete does not have access to first-rate equipment, they can certainly be at a physical disadvantage and most probably a psychological one – knowing that equipment is inferior.

Computer-aided design (CAD) is used by manufacturers to improve the design of rackets, sports shoes, racing bikes, skis and racing cars. Examples of the latest design methods and hi-tech materials include Chris Boardman's bike made by Lotus for the 1996 Olympics in Barcelona, and the rugby shirts made by Adidas for the All Blacks in the 1999 World Cup (see Unit 5A for more examples).

The application of high-tech materials, such as carbon fibre and titanium, has helped to reduce the weight of the prostheses used by amputee athletes. This has not only enabled disabled athletes to participate but to improve their sporting performance.

Training methods

Technology has been important in developing different **training methods**. Endurance athletes now incorporate high altitude training and environmental chambers into their training repertoire. Anaerobic athletes use threshold training, plyometrics and isokinetic conditioning equipment. Both types of athlete regulate their training intensity and frequency by the use of heart rate monitors.

However, the application of high-tech machines and equipment for resistance and cardio-vascular training is not exclusive to élite athletes. This equipment is now available in schools and sports clubs around the country.

The demand for **high technology nutrition** has led manufacturers to develop high energy foods, drinks and supplements.

Technology in performance evaluation

In addition to the contribution it has made to training analysis, technology has been prominent also in testing the outcomes of training. For example, aerobic power has been measured using Douglas bags or gas analysis machines in conjunction with treadmills, bicycle ergometers and swimming flumes. Strength can now be developed and assessed using variable resistance, hydraulic and computer-aided systems. Blood lactate measurements offer an additional valuable assessment of the effectiveness of anaerobic and aerobic training methods.

Video analysis is also employed to evaluate technique, provide statistical analysis on performance, tactics and patterns of play (see Unit 5A).

TASK

Using examples of sports in which you have been assessed, discuss the role modern technology has played in the preparation of élite performers.

The concept of sports science and support

The term **sports science** is used to describe the application of scientific methods, knowledge and principles from any branch of science to sport. Sports science is multi-disciplinary, incorporating areas such as sports medicine and psychology, exercise physiology and bio-mechanics.

National agencies

The political use of sport in the development of national identity and pride was analysed in Units 1, 4 and 6A and already reviewed on pages 461–62.

The adoption of scientific methods to improve sports performance has expanded rapidly since the end of the Second World War. This is a consequence of the increasing connection between politics and sport.

This was very evident during the Cold War in the 1960s, 70s and 80s. This was a period of great rivalry between the communist and capitalist superpowers, in particular the USSR and USA. At this time international sporting competition assumed significance beyond the realm of sport itself.

The Eastern bloc countries, particularly the Soviet Union and the German Democratic Republic (GDR), used success at the Olympic Games both as a symbol of national pride and as a clear demonstration of the superiority of communist politics over the capitalism of Western nations.

The outstanding successes of the GDR resulted from:

- the implementation of a pyramid system, funded by the state
- the creation of specialist sports schools with high-class facilities and coaching
- a process whereby talented sports performers were identified at an early age by extensive screening procedures and then filtered through the sports school system which culminated in attendance at the national training centre.

The role of sports medicine and the application of science to the study of sports performance and preparation (both ethically and otherwise) were also central to this success.

The United Kingdom Sports Institute (UKSI), based in London, is core to a regional network of centres providing facilities and support services. Through the lottery-funded World Class programme, Sport England supports sport and medical-related scientific research.

In the future, UKSI Research and Development will focus on priorities identified by sport. Until these services are ready, the gap will be bridged by the High Performance Coaching, Success in Sydney and ACE UK Career and Education programmes. The British Olympic Association provides sports science back-up for athletes through the British Olympic Medical Centre.

In Australia, the AIS now has one of the best sports science programmes in the world. Each of the twenty sports catered for at the centre has its own group of sports scientists who liaise with the coaches and athletes.

Influence of the media on sports performance

Sporting endeavours that were at one time local and possibly national news now reach a far wider audience. This is a reflection of, first, the growth in communications technology and second, the growth of a global audience across a wide range of activities.

The 'hype' that accompanies many of today's major sporting events is often media-generated. It boosts sales and audience figures and acts as a catalyst for the myriad of business ventures and industries for whom sport is a lucrative source of income.

The media and the individual

On an individual level, the media can elevate a sports personality to fame or banish them to anonymity almost overnight. This is particularly so in the USA. Whether such scrutiny elevates or depresses performance depends on how a sports star copes with being under the spotlight – in their private as well as their public lives. Increased media exposure can certainly influence the financial fortunes of an individual and/or a sport. Sponsorship and advertising deals can bring in money that permits better programmes of excellence, which can lead to elevated performance levels. Where, however, as in English premier league football, such income is spent on buying in players from other countries, levels of performance in a global context are merely 'shifted' rather than improved.

6. Strategies for training

This section will review the role of the leader (coach/manager) in the development of performance. To avoid duplication of information concerning bio-mechanical and physiological aspects, you should refer to short-term preparation (pages 458–61) and long-term preparation (pages 462–66). More information on the strategies for training covered in this section is provided in Unit 2A (pages 130–38) and Unit 5A (pages 335–36).

The leader's role in developing performance

Leadership can be defined as:

> ... *the behavioural process influencing individuals and groups towards set goals.*

> Barrow, 1977

There are a variety of leadership roles in the sporting arena:

- sports leader
- coach
- physical education teacher
- captain
- manager.

Although they all assume a leadership role, their aims and expectations differ. For example, the sports leader aims to create an organised, safe, fun atmosphere in which individuals and groups can take part in appropriate physical activity. The sports coach, on the other hand, concentrates on improving performance.

The sports coach

As we have seen in this Unit, the development of performance requires a synthesis of information from different sources. The NCF (1996) identified four areas of knowledge required by the successful coach:

- the sport which they are coaching: its rules, tactics, techniques and practices
- the performers in their charge: their goals, personalities, backgrounds
- the factors affecting performance: anatomy and physiology, skill acquisition, nutrition, sports medicine, sports psychology and bio-mechanics
- the factors affecting coaching: coaching skills, styles and methods.

At the highest level, delivery of specialised knowledge is not undertaken by the coach alone, but through a team of specialists. Former tennis star, Martina Navratilova, for example, employed a support team of nine specialists including two sports psychologists!

In its guidelines (1996), the NCF divides the coaching process into the three main areas:

- **planning**
- **conducting**
- **evaluating**.

Planning

Planning is concerned with identifying the needs and goals of the athlete, then devising suitable training strategies and programmes to achieve those goals.

Depending on the sport, a performer's goals will tend to be broken down into three key phases of the season or year: the off season, the pre-season and competition. We have seen from the sub-sections Short- and long-term planning that goals need to comply with the SMART principles (see page 167).

Once the performer's year has been separated into the long-term and the short-term preparation, the coach can then plan the content and programme of the training sessions.

An awareness of individual differences provides a key focus in developing the performer's routines and his or her training programmes. (Further aspects to consider here are referred to on pages 452 and 474 of Unit 6).

At this point we can refer back to the five key **principles of coaching** identified by Martens (1997) in Unit 5A on page 325 (Figure 6.166).

Under **coaching objectives**, Martens identified the balance that is required between the need to be successful and the physical, social and psychological development of the athlete. A synthesis of your knowledge of Units 1 and 4 should enable you to cite examples in global sport where this balance has stressed winning at the expense of the other objectives.

The other principles identified by Martens – **coaching styles**, **communication skills**, **reinforcement** and **motivation** – relate to the second fundamental

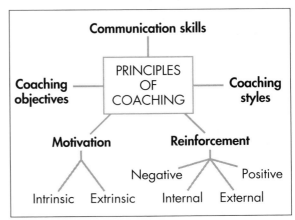

▲ *Figure 6.166* Martens' main principles of coaching

coaching process identified by the NCF – conducting coaching sessions.

Conducting

Unit 5A identified four key features of organisation required by the coach:

- coaching material
- time
- facilities and equipment
- the performer(s).

Coaching material refers to the identification of the appropriate physiological, psychological, technical and tactical components for the activity. More detail regarding the development of the physiological and bio-mechanical elements can be found on pages 454–66.

Technical training was covered in Unit 2A, Acquiring skill. In essence, this means setting up situations which facilitate the acquisition of skills necessary for good performance.

On a practical level, the coach must be aware of the three stages of learning (see also pages 122–24):

- **cognitive phase**
- **associative phase**
- **autonomous phase**.

Students of sports psychology (Unit 6B: Option B) will also be aware of the application and relevance of Bandura's model of observational learning (1997) to the first two stages of learning (see page 438).

Demonstrations play an important part in the learning process. However, a visual demonstration represents just one of three **forms of guidance** – the others are shown in Figure 6.167.

Guidance refers to the type of information presented to the learner to facilitate the learning process.

The second (associative) learning phase involves practice. Figures 6.168 and 6.169 summarise the factors involved in the structure and presentation of practices.

The **type of practice** used by the coach is important. They have to decide whether each skill should be performed continuously (massed), or whether to incorporate breaks (distributed) or whether to have a mix (variable) (Figure 6.168).

The **method of practice** a coach employs, that is, whether a skill is taught as a whole or in parts, will depend upon its complexity and organisation. For a fuller explanation of these factors, refer to Unit 2A, pages 109–10.

Learning cannot take place without **feedback**. Through feedback coaches can build upon strengths and help to eradicate weaknesses. Feedback in the form of **knowledge of results (KR)** or **knowledge of performance (KP)** forms an important part of conducting the session and is integral part of any evaluation (see also Unit 2A, page 112).

Evaluating

Evaluating performance is the last part of the coaching process. It involves assessing the extent to which goals have been achieved and identifying areas for improvement.

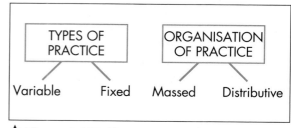

▲ **Figure 6.168** *The main types of practice*

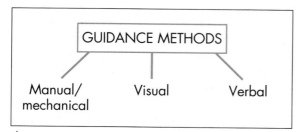

▲ **Figure 6.167** *Forms of guidance*

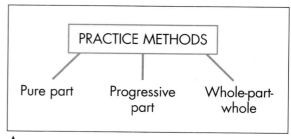

▲ **Figure 6.169** *Methods of practice*

Fitness testing is now seen as a reliable and objective means of assessing the physical conditioning aspects of the training programme. For recognised test protocols for assessing the skill and physical components of fitness see Unit 3, page 203.

A coach must be able to **analyse performance** to evaluate the effectiveness of training sessions. Unit 5A presented an overview of evaluation techniques for skill, positional and match analysis, and the types of data which can be collected to aid this process. A summary of the **methods of analysis** is shown in Figure 6.170.

TASK

Using examples from an activity you have been assessed in, identify the different ways in which a coach can evaluate the success or otherwise of a training programme.

Psychological considerations

Attitudes – the coach can play an important part in helping to change any negative attitudes of the performers in their care. Knowledge of the various strategies available, including Festinger's (1957) cognitive dissonance theory, would be useful here (see Unit 5A, page 301).

Attribution – the coach can use attribution to increase motivation, confidence, effort, and to reduce the pressure of the situation (see Unit 6B, pages 433–34).

Self-efficacy – knowledge of Bandura's theory of self-efficacy can help the coach to develop self-confidence in the athlete (see Unit 6B, page 435).

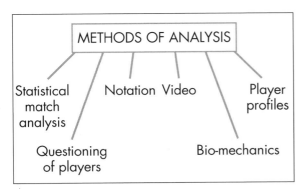

▲ **Figure 6.170** Methods of analysis

Aggression – knowledge of the causes and theories of aggression can help the coach to reduce the number and severity of aggressive acts both on and off the field (see Unit 6B, page 439).

Arousal, anxiety and **stress** – successful performance is dependent upon an athlete's ability to deal with the pressure of competition and to use the situation to positive advantage. A coach needs to be aware when the performer is showing signs of somatic anxiety and should be able to adjust it to the optimum level. Somatic and cognitive techniques must also be at hand to deal with the negative effects of stress (see Unit 6B, page 445).

Cohesion – in the sporting situation, the leader plays a key role in developing team cohesion and ensuring that the team plays to its true potential (group productivity). Knowledge of the task as well as the social make-up of a group can enable a coach to focus on strategies that foster greater cohesion and minimise 'faulty processes' (see Unit 5A, pages 332–3).

Cultural variations

In the UK the way in which organised sport emerged from the boys' public schools in the nineteenth century has had a profound influence on both the role of the coach and the pursuit of excellence.

With the exception of cricket, horse racing and golf, nearly all of today's sports governing bodies developed from the Oxbridge 'melting pot' in the last 35 years of the nineteenth century. Consequently, the dominant ethic that emerged was a **recreational ethic** rather than the 'win ethic' that is predominant in sports in the USA (see Unit 4A, page 222).

Since, originally, public schoolboys had rationalised these sporting forms, responsibility for organising and running sport was firmly in the hands of the participants, rather than with outside agencies such as coaches or managers. Consequently, until very recently, coaching in the majority of sports in Britain has developed as a voluntary and unpaid activity.

Since 1983, the needs of coaches in the UK has been addressed by the **National Coaching Foundation (NCF)**. The NCF has helped to boost the status of coaching at all levels, providing courses, information, products and support services through its regional structure. Although the NCF is sometimes referred to as the government's 'coaching arm', it is in fact an independent organisation.

The NCF is working together with the British Olympic Association to develop the **High Performance Coaching programme**. This aims to train world-class coaches through the creation of individual development programmes.

Coaching in the USA

The dominant concept in sport in the USA is the Lombardian 'win at all costs' ethic. This has developed through the interdependence of the capitalist system and the overt commercialisation of sport. Consequently, coaching has emerged as a specialised, full-time, high status profession, from high schools right through to professional sport. At the top level, the high media profile, the importance of winning and the accountability of coaches has meant that such appointments can be rather insecure.

Coaching in Australia

In Australia, top quality coaching forms a cornerstone of the development of excellence. The Australian Coaching Council (ACC) organises a professionally-run, centralised system with regional offices, funded from the federal budget. Coaches are identified and nurtured through the ACC's scholarship programme, which includes personal career guidance (mentors) and the opportunity to complete a Graduate Diploma of Elite Coaching.

The ACC also operates a National Coaching Accreditation Scheme, which culminates with the High Performance Programme. Australian coaches are kept up to date with the latest practices through workshops and seminars run by the ACC (see Unit 4A).

TASK

Using your knowledge of the scientific aspects of PE and sport, identify the advantages of having a fully professional coaching structure. Use examples to reinforce your points.

7. Sports medicine

Sports medicine developed largely but not entirely out of the expansion of the Olympic movement and the search for ways of improving athletic performance. It is now also regarded as an important aspect of preventative medicine and stands alongside other branches of medicine.

Issues relating to injury prevention and rehabilitation

One of the main questions relating to injury and rehabilitation is whether sport is good for one's health?

Whilst not relevant to individuals who take part in regular low-impact recreational activity, this does represent an issue for the competitive athlete. The ever-mounting pressures on top sportsmen and women to train harder and for longer periods of time increases their chance of suffering from injury.

This raises two important points:

- Most sports involve an element of risk.
- The training involved in the pursuit of excellence (of itself) increases the risk of injury. This concern is heightened when considering the training of young athletes.

Some sporting activities are open to more risk than others. For example, there is a greater risk of injury in a contact sport such as rugby than in a game of snooker. This raises the issue of **risk analysis** in sport.

Currently governing bodies are responsible for reducing the element of risk in their sport. A number of changes have been made in this regard. For example, the RFU has altered the scrummaging laws in junior rugby in an effort to reduce the chance of the scrum collapsing. They have also standardised the studs on players' boots, which has successfully reduced certain types of injury.

TASK

What rule changes or equipment changes that have been introduced in other sports in an effort to reduce injury can you identify?

In addressing the issue of injury reduction amongst young athletes, the governing body or coach can modify activities/rules in the following ways:

- **equipment** – any equipment used should be appropriate for the age/size of the performer, e.g. size of rackets, balls
- **playing areas** – the size of playing areas should be appropriate for the age and level of the performers
- **rules** – the duration and rules of matches/events need to be appropriate to the physical and psychological development of the players. The number of players on each team can also be reduced in an effort to increase involvement
- **age categories** – in competition, the coach and governing body must also ensure that age categories are strictly adhered to.

TASK

Identify a governing body of sport and analyse how successful they have been in adapting the adult game to suit the needs of younger participants.

Other issues

There are two other main areas for concern regarding the health of sports performers.

- The importance of winning has placed increased pressure on performers not only to recover from serious injury more quickly but also to continue performing when injured. The use of 'magic sprays' to aid short-term recovery whilst ignoring possible long-term consequences is increasingly becoming an issue.
- To succeed in modern sport athletes need to train longer, harder and start at an early age. Consequently a number of athletes are now suffering from the effects of over-use injuries. Research in this area is inconclusive but there is concern that the top sportsmen of today may become disabled from **arthritis** at a very young age.

Programmes for injury prevention/rehabilitation

Moyer (1990) identified two primary rehabilitative goals in sports medicine:

- **prevention of injuries** – athlete education and proper physical conditioning contribute to this
- safe return of the injured athlete to the previous level of competition as soon as possible.

Principles of injury prevention

The principles of injury prevention include:

- warm up/cool down
- flexibility training
- appropriate taping and bracing (for prevention or rehabilitation)
- protective equipment
- correct movement
- suitable footwear, clothing and other equipment
- appropriate surfaces for both training and competition
- appropriate training for the activity
- adequate post-activity recovery
- application of psychological techniques, e.g. relaxation exercises, imagery, self-talk
- appropriate and adequate nutrition.

Adapted from Brukner et al, 1993

The best means of injury prevention is education. If the athlete has knowledge of the above areas this not only helps in injury prevention but also aids the recovery process.

Principles of treatment

Thorough initial evaluation of injury, appropriate immediate treatment and a comprehensive rehabilitation programme can help achieve a safe return to fitness. As a general principle, treatment should be tailored to the individual athlete rather than a standardised treatment. The management of sports injuries is based upon five stages:

1 Minimise the extent of the damage.
2 Reduce associated pain and inflammation and promote healing of damaged tissue.
3 Maintain and restore flexibility, strength, proprioception and overall fitness during the healing phase.

4 Actively rehabilitate the injured athlete to enable a return to sport.

5 Assess and correct any predisposing factors in order to reduce the likelihood of re-occurrence.

Brukner *et al*, 1993

Stages of rehabilitation

There are four stages of rehabilitation (see also Table 6.2):

- Initial stage – as soon as possible after the injury, try to develop a pain free range of movement.
- Intermediate stage – resumption of normal activities and daily living with some sporting activity (skill-related). Fitness maintenance also included but not stressing the injured area.
- Advanced stage – commencement of functional activities related to sport.
- Final stage – return to sport. Full participation in training and competition.

Therapeutic modalities

Therapeutic modalities include the use of heat, cold, electric, light and sound (Figure 6.171). Treatments in the immediate post-injury and recuperative periods may include:

- **short-wave** machines – these emit electro-magnetic energy, increasing the temperature of the targeted area

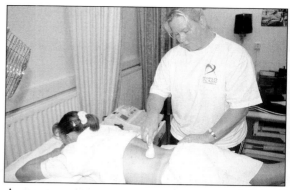

▲ *Figure 6.171 Expert medical support can help to speed up the recovery process*

- **ultrasound** – this can relieve pain and stimulates the repair of soft tissue injuries by producing heat
- **TENS** (Transcutaneous Electrical Nerve Stimulation) – this and interferential treatment transmits an electrical current through the injured area, causing muscle contraction and ion movement and also brings pain relief
- **Laser therapy** – decreases pain and inflammation.

The clinical use of heat and cold (**thermotherapy** and **cryotherapy**) is most effective in reducing the sensation of pain. If limited equipment is available, the best initial treatment is **RICE** (Rest/Ice/Compression/Elevation).

Table 6.2 *The stages of the rehabilitation process (Brukner, 1993)*

STAGE	FUNCTIONAL LEVEL	SPORT	MANAGEMENT
Initial	Poor	Nil suitable; substitute activities, e.g. cycling, swimming	RICE Electrotherapeutic modalities, stretches/isometric exercises
Intermediate	Good	Isolated skills, e.g. shooting in basketball	Electrotherapy (less) Stretches/strength work
Advanced	Good	Commence agility work Agility work Skills Games drills	Strength work Power work Proprioception Functional activity
Final	Good	Full participation	Continue strength work Power work Flexibility work

Techniques of reconditioning

These are commonly known as therapeutic exercise and include techniques to improve:

- **muscular strength**
- **cardio-vascular endurance**
- **flexibility.**

Techniques for improving muscular strength include: **isometric**, **isotonic** and **isokinetic** training. Programmes recommending the weight and number of repetitions include De Lorme's programme, the Oxford technique and Macqueen's programme.

Flexibility exercises can involve **static**, **ballistic** and **PNF** exercises. Cardio-vascular exercises can involve swimming, cycling and rowing.

The way in which exercise regimes are employed will depend upon the location and nature of the injury.

Manual therapy aims to restore optimal functioning of the body part by decreasing pain and increasing mobility through active or resistive exercise.

Nutrition and preparation

The importance of monitoring an athlete's diet has been discussed on page 458 and in Unit 6A.

The main points regarding nutrition and the performer can be summarised as follows:

- Athletic performance can be improved by good nutrition and hindered by poor nutrition.
- Carbohydrates, fats, proteins, minerals and water are essential for good performance.
- Carbohydrate is the main source of energy during exercise.
- The main difference between the diet of an athlete and a non-athlete is that the athlete has to consume more calories.
- Muscle glycogen stores can be increased in the build-up to an event by 'supercompensation' or carbohydrate loading.

The use of drugs in sport

The use of drugs to enhance performance has been evident since the ancient Olympic Games. Unit 1B (pages 80–82) reviewed the instances of drug use in the modern Olympic Games, starting with the death of the Danish cyclist Knud Jensen in 1960.

You should refer back to Unit 1 in order to set this against the wider context of deviance in sport. It is apparent that widespread drug use in élite and professional sport during the 1970s and 1980s occurred at all levels: individual, group and institutional .

Measures to counter the problem include random testing both in and out of season. Since 1994, testing procedures by the IOC's Medical Commission have expanded to include blood as well as urine samples. However, this practice has still not been universally adopted by all international governing bodies. Cases still occur where an individual athlete is cleared by their own governing body but found guilty by the IOC Medical Commission!

Legal and illegal drug usage

There are now over 150 substances on the IOC's banned list. This list is in constant flux as chemists supplying the drugs seem to be one step ahead of the testing agencies creating new preparations to beat the ban. The fine line between legal and illegal usage is becoming increasingly blurred. For example, the IOC permits the use of aspirin and local anaesthetic drugs where there is 'medical justification' but does not permit the use of decongestants for those same 'medical reasons'.

Sport now takes place in a 'global environment'. Whilst the European Charter for Sport underpins efforts within its jurisdiction to clear sport of doping through civil procedures and laws, there appears to be no equivalent body outside sport capable of enforcing such legislation at a global level.

The increased use of technology further confuses the issue of what is fair and unfair. For example, the use of environmental chambers and high altitude training to improve cardio-vascular fitness is legal but blood doping is illegal. Oxygen is now being used before and after an event, but should it be banned during the event?

TASK

a Discuss the use of altitude training, environmental chambers, creatine and oxygen in the improvement of performance.

b Explain whether or not you think they should be banned.

Justify your answers on medical and ethical grounds.

Current developments in genetic medicine suggest that the science of 'gene doping' will have replaced the culture of drugs by the year 2010. In the future, it might be possible that one injection of artificial genes could replace the weight-training machine as a means of building muscle!

We now live in a world where drug use in the wider social context appears to be rapidly increasing and the abhorrence of such practices is less marked than in previous generations. Such factors are likely to create very mixed messages to (largely) young sportsmen and women, for whom the concept of drugs is not an alien one.

Conclusion

This Unit has been concerned primarily with the application of scientific principles to the development of human performance. This has included the important role of sports medicine in the preparation of élite athletes.

It should be evident by now that success in élite sport in the modern age cannot be achieved in isolation. It requires a complex network of agencies providing funding, facilities, medical and physiological support, bio-mechanical analysis, nutritional advice and psychological training.

The increased use of science to enhance the preparation of the élite athlete is linked with a number of social processes at local, national and international levels. These include:

- the increased competitiveness of sport
- the growing relationship between sport and politics and the wish of governments to use success in sport to further their political aims (e.g. forging a sense of nationalism, national unity or stressing a particular ideology)
- the growing commercialisation of sport, emphasising the rewards for winning
- the technological revolution
- the increasing influence of the media
- the increased use of medication in everyday life, making it more difficult to isolate the unacceptable use of drugs within the sporting arena.

The interdependence of these factors has not only led to a dramatic improvement in athletic performance, but has reinforced the place of sport in popular culture. However, this inter-relationship has also resulted in the development of a number of unforeseen consequences, such as increased deviance in sport.

Key words and phrases

1. Introduction

(There are no key words and phrases in this sub-section.)

2. Individual differences

- **Nature** • **Nurture** • **Physiological** • **Psychological** • **Bio-mechanical** • **Time**
- **Space** • **Freedom** • **Physiological changes** • **Discrimination** • **WASPs**
- **Stacking** • **Centrality** • **Title IX** • **Cognitive domain** • **Psychomotor domain**
- **Affective domain** • **Feedback** • **Transfer** • **Personality** • **Imagery**
- **Mental rehearsal** • **Positive self-talk** • **Anxiety** • **Stress** • **Attribution** • **Size**
- **Body composition** • **Body mass**

3. Short-term preparation

- Competition phase   • Periodised year   • Acclimatisation   • Nutrition
- Carbohydrate loading   • Warm up   • Flexibility exercises   • Static   • Passive
- Ballistic   • PNF   • Performance-related planning   • Motivation
- Achievement motivation   • Intrinsic motivation   • Extrinsic motivation
- Cognitive evaluation theory   • Positive mental attitude   • Self-efficacy
- Goal setting   • Imagery   • Arousal   • Cognitive anxiety   • Somatic anxiety
- Self-directed relaxation   • Progressive relaxation training   • Self-talk   • Cohesion
- Social loafing   • Friction   • Fluid forces   • Air resistance   • Equipment
- Sportswear   • Adaptations to technique   • Morale   • National identity
- National unity

4. Long-term preparation

- Physical fitness components   • Skill-related components   • Fitness testing
- Training principles   • Progressive overload   • Specificity   • Reversibility
- Moderation   • FITT principles   • Training methods   • Continuous   • Interval
- Mobility   • Target training zones   • Self-motivated   • Long-term goals
- SMART principles   • Self-confidence   • Reduction of injury   • Sport England
- UK Sport   • Governing bodies   • Sports Aid   • British Olympic Association (BOA)
- National Coaching Foundation (NCF)   • Schools' sports associations
- United Kingdom Sports Institute (UKSI)

5. Technology in sport

- Ergogenic aids   • Training analysis   • Training enhancement
- Performance evaluation   • Injury prevention   • Rehabilitation   • Simulations
- Internal monitoring   • External monitoring   • Video analysis
- Pressure measurement   • Force platforms   • Accelerometers   • Electromyography
- Stroboscopy   • Electrogoniometry   • Flume tanks   • Computer-aided design (CAD)
- Training methods   • High technology nutrition   • Sports science

6. Strategies for training

- Planning   • Conducting   • Evaluating   • Principles of coaching
- Coaching objectives   • Coaching styles   • Communication skills   • Reinforcement
- Motivation   • Technical training   • Cognitive phase   • Associative phase
- Autonomous phase   • Observational learning   • Forms of guidance
- Type of practice   • Method of practice   • Feedback   • Knowledge of results (KR)
- Knowledge of performance (KP)   • Evaluating performance   • Fitness testing
- Analyse performance   • Methods of analysis   • Attitudes   • Attribution
- Self-efficacy   • Aggression   • Arousal   • Anxiety   • Stress   • Cohesion
- Recreational ethic   • National Coaching Foundation (NCF)
- High Performance Coaching programme

7. Sports medicine

- Risk analysis   • Equipment   • Playing areas   • Rules   • Arthritis
- Prevention of injuries   • Stages of rehabilitation   • Therapeutic modalities
- Short-wave   • Ultrasound   • TENS   • Laser therapy   • Thermotherapy
- Cryotherapy   • RICE   • Muscular strength   • Cardio-vascular endurance
- Flexibility   • Isometric   • Isotonic   • Isokinetic   • Static   • Ballistic   • PNF
- Manual therapy

REVIEW QUESTIONS

1 What are the advantages and disadvantages of the application of sports science in sport?

2 Using your knowledge of the scientific aspects of PE and sport, identify the main differences between the sedentary individual and a trained athlete.

3 Discuss the role that sports medicine plays in the preparation of élite athletes.

4 How does the preparation of sports teams differ during the 'on' and 'off' seasons?

5 How do individual differences affect the sports we choose to participate in?

6 A top UK athletics coach recently stated that drug-testing procedures should be withdrawn from athletics. Discuss the implications of this in terms of physiological, psychological and socio-cultural aspects.

7 You have been asked to develop a new coach education programme for the NCF. Identify and justify the areas of information to be included in the programme.

8 A number of top football clubs now have their own centres of excellence. Discuss the advantages and disadvantages of these.

9 A number of countries including the UK and Australia have implemented support programmes with the aim of achieving success in future Olympics. Discuss the necessary features of such programmes.

10 More countries than ever are trying to achieve sporting success in major global games. Suggest ways in which a nation can try to ensure that genetic potential for sport can be fully realised.

11 What strategies and methods can be used to maintain motivation during long-term injury?

12 Discuss and exemplify the importance of long- and short-term goals in the preparation of élite athletes.

13 What factors need to be considered when planning a training programme for élite female athletes?

14 The USA has traditionally had a strong 'win ethic' with regard to sports participation. What are the benefits and pitfalls of this?

15 It is often said that 'prevention is better than cure' when referring to sports injuries. Using practical examples, identify the main principles/techniques for injury prevention and possible programmes of rehabilitation.

Texts used in the writing of this section

❑ Bandura, A., *Social Learning Theory*, Prentice Hall, 1977

❑ Barrow, J. L., 'The variables of leadership', in *Academy of Management Review*, 1977

❑ Bartlett, R., *Introduction to Sports Biomechanics*, E&FN Spon, 1997

❑ Bernhardt, D. B., *Sports Physical Therapy*, Churchill Livingstone, 1986

❑ Brukner, P., & Khan K., *Clinical Sports Medicine*, McGraw Hill Book Co., 1993

❑ Deci, F. L., *Intrinsic Motivation and Self-Determination in Human Behaviour*, Plenum Press, 1985

❑ Dick, F. W., *Sports Training Principles*, A & C Black, 1997

❑ Elliot, B., *Training In Sport: Applying Sports Science*, John Wiley & Sons, 1998

❑ Gross, R., *Psychology: The Science of Mind and Behaviour*, Hodder & Stoughton, 1992

❑ Martens, R., *Successful Coaching*, American Sports Education Program, 1997

❑ Moyer, J. A., in Prentice, W. E. (ed), *Rehabilitation Techniques in Sports Medicine*, Times/Mirror/Mosby Publishing, 1990

❑ National Coaching Foundation, *The Successful Coach: Guidelines for Coaching Practice*, 1996

❑ Sage, G. H., *Introduction to Motor Behaviour: A Neurophysical Approach*, Addison Wesley, 1977

❑ Sharp, B., *Acquiring Skill in Sport*, Sport Dynamics, Eastbourne, 1992

❑ Williams, M. H., *The Ergogenics Edge*, Human Kinetics, 1989

Suggested further reading

❑ Muller, E., Ludesher, F. & Zallinger, G., *Science in Elite Sport*, E & FN Spon, 1999

❑ Reilly, T., Secher N., & Snell P., *The Physiology of Sports*, E & FN Spon, 1990

❑ Williams, M. H., *The Ergogenics Edge*, Human Kinetics, 1989

Index

Page numbers in *italics* refer to illustrations or tables.